Contents

KU-484-369

Preface

This book deals with terminal servers as central execution platforms for Windows-based applications. Users can access these terminal servers using clients that do not necessarily have to be overly intelligent. This might not sound terribly spectacular and might even remind you of the "good old days" of mainframes. You might also be wondering if the author of this book is an advocate of the old technologies who is seizing an opportunity to rebuff the current client/server concept. Quite the contrary! Terminal servers "adopt" an idea that has matured and developed out of the mainframe world and strengthens the client/server model. Widely distributed client/server environments will be re-centralized without changing the original goals that were set with their introduction.

> **Note**   I should emphasize that I have no wish to argue the success that mainframes have enjoyed. The more involved I get in terminal servers and large project environments, the deeper I venture into the mainframe world, which has much to teach about operational concepts and system stability.

In 1995, I first heard about a special multiple-user variant of Microsoft Windows NT. It was called *WinCenter Pro* and, through integrating additional functions, it allowed multiple users to log on simultaneously and even start their sessions using X11 clients. WinCenter was the perfect concept that I needed for a mixed UNIX –and Microsoft Windows environment with almost 800 computers. With WinCenter, UNIX users were finally able to work with the "killer applications" from the PC environment. Soon after the purchase of a 15-concurrent-user license and its installation on our first server, WinCenter Pro became one of the most frequently used services on the network at one of the world's largest research institutes for computer graphics, the Fraunhofer Institute for Computer Graphics, which has its headquarters in Germany and affiliated institutes in the United States, Portugal, and Singapore. In this way, approximately 200 UNIX graphics developers increasingly began to accept Windows NT. Unknowingly, I thus became one of the first system administrators in Europe to successfully establish a multiple-user server running Windows NT in a large, heterogeneous environment.

It was not necessarily easy to configure and run a PC with a multi-user Windows NT, especially on a network that could not deny its UNIX roots. The amount of time that I needed to set up (and understand) a stable system was quite substantial. But other administrators reported similar experiences, and the idea took root to modify the "hands-on training seminars" that I had been holding since 1996 on Windows NT administration to include WinCenter administrators. These seminars became so successful; they were quickly adapted to Microsoft Windows NT 4.0 Server, Terminal Server Edition, and Windows 2000 Terminal Services as soon as they became available. In view of the success of these seminars and my documentation on the WinCenter production environment, Thomas Pohlmann of Microsoft Press Germany and I had the idea to write a book about the terminal server for the German-speaking market, a book designed to be a real help for routine terminal server operation.

The first book was an unexpected and huge success; a second book followed when Windows 2000 and its Terminal Services were launched. The second book revealed the increasing relevance of Terminal Services for corporate environments. The third book, the one you are reading now, became an international edition and describes Microsoft Windows Server 2003 Terminal Services. Two additional, new areas of interest are also included: Web integration and application access portals. Much has changed since *Windows NT 4.0 Server, Terminal Server Edition*, Microsoft Press Germany, 1999 and *Windows 2000 Terminal Services*, Microsoft Press Germany, 2000 were released. This book draws on the experience gathered during eight years of terminal server projects with many customers in the United States and Europe. The individual project scope has changed from several dozens of users on individual servers to many thousands of users on several hundreds of servers. The terminal server concept has matured.

I would like to thank Martin DelRe, Valerie Woolley, and Florian Helmchen at Microsoft Press for their wonderful encouragement to publish a book whose target group might be somewhat different from the usual Microsoft readership. The contents of this book are not based solely on my own project experience and the limitless amount of "processed" information available in knowledge base articles, white papers, conference presentations, product manuals, tons of Help pages, and news groups. On the contrary, the knowledge and diligence of a number of specialists made invaluable contributions to this book and its quality.

- My special appreciation goes to Josef Zeiler at SBC-Consulting. As my German technical editor, he ensured that my imprecise or just plain wrong explanations did not find their way into this book. Furthermore, he supplied valuable information on the topic of licensing. Our technical discussions were often arduous, but always very productive.

- You would not be able to read this book in English were it not for the tireless efforts of the translators who met tighter-than-tight deadlines and made this mission impossible possible. Special thanks to Monika Schutz, who in addition to translating managed the first phase of the transcontinental translation project, Patricia Callow, Claire Jokubauskas, and Gabrielle Vernier.

- Pete Zeeb (technical reviewer) and Lisa Pawlewicz (copyeditor) with Microsoft Press, U.S., were essential players as they lent their skills to provide a nicely translated and technically accurate English version of *Microsoft Windows Server 2003 Terminal Services*.

- Sascha Goeckel is responsible for central Europe in his function as Technical Reseller Manager at AppSense Technologies Ltd. It was he, of course, who wrote the draft version describing the AppSense products in this book. Our discussions were always a great inspiration, especially on the topic of basic security in terminal server environments.

- Frank Seibert is the Director of Consulting Services at visionapp operating in Germany and in England. He is, in my humble opinion, a walking-talking encyclopedia on all topics even remotely connected to terminal servers. Many of the small (and great) configuration tricks described in this book are based on his vast knowledge, such as the optimized printer integration described in Chapter 14.

- *Andreas Mariotti* is a freelance consultant who works on many IT projects. He focuses on Windows terminal servers and Citrix MetaFrame, particularly on software distribution and automation. Andreas's knowledge about deploying terminal servers in large corporate environments is vast. He was one of my most important resources, especially when describing the application configuration in Chapter 5. He is also responsible for many minor, but important, improvements to almost all chapters. I have come to believe that Andreas probably knows every Knowledge Base article and white paper on terminal servers by heart.

- Thomas Goehring is the specialist for server and security infrastructure at visionapp. I am indebted to him for the detailed information about access control (Chapter 8) and the different encryption options for communicating with terminal servers.

- Christian Weyer was one of my students when I was working on my Ph.D. thesis. After successfully concluding his studies, he founded his own little company, which he named Eyesoft. He is now a Regional Director at Microsoft, MVP ASP.NET & XML Web Services, a successful book author, and a much-sought-after lecturer at many conferences. I owe it to Christian that Microsoft .NET technologies found sufficient recognition in this book. Without his help, I would have never understood the technical context, as described in Chapter 5, for instance.

- The topics relating to application access portals in Chapter 13 also involve the Citrix MetaFrame Secure Access Manager. Marc O. Borchert supplied this description. He is a Senior Strategic Systems Engineer at Citrix and draws his knowledge on this rather new product from the practical experience he has gained from customers and partners all over Europe. Additionally, he has a direct line to the product developers at Citrix.

I would also to like thank the following individuals for the detailed information, critical comments, corrections, tips, or test installations that contributed to this book: Mark Austin (AppSense), Peter Bergler (Microsoft), Christian Ferber (Fujitsu Siemens Computers), Christian Gehring (Citrix), Ralf Germowitz (BFE), Mark Gerrards (AppSense), Peter Ghostine (Emergent Online), Costin Hagiu (Microsoft), René Huebel (Fujitsu Siemens Computers), Christine Koch (Microsoft), Bob Kruger (Citrix), Jennifer Lang (Citrix), Daniel Liebisch (Citrix), Russ Naples (Citrix), Rizwan Pirani (Citrix), Mark Russinovich (WinInternals Software and SysInternals), Adam Overton (Microsoft), Enrico Schwalbe (Citrix), David Smith (Citrix), David Solomon (David Solomon Expert Seminars), Patrick Sommer (Software Spectrum), Oliver Schroeder (MCS), Edwin Sternitzky (Citrix), Mark Templeton (Citrix), and Walter Weinfurter (Microsoft).

Furthermore, I would express my thanks to my colleagues at visionapp, who are always ready to offer their advice and support: Petra Boeckmann, Chris Dittmar, Marc Freidhof, Klaus Friemann, Ulrike Gebhard, Thomas Gierich, Thorsten Goebel, Simon Hirth, Sascha Holzenthal, Sigfried Kienzel, Oliver Mahr, Klaus Mitter, Frank Roth, Dirk Schaefer, Ingo Schulz, Meik Schwind, Enis Sari, Perry Stanford, Michael Syre, Markus Thorwartl, Daniel Vollmer, and Daniel Winkler. Special thanks, of course, go to Joerg Krick and Jan Zirn, the managing directors of visionapp, for their generosity, giving me all the time and support I needed to write this book in addition to my regular job as Chief System Architect.

I would also like to thank the Ober-Ramstadt volleyball team for providing me with much-needed physical and mental balance during the writing of this book. They remained undeterred by my mood swings and continued to practice, celebrate, and live through unforgettable matches with me.

Last, but absolutely not least, my very special thank-you goes to my wife, Tina, and my sons, Luca and Tobias. They are the center of my personal universe. I'd also like to thank my parents and my parents-in-law, Erika and Dieter Liebschner. My family has always been and always will be my most valuable moral support. Every day, they show me what is truly important in this life.

Dr. Bernhard Tritsch
Ober-Ramstadt, Germany, October 2003

About This Book

Microsoft Windows Server 2003 was developed as the successor to the Microsoft Windows 2000 Server series, with special emphasis on use by IT professionals in corporate networks. It offers both exceptional stability and excellent performance. A computer system running Windows Server 2003 supports simultaneous execution of an almost unlimited number of processes for users interactively logged on to the system. It is, of course, possible to use several processors simultaneously to increase scalability. Specially adapted system components allow multiple users to log on to the system interactively (multi-user operation). Redirecting input and output operations to remote computers in application server mode is possible in the core Windows Server 2003 system using Terminal Services. However, this option first needs to be activated.

The multiple-user function of Windows Server 2003 Terminal Services should not be confused with the function that allows multiple users to be connected to the server through the network in a more general sense. Multi-user service without interactive logon to the server's user interface is frequently used for file, print, or directory services. In contrast, Terminal Services allows multiple interactive user sessions in parallel, with each of the sessions providing a desktop.

Terminal Services enables the connection of thin clients, also called *terminals*. Each client is assigned a session. Using this session, a logged-on user performs all operations on the server except keyboard, mouse, and monitor operations, which take place on the client itself. This design opens up interesting and powerful possibilities for Windows Server 2003 because it can be used in large corporate environments with extensive computer networks that are widely dispersed geographically. Windows Server 2003 with Terminal Services in application server mode allows simple centralization of administrative tasks and the use of low-maintenance clients. The technical term for this arrangement is *server-based computing*.

This book describes the installation, configuration, and administration of Terminal Services on Windows Server 2003. It not only presents the pure facts, but also describes how using Terminal Services affects administration and the outward characteristics of the system. Additionally, system extensions and third-party products are important to successfully deploy Windows Server 2003 Terminal Services. In particular, the MetaFrame product line by Citrix has an essential role.

Quick Start

Several requirements must be met before Windows Server 2003 Terminal Services can be used for the first time. To avoid a frustrating experience, please read the brief instructions found in the sections cited in the following list before connecting an independent terminal server on the network.

- For basic installation of the operating system on a network, see Chapter 2.

- For information on adding the terminal server functionality through the server configuration wizard in the Manage Your Server system tool, see Chapter 2.

- For information on setting up local users with a valid password as members of the Remote Desktop Users user group, see Chapter 4. Alternatively, you can use the predefined administrator account for the first logon.

- For information on supplying a suitable RDP client, see Chapter 3.

If a terminal server is located within a domain in the Active Directory, Chapter 4 supplies the necessary configuration information. When all requirements are *fully* met, you can proceed with testing Windows Server 2003 Terminal Services.

Windows Server 2003 comes with excellent information on Terminal Services, located in the Help and Support Center under Software Deployment\Terminal Services. It is highly recommended that you read these Help pages thoroughly before you work with a terminal server.

Book Structure

Microsoft Windows Server 2003 Terminal Services is divided into five major segments, each with a specific focus.

- **The basis of Windows Server 2003 Terminal Services**   Chapters 1 through 4 deal with the understanding the basics of Terminal Services, relevant network protocols and thin clients, configuration options, administration, and basic operation concepts.

- **Detailed operation concepts**   Chapters 5 through 8 examine in detail installing applications, using the registry, and using scripting mechanisms for the terminal server, as well as system security and stability.

- **System extensions for corporate environments**   Chapters 9 through 11 cover integrating and configuring the Citrix MetaFrame XP Presentation Server, managing MetaFrame environments, and running server farms in large corporate environments.

- **Web technologies for central distribution of Windows-based applications**   Chapters 12 and 13 focus on working with Windows-based applications on terminal servers that use Web technologies and application access portals.

- **Production environments**   Chapters 14 and 15 deal with optimizing, troubleshooting, and planning terminal server projects.

To understand this book, you should already be familiar with the basic concepts of Windows Server 2003 on a network. In particular, you should have at least basic knowledge of the standard administration tools, services, the registry, as well as network structures in domains and within the Active Directory Services.

This book is not intended to be a comprehensive textbook on installing and administering terminal servers. On the contrary, its aim is to present the essential concepts behind Windows Server 2003 Terminal Services. These concepts are then juxtaposed with realistic and tested reference scenarios that allow you to derive procedures for a real productive environment. It is also recommended that you read other publications by Microsoft and the different third-party manufacturers of extension tools.

Not all options of the tools and system components introduced are described in full. The author's intention is to fully cover one topic in each chapter, which means that descriptions of marginal areas of interest and the relevant system tools remain limited. This lends the chapters cohesiveness around one core topic. When necessary, the chapters refer to detailed descriptions in previous or succeeding chapters in this book.

Informational Notes

The following types of reader aids appear throughout this book:

Note   Additional notes on certain options or background information.

Tip   Interesting facts or techniques that allow a particularly elegant solution.

Important   Some functions are associated with a certain amount of risk. The "important" note is used to point those risks out to you at the appropriate place.

Caution   Contains valuable information about possible loss of data; be sure to read this information carefully.

Intended Audience

So who is the target audience of this book? First of all, the book addresses Windows Server and network administrators and experts who want to use Terminal Services. System integrators, technically savvy IT decision-makers, support staff, and security advisors are also part of the target group.

To get the most benefit from this book, you should at least have one copy of Windows Server 2003 that you can access as an administrator. You should also be able to install system extensions and applications on the server. An Internet connection is certainly helpful to download interesting tools and additional documentation.

In some chapters, we will look at the Microsoft .NET programming technique as it relates to .NET Windows Forms applications and .NET console applications. If you plan to copy the examples in your server environment, you should have available a Microsoft Visual Studio .NET development platform or the Microsoft .NET Framework SDK (Software Development Kit). You can download the latter free of charge from the Microsoft Web site or from the CD that accompanies this book.

Information Resources

It is essential for all administrators of a large computer network to have access to special information for their work. Microsoft and several other providers supply a full range of material and documentation for this purpose. Some of these resources will be cited repeatedly in this book. The most important resources are listed in the following sections.

Technical Network—TechNet

The subscription to TechNet gives you the complete collection of all available technical information on Microsoft products. The monthly CDs can be purchased directly from Microsoft or an authorized distributor.

Technical References

Resource Kits or technical references are books with accompanying CDs on Microsoft products. Resource Kits contain advanced information and special tools for administrators. Without the information and tools, it is much harder to manage systems in a professional environment. Selected tools included on the Microsoft Web site at *http://www.microsoft.com/windowsserver2003/techinfo/reskit/resourcekit.mspx* are mentioned frequently in this book.

Web Resources

The Internet is another source of information for Windows Server 2003 and Terminal Services. The following list includes a number of important URLs, although it is by no means comprehensive.

Label	Internet Address
Microsoft	
Windows Server 2003 Terminal Services site	*http://www.microsoft.com/windowsserver2003/technologies/terminalservices/default.mspx*
Support	*http://support.microsoft.com/*
Hardware Compatibility List	*http://www.microsoft.com/whdc/hcl/default.mspx*
Automated Deployment Service	*http://www.microsoft.com/windowsserver2003/techinfo/overview/ads.mspx*
Windows Logo	*http://www.microsoft.com/winlogo/default.mspx*
Platform SDK	*http://www.microsoft.com/msdownload/platformsdk/sdkupdate*
TechNet	*http://www.microsoft.com/technet/*
Developer Network	*http://msdn.microsoft.com/*
Office Resource Kit	*http://www.microsoft.com/office/ork*
Windows System Resource Management	*http://www.microsoft.com/windowsserver2003/downloads/wsrm.mspx*
Microsoft Press	*http://www.microsoft.com/mspress*
Citrix	
Knowledge Base	*http://knowledgebase.citrix.com/*
Portal/License Activation	*http://www.citrix.com/mycitrix*
Citrix Developer Network	*http://www.citrix.com/cdn*
Rick Dehlinger's TweakCitrix	*http://www.tweakcitrix.com*

Label	Internet Address
Client Solutions	
Tarantella	*http://www.tarantella.com*
New Moon	*http://www.newmoon.com*
Hob Soft	*http://www.hobsoft.com/www_us/home.htm*
UNIX RDP Client Rdesktop	*http://www.rdesktop.org*
WinConnect	*http://www.thinsoftinc.com*
Installation	
InstallShield	*http://www.installshield.com*
NetSupport	*http://www.netsupport.com*
OnDemand WinInstall	*http://www.wininstall.com*
Wise Solutions	*http://www.wise.com*
Desktop Management	
AppSense	*http://www.appsense.com*
AppLauncher	*http://www.applauncher.com*
TriCerat	*http://www.tricerat.com*
Softricity	*http://www.softricity.com*
Real Enterprise Solutions	*http://www.respowerfuse.com*
Emergent OnLine	*http://www.go-eol.com*
Load Tests	
Mercury Interactive	*http://www.mercuryinteractive.com*
Tevron	*http://www.tevron.com*
Scapa Technologies	*http://www.scapatech.com*
Macro and Script Tools	
KiXtart	*http://www.kixtart.org*
Insight Software Solution	*http://www.macroexpress.com*
Pitrinec Software	*http://www.pitrinec.com*
Wilson WindoWare	*http://www.winbatch.com*
TaskWare	*http://www.wintask.com*
Hiddensoft	*http://www.hiddensoft.com/autoit*
Script Horizon	*http://www.scripthorizon.com*

Label	Internet Address
Universal Printer Drivers	
ThinPrint	*http://www.thinprint.com*
UniPrint	*http://www.uniprint.net*
TriCerat	*http://www.tricerat.com*
Emergent OnLine	*http://www.go-eol.com*
Application Access Portals	
visionapp	*http://www.visionapp.com*
Panther	*http://www.pantherpowered.com*
Information	
WTS Technologies	*http://www.wtstek.com*
Technical Remote Computing	*http://dev.remotenetworktechnology.com*
SBC Hardcore User Page	*http://www.xs4all.nl/~soundtcr/*
SysInternals	*http://www.sysinternals.com*
TheThin	*http://www.thethin.net*
Thin-world.com	*http://thin-world.com/*
Daves Thinplace	*http://www.thinplace.de/*
Thin Planet	*http://www.thinplanet.com/*
SBC-Technet	*http://www.sbc-technet.com/*
Terminal Server Product Guide	*http://www.winntmag.com/Techware/InteractiveProduct/TerminalServer/*
Labmice.net	*http://www.labmice.net/terminalsrvcs/default.htm*

Service Packs, Updates, and Security Patches

Debugging is important for stabilizing a system. Microsoft, Citrix, and other manufacturers involved with Terminal Services under Windows Server 2003 provide *service packs* and *updates* free of charge on their Internet servers. Service packs usually replace a number of older system files and components with newer ones. Service packs and updates are for general troubleshooting and debugging; they also boost performance. Service packs are cumulative, which means that each of them contains the information and changes to its previous version. Before service packs are launched, it is recommended that you carefully read the experience reports published in the technical press. If a system runs properly with no obvious security gaps, it should not be changed.

> **Important**   Never touch a running system! This rule should also be observed under Windows Server 2003: Never install a service pack for no reason. Naturally, security gaps are always cause to install the related service pack, updates, or security patches.

Updates and security patches specifically remove certain sources of error in the run-time system, for instance, current security gaps. Updates and security patches should be installed when a server is directly affected by the danger created by an error or security gap. Knowledge Base articles often reference relevant updates and security patches.

About the CD-ROM

The CD accompanying this book contains additional information and software components, including the following files:

- **Scripts**   Sample scripts that are described in the book.
- **SpreadSheets**   A Microsoft Excel file containing the server resources calculation.
- **Tools**   Platform SDK, Microsoft .NET Framework SDK, Orca (Microsoft Installer Tool), and ACT (Microsoft Windows Application Compatibility Toolkit).
- **ValueAdd**   Additional tools and information by third parties on the terminal server market, such as SysInternals and AppSense.
- **Viewers**   Programs that display documents in different formats, for instance, Microsoft Word and Microsoft Excel.
- **Web**   Selected articles in HTML format, found in the Microsoft Knowledge Base.
- **White Papers**   Technical articles in Microsoft Word format.

Using the Companion CD-ROM

Insert the CD into the CD-ROM drive of your computer. If the *AutoRun* function is disabled on your computer, run the StartCD.exe file in the CD home directory to display the start screen. The menu items on the start screen reference the information on the CD.

Hardware Requirements

- Minimum 133 MHz in the Intel Pentium/Celeron family or the AMD k6/Athlon/ Duron family

- 128 MB memory

- 2 GB available hard disk space

- Display monitor capable of 800 x 600 resolution or higher

- CD-ROM drive

- Microsoft Mouse or compatible pointing device

Technical Support

Every effort has been made to ensure the accuracy of this book and the contents of the companion CD-ROM. If you have comments, questions, or ideas regarding this book or the companion CD-ROM, please send them to Microsoft Press using either of the following methods:

E-Mail *mspinput@microsoft.com*

Postal Mail Microsoft Press

Attn *Microsoft Windows Server 2003 Terminal Services: Editor*

One Microsoft Way

Redmond, WA 98052-6399

For additional support regarding the book and the companion CD-ROM (including answers to commonly asked questions about installation and use), visit the Microsoft Press Technical Support Web site at *http://www.microsoft.com/mspress /support/*. To connect directly to the Microsoft Press Knowledge Base and enter a query, visit *http://www.microsoft.com/mspress/support/search.asp*. For support information regarding Microsoft software, please connect to *http://support.microsoft.com*.

Chapter 1

The Concept of Terminal Services

Note This chapter introduces Microsoft Windows Server 2003 Terminal Services and includes a discussion of the basic features of Windows Server 2003 that play key roles in understanding Terminal Services. In this book, the term *terminal server* refers to Windows Server 2003 with Terminal Services in the application mode.

This chapter is designed to:

- Introduce you, through its history, to the possibilities that Windows Server 2003 Terminal Services offers.

- Familiarize you with the concepts of server-centered computing—the central topic of this book.

- Explain Windows Server 2003 and Terminal Services in detail.

- Describe the system architecture of Windows Server 2003, which allows multiuser operations without special modifications.

- Teach you the hardware selection criteria for terminal servers.

1

This chapter includes a detailed description of the operating-system architecture. The corresponding sub-chapter primarily targets experienced system architects and system engineers trying to optimize specific run-time environments. All other readers can safely skip that section and move on to the following chapters.

The History of Terminal Services

The Microsoft Windows Server 2003 product line includes Terminal Services, an optional extension of the operating system. It allows end-user applications or several Windows desktops to be used on different clients connected via a network. Applications are executed and data processed exclusively on the server.

Which server types support Terminal Services? For application servers, Terminal Services is provided with the Standard Server, Enterprise Server, and Datacenter Server. The following table lists important features of various server types. It also includes functions such as Remote Desktop to transfer the graphical user interface (GUI) to a remote computer for administration purposes, as well as the session directory to manage user sessions in server environments with capacity allocation mechanisms.

Table 1-1   Functions and System Requirements of Different Server Products (Enterprise Server and Datacenter Server Are Available in Both 32-Bit and 64-Bit Versions)

Function	Web Server	Standard Server	Enterprise Server	Datacenter Server
Terminal Services for application servers	No	Yes	Yes	Yes
Remote desktop for remote administration	Yes	Yes	Yes	Yes
Session directory	No	No	Yes	Yes
Number of CPUs supported	1–2	1–4	1–8	8–32
Maximum main memory supported (32-bit/64-bit versions)	2 GB	4 GB	32/64 GB	64/128 GB

Design Objectives

The primary design objective of Terminal Services was the display of many kinds of Microsoft Windows–based applications on multiple hardware platforms. To function properly, the applications must be able to run as is on Windows Server 2003 with Terminal Services enabled for application servers. By centralizing applications, the technology significantly reduces operating costs, especially in large corporate environments.

Moreover, Terminal Services under Windows Server 2003 provides a powerful option for distributing and updating software. It can replace or augment the Microsoft Systems Management Server and extends Windows capabilities, especially in large companies.

One secondary benefit of Terminal Services is the ability to eliminate so-called *dumb terminals* that are still in use at many companies. Windows Server 2003 in combination with Terminal Services opens up a migration path from a host environment to a more up-to-date environment.

In principle, a *terminal server* is a computer on which several users can work simultaneously while their screens can be displayed remotely. But is the platform a server or a client? The answer, as described in this book, is: An application server for several simultaneous users, who are logged on interactively to a single machine, is both a server *and* a client, depending on one's point of view.

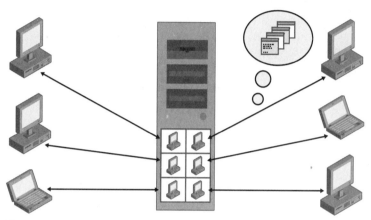

Figure 1-1   The terminal server multiple-user concept. A single server behaves like multiple Windows XP workstations whose output is redirected to multiple external devices.

The Development of Terminal Services

The Windows environment was developed in the 1980s to run on MS-DOS. The GUI was first introduced in November 1985. After the OS/2 initiative in cooperation with IBM to develop a successor to MS-DOS, Microsoft decided to work on a more progressive operating system that would support both Intel and other CPUs. The idea was to write the new operating system in a more sophisticated programming language (such as C) so that it could be ported more easily. In 1988, Microsoft hired David Cutler, the chief developer of Digital Equipment Corporation's VMS, to manage the Windows New Technology project.

In the early 1990s, Microsoft released Microsoft Windows 3.0. This gained a large user base and therefore played a key role in the development of the new Microsoft Windows NT system. The design work for Windows NT took two years; three more were required to write the related program code.

The first version of Windows NT was launched in May 1993. It was based on its smaller but very successful sibling, Windows 3.1. Windows and Windows NT had the same GUI. However, Windows NT was not based on MS-DOS; it was a completely new 32-bit operating system. From the very first version, Windows NT could run both text-based OS/2 and POSIX applications as well as the older DOS and Windows-based applications.

Over time, both Windows NT and Windows 3.1 continued to be developed. From the start, Windows NT was considered the more stable system, especially for professional environments. As companies introduced personal computers, Windows NT became the market leader due to its stability in spite of increasing hardware requirements.

When Windows NT versions 3.5 and 3.51 hit the market, Microsoft was not very interested in equipping its high-end operating system with multiple-user features like UNIX. Therefore, in 1994, Microsoft granted Citrix access to the Windows NT source code to develop and market a multiple-user expansion. The expansion was called WinFrame and was quite successful in several companies a few years ago.

Ed Iacobucci, the founder of Citrix, had already developed the WinFrame concepts. From 1978 to 1989, he worked on developing OS/2 at IBM. His vision that different computers be able to access OS/2 servers through a network led to the idea of a multiple-user system. IBM, however, did not recognize the potential such an environment held. Inspired by this concept Ed Iacobucci left IBM in 1989 to found Citrix. The first Citrix products were still based on OS/2 and enjoyed only modest commercial success. That changed only when the Windows NT source code was used.

WinFrame's great success and the increasing significance of thin client/server concepts led Microsoft on May 12, 1997, to license Citrix' multiple-user expansion, MultiWin for Windows NT. Part of the license agreement stipulated that Citrix would not launch a WinFrame version based on Windows NT 4.0. Microsoft provided this release on June 16, 1998, with the launch of Windows NT 4.0 Server, Terminal Server Edition (code name "Hydra").

> **Note**   Windows NT 4.0 Server, Terminal Server Edition, has been available only as an OEM version since August 2000. Due to the continued wide distribution of this platform, Microsoft made available the "NT 4 TSE Security Roll-Up Package" in April 2002.

One problem with Windows NT 4.0 was that the Terminal Server Edition was built on a modified version of the system kernel that required adapted service packs and hot fixes. This was addressed during the Windows 2000 design phase, when all needed modifications for multiple-user operation were integrated in the kernel from the start and corresponding system service and driver functions were realized—Windows 2000 Terminal Services. The single code base, designed to avert the obvious mistakes in UNIX and its many derivates, prevented a fragmentation of the Windows 2000 server market.

Unlike its predecessor, Windows 2000 did not require the purchase of an independent operating system for the multiple-user option. You simply enabled an integrated component. There was a single common system kernel for Windows 2000, regardless of the number of simultaneous users. The common kernel, of course, led to a standardization of service packs and hot fixes. All other system expansions or improvements immediately became available for terminal servers, too.

Compared to Windows NT 4.0, Terminal Server Edition, the new Windows 2000 Terminal Services included the option of using the clients' printer and clipboards from the server (printer redirection and clipboard redirection). Additionally, it was now possible to monitor sessions remotely; that is, one user could see another user's session and, with the corresponding permissions, could even interact with it.

To improve the integration of clients under Windows 2000, the Remote Desktop Protocol (RDP) protocol was optimized, a bitmap-caching option for raster images was introduced (bitmap caching), and access to client devices via virtual channels was created. A corresponding application programming interface (API) enabled the specific programming for multiple-user servers.

Before Windows Server 2003, Windows XP was launched as the new client platform on October 22, 2001. For the first time, client and server lines of the Windows NT code base were made available at different times. The standard installation of Windows XP also uses terminal server technologies for a number of tasks, such as the following:

- **Terminal server client**   Available in Windows XP Home Edition and Windows XP Professional. The new RDP client allows access to servers with activated Terminal Services.

- **Fast user switching**   Available in Windows XP Home Edition and Windows XP Professional. Users can run applications in the background while other users log on and work on the same Windows XP machine. Available in the Professional version only if the computer is not a member of a domain.

- **Remote assistance**   Available in Windows XP Home Edition and Windows XP Professional. A user can ask an expert for help and the expert can assume control of the user's screen. The objective is one-on-one support, generally in help desk environments. This technology allows shared access to the user's console. Access is configured through group policy. This feature is available at the Help and the Support Center Windows accessed through the Start menu by choosing the Help and Support option.

- **Remote desktop**   Only available in Windows XP Professional. The terminal server technology is available on the client platform. A user can operate a system under Windows XP Professional from another computer. The default setting allows only administrators to use this function. Additional users can be added through the integrated Remote Desktop User Group via the Control Panel.

During the installation of Windows Server 2003, Terminal Services is automatically set to Remote Desktop mode. To use Terminal Services, however, it must be activated via Workstation | Properties | Remote or the group policies. This allows the administrator easier access to the server over the network. Under Windows 2000, this mode was called *Remote Administration*, even though the basic function remains the same.

If Terminal Services is used in application server mode, it needs to be configured accordingly. Compared to Windows 2000 features, several changes and improvements were made.

- **Administrative tools**   Improved tools for Terminal Services administration.

- **Printing**   Improved printing via terminal servers. Local printers can now be integrated and reconnected automatically.

- **Redirecting drives and file systems**   Users can now see and use the local drive of their client during terminal server sessions.

- **Redirecting audio streams**   The audio output of a terminal server session can be redirected to the client platform.

- **Redirecting the clipboard**   Users can copy and paste between local and server-based applications.

- **Group policies**   Almost all Terminal Services features can now be managed with the help of the group policies.

- **WMI provider**   Most Terminal Services configurations can be executed by means of WMI (Windows Management Instrumentation) scripting.

- **Access rights**   Expansion of security features through new user groups and permission allocation.

- **Session directory**   Redirection of a user logon to an existing disconnected connection within a farm of terminal servers. This requires the installation of a corresponding service.

The RDP protocol also was considerably reworked and improved during the development of both Windows XP and Windows Server 2003.

All these expansions and improvements optimized Terminal Services for use in corporate environments. This book presents all its related functions and features in detail.

Server-Based Computing

The terminal server concept does not follow the usual approach to operating systems at Microsoft. It does not fit the notion of a "rich client" with local applications integrated into a network of high-performance servers that use a massive amount of resources. Neither does a terminal server match the typical environment of .NET-connected applications with components running on different platforms. On the other hand, the terminal server does support the concept of "server-based computing." It is based on a centralized, well-equipped server—which we could call the host—which many users log on to simultaneously to work interactively with the applications installed on that server. All the application components run exclusively on the server. The server is accessed via the network from low-maintenance clients equipped with basic functions only. These clients are also called *terminals*, which is how the term terminal server came about. The clients merely provide visual access to applications and a means to interact with them by keyboard and mouse. Depending on the clients' characteristics, additional input and output devices can be added.

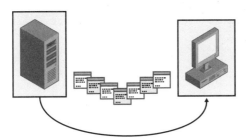

Figure 1-2   Schematic representation of the transfer of screen content from a Windows Server 2003 terminal server to a thin client over the network.

If this brings the world of mainframe computers to mind, you are not far from the mark. The terminal-host concept is not new and is now enjoying a revival in the terminal server. The basic idea was simply set on a new, state-of-the-art foundation, thus enabling access to modern, graphics-oriented applications without the need for modifications.

Different Client-Server Architectures

Even if terms such as terminal and host are often associated with it, the terminal server remains a special variant of the pure client/server environment. In a client/server architecture, certain resource-intensive tasks such as user authentication, printing, e-mail administration, database operations, or applications execution are limited to the server (the supplier). The clients (the customers) are linked to the server and provide a conduit for requesting services from the server. As a result, network traffic is usually quite low compared to other types of architectures. However, the server often demands high-end processing power, hard-drive capacity, main memory, and data throughput.

There are different levels of client/server options. They vary in their handling of the distributed application and data management, which in turn affects the efficiency of the server or client.

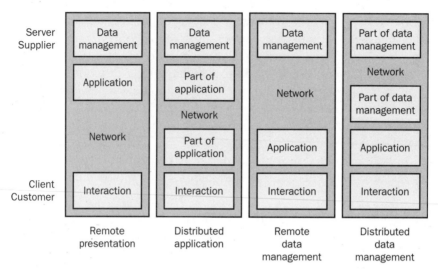

Figure 1-3   Different client/server options.

- **Remote presentation**   Remote presentation corresponds to a thin client having little native intelligence that depends directly on its server. The server is responsible for running all applications and managing data, whereas the client handles display, keyboard and mouse connections. X terminals, "green terminals" on mainframe computers, or terminal server clients are examples of this type of client. You could also include a Web browser that displays HTML pages in this category because all the "intelligence" needed to create these pages resides on the Web server.

- **Distributed application**   The concept of a distributed application is realized in many network systems where the client needs a certain amount of native intelligence to optimize the processing of complex tasks. For instance, database requests are created on the client to be run on a database server. Seldom-used or computation-bound components of a client application can be transferred to a server. The latter option exploits the strengths and available resources of both the client and the server. However, due to their high degree of distribution, these applications often require a major human effort to develop and maintain, such as SQL databases or Siebel systems. A Web browser also falls into this category if, in addition to HTML pages, it runs local scripts that transfer specific application logic to the client. These scripts can be loaded with the HTML data stream and are usually based on Visual Basic Script or JScript (or JavaScript).

- **Remote data management**   Remote data management is used by many companies that have a PC infrastructure: all the application programs are found locally on the client, and only data is saved in a central location. This permits simple strategies for backing up and managing user data, thus requiring a less complex server structure. One clear disadvantage, however, is the level of management required to install and administer applications. Experienced users and developers favor this model because they in large part retain control over their clients.

- **Distributed data management**   The distributed data management model is every central administrator's nightmare. Not only are applications stored on the client, but also some data as well, which makes it very difficult to manage and secure. Even though the user retains most control over the client computer, he or she would be at a loss in the event of a hardware or software error. The loss of a local hard drive could cause damage to the company due to un-recoverable data. The connected servers are only used for occasional data archiving and perhaps accessing e-mail or the Internet.

Terminal Servers in Client/Server Environments

A terminal server requires the integration of thin client software, thin clients, or terminals. It corresponds to the first of the client/server options (remote presentation) mentioned earlier and therefore has the advantage of central administration. The other client/server options can be associated with different popular computing concepts as well, which helps classify them. For example, a PC in a local area network (LAN) falls under remote data management, whereas a classic client/server solution is a distributed application.

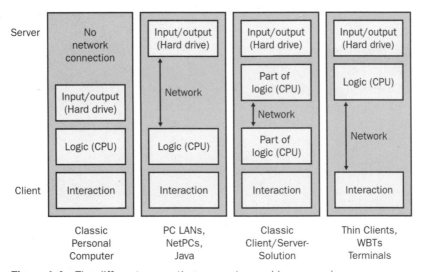

Figure 1-4   The different computing concepts used in companies.

Nevertheless, a bi-level client/server model is inadequate and falls short of reality. Most of the time real environments have several layers. A client accesses an application or the Web server on the intranet, which in turn accesses a file server, a print server, a database server, or an e-mail server. In this way, the multilevel model meets the not-so-new requirement for complex application programs: the separation of presentation/interaction, program logic, and data management.

The real challenge for system administrators lies in providing and controlling such a complex environment. The reason is that often several client/server models are combined in corporate terminal server environments. For instance, Microsoft Outlook, a client application, accesses an Exchange server which is a distributed application. If, however, Outlook is not installed directly on the client PC but on the terminal server, this model would resemble a remote presentation. The processing logic for the Exchange data in Outlook is separate from its display on the terminal server client. Even though it seems awkward at first, this method has definite advantages over other models.

Windows Server 2003 and Terminal Services

Terminal Services is available for all members of the latest Windows server family and can be activated at any time. It can be accessed on the Web Server only in remote desktop mode, so it is not a terminal server in the usual sense. The terminal server component provides the graphical user interface to a remote device via the LAN or an Internet connection.

The Different Terminal Server Modes

In Windows Server 2003, Terminal Services is available in two varieties: application server mode, which must be installed as a component, or remote desktop mode, which is used for remote administration of the server and requires special permissions to access.

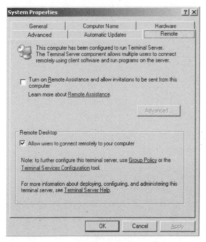

Figure 1-5   Ability to activate remote desktop connections via My Computer | Properties | Remote.

Application Server

A terminal server running in application server mode is an efficient and reliable way to furnish Windows-based applications on a network. This terminal server represents a central installation point for applications that are accessed simultaneously by several users from their respective clients.

> **Note**   If applications are already installed on Windows Server 2003 and Terminal Services is later activated in application server mode, some of the applications might not work properly. A multiple-user environment has special configuration requirements. These requirements are described in Chapter 5.

Terminal servers in application server mode also allow Windows-based applications to run on clients that are not running the Windows operating system. However, additional third-party (for example, Citrix) products must be used to realize this option.

> **Note**   The central topic of this book is operating a terminal server in the application server mode.

Remote Desktop

The remote administration mode was first introduced under Windows 2000 Terminal Services. Under Windows Server 2003, this mode was renamed *remote desktop* due to its relation to Windows XP. It was developed mainly to allow remote access to a server running on Windows 2000 or Windows Server 2003. This enables the administrator to access all graphical user interfaces across the network, including all their administrative tools for installed Microsoft BackOffice applications or other server applications.

A server's performance or BackOffice application compatibility should not be compromised by remote administration. Therefore, remote desktop mode should use only a minimum of memory and processor resources. This allows for a maximum of two remote administrator sessions per console session. These administrators do not need special licenses.

Some programs require a direct logon to the console for administrative tasks. Under Windows 2000, it was not possible to invoke the console remotely via Terminal Services. Windows Server 2003 allows you to run a console remotely by using the */console* parameter. Installing Microsoft Office 2000 in a "normal" session may cause MSI error 2577, whereas installation via a console session runs smoothly.

> **Note** *Consoles* are input and output devices physically connected to the server hardware with Windows Server 2003 installed that has Terminal Services activated.

Required Components

Terminal Services and its two modes represent a high-performance approach to reducing operating costs and administration of a Windows environment. Thin clients connected over the network are the main factor. A multiple-user environment, therefore, consists of the following three groups of components:

- **Terminal server** Windows Server 2003 with Terminal Services installed that permits simultaneous user sessions. Standard applications can be used in each session.

- **Communications protocol** A key component is the protocol enabling remote clients to access the terminal server. The standard protocol is RDP (remote desktop protocol).

- **Access software on a client** Software on a thin client, a Web browser, or a standard PC that enables access to a terminal server over the network. Client hardware and software display the user interface (desktop) and allows input by keyboard and mouse.

This book introduces and describes in detail all three groups of components.

System Architecture

To enable Windows Server 2003 to support multiple simultaneous users, the operating system must meet several basic prerequisites. This includes the standard components of Windows Server 2003 such as memory management and very specific Windows components and services, such as Windows Terminal Services. The following provides a detailed description of the system architecture with a view toward support of multiple users.

The Windows Server 2003 architecture still corresponds to the first model of Windows NT. It combines the attributes of several operating system models, including a layer-oriented approach and a client/server concept. The internal system structure of Windows Server 2003 is divided into a series of components. Some parts of the operating system run in a highly privileged and protected mode (Executive), whereas others run in an application mode. It is extremely interesting to look closely at the individual modes to gain a better understanding of terminal servers and how they support simultaneous users.

The structure of Windows Server 2003 is based on a kernel architecture that is divided into a privileged core mode and the less protected user mode. This characteristic feature of Windows architecture is also evident in each mode's strictly separate address area and is based on the processor's ring structure. This design allows each program module to be categorized by priority level.

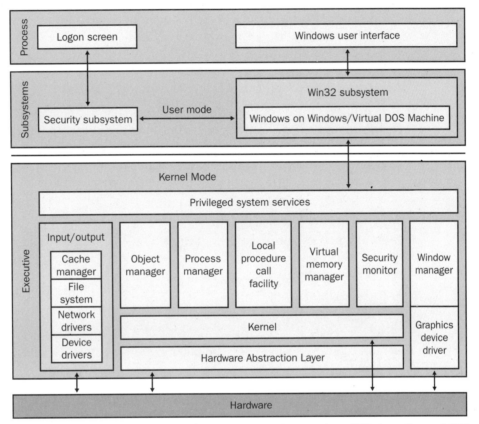

Figure 1-6   The operating system structure of the 32-bit version of Windows Server 2003.

An Intel CPU (as of generation 80386) or compatible processors normally offer four priority levels. The top priority, that is, the highest level of protection with permissions to execute privileged operations and to communicate with the hardware, is assigned priority level zero. Windows Server 2003 uses only ring (level) zero for the core mode (core and system services) and ring three for the user mode (all other processes). Rings one and two are not used at all.

If we compare Windows Server 2003 with other operating systems, we encounter numerous terms that serve to characterize as well as differentiate. Let's look briefly at the terminology and how it relates to Terminal Services to establish a common basis for the following chapters.

- **Cooperative multitasking** This type of operating system allows the simultaneous execution of different applications. The applications must cooperate with each other by frequently relinquishing processor control to another application. This concept is the basis of older Windows systems, for example, Windows for Workgroups 3.11. On a modern terminal server under Windows Server 2003, we can now run programs developed for cooperative multitasking. However, many features of the historic run-time environment must be simulated and extended to enable the simultaneous execution of the corresponding applications. These applications often tend to consume vast resources on the host system because they were never designed for such a high degree of process control.

- **Preemptive multitasking** This type of operating system provides strict allocation control of applications that run simultaneously. The time allowed for accessing the processor or processors can be determined exactly and does not depend on the current status of each application. The application status is saved when the application relinquishes processor control. The status is restored when the application resumes control. A terminal server is optimized to run programs developed for this kind of operating system.

- **Memory protection** Windows Server 2003 includes mechanisms that successfully keep an application from accessing the memory of the operating system or another application. When using Terminal Services, it is also important to strictly separate processes of one user from those of another to avoid mutual interference.

- **Multiprocessing** This is the ability of an operating system to use several processors (CPUs) within one computer at the same time. This feature is crucial for a terminal server because it directly influences the terminal server's scalability in terms of the number of simultaneous users. Unlike many other server scenarios, a terminal server often needs to execute many simultaneous processes, which makes its ability to evenly distribute the load among several processors extremely important.

- **Multithreading** This is the ability of an operating system to execute several program threads (subprocesses) within one application. If a system has the corresponding equipment, the programs can be run on different processors, contributing to the scalability of the system. However, this only works if highly resource-intensive processes of a server application (such as a database or a Web server) are divided into smaller units (threads) allowing distribution to several processors. This is usually not the case with terminal servers because relatively small user applications are normally run on them. Their performance is enhanced because all threads of an application instance are then bound on one processor, which reduces the thread synchronization efforts required for executing a common task.

> **Note**   The term *hyperthreading* has been introduced in connection with modern Intel processor generations. Hyperthreading refers to separating one physical processor into two logical processors. In certain scenarios, this technology improves the execution of parallel tasks, especially at the thread level.

The Privileged System Components

Processes running in core mode have the task of ensuring that the basic functions of the operating system work. Therefore, they need to be prioritized according to their importance and complexity. High-priority kernel processes control access to the hardware, manage the available memory, and provide resources to processes running in user mode.

Here are the executive-mode components in ascending order.

Hardware Abstraction Layer (HAL)

The hardware abstraction layer is a component named Hal.dll. It must be modified when Windows Server 2003 is ported to a different processor, bus architecture, or any other computer architecture. The Terminal Services functions do not require a modified hardware abstraction layer.

Kernel

The kernel is a highly protected component of the operating system and is considered the central monitoring instance of the operating system. The kernel processes interruptions, handles exceptions, determines the runtime of threads (subprocesses), allocates processor time, synchronizes processors, and makes objects and interfaces available.

The so-called "scheduler" is an important part of the kernel. It allocates processor time and determines the sequence in which threads are executed. The next thread in line receives a certain amount of time. When its time is up, the scheduler checks if another thread with the same priority level needs to be run. If so, all attributes of the current thread are saved and the next thread and its attributes proceed. Threads are grouped by priority level and handled accordingly by the scheduler.

Object Manager

The object manager creates, manages, removes, and protects operating system objects. These objects usually include interfaces, memory, processes, threads, files, directories, and so on. All objects have their own properties, methods, access information and identification. Processes under Windows Server 2003 use object identification to manipulate the objects.

The object manager also monitors the Windows Server 2003 namespace. The namespace is responsible for identifying objects in the local computer environment in a hierarchical organization. Object names are saved to a location depending on the object type. Only selected object types are visible for user applications.

Because of Terminal Services, there are two namespaces for creating objects in a system running Windows Server 2003. Regardless of the session context that created an application, the system-wide namespace is visible to all applications across the system. The user-specific namespace, however, manages the objects related only to the applications that originated in the same session.

To simplify the management of namespaces under Windows Server 2003, the system-wide namespace and the console-session namespace (mostly, but not necessarily, session ID 0) are linked. All objects created in the console session are automatically assigned to the system-wide namespace. In this way, Windows services or generally accessible applications do not need special handling for all users to access them. They only need to be installed or started within the console session.

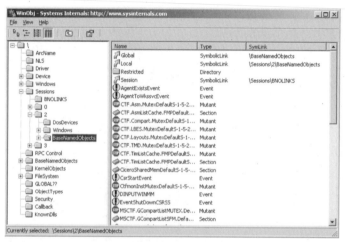

Figure 1-7 The objects on a terminal server displayed by WinObj by Systems Internals. One console session (0) and two user sessions (2 and 3) are shown.

Process Manager

The process manager manages process and thread objects. A process is defined as an address space, a set of resources, and a set of threads that run within the context of the process. A *thread* is the smallest time-controlled unit that can run within the system. The process manager provides all standard services for creating and using processes and their threads within the context of a subsystem.

Local Procedure Call Facility (LPC)

Local Procedure Calls (LPC) are used for inter-process communication on a local computer running Windows Server 2003. Local Remote Procedure Calls (RPC) are built on LPC. Processes can directly access each others address spaces so long as the security on a target process object allows it. All processes running under a given user account can access each others memory and many applications rely on shared memory for inter-process communication.

Virtual Memory Manager

The Virtual Memory Manager manages memory and swap files. It is a popular method of expanding physical memory by reserving space on the disk for physical memory areas not currently in use so that other programs can use it. Swapping allows the total memory required by all the applications to exceed actual physical memory.

The 32-bit variant of Virtual Memory Manager under Windows Server 2003 occupies a default virtual address space of 4 GB for each process started on a terminal server. The virtual addresses are then mapped to the physical pages of the main memory. Two GB each of virtual address space are reserved for user-specific and system-specific data. The user-specific part offers an individualized view of the memory area for the process. This allows a thread to access its own memory within a process, without allowing access to the memory of a different process. The system-specific part is available to all processes, allowing consistent access to all kernel services.

> **Note**   The information on available memory focuses on the use of "normal" application programs and does not apply to the special server applications, such as relational database systems. Standard applications for end users usually do not have routines that require using memory resources in this way. Therefore, all special techniques used to virtually expand the 32-bit address space and modify the memory allocation between user-specific and system-specific data are not discussed here.

The common system-specific portion of memory is naturally problematic where multiple simultaneous user sessions are concerned. Each session needs its own subsystems and drivers. Windows Server 2003 provides an individual kernel address space for each user session, the so-called *session space*. This is where the image of each session's Window Manager and the graphics and printer drivers are stored.

To manage this allocation, the Virtual Memory Manager assigns each new user session an identification—the session ID. Each process is now linked to its session space through its session ID. In this way, an application does not differentiate between a terminal server session and a Windows XP computer session. In a nutshell, a terminal server uses session space to create a virtual computer for each session.

Security Reference Monitor

The security reference monitor controls the security standards on the local computer. It provides its services for both the privileged system components and the subsystems running in user mode. Whenever a user or a process attempts to open an object, the security reference monitor checks for the required permissions. If the user or process ID indicates that the required permissions appear in the access control lists (ACLs), the object can be opened and used.

The security reference monitor also generates security-related administrative messages. These messages are stored in the event log.

Input/Output system

The input/output system coordinates and manages the data streams received and sent by Windows Server 2003. It's main task is to link different input and output drivers with standardized interfaces.

Generally, the input/output system consists of the following components:

- **Device driver**   Supports all peripheral devices such as printers, hard disks, mice, and scanners.

- **Network driver**   Connects network cards and protocols. Also provides a redirector mechanism enabling access to resources such as files or printer queues via the network.

- **File system driver**   Provides access to various file systems such as NTFS, FAT32, or FAT. Combined with the redirector, it allows connections to other file systems in the network, such as Novell NetWare.

- **Cache manager**   Handles intermediate storage of frequently used files in the main memory for the input/output system.

Graphical Output System

The Windows Server 2003 graphical output system is based on a window manager. The window manager represents the system components that display all graphical screen elements and manage the windows (filename: Win32k.sys). The Graphics Device Interface (GDI) provides the functions required to display graphical elements for unmanaged code (that is, traditional 32-bit Windows programs) on the monitor and to communicate with printers. For managed code, as deployed in .NET, the graphical interface to create local, Windows-based applications is called GDI+. The operating system manages both GDI and GDI+ in parallel. The GDI-DLL is located in the System32 subdirectory of the installation folder (such as C:\Windows). The components of GDI+ (filename: GdiPlus.dll) can be found in the WinSxS subdirectory of the installation folder. The .NET runtime environment is able to support several versions in parallel.

Under Windows NT or Windows 2000, the graphical elements of the user interface could be modified only slightly. A Windows Server 2003 with a Windows XP base, however, offers more options. For instance, by selecting alternative "themes," the user can customize the basic appearance of windows and other graphical elements. This does not alter the function of the graphical elements, just their attributes, such as shape, color, and position.

When executed, all applications call Win32 or .NET standard functions for graphical display. These functions are forwarded as requirements to the window manager. The window manager responds by invoking the corresponding internal graphical functions. The graphical system then communicates with the corresponding operating system drivers without needing to know anything about the physical hardware. It is actually the drivers that modify the data stream, enabling the data to display on the output device. The GDI and GDI+ drivers form a layer between the applications in user mode and the graphics drivers in privileged mode.

OpenGL and Microsoft DirectX define two additional graphical interfaces for Windows Server 2003. They are independent of GDI/GDI+ and handle special tasks that do not usually play key roles on terminal servers. Conceptually, both interfaces can be used on terminal servers, but they would consume too many resources and significantly slow the output speed on remote clients. We only mention them to round out the list.

- **OpenGL**   Functional interface to create professional 3-D applications (CAD, Virtual Reality, etc.).

- **DirectX**   Direct and very quick addressing of multimedia input and output devices for applications with real-time character (particularly games).

A terminal server significantly increases the complexity of a graphical output system. Because multiple interactive users are supported, each corresponding output must be treated differently. Therefore, there is not just one output system; several (virtual) output channels to clients must be established.

The Subsystems in User Mode

In user mode, Windows Server 2003 provides several closed subsystems for executing applications. They are part of the operating system and communicate with the kernel components in the layer underneath. Their screen output is regulated via the Win32 graphical interface.

- **Win32**   This subsystem (called Csrss.exe) controls the execution of 32-bit Windows processes and threads. It also includes the (Windows-on-Windows (WoW) module. This module represents a 16-bit Windows system that runs corresponding programs. Another module is the Virtual DOS Machine (VDM), which runs DOS programs. However, direct access to the hardware is not granted.

- **Security**   A subsystem to authenticate users and monitor the degree of security of the other subsystems (filename: Lsass.exe).

In addition to the subsystems, there are always a number of other system processes in user mode on a Windows Server 2003.

These are the most important additional system processes:

- **Windows administration**   This process controls the graphical interface presented to the user after logon (filename: Explorer.exe). It positions the individual application programs on the desktop. Along with the underlying software layers of the graphical system, this process determines how the user moves through the window system and the functions that open, change, move, and refresh windows and their contents.

- **Session manager**   This process manages sessions and is the first process in user mode created after system start. It takes care of several initialization activities related to, for example, the local procedure calls, environment variables, the window manager, subsystems, and the logon process (filename: Smss.exe). While the system runs, the session manager also handles the creation of new user sessions.

- **Logon process**   This process controls the interactive user logon and communicates with the security subsystem (filename: WinLogon.exe).

- **Service controller or service manager**   The administrative instance for background processes that run even if no user is logged on to the system (filename: Services.exe). Several Windows components are realized as background processes, such as printer spoolers, event protocols, remote procedure calls, and many network services.

Adaptations to Multiple-User Operation

To better understand the system's behavior and Windows Server 2003's multiuser capability, we need to take a detailed look at several key components and how they interact. On the one hand, there is the connection of keyboards, mice, and monitors on remote clients. On the other hand, a strictly separate session for each user on the terminal server needs to be managed.

As described in the introduction to the Virtual Memory Manager, each user session has its own address space within the system. This space is used to virtualize the required kernel components of the 32-bit subsystem (Win32k.sys) and the system drivers for each user. The operating system was optimized for terminal services so that several instances of adjusted kernel components can be started. All processes still need to be linked to a user session, which also affects the administration of the virtual memory. The central system resources (memory, CPU, and kernel objects) are allocated according to individual users.

> **Note**   In general, the 32-bit subsystem (Win32k.sys) is suitable for multiple-user operation, even if Windows Server 2003 has not been configured as a terminal server in application mode.

Services and Drivers

The Windows Server 2003 multiple-user function is primarily based on a special Windows service (Terminal Services) and on the corresponding device drivers. Terminal Services allows users to establish an interactive connection to a remote computer. Remote desktop, remote support, and terminal servers work only when supported by this Windows service.

If a client is connected via Terminal Services, it receives an individual virtualized user session. This session has its own *Csrss* and *WinLogon* processes in user mode and access to both the kernel and the display driver. The monitor, mouse, and keyboard respond via the network instead of locally. The following drivers are installed on the system to make this work:

- **Termdd.sys**   General terminal server driver
- **Rdpcdd.sys**   RDP Miniport
- **Rdpdr.sys**   RDP device redirection
- **Rdpwd.sys**   RDP stack driver for TCP/IP

The configuration of each user session on a remote client enables it to load its own drivers to connect the monitor, keyboard, and mouse. Mouse and keyboard drivers communicate with the network protocol via a multiple-use instance of the general terminal server driver and of the RDP drivers. All client sessions provided through the RDP protocol are either available (waiting) or interactive (bound). The waiting thread of a potential RDP session listens via TCP port 3389 for a connection request from the client side.

The following processes are started for each user session:

- **Winlogon.exe**   Manages the users' logon information. (The process runs within the system context.)
- **Csrss.exe**   Handles the individualized graphical output. (The process runs within the system context.)
- **Explorer.exe**   Manages the graphical output in user mode. (The process runs within the context of the interactive user.)

What makes the graphics system of a terminal server special is that the graphics requests of a user session are not forwarded to the console's display driver (unless the user is working directly at the console). Instead, the requests are sent to the virtual graphics driver that can communicate with the client via the RDP protocol.

Connections and Sessions

Together with Terminal Services, the session manager (Smss.exe) handles the individual connections between a terminal server and its clients. The two generate and dispose of session objects that are responsible for the individual copies of Csrss.exe and WinLogon.exe. This concept is completely independent of the communications protocol used.

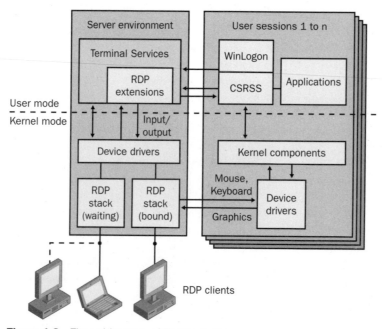

Figure 1-8   The achitecture of Terminal Server.

Process Priorities

Of particular interest are the priority levels of processes and threads related to system responses and started applications. Processes in user mode can have six different priority levels: low, below normal, normal, above normal, high, and real-time. Within these process classes, the individual threads can take on seven different levels: idle, low, below normal, normal, above normal, high, and real-time. With regard to the system, a thread has a basic priority of 0 through 31, which is a combination of process class and thread class priorities.

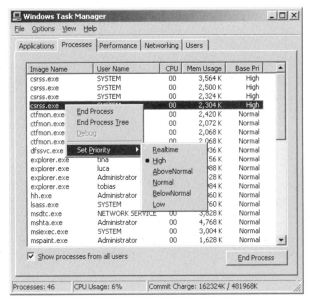

Figure 1-9   Basic priority levels of processes as shown in the Task Manager.

In most cases, the basic priority of a process is selected so that it runs in one of the standard priorities. These priorities range from 24 (real-time), 13 (high), 10 (above normal), 8 (normal), 6 (below normal) to 4 (low). Some system processes, however, have a slightly higher priority on start-up to optimize overall system behavior. This goes for all current foreground processes, that is, those applications with a focus on input. On a terminal server, these are always multiple applications when multiple users are logged on interactively. In the Windows Server 2003 default setting, foreground processes have priority level 8, as do background processes.

The *Smss* session manager establishes new user sessions. Therefore, its performance is key to the terminal server, thus its high priority level of 11. The Services.exe service manager that handles background processes (the Windows services) also has a slightly higher priority level (9).

The *Csrss* Win32 subsystem and the *WinLogon* process are created individually for each user session. Together with the *Lsass* security subsystem, they are the critical components in terms of a terminal server's ability to respond. Therefore, these components have a high priority level (13).

The .NET Runtime Environment

Up to this point, we have considered Windows Server 2003 solely as the successor to Windows 2000 Server, with some additional functions and improvements. But some of the puzzle pieces are still missing, such as the link to the .NET Framework. What exactly is the basic idea behind the .NET concept for Windows Server 2003?

Looking at .NET from the operating system perspective in providing applications, there is a fundamental difference between it and its predecessors: .NET allows a *different* type of program execution. While the previous 32-bit Windows-based applications were able to communicate directly with the operating system, the new Framework applications require an intermediate layer—the .NET runtime environment (common language runtime). The runtime environment represents the instance where all .NET applications are executed. Only the runtime environment communicates with the operating system once it has translated the .NET application's byte code, and then it controls execution. To display a windows-oriented application (Windows Form), the .NET runtime environment basically requests the same graphics information from the operating system as a 32-bit application.

Any compiler that writes Microsoft Intermediate Language Code (MSIL code) can be used to create a Framework application. The .NET runtime environment executes the MSIL code on application start-up. Code that is executed within the .NET runtime environment is called *managed code*, while code that is executed beyond these limits is called *unmanaged code*.

What is the advantage of this type of construct? The .NET runtime environment serves as an abstraction layer for a virtual machine that represents the only relevant target environment for the developer. If the .NET runtime environment is available for different hardware platforms, a program created once does not need to be modified. The runtime environment provides the translated requests to the operating system. It also carries out other important tasks, such as monitoring security guidelines, isolating memory areas, managing memory resources, and handling exceptions. .NET programs can be developed in all languages that adhere to a standard schema for the definition of data types and whose compiler generates valid MSIL code.

How do Framework applications behave on terminal servers? They behave no differently than 32-bit programs optimized for running on terminal servers. The .NET runtime environment is perfectly able to handle multiple users who simultaneously use Framework applications on the server. Thus, Windows Server 2003 with Terminal Services activated and running in application server mode is able to execute both managed and unmanaged code for multiple users and to send the graphical output of the applications to the corresponding clients via RDP.

How the Components Interact

If Windows Server 2003 with Terminal Services activated is started in application server mode, all components need to interact seamlessly. Only then is multiple-user operation with all its functions possible. So what exactly happens between boot-up of the terminal server and connection to a remote user?

1. When the terminal server is booted up, some system components are individually initialized.

2. The console session of the server is started. This includes connecting local resources, such as keyboard, mouse, and monitor, via the corresponding device drivers.

3. The Windows Service Terminal Services is started. It manages future user sessions.

4. Terminal Services initiates the session manager that handles all user sessions except the console session.

5. When the session manager start-up phase is complete, monitoring threads are generated for each communications protocol and every network card so configured.

6. The connection request of a client is received by the thread in charge and forwarded to the session manager. The thread immediately resumes listening for connection requests.

    Upon a connection request, the session manager and the Virtual Memory Manager generate a user session with a unique ID. The user session has an individual WinLogon.exe, Csrss.exe, and Explorer.exe. The Terminal Services drivers redirect input and output of keyboard, mouse, and monitor.

7. The user sees the logon screen for Windows Server 2003 on the client. Logging on enables interactive use of the desktop during the session.

8. When a user starts an application, the process manager is always able to map it appropriately based on the unique session ID.

This description, however, is greatly simplified. Some things are still missing, such as all the processes for negotiating protocol parameters, assigning session IDs, and licensing. All these details are discussed in the chapters that follow.

System Resources

Windows Server 2003 is still a standard server, even with Terminal Services activated in application server mode. However, some characteristics do distinguish it from a standard installation, especially in terms of services, drivers, devices, modules, and environment variables. All these components can be monitored via Control Panel and can be modified, if necessary.

Figure 1-10   The Administration Tools in the Control Panel.

Windows Services for Terminal Servers

On Windows Server 2003, background processes that run even when no users are logged on are known as *Windows services*. On other systems, they are often called *daemons*. These services can run within the context of a certain user and therefore, the corresponding security guidelines apply. Several services are included in Windows Server 2003 and many of them must be activated for the system to operate properly. The services manager controls these services. Only administrators have full access to this function, either through the services icon on the control panel, computer administration, or through command line interface.

Many of the basic services are executed within the context of the Services.exe program. This program is directly linked to the services manager. Other services have their own executable file but can directly depend on the existence of other services. Some services can be bundled in a service host. This has the advantage that separately managed services are not interrupted if one service malfunctions. Only a service makes Windows Server 2003 a "real" server.

A terminal server has two special Windows services that are used for multiple-user operation.

- **Terminal Services**   Allows multiple users to create interactive connections, display the desktop, and see applications on remote clients. This service is the basis for remote desktops, remote support, and terminal servers.

- **Terminal Services Session Directory**   Forwards a connection request to a terminal server in a load-sharing system. If this service is stopped, all connection requests are directed to the first available server.

Additionally, the following service is necessary on at least one computer involved in this interaction:

- **Licensing logging**   Monitors and logs the client access-licensing process for some parts of the operating system (such as Internet Information Services, terminal server, and file/print server) and for products that are not part of the operating system, such as Microsoft SQL Server and Microsoft Exchange Server. If this service is interrupted, licensing is forced but not monitored.

Right after its start, the Terminal Services Windows service waits for a connection request from a suitable client. Together with the Virtual Memory Manager, it assigns each user session generated during a client connection a unique identification number (session ID).

When a terminal server is rebooted, the session ID numbers start at zero and increment from there. As the console session is always first, its session ID is 0. If no other users log on to the system interactively, the terminal server initially behaves like a "normal" Windows server, even though it has been optimized for multiple-user operation.

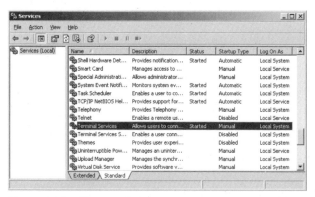

Figure 1-11   Display of services.

Note   Terminal Services is also loaded on a server not running in application server mode. This is done because besides managing the console session, Terminal Services enables administrative access to the server, that is, using the remote desktop. This explains why Terminal Services is launched when the console session is initialized, even though its auto start type is set to Manual. It is not easy for the administrator to interrupt it and deactivation of this service is strongly discouraged.

Terminal Server Drivers and Devices

A driver is a program used by certain devices—such as modems, network adapters, and printers—to communicate with Windows Server 2003. Even if a device is installed on the system, Windows Server 2003 can use it only after the corresponding driver has been installed and configured. If a device appears in the Hardware Compatibility List (HCL), Windows Server 2003 usually has the appropriate driver. On start-up of the computer, the device drivers (for all activated devices) are loaded automatically and run invisibly in the background.

Terminal Services clients also have devices, such as the keyboard, mouse, and monitor, that must communicate with the server. Because they are not physically located on the server, they are called *virtual devices*. These devices are managed via a corresponding terminal device driver.

In concept, the terminal device driver converts command sequences to and from the virtual device into network calls, thus enabling communication with the physical device on the client. This is comparable to the redirector of the file system under Windows Server 2003 when accessing files on the network.

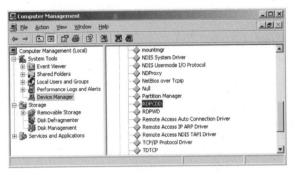

Figure 1-12   Device manager for non-PNP drivers.

Device redirection for the terminal server is therefore also displayed in the device manager for computer administration.

> **Note**   Some devices display in computer administration only when the option Show Hidden Devices is selected under the View menu.

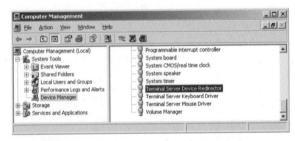

Figure 1-13   Device Manager for system devices.

The device manager is an administrative program that enables you to manage the devices in a computer. It allows you to display and modify device characteristics, update device drivers, configure device settings, and remove devices.

If you select the device redirector properties in the device manager, the provider, the date, the version, and the digital signer of the corresponding driver are displayed.

Figure 1-14   Device redirector properties in a terminal server.

The driver details of device redirection display the path and the name of the corresponding file. The file version is of interest for verifying possible modifications. Under Windows Server 2003, however, system file protection (SFP) should prevent any such modifications.

Figure 1-15   Driver details on terminal server device redirector.

> **Note** All currently loaded kernel drivers can also be displayed through the **driverquery** command in the command line.

Environment Variables

Windows Server 2003 defines various environment variables that are available to each user and his or her applications during run time. In particular, these variables are used for global administration of both logical name allocations and directories. The user may also define additional environment variables.

An environment variable is referenced by its logical name surrounded by percent (%) signs. For instance, the computer's name can be referenced by the *%ComputerName%* variable. Upper and lower case rules are of no importance here. Environment variables are often used on terminal servers to perform an evaluation during logon scripts to adapt a terminal server session when a user logs on.

These are the most important environment variables for a terminal server:

- **%AllUsersProfile%**   Was introduced under Windows 2000; includes the path to the generally valid "All users" profile.
- **%AppData%**   Another recently introduced environment variable; includes the user-specific path to the application data.
- **%ClientName%**   Name of the client; the user works interactively on the terminal server via this variable.
- **%ComputerName%:**   Name of the computer onto which the user is logged on interactively.
- **%HomeDrive%**   Drive letter of a user's individual home directory.
- **%HomePath%**   The complete path to the user's individual home directory.
- **%LogonServer%**   The server responsible for the user's authentication.
- **%OS%**   ID of the operating system ("Windows_NT" under Windows NT, Windows 2000, and Windows Server 2003).
- **%SessionName%**   Name of the user session on the terminal server.
- **%SystemDrive%**   Drive letter of the folder containing the operating system.
- **%SystemRoot%**   The directory containing the operating system.
- **%Temp% and %Tmp%**   Path to the user-specific temporary folder.
- **%UserDNSDomain%**   DNS name of the domain where the user account is located.
- **%UserDomain%**   The domain where the user account is located.
- **%UserName%**   Name of the current user.

- ***%UserProfile%***   Complete path to the profile of the current user.
- ***%WinDir%***   Path for access to .ini files.

Some environment variables can be modified via the System tool in the Control Panel. The *Set* command without additional parameters permits the output of all environment variables at the prompt.

> **Note**   In the following chapters, the environment variables are used to name specific folders, such as the SystemRoot folder.

Hardware Requirements

The quality of the hardware for a terminal server is key to the performance of the overall system. Every operation of all connected thin clients takes place on the server. Therefore, the server must be quite powerful. Normally, its hardware is among the most powerful in the server room. New hardware concepts, such as Blade Server, allow the distribution of the overall system performance (if load-sharing mechanisms are used) to several, relatively inexpensive servers. Thus, the proper dimensioning of a server is often a balance of price, manageability, and application requirements.

> **Note**   This part of the book describes the hardware requirements only for the installation of a terminal server without applications. Therefore, the following remarks apply only to the hardware needed for the operating system and the necessary terminal server components. You will find more information on dimensioning a terminal server with applications for a large number of users in Chapter 5.

Selecting the Server Hardware

Consider the following criteria when selecting terminal server hardware (keeping in mind that this is a preliminary list).

- The selected server platform needs to be certified for operation under Windows 2000 or Windows Server 2003. If not, you must at the very least ensure that only standard components with sufficiently tested drivers are used.

- Special attention should be paid to processor capacity. It needs to be as high as possible to accommodate the simultaneous start of multiple applications at peak times (for example, when many users start working), when terminal servers are often pushed to the edge of their ability. These situations should be avoided. The minimum processor speed of a terminal server should be 733 MHz. In Chapter 5, we will describe in detail the capacity requirements of individual applications in relation to processors.

■ The operating system alone needs a minimum of 128 MB of main memory. The optimal amount of main memory for an operating system without applications is 256 MB. Any additional memory requirements for individual applications are discussed in Chapter 5. In principle, the server platform should allow for at least 2GB of memory expansion. Maximum values are 4 GB for a Standard Server, 32 GB for an Enterprise Server, and 64 GB for a Datacenter Server.

■ The server needs to have a high-performance hard drive subsystem (if applicable, a hardware RAID system via SCSI bus). Alternatively, you could also use Storage Area Networks with corresponding adapter cards for terminal servers. The hard drive must provide at least 1.5 GB for the operating system. Additionally, there will be swap space for virtual memory, memory for locally saved user profiles and the necessary system resources for the applications. In total, the hard drive space for a terminal server should comprise at least 10 GB. An additional hard drive or a devoted RAID channel for swap space can sometimes increase system performance. However, it is preferable to have a sufficient quantity of real memory to avoid, as much as possible, swapping data to the hard drive.

■ The speed and capacity of the network connection depends on the potential number of users. The network connection should support a continuous data stream of 50 to 100 KBit/s per user to the clients. In the direction of the file servers, a network adapter with at least 100 MBit/s is required. In many switch-based environments, one network adapter per server with a throughput of 100 MBit/s is usually sufficient. However, no more than 50 users should work interactively on each server (see also Chapter 3). Several redundant network adapters can be employed per server so that the failure of one network connection does not bring down the entire server. Such an arrangement requires a much more complex network configuration. To work properly, other network components (such as switches, power supply for servers and network components) must also be redundant.

■ The server hardware should have a fast system bus so that internal data communication is not impeded.

■ It is recommended that the server be "free" of all components that are not needed for productive operation. For example, this would include audio cards or peripheral devices that might produce unwanted side effects when deployed.

A terminal server in Windows Server 2003 is scaled better than its predecessors because it is optimized for multiuser operation in terms of process administration, memory virtualization, and the registry database.

Terminal Servers and BackOffice Applications

Standard high-performance terminal server hardware lures many administrators into installing BackOffice, server applications, or Windows services on top of the applications for interactive users. This, however, is usually counterproductive.

The foreground applications on terminal servers are optimized to behave in a way familiar from client platforms (such as Windows XP or Windows 2000 Professional): they are prioritized to respond as quickly as possible to user access. A BackOffice server, however, is optimized for quick allocation of system resources for server applications and Windows services. This type of application (such as database system, a Web service, an e-mail program, or a directory service) is usually invoked as a high-priority background process that is completely different from an interactive foreground application. The server applications should respond as quickly as possible to the network calls from the corresponding client program, whereas the interactive applications on the BackOffice server console are substantially delayed.

If server applications and interactive desktop applications are installed on a terminal server and operated in parallel, they interfere with one another because they each demand preferred handling. If all applications demand preferred handling, a critical bottleneck results. This substantially lowers performance in both types of applications. When terminal server and BackOffice server are strictly separated, both perform much better.

> **Note**   For test installations, it is perfectly fine to combine terminal server and BackOffice server on one hardware platform. Such configurations, however, are limited in scale, quickly become saturated, and do not allow a realistic assessment of the power of neatly separated server systems. Combination servers are best used in demonstration environments.

Chapter 2

Installation and Configuration

Now that you have been introduced to the concept of Terminal Services for Microsoft Windows Server 2003, you will learn how to install and configure the system. Related topics include:

- The basic installation of Windows Server 2003 and Terminal Services, the requirements, and the different installation options (CD-ROM or network).
- Details on licensing terminal servers and their system tools.
- The tool for setting up Terminal Services—Terminal Services Configuration.

System Installation

This chapter describes the requirements for installing Windows Server 2003 and activating Terminal Services. Before you install the software from CD-ROM or via the network, you need to make several basic decisions. You can manually install the software, but there are also several options to automate the process. You will find the necessary information in this section.

Installation Requirements

To successfully install Windows Server 2003, the target platform must meet the requirements of the operating system. This will help prevent installation problems and correct errors after installation. To set up the optimal system based on the requirements, it is very helpful to have a basic grasp of the most important configuration options.

To install Windows Server 2003, a suitable hardware platform is essential. The following list includes the recommended features for different hardware components. It is assumed that the Standard Server and Enterprise Server are the most widely used options of terminal servers. The Datacenter Server is mentioned only for the sake of completeness.

- **Processor**   For the Standard Server, Enterprise Server, and Datacenter Server, x86-based processors (32-bit) are supported. The Enterprise Server and the Datacenter Server also supports Itanium-based processors (64-bit). The minimum recommended clock rate for the Standard Server is 550 megahertz (MHz) and 733 MHz for the Enterprise Server and the Datacenter Server.

- **Main memory**   The minimum is 128 megabytes (MB); however, 256 MB is recommended. The maximum for Standard Servers is 4 gigabytes (GB), 32 GB for Enterprise Servers with 32-bit systems, and 64 GB for 64-bit systems. Datacenter Server requirements are significantly higher: the minimum is 512 MB; the maximum is 64 GB for Datacenter Servers with 32-bit systems, and 128 GB for 64-bit systems.

- **Hard drive**   The hard drive should provide 1.5 GB of available space for a 32-bit system. 64-bit systems require 2 GB. These figures represent the hard drive space for the operating system only and do not include memory for swap space, applications, potential local user profiles, and local user data.

- **CD-ROM drive**   The recommended minimum speed for the CD-ROM or DVD drive is 12x. If the installation is performed via the network, no CD-ROM drive is necessary.

- **Network**   At least one available network adapter is required to install Windows Server 2003.

- **Input devices**   A keyboard and a mouse are usually required to install the operating system.

- **Output device**   A monitor with a minimum resolution of 640x480 pixels should be connected to the server. The recommended minimum resolution is 800x600 pixels.

If you use hardware components only from the hardware compatibility list (HCL), your chances of obtaining a fully functional system improve markedly. The updated list is available on the Internet at *http://www.microsoft.com/hcl*.

During the installation of Windows Servers 2003, you will be prompted to select the desired file system. We strongly recommend the NTFS file system. It includes the following important options that set it apart from other file systems, such as FAT or FAT32:

- **File-level and folder-level security** Access to files and folders can be strictly controlled via NTFS.

- **Compression** NTFS allows compression of hard drive partitions and files, thus reducing space requirements for data on the hard drive. However, compression does require additional system capacity and should not be used on terminal servers.

- **Quotas** Allocates a maximum amount of space per user on selected hard-drive partitions.

- **Remote storage and mounting partitions to folders** These features are supported only under Windows Server 2003, although Microsoft Windows 2000 did support them to a very limited extent.

> **Note** A local hard drive formatted with NTFS can be accessed only by systems running Microsoft Windows NT, Windows 2000, Windows XP Professional, or Windows Server 2003. Due to the new NTFS properties for Windows Server 2003, there could be incompatibilities in handling the file system using older tools, for example, imaging and cloning programs.

In addition to selecting the file system, during installation you also need to decide whether to join a Windows domain or a workgroup. If you decide to join an existing domain, you need a domain name and an account for the server you want to install. The former can be obtained from the administrator of the domain name system (DNS), the latter from the domain administrator. You need both before you can install your new system. You can generate a domain name and a server account during installation only if you have domain administrator rights. (See also Chapter 4.)

> **Note** To join a domain, you need to make sure that a domain controller is available and that a server with DNS service is activated on your network. In principle, a terminal server running Windows Server 2003 works just as well in an NT4 domain.

If you are on a small network that has no domain or if you prefer to join the domain later, you can join a workgroup. You can select the name of an existing workgroup or create a new workgroup.

Before you install the server, you should also decide on a password for the local administrator account. The password should conform to general security guidelines to protect your server from potential attacks right from the start. If you enter a noncompliant password, a corresponding message will appear. If you leave the password blank, you will not be able to access the server later using Terminal Services from a remote client.

Installation Options

Windows Server 2003 can be installed from CD-ROM or via the network.

Installation from a CD-ROM

The Windows Server 2003 operating system is delivered with all necessary components on one CD-ROM. There are four different installation methods, depending on the current configuration, Boot from a bootable CD-ROM drive. The computer system must have the corresponding hardware to support this option.

- Create installation disks and use them to reboot the system. In addition to a disk drive and a hard drive, you need a CD-ROM drive supported by the drivers on the startup disks.

- Manually execute the Winnt.exe or Winnt32.exe installation program on the CD-ROM using an existing operating system.

- If the CD-ROM drive is incompatible with Windows Server 2003, copy the installation directory to the hard drive using another operating system. Then manually execute the Winnt.exe or Winnt32.exe installation program from the hard drive.

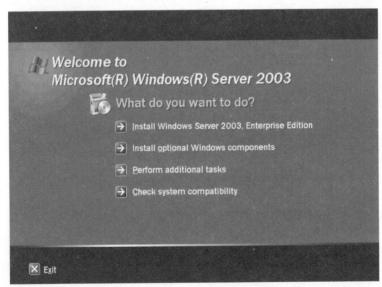

Figure 2-1 The startup screen for installing Windows Server 2003 on an existing 32-bit Windows operating system.

Installation via the Network

Windows Server 2003 can be directly installed over the network. This option is especially appealing for corporate environments in which software is distributed via central file servers.

Three requirements must be met for a network installation to work:

- The distribution server uses the same files as the i386 folder on the CD-ROM to install the 32-bit version of the operating system. The 64-bit version requires access to the ia64 folder.

- There must be sufficient memory on the local hard drive of the target computer.

- The target computer must have network software installed that allows access to the distribution server.

After connecting to the distribution server, you only need to run the Winnt.exe installation program on the target platform. Winnt.exe generates a temporary folder called Win_nt.~ls on the target platform. Installation files are copied to this folder. The local computer is then rebooted and the installation executes from the temporary folder.

> **Tip**   The Microsoft Windows Pre-installation Environment allows a client to connect to a distribution server. As this book was being written, Microsoft announced the coming release of the Automated Deployment Service tool, which will support the rollout of new servers. Further information is located at *http://www.microsoft.com/windowsserver2003/techinfo/overview/ads.mspx*.

Installation Programs

Windows Server 2003 has two installation programs. Each is linked to a different type of existing infrastructure:

- **Winnt**   Local or network-based new installation executable under MS-DOS, Windows 3.1, or Windows for Workgroups.

- **Winnt32**   Update for Windows 95, Windows 98, Windows Millennium Edition, Windows NT, Windows 2000, Windows XP, or Windows Server 2003.

The behavior of the Winnt.exe installation program can be modified using arguments and parameters. The syntax of the Winnt command is described in Table 2-1.

Table 2-1 Winnt Command Arguments and Parameters

Arguments	Description
/a	Activates accessibility options.
/c[:Command]	Defines a command to be executed after the graphics-mode portion of the installation is finished.
/r[:Folder]	Creates an additional, optional folder in the Windows installation folder. The /r argument can be used several times to create multiple folders. They will not be deleted after the installation is complete.
/rx[:Folder]	Creates an additional, optional folder in the Windows installation folder. The folder is deleted after the installation is complete.
/s:Source	Specifies the location of the system files for installation. The full path in the form of x:\[\Folder] or \\Server\Share[\Folder] must be specified. The current folder is the default path.
/t[:Tempdrive]	Instructs Setup to save the temporary files on the specified drive and to install Windows Server 2003 there. If no drive is given, Setup will try to find one.
/u[:Answerfile]	Performs an unattended installation using an answer file (requires /s). The answer file contains the answers to some or all of the prompts that the user normally responds to during installation.
/udf:Identifier[,UDF file]	Indicates an identifier that Setup uses to specify how a UDB file (uniqueness database file) modifies the answer file. (See /u.) The /udf parameter overwrites values in the answer file, and the identifier determines which values in the UDB file are used. If no UDB file exists, Setup prompts the user to insert a disk containing a file called $Unique$.udb.

The behavior of the Winnt32.exe installation program can also be modified using arguments and parameters. However, the Winnt32 command syntax is much more complex than that in Winnt, as you can see from Table 2-2.

Table 2-2 Winnt32 Command Arguments and Parameters

Arguments	Description
/checkupgradeonly	Checks if the computer is compatible for upgrade to Windows Server 2003. For Windows 95 or Windows 98 upgrades, Setup generates a report file called Upgrade.txt in the Windows installation folder. For Windows NT 4.0 or Windows 2000 upgrades, Setup saves this report in Winnt32.log in the installation directory.
/cmd:Commandline	Instructs Setup to execute a certain command before its final phase, that is, after the second reboot of the computer and after Setup has collected the necessary configuration data, but before Setup is complete.

Table 2-2   Winnt32 Command Arguments and Parameters

Arguments	Description
/cmdcons	Installs additional files and adds the recovery console option for repairing a damaged system to the OS selection screen. Used only after Setup is complete.
/copydir:[i386\ia64]\ Folder	Creates an additional folder in the folder that contains the Windows Server 2003 system files. The folder can include site or company-specific data or drivers. For example, to create the folder Private_Drivers on a 32-bit system, you would type: **/copydir:i386\Private_Drivers**. The argument */copydir* can be used several times to generate multiple new folders in the system root.
/copysource:Folder	Creates an additional folder in the folder that contains the Windows Server 2003 system files. Setup can use this folder and its files for configuration. In contrast to the folders */copydir* creates, */copysource* folders are deleted after Setup is complete.
/debug [*Level*]:[*Filename*]	Generates a debug log on the level specified, for example, */debug4:C:\Win2000.log*. The standard log file is C:\%Systemroot%\Winnt32.log and the debug level is 2. The log levels are defined as follows: 0: Severe errors 1: Errors 2: Warnings 3: Information 4: Detailed information about debugging Each level includes the levels below it.
/dudisable	Prevents execution of Dynamic Update. Only original installation files are used, even if an answer file specifies Dynamic Update.
/duprepare:Foldername	Prepares an installation folder on a network share for Dynamic Update files from the Windows Update site. The share can then be used for multiple clients.
/dushare:Foldername	Specifies a common resource (for example, folder share in the network) where the files for Dynamic Update are located. They were previously created using the */duprepare* argument.

Table 2-2 Winnt32 Command Arguments and Parameters

Arguments	Description
/emsport:{com1\com2 \ usebiossettings\off}	Activates or deactivates Emergency Management Service (EMS) during and after the installation. This service allows remote server access in critical situations via the port specified. EMS is typically needed when a local keyboard, mouse, or monitor is required but not available. EMS requires special hardware and is available only under Windows Server 2003.
/emsbaudrate:Baudrate	Specifies the data transmission rate for EMS communication (9600, 19200, 57600, or 115200). This argument can be used only in combination with /emsport:com1 or /emsport:com2.
/m:Folder	Specifies Setup to copy replacement files from an alternate location. Instructs Setup to look in the alternate location first, and if files are present, to use them instead of the files from the default location.
/makelocalsource	Instructs Setup to copy all source files onto the local hard drive for installation. This ensures access to installation files even if the CD-ROM is not available for the rest of the installation.
/noreboot	Instructs Setup not to reboot the computer after Winnt32 has completed the file copy phase so that another command can be executed.
/s:Source	Specifies the source of system files for the installation. Several /s sources can be specified to simultaneously copy files from several servers. If multiple /s arguments are used, the first server listed must be available. Otherwise, Setup cannot run.
/syspart:Drive	Specifies that the Setup startup files can be copied to a hard drive, the hard drive marked active, and files ready to install on another computer. That computer starts with the next phase of Setup. The /syspart parameter must always be used in combination with the /tempdrive parameter. The /syspart argument for Winnt32.exe can be executed only on a computer that is already running Windows NT 4.0, Windows 2000, or Windows Server 2003. It cannot be executed under Windows 9x.
/tempdrive:Drive	Instructs Setup to store temporary files on the partition specified and to install Windows Server 2003 on this partition.

Table 2-2   Winnt32 Command Arguments and Parameters

Arguments	Description
/udf:id [, *UDB file*]	Identifies an ID that Setup uses to specify how a UDB (uniqueness database) file modifies an answer file. (See */unattend*.) The UDB overwrites information in the answer file. The ID determines which values are used in the UDB. For instance, */udf:RAS_User,Company.udb* overwrites settings specified for the RAS_UserID located in the Unsere_Firma.udb folder. If no UDB file is specified, Setup prompts the user to insert a disk containing the *$Unique$.udb* file.
/unattend	Updates earlier versions of Windows Server 2003, Windows 2000, or Windows 4.0 from Service Pack 5 in unattended Setup mode. All user settings are taken from the previous installation so that Setup can be executed without user interaction.
/unattend [*Number*]:[*Answerfile*]	Performs a reinstallation in unattended Setup mode. This works with computers running Windows 98, Windows Millennium Edition, Windows NT, Windows 2000, Windows XP, or Windows Server 2003.
	Setup imports the user-specific information from the answer file. *Number* is the number of seconds between the end of the file copy process and reboot by Setup. *Answerfile* is the file name of the answer file. The default answer file is Unattend.txt.

Unattended Installation

One of the most striking improvements to Windows Server 2003 is automated installation via scripts. The setup manager wizard simplifies script generation for customer-specific installations. It is no longer necessary to learn complex script syntax to automatically set up the operating system according to set requirements.

Unattended installation of a basic system is based on *Remote Installation Services* (RIS). The target platform for the server installation connects with an RIS server during the initial startup phase. The RIS server has all the source files and automation data. In contrast to a network installation using Winnt.exe, you do not need any knowledge of source files' physical memory, and you might not even have to complete any dialog boxes. A RIS server can provide several operating systems in different sizes. For example, you can save both the minimum configuration of Windows Server 2003 on the RIS server and, in parallel, a special Windows Server 2003 configuration in application server mode.

Both Windows Server 2003 installation images can be made available for all users of a network for new installs. It is, however, more reasonable to limit access to administrators through adjusting the corresponding NTFS security settings for the answer file on the RIS server.

An operating system can take many forms on an RIS server. For instance, it is possible to install the Windows Server 2003 minimum configuration and, in parallel, a special Windows Server 2003 configuration in application mode. The images of both Windows Server 2003 installations can then be provided to all network users. However, it would make more sense to limit this option to administrators by selecting certain NTFS security settings concerning the answer file on the RIS server.

What are the necessary steps to set up an environment for an unattended installation?

1. Install remote installation services on a network server.

2. Configure the optional components and applications to be installed on the target platforms. An answer file for the automatic installation is also generated.

3. The images of the different configurations are stored on the RIS server.

4. The target platform connects to the RIS server via a PXE-capable network adapter or a startup disk created using RIS.

5. The operating system is installed on the target platform with little or no interaction from an authorized user.

With the help of scripts and answer files, you can control the amount of interaction needed during installation. The setup manager wizard plays a key role in this task. It allows you to generate or modify answer files for Windows Server 2003.

You can, of course, continue to use answer files that you created or adapted with a standard text editor. For this purpose, a template file called Unattend.txt is located in the i386 folder of the installation CD-ROM. To install Terminal Services in application server mode, you need to add the following lines to the answer file:

```
[Components]
TerminalServer = On
```

You can also configure Terminal Services by entering the following lines in the [TerminalServices] section of the Unattend.txt answer file. Table 2-3 lists the corresponding options.

Table 2-3 Possible Input for [TerminalServices] in the Unattend.txt Answer File

[TerminalServices] Settings	Description
AllowConnections	Specifies whether clients on the network can access the terminal server.
	0: Remote desktop deactivated (default setting)
	1: Remote desktop activated

Table 2-3   Possible Input for [TerminalServices] in the Unattend.txt Answer File

[TerminalServices] Settings	Description
LicensingMode	Specifies how Terminal Services handles client access licenses (CAL).
	PerDevice: Configures the terminal server so that each connected device requires a valid CAL for the terminal server (default setting).
	PerUser: Configures Terminal Services so that it supplies a valid CAL for each active user.
PermissionsSetting	Allows the selection of security settings for users of terminal server sessions.
	0: Sets the permission compatibility in line with the Windows 2000 or Windows Server 2003 security guidelines. Some applications that were originally developed for Windows NT 4.0 or older operating systems might not function properly in this mode (default setting).
	1: Sets the permission compatibility in line with Windows NT 4.0 security policies. Users are granted access to critical areas of the registry database.

The following lines might appear in an answer file:

```
[Components]
TerminalServer = On
...
[TerminalServices]
AllowConnections = 1
LicensingMode = PerDevice
PermissionsSettings = 0
```

To further automate the installation, you can use the Sysprep.exe tool. It duplicates the operating system and applications already installed on a reference platform. However, it is important that the target devices have the same hardware configuration as the reference device.

Installation Phases

The objective of the Windows Server 2003 installation process is to load the operating system to the target platform so that, by that time the installation is complete, the entire system is completely functional. In particular, that means that all the different motherboards, chip sets, hard drive controllers, USP ports, graphics cards, and network adapters should support the conventional hardware. To further complicate matters, processors are made by a number of manufacturers. There are different system busses. Moreover, you are able to select any number of options for the individual components of the operating system. Therefore, to simplify the overall installation process, it is divided into several easily identifiable phases.

Preparation Phase

The preparation phase is needed only if you start the installation from another operating system. This is when you can update or newly install Windows Server 2003, perform additional tasks, or verify system compatibility. The licensing agreement and license key query follow, as well as setting further options such as the source directory, accessibility options, language, or dynamic update. The preparation phase is omitted if you boot the target computer directly from boot disks or the installation CD-ROM. At the end of this phase, files are copied to a temporary area and the system reboots.

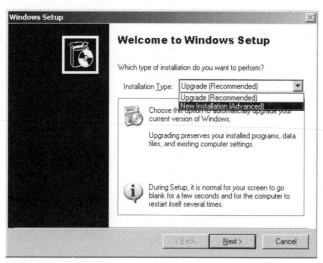

Figure 2-2   Selecting the installation option.

Text-Based Phase

The text-based phase loads the operating system's kernel, as well as a number of drivers, but it does not launch the graphical user interface. From the welcome screen, you can choose to continue with the installation, repair a damaged installation, or abort.

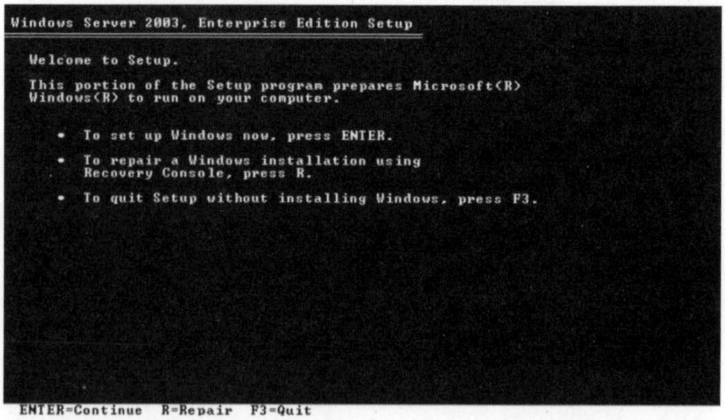

```
Windows Server 2003, Enterprise Edition Setup

    Welcome to Setup.

    This portion of the Setup program prepares Microsoft(R)
    Windows(R) to run on your computer.

        • To set up Windows now, press ENTER.

        • To repair a Windows installation using
          Recovery Console, press R.

        • To quit Setup without installing Windows, press F3.




ENTER=Continue   R=Repair   F3=Quit
```

Figure 2-3   Welcome screen of the text-based installation phase.

Note   At the beginning of the text-based phase, you can press F6 to load a hard-drive subsystems driver that is not part of the standard scope of installation files. If you want to use an alternate hardware abstraction layer (HAL), press F5. To start Automated System Recovery, press F2 when prompted on the F6 screen.

After the welcome screen is displayed, the hard drives are checked and the licensing agreement appears. Next, the system is checked for previous versions of Windows NT, Windows 2000, or Windows Server 2003. Then, all the hard drives are listed with their partitions. You select the partition (existing or new) where you want to install the operating system files and the installation proceeds automatically. One new feature of Windows Server 2003 is quick formatting of empty areas of the hard drive, which really reduces installation time.

Note   It is usually a good idea to install Windows Server 2003 on a newly formatted partition. Thus, you will have a clean system with no old versions of executable programs or DLLs. NTFS is recommended for formatting the file system.

After selecting and preparing the target partition, the installation process creates a list of files that are then copied into an installation directory. Finally, the initial configuration of Windows Server 2003 is created and saved. Now the graphics-based phase of the installation begins.

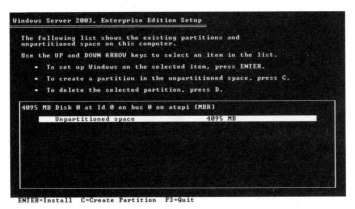

Figure 2-4   Selecting the target volume for an installation.

Graphics-Based Phase

Graphical dialog boxes guide you through the following steps. The dialog boxes help with the intricacies of hardware recognition and setting regional and language options (numbers, currency, time, and keyboard layout, if not already defined).

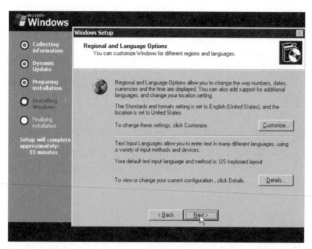

Figure 2-5   Selecting regional and language options during the installation.

You then enter the user name, the company, and the license key, if you did not already do so during the preparation phase. Subsequently, you select the licensing mode and computer name, and choose a password for the administrator account.

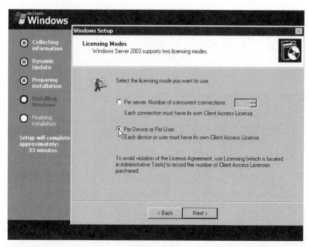

Figure 2-6   Selecting the licensing mode during the installation.

The following dialog boxes allow you to set the date and time as well as configure the network. This includes optionally configuring the client for Microsoft networks, file and printer release, and the TCP/IP protocol. After you select a domain or workgroup, a few closing tasks remain: set up the start menu, register all components, save all settings, and delete all temporary files. The Windows Server 2003 installation is now complete and it is time to reboot the system.

Post-Installation Phase

When you first log on as administrator, the server configuration dialog box is displayed. You can add more server functions (listed in Table 2-4) with the help of the server configuration wizard. This is essential to the terminal server function described in this book, which requires the special setup of an application server. The remote administration option is included in the standard functions of Windows Servers 2003 and does not need to be specifically installed.

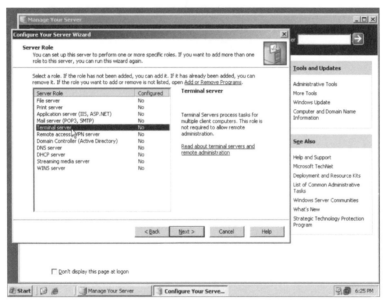

Figure 2-7   Installation of the terminal server function through the server wizard.

Table 2-4   Windows Server 2003 Server Functions

Server Function	Description
File server	File servers manage user and application access to files and allow files to be saved to the file share.
Print server	Print servers allow access to network printers and manage printer settings and drivers.
Web application server	Web application servers provide the core technology required to create, distribute, and operate XML Web services and Web applications. This includes Microsoft ASP.NET, COM+, and Internet information services (IIS).

Table 2-4   Windows Server 2003 Server Functions

Server Function	Description
Mail server	Mail servers use the POP3 and SMTP services to enable e-mail delivery.
Terminal server	Terminal servers allow multiple interactive users to log on and work with the system via client computers. This function is not necessary for remote administration.
RAS/VPN server	RAS/VPN servers enable remote clients to connect to the network over telephone lines or a secure VPN link. They also provide network address translations that allow computers on smaller networks to share one Internet connection.
Domain controller	Domain controllers store directory data and manage user login processes as well as searches in the directory hierarchy.
DNS server	DNS servers translate domain and TCP/IP host names into IP addresses.
DHCP server	DHCP servers dynamically assign IP addresses to network clients.
Streaming media server	Streaming media servers store digital multimedia presentations that can be transmitted via intranet or Internet.
WINS server	WINS servers translate NetBIOS computer names into IP addresses.

After all the desired options are selected, the server configuration wizard installs the required files and components. The computer might also reboot. The installation and basic configuration is now complete.

The Windows Servers 2003 Help pages provide further information on Terminal Services, including checklists for setup, recommendations for use, notes on administration, and troubleshooting instructions.

Framework Conditions

Several critical framework conditions must be met during installation.

- The installation partition must be formatted with NTFS. Otherwise, the security settings for the file system cannot be established.

- Do not install graphical screensavers on a terminal server. They consume too much CPU even if the graphical elements are minimal.

- Avoid intricate wallpaper or desktop designs (themes). They need to be restarted every time you resize the window, and on terminal servers, this leads to an increased net load.

Upgrade Paths

For the most part, it is advisable to install Windows Server 2003 on a clean, suitable hardware platform. It is, however, also possible to upgrade a Windows NT or Windows 2000 installation. The prerequisites for an upgrade follow.

- Standard Server

    - Windows NT 4.0, Terminal Server Edition, with Service Pack 5 or later

    - Windows 2000 Server on a computer with one or two processors

- Enterprise Server

    - Windows NT 4.0, Terminal Server Edition, with Service Pack 5 or later

    - Windows 2000 Server on a computer with three or four processors becomes an Enterprise Server

    - Windows 2000 Advanced Server

Licensing

In the deployment of a terminal server, the question of licensing policy is far from trivial. In corporate environments in particular, terminal servers have hundreds or even thousands of users. For this reason, it is very important to examine licensing in detail.

Types of Licensing

Several types of licenses must be obtained for normal operation of Windows Server 2003 with Terminal Services activated in application server mode. They are:

- Windows Server 2003 Server License

- Windows Server 2003 Client Access License (CAL)

- Windows Server 2003 Terminal Server Client Access License (TS-CAL)

> **Note**   This section does not discuss licenses for applications (for example, Microsoft Office, CorelDRAW, Acrobat Reader, or Oracle Client). These licenses must be bought separately, and they might be based on completely different models.

Windows Server 2003 Server License

When you acquire the server operating system, the Windows Server 2003 Server license is included. It allows you to install and operate Windows Server 2003 and comes with a unique license key. You will be asked for this key when installing the operating system.

Windows Server 2003 Client Access License

Every computer or Windows terminal that establishes a connection to Windows Server 2003 requires the Windows Server 2003 Client Access License. Client access licenses permit clients to use the file, print, or other network services provided by Windows Server 2003. In the past, these licenses were offered as either *Per Client* or *Per Server* licenses.

Under the new Windows Server 2003, the Per Client licenses were renamed and can now be purchased Per Device or Per User. A Per User license does not include *concurrent users* but *named users*. This means, for instance, that a company does not have to pay license fees for each client that employees use (for example, for access to the intranet). A company in which several employees share a device can also save money by using the Per Device license.

> **Note**   As mentioned earlier, a client can still access any Windows Server 2003 on the common network with a Per Device or Per User license.

Though seldom used in companies now, a Per Server Client Access License still requires the number of licenses to equal the maximum number of simultaneous server connections. Each device or user can access the server, but the number of simultaneous connections cannot exceed the number of installed Per Server licenses.

Windows Server 2003 Terminal Server Client Access License

Client computers or Windows terminals with a Windows Server 2003 Terminal Server Client Access License are allowed to access Windows Server 2003 Terminal Services. For example, this license is needed to launch a terminal session and execute Windows applications on the server.

Similar to the Client Access License, the Terminal Server Client Access License is available Per Device or Per User. There are no plans to offer a Per Server License.

- As under Windows 2000, a Per Device license is associated with a terminal device. Each terminal using Terminal Services must have such a license.

- A Per User license grants a known user an access license for any terminal device. The user can then access the company's terminal servers from his or her office workstation or handheld device, from a notebook on the road, or from a personal computer from home.

It is possible to mix licensing modes so that both types of licensing are provided on a Terminal Services license server. The home version of the Terminal Server Client Access License that was available under Windows 2000 is no longer offered under Windows Server 2003 because Per User licensing rendered that license superfluous.

> **Note**   At the time of this writing, Microsoft was not offering Per User licenses for Terminal Services, although Windows Server 2003 is technically capable of handling them. However, all available information available indicates that this licensing mode will be available with a future version of Windows Server 2003.

Operating System Equivalency

Operating system equivalency as it existed under Windows 2000 Server has been scaled back under Windows Server 2003. Under Windows 2000, operating system equivalency allowed clients with the same or with a higher version than the server legal access to Terminal Services without a Terminal Server Client Access License. For example, this applied to combinations of Windows 2000 Professional with Windows 2000 Server or Windows XP with Windows 2000 Server.

Microsoft offers its customers the following options for Windows Server 2003:

- Customers who signed a Platform or Enterprise Operating System Agreement (EA), or an Upgrade Advantage (UA) or a Software Assurance (SA) agreement, with Microsoft, will receive one Windows Server 2003 Terminal Server Client Access License including Software Assurance for each licensed Windows desktop. As a precondition, the Windows desktops must be covered by these agreements at the time of Windows Server 2003 release. Windows desktop licenses purchased subsequently do not include the Terminal Server Client Access license.

- Customers holding licenses for Windows XP Professional without upgrade rights (by EA, UA, or SA) at the time of Windows Server 2003 release receive for each of their licenses one Windows Server 2003 Terminal Server Client Access License. This license will exclude upgrade rights that would result from an ES, UA, or SA.

If this licensing model is retained, a Terminal Server Client Access License will have to be obtained for each client device. The only alternative would then be the Per User license.

External Connector License

Another licensing change under Windows Server 2003 relates to the access licenses for anonymous users outside the licensing company. By means of an *external connector license* (EC), a company can grant external users access to server resources. External users are employees that are not employed by the licensee or associated companies.

This type of license is purchased per accessible server. The external connector license is valid for both server services (Client Access License) and terminal server services (Terminal Server Client Access License). If Windows 2000 Internet connector licenses or terminal server Internet connector licenses are present, they will be replaced by the corresponding external connector licenses.

> **Note**   Companies can purchase normal licenses for users outside of the company. It can, for example, be more economical to purchase Windows CALs or TS CALs instead of an external connector license for users requiring access to server or terminal server services on the company's network.

Licensing Method

Terminal Services has its own licensing method for clients logging on to terminal servers. This method differs from the licensing method for "normal" Windows Servers 2003 clients. Clients can log on to a terminal server in application server mode only after they receive a valid license from a license server. If Terminal Services is running in remote desktop mode, two simultaneous logon connections are permitted, and no license server is required.

To use Terminal Services in application server mode, you need an activated license server. After the license server is activated, you can safely install client licenses and assign them to the clients. The first time an unlicensed client attempts to log on to a terminal server, the server contacts the license server and requests a license for this client. (See also the section "License Servers" later in this chapter.) Before licenses can be issued for clients, a licensing server must be installed on the network. This license server must have been activated by Microsoft Clearinghouse and provides encrypted key packages for the client licenses.

Whereas installing the license server on a domain controller was recommended under Windows 2000, this service can now be installed on each member server of a domain or workgroup. The terminal server license server can supply licenses either to its domain or the entire organization. The latter is naturally recommended only if the Active Directory directory service structure has more than one domain.

Microsoft Clearinghouse

Microsoft Clearinghouse is the Microsoft-managed database used to activate license servers and to install, upon request, key packages for the client licenses on license servers. The Clearinghouse stores data on all activated license servers and all key packages issued. In this way, it is easy to track which client licenses are used in an organization that uses terminal servers and to ensure that the organization has purchased enough client licenses. Microsoft Clearinghouse is accessed via Terminal Services licensing.

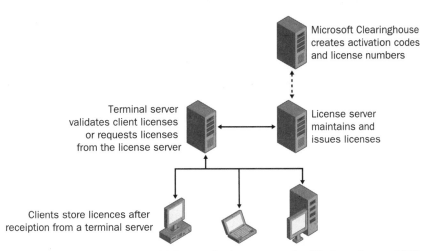

Figure 2-8   The licensing model for terminal servers under Windows Server 2003.

License Servers

The license server stores all client licenses available in the domain or on the entire network and tracks licenses issued to clients. Before a client receives a license, the terminal server must be able to connect to the activated license server. One license server can support several terminal servers simultaneously.

As an option, the group policies allow controlling the access of individual terminal servers to the licensing service. In this case, only members of the terminal server computer local domain security group can obtain licenses from the terminal server license server.

Installation

When setting up Windows Server 2003, you can optionally install a license server on the computer. However, you can also install it later via Add/Remove Windows Component in the dialog box under Start\Control Panel\Add or Remove Programs.

Figure 2-9 Later installation of Terminal Services licensing.

Because Terminal Services should be installed on member servers specifically set up for these services, it might be better to put the license server on an independent computer. However, if you use the terminal server as an independent server, or if this is the only Windows Server 2003 in a Windows NT 4.0 domain, you can install the terminal server licensing service on the same server.

If you plan to migrate a workgroup or Windows NT 4.0 domain to an active directory domain at a later time, it is recommended that you install the license server on a computer that will also be migrated to that new domain.

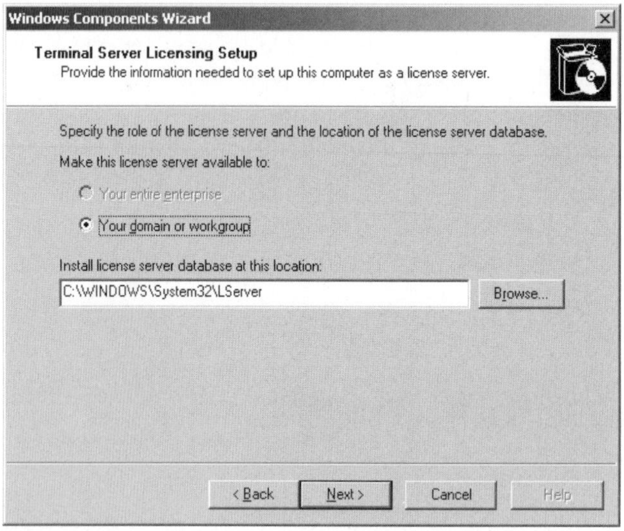

Figure 2-10 Determining the role of a license server.

A license server is installed by default as a domain license server and is the best option if each domain is to have its own license server. It is also possible to install a license server as a company license server. This type of license server is recommended if several domains need to be managed.

A terminal server can grant nonlicensed clients a connection for 120 days. After this time, the terminal server will not allow these clients to connect unless a license server is found to provide a client license. A license server that is not yet activated can issue temporary licenses valid for 90 days.

After installation, you can find the license server's administration interface under Start\Administrative Tools\Terminal Server Licensing.

Figure 2-11   Terminal server licensing right after installation and before activation.

Activation

Before a license server can issue permanent licenses for Terminal Services clients, it must first be activated by Microsoft via Terminal Services licensing. Upon activation, Microsoft issues a digital certificate for a license server. This certificate is used to verify the ownership rights and the identity of the server. A license server with this certificate can conduct transactions with Microsoft and receive client licenses for the terminal servers. There are three ways to activate a license server: automatically over the Internet, manually via a Web browser, or over the telephone. As soon as the license server is activated, it confirms the server's identity and enables it to receive licenses and issue them to clients.

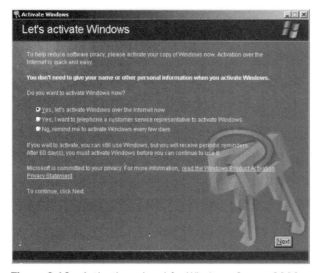

Figure 2-12   Activation wizard for Windows Server 2003.

After license server activation, key packages for client licenses can be installed on the server. These packages allow the server to issue licenses upon request by terminal servers on the network. The corresponding key packages are stored and tracked on the license server. Microsoft installs key packages for client licenses using the Terminal Services licensing procedure. When Microsoft receives a request to install client licenses, it issues the requested number of key packages to the license server. You can use the same methods to install client licenses as you do to activate a license server.

Under Windows Server 2003, the way access licenses are granted depends on the type of license. The following method is used for a Per Device license. When the client licenses are installed on a license server, the server can issue licenses. When a client attempts to log on to a terminal server, the terminal server recognizes that the client does not have a license. It looks for a license server that can issue a new license to the client. For the first session, the new license is a temporary Per Device license.

If the client logs on again after terminating the first session, an attempt is made to convert the temporary license into a full Per Device license. If no Per Device licenses are available, a temporary license valid for 120 days is issued to the client. After this time, the client will no longer be able to log on to a terminal server.

An issued client license is permanently assigned to a certain computer or terminal and cannot be transferred to another device without manual intervention. A client license is a digitally signed certificate that is stored locally on the client.

The following rule was valid under Windows 2000 up to Service Pack 3: If the certificate was lost, possibly due to hard drive damage, the license could be reactivated only by Microsoft and would be reissued to the client after the system was reinstalled. Windows 2000 Service Pack 3 includes a new function that is valid for Windows Server 2003 terminal server licensing. It is a significant improvement over the licensing process described earlier. If a Terminal Server Client Access License is issued as a Per Device license, it is valid for a random period between 52 and 89 days. Its validity is verified upon each connection. If the license is due to expire within the following 7 days, it is renewed for another period ranging from 52 to 89 days. If there is no license server available when the client logs on, the client can still connect to the terminal server.

If a client does not log on again during the valid period, the license is returned to the pool of available licenses on the license server. This eliminates the danger of losing licenses because of hard drive damage, reinstallation of clients, or test connections to the terminal server. You will find a more detailed description of this procedure at *http://support.microsoft.com/* under Knowledge Base article 287687, "Before a license server can issue permanent licenses for Terminal Services."

Terminal Services Configuration

Windows Server 2003 Terminal Services is configured after installation and, if necessary, during operation using a specific tool: Terminal Services configuration. This tool allows you to modify the parameters for connections and server settings.

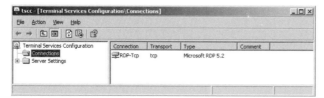

Figure 2-13   The Terminal Services configuration console.

> **Note**   Terminal Services settings have a relatively high priority level and can overwrite the corresponding client or user account options. Only Group Policies have a higher priority level than Terminal Services configuration. The hierarchy (descending) is clear: Group Policies—Terminal Services configuration—User configuration—Client configuration. User configuration and client configuration details are discussed in the following pages.

However, before we introduce you in detail to Terminal Services configuration, it is important that you understand the meaning of *Connection* and *User session* in terms of terminal servers.

> **Note**   Unlike many other administration tools, Terminal Services Configuration is explained in great detail in this book because it is central to the administration of a terminal server. Furthermore, this tool can serve a vital role in explaining the basic mechanisms of terminal servers.

Connection Configuration

A connection between the client user session and the terminal server can basically be realized at three different points in the system. The selected settings must be valid for a type of protocol, an individual user, or an individual client. There are special tools for each of these tasks.

Connection-Specific Settings

This configuration affects all users who connect from network clients to a Windows terminal server over a specific connection (in this case, Microsoft RDP 5.2). The corresponding tool is Terminal Services configuration. Only an administrator on the Terminal Services Machine has access to this tool. It is also possible to copy certain options from the individual configurations for users or clients.

> **Important**   Even if Terminal Services configuration appears to be the strongest way to set parameters for Terminal Services connections, there is one authority with a higher priority level: Group Policies!

User-Specific Settings

This configuration affects an individual user account and is performed by the administrator through user administration. It is important to keep in mind that the corresponding options were added for local user-specific components of computer administration with Terminal Services installed and user administration on the domain level.

Moreover, these user-specific settings are active only if they were approved during the configuration of the connection-specific settings. If they were not approved, the connection-specific settings overwrite the user-specific settings. Terminal Services configuration is therefore stronger than user administration.

Client-Specific Settings

This configuration applies to an individual client and can be performed on the client hardware or the client software. The client user might even have permission to select setting options. These client-specific settings are active only if they were approved during the configuration of the connection-specific settings. If they were not shared, only the connection-specific settings apply. User administration is therefore stronger than client configuration.

User Sessions

Every user of a terminal server is assigned his or her own session. Each session has its own life span that is independent of all other activities on the server. The following paragraphs describe the different phases of the life of a user session.

Connecting

When Terminal Services is started, it first initializes two user sessions in idle mode. A monitoring thread is launched and waits for a connection request via a certain TCP/IP port. As soon as a user connects to the terminal server through his or her client, the connection request is immediately accepted and forwarded to the kernel driver of the appropriate protocol (for example, RDP). The kernel driver transmits the request to Terminal Services. Terminal Services initializes a special thread to handle the request.

This new thread handles the negotiation between server and client regarding cache size, compression, encryption, client version number, license details, and virtual channels. If the connection is successful, it is assigned to one of the idle sessions. Then the session space is initialized (Csrss, WinLogon, and kernel driver) and a new idle session is generated. Finally, the user is authenticated by means of an interactive dialog box or automatic forwarding of the identification information on the client. As soon as the user is identified, he or she can start the interactive session.

Disconnecting

The user can terminate the connection between client and terminal server without logging off. The connection can also be terminated when a predefined time limit is reached. The session's graphical image and user processes are stored on the server just before disconnecting. Therefore, the user can reconnect to the session on the terminal server and resume work. The IDs of disconnected sessions and the corresponding user IDs are stored in memory. They can be reused at any time on reconnection.

From a technical perspective, only the RDP and TCP/IP drivers are removed from memory when a connection is terminated without logging off. The kernel element of the 32-bit subsystem handles interrupting all graphical output to the system driver. This means that the session becomes invisible until the user reconnects or on reaching the predefined time limit for automatic removal of the disconnected session from memory.

The applications that were open when the session was disconnected continue to run without interruption. For instance, an FTP client can continue downloading a document from the Internet without a problem in a separate user session, even though the user is no longer connected interactively.

Reconnecting

When a user requests a new connection to the terminal server after disconnecting, a new session is generated. The logon screen prompts the user for authentication if the user ID was not automatically transmitted. If the system detects a separate session for this user from the logon ID and password, the user is reconnected to that session. The required drivers are loaded and the graphical subsystem is invoked to display the current session contents.

If configured to do so, disconnecting and reconnecting can also be used on the server side for unstable network connections. If a client loses the connection to the server, the server detects the interrupted data flow and saves the session for a preset period. Even if a client is accidentally switched off, no data is lost to the user. When the client is switched on again and the user logs on to the terminal server, the user is reconnected to the previous session.

Logging Off

Of course, a user can log off a terminal server session, that is, terminate the session. The result is the same as logging off the local Windows XP or Windows Server 2003 console. All resources that the session was using are released on the server.

Server Connection Options

After launching the Terminal Services Configuration tool under Start\Administrative Tools, you will see two menu items in both panels: Connections and Server Settings. If you select Connections in the left panel, the right panel displays the protocols installed. If Windows Server 2003 with Terminal Services is installed with no add-on products, you will see only Microsoft RDP 5.2.

> **Note** To modify all settings in Terminal Services configuration, you must be logged on as a user with administrative rights. If you installed Citrix MetaFrame XP Presentation Server on your terminal server, you will see several protocols in Terminal Services configuration. You can find a detailed description and scope of Citrix MetaFrame XP Presentation Server starting in Chapter 9.

Right-click the mouse to open the Connections context menu. The following options are displayed:

- **Create New Connection** A wizard helps you set up a new connection. You need to enter the type of connection (for example, RDP 5.2), data encryption, remote monitoring options, type of transmission (for example, TCP), and network adapter. To set up a new connection, at least one of the parameters for connection type and transmission type, or for the network adapter, must differ from those for an already existing connection.

- **View** Adjusts the MMC console to the user's preferences. Adds or removes columns, sets the view to display large icons, small icons, lists, or details.

- **Refresh** Redraws the graphical user interface to display changes in values.

- **Export List** Saves the names of the Connections columns in a text file.

- **Help** Displays Help information related to the MMC console and Terminal Services Configuration.

You initiate the setup of a new connection in Terminal Services configuration using the context menu of the Connections option on the console tree (that is, in the right panel) or via the Action\Create New Connection menu item. This will start the connection wizard for Terminal Services.

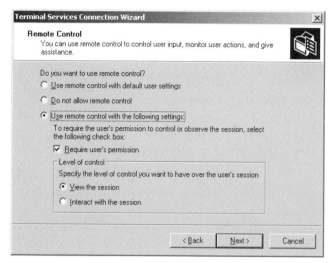

Figure 2-14   Connection Wizard dialog box for Terminal Services to create a new connection. The parameters for remote control are set here.

By selecting a connection protocol in the right panel of Terminal Services configuration and opening its context menu, you can enter several global settings. One of them is especially important: the deactivation option under the All Tasks menu item. This option prohibits any other user from logging on to the terminal server using the connection protocol you selected. It is often needed to begin maintenance work on the server.

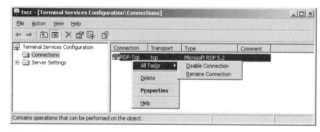

Figure 2-15   Connection context menu, allowing the deactivation or renaming of the connection.

When you select Properties for the connection protocol, the right panel displays a dialog box with eight tabs. These tabs allow you to configure the connection parameters.

General

The first tab is labeled General. Use this tab to enter an optional comment to describe the connection, the degree of encryption, and the standard authentication method you selected. The transport protocol to transmit data streams over RDP 5.2 is always TCP/IP and cannot be modified. The RDP 5.2 connection type is also a default value that cannot be changed.

For the server, you can choose between four degrees of encryption for data transmission between server and client for RDP 5.2.

- **Low**   All data sent from the client to the server is protected with 56-bit encryption. Data sent from the server to the client is not encrypted.

- **Client-compatible**   All data transferred both from client to server and server to client is protected using the maximum encryption supported by the client. The client thus determines the degree of encryption. However, this could allow unencrypted data to pass through the network, depending on the client configuration.

- **High**   All data sent from the client to the server and vice versa is protected by an encryption using the maximum encryption supported by the server. For a standard terminal server, this is 128 bits. International clients that do not support this encryption cannot connect to the server.

- **FIPS-conform**   All data exchanged between client and server is verified according to Federal Information Processing Standard 140-1.

Note   In some countries, the law limits the level of encryption; for example, the level might be limited to 64 bit. Therefore, the specific language versions of Windows Server 2003 Terminal Services do not support higher encryption in these countries. Clients that must request a higher encryption cannot connect to the language-specific terminal servers with lower degrees of encryption.

If you activate the Use standard Windows authentication option, you cannot use any third-party security components for user authentication. In this case, Microsoft GINA-DLL is used exclusively.

Note   In many countries, encryption under the Windows NT 4.0 Terminal Server Edition was limited to 40 bits on all levels. If you use older-generation RDP clients, they might support only 40-bit encryption keys. If the degree of encryption is set to client-compatible, Windows Server 2003 Terminal Services will automatically adjust the encryption downward.

In production environments, you use this tab only to adapt the level of encryption to the corresponding requirements. Other options are usually not as important here.

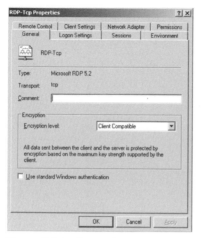

Figure 2-16   General settings of a connection protocol in the Terminal Services Configuration.

Logon Settings

The Logon settings are configured under another tab. On the client, you enter the logon information (including the password, if required) into the fields under the corresponding radio buttons. The data is passed on to the server at logon. Be careful not to confuse this with the single sign-on solution in which the information the user enters at logon is automatically used to establish a session on the client. Even though this option is convenient for logging on to a terminal server session, it does present security problems. Furthermore, not all clients support this option.

Alternatively, you can input a user name, domain, and password for logging on to the terminal server. This enables an automatic logon, too, and is valid for all user sessions requesting a connection over this type of protocol. In many environments, however, there might still be security concerns regarding user access. Nonetheless, this is a very powerful option that allows anonymous users to access a terminal server running noncritical applications, for example, information terminals in a department store.

You can make both logon options more secure by requiring the user to enter the password manually. To activate this option, select Always request password option. This prevents the stored password from being used, no matter where it resides (client side or server side). Regardless of the logon option, users will be required to enter their password each time they log on to the terminal server, thus significantly increasing security.

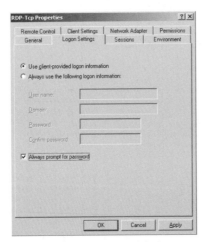

Figure 2-17   Connection protocol logon settings.

In production environments, always select this option button, unless the user is authenticated in a special secured environment that is safe for password transmission.

Sessions

The configuration of sessions on this tab sets the timeout limits for Terminal Services and determines the reconnection settings. The timeout limits are set using three counters. You have the choice of three predefined settings:

- **End a disconnected session**   This counter sets the maximum time a disconnected user session remains in memory. When the interval specified is completed, the session is ended; that is, the session is physically removed from memory, the user's applications are terminated, and the user is logged off. Terminal Services configuration allows you to set the value for the protocol in question (only RDP in the default installation) only if you select Override user settings. In this case, the setting you define here overrides the corresponding setting in the terminal server-specific expansions for local users and groups or users and computers in the Active Directory directory service. In this way, the terminal server administrator can set a generally valid standard for the behavior of Terminal Services for separate sessions.

- **Active session limit**   This counter sets the maximum duration of a user session. When the time is up, the session is either disconnected or ended, depending on the settings specified in the following paragraph. To set the active session limit value, you also need to override the user settings.

- **Idle session limit**   With this counter, you set the time that a user can remain inactive. If this time limit is exceeded, the session is either disconnected or ended, depending on the settings described in the following section. This is yet another value that you can set only if you override the user settings.

Setting session limits does involve a certain amount of risk. For instance, if the idle session limit is set to 60 minutes, a session might be disconnected or ended when the user is simply on an extended lunch break. In the worst case scenario, data might be lost. On the other hand, setting a time limit is sometimes the only way to prevent inactive users from wasting server resources.

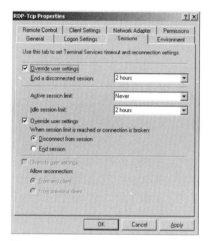

Figure 2-18   Configuring user session limits.

The following settings relate to system behavior when the session limit is reached or the connection is broken. Selecting Override user settings combined with Maximum Idle Time overwrites the settings in the terminal server-specific settings for local users and groups or users and computers in the Active Directory. Thus, the configuration settings chosen here turns an individual user request into a generally binding system behavior preset by the terminal server administrator.

When the session limit is reached or the connection is broken (for example, by switching off a client), there are two options:

- **Disconnect from session**   The network connection is interrupted but the session remains stored in terminal server memory. This applies to all open applications and the corresponding user data.

- **End session**   The user session is completely removed from memory. Unsaved application data is lost if the user did not save it and no automated backup processes were activated.

On closer examination, one combination of settings seems completely useless at first: A disconnected session is ended after 10 minutes, yet the session also ends when the session limit is reached. Can a disconnected session remain in memory? The answer is yes. A user can explicitly ask the client to disconnect from a session. This disconnection does not result from a session limit or an interrupted network connection. In this case, the 10-minute time limit is valid for the disconnected session until it is ended, if the user does not reconnect to it.

A disconnected session can be reestablished by any client under the RDP protocol. The user account and the corresponding password are essential to establish a new connection. This option is particularly helpful if the terminal server is protected by an uninterruptible power supply, but the clients are not. In this case, a short power failure does not result in the loss of user data or application statuses. The user can then continue working with his or her session from any client.

This setting cannot be changed under the RDP protocol. Other protocols might allow limiting reconnections to the previous client. Therefore, this configuration option does appear in the dialog box. Here, too, selecting Override user settings overwrites the corresponding setting in the terminal server-specific expansions for local users and groups, or for users and computers in the Active Directory.

> **Note**   If the user is allowed to reestablish the connection to a disconnected session from the same client only, this can result in problems if the physical client fails. Even if an identically configured client replaces the original client, the user will not be able to use his or her session again.

In production environments, the time limits for user sessions are usually set in this tab and can overwrite previously set, different user settings. In particular, this applies to ending a disconnected session after several minutes or hours and after the idle session limit. Therefore, it is strongly recommended that these values be thought through and communicated to users well in advance. When sessions disappear without sufficient warning, users often reject the technology, unjustifiably. It is not the technology that creates the problem, but the organization or, in some cases, the communication involved.

Environment

The Entering two strings in the tab Environment enables the configuration of an exclusive program that is started automatically upon user logon. An entry at the Program path and file name specifies the program desired. The Start in prompt determines the default directory allocated to the program.

When a user logs on, the program inside a full-screen session window is displayed instead of the normal desktop. When the user ends the program, the terminal server session is terminated, too. This leads to a basic form of environment where only one application is able to run.

This option becomes active only if the Override settings from user profile and Remote Desktop Connection or from Terminal Services client option were activated. This overwrites the corresponding setting in the terminal server-specific settings for local users and groups or users and computers in the Active Directory, including the client side as well. In this instance, too, the Terminal Services configuration takes precedence over the user or client-specific settings.

> **Important**   In general, specifying a start program does not prevent the user from running another program. Some desktop functions could still be misused behind the active application. For a strict single-application environment, the terminal server administrator needs to add further security settings.

> **Note**   Problems that arise when starting the program over the network might indicate improper timing. For example, the terminal server might be trying to start a program before a required network drive in a logon script is connected.

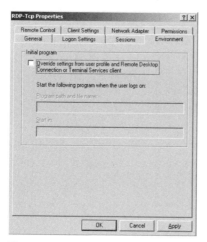

Figure 2-19   Configuring environment settings.

The options in this tab are usually not modified in production environments. In general, a different technology is used to display individual applications. We will describe this technology in detail later in this book.

Remote Control

The Remote Control tab allows a user session to be "mirrored" on another client. This function is for administrative tasks, for example, help desk tasks. The remote control configuration allows you to use user-specific default settings, as well as to fully deactivate and configure the following settings:

- Use remote control with default user settings means that the user settings of a local user or in the Active Directory are used to determine the following options.

- Do not allow remote control prohibits the takeover of a user session thus configured.

- Under Use remote control with the following settings in the dialog box, the administrator can determine if a user must approve of remote control when the administrator assumes control over a session. Additionally, it is possible to define whether the remote session can be viewed only under remote control, or if the administrator can also interact with the session by assuming control of the keyboard and the mouse.

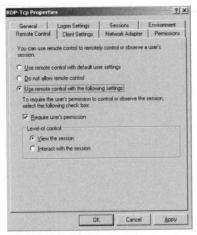

Figure 2-20 Configuration of remote control, where the user must give his or her permission, and the remote session can only be viewed.

Note Labor-law restrictions in some countries prohibit monitoring users without their knowledge. It is therefore mandatory to obtain the user's permission. For this reason, remote control behavior in production environments is usually preconfigured under this tab and not under user settings.

Client Settings

Client settings allow an administrator access to several options related to the integration of client resources in the user session. Integrating these options supports the intuitive assumption by the user that he or she can continue to use local resources even though the application on the screen is physically running on a remote server. Furthermore, this reduces the time it takes a user to become familiar with the system. For example, during a Terminal Services session, a user can issue the print command without first having to correctly allocate the appropriate resources.

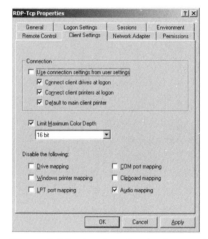

Figure 2-21   Settings for the integration of client resources.

In principle, the following options can be preconfigured for a connection protocol such as RDP 5.2. The first three options can also be defined through the user settings.

- **Connect client drives at logon**   At logon, this option displays the local client drives as network drives in the corresponding terminal server session. These network drives are labeled \\TSCLIENT\A, \\TSCLIENT \C, or \\TSCLIENT \D. This option is activated by default.

- **Connect client printers at logon**   At logon, this option displays the local client printers as network printers in the corresponding terminal server session. This option is activated by default.

- **Default to main client printer**   This option determines whether a print job is forwarded automatically to the terminal server default printer or to the main client printer. This option is activated by default, which sends the print job automatically to the default client printer.

- **Limit maximum color depth**   With this option you determine whether you want to limit the maximum color depth for a terminal server client using this connection. If this option is active, you can select 8-bit, 15-bit, 16-bit, or 24-bit. The default setting is preconfigured to 16-bit.

Printer connections will take the most time because numerous driver combinations can apply. The other interfaces are a bit easier to integrate, although you can always disable them again as well.

The following options can be disabled regardless of how you initiated the connection to the client drives or printers, that is, either via the options described earlier or via the user settings in the system tool Computer Management.

- **Drive mapping**   If you check this box (that is, you disable it), you will not be able to connect to the local client drives from a Terminal Services session. You can also override the Connect client drives at the logon option described earlier. This option is disabled by default, that is, you will connect to the client drives at logon.

- **Windows printer mapping**   If you check this box (that is, you disable it), you will not be able to automatically connect to the client printers at logon. However, you can still manually initiate a connection to a client printer from a Terminal Services session if the LPT or COM port options are enabled. This option is disabled by default, that is, you will connect to the client printers at logon.

- **LPT port mapping**   If you check this box (that is, you disable it), the list of available printers will not include any client printer connected via the LPT port. This option is disabled by default, that is, you can manually integrate all printers that are connected via the LPT port on the client. When you log on again, printers you mapped manually will be restored only if Windows printer mapping is enabled.

- **COM port mapping**   If you check this box (that is, you disable it), the list of available printers for Terminal Services sessions will not include any client printer connected via the COM port. This option is disabled by default, that is, you can manually integrate all printers that are connected via the COM port on the client. When you log on again, printers you mapped manually will be restored only if Windows printer mapping is enabled.

- **Clipboard mapping**   If you check this box (that is, you disable it), no data exchange between terminal server and terminal server client is possible via the clipboard. This option is disabled by default, that is, the clipboard does allow data exchange.

- **Audio mapping**   If you check this box (that is, you disable it), it is not possible to transmit audio data streams from terminal server to terminal server client. This option is enabled by default, that is, system sounds and other audio signals of the user session will not be transmitted to the client.

Important   LPT and COM mapping support only the connection of printers via the respective ports. Other local client devices, such as serial bar code readers, cannot be contacted using RDP 5.2.

The network bandwidth required can be heavily influenced by the combination of client and server clipboards and the client printer mapping. For instance, when you copy a large graphic from an application running on the client and place it into an application running on the server, all the data on the clipboard must be transmitted via the network. Printer mapping is another critical issue, because a print job of several megabytes can put quite a load on a narrowband WAN connection for some time. This, of course, affects the operating speed of the clients connected via remote access server (RAS).

The configuration options are very comprehensive. Therefore, it is easy to make mistakes. Please make sure that you determine in advance the options you need for productive operations in the target environment.

Network Adapters

On the next tab, you select one or more network adapters to allocate to the connection protocol. Allocating a certain network adapter to a protocol can make a lot of sense in some environments. This is especially true for complex networks in which clients are connected via LAN and WAN lines.

The tab provides an additional configuration option: the number of possible connections. That number can be unlimited or clearly limited to a certain quantity of simultaneous RDP connections over the network adapter selected. In this way, you can determine the number of network connections and thus the RDP bandwidth used for one network adapter. The remaining bandwidth can then be reserved for other services. See Figure 2-22.

Note   The maximum number of connections is not linked to the license configuration. Licenses are monitored using an independent tool.

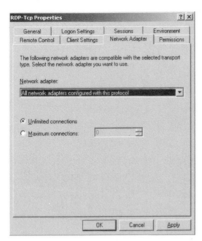

Figure 2-22   Selecting the bound network adapter and the maximum number of connections.

Permissions

When it comes to user access, security plays a major role on a terminal server. For this reason, the Permissions tab provides access to the security settings of individual protocols.

Permissions control what a user or a group may or may not do. Only an administrator can modify the standard access types: Guest access, User Access, and Full Control. They are listed in Table 2-5.

Table 2-5   Standard User Access Permissions

Permission	No Access	Guest Access	User Access	Full Control
Request information on the session	No	No	Yes	Yes
Set information or connection parameters	No	No	No	Yes
Use remote monitoring	No	No	No	Yes
Log on to server	No	Yes	Yes	Yes
Log off sessions	No	No	No	Yes
Send messages	No	No	Yes	Yes
Connect to forced-off sessions	No	No	Yes	Yes
Disconnect a session	No	No	No	Yes
Use virtual channels	No	No	No	Yes

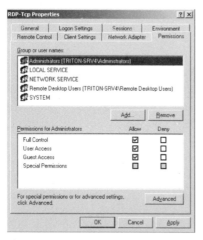

Figure 2-23   Setting permissions.

Access to Terminal Services or starting a Terminal Services session is usually regulated by Remote Desktop Users, a particular user group. New users who are to work on the terminal server are therefore added to this group. You should not modify this permission structure without a good reason to do so.

> **Tip**   Use the Advanced button to configure how you want to monitor the selected connection protocol in the Event Viewer.

> **Important**   Before you can use Terminal Services, the server must be released under Control Panel\System\Remote\Remote Desktop. Normally, this happens automatically during the installation of a terminal server. Furthermore, users who access Terminal Services must have a valid (not blank) password.

Server Settings

Fundamental changes to the runtime environment can be performed through the Terminal Services Configuration server settings.

- **Delete temporary folders on exit**   Determines whether the directories for temporary files are deleted upon ending the session or not. This option is enabled by default to save resources on the terminal server.

- **Use temporary folders per session**   Each user has a personal directory for temporary files, or all users access one common temporary directory. By default, each user has a personal temporary folder.

- **Licensing**   You can choose between licensing per device or per user. The former requires a license for each client computer that connects to the terminal server. The latter requires a license for each user who connects to the terminal server. The license per device option is active by default. Licensing per user is not currently supported.

- **Active Desktop**   You can enable or disable use of the Active Desktop. The option to support Active Desktop is disabled by default.

- **Permission Compatibility**   The Full Security option for running applications is compatible with Windows 2000 and Windows Server 2003. However, this prevents older applications from being executed (for example, SAPGui 4.6x or Microsoft Access 97). Therefore, the Relaxed Security permission compatibility setting offers reduced security control and provides full access for all users to the registry and system directories. The Full Security option is enabled by default.

- **Restrict each user to one session**   If this option is selected, there can be only one session per user. This way, you can save resources on the terminal server and reconnection to existing sessions is easier. Each user is restricted to one session by default.

- **Session Directory**   This option allows integration of an instance that centrally manages the directory of a user session, which enables reconnecting to a session even in server farms. This option is disabled by default.

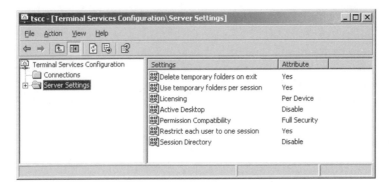

Figure 2-24   Terminal Services configuration server settings.

Chapter 3

Communication Protocols and Thin Clients

An environment built on the concept of server-based computing is not made up solely of terminal servers. The network, communication protocols, and clients play an equally important role. This chapter is designed to shed more light on the following topics:

- Connection of terminal servers to existing networks with their various protocols and services.

- The RDP protocol for communication between terminal servers and clients.

- The different types of clients, such as Microsoft Windows–based terminals, PCs on a LAN, or network computers.

- The myriad details on the RDP clients that come with the terminal server, including information on installation, configuration, use, and the options to connect clients to a terminal server session.

- Structured planning for the installation of terminal servers and Terminal Services clients in different network environments.

A terminal server cannot function properly without a network. Each terminal server client needs a network to access the multi-user system. The network is also essential for connecting other server services to the terminal server environment.

Therefore, planning, sizing, and configuring the network components play key roles in the proper functioning of a terminal server under Microsoft Windows Server 2003.

Before we examine the Microsoft Remote Desktop Protocol (RDP), let us first turn to the basics of conventional Windows server network mechanisms. Experienced network administrators can safely skip the first section on network connections and protocols and move directly to the RDP functions.

Network Connections and Protocols

In order to improve the structure of networks, the International Standardization Organization (ISO) developed a so-called reference model for Open Systems Interconnection, the OSI reference model, in 1977. This model comprises seven well-defined layers: the transport functions are distributed over four layers and the data-processing layers comprise the topmost three. The data-processing layers are often bundled and are known as the *application layer*.

The basic idea behind this model is that each layer provides certain services for the one above. A layer thus shields the higher layers from details, such as how the corresponding services are realized. Between every two layers, there is an interface that allows defined operations and offers services.

Modern protocols are still viewed from the perspective of this tried-and-tested model, even if they have not been implemented in five or seven layers. It allows them to be compared and differentiated from other protocols.

In this book, the protocols used are divided into two basic categories derived from the OSI model. Both are crucial to terminal server operation:

- **Transport protocols** Conventions for handling and converting data streams for exchange between computers over a physical network cable, a fiber optic cable, or a wireless network. These protocols correspond to the transport-oriented functions of the OSI model. Examples of transport protocols include TCP/IP, IPX/SPX, or NetBEUI.

- **Communication protocols** Encryption of function calls for certain tasks to be run on a remote computer. Corresponds to some of the functions that can be attributed to the application layer of the OSI model described in the preceding bullet. These functions include interprocess communication methods and the terminal server protocols Microsoft RDP and Citrix ICA. Even though the X11 protocol is used mostly under UNIX operating systems for remote access to applications, it belongs in this category as well.

Terminal servers on a network can support several transport and communication protocols in parallel. It is thus important to know which protocols exist with the corresponding communication mechanisms and for what purpose they are used. If required, you can install missing protocols later or remove superfluous protocols anytime to adapt to a changing network environment.

The communication protocols for the terminal server listed earlier are all described in detail in this book. Let us briefly touch upon transport protocols and interprocess communication.

Transport Protocols

A transport protocol refers to the four bottom layers of the OSI model, that is, the transport functions. These functions include determining the right path to the target computer and adapting the format of the data packet for transport to another network, as well as establishing the end-to-end connection between two or more communication partners.

TCP/IP

The TCP/IP transport protocol has become a standard over the past 10 years and is therefore very important for Windows Server 2003 in general, and for a terminal server in particular. This transport protocol is most often the basis for the connection to terminal server clients via the various communication protocols.

TCP/IP consists of a set of subprotocols arranged in a layer model. The communication can either be connection-oriented (TCP) or connectionless (UDP).

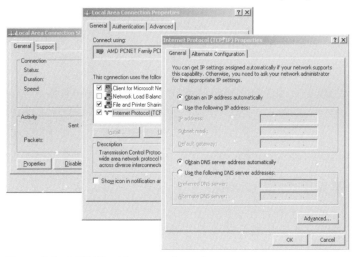

Figure 3-1   TCP/IP address configuration.

Under Windows Server 2003, you configure the TCP/IP protocol in the Control Panel using the Network Connections icon. As administrator, you can set the properties of the local area connections and the TCP/IP protocol.

NWLink and IPX/SPX

The NetWare-compatible protocol NWLink was introduced under Microsoft Windows NT 3.5. It corresponds to Novell's IPX/SPX and can transport data over a network in a way very similar to TCP/IP. Windows Server 2003 add-on products such as

Citrix MetaFrame allow the use of IPX/SPX as an alternative to TCP/IP for communication between Terminal Services and specially adapted clients.

You install the NWLink protocol on Windows Server 2003 through Start\Control Panel\Network Connections and then select the network card to configure. In the LAN connection properties, select the Install button to open the new network components dialog box. Select NWLink IPX/SPX/NetBIOS Compatible Transport Protocol.

The NWLink protocol is no longer supported in the 64-bit version of Windows Server 2003. However, this does not affect Microsoft's remote desktop protocol for connecting terminal servers, because it cannot use this protocol as a transport medium. This is not the case for Citrix ICA: it can use various transport protocols—for example, the NWLink protocol.

NetBEUI

The former standard protocol used by Microsoft and IBM in their network operating systems was NetBEUI (NetBIOS Enhanced User Interface). NetBEUI was also supported by Windows 2000, Windows NT, Windows 98, and OS/2, but it did not allow routing on the network. However, this protocol was very easy to install and manage. Before the success of TCP/IP, NetBEUI was the preferred protocol, particularly for smaller networks. Now, under Windows Server 2003, NetBEUI is no longer used and does not exist in the system.

> **Note**   The starting point for the development of NetBEUI was the NetBIOS interface (Network Basic Input/Output System). NetBIOS applications do not necessarily need the NetBEUI protocol and can run via TCP/IP or IPX/SPX.

Interprocess Communication

In a distributed environment, data must be exchanged bi-directionally between different server and client components. Windows Server 2003 offers nine possibilities for this process: named pipes, mail slots, Windows sockets, remote procedure calls, NetBIOS, NetDDE, server message blocks, DCOM (COM+), and SOAP.

Although some of these options are already dated, they often play an important role on a terminal server, even if the terminal server is running under Windows Server 2003. Why are they still important? Because the modern terminal server must still run several older Windows-based applications. Large companies often need to support many self-developed and critical applications for a long time. For them, it is essential that as many conventional interprocess communication methods as possible work properly. For this reason, we will now describe the most important methods (except for named pipes, mail slots, and NetDDE).

Windows Sockets

The Windows socket interface allows communication between distributed applications via protocols with different addressing systems. The types currently supported by Windows Sockets include TCP/IP and NWLink (IPX/SPX). Originally, they were derived from the Berkeley Sockets, a standard interface to develop client/server applications under UNIX and many other platforms.

> **Important**   A terminal server communicates with its clients via Windows Sockets and not via the server service.

Remote Procedure Calls

The remote procedure calls (RPCs) concept was originally developed by Sun Microsystems to invoke processes on a remote computer as if they were executed locally. It was designed so that the developers did not have to take care of network communication details. Therefore, RPCs use different basic methods, such as Windows Sockets, and they encapsulate the actual communication in a simpler schema.

Under Windows Server 2003, remote procedure calls and their local variant, local procedure calls, play a very important role. However, these calls usually run in the background and offer administrators an indirect means of influence only. Higher services for interprocess communication use RPCs quite often.

NetBIOS

The NetBIOS interface has been used since the beginning of the eighties to develop distributed applications. NetBIOS applications can communicate via different protocols:

- **NetBIOS over TCP/IP–NetBT**   Communication based on the TCP/IP protocol.

- **NWLink NetBIOS–NWNBLink**   Communication based on the IPX/SPX protocol.

The NetBIOS interface consists of fewer than 20 simple commands that handle data exchange. In particular, NetBIOS handles the request and response functions between client and server components. This applies to Windows Server 2003, as well. Therefore, seamless support of NetBIOS functions on a terminal server is necessary, especially for older applications because they were usually not developed using current Internet standards.

Resources for the NetBIOS interface are identified via their UNC names (Universal Naming Convention) with the format \\Computer\Share. You can now access the files, folders, and printers released under these names.

Important The NetBIOS name (also known as *Microsoft computer name*) does not need to be identical to the TCP/IP name (also known as *TCP/IP host name* or *DNS name*) that might exist on the same computer. However, you are strongly urged not to use different naming conventions for the two services. This often leads to confusion for both users and administrators. Starting with Windows 2000, however, the difference between the two name spaces has been virtually eliminated.

CIFS and SMB

The Common Internet File System is for remote access of PCs running a Windows OS to the file system of another computer. The basic mechanism has been better known as *Server Message Blocks* (SMB) since the early eighties. The SMB functions include session control, file access, printer control, and messages. Groups of requests to the NetBIOS interface are bundled and transmitted to a target computer.

Only when SMBs were ratified as an open X/Open standard called CIFS was the concept accepted on a wider basis. Since 1996, Microsoft has used official specifications and publications to actively promote the use of CIFS.

Unlike other file systems, CIFS provides its data to users, not computers. The user is authenticated on the server and not the client. Special authentication servers (for example, domain controllers) can be used for this across the network.

Note On a terminal server, SMB functions are often used to link users' basic directories and to print documents on network printers.

DCOM and COM+

The basic idea behind a distributed environment is to develop applications and services as components. By using the component principle it is possible to break down monolithic applications into predefined components based on standards that are simpler to build and maintain. If you adhere strictly to this principle, you will end up with small, independent, reusable, and self-contained units. Before the Microsoft .NET strategy was introduced, this procedure was possible through the Component Object Model (COM). COM enabled the development of binary software components and led to uniform communication between several of these components. A developer would be able to put together an application by reusing certain components according to the modular design.

So-called middleware such as COM relieves the developer of communication mechanism details, enables the use of familiar techniques, and offers a uniform application programming interface (API). Middleware therefore represents an abstraction layer between the application and the operating system, and it allows the modules of a distributed application to communicate with each other.

The COM components are anchored directly in the operating system. They are thus available for each application with defined interfaces and can be used freely. The problem, however, is that an application might no longer function or might have only limited function if the required COM components are no longer installed on the system.

COM is still widely used today. For years, it has been the basis for the historical Object Linking and Embedding (OLE) and for the ActiveX technology. It was expanded by Distributed COM (DCOM), the corresponding standard for communication across computer boundaries. Before the .NET Framework was introduced, the entire distributed-applications strategy was based on the DCOM model and its successor, COM+. It is therefore found in many established software products.

On a terminal server, the DCOM model places high demands on the system architecture it is built on. Different users communicate with their applications via DCOM, if required. All communication channels are safely allocated to their corresponding user sessions at all times on Windows Server 2003.

SOAP

The simple object access protocol (SOAP) is a protocol based on XML. SOAP exchanges data in a decentralized and distributed environment and consists of two core components: an envelope for supporting expansions and modular requirements, and an encryption mechanism for managing data within the envelope. It does not require a synchronous execution or direct interaction based on request/response mechanisms, but it allows the use of different protocols normally used for communication between distributed software components.

SOAP is one of the basic elements of the .NET strategy and thus plays a dominant role in Windows Server 2003.

Names and Name Resolution

How do computers obtain their unique names? How do they find each other on the network? How does a user identify required resources on a network? How does a terminal server communicate with other network computers? These issues are resolved through varying concepts, all of which are based on attributing logical names to individual computers and resources.

In the course of development of TCP/IP, two techniques emerged for converting logical TCP/IP names to IP addresses:

- **Hosts file**   This file exists on all computers. It contains a simple line-by-line list in the form of IP address = Computer name. Because this table needs to be updated for each computer in case of any modification (for example, a new computer is installed), this type of name resolution is very time-consuming, labor-intensive, and error-prone.

- **DNS (Domain Name Service)**   A central name server hosts a database containing TCP/IP names and the corresponding IP addresses. Clients or specially configured servers request and receive the IP address of a certain TCP/IP name from this name server.

> **Note**   There are also corresponding name resolution mechanisms for NetBIOS: the Lmhosts file (LAN manager hosts file), or WINS (Windows Internet Name Service). These mechanisms are obsolete today.

Domain Name Service

Programs and users rarely reference computers and other resources by their binary network addresses. Instead, they use logical ASCII character strings, for example, www.microsoft.com. A computer on a network, however, understands only addresses such as 192.44.2.1. Therefore, we need mechanisms to convert from one convention to the other. This is particularly true for connecting clients to their terminal servers.

In the beginning, the Internet predecessor DARPANET needed only one simple ASCII file that listed all computer names and IP addresses. This soon became obsolete as thousands of computers became linked over the Internet. A new concept was needed that addressed, in particular, increasingly large file sizes and name conflicts when connecting new computers. This concept resulted in the *Domain Name System* (DNS).

The essence of DNS is the introduction of a hierarchical, domain-based name schema and a distributed database system for implementing that name schema. It is used primarily for mapping computer names to IP addresses. If configured accordingly, DNS can also map IP addresses to their logical names (reverse lookup). A globally registered computer name is called a *Fully Qualified Domain Name* (FQDN).

In this context, a domain consists of a logical structure of computers. Within a domain, there can be subdomains that are used for structuring comprehensive networks. The owner of a domain is responsible for the administration of subdomains by means of a domain name server.

If a network is very extensive, it is further divided into zones. A zone defines which Internet names are physically managed in a certain zone file. A DNS server can manage one or more zones. A zone does not necessarily contain all subdomains of a domain. Accordingly, a large domain can be divided into several zones that are managed separately. All modifications to a zone are performed on an assigned DNS server.

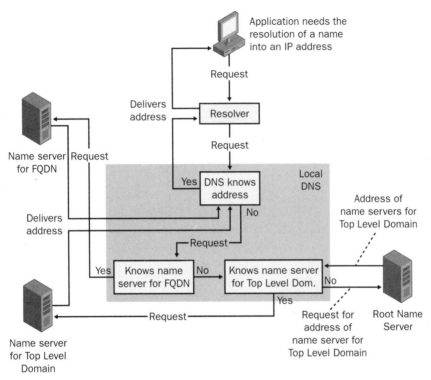

Figure 3-2 Name resolution through DNS.

Most network concepts, including Active Directory directory service under Windows Server 2003, are based on DNS. An expansion allows mapping and registering new IP addresses to logical computer names automatically at runtime. This so-called "dynamic DNS" is used mainly in combination with DHCP.

Important Whether a terminal server functions properly or not is highly dependent on an adequate DNS infrastructure. It is often the correct configuration of the DNS server, not its platform, that makes the difference.

DHCP

Because IP addresses must be unique, an administrator cannot arbitrarily map them. As a result, managing address mapping for terminal server clients on a corporate network can require significant personnel and time. For this reason, the dynamic host configuration protocol (DHCP) is often used in terminal server environments. It is a simple procedure that dynamically configures computers on TCP/IP networks from a remote location. With each logon, DHCP maps preset IP addresses and assigns IP addresses from a pool.

Three values are essential for successfully sending and receiving TCP/IP data packets between two computers:

- **IP address**   Unique identification of the network device, for example, 192.168.1.2.

- **Subnet mask**   Bit pattern used to distinguish network ID and host ID within the IP address, for example, 255.255.255.0.

- **Standard gateway**   Router that receives a data packet if the target computer is not in the same subnet as the source computer. The router forwards the data packet via routing tables to its destination.

So how can a client that does not have these values be configured over the network? The client sends a broadcast TPC/IP packet over the network that always contains the MAC address of its network adapter. This broadcast is received by one or more DHCP servers, and one or more of the DHCP servers replies to the client with a message that they can provide IP configuration data. The client then sends a broadcast requesting the desired configuration data. This request contains the MAC address of the DHCP server that answered first. This prevents the other servers from sending configuration data as well. The client receives its configuration data from the selected server, confirms receipt, and configures itself at runtime. The amount of data exchanged is usually less than 2 KB, and the entire communication usually takes under a second.

The DHCP configuration values may not be allotted to a client permanently, only for a certain amount of time. This allows IP addresses to be mapped from a pool. This pool can be smaller than the potential number of client computers. If a client is still active on the network after half its allotted time has passed, it can request an extension from the DHCP server. If the original DHCP server is unavailable, the client attempts to contact another DHCP server after 87.5 percent of its allotted time has passed.

If the configuration values of an IP address have changed since they were last assigned to a client, the DHCP server can deny an extension. Usually, however, the server instructs the client to release the address and requests new configuration data. In this way, configurations on the entire network can be modified without modifying the clients themselves. The administrative effort for clients is therefore minimal. All active DHCP clients on a corporate network can be reconfigured remotely within a predefined amount of time. This is especially useful for terminal server environments, because maintenance work for their clients is greatly reduced.

You can implement the dynamic DNS concept under Windows Server 2003 combined with the DHCP service. After a DHCP server maps an IP address, the data is forwarded to the DNS server, at which point it is automatically entered in the appropriate database. Because this technique eliminates the need to manually configure name resolution, it is often used with terminal server clients.

Routing

The IP schema for network addresses allows mapping an identity to each connected computer. However, to manage network routing, you need one additional identification, the network Media Access Control (MAC) address. A MAC address is globally unique and therefore unmistakable, and it is usually predefined in the hardware of each network adapter.

The pathway from one terminal server on the network to a remote client is known as routing. It is usually realized by tables on a host or by routers as special network components. Routers can connect IP subnets, use several protocols, and forward data packets to their target subnets (for example, a workstation at home or a remote terminal server). A router supports only packets with a specific target address. The routing tables can be manually predefined or dynamically generated at runtime. Dynamic routers use a series of standardized protocols for different requirements.

The router components include, at a minimum, a table with IP addresses of subnets and information on how to forward the packets of these subnets. Broadcasts that might overload the network are filtered out upon transfer from one subnet (segment) to the other.

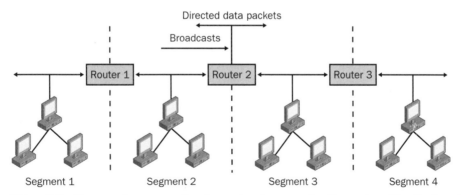

Figure 3-3   Three routers separating four network segments. The routers filter the broadcasts.

Therefore, a data packet transversing a router can be:

- Forwarded to a local network, if it belongs to the subnet

- Forwarded via another network card to another network over another router

- Rejected at the router, if the router does not have any information on how to forward this packet

Furthermore, many routers can be configured so that, in spite of their original function, they allow broadcasts on certain TCP/IP ports. This enables several broadcast-based functions to be used on a large and structured network (for example, DHCP).

> **Important**   You should open only those TCP/IP ports on routers within intranets that are sufficiently protected by a firewall. Otherwise, the danger of illegal access from the Internet is too great.

Therefore, correct router configuration is vital, especially for terminal servers on large local networks or over long distances. The settings of an ISDN router determine the network's capacity and the services provided for a connected workstation at home. However, communication paths over too many router components can cause timeout problems.

Remote Desktop Protocol (RDP)

In May 1997, Microsoft began developing a protocol for exchanges between terminal servers and their Windows OS clients. This protocol is called *RDP* (remote desktop protocol) and is based on International Telecommunication Union (ITU) standards. In particular, RDP is based on the standards of the T.120 protocol family, especially on T.125 Multipoint Communication Service–Protocol Specification (MCS) and T.128 Application Sharing. RDP is also strongly aligned with communication mechanisms that were already in use for data exchange under Microsoft NetMeeting.

Any device can be a client as long as it has an output medium, a mouse, and a keyboard. It also needs to be able to communicate over the network using RDP. Further intelligence is not needed on the client side. The currently available Microsoft RDP clients support only Windows CE, the 32-bit and 64-bit Windows operating systems, an ActiveX control element for Microsoft Internet Explorer, and Apple Mac OS X.

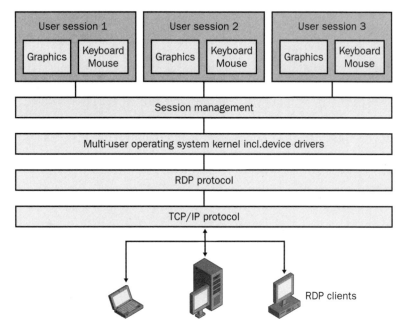

Figure 3-4   RDP protocol integration under Windows Server 2003.

RDP Architecture

The RDP protocol allows communication via up to 64,000 channels. The screen is transmitted as a raster graphic (bitmap) from the server to the client or terminal. The client transmits the keyboard and mouse interactions to the server. The communication is extremely asymmetric. Most data is transmitted from the server to the client.

RDP was originally designed to support different network topologies. In its current state, it can be executed only via TCP/IP networks and is internally divided into several layers. The reason for this, at the lowest level, is that the T.120 protocol family, on which RDP is based, was optimized in accordance with some rather complex specifications of the ISO model. These were mostly grade-of-service mechanisms. Because these cannot be mapped to the TCP/IP protocol, an X.224-compatible adaptation layer handled mapping the specified service primitive of the ISO layer to the service primitive of the TCP/IP protocol.

Basically, only four service primitives are needed, three of which are for connection administration: connection request, connection confirmation, and disconnection request. Connection and disconnection come from the client. When the server ends the connection, the client is not specially notified. In this case, the client implementation needs to address the defined behavior through corresponding exception handling. The fourth service primitive handles data transmission.

The layer above this one provides multicast services. Multicast services allow both point-to-point and point-to-multipoint connections. This is the only way to implement functionality with several endpoints, for example, remote control.

A special security layer comprises all encryption and signature services. It keeps unauthorized users from monitoring the RDP connection and prevents the transmitted data stream from being modified. The RC4 algorithm by RSA Inc. is used for encryption. A signature that consists of a combination of the MD5 and SHA-1 algorithms prevents data manipulation. Additionally, the security layer manages the transmission of the user authentication and the relevant licenses.

The truly relevant layer handles the transmission of mouse and keyboard input and display output. This mechanism is relatively complex. It negotiates the operations used during connection, and it manages the caching information of some data, which reduces the network load significantly.

Over the course of its development, the RDP protocol was further adapted to Windows NT, Windows 2000, Windows XP, Windows Server 2003, and their applications. Many expansions of the protocol relate to this specific type of environment. The original program transmits data over the RDP protocol stack to the TCP/IP protocol stack. Through the layer model described earlier, the data is directed to a channel, encrypted, divided into predefined sections, adapted to the network protocol, addressed, and sent on its way. On the receiving end, this process occurs in reverse, making the data available to the target program. Licensing modalities are monitored here and encryption methods selected. Additional services manage the protocol-specific adjustments in user mode.

Windows Server 2003 Terminal Services is independent of the RDP protocol. The protocol is basically exchangeable; Terminal Services provides a flexible platform for multi-user mode. This platform allows other manufacturers to develop alternative protocols that use Terminal Services functions.

Due to its higher capacity, a kernel driver provides the remaining runtime environment to generate the RDP data stream. (See Chapter 1.) The kernel is subdivided into a section for the transport protocol (TCP/IP) and a section for the session-specific communication protocol (RDP). The latter is executed by the Termdd driver, which transfers mouse and keyboard input from the remote clients to the kernel.

RDP Capabilities

A terminal server does not know which type of client will contact it next. Therefore, all parameters that characterize the client and describe its functions need to be transmitted when connecting. A set of predefined capabilities is used for this purpose.

Knowledge of client capabilities allows a terminal server to respond flexibly to a client's requirements. The capabilities are divided into several groups:

- **General abilities**   Client platform and operating system used, protocol version, and data compression supported.

- **Bitmaps**   Desktop size, preferred color depth, supported color depths, and bitmap compression.

- **Character commands**   Support local character operations, for example, text output or administration for overlaying and redrawing panels.

- **Bitmap cache**   Temporary or persistent caching of frequently used bitmaps on the client.

- **Color table**   Supports a palette for drawing pixels in bitmaps.

- **Panel activation**   Controls the active application window when viewed singly versus in the context of a complete desktop.

- **Remote control**   Supports remote administration, allowing a client to be controlled from a remote location.

- **Cursor**   Defines mouse-cursor color properties.

Some of these properties are vital to the performance of the RDP protocol and warrant a closer look.

Graphics Display Under RDP

If you view a user interface or a dynamic Windows application on a remote client, it is reminiscent of a digital movie. The action might be a bit abstract, and the cutover as application windows change or start is very abrupt. Displaying a graphical user interface on a remote client mainly requires the transmission of huge amounts of data. If modified screen sections were always transferred as a complete set from server to client, the data would easily total from several hundred kilobytes to more than a megabyte. For this reason, starting or ending a full-screen application is particularly expensive in terms of the required network bandwidth.

Therefore, optimizing the RDP protocol and its handling of graphical elements has been given the utmost attention and effort. The most efficient compression algorithms and administration mechanisms have been used, supporting almost all graphics operations of both a Windows desktop and Windows-based applications. The intended result is to keep computational effort and required network bandwidth at the lowest possible level.

The RDP graphics driver receives the graphics commands from the applications via the graphics device interface (GDI or GDI+, discussed in Chapter 1). The application instructs the GDI(+) where and what to draw. The GDI(+) forwards the instructions to the RDP driver. Nevertheless, the GDI(+) does not recognize that the graphics elements are not output on a local screen. The RDP driver transmits that data to a remote client. This is exactly when optimization must occur. Most graphics operations focus on producing raster images (*bitmaps*), drawing graphics primitives, and displaying text characters.

A bitmap is a rectangle consisting of pixels of different colors, thus creating a specific pattern. For instance, an application symbol (icon) is such a bitmap. The display of a static bitmap can be accelerated using compression when transmitting. Compression is possible at low color depth through a simple temporary encryption scheme that transmits only one color value if several pixels of the same color appear in a row. The rates of compression can also be influenced by the applications used and by the design of the graphical user interface. For example, using many colors and horizontal color transitions is very critical. This is why the decoration of panels in a remote client session is much simpler than on the console. The total number of colors used, as defined under bitmap properties, is also very important in the selection of the compression algorithm and the resulting compression rate.

Color palettes can further optimize bitmap use. A table containing color values is created and transmitted to the client. If individual pixels in a bitmap need coloration, the position coordinates in the table are transmitted, not the color value. The amount of data is always smaller when the color depth is high but the number of simultaneously used colors is relatively low. Thus, an individual color value requires up to three bytes, whereas the color position in a table with a maximum of 256 entries needs only one byte.

Even more problematic are animated images, that is, animated bitmaps. They result in significantly higher transfer rates on the network, even if they are very small (for example, animated or blinking mouse cursor). In this instance, we need another mechanism to limit the data volume: *caching*.

How can the output of graphics be realized, for example, lines or rectangles that make up many elements of the user interface? The easiest solution is to draw a line by transmitting each and every pixel. A much more efficient method is a command that defines the start and endpoint, thickness, and color of a line. The rest can be calculated by the output device. Naturally, this feature also uses much more complex commands, such as redrawing a window after it has been overlapped. Here, caching also plays a key role in temporarily storing data of all panel elements and contents.

Individual letters in character strings are managed by a special kind of bitmap, the *glyph*. In principle, the output of characters using glyphs is much easier than the transmittal of letter bitmaps. A command requests only the output of a glyph at a set screen position. However, the number of different fonts and font sizes of the current font sets is quite problematic, as is the initial transport of the glyphs to the client.

Caching

We already mentioned another mechanism to reduce the amount of data transmitted. It is called *caching*, or temporary storage. In this process, the client reserves memory that houses frequently used image fragments that can be displayed again without any network transmission taking place. Some character operations do not work at all without caching, due to technical reasons.

Caching functions are not realized solely through the client's main memory. If local hard drives exist, they can permit so-called persistent caching, in which the cached data is still available even after a client reboot. In principle, special network components can store RDP data and thus provide a global caching space on a LAN segment.

RDP supports the following caches:

- **Bitmap cache**   Cache for different kinds of bitmaps. Size and number of these caches is determined upon connection.

- **Font cache**   Cache for glyphs (character bitmaps). The cache size must be sufficient for storing all characters of a defined character set.

- **Desktop cache**   Cache for a desktop screenshot. A character command stores or outputs this special bitmap.

- **Cursor cache**   Cache for mouse cursors that need special handling. Special graphics algorithms ensure that the correct mouse cursor is displayed on the desktop without generating a lot of network traffic and overloading the local processor resources. Drag-and-drop operations with the mouse therefore do not require the transmission of new graphical elements, but only the transmission of the new coordinates.

- **Text cache**   Cache for frequently used character strings and the corresponding formatting information. Glyphs from the font cache are used to generate a complete character string.

Virtual Channels and Mirroring

An RDP client or application can use a *virtual channel* to transmit specific information. Virtual channels thus help add functions that are not yet specified in the RDP protocol. They represent a platform that future developments can be based on without having to modify the communication methods between a terminal server and its clients. With Windows Server 2003 and RDP 5.2, virtual channels are used for joint client and server clipboards and for redirecting print jobs to local client printers.

Basically, the RDP protocol allows distribution of data streams from one source to many destinations without having to send the data separately. An application can therefore be mirrored on another client. Even the point of input can be transferred from one user to another.

RDP Protocol Features

The features of the RDP protocol play a key role in the wide acceptance of terminal servers. RDP 5.0, deployed under Windows 2000, already set the direction for the future. The most important RDP features follow:

- 256-color (8-bit) support

- Remote monitoring

- 56-bit and 128-bit encryption options

- Improved compression and caching to reduce network traffic

- Option to restore the connection to an existing user session

- Connection to printers and the clipboard on the client

RDP 5.1 was established as an integral part of Windows XP when it was launched. Overall, this version's improved and new properties strengthened Terminal

Services significantly. However, without a suitable server, Windows XP and RDP 5.1 could not exploit the full potential the new technology offered.

So which new properties did RDP 5.1 offer? The following list provides an overview:

- Supports up to 16 million colors (24 bit)

- Provides increased screen resolution of 640 x 480 up to 1600 x 1200 pixels

- Maps predefined, local key combinations to the user session

- Connects to the client's local file system

- Provides improved support of client and network printer integration

- Transmits audio data to the client. The required bandwidth can be controlled. MIDI data integration is not supported.

- Redirects serial ports from the client to the user session on the terminal server

- Permits use of the console session from a remote client. All administrative tasks can be performed without physically accessing the peripheral server devices.

- Requests time-zone information from the client and adjusts the user session accordingly.

- Supports smart cards if a corresponding reading device was installed on the client

- Optimizes bandwidth settings to support different network scenarios (intranet, modem, etc.)

Windows Server 2003 RDP 5.2 has all properties of its predecessor with a few minor additions, such as automatic reconnection of ended sessions.

Required Network Bandwidth

It is very important to know how much bandwidth the RDP protocol uses on the network. Unfortunately, there is no universal answer to this question because it is influenced by so many external conditions, such as:

- Color depth and screen resolution set and supported on the client

- Encryption and compression

- Desktop backgrounds allowed or prohibited, window contents displayed while dragging, animated menus and windows, designs, or bitmap caching

- Client and server platform capacity

- Type and combination of applications used

- User behavior

RDP is usable at a bandwidth of 20 kilobits per second (Kbps), and most efficient at 50 Kbps. If there is sufficient bandwidth, the RDP protocol can use up to 500

Kbps. For instance, it uses more bandwidth if a program produces large graphics quickly in series, and if it is limited only by the output channel's capacity. This situation occurs when computer games, videos, animations, or certain benchmark programs are launched via an RDP client. Therefore, these programs are normally not suitable for running on terminal servers.

Only comprehensive tests, as described in Chapter 11, can give us more detailed information on the bandwidth required in a target environment. Just be prepared for some surprises! The RDP protocol does not always behave as expected. For instance, it is not necessarily true that increasing the supported color depth from 8 bits to 16 bits inevitably results in poorer performance. An 8-bit color space was supported in the past, and for compatibility reasons, the algorithms used then are still available. Modern algorithms are generally faster and optimized to a larger color space. So using more colors could actually improve performance.

Client and server platforms play a key role, too. Network bandwidth can be reduced through compression. However, if the client is too slow to process the received data stream and simultaneously encrypt it, the sessions will not run smoothly. Therefore, optimizing the transmission rate by prohibiting desktop backgrounds or animated menus is of little use.

Figure 3-5 shows a great example of a measurement with limited validity. Six RDP sessions, each configured differently, were executed in a sequence on one client. The bandwidth required by a 16-bit program for graphical load tests was measured for each session. During the measurement, both computer platforms had exclusive use of a 100-megabit network. Each session had its own user account in order to prevent mutual influence. The 16-bit test program was run within each user session in the 16-bit emulation environment. (See the discussion of WoW and VDM in Chapter 1.)

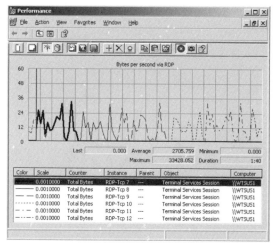

Figure 3-5   Result of a bandwidth test with several RDP sessions, all configured differently, on the system monitor. (See also Chapter 4.)

The results are very similar, and peak loads are all between 25 kilobytes per second (Kbps) and 35 Kbps. This is even more surprising when we review the individual RDP session parameters, as shown in the following table:

Table 3-1   Configuration of the Individual RDP Sessions for the Bandwidth Test

Session ID	Resolution	Color Depth	Bitmap Caching	Network Optimization
7	1024 x 768	16 bit	Yes	LAN (10 Mbps)
8	640 x 480	16 bit	Yes	LAN (10 Mbps)
9	1024 x 768	8 bit	Yes	LAN (10 Mbps)
10	640 x 480	8 bit	Yes	LAN (10 Mbps)
11	1024 x 768	16 bit	No	Modem (28.8 Kbps)
12	640 x 480	16 bit	No	Modem (28.8 Kbps)

We see that the different RDP session configurations resulted mainly in different run times of the test program. The run times differed by up to 50 percent, depending on the parameters selected. However, the values for the network peak loads did not differ very much. It is rather noteworthy, though, that the highest peak load occurred during session 9 configured with only 256 colors (8 bit). In this case, the display speed on the client had the highest value, which correlated with the corresponding demands of the network.

In contrast, Figure 3-6 shows a normal RDP session whose parameters match the ones used in session ID 40 from Table 3-1. Again, both computer platforms had exclusive use of a 100-megabit network without bandwidth limitations. The user of the measured session first started the Paint program and opened a large graphic. The user then started WordPad, opened an existing document, and started adding to it. The application windows were continuously dragged on the desktop. Short-term network load peaks of more than 10 Kbps were observed only when a new application was opened and the window needed to be transmitted for the first time. The processor load was also moderate during these actions, which could be attributed to the fact that the user was the only one on the terminal server.

The average bandwidth measured was 2.6 Kbps, which corresponds to approximately 20 Kbps. If the session were run over a 56 Kbps modem, the bandwidth would definitely suffice. The only difference observed was a short delay in the initial construction of the application windows. Optimizing the transmission rate in the client settings would further reduce the bandwidth required. This scenario would result in relatively smooth operation even on very slow network connections.

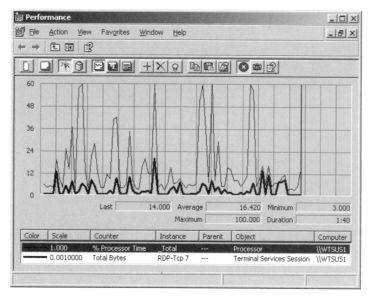

Figure 3-6   An RDP session with normal user actions is measured. The thick line represents the corresponding network bandwidth in Kbps; the thin line displays the processor load.

Latency

User satisfaction in a terminal-server environment is even more influenced by network delays (latency) than by nominally available bandwidth. For instance, a wide area network (WAN) is usually unsuitable for a terminal server, despite its extremely high bandwidth. Signal transmission from user input to client response can take up to one second, because the signal has a long way to travel: from mouse or keyboard to the server, eliciting a graphical response from the corresponding user session, which is then transmitted back to the client.

In addition, not every keystroke made on the RDP client is immediately sent to the server. An input buffer first collects user input to send it as a package. This can also lead to obvious delays in the response behavior of application programs. However, the problem can be resolved by modifying the parameters for buffering RDP data streams. This functionality is described in detail in Chapter 6 and Chapter 15.

If you have ever tried to run a highly interactive application program smoothly, you know it can be rather problematic. Users often also insist on a certain grade of service in terms of maximum response limits and mask change times. Therefore, latency in production terminal server environments should be less than 100 milliseconds (ms). At 150 to 200 ms, delays are very obvious, and at 300 to 500 ms, users normally no longer tolerate system behavior.

A simple method to measure latency between two network nodes (for example, RDP client and terminal server) is the **ping** command. This command invokes a service program for measuring connections to a remote computer. Through echo request and echo reply packages, **ping** determines whether a certain IP node (that is, a certain computer system) within a network is operational.

A typical **ping** command contains a number of parameters that further specify the command's behavior. Checking latency between RDP clients and terminal server would look like this:

```
ping -t -n 20 -1 200 <Servername>
```

Table 3-2   Selected Parameters of the Ping Command

Parameter	Description
-t	Continuously sends **ping** signals to the computer specified.
-N number	Sends the *number* of echo packages defined. Default = 4.
-l length	Sends echo packages with the amount of data specified by *length*. Default = 32 bytes, maximum value = 65,527 bytes. The typical length of an RDP package is between 50 bytes and 1000 bytes.

RDP and the Network Monitor

The network monitor is a system tool included in Windows Server 2003. It is used for complex operations on the network, especially for network analysis and trouble-shooting. The network monitor or an agent connected to it collects all the data on a network adapter.

Both Windows Server 2003 and Microsoft Systems Management Server include the network monitor. At first glance, both tools appear to be identical. However, the operating system variant has some functional limitations. Only the full-fledged Systems Management Server network monitor can receive data packages from other network monitor agents, which allows a more global view of the full system. This is also valid for the network connections between two remote computers. The network monitor delivered with the terminal server can log only the connections of the local network adapter(s).

Note   The network monitor is not included in the predefined Windows Servers 2003 installation routine. It can be installed by adjusting the installation options, or subsequently in the dialog box under Control Panel\Add or Remove Programs\Add\Remove Windows Components in the Start menu.

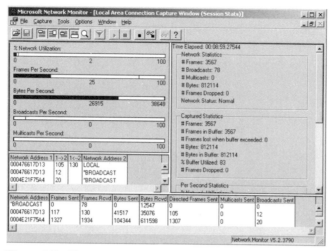

Figure 3-7   The network monitor logs the data traffic between a terminal server and an RDP client.

Network Monitor Functions

The network monitor allows you to define capture filters so that only certain network data is stored for analysis. The filter options can be based on source and destination addresses of the network adapter, source and destination addresses of the protocol, and on pattern matching in the network data stream. As soon as a capture is complete, further filters can restrict the display or limit it to certain protocols.

To simplify the analysis, the collected binary network data streams are interpreted based on their protocol, edited, and displayed. Protocol headings are clearly separated from usable data. They are easy to read and, with a little practice, to understand.

If problems originate in the network during a terminal server session, the network monitor captures all the corresponding information. If you save the collected data in a file, you can analyze it later with the help of the network monitor. Sending this file to a remote specialist allows remote troubleshooting, too.

Caution   The network monitor is a powerful tool for collecting and displaying data streams in corporate networks. It is also an excellent means of targeting, capturing, and displaying unencrypted data. This also applies to unencrypted passwords. Therefore, an administrator should understand how a network monitor works in his or her corporate environment. The Microsoft Systems Management Server network monitor can trace all other network monitors operating on the network.

Network monitor agents greatly simplify terminal server management. All you need is an available network monitor and a basic understanding of the communication mechanisms to the different clients. With network monitor agents, you can also monitor data transmission between terminal servers and domain controllers, and between file and print servers. As you see, this is a valuable tool, especially for solving broadcast problems in complex, structured networks using routers and switches.

Analysis of the RDP Data Stream

The following system structure allows easy measurement of an RDP data stream:

1. A terminal server called WTSUS1 is waiting for a connection request from an RDP client.

2. The user of a client platform called STETBACH and an installed RDP client connects to the terminal server.

The network monitor is launched on the administrator console of the terminal server. Data collection begins just before connecting to the client. Now, the RDP session can be easily monitored in the network monitor. After the user of the RDP client has logged on and performed several standard actions on the desktop of the terminal server session, data collection can be stopped. You can now analyze the data by displaying it in a special window by pressing the F12 key. Alternatively, you can save the data in a file and reload and analyze it at a later time.

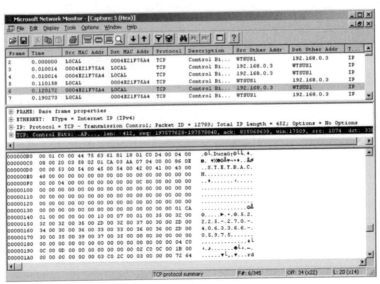

Figure 3-8 The network monitor analyzes an RDP data stream.

You will see a summary of the individual packages at the top of the analysis window of the network monitor. The protocol information recognized appears in the middle, and the raw data is displayed in hexadecimal form at the bottom. The summary includes an item number, the time the collection process started, the hardware's source and target address, the protocol, a description, and the network's source and target address. Because the network monitor does not have a module for recognition of RDP, all packages are labeled with the TCP protocol.

The first three frames of the RDP sequence contain the TCP connection (this corresponds to item numbers 1 to 3 in Figure 3-8). If you analyze the first two rows in detail, you can recognize the TCP connection by the set synchronization bits (S in the TCP protocol information flags in the middle part of the window panel). Frames two and three contain the acknowledgement A for the previous frame. With frames four and five (item numbers 4 and 5), you establish an ISO-over-TCP/IP connection according to Internet standard RFC 1006. This is necessary because the T.120 protocol family, on which RDP is based, requires an X.224-compatible transport protocol.

Frame six (item 6 in Figure 3-8) initializes the T.120 connection and transmits the first parameters for the RDP protocol. You can clearly see the client's name here (from byte D2, the string reading STETBACH). It is a bit more difficult to find the client's resolution of 800 x 600 pixels. You can find it from position C2 in hexadecimal form as 0320 x 0258 pixels with exchanged bytes. In the following frames, encryption is negotiated, the client user logon name is sent, and the logon screen is transmitted.

If you are willing to spend some time on this, you can decipher the basic mechanisms of the RDP protocol as described earlier. This can be very helpful for diagnosing errors and solving problems in network communication.

Different Client Types

Now that we have looked at transport and communication protocols in general and RDP in detail, let us shift our focus to client devices. What do users and administrators expect from clients? First, clients should execute applications and enable connection to the network. Providing a suitable user interface is, of course, another client task. This interface should be as intuitive and ergonomic as possible to optimally support the user. The client should also be as cost-efficient as possible, which is of vital importance, especially in corporate environments. For these reasons, the central administration functions of the client should be comprehensive and include administration of any local applications.

The number of the above-mentioned requirements means a wide variety of clients can be used in a terminal server environment. The product range begins with Windows-based terminals and works its way up through handheld PCs, portable PCs (notebooks), and desktop PCs on a LAN, all the way to UNIX workstations on a LAN. There are platforms that do not quite belong in the list because they are based on special hardware or a particular Internet browser.

It is difficult to characterize all these platforms as thin clients, because their design objectives are quite different. They all belong to the different thin or rich client options that are described in Chapter 1. That is not to say that you can lump all of these client types together for comparison. The resulting numbers would not be realistic. The fact is that the traditional Windows-based PC in its current form is very flexible, but it is also expensive in comparison to a Windows-based terminal. The different types of clients can still be reduced to a common denominator through suitable client software.

The issue of access to the terminal server should also be addressed at this point. One option is to map the user interface of a terminal server session completely to the client. This means that a terminal server remote desktop could be displayed on an existing client local desktop. In this case, a user would have to know which desktop has the applications he or she needs. This situation is mitigated only if the local desktop has very limited functionality and the fewest possible local applications are installed. The remote desktop then becomes the actual user interface.

Another option is to directly display only the remote applications of a terminal server on the local desktop of the client. To realize this option, you need a high-performance desktop on the client platform. Yet with this option, the difference between local and remote applications is negligible.

A terminal server with no other expansion components usually uses the first option; that is, the terminal server desktop is fully mapped to the client platform. Individual applications can be run on the client desktop only by greatly reducing standard terminal server functions.

Client Categories

The time has come to sort out the numerous terms used for all the possible clients. We will focus on the various clients deployed with terminal servers.

Windows-Based Terminals

The hardware of a Windows-based terminal (WBT) consists of keyboard, mouse, monitor, network adapter, and parallel and serial interface. It does not include a local hard drive. Small areas of RAM and ROM house the operating system (for example, Windows CE .NET or Embedded Windows XP) and the access software for one or several server platforms. Different modules of access software enable access to terminal servers or other types of multi-user servers.

No local processes should be run on the WBT, which, technically speaking, also excludes the .NET runtime environment or a Java Virtual Machine. Only scaled-down Internet browsers are an exception. The operating system makes remote administration of WBTs very easy. Windows-based terminals are therefore ultra-light clients that require only minimal administration.

The local WBT desktop provides only basic functions and therefore remains mostly in the background. The user normally works with the remote desktop of the terminal server. This makes the WBT a perfect platform for RDP.

Windows-based terminals are available from numerous manufacturers, the most important being Wyse, Neoware, Fujitsu-Siemens, and Hewlett-Packard. LAN-based PCs running Linux or Windows XP Embedded are also good options in place of WBTs.

Network Computers

In 1996, Apple, IBM, Netscape, Oracle, and Sun Microsystems introduced the profile of a network computer (NC) that required the following hardware: a monitor with a minimum resolution of 640 x 480 pixels, a mouse, a keyboard, and audio output. A hard drive system was not necessary. An NC must support the TCP, FTP, Telnet, NFS, UDP, and SNMP network protocols as well as HTML, HTTP, Java, SMTP, IMAP4, and POP3 Internet standards. DHCP and BOOTP load and start an operating system over the network. DHCP assigns the IP address; BOOTP loads the operating system over the network and uses it to boot the client platform.

For the most part, an application's procedural logic can run on the network computer's local platform. The necessary program resources are normally loaded over the network or stored in local, nonvolatile memory. The local programs can therefore become quite voluminous, for example, when executing Java applets. This differentiates the NC concept from the original idea of the Windows-based terminal.

Even though pure network computers can be used to access terminal servers and their applications over a suitable RDP client, they have all but vanished from the market. This is mainly because the difference between Windows-based terminals and network computers has become negligible. Another reason is that the NC concept has significantly improved through modern operating systems (such as Linux). However, these new devices are not being named consistently. In fact, the manufacturers are trying to establish their own brand names on the market for this class of device.

Mobile Devices

The mobile device category includes small computers to run very thin, local applications. They are often called *handheld PCs* or *palm-size organizers* and have only limited local logic. Many of these devices are equipped with a very small monitor, and you enter data with a stylus instead of a keyboard. Windows CE or Pocket PC are two common operating systems for handheld PCs. They are stored in ROM together with the applications.

Mobile devices can run on batteries for 8 to 12 hours, which makes them extremely flexible and locale-independent. If wireless network connections are brought to bear (for example, radio or infrared), these devices can be used almost anywhere. Access to a terminal server through an installed RDP client is always possible, allowing almost any application to be used. It would not make a lot of sense to map the entire desktop of a terminal server session to such a device. The local screen resolution is usually much too low.

Notebooks

Notebooks or laptops are the most sophisticated mobile computers. These devices are fully equipped clients and provide the same peripheral components as a stationary PC. The entire configuration is, of course, very small and light. Notebooks have rechargeable batteries, so they do not need a stationary power supply. Windows XP is the operating system of choice for notebooks. Newer versions of this device class are designed like a notepad and allow input via a special monitor and stylus.

If a network adapter and an RDP client are installed on a notebook, you can use remote applications without consuming too many local resources. Nonetheless, the notebook as a thin client is not without problems. Because the notebook is not always connected to the network, central administration is more difficult.

PCs or Workstations on the LAN

PCs or workstations on the LAN are stationary, fully equipped clients based on operating systems such as Windows 2000 Professional, Windows XP, Mac OS, or UNIX and Linux. However, they can still be considered thin clients if they have the right software installed to access the server platforms on the network. An RDP client or an ICA client are options for selecting the access software. (See Chapter 9.) The applications launched in this way run exclusively on the server.

A special configuration option enables access to local client resources such as hard drives or printers. Local applications can still run in parallel. This makes the system both flexible and more difficult to manage.

This client category can be operated using two different configurations:

1. The PC or workstation has very limited functions and is mainly a carrier platform for an RDP client. Even with minimal use of local resources (for example, processor, main memory, or hard drives), acceptable results can still be produced. For this reason, even older machines can be used for this purpose. It is also possible to reduce user access to existing local resources for security reasons. For instance, it is possible to prevent writing data to the local hard drive to enforce using a central memory instance.

2. The PC or workstation can access terminal servers only to integrate a few central applications in a well-designed local environment. A device used in this way is usually based on a relatively current hardware generation.

> **Note**   Many of the statements made here also apply to notebooks, but to a lesser degree.

Planning of the Client Platforms

Users' acceptance of the terminal server environment is often based on their experience with the client. Before selecting a client, it is important to understand its purpose.

Purpose

Clients fall into one of several categories in a terminal server environment:

- **Replacement for the local desktop** This includes clients running no local applications except the RDP client. The user does not have contact with the local desktop. This type of client is best for users who need to work with only a few applications that all run on terminal servers.

- **Supplement to the local desktop** This environment combines a local and a remote desktop. This combination makes sense especially when the client and server operating systems are very different or when local applications cannot be moved to terminal servers. This configuration is also suitable if the client is specifically configured for a certain user group. However, the user might find it difficult to be confronted with two different desktops and then have to look for the desired application. Normally, only experienced users should work in this kind of environment. Highly asymmetric environments, with a very small number of local applications versus a large number of remote applications on terminal servers, are the exception. This environment is practical only if the needed local applications cannot run on terminal servers.

- **Local display of remote applications** In this category, applications on the terminal server are displayed on the local client desktop. This configuration creates the most natural impression for the user when accessing applications. The user cannot tell the difference between local applications and remote ones. The necessary functions are configured using a predefined boot program for connecting to a terminal server or through third-party components.

These categories and their transferability to target environments are the primary factors in selecting the client.

Selection Criteria

How do you select the right client for terminal servers? First, you need to analyze existing devices to see whether you can use them for the intended purpose. If you need to acquire new clients, the above-mentioned client categories, the intended purpose, and hardware-specific parameters are essential.

- **Category by purpose** Windows-based terminals and network computers are always the preferred solution for replacing the local desktop. Notebooks and PCs on a LAN are the right choice for supplementing the local desktop. Local display of individual remote applications is best for mobile devices and PCs on a LAN.

- **Processor**   Type, speed, and long-term availability of the processor are crucial because the processor determines performance and its long-term viability.

- **Memory**   Size of RAM and ROM and a Flash-ROM card to manage the local operating system and other system components to access the terminal server.

- **Keyboard and mouse**   Input devices suitable for multiple languages and specific user requirements.

- **Monitor**   Maximum resolution, color depth, and refresh rate of the output device. In addition, you need to select either analog or digital monitor control.

- **Multimedia**   Audio and video support options.

- **Interfaces**   Ability to use local serial and parallel interfaces, adapters for different network topologies and USB ports.

- **RDP client software**   Availability of current RDP client software for the platform.

- **Central management**   Central management is very important if you do not want to change client configuration locally. Only authorized persons can modify configuration. Users should not have uncontrolled access to clients' configuration parameters. This is the only way to substantially reduce the client administration effort.

- **Modem dialup**   Options to dial up the existing network structure via the point-to-point protocol (PPP) or the point-to-point tunneling protocol (PPTP).

- **Security**   Support of current encryption options and integration of smart cards or biometric authentication procedures.

- **Web browser**   Option to integrate a local web browser and the corresponding functions (for example, client-side scripting or Java).

- **Additionally required terminal emulations**   Additional system components that can be integrated to access central systems (for example, VT emulation and host connection).

> **Tip**   RDP clients exist for platforms other than the ones supported directly by Microsoft. For instance, Tarantella, a middleware product, allows implementation of the RDP protocol on the Tarantella Adaptive Internet Protocol (AIP). The corresponding AIP clients can therefore integrate terminal server sessions into UNIX environments. (See *http://www.tarantella.com*.) HOB developed a Java client for RDP. (See http://www.hobsoft.com/www_us /home.htm.) The Linux developers offer several solutions for their operating system, for example, Rdesktop (*http://www.rdesktop.org*) or WinConnect (*http://www.thincomputinginc.com*).

Before you finalize your selection of new clients, you might want to compare the requirements to a list of properties of the different brands. In addition to model options and prices, the client type figures largely in calculating administration costs.

Terminal Services Clients

Now that we have addressed Terminal Services, the RDP protocol, and different client types in the last few sections, we can move on to the details of RDP clients for Microsoft operating systems. Only these clients allow remote work on the terminal server and are therefore an essential part of the overall system. The basic precondition for networking clients is the integration of monitor, mouse, and keyboard, as well as the support of the RDP protocol.

In principle, the potential target platforms for Terminal Services clients can be divided into the following categories:

- Windows-based terminals under Windows CE
- Apple Macintosh computers under Mac OS X
- Personal computers under Windows 95, Windows 98, Windows NT, Windows 2000, and Windows XP

> **Note**   The name *Terminal Services client* refers only to RDP clients offered by Microsoft. This section deals exclusively with the Terminal Services clients for the 32-bit variants of Microsoft Windows. Windows-based terminals or Macintosh platforms will not be addressed in any depth here.

Terminal Services clients initiate the connection to a terminal server via TCP port 3389. A waiting RDP thread receives the connection request and starts a user session. The user session is taken over by another RDP thread that handles interaction between client and server. The waiting RDP threads then continue listening for new connection requests on the network.

Two standard clients exist for this type of access to Windows Server 2003 Terminal Services: the *Remote desktop connection* and the *remote desktop MMC Snap-in*. Both use the *Mstscax.dll* terminal server client ActiveX control element and will be described in detail in the following section.

Remote Desktop Connection

The remote desktop connection is the default RDP client installed on every terminal server. It is stored under Start\All Programs\Accessories\Communications.

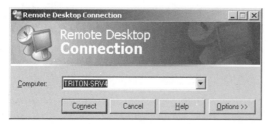

Figure 3-9   Remote desktop connection start window.

The remote desktop connection allows input of data required to connect to a terminal server. You can enter the computer name and other optional values as parameters.

> **Note**   The remote desktop connection replaces the Windows 2000 Terminal Services client and Client Connection Manager.

Installation

On another 32-bit Windows version (for example, Windows XP or Windows 2000 Professional), you can install the remote desktop connection from a source folder on Windows Server 2003. This folder is located at %SystemRoot%\system32\clients\ tsclient\win32 and contains all files required for the installation. If need be, this folder can be released, that is, it can be accessed over the network. The installation itself is very easy and is supported by a wizard.

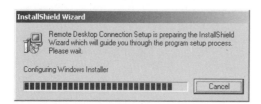

Figure 3-10   Initializing the remote desktop connection installation wizard.

After the welcome screen is displayed, you are asked to accept the license agreement and enter the user name and company. Then you decide if the remote desktop connection should be installed for the current user or for all system users. After you enter that information, the installation takes a few minutes to finish. The necessary files are saved to the local hard drive and the start menu is updated. The ActiveX control *Mstscax.dll* terminal server client is integrated into the system.

> **Tip**   You will find information on using *Mstscax.dll* for developing your own applications in the Platform SDK documentation.

When you are done, the remote desktop connection is operable and its application icon can be found under Start\All Programs\Accessories\Communications.

Connecting

With the help of the remote desktop connection, it is quite easy to launch a user session on a terminal server. All you need is network access and the required access permission. To connect, you can select the computer name and other logon settings on the advanced screen that appears when you click the Options button. In this mode, the remote desktop connection user interface displays five tabs. With these tabs, you can choose several settings in different categories.

The first tab is the General tab, which is an expansion of the initial user interface that you see when you connect. It allows you to set basic logon settings:

- **Computer**   Enter a computer name or select one from a list of identified terminal servers.

- **User name**   A user's logon name.

- **Password**   Optional input of the password, which is used with the user name to log on, if accepted by the terminal server.

- **Domain**   Name of the domain or the local computer that is responsible for authenticating the user.

If desired, the password can be encrypted and saved in the user's profile so that it can be used for the next logon. However, this might cause system security problems.

The General tab also allows you to save and open connection settings in files. The corresponding format is described in detail below.

Figure 3-11   The remote desktop connection General tab.

You select Display options in another tab. You can predefine the remote desktop size, which ranges between 640 x 480 and 1600 x 1280 pixels. The highest setting depends on the maximum resolution of the local graphics card. Alternatively, you can select the full-screen mode that covers the entire client screen and completely hides the local desktop.

You also use this tab to select the number of colors used. The range lies between 256 colors and full-color mode (24 bit). As with desktop size, the number of colors depends on the settings of the local graphics card. However, these settings can be overridden by other settings on the terminal server because the server configuration takes precedence.

At the bottom of the tab, you will find the option for displaying the connection toolbar in full-screen mode. The connection toolbar contains window control elements, such as minimize or maximize. These control elements greatly simplify reactivating the local desktop because it is fully covered by the remote desktop in this mode. If you deactivate this option, the toolbar is displayed for five seconds after logon and then disappears.

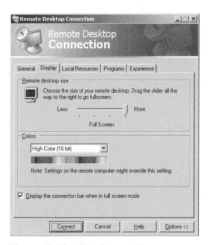

Figure 3-12 Display settings.

The third tab deals with Local Resources, that is, audio data streams, keyboard, and other local devices. For audio data streams (sounds), you can select options for playing sounds on the remote computer, on the client, or not at all. In a terminal server environment, only the last two options are reasonable, because sound output on the server is either impossible or undesirable.

For the Windows keyboard shortcuts, you select the option of using them locally or remotely and whether you want them in full-screen mode. This is the only way to clearly allocate the keyboard shortcuts to the predefined target devices. Sessions within the remote desktop connection are controlled using the following keyboard shortcuts. They differ from the local desktop shortcuts to avoid colliding with the client system.

Table 3-3   Predefined Keyboard Shortcuts of the Remote Desktop Connection for Frequent User Actions

Keyboard Shortcuts	Description
Alt + Page up	Toggles programs from left to right as displayed in the list in the dialog window
Alt + Page down	Toggles programs from right to left as displayed in the list in the dialog window
Alt + Insert	Cycles through all programs in the sequence in which the programs were started
Alt + Home	Displays the start menu on the client desktop
Ctrl + Alt + Pause	Toggles between window and full-screen client mode
Ctrl + Alt + End	Opens the security settings Windows panel
Alt + Delete	Displays the Windows menu
Ctrl + Alt + Minus (-)	Saves an image of the active client session window on the terminal server clipboard. Produces the same behavior as the Alt + Print shortcut on a local computer. However, you must use the minus key on the numeric keypad.
Ctrl + Alt + Plus (+)	Saves an image of the entire client session window on the terminal server clipboard. Produces the same behavior as the Print shortcut on a local computer. However, you must use the plus key on the numeric keypad.

In addition to audio output and shortcuts, the third tab defines the automatic connection to local drives, printers, and serial ports. All this helps to integrate the local resources with the remote user session. The user thus gains intuitive access to the client devices even though the user is active only within the terminal server session.

Note   The smart card reader option appears in this tab if the client has a smart card reader. This reader can be used in the terminal server session.

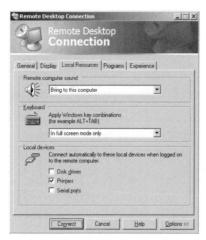

Figure 3-13   Local resources configuration.

If you enter two character strings in the fourth tab, called Programs, you can configure an exclusive program that starts automatically when you log on. The string in Program path and file name specifies the desired program, and the string in Start in the following folder defines the default directory assigned to the program.

When you log on, the normal desktop is not displayed; instead, you'll see the program in full-screen mode within a remote desktop connection window. This lays the foundation for an environment that runs only one application.

Note   This configuration will not take effect if the settings on the terminal server differ. The terminal server configuration always overrides client settings.

Figure 3-14   Start options configuration of a selected program.

By using the last tab, Experience, you optimize transmission performance. The higher the available network bandwidth, the more graphical functions can be used. The optional properties are listed in descending order by requirements. Managing a desktop background (wallpaper) requires the most network bandwidth, whereas a slow connection will still support themes. Caching should always be enabled because it significantly reduces the data rate without degrading performance. However, this is valid only if the client's memory resources are fast and large enough. Otherwise, caching can have a negative impact on system performance.

The last option in this tab allows you to determine whether the connection will be reestablished if it was ended. Selecting this option ensures continuous communication, even if the lines are unstable.

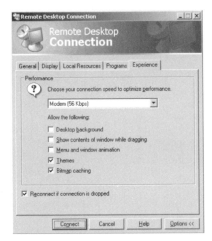

Figure 3-15   Configuring performance parameters.

Within its graphical user interface, the remote desktop connection offers access to all essential settings that you need to configure and optimize communication with terminal servers. However, you have to use the command line to get to a number of expanded options.

Mstsc Command-Line Options

Instead of invoking the remote desktop connection via the Start menu, you can also use the command line to do just that by calling up **Mstsc.exe** and several arguments. In this way, you can reuse connection options saved in RDP files.

The **Mstsc.exe** command syntax:

```
Mstsc File /v:Server[Port] /console /f /w:Width /h:Height /edit /migrate
```

Table 3-4   Arguments and Parameters of the Mstsc Program

Argument	Description
File	Specifies the RDP file name for connecting
/v:Server[Port]	Specifies the DNS name or IP address of the server to which you want to connect. You can enter the desired port here.
/console	Connects to the console session of the terminal server
/f	Starts the client in full-screen mode
/w:Width	Specifies the width of the remote desktop in pixels
/h:Height	Specifies the height of the remote desktop in pixels
/edit	Opens the RDP files specified for editing
/migrate	Transfers the configuration files generated under Windows 2000 using the Windows Connection Manager to the new RDP file

You can connect to the terminal server's console session only by using the command-line option. A referenced RDP file, however, offers more flexibility.

Using an RDP File

By using the remote desktop connection General tab, you have the option of saving the configuration settings selected for connecting to a terminal server. The settings are saved in Unicode text files with the extension .rdp. You can use them either in the graphical user interface or with the command-line option of the remote desktop connection.

RDP files are therefore well-suited for defining default configurations to access terminal servers or individual applications on terminal servers. What other information lurks in RDP files? Here is a closer look at a sample RDP file:

Listing 3-1: Contents of a Sample RDP file

```
screen mode id:i:2
desktopwidth:i:1024
desktopheight:i:768
session bpp:i:16
winposstr:s:0,1,0,0,800,600
full address:s:TRITON-SRV1
compression:i:1
keyboardhook:i:2
audiomode:i:0
redirectdrives:i:1
redirectprinters:i:1
redirectcomports:i:1
redirectsmartcards:i:1
displayconnectionbar:i:1
autoreconnection enabled:i:1
username:s:test
domain:s:TRITON-SRV1
alternate shell:s:C:\Windows\system32\notepad.exe
shell working directory:s:C:\Documents and Settings\tritsch\My Documents
```

```
disable wallpaper:i:1
disable full window drag:i:1
disable menu anims:i:1
disable themes:i:0
disable cursor setting:i:0
bitmapcachepersistenable:i:1
```

Most lines correspond to settings that can be defined via the graphical user interface. Nevertheless, some of these options need to be explained in detail. The following table provides a detailed description of all lines in the RDP file.

Table 3-5   The Most Important Lines of an RDP File

Option	Description
screen mode id:i:	Integer that determines whether the remote desktop is started with a set resolution or in full-screen mode. 1: Set resolution 2: Full-screen mode
Desktopwidth:i:	Integer that specifies the width of the remote desktop. Values other than 640, 800, or 1024 are possible.
Desktopheight:i:	Integer that specifies the width of the remote desktop. Values other than 480, 600, or 768 are possible.
session bpp:i:	Integer that specifies the color depth in bits. Possible values: 8, 15, 16, and 24.
winposstr:s:	Character string containing position and size of the client window on the remote desktop. Values three and four of the character string determine the position of the top left corner of the window on the client desktop, five and six the position of the bottom right corner. Example of a valid value: *winposstr:s:0,1,100,100,920,750.*
full address:s:	Character string that contains the DNS name or IP address of the target server.
compression:i:	Integer that specifies the client's compression standard.
keyboardhook:i:	Integer that specifies where the Windows keyboard shortcuts are used. 0: Use on local computer 1: Use on remote computer 2: Use only in full-screen mode
audiomode:i:	Integer that handles sound events on the remote computer. 0: Play on this computer 1: Do not play at all 2: Play on remote computer
redirectdrives:i: *redirectprinters:i:* *redirectcomports:i:* *redirectsmartcards:i:*	Integers that specify if local drives, printers, serial ports, or smart cards automatically establish a connection to the user session on the remote computer. 0: No 1: Yes

Table 3-5   The Most Important Lines of an RDP File

Option	Description
displayconnectionbar:i:	Integer that specifies whether the connection toolbar is displayed in full-screen mode. 0: No 1: Yes
autoreconnection enabled:i:	Integer that specifies whether the connection is automatically reestablished if ended. 0: No 1: Yes
username:s:	Character string containing the user name.
domain:s:	Character string containing the domain or server name that is responsible for user authentication.
alternate shell:s:	Character string containing path and name of a program that is started on connection.
shell working directory:s:	Character string containing the working directory for the program that is started on connection.
disable wallpaper:i: *disable full window drag:i:* *disable menu anims:i:* *disable themes:i:* *disable cursor setting:i:*	Integers that specify how many options for optimizing network performance are disabled. This affects desktop background, display of the window content when dragging, menu and window animation, themes, and bitmap caching. 0: Allow option 1: Disable option
bitmapcachepersistenable:i:	Integer that specifies if the cached bitmaps persist on the local hard drive. This would make them available for the next session. 0: No 1: Yes
auto connect:i:	Automatic user logon. 0: No (password is not saved) 1: Yes (password is saved)
connect to console:i:	Integer that specifies whether you open a console or a user session. This line is not automatically generated when you save the remote desktop connection parameters. Therefore, you need to insert it manually, if necessary. 0: User session (default) 1: Console session

Tip   The default values of a remote desktop connection are also saved in an RDP file. This file is called Default.rdp and is a hidden file in the Documents and Settings\<User Name >\My Documents folder. When distributed in the standard profile to users' desktops, this type of file opens up new possibilities for accessing applications over terminal servers.

Remote Desktop MMC Snap-In

The Remote Desktop Snap-in in the Microsoft Management Console allows management of connections to terminal servers. In combination with Terminal Services, it also administers the connections to other forms of Windows Server 2003. The snap-in is ideal for administrators who need to maintain simultaneous connections to multiple servers.

> **Important**   The Remote Desktop Snap-in is not an RDP client for normal users, but a tool for administrators. For this reason, the default setting of the Remote Desktop Snap-in always establishes a connection to the console of the target server. Additionally, most tasks from the Remote Desktop Snap-in can be executed only if you are logged on as the administrator. Nonetheless, networkwide guidelines might prohibit certain tasks.

To use Remote Desktop Snap-in for the first time, start the Microsoft Management Console (Mmc.exe). A dialog box is displayed, allowing you to add standalone Snap-ins via File\Add\Remove Snap-in. Select Remote Desktop from the list of available snap-ins and add it to the console.

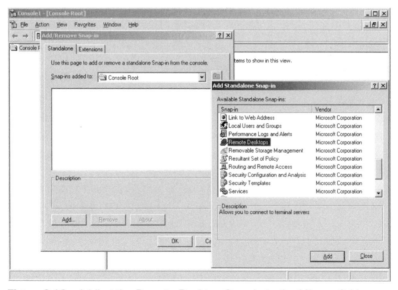

Figure 3-16   Adding the Remote Desktop Snap-in to the Microsoft Management Console.

On terminal servers, this type of predefined console can be found under Start\All Programs\Administrative Tools\Remote Desktop.

When you start the Remote Desktop Snap-in for the first time, you need to generate connection configurations to the servers desired. On the left side of the console panel, select Remote Desktop with the right mouse key. In the resulting context menu, select the first list item, Add New Connection. In the dialog box, enter the desired server name or IP address, a connection name, and—optionally—logon information, password, and domain.

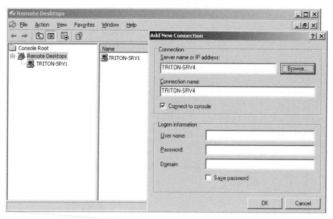

Figure 3-17 The Remote Desktop Snap-in with one connection configured and a new connection being added.

The default setting for initial configuration creates a connection to the console of the server desired. This is particularly helpful for administrative tasks, but only authorized users may access the server. It is not a multiple-user option, and is used exclusively for remote administration. Only if the appropriate option is disabled can multiple Remote Desktop Snap-in users access the same server.

> **Note** The Remote Desktop Snap-in allows you to enter your user information for automatic logon to the terminal server. After entering the password in the connection dialog, the password is encrypted and saved in the MSC file. The encrypted password is protected and can be modified only with the logon data of the user who entered it in the connection dialog. If you do not enter the password in the connection dialog, the default Windows logon dialog appears when the session starts and prompts you to enter the password manually. In this way, the password is not saved on the local computer.

After setting up the connections desired, you can access one or more selected servers by choosing the corresponding connection name from the Remote Desktop list. If this does not work right away, you can reinitiate the connection using the context menu of the connection name (that is, the server) at a later point in time.

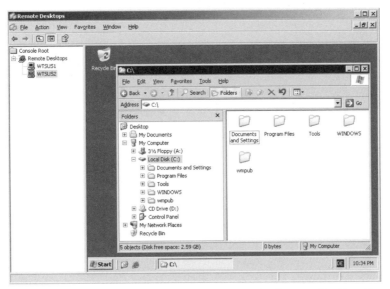

Figure 3-18   Existing connection to a server in the Remote Desktop Snap-in. The desktop size depends on the dimensions of the Result Pane on the right.

Other important options in the context menu of a selected server include ending an existing connection and displaying the connection properties. The latter, in particular, provides options beyond those in the initial setup of a connection.

> **Note**   Unfortunately, some other helpful options have not (yet) found their way into the tool. For instance, there is neither an option to disconnect a session in the context menu of a server nor the ability to log off. Established connections cannot be sorted by name or grouped. This is especially troublesome if you want to manage a large number of servers with the Remote Desktop Snap-in.

When you open the properties of a preconfigured connection, a dialog box with three tabs is displayed. The options under the General tab relate to the same parameters as for setting up a new connection: server name, connection name, and logon information.

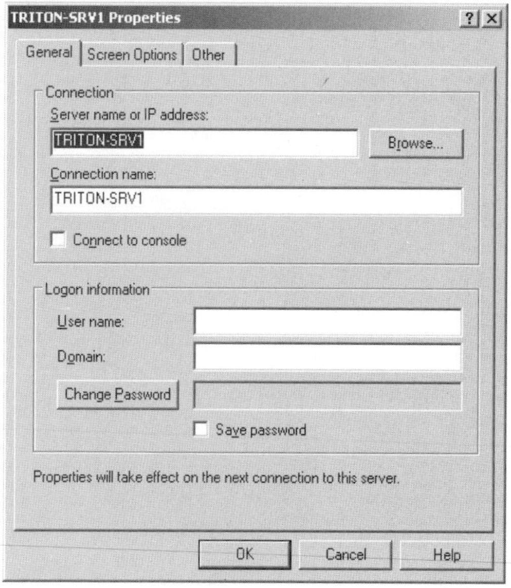

Figure 3-19 Later adjustment of general properties in Remote Desktop Snap-in.

On the Screen Options tab, you can choose to display the desktop as the MMC Result Pane is displayed, in a standard size (640 x 480, 800 x 600, or 1024 x 768), or you can opt for a custom size. However, the new settings will not take effect until the next connection. Similarly, changing the MMC pane size does not modify the size of the desktop if the corresponding connection was initiated with MMC Result Pane option selected.

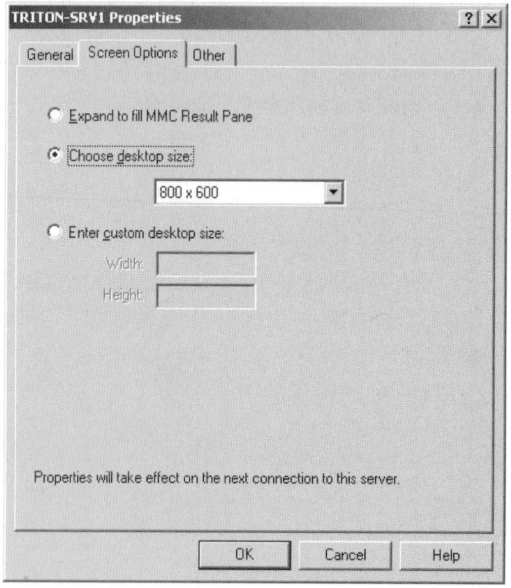

Figure 3-20 Adapting the screen options under Remote Desktop Snap-in.

On the Other tab, you configure a program to automatically start on logon, along with its default directory. When a user logs on, the selected program completely fills the desktop. Ending the program also ends the user session.

Another option on this tab allows you redirect local client drives to the user session on the remote server. You cannot redirect printers or serial ports or control network bandwidth and encryption options.

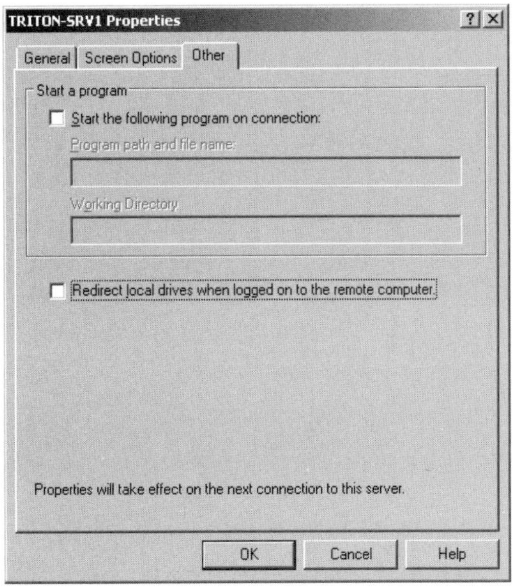

Figure 3-21   The Properties tab under Remote Desktop Snap-in.

Connection Options

The connection configurations between terminal server and RDP clients are not static or identical for all scenarios. Instead, they must be able to adapt to dynamic user behavior and to the varying standards of an administrator. Many parameters control and configure such connections. These parameters can be set in different places.

We already learned about two of them: the Terminal Services configuration on the terminal server and the RDP client remote desktop connection and the Remote Desktop MMC Snap-in on the client. It is probably easiest for a system administrator to treat all user settings for a certain connection type of Terminal Services configuration in the same way. In some cases, however, it might be necessary to allow special settings through user entries on the client.

In principle, it is possible to set certain options either on the server only or the client only. This is a lot less problematic than configurations that can be set on both sides. Which one is relevant? The basic rule is that terminal server settings prevail over differing settings on the RDP client. In other words, the terminal server administrator is stronger than the end user.

To get a feeling for the capabilities of each, compare the connection options of the Terminal Services configuration, the Remote Desktop connection, and the Remote Desktop MMC Snap-in in the following table.

Table 3-6   Comparison of Configuration Options for Terminal Servers and RDP Clients

Option	Terminal Services Configuration	Remote Desktop Connection	Remote Desktop MMC Snap-in
Configure the LAN adapters used	Yes	No	No
Counter for maximum connections per LAN adapter	Yes	No	No
Select level of encryption	Yes	Preset	Preset
Automatic logon	Yes	Yes	Yes
Always request password	Yes	No	No
Connection timeouts	Yes	No	No
Timeout for ended connections	Yes	No	No
Timeout for idle time	Yes	No	No
Handle interrupted connections	Yes	No	No
Start an initial program	Yes	Yes	Yes
Redirect local drives	Yes (non-binding)	Yes	Yes
Redirect local printers	Yes (non-binding)	Yes	No
Redirect local serial ports	Yes (non-binding)	Yes	No
Redirect local clipboard	Yes	No	No
Redirect local audio streams	Yes	No	No
Preset/select desktop size	No	Yes	Yes
Preset/select color depth	Yes	Yes	No
Connect to the console	No	Depends	Yes
Automatic reconnections	No	Yes	No
Control network bandwidth	Yes	Yes	No
Control full screen options	No	Yes	No
Logs	Yes	No	No

Network Planning

After introducing the server component in the previous chapter and the network protocols and client components in this chapter, all we need to complete our description of the terminal server environment is a basic estimate of the required bandwidth and network structure options.

So how can terminal servers, RDP clients, and the RDP protocol be used in different network environments? To answer this question, let us look at some basic configurations in detail. We can use these configurations to derive benchmark data to plan, dimension, and configure the network environment. This fundamentally qualitative data will be refined in later chapters to develop precise quantitative estimates.

Minimal Configurations

The simplest scenario for a networked terminal server is to connect it to a number of thin clients or terminals. Windows Server 2003 with Terminal Services in application mode must be installed on suitable hardware. On the same platform, applications must be installed, user accounts set up, and basic user directories created. (See also Chapter 4 and Chapter 5.) For this reason, all application data, user data, user accounts, and user profiles are found on the terminal server. A local printer connected to the server provides the frequently needed print function.

You can link the terminal server to the clients over a relatively simple TCP/IP network structure. This configuration allows the terminal server to handle several dozen users and clients simultaneously.

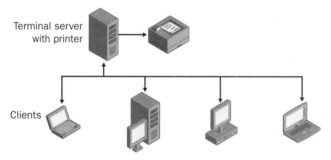

Figure 3-22   Stand-alone terminal server with local printer and RDP clients on the network.

The network bandwidth required between the terminal server and clients is relatively low. It usually ranges from 20 Kbps to 50 Kbps for each client. The exact bandwidth depends on the applications used and the users' working style. A more exact basis to calculate the required network resources is described in Chapter 5. Certain graphics applications and intense printer use increase the bandwidth demand, whereas reduced user activity can virtually silence data traffic.

If you want to deploy Windows-based terminals or other relatively simple clients, you might want to assign IP addresses automatically via DHCP. This significantly reduces the installation and administration effort for the clients' individual configuration. The necessary DHCP service needs to be installed on the terminal server (if required, in combination with a DNS service).

Integrating Local Devices

Within a corporate environment, there are often clients with their own peripheral devices connected to a terminal server. Physically, all applications can run on the server in this configuration. From the user's point of view, it looks as if the applications are running on the client. This is because monitor output and interaction look exactly like local applications. Therefore, it seems natural to use the client peripherals for remote applications, too.

Of course, this contradicts the pure terminal server model in which clients must be as simple as possible. The RDP protocol, however, transfers and maps client interfaces to the server environment (port remapping). This way, many of the local peripheral devices and resources connected to the client are available for terminal server sessions. This particularly includes local drives and printers connected to the client's serial or parallel interface and devices that are connected to the serial interface. Please note that only USB printers are supported for USB ports.

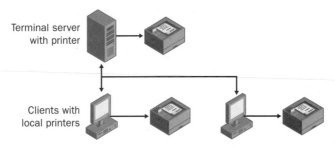

Terminal server with printer

Clients with local printers

Figure 3-23   Clients with local printers that can be mapped to the corresponding user sessions on the terminal server.

There are two ways to configure local devices for use with client devices. Certain types of local devices can be made available to all terminal server users or only to individual users who logged on interactively over a suitably configured client. In the first case, the client device is displayed on a specific interface of the entire terminal server. In the latter case, the device appears in the user session only.

Both methods seem logical because the client device can be contacted using the IP address or the logical name and its local interface name (for example, local drive C:). If redirected to a logical terminal server interface (for example, *TSCLIENT**C*), the device becomes available to all affected users through a corresponding driver. The resulting behavior is similar to a peripheral device that is contacted over a network connection. However, the many different client device drivers could pose a problem because they must seamlessly appear in the user sessions on the terminal server.

Client interface redirection can also be used for other peripheral devices that are very important to the corporation. For instance, it is possible to integrate fingerprint scanners into the existing interfaces of an RDP client so that the scanners can be used by the applications running on the terminal server. You might need special drivers to support the virtual channels that allow expanded communication between terminal servers and clients.

Note   When you use client devices over a terminal server, the network traffic might increase significantly. On the one hand, the data stream that displays the application and enables user interaction must be sustained. On the other hand, data for client device control is transmitted over the same pathway. This is particularly noticeable when printing large documents or graphics.

Uses for Individual Terminal Servers

What is the minimal configuration of one stand-alone terminal server and a few clients good for? Unfortunately, the answer is rather sobering. A terminal server with this configuration should be used only in testing environments or environments with a very low availability requirement. You could, of course, connect several dozens of clients over an older 10-megabit network without running into problems. But if the terminal server fails, no one will be able to work with the central applications. Because user data and profiles are also located on the terminal server, they could be lost if the system fails.

Important   If you also configured the terminal server as a domain controller in order to later expand the environment, you might experience even more difficulties. For instance, users cannot interactively log on to a domain controller if they are not members of the administrator group. This applies to logging on over Terminal Services as well. Only if you modify the local security guidelines will users be able to log on to the server's desktop interactively via Terminal Services.

Corporate Configurations

The terminal server configurations examined thus far are based on a simple, two-layer model. The model consists of a number of clients that access the network over one terminal server. This type of environment is rather limited with respect to the number of potential users and system availability. In the following section, we will introduce models that overcome these limitations and that therefore work especially well in corporate environments.

Basic Models

It is not enough to simply add another terminal server to a single-server environment to accommodate more users. The formula for incrementing terminal servers is actually "one, four, many."

The reason is as follows: when users log on to the only existing terminal server and use those applications, a profile for each user is created. If a second terminal server were added, users would be able to log on to both servers, creating a different user profile on each server. Users would definitely complain. The only concept that makes sense in this environment is the principle of Microsoft server-based profiles. Because this concept is closely tied to domain concepts, the solution is to install a domain and the corresponding domain controller, or to use an existing domain.

There should always be a second domain controller to prevent any potential errors that, for instance, keep users from logging on. The second domain controller can offset the failure of the first. You can also use one of the domain controllers to save user profiles centrally. If you frequently replicate user profiles on the second domain controller using the appropriate recovery procedures, you increase system availability in case of failure. Therefore, the minimum number of servers needed to implement a fail-safe and load-balanced solution is four.

Due to the problem described earlier, the domain controller should not be put on a terminal server if it can be avoided. It is possible to do so without reinstalling the entire system; however, domain administration and multiple-user processes affect each other so much that the performance of the entire system significantly declines. For this reason, an expanded multi-user system consists of two terminal servers and two domain controllers. Because of redundant components, the four servers and a properly dimensioned network build a relatively secure and capable environment. If you install load-sharing mechanisms on the terminal servers, you will improve availability.

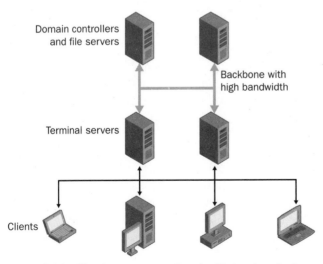

Figure 3-24 Simple corporate network with two terminal servers and two domain controllers.

Note   By comparison, you can use lower-performing PCs for domain administration. The only requirement is a good network connection between the four servers. Another option is to integrate terminal servers into an existing Windows 2000 or Windows Server 2003 domain with a powerful domain controller.

Conceptually, it is just as easy to integrate additional servers into this environment. This applies to both additional terminal servers and domain controllers, and to file, print, and database servers (back-end servers). Everything can be tied to a three- or four-layer model that takes into account all servers involved. From a technical point of view, however, it takes a good deal of experience working with complex network structures to realize this type of multiple-layer environment.

Nevertheless, a global network-bandwidth rule does exist for multi-layer models: The bandwidth needed between terminal servers and each Terminal Services client is relatively low, whereas the network between terminal servers and the supporting servers (for file, print, and directory services, or databases) should be as powerful as possible.

The reason for this is clear. The RDP protocol is optimized to use low-bandwidth connections to transport the graphics contents of a user session from a terminal server to the client, and user actions (keyboard and mouse) from the client to the terminal server. Typically, this requires data throughput of 20 to 50 Kbps. Therefore, one terminal server with a 10-megabit network card can theoretically supply data to more than 200 clients of one user session each. Of course, you cannot use a TCP/IP network at 100 percent capacity, nor can a typical terminal server manage 200 simultaneous sessions. Furthermore, the same network connection is used to exchange even more data with other computers on the network. These figures demonstrate that the throughput to individual clients is rarely the bottleneck. The highest likelihood for a problem in this case might stem from pooling many client connections in routers or switches before they reach the terminal server. Pooling can cause problems in selecting optimum routes for data packages, which in turn results in transmission delays (latency). Faulty resolution of computer names to IP addresses can also cause significant slowdowns that are unrelated to the nominal network transfer rate between terminal server and clients. Networks with the fewest intermediate stations ensure optimum communication between terminal servers and Terminal Services clients and guarantee a continuous rate per client within the 50 Kbps range.

The communication between a terminal server and other servers follows a completely different model. The throughput rate must be as high as possible to quickly respond to user-specific requests for file services or databases of the applications on the terminal server. For this reason, terminal servers should be placed on an internal high-speed network and, if possible, logically close to the back-end servers whose services they need. This can be accomplished by arranging all servers, including terminal servers, in a computer center, or at least on the same network segment. This type of setup is known as *server consolidation*.

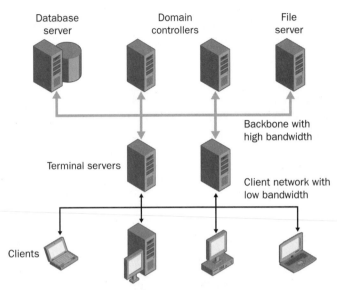

Figure 3-25   Terminal server in a consolidated environment.

So how does a terminal server behave in a consolidated environment? For example, a user starts Microsoft Word on the terminal server, but the application is mapped only to the client. Only when the window for Word is created does the 50 Kbps data stream flow from the terminal server to the client. If the user opens a large document in his or her base directory on the file server, the corresponding data is transferred to the terminal server. Only changes to the graphical user interface, that is, the graphical elements on the currently displayed page in Word, are transferred from the terminal server to Terminal Services client. The document itself does not leave the terminal server to travel to the client! Therefore, the faster the connection between the terminal server and file server with the document, the faster the document is displayed in the user session on the client computer.

Server Farms

Time and again this book refers to the term *server farm* in connection with terminal servers. A server farm is a group of terminal servers bundled into one logical unit. This unit provides a common set of applications that corporate users can access via Terminal Services clients. This is why the servers in a server farm are usually identical.

To hide the number and identities of a server farm's members, the servers are often consolidated on a load-balancing system. To users, load balancing is accomplished by a logical device that uses predefined criteria to decide at user logon which physical server will support the user's session.

> **Important**   A load-balanced server farm is not a cluster that transfers processes from a failed server to another server in that cluster. If a server that is part of a server farm fails, the processes on that server are lost. This also applies to the unsaved data being processed when the failure occurred. Users of the server lose their sessions and application data. However, users can immediately log on again to the server farm and continue their work on another load-balanced server. They can use the data file that was created the last time they saved their user-specific application files. The precondition, of course, is that the corresponding file server be completely independent from the server farm.

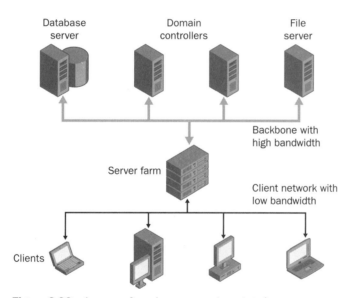

Figure 3-26   A server farm in a corporate network.

A load-balanced server farm optimally fulfills the scalability requirements of terminal servers in corporate environments. Users no longer use the name or IP address of individual servers, but connect to the terminal servers through load balancing. Either a hardware component or several software solutions can be used for load balancing. When administrators discover that servers no longer meet user requirements, they can either upgrade individual servers (scale up) or add servers to the server farm (scale out). Both procedures go unnoticed by users because they normally do not know what physical components comprise a server farm.

Regardless of whether a company decides to scale up or scale out, all a user sees is that more resources are available, which benefits overall system performance and the user experience.

A server farm can be operated with dozens or even hundreds of terminal servers if the load is distributed evenly. This is accomplished using completely separate servers for file and print services, directory services, databases, or e-mail services.

Note   You will find a more detailed description of the mechanisms and solutions behind the load-balancing concept in Chapter 11.

At first, a company usually sets up a server farm to provide certain groups of applications to predefined groups of users under strict security standards. Separate server farms should be used only if the company has two clearly delimited environments, such as two divisions with individual cost centers and separate infrastructures.

Integrating Back-End Servers

The integration of back-end servers is critical to the server farm because all user and machine-specific data must be managed independently of the terminal servers to achieve optimum scalability and failure protection. This applies especially to the following data categories, which can be allocated to specialized back-end servers:

- **User Data**   User name, password, and other user-specific parameters that are managed on domain controllers. For availability reasons, this data is usually saved on several domain controllers.

- **Group Policies**   Binding guidelines for computers and user groups. Also managed by domain controllers.

- **User Files**   User profiles and user-specific application files are usually saved on file servers. If a file server is highly available, it can be combined with another physical server to form a *cluster*. If a server within a cluster fails, the other server assumes its tasks. The data itself is saved on a redundant hard drive system that can be accessed by all servers of the cluster. Other platforms that you can use with file servers are *network- attached storage* systems or *storage area network* systems.

The file server setup has a significant influence on overall system performance. If the file server is optimally adjusted for file access over a fast network, the terminal servers are faster. It also allows you to establish a plausible access control and security strategy. Print, database, and e-mail servers play key roles in realizing certain functions on the terminal servers as well.

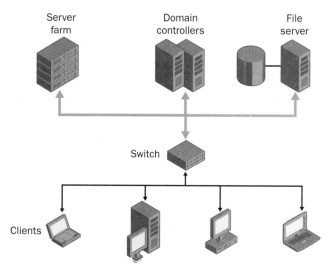

Figure 3-27   A server farm and several back-end servers.

For Terminal Services clients to operate well in corporate environments, a certain infrastructure is needed. In addition to a stable network, you need a properly functioning name resolution mechanism (DNS server) and an instance for dynamic client ID assignment (DHCP server).

Everything thus far is a clear indication that terminal servers and Terminal Services clients depend heavily on back-end servers. A perfectly functioning server farm is worthless if one of the relevant back-end servers causes problems. For this reason, the consolidation of back-end servers is a prerequisite for successful terminal server projects.

Terminal Services on the LAN

How can we transfer the concepts and models described to a real network? Figure 3-28 shows a typical corporate Local Area Network consisting of a server farm with several terminal servers. The server farm is located in the computer center and is integrated into the same network segment as the company's back-end servers. If the infrastructure is decentralized, the back-end servers must first be centralized to achieve the necessary environment.

The departmental clients now access the central terminal servers via the RDP protocol. The bandwidth required is relatively low (around 50 Kbps). It is very important that the network be available and the bandwidth constant. One should definitely avoid clients that occasionally transfer large volumes of data independently of the RDP protocol or a large number of simultaneous massive print jobs.

The administration department should use only Windows-based terminals, which excludes the use of local applications. This reduces the client tasks to presentation and interaction and shifts all application logic and data maintenance to the computer center. By consistently implementing the server-centered model, you achieve the best savings in terms of client administration costs.

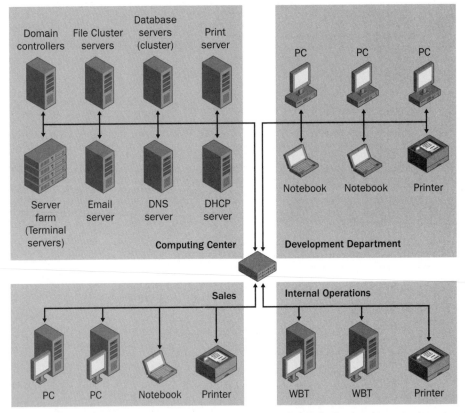

Figure 3-28   Terminal servers and Terminal Services clients in the local corporate network.

There are, of course, negative aspects to this type of environment: an environment that is based on terminal servers certainly does *not* optimally support mapping high-resolution video sequences, intense use of animation, or work on sophisticated CAD documents. This also goes for scenarios that require local real-time use of large amounts of data, such as scanning documents or generating multi-media content. These tasks should therefore be processed using local applications on clients with adequate resources. However, subsequent transfer of the resulting data to central servers can also become an issue in large corporate networks.

Terminal Services on the WAN

The next question is how to transfer the model of terminal servers on a local network to the integration of remote offices over wide area networks (WANs). The difference between a structured local network and a WAN is not very great. Several routers connect the individual company sites via dedicated or leased lines. The resulting network is highly suitable for terminal servers. The bandwidth required for communication between the sites is usually significantly lower than in a conventional environment.

One critical parameter for the successful deployment of terminal servers is latency during the transmission of data packages between sites. Latency determines the delay in displaying graphics elements on the user interface in response to user input. If this time is too long due to gaps in router configuration or the WAN, users are quick to reject terminal server technology.

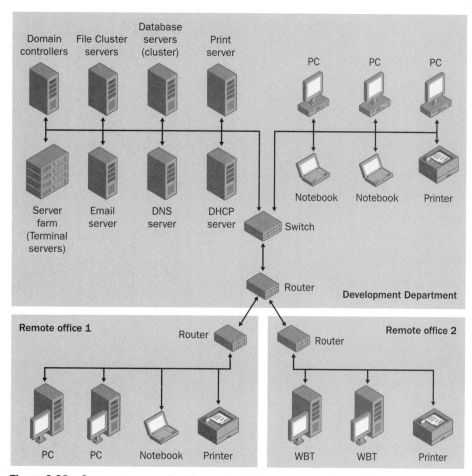

Figure 3-29 Corporate network with remote offices connected on a WAN.

Figure 3-29 illustrates a corporate network with two remote offices connected to the company headquarters via routers. The headquarters computer center hosts a server farm with several terminal servers. They provide applications to the users who can either be at the headquarters or at their remote offices.

For technical or policy reasons, it is possible that not all corporate server resources will reside at one site. Therefore, terminal servers might need to be operated at several sites. This setup is practicable only if the terminal servers primarily access resources (for example, databases or file servers) located at the same site.

Figure 3-30 depicts a setup in which terminal servers in remote office 1 provide applications that use the data from a database server at the same site. The clients can access both terminal servers in the company headquarters and remote office 1.

However, the terminal servers do not have the same configurations and therefore provide different applications. A domain controller is recommended in the remote office so that user profile data does not have to be downloaded from headquarters upon logon.

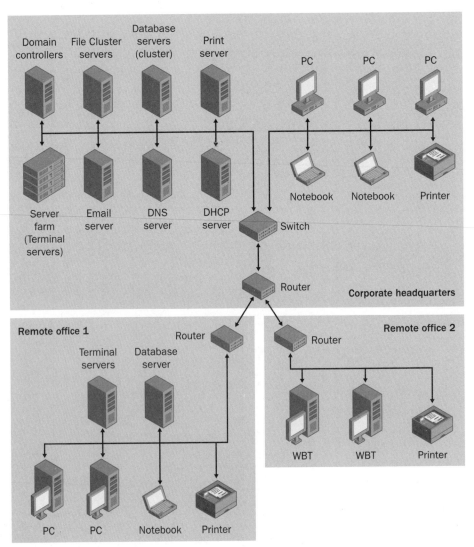

Figure 3-30   Corporate network with terminal servers in the corporate headquarters and remote office 1.

In the extreme case, the same server infrastructure is available for both remote office 1 and company headquarters. This is often true for large companies that set up a backup computer center at a secondary site for security reasons. A lack of available bandwidth between continents can cause a global company to work with several computer-center and terminal-server sites. However, planning infrastructure and user access paths is extremely difficult under these circumstances.

What typical mistake should be avoided at all costs in a corporate environment with terminal servers? Never put terminal servers where the clients are if there are no back-end servers, which are the most important resource. Communication between terminal servers and their clients usually consumes far less bandwidth than accessing resources such as documents or data in databases. For this reason, a setup as shown in Figure 3-31 does not make full use of the advantages that terminal servers offer. On the contrary, in this instance investments in terminal server infrastructure could actually lead to negative effects.

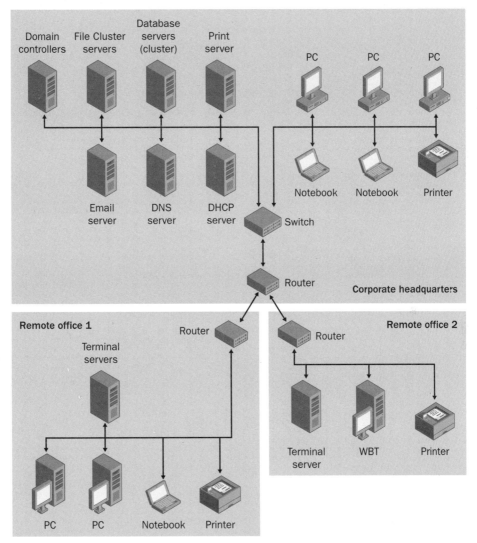

Figure 3-31   The wrong configuration of a terminal server environment. The terminal servers are no longer located in the computing center of corporate headquarters, but in remote offices.

Integrating Individual Home Offices

It is relatively easy to integrate Terminal Services clients in companies as described earlier if the employees work in buildings connected via a common network infrastructure. The situation is quite different if you want to establish a configuration for home offices or very small sales offices. Users access the terminal servers in the company headquarters through modems (analog, ISDN, or DSL) or small telecommunication routers. They can direct their documents to a printer that is locally connected to the server inside the company. It is, of course, possible to use printers that are locally connected to the client, as described earlier.

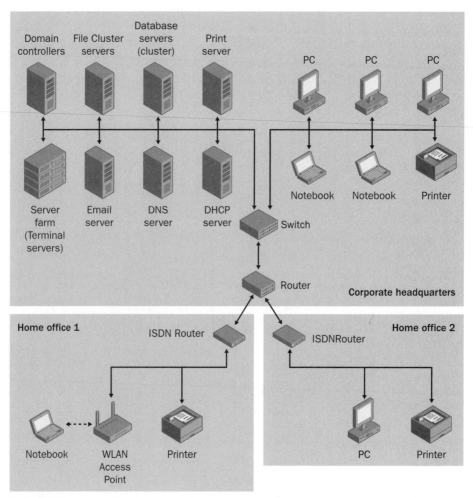

Figure 3-32   Integration of home offices or small remote offices.

To integrate home or small remote offices, the company needs a high-performance router. This router translates communication over telephone lines to the local corporate network standard. The bandwidth required is between 56 Kbps and 64 Kbps per client, or possibly less.

You need to note some peculiarities for using terminal servers on telecommunication networks. For one thing, the telecommunication infrastructure must be designed so that the terminal server sees it as the local network. This is not really a problem with the current telephone systems and dial-up routers. Another condition is that the connections between terminal server and clients must always be reliable, stable, and maintained. If the connection is interrupted for only a few seconds, the user session is terminated. It is highly possible that user data will be lost in this case—despite the terminal server option to reconnect a user session.

> **Note**   If you establish a configuration for home offices, you definitely need to think about security. Should company documents be printed on the client side? Should data be exchanged between client hard drives and the terminal server? Should logon information be saved on the client? Does the data exchanged need to be encrypted?

A well-placed note here about modem and ISDN configuration can dismiss false expectations: an existing ISDN connection will not be terminated if the user of a terminal server session is no longer working interactively, that is, if the user is no longer generating direct network traffic with the Terminal Server. The Terminal Server connection will be maintained until the user logs off, disconnects, or reaches a time limit. Special administration packages are sent automatically over the network to ensure that the connection is kept open to prevent possible data loss in application programs that are open in the user session.

Chapter 4

Administration and Operation

Now that we have covered the basic concepts of Terminal Services under Microsoft Windows Server 2003 and the corresponding network and client options, it is time to move on to the subjects of administration and operation. We will introduce special system tools and expansions to the standard Windows Server 2003 environment. This chapter focuses on the following:

- Terminal Services Manager as a powerful and centralized administration tool for multiple-user expansion of Windows Server 2003.

- Windows Server 2003 standard tools and their specific adaptations for optimum support of Terminal Services, including Task Manager, System Monitor, Event Viewer, and Control Panel.

- The specific terminal server properties included in user and group administration and how to set them up for standard operation. The settings for user and Terminal Services configuration and remote desktop connections will also be compared.

- Domains and Group Policies that allow comprehensive configuration and control of more than one terminal server.

- The significance of central user profiles in administering individual user settings in a terminal server environment, including other user profile information and background information on INI mapping and temp mapping.

- Various integration concepts for client and network printers in a terminal server environment.

Many of these topics are also important for operating a normal Windows Server 2003 on a network, particularly domains, Group Policies, central user profiles, print concepts, and, of course, the Control Panel tools. This book, however, examines them through the lens of the terminal server.

Terminal Services Manager

The Terminal Services Manager program is the central tool for managing users, sessions, and processes on individual terminal servers and for server farms. You invoke the program via the Start menu under Administration\Terminal Services Manager. Alternatively, you can start Terminal Services Manager by typing **Tsadmin.exe** on the command line. For some functions, such as remote control, Terminal Services Manager needs to be invoked from a Terminal Services client session. This function is disabled in a console session.

Figure 4-1   Terminal Services Manager.

The Terminal Services Manager application window has two panels. The left panel contains server and user session lists. If the servers are part of a domain, this information is integrated as well. The right panel shows information on each item selected on the left.

The data displayed depends on whether you selected all the servers in several domains, one domain, one server, or one session. The following table lists the possible combinations.

Table 4-1   The Information Displayed in the Terminal Services Manager Tabs Depends on the Object Selected, Such as Domain, Server, or Sessions

Tabs	All Servers	Domain	Server	Session
Users	Yes	Yes	Yes	No
Sessions	Yes	Yes	Yes	No
Processes	Yes	Yes	Yes	Yes
Information	No	No	No	Yes

In addition to displaying information, this tool allows you to perform several different administrative tasks. The Actions menu item in the application window or the context menu of the individual information elements offers the following options:

■ Managing terminal servers involved

■ Connecting to a client

■ Ending the connection to a client

■ Sending messages to user sessions

■ Monitoring activities of individual user sessions (remote control)

■ Resetting individual user sessions

■ Terminating a user session, such as logging off a user

■ Displaying user and system processes

■ Terminating individual processes

■ Ending the connection with all servers in the domain

■ Connecting to a computer

■ Updating servers in all domains

■ Ending the connection to all servers

■ Displaying the client status

Servers, Sessions, and Users

One of the Terminal Services Manager views relates to the server that executes the program. If a user creates a session by connecting to the displayed terminal server via a Terminal Services client, the session appears in the Session tab. The tab also contains information on the session and user name, ID, status, client name, idle time, logon time, and a comment.

The names of the users who are logged on to the selected server are listed in the Users tab. This tab also includes session name, ID, status, idle time, and logon time. Each application that runs on a server can be monitored in the Processes tab. It also shows the user and session name, ID, process ID (PID), and program name. The default view also displays system processes. You can change this setting via the View\Display System Processes menu option.

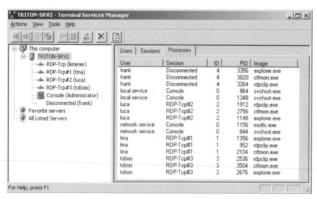

Figure 4-2   Displaying all processes on a terminal server.

You can add more terminal servers to the All Listed Servers group by selecting Actions in the tool bar and then selecting Connect To Computer.... If needed, you enter the name and the password of an authorized user. In this way, an administrator is able to monitor all users, sessions, and processes on multiple terminal servers from one location.

Note   If a server icon is grayed out, it is not possible to access the related information.

If you want to display certain server lists in the future, you can integrate the servers using Add to Favorites in the context menu of your Favorite servers list.

Many tabs show the status of current sessions. The options are as follows:

- **Active**   The session is connected, and a user is logged on to the server.
- **Connected**   The session is connected, but there is no user logged on to the server.
- **ConnectQuery**   The session is in the process of connecting. If this state continues, it indicates a problem with the connection.
- **Listen**   The session is ready to accept a client connection.

- **Disconnected** The user is disconnected from the session, but the session is still attached to the server and can be reconnected at any time.

- **Idle** The session is initialized and ready to accept a connection.

- **Down** The session failed to initialize correctly or could not be terminated, and it is not available. If this state continues, it indicates a problem with the connection of the session.

- **Init** The session is in the process of initializing.

- **RemoteControl** The session is in the process of remotely controlling another session.

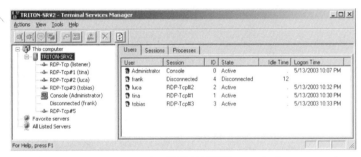

Figure 4-3 Five users on the TRITON-SRV2 terminal server and one connection request from a client (RDP-Tcp#5).

In Terminal Services Manager, the system console session (named *Console*) is automatically listed in the Sessions list. The console represents the keyboard, the mouse, and the monitor of the computer on which the terminal server is installed. If you are authorized, you can log on to a terminal server from console session just as from a client session. You can send messages to the console session but perform no other administrative tasks.

The "listener threads" differ from regular sessions. The threads monitor the network protocol and accept new RDP client connections that create new sessions for client requests. If you configured more than one connection type in the Terminal Services configuration, you will see several listener threads for the different connection types.

It is possible to reset a listener thread. However, this is not recommended because all sessions using the same terminal server connection will also be reset. Resetting a session without notifying the user can cause data loss on the client.

Each user session can be viewed in detail, including processor ID (PID) and program names, in the Processes tab. You will also see Csrss.exe, Winlogon.exe, Rdpclip.exe, and Ctfmon.exe. These processes are part of each terminal server session, just like Explorer.exe.

> **Note** In a Microsoft Windows 2000 terminal server, all processes were started for two user sessions. This default setting was changed for Windows Server 2003. There are no longer any idle sessions. Nevertheless, idle sessions can still be established through corresponding entries in the registry database. (See Chapter 6.)

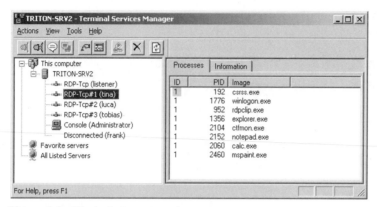

Figure 4-4 Displaying user session processes.

The Information tab allows you to request information about the individual user sessions, including user and client name, client build number, directory, product ID, address, server buffer, color depth, modem name, encryption level, client license, client hardware ID, client buffer, and client resolution.

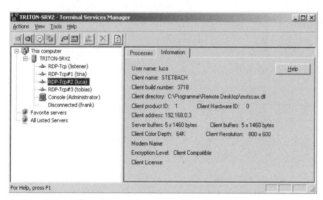

Figure 4-5 Information about a selected user session.

Possible Actions

When you select one of the servers, you can access further information about logged-on users, sessions, processes, and client configuration. You can choose from all the possible actions from the main menu of the Terminal Services Manager or the corresponding context menu accessible via the right mouse button.

Terminal Services Manager actions include connecting and disconnecting, sending messages, remote desktop, resetting user sessions, displaying status information, and logging users off an existing session. You can also terminate processes, connect to or disconnect from computers, and update servers in the domain. If you added favorites in the Preferred Servers menu, you can delete them here as well.

One of the most frequent actions is sending messages to users or groups. Administrators use this option to forward instructions to users in the event of problems.

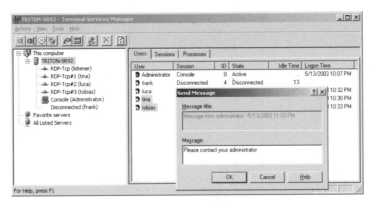

Figure 4-6 Sending a message to multiple users.

You should perform actions such as disconnecting, resetting user sessions, logging off users, or terminating processes only for a good reason, such as terminating hung application processes, handling orphaned user sessions, or preparing for administrative tasks. If you disconnect a user from a session without prior notice and the user loses data, acceptance will quickly wane.

Remote control is a powerful option that supports users in problem situations. An authorized user (for example, an administrator) can connect to the session of a user who needs help. The user sessions are then linked so that the administrator can view the user's session screen. The administrator's desktop is completely synchronized to the user's desktop. This works correctly only if the video resolution of the client device on which the administrator is working meets the requirements of the connected user session.

Note An alternative term for Remote Control is *Remote Desktop*. The latter is used when the administrator actively assumes control of a user session. In the command line, *shadow* invokes remote control as an alternative to the similar action in the Terminal Services Manager.

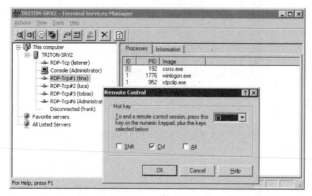

Figure 4-7 Invoking remote control in the Terminal Services Manager.

Depending on the Terminal Services configuration settings (described in Chapter 2) or the user account settings, the framework conditions for remote access to a user session are set here. In particular, two settings are involved:

1. Will the user be asked for permission to connect?

2. Is the session only displayed (mirroring or remote desktop) or is interactive access possible (remote control)?

Note Usually, only an administrator has permission to connect to another user session via remote desktop (as described later in this chapter in the User and Group Administration section). Remote desktop cannot be started from the server console. The authorized user needs to be in an RDP session. You cannot access the console session via remote desktop, either. There is only one exception: if the administrator's console session is displayed on a Terminal Services client using the */console* parameter, the session can be controlled through remote desktop.

A user requesting help sees the remote desktop session as shown in Figure 4-8. The user selects Yes to allow remote desktop or No to refuse. If the user does not respond at all, the system automatically denies the request after a few seconds. In this way, an administrator can never access a user's desktop without permission if the environment was configured accordingly.

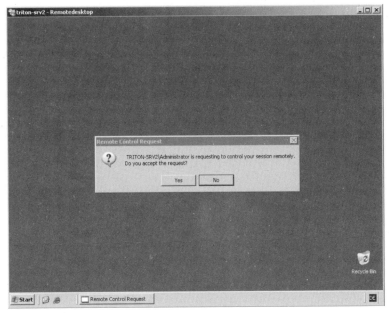

Figure 4-8   Accepting a remote desktop request.

> **Important**   Terminal Services Manager is a powerful tool that can influence the work of many users at the same time. Before using this tool in a production environment, you should first test its behavior and carefully run through standard operations. This certainly includes targeted identification and termination of applications in a user session, logging off users, and interrupting and resetting a client connection.

Adapting the Standard Environment

In addition to the special terminal server tool described in the previous section, several standard tools have been adapted to the multiuser environment. Table 4-2 offers you a quick overview. The tools that are executed from a remote computer over the network are labeled accordingly.

Table 4-2 Modifications to Standard Tools for Use in a Terminal Server Environment

Tool	Specific Function	Remote Execution
Task Manager	Display of process allocation of user accounts under the Processes tab. Shows all current user sessions under the User tab.	No
System Monitor	Additional objects for monitoring a terminal server.	Yes
Event Viewer	Additional event sources.	Yes
Control Panel	For setting of specific system properties and custom installation of applications.	No

Task Manager

Right-click the desktop taskbar, and select Task Manager from the menu. You can alternatively invoke the Task Manager from the security screen. The first tab of the main window displays all programs currently running for the logged-on user and their status. If a programs stops responding, you can remove it from memory using the End Task button. This tab is not especially important to terminal server administrators, whose interest lies more in the current programs and processes of other users.

The Processes tab gives you a more detailed look at current processes as well as Windows services. This tab is unique because it lets you see who is using which process, providing you a differentiated perspective of system activity. An administrator can see all the current system processes if the Show processes from all users option is checked. All other users see only their own processes.

The memory requirements of the individual application processes are of particular interest to terminal server administrators. It is easy to see that different instances of the same application can have very different memory requirements. For example, Figure 4-9 shows this quite clearly for Explorer.exe, the process responsible for managing windows during a user session.

You can right-click one of the processes to set its priority level (low, below normal, normal, above normal, high, or real-time). However, changing the priority level of a process can produce unwanted side effects in terms of system stability and process response times. Thorough testing is recommended before you change a priority level.

Tip You can start a process at High using the **Start /high** <*Program Name*> command. The other priority levels are available using the **/low**, **/belownormal**, **/normal**, **/abovenormal**, or **/realtime** arguments. However, use the **/realtime** argument only with the utmost caution.

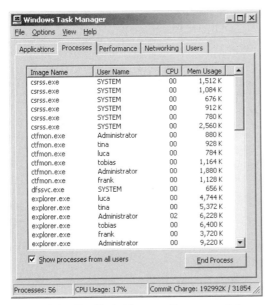

Figure 4-9   The Task Manager Processes tab.

The Performance tab displays the utilization of all physical or virtual processors (supplied by hyperthreading), swap-file utilization, and detailed information on memory usage. Unlike an administrator, users cannot see all the available memory. They see only the amount of memory that is allocated to their current sessions. The most important information in this tab for terminal server administrators is total physical memory versus available physical memory. Terminal servers tend to experience abrupt performance bottlenecks when they are very low on physical memory. This happens whenever the current reserved memory (that is, the virtual memory used) significantly exceeds existing physical memory.

The Windows Server 2003 Task Manager has another two tabs beyond those in Windows 2000. One is the Network tab, which allows you to observe the network load, the transmission rate, and the status of available network adapters. You can verify in this tab that the required network bandwidth is not pushed to its limits. For instance, an Ethernet network adapter should not constantly exceed 30 percent to 50 percent capacity.

The second tab is Users, and like Terminal Services Manager, it displays the user name, the session ID, the status, and the session name of each user session. Task Manager is therefore an excellent tool for gaining a general overview of a terminal server's utilization.

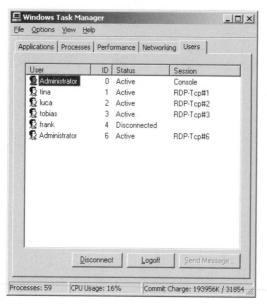

Figure 4-10   The Task Manager Users tab.

System Monitor

Another essential administration and analysis tool included in Windows Server 2003 is the System Monitor. It displays available and used system resources, which Windows Server 2003 manages with internal counter variables. This tool helps you identify system bottlenecks and trace results during manual system optimization.

There are three types of performance indicators or counters in System Monitor:

- **Instantaneous counters**   which display the most recent measurement.

- **Average counters**   which measure the value over time and display the average value of the last two measurements.

- **Difference counters**   which subtract the last measured value from the previous one and display the difference.

Using counters, the System Monitor oversees the entire system and the network. With the proper permissions, you can also access remote computers. Practically all data measurable at run time can be recorded and displayed as a counter. The data can be processed in several ways.

- Collect and display real-time performance data for a local or several remote computers. Display current or previous data recorded in a performance log.

- Present data in a printable diagram, histogram, or report view.

- Create reusable performance-monitoring configurations that can be applied to other computers running Microsoft Management Console.

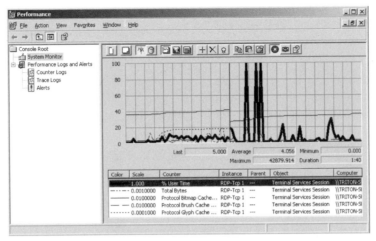

Figure 4-11   The System Monitor analyzing a user session.

The System Monitor thus supports manual, demand-driven, and automatic sampling at predefined intervals. You can select the start and end times to display log data for a certain period of time.

Counters

The System Monitor offers an overwhelming array of options for displaying local and remote system information. Administrators have any number of ways to approach system analyses on a local or remote computer under Windows Server 2003.

The following are the most important counters that can point to a performance bottleneck in a terminal server:

- **Network interface—Total Number of Bytes/s: The rate at which bytes are sent and received over the interface**   If this value approaches the physically available network bandwidth, the network should be segmented and/or an additional network card installed.

- **Processor—%Processor Time**   Percent processor time needed to execute a non-idle thread. This performance measure is the primary indicator of processor activity. The time span that the processor needs to execute the idle-process thread in each sampling interval is subtracted from 100 percent. Each processor has an idle thread that consumes cycles during which no other threads can be executed. The performance indicator shows the average consumption during the sampling interval in percent by subtracting the time the service was inactive from 100 percent. If the processor time value is consistently high (more than 80 percent) while the network load is low, the processor is too weak.

- **Processor—Interrupts/s** The number of hardware interrupts that the processor receives and processes per second. This value is an indirect indicator of the activity of devices that generate interrupts, such as the system clock, mouse, disk drivers, network cards, and other peripherals. These devices usually generate a processor interrupt when they finish a process or require intervention because normal thread execution is suspended during the interrupt. This performance indicator shows the difference between the values of the last two sampling intervals divided by interval duration. If this value is high (more than 70 percent) for an extended period, a network card might be receiving faulty network packages.

- **PhysicalDisk—%Disk Time** The percentage of time needed by the selected drive to process read and write requests. If this value is consistently high (more than 25 percent), the access speed of the hard-drive system is insufficient. In this case, you might want to consider using RAID systems with ample cache memory.

- **Redirector—Server Sessions** The number of security objects that the redirector manages. A large number of these objects on terminal servers is often an indication of how frequently user sessions access file server shares (for example, home folders). Above-normal values for this indicator in conjunction with terminal server bottlenecks often point to the problem. Usually, reducing the number of connected drives per user session improves the situation.

- **Server Work Queues—Queue Length** The current length of the server queue for this CPU. A sustained queue length significantly above four indicates processor overload. This is an instantaneous value, not an average count over time.

- **Memory—Available Bytes** Physical memory available for processes (in bytes). This value is calculated by adding up zeroed, free, and standby memory. *Free* memory is available memory. *Zeroed* memory consists of memory pages filled with zeros. This type of memory prevents subsequent processes from accessing data of previous processes. *Standby* memory is memory that is still available but has been removed from the working pages of the process. This indicator shows only the last measured value, not an average. If you constantly have little free memory in relation to entire memory, the physical memory is undersized. System performance suffers significantly in this case.

- **Memory—Committed Bytes** Committed virtual memory in bytes. *Committed virtual* memory is physical memory for which memory space is reserved in the swap file so that it can be rewritten to the data carrier. This indicator shows only the last measured value, not an average. If its value approximates the available physical memory, the system begins a lot of read/write operations, resulting in significantly reduced performance. The solution is to add memory to the system.

- **System—Processes**   The number of system processes at the time of data collection. This is an instantaneous indicator, not an average over time. Each process represents the execution of a program.

- **System—Processor Queue Length**   The number of threads in the processor queue. Even if you have several processors, there is only one queue for processor time. This performance indicator counts only finished threads, not threads being executed. If this value is consistently higher than 10 threads per available processor, the processors are overloaded. If this value is significantly higher than 20 threads per processor, you definitely have a bottleneck. This indicator shows the last measured value only, not an average.

A terminal server provides additional performance indicators offering specific types of analysis.

- **Terminal Services**   A specific System Monitor object with three performance indicators for active and inactive sessions and for the total number of sessions.

- **Terminal Services Session**   A specific System Monitor object with some 100 performance indicators for the RDP protocol, processor load, necessary memory resources, input and output buffer, compression, swapping activity, error rate, caching behavior, and asynchronous communication. Each user session can be monitored and analyzed individually.

Performance Logs and Alerts

When you start System Monitor, it is displayed as a snap-in on the Microsoft Management Console, like so many other tools in Windows Server 2003. The Performance logs and alerts option lets you automatically record performance data of local or remote computers. The System Monitor can display the performance data that was logged. As an alternative, you can export the results to spreadsheet programs or databases to generate reports or analyze the data. This is a good option for regular long-term analysis of the performance indicators listed in the preceding section in a terminal server environment (much like a long-term ECG).

Performance logs and alerts provide the following functions:

- Data is recorded in a comma-delimited or tab-delimited format for easy export to spreadsheet programs. In addition, a binary log file format is used for continuous logging, where new data overwrites old.

- You can display the data recorded in performance logs and alerts both during and after the recording process.

- Because logging is performed as a service (SysmonLog service with the display name Performance logs and alerts, Smlogsvc.exe), data is collected regardless of whether a user is logged on or not.

- You can define start and end times, file names and sizes, and other parameters for automatic log creation.

- You can define an alert that sends a message, executes a program, or starts a log if the performance indicator value exceeds or drops below a certain setting.

Event Viewer

The Event Viewer allows you to monitor Windows Server 2003 events. It replaces the windows that display administrative message to users, who normally have no idea what to do with them. The messages contain information on system events and are therefore more interesting to administrators. A special system service saves these messages as logs.

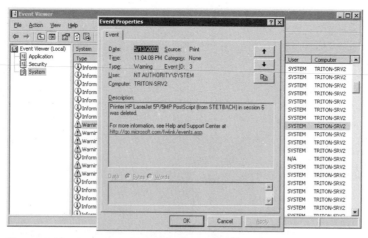

Figure 4-12 The Event Viewer analyzes the system log. In this example, the warning message indicates that a printer was deleted in a user session.

Event Logs

The event log service records three types of logs:

- **Application** The application log contains events recorded by applications or programs. A database, for instance, could record a file error in the application log. The program developer decides which events will be recorded.

- **Security** The security log contains events dealing with security, such as valid and invalid logon attempts, and events involving resource use, such as creating, opening, or deleting files. The administrator decides which events will be recorded in the security log. If the security log option is enabled, you can record all system logon attempts, for example.

- **System** The system log contains events that were recorded by Windows Server 2003 system components. For instance, failure to load a device driver or other system component on startup is recorded in the system log. The types of events that can be recorded are determined by the system components used.

> **Note**   All users can view the application and system logs. However, only administrators can access the security log.

Creating security logs is enabled by default only for the most important options. You can change this setting under the local security settings or Group Policies (as discussed later in this chapter).

Figure 4-13   Default values of the local security settings.

The administrator can also set the audit policy for the Event Viewer to stop the system when the security log size is exceeded.

Event Types and Related Information

The Event Viewer displays the following events:

- **Error**   A major problem, such as data loss or function failure. This error is logged if, for example, a required service was unable to load on system startup.

- **Warning**   An event that is not necessarily major but could indicate future problems. A warning is recorded if there is little memory available on the hard drive, a user-session printer is deleted, or there is no license server in the network environment.

- **Information**   An event that reports the successful execution of an application, a driver, or a service. An example of an information event is if remote control of a user session on this computer has been requested or if the terminal server cannot assign a client license.

- **Success Audit**   A successful, audited security access. If, for instance, a user logs on to the system, it is recorded as a success audit event.

- **Failure Audit**   A failed, audited security access. If, for example, a user fails to access a network drive, it is recorded as a failure audit event.

The main Event Viewer window displays the following data for the selected log category:

- **Type**   Classification of the event by Windows Server 2003 (error, warning, information, success audit, or failure audit). An icon at the beginning of the event line marks this data.

- **Date**   System date when the event was generated.

- **Time**   System time when the event was generated.

- **Source**   The software component that produced the event (for example, TermService).

- **Category**   Classification of the event by the source.

- **Event**   Number identifying the event (for example, 1004 for TermService information or 1027 for a TermService warning).

- **User**   Identification of the user at the time the event occurred.

- **Computer**   Name of the computer on which the event occurred.

A terminal server logs some very specific events, most of which relate to the runtime system, security settings, and licensing. The following is a list of some basic log entries that might appear in the Event Viewer and require action by the system administrator:

- The terminal server could not assign a client license.

- No license server that can assign valid terminal server licenses was found in the working group or domain.

- The connection to a local printer was set up or removed within a user session.

- A tool requires Terminal Services to function.

- Terminal Services was unable to authenticate a user because the user does not have the required permissions or Terminal Services is no longer running.

- An error occurred on setting up a new connection type that requires a unique combination of communication protocol, transport protocol, and network adapter.

- Changes currently being made to the registry cannot be applied for the current user. All users must be logged off.

- Registry settings could not be saved in the user profile because they have just been changed by another program or service.

Handling Logs

The Connect To Another Computer... context menu item with Event Viewer (local) activated allows you to call up log information of other systems on the network running Windows Server 2003. This is very practical, especially when a user reports that the system is unstable and the administrator wishes to make an initial diagnosis remotely.

Filter functions help if the log volume becomes too large for a targeted analysis of certain events. Activate the corresponding dialog box via the Properties menu item of the selected log and use the Filter tab.

You can archive, analyze, and process the logs in files. Corporate policy often requires storage of log information. Stored log files help reconstruct security violations after the fact.

If logs are to be saved frequently, data must not be lost: select the appropriate log-size settings and define how old log entries should be handled. If you choose the option never to overwrite events, normal users might receive messages intended for an administrator. The message might report that the event file is full and must be saved by an administrator. When this happens, the user usually informs the administrator so that such messages will be dealt with appropriately.

Note   If security events are logged, it is also possible to monitor the deletion of log data. This is absolutely necessary if administrators need to trace possible unauthorized actions by other administrators attempting to remove incriminating data. In this case, all administrators must have and use their own uniquely named administrator accounts.

Control Panel

The Control Panel provides a comprehensive set of specialized administration tools for operating system configuration, applications, and Windows services. The main Control Panel and its Administration window contain a number of icons. Each icon is assigned to a tool for setting different parameters. The tools in the Administration window are identical with the tools under Start\Administration.

How do you display and launch the Control Panel tools? This depends on the configuration of the Start menu. You can choose the new Category View or the familiar Classic View. In the new Category View menu, the Control Panel is displayed as a link to a separate window containing the Control Panel tools. Within this window, the tools are displayed in the Classic View or the more tightly structured Category View.

Under the Start menu properties, you can also completely fade out the Control Panel or display it as a complete menu. In the latter case, all Control Panel tools can be invoked directly from the Start menu—there is no Category View.

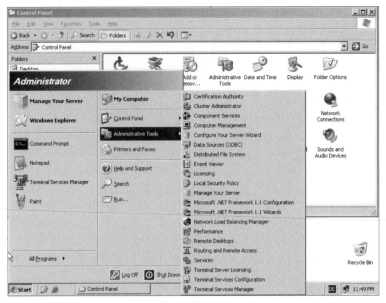

Figure 4-14 Control Panel tools displayed in the new style of Start menu and in Explorer.

If you selected the Classic View of the Start menu, you access the Control Panel via Start\Settings\Control Panel. The expanded Start menu options allow you to choose whether the Control Panel tools are launched directly from the Start menu or in a separate window.

> **Tip** If you would rather not configure the Start menu bar for Control Panel access, you can just as easily open it from Explorer. It is always located under Desktop\My Computer\Control Panel.

Some tools are used for system-wide settings by an administrator, and some are intended for user-specific settings. You will find not only the standard icons for Windows Server 2003 tools in the Control Panel. Some system or application programs that are installed later add their own icons.

Even the standard Control Panel tools offer so many settings that to describe each would go well beyond the scope of this book. Some tools, however, allow the modification of parameters that are important to a terminal server runtime system. These tools and their options are the focus of the following section.

System

If you select the System tool under Control Panel, a dialog pops up in which you can select the view and modify system properties. You have to be in a user group with administrator privileges to take advantage of this option. The dialog has the following tabs: General, Computer Name, Hardware, Advanced, Automatic Updates, and Remote.

The first three tabs apply to general settings and are not particularly significant for terminal servers. The General tab offers information on the system, the registered user (including the license key), and the computer. The Computer Name tab allows you to modify the computer description, name, and working group or domain. The Hardware tab enables you to install new hardware, change device driver properties, and set up different hardware profiles. The latter option is not particularly relevant to terminal servers.

The Advanced tab, however, is extremely relevant. It contains options for adjusting system performance and user profiles, and for system start and recovery.

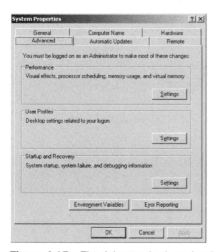

Figure 4-15   The Advanced tab under the System tool of the Control Panel.

Clicking the Settings button under Performance opens a new window named Performance Options that has two tabs. The first is the Visual Effects tab, and it allows you to change settings relevant for desktop display. The default setting on a terminal server is automatic selection of the optimum setting. This ensures the performance-friendly display of graphics elements, which means that some visual effects are no longer used, such as animation, shadowing, or displaying window contents while dragging.

If an authorized user changes the default setting, RDP user sessions can significantly burden the terminal server's resources with visual effects. For this reason, it might be practical to predefine the option for optimum performance on terminal servers or allow only a few user-defined options (for example, through

Group Policies). Generally, the default setting is suitable for most terminal server environments.

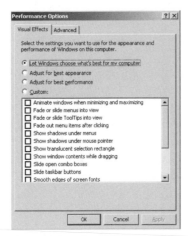

Figure 4-16   Setting visual effects under System Performance options.

The second tab in the Performance Options window is named Advanced, and it lets you define processor time, memory use, and virtual memory. The processor resources on a terminal server should be optimized for programs, not for background services. Background services mainly play a key role on back-end servers (for example, database or e-mail servers) and should therefore have priority there.

Important   A terminal server's primary task is executing as many end-user programs as possible. Optimizing processor resources for programs involves both foreground and background applications. Therefore, this is the best setting to fulfill terminal server requirements.

The question of the optimum setting for memory use has no easy answer. The Windows Server 2003 default setting of best performance of system cache favors the terminal server as the server platform. If the terminal server users work mostly with the same applications, a large cache is certainly advantageous because it provides faster access to already loaded data structures (for example, start screens or generally valid dialog windows).

By modifying the memory usage settings to optimize programs, the server assumes more of a workstation role. The programs run more quickly, but the entire system might reach its saturation point too soon because the data structures are not sufficiently reused. Comprehensive testing is needed to determine the best setting because it clearly depends on the combination of installed applications.

The Change button in this window opens the dialog for setting virtual memory. The initial and maximum size of the swap file and its physical location on the local hard drive are configured here. The swap file should not be limited to one partition because it can extend over several partitions or even hard drives. For the best results, these drives should each have their own channels on the hard-drive controller. This, in combination with a sizable initial swap file, increases system performance. To avoid dynamic growth in swap-file size, the start and end size should always match in a terminal server environment. These settings are not the same after installation, so they require manual adjustment.

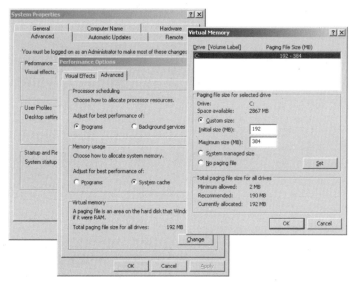

Figure 4-17   Unmodified default setting for virtual memory under Performance Options.

After a standard installation, the predefined initial swap-file size for the virtual memory is about 1.5 times greater than the physical memory. The maximum size is approximately triple for physical memory. It is recommended that you set both the initial and maximum swap-file size to twice the size of the physical memory. For servers with substantial physical memory (greater than 2 GB), you may reduce this factor to 1.5. Increasing the file size is not the best approach for productive environments. So much hard-drive maneuvering is needed to access swap that is equal in size to physical memory that the server cannot keep up. Only thorough testing in a concrete target environment will reveal the optimum swap-file size.

The next setting on the Advanced tab is User profiles. Click the Settings button to open a new window. This is where individual user session profiles are managed. (See also later sections in this chapter.) All changes to user profiles must be made in this window. Manually copying, deleting, or moving profile directories in Explorer is not recommended.

The Change Type button allows you to assign either the local or the server-based profile to users logging on to this computer. A server-based user profile permits users to log on to other computers using the stored profile. This option is essential for terminal server farms. However, it is recommended that you implement this option under user administration by entering a terminal server profile or by configuring the profile path as a Group Policy.

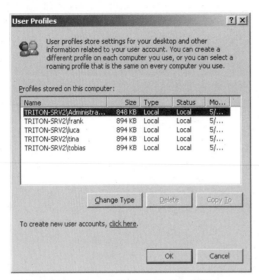

Figure 4-18   The dialog box for modifying user profiles.

The Settings button under Startup and Recovery allows administrators easy access to the start options in the Boot.ini file. Furthermore, the administrator can configure the system response to a STOP state, that is, a blue screen. By default, terminal servers automatically reboot in the event of a system error. If a system crash does not involve a hardware failure, the server will be back up relatively quickly. Debug information should be confined to a small memory dump or a kernel memory dump because a full memory dump would take up more hard-drive space than the additional data is worth. Therefore, this option is reserved for troubleshooting under the guidance of experienced support staff.

Note   If you would like to save a full memory dump in the event of a system error, you need sufficient space on the partition with the %SystemRoot% folder. Even if the final target of the backup file is elsewhere, it will be generated on the system partition first.

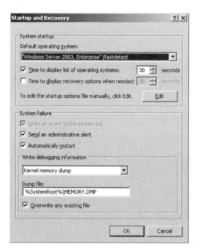

Figure 4-19   Startup and recovery options.

The Environment variables button on the Advanced tab of the system tool allows you to modify the environment variables for the entire system and the current user. Only an administrator can add, change, or delete system-wide environment variables.

Figure 4-20   Modifying environment variables.

The Error reporting button automatically reports software errors to Microsoft. This option helps improve future products. Of course, you can disable this option as well.

Now that our extensive tour of the Advanced tab is complete, let us advance to the simpler Automatic Updates tab. This tab has no specific relevance to terminal servers; it ensures that the computer is kept up to date, if required. If you enable this option, you have the following choices for downloading and installing Windows update software:

- Notification before each download and each installation
- Automatic download and notification before installation
- Automatic download and installation according to a preset schedule

Tip   Automatic update should not be activated for terminal servers because unmonitored software installations might be performed when the system is not in installation mode. (See Chapter 5.)

Finally, the Remote tab is directly tied to terminal server functions. In this tab, you can enable or disable remote control for support tasks and access over remote desktop connections.

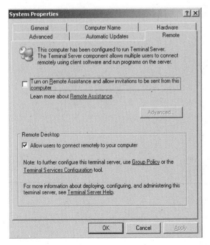

Figure 4-21   Configuring terminal server options.

Software

The Add or Remove Programs tool on the Control Panel is a convenient and powerful means of installing software. The Add New Programs button is used for this purpose. On a terminal server, the software tool changes the system environment to a special installation mode. After the installation is complete, the system is reset to application mode. (See Chapter 5.)

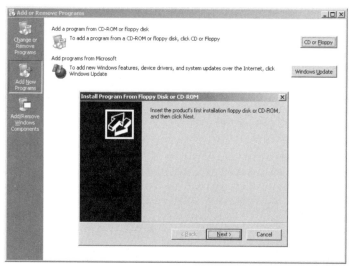

Figure 4-22   Adding a new program using the tool Add or Remove Programs.

You can also set the different modes at the command line, a fact frequently overlooked by administrators and resulting in massive disruptions in the runtime behavior of the terminal server and its applications.

> **Note**   Applications should always be installed at the console, that is, in the 0 session. An installation within a client session could produce unwanted results. However, this issue is better addressed under Windows Server 2003 than under its predecessors. You can now redirect the console session to a Terminal Services client using the */console* parameter.

User and Group Administration

Each user who frequently accesses a multiple-user server over the network needs a user account. This account contains information about the user, such as name and password, and all permissions regulating the user's network access. It can be set up locally on the terminal server or centrally in a domain using Active Directory.

Users who have similar functions or need the same resources can be grouped. Grouping makes management and assigning privileges easier because functions are no longer tied to individual users. Instead, they can be assigned to the entire group of users.

User Account Concept

Local users and groups are managed in a Computer Administration snap-in under the Start\Programs\Administration menu. A user account is always based on data such as the unique name, password, group membership, basic directory, user profile, or logon script. Additionally, there are user properties that have the attribute *true* (= yes) or *false* (= no), which are needed, for example, to specify if the user needs to change his or her password on the next logon or if the account is deactivated.

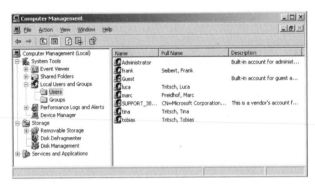

Figure 4-23   Computer administration with local user accounts.

Each user account is defined throughout the system by a *security identifier* (SID). The SID is generated by an algorithm and is based on the network adapter's hardware address and the current system time. As such, it is globally unique and remains actively linked to certain objects (for example, files) as security information if a user account is deleted. If a user account is created, deleted, and then re-created using the same name, the new user account does not have the same rights as the old one because it has a new SID.

Note   The tool for managing users within an Active Directory domain is called Active Directory Users and Computers and is located in the Start menu under Administration Tools. Terminal server properties can also be set from options within Administration Tools. In addition, several user properties can be configured centrally under Group Policies.

Terminal Server Expansions

Managing users and groups is essential for smooth operation both on individual terminal servers and within a domain. Only an administrator or a member of the Account Operators user group has the permissions needed to create new users or modify data of existing users.

The properties dialog box for local users on a terminal server contains tabs for configuring multiple-user options. The following sections give details on each tab.

Member Of

The Member Of tab is needed to add a user to the Remote Desktop Users group. Only members of this group have permission to access the server via a Terminal Services client.

Use the following procedure to add a user to the Remote Desktop Users group:

1. Click Add... in the Member Of tab.

2. Click Advanced... in the first Select Groups dialog box.

3. Click Find Now in the second Select Groups dialog box.

4. Select Remote Desktop User from the search results, and click OK. The second Select Groups dialog box closes.

5. Click OK in the first Select Groups dialog box. This dialog box also closes.

6. The user becomes a member of the new group when you click Apply to confirm the new properties.

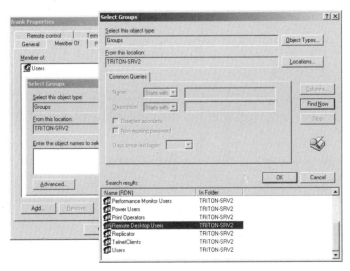

Figure 4-24   Adding a user to the Remote Desktop Users group.

Environment

The Environment tab is used to configure the Terminal Services startup environment for executing an initial program and connecting client devices.

To configure a program, you enter the path to the executable (for example, C:\Program\Microsoft Office\Excel.exe) and an optional start directory (for example, C:\User) for the application data. The program, which starts when the user logs on, becomes an alternative display to the normal Windows 2000 user interface.

Figure 4-25 The Environment tab for user properties.

The client device connections apply to the existing drives and printers. If required, they can be blended with the existing terminal server resources. In this way, the terminal server can use the printer that is physically attached to the client device as its default printer.

Similar settings can be selected for Terminal Services configuration (described in Chapter 2) and Terminal Services clients (described in Chapter 3). The local user administration settings override the client settings but have a lower priority than the Terminal Services configuration settings.

Sessions

Time limits for Terminal Services and reconnection settings are entered under the Sessions tab.

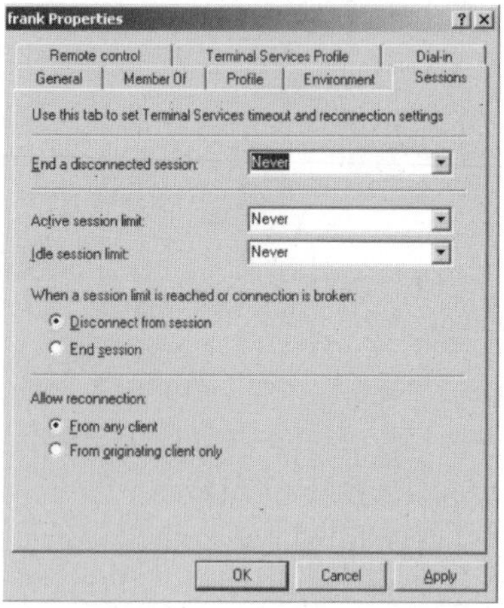

Figure 4-26 Configuring session parameters.

Time limits define the maximum duration of certain activities. The time period you choose is completely optional; however, the drop-down menu suggests the following discrete values: Never, 1 minute, 5 minutes, 10 minutes, 15 minutes, 30 minutes, 1 hour, 2 hours, 3 hours, 1 day, and 2 days.

- **End a disconnected session**   This time limit specifies the period that a disconnected session is stored in terminal server memory. The user can reconnect to the session within that period of time. A session can be disconnected for many reasons: active session limit, idle session limit, interrupted modem connection, network failure, switching off the client, or selecting the Disconnect option on a Terminal Services client.

- **Active session limit**   Here you enter the period after which a client is disconnected from the terminal server or the active session ends. Measurement begins on connection and is not affected by any other limits (for example, idle session limit).

- **Idle session limit**   This time limit defines when a session is disconnected or ended if the user has been completely inactive, that is, has not touched the mouse or keyboard for the entire session.

Select the Disconnect from session or the End session radio button to determine what happens when a session limit is reached or the network connection is broken. Users may reconnect to a disconnected session still stored on the terminal server as selected in the From any client or From originating client only radio button. The corresponding protocol must support this property; RDP 5.2 does not (but Citrix ICA does). This option is only supported if you install Citrix MetaFrame XP Presentation Server as described in Chapter 9.

It is possible to overwrite the properties in this tab with different corresponding parameters under Terminal Services configuration and Active Directory settings.

Remote Control and Remote Assistance

Remote Control is an interesting option for the support of terminal server users. This function is often referred to as *mirroring* and redirects a user session to another client. As soon as an authorized user can interact with the mirrored session, the function is referred to as *remote assistance*.

The remote control and remote assistance concepts represent, of course, a major encroachment on the Windows Server 2003 security concept. In some countries, the law forbids mirroring without the user's knowledge or consent. Additionally, legal regulations might require that the user being observed receive continuous notification for the duration of the mirrored session. For this reason, remote assistance can be disabled for a user account. At a minimum, you should always ask the user for permission to mirror his or her session. If you activate the corresponding remote assistance option, a dialog box is displayed that notifies the user of the administrator's need and requests the user's permission. If the user denies permission, the user session cannot be mirrored.

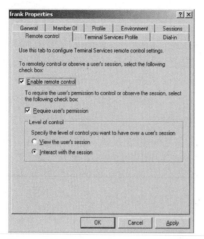

Figure 4-27 Remote desktop configuration.

During remote assistance, there are two basic options for the administrator's level of control in the user session: the administrator can simply view the session or may interact with the session using the mouse and keyboard. These options can be set individually for each user account.

These options can also be set under Terminal Services configuration or Active Directory Group Policies, where they have higher priority.

Terminal Services Profile

The Terminal Services Profile tab allows you to assign a special user profile for logging on over a client session. Notice that the Terminal Services profile depends to a certain extent on the user's default profile.

- If only a default profile (Profile tab) is defined, it is valid regardless of where the user logs on (workstation or Terminal Services client).

- If only a Terminal Services profile is defined, it applies only if the user logs on through a client session (that is, by using the multiple-user option of a terminal server).

- If both default and Terminal Services profiles are defined, the user receives different profiles depending on the user's client type. The user is assigned a default profile for a normal logon under Windows 2000 Workstation or Windows XP and a Terminal Services profile for logon through a Terminal Services client.

This tab also allows you to assign each Terminal Services user a home folder, which is used only when logging on to a terminal server. It is also possible to revoke a user's logon privileges to a terminal server, which renders all his or her other configured multiple-user options useless.

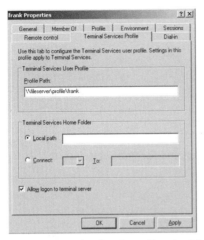

Figure 4-28   Configuring a Terminal Services profile and a home folder.

Home folders are usually created on file servers that are subject to relatively simple rules. First, the file server must have enough memory to meet the users' requirements. Second, good data-access and network-connection speed are essential. Finally, file servers need to be as fail-safe as possible. Therefore, they are often configured as cluster systems to ensure the highest availability.

> **Note**   In addition to domain controllers, file servers are among the most critical elements in a network environment. If they fail for a longer period, work is severely limited, especially in terminal server environments.

Connection Options—A Comparison

As already described in Chapter 3, the options for connecting terminal servers to their clients are flexible rather than fixed, to adjust to certain general conditions. The corresponding settings can be selected in not just one, but in several different places, each with its own focus.

- System-wide settings are defined under Group Policies; these settings override all others.

- Connection-specific settings on the terminal server are defined using the Terminal Services configuration tool. These settings have a lower priority than Group Policies, provided they can also be modified there.

- User-specific settings are defined through user accounts; these settings have a lower priority than Group Policies and Terminal Services configuration.

■ Client-specific settings are defined on Terminal Services clients (for example, through a remote desktop connection under Windows XP). These settings have the lowest priority.

However, not all connection options can be changed everywhere. To determine exactly where to configure certain properties, consult the following table, which compares Terminal Services configuration, user accounts, and remote desktop connection.

Table 4-3 Comparison of Configuration Options for Terminal Servers, User Accounts, and RDP Clients

Option	Terminal Services Configuration	User Account	Remote Desktop Connection
Configure the LAN adapters used	Yes	No	No
Set a counter for maximum connections per LAN adapter	Yes	No	No
Select encryption level	Yes	No	Preset
Enable automatic logon	Yes	No	Yes
Always request password	Yes	No	No
Time limits for connections	Yes	Yes	No
Time limit for disconnected sessions	Yes	Yes	No
Idle session limits	Yes	Yes	No
Handle interrupted connections	Yes	No	No
Start initial program	Yes	Yes	Yes
Redirect local drives	Yes (nonbinding)	Yes	Yes
Redirect local printers	Yes (nonbinding)	Yes	Yes
Redirect local serial ports	Yes (nonbinding)	No	Yes
Redirect local clipboard	Yes	No	No
Redirect local audio streams	Yes	No	No
Predefine/select desktop size	No	No	Yes
Predefine/select color depth	Yes	No	Yes
Connect to the console	No	No	Depends
Automatic reconnection	No	No	Yes

Table 4-3   Comparison of Configuration Options for Terminal Servers, User Accounts, and RDP Clients

Option	Terminal Services Configuration	User Account	Remote Desktop Connection
Control network bandwidth	Yes	No	Yes
Control full-screen options	No	No	Yes
Activate remote desktop	Yes	Yes	No
Define Terminal Services user profile	No	Yes	No
Define Terminal Services home folders	No	Yes	No
Logs	Yes	No	No

A terminal server is rarely set up in isolation, and a corporate network is not built around new terminal servers. Normally, new servers are integrated into already existing and established network structures. This next section deals with domain integration and Group Policies for terminal servers.

Domain Integration

Once they reach a certain size, computer environments based on Windows 2000 and Windows Server 2003 are usually organized into domains. A domain on a terminal server functions primarily as central instance for authenticating users and assigning shared printer and file resources. Together with the domains, Active Directory is the directory service for Windows 2000 and Windows Server 2003. It saves information on network objects, such as users, groups, servers, or printers. Users and administrators can call up this data using simple search functions. The Active Directory service uses a structured data memory on which the logical and hierarchical order of directory information is based.

> **Note**   This book does not explore in detail the complex design objectives and models of domains and the Active Directory service. However, we cannot ignore these topics completely. We will indeed examine them, always in the context of terminal servers.

In principle, a terminal server within a domain behaves just like a "normal" system running Windows 2000 Professional or Windows XP. The only difference is that one computer name is valid for multiple users. Therefore, a terminal server is integrated into a domain structure normally, that is, by using the System Properties window accessed through Control Panel. Within the System Properties window you select the file tab Computer Name and change the membership to a domain or working group by using the Change... button.

The More... button opens another dialog box in which you can add a suffix to the DNS name and see the NetBIOS computer name. The NetBIOS computer name is used for interoperability of older computers and services.

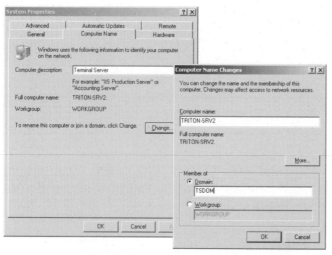

Figure 4-29   Adding a terminal server to an existing domain.

A terminal server should never assume the function of a domain controller. The Terminal Services design objective is clearly to provide optimally performing applications to interactive users. This, of course, strongly contradicts the highly prioritized processes needed for database synchronization and preferred handling of logon requests. Therefore, we recommend using at least two dedicated domain controllers.

Group Policies

Under Microsoft Windows NT 4.0, the Group Policy Editor was introduced. With the help of this editor, system policies could be created to manage the work environment and user actions. These policies were also used to enforce system configuration settings for all computers under Windows NT 4.0. This concept was significantly enhanced under Windows 2000 through the introduction of Active Directory. Many familiar tools were standardized and replaced by the new Active Directory integrated Group Policy tools and the attendant extensions. Windows 2000 offered other completely new functions, such as setting policies at different locations and predefining the scope of policies through security groups. For an administrator, Group Policy has been one of the most important enhancements in the Windows network management environment.

If computers and user accounts under Windows Server 2003 are combined within domains and organizational units, their properties and restrictions are controlled via Group Policies. Group Policy is a great tool for fine-tuning a Windows Server 2003 network environment and its computers. This especially applies to user interface functions, software installation, administrative templates, redirecting access to folders, security settings, Microsoft Internet Explorer administration, as well as Terminal Services configuration and terminal server session administration. However, bear in mind that problems are inherent in mixed terminal server environments running different Windows versions with a common Group Policy.

Basically, Group Policies can be applied to user or computer objects within sites, domains, or organizational units. Computer objects are not limited to client computers, but can also include domain controllers and all servers (Windows 2000 Server and Windows Server 2003) in a domain. Settings are passed from one Active Directory level to the underlying levels if not expressly prohibited. At a minimum, you can even configure a standalone server through Group Policies. This is known as a local group policy.

Group Policies is a powerful administrative tool for Windows Server 2003. We will encounter it often in this book.

Note   To invoke the tool for managing the Group Policy on a domain controller, select Administration\Active Directory Users and Computers. Use the **Gpedit.msc** command to open the local group policy object on a standalone terminal server. To differentiate the options for the various operating systems, you can filter the administrative template policies by various criteria under View\Filtering....

Using Group Policies

With Group Policies and the corresponding expansions, you can perform the following tasks essential to terminal servers:

- **Policy administration**   A file is generated for Group Policies that contains registry settings. These settings are written to the registry database in the area for individual users or local computers. The entries in the registry database determine system behavior for users or the computer. (See also Chapter 6.)

- **Script assignment**   Executing scripts to boot up and shut down the computer and log users on and off. It is possible to enter several scripts to be executed in a predefined sequence. In so doing, however, you might disable scripts that were set in user configuration. It is therefore not possible to combine both script configurations.

- **Directory redirection** The Application Data, Desktop, My Documents, My Pictures, and Start Menu directories on a local computer can be moved to one network resource.

- **Application management** Assigning, publishing, updating, and repairing applications, which requires an additional expansion of the software installation. However, please make sure that you really want to distribute software from a terminal server. Performance bottlenecks are likely to occur due to the potentially large number of simultaneous users who can be assigned software.

- **Security options** Override local security settings with centrally managed policies.

A Group Policy always consists of two parts, user configuration and computer configuration. They represent two different categories of configuration. If needed, you can set an object within Active Directory to only load one of the two parts. This is useful if the other part is not relevant for the object and optimizes the communication effort on loading the Group Policy.

As you can see, users and computers are the only types of Active Directory objects that contain policies. Policies are not used with security groups, in particular. For performance reasons, security groups filter the policies through Accept Group Policy for access control. This entry can have the value *Enabled* or *Disabled* or is not configured at all. (See also Chapter 8.)

Policies can thus be set locally and centrally. But which setting takes precedence if there are different values for one property? There is a clear hierarchy in applying Group Policies.

1. **Local Group Policy object** Exactly one group policy object is saved locally on each Windows Server 2003. This object can be found under %System-Root%System32\GroupPolicy.

2. **Site (Location)** In the next step, all Group Policy objects assigned to one Site are processed. This process follows the sequence defined by the administrator. A site is defined within Active Directory by the Administrator and allows definition of synchronization between sites and local logon rules.

3. **Domain** Several Group Policy objects assigned to one domain are processed in the sequence defined by the administrator.

4. **Organizational units** Organizational units can be nested within other organizational units, and an object (computer or user) may only exist in one organizational unit. Thus, rules defined within Group Policy at the top level of the Active Directory organizational unit hierarchy are applied first. Then the Group Policy rules in the subordinate levels are applied, until finally those Group Policy levels that contain the users or computers objects are processed.

If policies differ, the policies applied at a later point in time overwrite the previous ones by default. If there are no differences in the settings, both previous and later policies are followed.

Note   A Group Policy has priority over local administration tools or applications. Thus, terminal server settings established under Terminal Services configuration or computer administration will be overwritten by a differing Group Policy. The same applies to the remote desktop connection on a client computer controlled by Active Directory. This enables you to establish company-wide settings for terminal servers, their applications, and users. The ability to perform subsequent administrative tasks centrally is usually well worth the initial configuration effort.

Tip   The Administrative Templates source files, which make up a large part of the Group Policy, can be found in the %Systemroot%\INF folder. The corresponding local working copies are saved in the hidden %Systemroot%\system32\GroupPolicy\Adm. folder. If the terminal server is member of a domain, the working copies are always located in the domain controllers' SYSVOL folder. After a standard installation, this is also where you will find System.adm for system configuration (also for Terminal Services), Inetres.adm for Internet Explorer, Conf.adm for Microsoft NetMeeting, Wmplayer.adm for Microsoft Windows Media Player, and Wuau.adm for automatic updates. The hidden Admfiles.ini file determines which of the administrative templates will actually be used. You can, of course, add more administrative templates if the files use the standard format.

Computer Configuration

A computer configuration is applied to a computer on startup, regardless of who logs on. Computer configuration is divided into the following basic extensions, which can be further delineated:

- **Software Settings**   Computer-specific settings for the software installed through Group Policy.

- **Windows Settings**   Scripts for startup, shut-down, and security settings.

- **Administrative Templates**   Windows components, system, network, and printer.

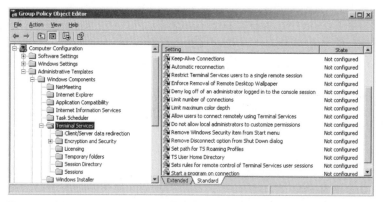

Figure 4-30 Setting computer-specific Group Policies for Terminal Services.

The following list specifies the key locations where the computer configuration can be adapted for terminal servers.

- **Computer Configuration\Windows Settings\Security\Local Policies\ User Rights Assignment** This comprises numerous settings, including an option to allow or prohibit individual user groups from logging on through Terminal Services. For this reason, this configuration is essential for terminal servers.

- **Computer Configuration\Windows Settings\Security\Local Policies\ Audit Policy** Settings for logged system events.

- **Computer Configuration\Windows Settings\Security\Local Policies\ Security Options** Security Settings for domains, connected devices, interactive logon, network, system objects, and monitoring. One of the settings relevant to terminal servers is whether users may install printer drivers or not.

- **Computer Configuration\Windows Settings\Security Settings\Software Restriction Policies** Central definition for application options of installed software.

- **Computer Configuration\Administrative Templates\Windows Components\ Application Compatibility** Options to enable and disable mechanisms related to application compatibility and handling 16-bit applications. The settings you select here might limit the use of a terminal server (for instance, if it can no longer execute 16-bit applications).

- **Computer Configuration\Administrative Templates\Windows Components\ Terminal Services** General Terminal Services parameters, to some degree similar to the ones definable in Terminal Services configuration or user accounts.

- **Computer Configuration\Administrative Templates\Windows Components\ Terminal Services\Client/Server Data Redirection** Configure device and port redirections because they can also be defined under Terminal Services configuration, user administration, or a terminal services client.

- **Computer Configuration\Administrative Templates\Windows Components\ Terminal Services\Encryption and Security**   Select parameters for password entry, RDP encryption, and RPC security.

- **Computer Configuration\Administrative Templates\Windows Components\ Terminal Services\Licensing**   Settings for licensing over license servers and license updates for terminal servers and Terminal Services clients.

- **Computer Configuration\Administrative Templates\Windows Components\ Terminal Services\Temporary Folders**   Using temporary folders per session and deleting temporary folders when a user session on a terminal server ends.

- **Computer Configuration\Administrative Templates\Windows Components\ Terminal Services\Session Directory**   System behavior when using a session directory (starting with Windows Server 2003 Enterprise Edition only).

- **Computer Configuration\Administrative Templates\Windows Components\ Terminal Services\Sessions**   Configure time limits just like under Terminal Services configuration and user administration. If the settings also apply to user configuration, computer configuration has priority in case of conflict.

- **Computer Configuration\Administrative Templates\Windows Components\ Windows Installer**   Configure installation environment; if at all possible, prohibit uncontrolled installations by users for terminal servers. You also decide if administrators may perform installations from Terminal Services sessions.

- **Computer Configuration\Administrative Templates\Windows Components\ Windows Update**   Settings for automatic system updates, which must be very restrictive for many terminal server environments. These settings prevent unsynchronized system updates that could cause inconsistent conditions in server farms.

- **Computer Configuration\Administrative Templates\System\User Profiles**   System settings for user profiles. Contains time limits for centrally saved profiles and options for local, cached profiles. These parameters are essential for terminal servers that are organized in farms.

- **Computer Configuration\Administrative Templates\System\ Scripts**   Configure waiting times, synchronization conditions, and visibility of system-relevant scripts (for example, logon script or start script). Because logon scripts often a play key role on terminal servers, the settings you select here are very important. If the settings also apply to user configuration, computer configuration has priority in case of conflict.

- **Computer Configuration\Administrative Templates\System\Logon**   Among other options, choose to execute certain programs when a user logs on or process the usual lists. Initialization of customer-specific applications for terminal servers can depend on these settings.

- **Computer Configuration\Administrative Templates\System\Group Policies**   Settings that influence the behavior of Group Policies updates on affected computers and which policies apply.

- **Computer Configuration\Administrative Templates\System\Remote Assistance**   Basic settings for remote assistance options based on Terminal Services.

- **Computer Configuration\Administrative Templates\Printers**   Settings on printer use and setup.

Many of the above configuration elements are described in much more detail later in this book.

> **Tip**   All relevant computer configuration files are located on the server in the %Systemroot%\system32\GroupPolicy\Machine folder. This folder contains the Registry.pol file with the selected computer-specific settings of the administrative templates that are taken directly from the Group Policies Editor. You can also save script files here to be executed when the server boots up or shuts down.

User Configuration

A user configuration is applied to a user at logon, regardless of where the user logs on. It is divided into the following basic extensions, which can be delineated in even greater detail:

- **Software Settings**   User-specific settings for the software installed.

- **Windows Settings**   Remote installation services, logon and logoff scripts, security settings, and Internet Explorer maintenance.

- **Administrative Templates**   Windows components, start menu and taskbar, desktop, Control Panel, released folders, network, and system.

The computer configuration has priority over the user configuration where the options are the same.

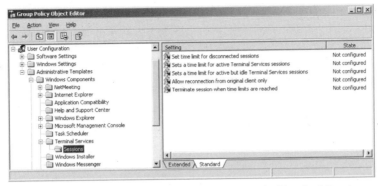

Figure 4-31 Setting user-specific Group Policies for Terminal Services.

The following list specifies the key locations where the user configuration can be adapted for terminal servers:

- **User Configuration\Windows Settings\Scripts** Select scripts to be executed upon user logon and logoff. Logon and logoff scripts are critical for smooth operation of a terminal server environment.

- **User Configuration\Administrative Templates\Windows Components\ Application Compatibility** Option to prevent user access to 16-bit applications.

- **User Configuration\Administrative Templates\Windows Components\ Windows Explorer** Numerous options for Windows Explorer settings. Restricting them can significantly improve terminal server security.

- **User Configuration\Administrative Templates\Windows Components\ Terminal Services** Select a program that is automatically executed when a user session is established and determine remote monitoring settings.

- **User Configuration\Administrative Templates\Windows Components\ Terminal Services\Sessions** Configure time limits just like under Terminal Services configuration and user administration.

- **User Configuration\Administrative Templates\Windows Components\ Windows Update** Eliminate access to all Windows Update functions. This prevents users from modifying the terminal server configuration.

- **User Configuration\Administrative Templates\Start Menu and Taskbar** Comprehensive configuration options for start menu items and taskbar elements to control user access.

- **User Configuration\Administrative Templates\Desktop** Modify desktop icons and context menu items. Additional settings for Microsoft Active Desktop and user access to the Active Directory service.

- **User Configuration\Administrative Templates\Control Panel** Control access to the entire Control Panel and some individual tools. Prevent installation of new software or printers or set standards for desktop design. These options help improve terminal server stability.

- **User Configuration\Administrative Templates\System\User Profiles** Link a user's home directory with the root of a share, set profile size, or exclude directories from profiles saved on a server.

- **User Configuration\Administrative Templates\System\Scripts** Configure synchronization conditions and logon script visibility. Because logon scripts often play a key role for user sessions on terminal servers, the settings you select here are very important.

- **User Configuration\Administrative Templates\System\Logon** Choose to execute certain programs when a user logs on or process the usual lists.

- **User Configuration\Administrative Templates\System\Group Policies** Settings that influence the behavior of Group Policies updates for affected users and which policies apply.

Many of the above configuration elements are described in much more detail later in this book.

> **Tip** All relevant User Configuration files are located on the server in the %Systemroot%\system32\GroupPolicy\User folder. The folder contains the Registry.pol file with the selected user-specific settings of the administrative templates that are taken directly from the Group Policies Editor. You can also save script files here that are executed when a user logs on or off.

Configuration Within an Organizational Unit

Group Policies is an excellent tool for managing multiple terminal servers within Active Directory. It manages users and groups in the predefined Users container. There is a separate container for the computers, including the corresponding settings. However, terminal servers can also be bundled into individual organizational units, each with its own Group Policies. In principle, an Active Directory object (for example, a computer, a user, or a group) can be in only one container or organizational unit.

When implementing Group Policies on terminal servers, keep the following in mind: Usually, terminal servers are combined into one organizational unit to enable uniform configuration using Group Policy. User settings should definitely be defined as well. However, as already mentioned, the settings apply only to objects that are part of the related organizational unit. User settings for accounts in other organizational units are therefore not carried over.

To solve this problem, there is a very important setting under Computer Configuration\Administrative Templates\System\Group Policies: Loopback Processing Mode for User Group Policy. Here you can activate the User Configuration that is part of the organizational unit for the server in question. If a user logs on to the server, the settings of his or her organizational unit will be replaced by or combined with the user settings of the server's organizational unit. If they are combined, the user settings in the server's Group Policies take precedence over the normal user settings in conflict situations.

Here is a practical example of this mechanism: users who work in a company's subsidiary have local, conventional clients running Windows XP with their Internet Explorer proxy settings pointing to the subsidiary's proxy server. If the users log on to a terminal server located at headquarters, the headquarters' proxy server should be used. This can be configured using the loopback processing mode.

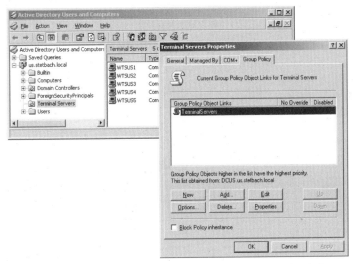

Figure 4-32   A Group Policy object of the organizational unit for terminal servers.

So how can multiple terminal servers within one domain be made available to a user group?

1. Install the terminal servers and add them to a domain.

2. On one of the corresponding domain controllers, create a new global group for the terminal server users in the Users container of the Active Directory Users and Groups tool. The group should have a meaningful name, such as *WTS users*.

3. Add the newly created or existing user accounts in the Users container to the new group of terminal server users.

4. Create a new organizational unit for the terminal servers in the domain, named,

for instance, *Terminal Servers*. Add all involved terminal servers to this organizational unit. The organizational unit receives a new Group Policy object for which you activate the loopback processing mode (preferably using **Replace**). At this level, you can also define any additional Group Policies for terminal servers.

5. On each terminal server, add the global terminal server user group you created to the local Remote desktop users default group.

Now all users in the global terminal server user group can log on to all terminal servers in the corresponding organizational unit.

> **Note** The Group Policies for computer and user configurations will be updated after a preset time and hence are often not valid immediately. Updates take place every 90 minutes with an additional random delay of 0 to 30 minutes. You can change the update rate under Computer Configuration\Administrative Templates\System\Group Policies.

User Profiles

Profiles represent user settings on Windows Server 2003. They include desktop settings or user preferences for conventional Windows applications. A standard Windows Server 2003 saves these settings for each user in an individual data structure that you can find in the systems folder under \Documents and Settings*<Logon Name>*. Each user logon name, and thus each user profile, is unique. If a local logon name and a domain logon name are identical, the domain name is added to the logon name (Logonname.domainname), thus creating two different profiles.

Folder Hierarchy

A user profile's folder hierarchy contains application data, desktop settings, information on the print environment, user files, local settings, neighborhood computers in the network environment, individual start menu expansions, and specific information about installed applications, such as Internet Explorer.

Let us first take a closer look at this folder hierarchy and a typical user profile.

- **Application Data**   Hidden folder with application-specific information.
- **Cookies**   Internet Explorer cookies.
- **Desktop**   Configuration of the graphical user environment.
- **Printhood**   Hidden folder for printer configuration.
- **My Documents**   Default location to save user files.

- **Favorites**   Windows Explorer favorites.

- **Local Settings**   Hidden folder containing application data, temporary files, and history.

- **Nethood**   Hidden folder containing network information about neighboring computers.

- **Send To**   Hidden folder containing links for the Windows Explorer Send To context menu.

- **Start Menu**   User-specific files and start menu application links.

- **Templates**   Template files.

- **Windows**   Special folder for terminal servers, usually containing application-specific configuration and log files.

> **Note**   Some user profile folders are hidden, which means that they are not displayed in Explorer. However, this is no real obstacle to the experienced user and should not be seen as a strict security measure.

Another essential user profile element is a hidden file named Ntuser.dat in the profile directory root. At logon, Ntuser.dat is the data container for individual entries in the Windows Server 2003 registry database. (See also Chapter 6.)

Ntuser.ini, another hidden file, contains the list of files excluded from the user profile. These folders are excluded if the profile is saved centrally on one server. For this reason, it is possible to limit the amount of data transferred to the server. Entries in this file are usually generated through a Group Policy under User Configuration\Administrative Templates\System\User Profiles: Exclude directories in roaming profiles.

So exactly how is a profile generated? When a user logs on for the first time (or after his or her prior profile has been deleted), a new profile is generated using the general Default User template. When the user logs off, the profile and its individual settings are saved under \Documents and Settings\<*Logon Name*>. At the next logon, the profile is reloaded and provides the settings of the user's previous session.

Roaming Users

A user who normally works with Windows 2000 Professional or Windows XP will arrange views, icons, and links to applications according to his or her personal taste. All this individual information is saved in a local profile and is applied the next time the user logs on.

Administrators of domains with "roaming users" are aware that these settings are no longer available if the user logs on to another workstation. To get around this problem, the developers of Windows NT created the option to save user profiles in one central location of the network. When a user logs on, his or her individual profile is invoked through a server. The path to the server-based profile can be configured through user administration.

> **Tip**   It is recommended that profiles for roaming users be kept as small as possible, for example, by excluding the temporary directory from the profile and shifting the My Documents and Application Data files to a network drive.

When a roaming user logs on to a terminal server, the server-based profile would become valid for the remote session's desktop. This, however, can result in invalid links to programs installed locally on a Windows XP workstation that are not available in the terminal server session. This in turn leads to problems such as incorrectly displayed icons or error messages on application start.

To avoid these problems, you can enter a special profile path on the terminal server that is not linked to the normal profiles (as mentioned earlier in this chapter). This procedure ensures that a user's profile settings for logon to a terminal server are different from the ones for logon under Windows XP. It also simplifies using different paths to the required applications in a corporate environment.

When a user logs on to a terminal server, profiles are loaded in a predefined sequence, as follows:

1. If a corresponding configuration was established in user administration, the Terminal Services profile is loaded.

2. If there is no Terminal Services user profile, the server-based profile for a roaming user is loaded. If a locally cached and current server-based profile exists, it is loaded. Otherwise, the user session loads the server-based profile from the network share.

3. Only if the user does not have a server-based user profile is the local profile loaded (which is not identical to the cached server-based profile). However, in this case, the user is no longer a roaming user.

After the server-based profile has been loaded from the network, it is cached locally on the terminal server's hard drive. All changes to the user profile are managed through the local copy. When the user logs off, these changes are transferred to the corresponding, centrally managed profile. Under certain circumstances, it is recommended that the local information be deleted as soon as the user logs off. One such circumstance is if several load-balanced terminal servers provide sessions for a large group of users. In the course of time, all user profiles are collected on all terminal servers without necessarily representing the most current status. Required disk space is quite large without really being advantageous—the user profiles probably have to be transferred time and again from the central server. With voluminous profiles and low network speed, logon takes a lot longer when copying a complete profile instead of accessing locally saved ones.

The most effective way to avoid getting cached profiles is to delete them through a Group Policy as soon as the users log off the terminal server. The central version of the profiles should be saved on a file server with sufficient hard-drive space. You access the file server through an exported directory. One condition is, however, that it be integrated into the domain. Furthermore, the terminal servers must be configured largely the same in terms of operating system and applications to share profiles.

Mandatory Profiles

A mandatory profile is a variant of the server-based profile. You just need to rename the Ntuser.dat file of an existing profile to Ntuser.man. This type of profile can now be allocated to one user or even a group of users. The data contained in a mandatory profile is loaded from the server when the corresponding users log on. However, they cannot change the mandatory profile data when they log off. This means that all individual changes made during a user session are lost on logoff.

What does this concept have to do with terminal servers? It can help solve a problem that occurs quite frequently in larger terminal server environments: if one or two terminal server farms are set up with different sets of applications, profile conflicts are sure to follow. When a user with a single server–based profile logs on to one terminal server on each of the two farms, the individual settings on both servers might be modified. When the user logs off the first terminal server, the related profile is saved on the profile server. When the user logs off the second, differently configured user session, this profile is saved as well—and might overwrite some of the data changed in the first user session. Therefore, the easiest solution is a mandatory profile that contains all information relevant to both server farm configurations. To avoid losing individual setting changes (for example, changing the default printer), logon and logoff scripts must manage all corresponding data.

Using mandatory profiles and script mechanisms for differently configured server farms is one of the less trivial tasks of an administrator. This type of concept requires thorough planning and implementation. You will find further information on this topic in Chapter 6, Chapter 7, and Chapter 11.

Ini Mapping and Temp Mapping

The profile folder structure comprises another folder that is essential for using Terminal Services. This folder is named WINDOWS and contains user-specific versions of ini files that are mostly used by 16-bit and older 32-bit Windows applications. A terminal server session prompts this type of Windows application to load its configuration data from the user profile WINDOWS folder. If the data is not there, it is loaded from the usual place, the system directory (normally C:\WINDOWS for Windows Server 2003). The configuration that was changed during a Terminal Services client session is always saved to the user's profile folder. The original ini file never changes. Thus, ini files are individualized even though the corresponding application was not developed for a multiuser environment.

Important   The procedure described above is referred to as *ini-mapping* and is an effective method for making older applications usable for multiple users. The default path to the ini files can vary in the available Microsoft operating systems. The applications usually invoke it through the *%WinDir%* environment variable for installation procedures and all ini file accesses. Nevertheless, ini mapping and the resulting user profile access lead to a slightly different behavior in terminal servers. The path in *%WinDir%* is used only when the application is installed and first used.

This type of user-specific ini file administration is maintained under Windows Server 2003 using the *%Temp%* and *%Tmp%* variables. In a terminal server's %Temp% folder, you will never find the "wild mix" of all the users' temporary files, as in Windows NT 4.0. Starting with Windows 2000, temporary files have been managed by the user profile and its \Local Settings\Temp folder. The complete temp path for a user who is an administrator might therefore be C:\Documents and Settings\Administrator\Local Settings\Temp. Depending on the terminal server's configuration, the temporary directory path may be supplemented by a session ID. This allows a user to log on several times and use temporary files for each individual session.

Important   Setting up individual temporary directories is very important if you want to run standard applications securely. For instance, the documents loaded last by Microsoft Office Word can be rebuilt from the temporary data after a runtime error. If it were possible to inadvertently access other users' temporary files on a terminal server, the documents would end up with the next user who logs on and not with the actual document owner.

Printing

Hassle-free printing is a central requirement in a corporate environment and requires an appropriate infrastructure. Using print servers and connecting local printers to clients are two ways for providing printers concurrently to multiple users. However, planning, configuring, and maintaining this type of remote printer environment requires significantly more know-how of the basic mechanisms than using a direct printer connection to the terminal server.

Print Clients and Printer Drivers

Printing a document seems trivial at first glance: the computer transfers all graphical elements of the document to a device that outputs the graphics on paper. Unfortunately, there is a lot more to the process than is apparent. The ludicrous array of document formats, graphical elements, and printer types generates problems.

The source of a print job is referred to as the *print client*. If a user enters the command to print a document or a document area, an image of the document to be printed is generated in an *enhanced metafile format*. Because this format is independent of the target printer, it needs to be adapted to the correct format for that printer. To achieve this, the corresponding printer driver must be installed and registered on the print client. The printer driver generates the specific data stream from the enhanced metafile format to contact the target printer.

Spooling is the administration and processing of print jobs for all connected printers. This task is performed by a special service that is referred to as a *spooler*. It accesses printer drivers for processing print jobs. When this service is terminated, you can no longer print on the local computer, regardless of the printer drivers installed.

When a printer driver is installed, the applicable files are saved in the %Systemroot% \system32 \spool \drivers \w32x86 \3 folder. The *3* at the end of the path defines the printer driver's version, which corresponds to Windows 2000 and Windows Server 2003. A *2*, however, indicates a printer driver that was developed for Windows NT.

> **Important**   Printer drivers that were developed according to Windows NT conventions run as kernel drivers in the operating system's executive layer. (See also Chapter 1.) As a result, they often end up in the notorious blue screen, the color of the screen when the system fails. The newer printer drivers that were developed according to the specifications for Windows 2000 and Windows Server 2003 run in user mode and do no harm in case of failure. Due to downstream compatibility, Windows Server 2003 can still use the old printer drivers. However, this is not recommended on terminal servers and is therefore prohibited through the default setting. You can change this behavior through Group Policies.

The concept of automatically installed printer drivers was developed for Windows operating systems to simplify network printing. A central instance transfers the printer drivers to a computer with the proper OS and permissions to use this printer. Oftentimes, installation is initiated automatically by the first user who requests the corresponding printer on the network. However, this behavior might be problematic for terminal servers. An administrator is no longer able to control which drivers are currently on the terminal server. You can regulate behavior more strictly only through modifying the registry database. (See also Chapter 6.)

So how does the system decide which printer driver to use for which printer? The %Systemroot% \inf folder contains a file named Ntprint.inf. Among its other tasks, this file enables exact allocation of the known printer types to the existing printer drivers. The file's syntax is relatively simple:

```
[HP]
"HP LaserJet 5MP"    = HPLJ5MP.GPD
```

Print Servers

If network printers are used in corporate environments, it is not very efficient if each computer handles its own local print jobs and sends them to the target printer. A dedicated server should perform this task, and in so doing becomes a print server. All computers on the network send their print jobs to the print server. In case of frequent changes to the printer constellation, this procedure ensures a minimum of necessary changes to the client system. Spooling is again key here, that is, receiving, processing, caching, sequencing, and distributing print jobs.

It is possible to divide the processes during a print job on the network into several individual steps. A terminal server assumes the same role in this example as a normal client.

1. A user prints a document from a terminal server. The GDI/GDI+ graphical interface generates an output data stream using the selected printer driver. The driver is transferred to a spooler, the source of the following network commu-

nication. Often, the data stream is transferred directly to the print server that then assumes the task of spooling. In third-party systems, the process is similar but excludes the use of the GDI interface.

2. The terminal server sends the print job to the print server. The generated data stream is sent through a "remote procedure call" to the server's router. The print server receives the print job and processes the data received. With Windows operating systems, the print job is handled by the Redirector, where the server service transfers the data to the print server. If the client is a UNIX computer, the print server's LPD service is needed to accept the print job.

3. The router or print-server services forward the print job to the server's local print support. The spooler on the server processes and carries out the print process. It saves that data on the hard drive until the data can be further processed in the print process.

4. The print job is forwarded to a separator page processor and the print monitor. Either the printer or another print server receives the print job via the physical interface and converts it to individual pages.

The printer drivers play a key role in the preceding process. They allow a generic communication between an application and the different printers, regardless of device type or language that was used to write the page.

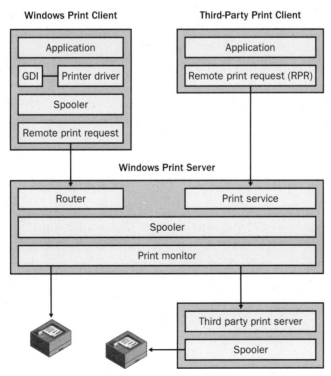

Figure 4-33   The basic architecture of a print server environment. The Windows print client runs on the terminal server.

Network Printers

Terminal servers, print servers, Terminal Services clients, and network printers frequently do not run on the same network segment. Which setups exist in a comprehensive network with terminal servers and Terminal Services clients on different segments?

- The Terminal Services client and a network printer are on one network segment, and terminal servers and printer server are on another. This is a typical setup for home offices and small remote offices connected to the company headquarters' network via an ISDN router. The user works on a terminal server and starts some applications. A print job is generated in the computing center on the terminal server and sent to the print server on the logical, "short" path. Subsequently, the print data is sent to the printer on the other network segment via routers. This scenario is problematic if, in addition to Terminal Services client, local applications are used on the client computer. These local applications generate a print job on the client, send it the long way to the print server, and again from there the "long" way to the printer. Due to this redundant data transfer per print job, the line between the network segments is frequently heavily loaded. It is therefore recommended that a local print concept be used for local applications, although it does make the environment's configuration a bit more complicated and requires user expertise. A fast connection between the two network segments makes this configuration an excellent option.

- Terminal Services client, a print server, and a printer are on the same network segment, the terminal server on another. This is a rather unusual combination if there is only one, very powerful print server. Both server types are not on the same, central segment, which is not very practical. Only if the concept is supported by small, decentralized print servers is the scenario slightly more realistic. This arrangement does have an advantage, though: the print-data stream needs to be transferred only once between the network segments for both terminal server sessions and local applications.

- The Terminal Services client is on one network segment, and terminal servers, print server, and printer on another. This is a network arrangement that meets increased transfer and security requirements. A print job from a terminal server session does not traverse any segment borders, that is, the environment can achieve an optimum print-data transmission rate. Furthermore, this combination allows company data to be printed to just one single network segment. If the network segment with the Terminal Services client is external and the network segment and other components are inside a monitored company building, it is relatively safe to print sensitive data. The data never leaves the internal network segments; only transient monitor images get out. These statements do not apply to local applications on the client, where such a solution is unsuitable.

We could, of course, look at some other arrangements based on more than two network segments. However, they are mere extensions of the above examples and would not yield any new features.

Redirected Client Printers

The RDP protocol from version 5.0 supports printers that are physically connected to the client. Interfaces and print queues are redirected to the terminal server and thus become visible within a user session. You can even set the user session's default printer to the client printer. In this way, all print jobs from a user session on a terminal server are automatically sent to the client printer.

The user generally expects to use the redirected client printer even though the applications are physically running on the remote server. The technical implementation of this behavior is supported by applications that do not communicate directly with the printer but via the GDI interface and spooler.

On a terminal server, the client printer has one more instance for handling print jobs. This instance is named RDP Port Redirector (RDPPR). It creates an administrative unit for virtual printers that are each associated with the physical client printers. The number of virtual printers depends on the currently active user sessions. A virtual printer's properties correspond to those of a real printer that is connected to the terminal server either directly or through a print server. Therefore, applications or their GDI requests cannot discern any differences between the two printer types.

When a user logs on, the RDPPR automatically establishes all existing serial, parallel, and USB ports as well as the printer queues of the corresponding client. This process dynamically generates virtual printers and interfaces on the terminal server through Plug and Play API, which are then integrated into the user session. Possible changes to the print queues are also conveyed to the terminal server this way, which enables runtime adjustment. The user session on the terminal server also handles default printer settings (for example, double-sided printing).

The print queue terminates when the user session ends. All incomplete or suspended print jobs are lost. The settings of the corresponding client printer are saved on the client and reloaded for later sessions.

An event is created in the Event Viewer if a necessary printer driver is not available on the terminal server. If you still want to use the printer, you need to install the driver manually. However, you need administrator rights on the terminal server to do this. After you install the printer manually, you can delete the printer object connected to the serial, the parallel, or the USB port. Upon user logon, the integrated user session printer is mapped to the redirected client interface. Thus, local USB printers are supported, too.

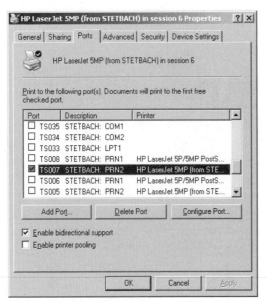

Figure 4-34   List of redirected and automatically generated print queues on a terminal server.

Note   Redirected printers are available for all applications running on the terminal server. These printers appear in the Printers menu of the Control Panel and have the following format: *Client printer name/Client computer names/Session ID*.

If a data stream is sent from a user session to a virtual printer, the RDPPR forwards the print job to the corresponding client. The client communicates with the physical printer. All data used for connecting a client printer is transferred using a separate, virtual RDP channel.

Chapter 5

Integrating Applications

This chapter provides all the information required to install and adjust user applications on a terminal server. It not only describes pure installation procedures, but also the prior gathering of all the relevant data that will affect the server infrastructure and the applications used.

- Applications used simultaneously by multiple users need to meet certain criteria and be compatible with terminal servers. This chapter describes the relevant technical requirements.

- A terminal server needs to run in a certain mode when applications are installed. This chapter explains why and describes the correct application installation procedures.

- Manual installation of applications is untenable in large terminal server environments. This chapter presents the key arguments for special installation tools.

- Several examples are cited to illustrate the installation of frequently used applications.

- In the past, companies and individuals developed Microsoft Windows–based applications themselves. This will likely continue as long as the functionality needed is not built into the off-the-shelf product. This chapter describes what you need to bear in mind if you want to commission or code your own customized applications for terminal servers.

- At the end of this chapter, you will find out how the application mix influences the sizing of your terminal server.

Applications in Multiple-User Mode

Thus far, this book has focused on Microsoft Windows Server 2003 multiple-user options and Terminal Services clients. We looked at all key concepts and tools for Terminal Services, user administration, and network connection of clients from the point of view of an administrator. We did not elaborate on applications until now. In the final analysis, a terminal server relies on user acceptance and effective delivery of applications.

Ideally, no problems should arise when you install and run any program on a terminal server without special configuration. Unfortunately, this is the exception rather than the rule. Many older applications or their installation routines might already behave badly on a standard Windows 2000 workstation or in Windows XP. Even more applications were designed in a way that does not allow their default settings to handle simultaneous multiple users. Consequently, such applications often make assumptions about the operating system that do not apply to a multiple-user environment.

Basically, the Microsoft programming principles for 32-bit applications should ensure proper functioning of programs that are used in multiple instances by multiple users. In the past, however, many application developers did not adhere to these principles, making subsequent improvements necessary to run within a terminal server environment. The adjustments involve registry settings as well as directory structures and file access permissions.

Multiple-User Operation Requirements

In a terminal server–based environment, applications run on the server platforms only. The clients do not execute any type of local application logic. They display only the user interface and accept input. Of course, applications on the server do need to support this scenario.

The design of conventional Windows-based applications had already been specified for Windows 2000 Server, and the result was a standard that set important design guidelines for applications. This standard formed the basis for certifying an application for its use with Windows 2000. A similar certification program exists for Windows Server 2003 as well. The applicable logo is Certified for Windows Server 2003. Find more information on this topic at *http://www.microsoft.com/winlogo*.

> **Note**   A conventional application is an application based on *unmanaged code*. Therefore, statements made in this connection do not apply to Windows-based applications that are built on the .NET Framework and based on *managed code*. They will be addressed separately.

A conventional application that meets the Certified for Windows requirements can be used freely in Windows 2000 and Windows Server 2003 multiple-user environments. If an application strictly follows all the guidelines, it has several predefined properties. The installation is robust and self-repairing, minimizing any conflicts between shared components (such as DLLs). This allows different applications to peacefully coexist on one platform.

Furthermore, a "clean" application is easily distributed in a networked environment and ensures easy administration within organized structures. It can also save user and computer settings in one central profile and thus allows you to manage roaming users. It supports multiple users per computer and recreates application settings if a computer needs to be physically exchanged. Global and user-specific data is strictly separated. Optimally, this type of application also supports several different clients with their own customized user interfaces (for example, logos, colors, or fonts).

Naturally, the application should be able to run in a strictly controlled network environment and allow administrators to set the security and user interface parameters according to company regulations. Finally, an application must be able to provide a clear path for converting from an earlier version of Windows to Windows Server 2003.

When evaluating applications, you need to look at several categories that are based on different fundamental technologies or require different conditions.

- Conventional Windows-based applications that access the 32-bit API of the operating system. These are typical, frequently used applications such as Microsoft Office XP, CorelDRAW, or Adobe Acrobat Reader.

- Applications that are based on the Microsoft ASP.NET Web Forms concept or XML Web services and behave like Web applications. Web servers such as the Microsoft Internet Information Server control their processing logic.

- Applications that are based on the .NET Windows Forms concept and generally behave like conventional 32-bit Windows-based applications.

Let us now look in detail at each of these categories.

32-Bit Windows Applications

A terminal server environment allows different users to simultaneously execute several application instances. Therefore, an application's components (.exe files or DLLs) need to be programmed in a way that several users can work with them at the same time. Consequently, the following special conditions for user data and files need to be met:

- **Separate memory areas**   Several application instances executed by different users should not access common memory areas containing user-specific data to prevent unwanted data exchange between two user sessions.

- **File access lockout**   When one user accesses a program file, file access should not be locked for other users. Otherwise, only one application instance can be executed.

- **File access permission**   Non-administrative users should probably not have access to system files or have the same permissions as administrators. Avoid setups that would, for instance, prevent users who did not install an application from starting it.

- **File saving location**   User-specific data and configuration files must be saved in separate, user-specific locations to avoid collisions and to manage access permissions.

At first glance, this does not seem complicated. However, in reality, older applications usually do not expect to be used in a multiple-user environment. They therefore make certain assumptions about their living space and behave accordingly. If this type of application is further developed, legacy design decisions often survive, even though they are not in keeping with the terminal server requirements previously discussed.

Through a corresponding API (Application Programming Interface), conventional applications are able to access specific system functions and data structures on terminal servers. This allows the development of applications that recognize they are running on terminal servers. In this way, developers can predefine certain program behaviors that apply only to terminal servers. A great example is an application that unambiguously identifies its user through a computer property, such as the IP address on a server running Windows Server 2003 without Terminal Services installed. On a terminal server, this property is not unique and might prevent simultaneous use of the application by several users. However, if the application recognizes that it is running on a terminal server and is so configured, it can switch to a mode that recognizes the user name as the unique differentiating feature. It is, of course, preferable to avoid such dependencies right from the start, when the application is being developed.

Conventional 32-bit applications that run on a terminal server present potential problems.

- **Dynamic link libraries**   Frequently, applications running on terminal servers use dynamic link libraries (DLLs). DLLs are software components, and they can be used by several applications. There are no general mechanisms to manage different DLL versions. For this reason, an application that accesses DLLs is not guaranteed to work properly. Under Windows 2000, side-by-side DLL (SxS DLL) support was introduced. It allows parallel use of several DLL versions on one system. However, SxS DLL did nothing to make DLL management easier, which is why the term *DLL hell* evolved with respect to the susceptibility to failure of complex Windows environments. This, of course, is not a terminal server–only problem; the multiple-user environment just highlights it more.

- **Registry**   The registry manages system and user configurations. (See Chapter 6.) Unfortunately, not all programs handle the differences between system and user settings as carefully as they should. This might be acceptable for systems that are used by a single individual. For terminal servers, this could mean a mixing of information from different users.

- **.Ini files**   From a historical point of view, .ini files were used before the registry was introduced. They were used to save and reload system and configuration data. All this happened at a central system location and therefore did not support differentiation between users. Older applications that use .ini files are therefore a special challenge when working with terminal servers.

- **User-specific application data**   An application should be able to save all user-generated data within files in a user-specific folder. The application should be configured to point to the user's home directory as the default archive directory. This requires the application to handle certain conventions, such as file access over the network or home directories with long names. User-specific application data is essential for terminal servers because terminal server users usually save user data on file servers on the network, not locally.

- **Temporary data**   Applications often create temporary data in temporary system folders. However, if several users are working on the system simultaneously, the temporary data must be strictly separated. Otherwise, data might get mixed up and possibly result in unauthorized data access. If user-specific temporary directories are used properly, such problems will not occur.

Due to the potential problems described above, some applications' installation routines need to be adapted for terminal servers to establish a working system environment without having to change the applications and installation programs themselves.

Framework Applications

In the summer of 2000, Microsoft announced the development of the .NET Framework, which allows completely new types of applications for Windows platforms. The .NET Framework has been on the market since the beginning of 2002 and supports three different types of applications.

- **ASP.NET Web Forms**   This type of application runs on Web servers (that is, Internet Information Services under Windows Server 2003) and generates output in HTML format (as Web forms). To display the graphical user interface (GUI) and interact with the application, the client requires a Web browser. The application logic is encoded with a technology called ASP.NET. Web forms do not usually have a role on terminal servers, but they can have an indirect impact if they are used to implement an application access portal.

- **XML Web Services** These applications also run on Web servers, but they interact with programs instead of with users. Web services thus represent a new generation of technology for developing modular software components that can be distributed on the network by means of a formal description and standard protocols. Web services are normally based on eXtensible Markup Language (XML) for data and document formats, Web Services Description Language (WSDL) to describe messages and services, and the Simple Object Access Protocol (SOAP) for communication among the software modules. XML Web services do not usually run on terminal servers.

- **.NET Windows Forms** Windows Forms are the descendants of conventional 32-bit Windows programs. They normally run in one window on the Windows desktop and can therefore be installed on terminal servers. If so programmed, Windows Forms can access Web services via the default interfaces and use their functions. The .NET Framework offers class libraries that can be used to develop Windows Forms applications.

The three Framework application types have one thing in common: they do not communicate directly with the operating system. They need a runtime environment as an intermediate layer, the *common language runtime* (CLR), which is able to process any application code written in *Microsoft Intermediate Language Code* (MSIL code). This platform-independent code is also known as *managed code* because it is strictly controlled by the runtime environment instance. For an application developed in a .NET language per common language runtime guidelines (for example, C# or Microsoft Visual Basic .NET), a *compiler* translates the source code into MSIL. The result in MSIL is then bundled into executable and transportable packages called *assemblies*. In rough terms, MSIL is like the assembler code of a Framework application and as such can be modified directly. However, a developer usually uses one of the .NET programming languages, not MSIL.

> **Note** The .NET common language runtime was developed primarily for security and to be independent of any programming language. Because the CLR controls the code in MSIL, it is easier to control security than in conventional 32-bit applications. Windows Server 2003 comes with .NET Common Language Runtime version 1.1 and can run Framework applications without any modifications.

An assembly is a self-contained unit that contains all the metadata, resources, and data it needs. A complete Framework application consists of at least one assembly, which you can install on a platform simply by copying it. No registration is required. Additional functions can be encapsulated in further assemblies. These assemblies must be located in the same folder or in a subfolder. You can also use an

XML file to determine where the runtime environment should look for additional assemblies. Assemblies used by more than one application are an exception. They are saved in a special folder, the %SystemRoot% \Assembly folder, also called the *Global Assembly Cache* (GAC). All assemblies in the GAC need to have a name, a version number, a public key, and a signature for unambiguous identification. All these elements comprise the strong name. The combination of assemblies, pre-defined folders, and strong names wards off the DLL hell of conventional 32-bit applications.

What happens if you want to run a Framework application that is an assembly in Microsoft Intermediate Language Code? In the case of .NET Windows Forms, the assembly is packed into an executable file that you can launch. Special header entries in the .exe file identify it as a .NET program that the operating system recognizes. This file first needs to be converted from the correct version of the common language runtime to a platform-specific byte code, either a 32-bit x86 code or a 64-bit Itanium code, depending on the platform. A just-in-time compiler is launched automatically after the .exe file with a Framework application is started and helps with the translation. This process runs every time the application is started. After the first time, the applications generally start a lot faster because the files are still in the main memory cache.

> **Important**   Why not install a platform-independent version of the Framework application in the target environment? The just-in-time compiler might know certain details about its computer such as number of available processors, memory, and other resources. It uses that information to optimize the application for the target environment when it translates the Microsoft Intermediate Language Code to platform-independent byte code. If a developer starts the just-in-time compiler on his own computer system to pre-compile the code and later transfers the code to another target machine, the result might not be optimized for a terminal server.

When terminal servers are the target platform, what exactly are the requirements for .NET Windows Forms applications?

- Configuration data that might be necessary for the runtime behavior of the application is usually in XML format. If these configurations affect user-specific settings, they need to be managed individually.

- User-specific application data should be saved in the user's home directory.

- .NET programs can also access the registry, although usually they do not. They are nonetheless subject to the same rules as conventional 32-bit applications. Because Framework applications rarely access .ini files, we can forego a detailed explanation on this point.

- To keep the system in a consistent state, you need to disable all options for user-initiated installations of Framework applications. Only administrators should have the right to install new Framework applications.

- One recommendation is to translate future Framework applications with the just-in-time compiler before a user invokes them for the first time. The Ngen.exe tool from .NET Framework SDK allows an administrator to translate the MSIL code of the assembly into platform-specific code and save it in the GAC. This needs to happen on every server where the application will be installed (for example, with a specific installation routine). However, performance improvements occur only while loading the application. Code created by the user by automatically evoking the just-in-time compiler is usually faster than code created by the Ngen.exe tool.

It is best for the application's installation routine to make some of the modifications, whereas other settings must be taken into account during the application's development. Overall, the basic structure of .NET Windows Forms application is clearly better than most conventional 32-bit applications and is certainly just as compatible with terminal servers. So far, there are too few .NET Windows Forms applications on the market to make a qualified statement. However, the simplified programming model and excellent development tools will quickly change this.

Finally, we will briefly review the GDI+ graphical interface and how it interacts with Framework applications. GDI+ is not part of the .NET Framework, as often assumed, but rather is part of the Windows XP operating system and Windows Server 2003. However, the graphics requests through the related class library of the .NET Framework use GDI+. All GDI+ classes are located in the *Gdiplus* namespace and can easily be used in Windows Forms applications because they tend to be programmed in C# or Visual Basic .NET.

Application Installation Procedures

As often mentioned in this chapter, how applications are installed under Windows Server 2003 depends on whether the server is configured as a terminal server or a normal server. The reasons were outlined previously in this chapter: the two types of servers differ in their handling of the registry and .ini files.

Important Before you install an application, you should block user access to the server. You can completely disable the RDP protocol using Terminal Services configuration or selectively block certain user groups from accessing RDP. Once that is done, an administrator can perform the required work on the console. If the RDP protocol is blocked to selective users, an administrator may use a remote RDP console session.

What problems can occur in the registry as the central instance of system configuration?

- If an application is installed and configuration data that all users need is written to the installing user's individual area instead of to the global area of the registry, then the application will work perfectly for that user, but not for anyone else. Important application data will be stored in that user's profile only (usually an authorized administrator).

- When an application is installed, user-specific data may be deliberately omitted from the user-specific area of the registry. Instead, the data is entered when the user opens the application for the first time. Some values, however, might have to be predefined by the administrator.

Creating .ini files can also cause massive problems during installation. True INI (initialization file) mapping allows redirection of individual .ini files to any user's profile. (See Chapter 4.) Yet this approach makes sense only when the terminal server is in normal mode. During an installation, the administrator should be able to store a default .ini file in a central location. If a user later starts the application for the first time, the central .ini file can be used to initialize the user's own .ini file, which is then saved in his or her profile.

> **Note**   These problems should no longer arise with .NET programs because they do not use .ini files and therefore do not access the wrong areas in the registry. Nonetheless, we recommend using the following procedures for Framework applications, too.

Installation Mode

To overcome the above-mentioned problems, you need to change the terminal server from normal execution mode to special installation mode before installing an application. You can use the Add or Remove Programs Software tool in the Control Panel or type the following command at the prompt:

change user /install

If the terminal server is not running in installation mode, it automatically switches to installation mode when the default **Setup.exe** command executes the installation program. However, this offers no real protection against installation errors. If the installation routine naming convention does not use the **Setup.exe** command, the installation will probably run in the wrong mode. We recommend using the Add or Remove Programs Software tool in the Control Panel because this insures that the terminal server will be in proper mode during application installation.

> **Tip**   You can check the terminal server's current mode at any time using the **change user /query** command.

Figure 5-1   Changing a terminal server to installation mode and checking the mode from the command prompt.

After you switch to installation mode, install the application as usual, which involves several processes. All user-specific registry entries are automatically mirrored to a system-wide registry area. The path is HKLM\Software\Microsoft\Windows NT \CurrentVersion\Terminal Server\Install\Software. (See Chapter 6.)

If a user other than the administrator needs the information, the data is supplied through the previously mirrored, system-wide registry path. This is called *registry mapping*. The data saved in the Terminal Server\Install registry path are overwritten by the user profile. Only Terminal Services running in application mode activates these minor modifications to the Windows kernel. This easily solves the first of the two registry problems discussed earlier.

If the application requests the Windows directory during installation (for example, using system requests such as *GetWindowsDirectory*), the terminal server returns the system's root directory. This directory is clearly defined in the %WinDir% environment variable. If you add entries to existing .ini files (with system requests such as *WritePrivateProfileString*), you access the .ini files in the system's root directory if the system is running in installation mode. The same goes for creating new .ini files. INI mapping is disabled while the terminal server is running in installation mode. This modification to the Windows kernel takes effect only if the system is a terminal server.

The previous explanation of the installation mode points us to the solution to the second registry problem: How do we create central application parameters in the registry when the application is used for the first time? In execution mode, all registry entries are saved in the administrator's profile—after all, the terminal server is designed to keep user data separate. The solution is that the administrator installing the application should invoke it for the first time with the terminal server still in installation mode. Mirroring the user-specific entries saves the application configuration to the registry's system-wide area. These entries are then copied to each user's profile when the system resumes running in execution mode.

> **Note**   It is now clear why applications might not function correctly if they were installed before Windows Server 2003 was made a terminal server. Neither registry mapping nor INI mapping work properly in this instance.

If the administrator has already invoked the application in execution mode, a temporary administrator should be set up to launch the application in installation mode and configure it such that all users later have access to the needed information (such as path, colors, font size, and so on). When other users launch the application for the first time, the associated data are also saved in the system-wide registry hive named HKLM\Software\Microsoft\Windows NT\CurrentVersion\Terminal Server\Install. Once this process is complete, the administrator account can either be deleted or temporarily disabled until it is needed again for similar tasks. If entries containing the user name were made in the system-wide registry area when the application was first used, the name might need to be globalized. You can use the %UserName% environment variable to modify the registry manually. (See Chapter 6.)

> **Important**   When installing an application on a terminal server, never start a previously installed application, such as Microsoft Internet Explorer, unless absolutely necessary. In installation mode, *all* changes to your personal settings will be mirrored to the system-wide registry area and included in other users' profiles. Many applications change their registry settings when they are started, or, at the latest, when they are terminated. The settings you unintentionally bequeath to other user sessions on the terminal server might have unforeseen ramifications.

Restoring Execution Mode

Once an application is installed, you need to return the system to normal execution mode. If you used the Add or Remove Programs tool in the Control Panel or **Setup.exe** to install the program, you will be prompted to do so in the final dialog box.

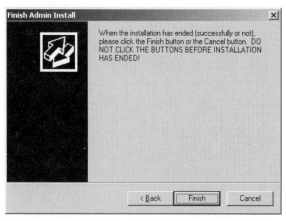

Figure 5-2 Final dialog box after installing an application on a terminal server.

Alternatively, you can reset the system to execution mode by entering the following command at the command prompt:

change user /execute

> **Important** You should always finalize an installation properly, even if it was unsuccessful. Use the dialog box shown in Figure 5-2 or the command prompt. Otherwise, the system will remain in installation mode and therefore mirror individual settings by the administrator to the system-wide area of the registry.

Supporting Tools

Administrators often face great challenges in successfully installing applications on a terminal server. Some companies require many applications to be installed on terminal servers. Furthermore, the growing user base demands these installations be distributed to dozens or even hundreds of servers combined in farms. It is therefore important for the installation procedure to be predictable and reproducible.

A good administrator begins to structure and optimize the procedure early on. Because prior planning is so important for creating repeatable installation procedures, this topic will be our focus in the following section.

Microsoft Installation Tools

Simplified administration was one of the key goals in developing Microsoft Windows 2000 and Windows Server 2003. Installing software was supposed to become easier and more transparent to the user as well. These goals were met by Windows Installer, which makes installing software on workstations almost fully automatic. Group Policies distribute the software in the form of an installation package, or the software can be manually installed by double-clicking a file with the .msi suffix.

An .msi file is a clearly defined package that contains all information required to install software in an embedded database such as copied files or previously created registry entries.

> **Note**   You can easily provide Framework applications using Windows Installer. Framework applications are generally more simple than conventional 32-bit applications, because Framework applications do not directly depend on other applications or have uncontrolled components. Moreover, they are easy to install. Just copy them to the target system; no registration is required. You need to call on special installation tools only if you want to install a .NET assembly into the GAC.

Windows Installer

Windows Installer version 2.0 is integrated into the Windows Server 2003 operating system. Msiexec.exe, a Windows Installer service, enables you to automatically add applications and application components that are offered as .msi packages. This service can assign delegated rights that surpass the permissions of the installing user. Users interact with application-specific dialog boxes.

> **Note**   It is, of course, possible to install a Terminal Services client on the target platform with an .msi package and Windows Installer. However, the target platform must support this method, which is usually true for Windows XP and Windows 2000 Professional.

Microsoft Windows Server 2003 can use Windows Installer to distribute programs in a company. Computers or users can be assigned certain programs, or they might be released for general use. Because several users can access programs simultaneously in terminal server environments, special preparation is needed.

For terminal servers, applications must be installed per computer so that they are available for every user who can access them. Assigned programs can be installed from the console or via a remote console session. In the latter case, several problems might arise.

- Installing an application requires that the system be switched to installation mode and possibly rebooted. The administrator should confirm that no users are logged on to the terminal server interactively before starting the installation.

■ If the application is installed via a remote console session, the session might end or reset if the system needs to be rebooted. When the server reboots, the session is reset and the administrator might have to log on to the terminal server again to make sure that the program was installed properly.

Windows Installer installs programs on different levels, depending on how the .msi package was created. Many .msi packages perform a minimum installation, that is, of just a few program components. This technology is known as *application advertisement*. When a user invokes an application, Windows Installer determines which parts of the program are already there and then installs any needed advertised components. Because advertised programs and components are advertised per user, however, terminal servers cannot accept them. If a user tries to install an application component after another user has already started the same application, the system will behave inconsistently.

Furthermore, non-administrators typically cannot launch installations directly from Windows Installer if Terminal Services is running in application server mode. Only administrators can do so. Therefore, it is important from the beginning to install all applications locally so that they run properly on terminal servers.

Some applications require different options for installation on a terminal server versus normal workstations. During an installation, the application must recognize that its target platform is a terminal server—that is, become *terminal server-aware*. Alternatively, a transformation file (.mst) can be used during installation to adapt the logic of the .msi package to the target platform. Likewise, the .mst file can be used to let Windows Installer know about the additional program components to be installed locally. One example is Microsoft Office 2000, which has certain functions that must be modified in just this way or they are simply not installed.

If the applications to be installed on the terminal server are not terminal-server-aware and if there are no associated .mst files (called *transforms*), the administrator must ensure that all required components are fully installed or create transforms. If the applications were installed on a terminal server with the correct .msi and .mst files, uninstalling is straightforward, including reversing specific installation steps.

Windows Installer SDK

Windows Installer SDK is indispensable for creating professional installation packages for Windows Server 2003 applications. It is part of Microsoft's Platform SDK and contains documentation, different Windows Installer database tools, examples for user-defined actions (written in C and VBScript), header files and libraries for C, empty .msi databases, and so on.

Tip   You can download Platform SDK from this Web site: *http: //www.microsoft.com/msdownload/platformsdk/sdkupdate.*

Windows Installer SDK contains a number of tools for creating and managing installation packages. The foremost and most essential is Windows Installer 2.0 Table Editor (Orca). This tool helps create and manage installation packages that are based on Windows Installer. Orca lets you open .msi files to view and work on database tables directly. In addition, Orca is an excellent tool for learning about .msi packages.

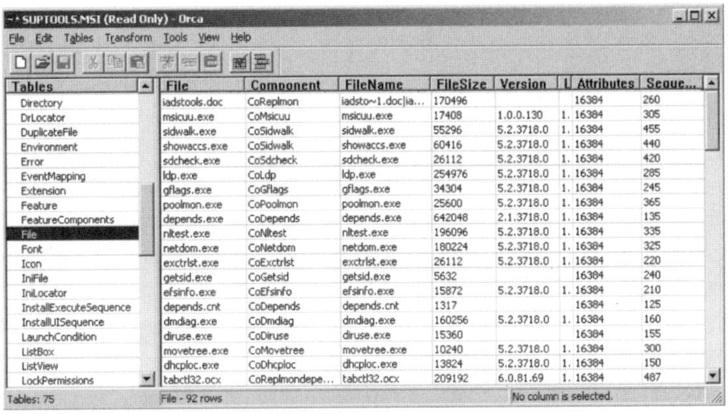

Figure 5-3   Windows Installer 2.0 Table Editor (Orca).

Microsoft Visual Studio.NET

Microsoft Visual Studio .NET is not only an environment for developing cutting-edge programs. It also allows you to create .msi installation packages through associated project types. The installation package is created when projects are translated and is available immediately.

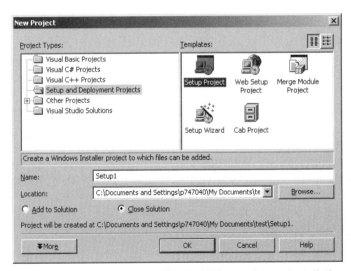

Figure 5-4   Microsoft Visual Studio .NET: creating an installation package.

If the application being developed using Visual Studio.NET was designed specifically for use on a terminal server, you can also adjust the corresponding installation routines here.

Installation Tools from Other Manufacturers

Microsoft tools alone do not always suffice to create installation packages. This is especially true in large corporate environments where highly automated installation processes are required to keep costs down. This is particularly true when introducing terminal servers. Consequently, a market for powerful installation tools has developed. Microsoft closely cooperates with InstallShield Software Corporation and Wise Solutions, Inc., to support their tool development.

These programs often work with a so-called "snapshot" mechanism. This means that the system status is recorded before software is installed. Subsequently, the software is installed. Finally, the old status and the new status are compared. The results of the monitored installation and the difference between old and new status are bundled together in an installation package, which is easy to copy to other computers.

Alternatively, you can manually create an .msi package. This requires detailed knowledge of the application being installed. Most commercial installation tools support this procedure as well.

Some companies also offer installation mechanisms that are not based on .msi packages, but are instead based on their own installation engines or script engines. These support platforms that do not have Windows Installer, or that encapsulate the installation logic to prevent it from being viewed or modified with third-party tools.

InstallShield

InstallShield offers several products that focus on software installation. InstallShield Express and InstallShield Developer are based on Windows Installer. InstallShield Professional uses its own installation technology, called InstallScript Engine. The related script language is suitable for creating dialogs and can be used in InstallShield Developer and InstallShield Professional. All InstallShield installation tools can distribute Framework applications and, if required, the .NET Framework. The target platforms of these tools include Windows Server 2003, Windows XP, Windows 2000, Windows NT 4, Windows ME, Windows 98, and Windows 95.

InstallShield Express and InstallShield Developer create .msi databases appropriate for end users. Windows Installer processes these databases when the installation program is executed. InstallShield Help describes where and how to make the project-specific settings in the development environment. By contrast, .msi Help documents all .msi actions and database tables that can be accessed by InstallShield's Direct Editor or by Orca.

You will find detailed information on InstallShield at *http://www.installshield.com*.

NetSupport

In its NetInstall product, NetSupport relies on a technology that is completely independent of Windows Installer. This product offers many more functions than Windows Installer. It requires a special agent that needs to be saved to the target platform before any type of installation starts.

Installation and uninstallation procedures are triggered as needed by time, events, or profiles. No manual intervention is required. Automating all installation procedures is key and can even include installing the operating system using an additional tool: Operating System Deploy (OSD).

Before installation comes packaging. Corresponding tools and an independent script language are used, creating a package with the application software files and all definitions for installation and configuration.

NetSupport NetInstall explicitly supports the terminal server as a target platform. NetSupport developed special mechanisms for setting installation schedules, controlled deactivation of the terminal server, user access before installing new software, and reactivation after all installations and reboots have finished. The installation logic also features the separation of computer and user-specific settings, just as terminal servers require.

You will find detailed information on NetSupport at *http://www.netinstall.com*.

OnDemand

WinINSTALL from OnDemand allows you to create distribution packages by recording changes that are created during each installation procedure. Later adjustments to the resulting package can be made via graphical user interface; no script language is required.

WinINSTALL also allows automatic synchronization of installation packages between distribution servers on the network. The distribution mechanisms are varied: time-controlled, via a Windows service, logon scripts, e-mail, or CD-ROM, or through a hidden partition.

The Windows 2000 Server installation CD-ROM did contain a version of WinINSTALL with reduced functionality. You will find updated information on WinINSTALL at *http://www.wininstall.com*.

Wise Solutions

Wise Solutions offers several products to create and manage installations. Wise for Windows Installer allows you to create .msi packages, whereas Wise Installation System uses its own installation technology. Both products are based on a specific script language that allows you to freely define the installation logic to a great extent. Furthermore, a debugger supports creating dialog boxes to guide users and validate results.

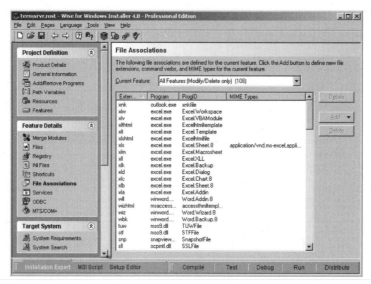

Figure 5-5 Wise for Windows Installer analyzes an installation package.

You will find detailed information on Wise Solutions products at *http://www.wise.com*.

Cloning Hard Drives

Cloning or imaging programs are used to write all data on a hard drive to another data carrier, regardless of the operating system installed. Cloning creates an image of the source system that can be replicated on any number of targets. With this method, you can quickly distribute complete reference installations to many servers as well as conserve production systems before making a change.

Many cloning programs are based on MS-DOS and the corresponding drivers for hard drives, SCSI adapters, CD drives, backup drives, or network cards. As a result, these programs are quite small and usually fit on one disk. The disk is used to start up and secure a computer. The hard drive image is copied to an empty computer the same way, except that the data is written to the local hard drive from the backup data carrier. Most cloning programs have an optional additional Windows-based application only for backup purposes.

The cloning process might sound relatively easy, but there are several problems that related programs need to address.

■ If source and target drives are not 100 percent identical in terms of size, partitions, and sectors, the cloning program must adjust the data structure accordingly. Target partitions must not be smaller than source partitions.

■ Boot managers and master boot records (that is, operating system starting areas) must not be deleted, damaged, or modified.

- MS-DOS file limit sizes defined by the file allocation table (FAT) file system must be observed. The maximum size is often only 2 GB for downward compatibility with older DOS versions. For this reason, images of larger partitions must be distributed to several files.

Important   Some manufacturers offer only limited support if their systems or applications were installed through cloning. You should therefore check whether the installation you are planning affords you the support that you are used to.

Even though a cloning program can read and write partitions by sector, it helps if it recognizes the NTFS file system. This way, only occupied sectors are considered, often reducing the size of the image significantly. Data compression is another way to reduce the backup space required.

The security identifiers (SIDs) that uniquely identify an installation are a specific problem in Microsoft Windows NT, Windows 2000, and Windows Server 2003. Duplicate SIDs can severely hamper network operation, especially under Windows 2000 and Windows Server 2003. Either the cloning program must change the SID, or the free NewSID tool from Systems Internals (*http://www.sysinternals.com*) can be used for this purpose.

Important   When you clone a terminal server installation to distribute to other servers, the source and target hardware should be identical. Otherwise, hardware recognition errors might occur on the target system during system start.

In spite of all these obvious issues, several successful cloning programs for terminal servers have become established on the market. Among the best known are PowerQuest DriveImage and Symantec Ghost.

Tip   Cloning programs are excellent for protecting a production system from disasters that even RAID systems or backup strategies cannot prevent. Examples include large-scale virus attacks or willful manipulation of server installations. The image of the clean installation stored in a safe place can be rewritten to the original system in very little time.

Installing Applications—Examples

What makes an application terminal server–compatible and easy to install? This is not an easy question to answer. Even "standard" applications need some adjusting before they can run on terminal servers. Hence, installing any application on a terminal server requires detailed planning. The following questions should be answered beforehand to uncover any issues, giving you an opportunity to prevent them right from the start.

- Does the installation of this application differ from the standard procedure?

- How is the application's user-specific information managed? In XML files, the registry, .ini files, a database, program-specific files, or only in global system areas? Does the application happen to assume a single user only?

- What are the interdependencies between the application and software components (such as DLLs) or other applications (such as Internet Explorer)? Do other applications depend on the one being installed? This determines the installation sequence.

- Are certain system requirements mandatory for the application to function, such as system components, peripherals, screen resolution, or runtime environments?

- Does the application need special drivers or Windows services installed first?

- Do tools exist (besides the normal installation routines) that allow you to adjust the installation in advance?

- Is the software installed in the default directory as defined in the %ProgramFiles% environment variable? Can the target directory be changed during the installation?

- Are there application-specific templates for adjusting Group Policies?

- Does the application use large start screens, sound, animation, or other resource-intensive multimedia effects that are not suitable for terminal servers? Can these effects be disabled in the configuration?

- Can you start more than one instance of the application on one computer? Does this work on a terminal server with several users? Does the application use exclusive access to files or registry areas?

Let us go through installing several applications step by step and use that as a basis for a general installation procedure.

Note The following applications are simply representative of various applications often requested in terminal server environments. No endorsement is implied.

Microsoft Office 2000

Installing Microsoft Office 2000 is relatively straightforward and requires attention to a few general parameters, in particular the Office 2000 option that allows a user to install some components later. This option is not recommended for terminal servers. Therefore, the "normal" installation of Office 2000 via .msi file does not work, and you need an alternative method. The steps for installation follow:

1. Switch to installation mode. Always use the Software tool in the Control Panel or the command prompt.

2. Optional: modify the Office 2000 transform file for terminal servers. The file is named TermSrvr.mst and is located in the Office 2000 Resource Kit (ORK) or on the Internet at *http://www.microsoft.com/office/ork*. If you do not want to install the entire program package, you can make your choices in the file and mark the Office components as local or not to be advertised. Only these two options ensure that the installation will work as intended and cannot be altered later. Users will not be able to make future changes.

3. Install Office 2000 with the setup command and the *TRANSFORMS="<Path> \TermSrvr.mst"* parameter. In the absence of the transform file, the installation aborts and a corresponding message is displayed.

4. Switch to execution mode.

5. Configure default settings using profiles or policies.

> **Note**   Because Termsrvr.mst was created for the English version of Office 2000, minor problems might occur when installing international versions. The individual animated assistants are marked "do not install," even though the Show Office Assistant setting might be enabled. Because of the transform file, the individual assistant files (*.asc) do not exist. Error messages appear because the names of the assistants differ in the various languages. To solve this problem, check the entire group of assistants as "do not install"—with one exception. The Motionless Office Assistant is an unanimated assistant and uses few system resources on terminal servers. To install it, copy the Stillogo.asc file to %ProgramFiles%\Microsoft Office\Office 11.

With the help of the Custom Installation Wizard from the *Microsoft Office 2000 Resource Kit*, you can modify the Termsrvr.mst file to suit your needs. The following options can be modified:

■ Installation path and name of the organization

■ Office components that are to be installed or remain unavailable (for example, text converters or graphics filters)

- Microsoft Outlook options (for example, name of the Exchange Server, mailbox-naming conventions, personal folders, name and port of the LDAP directory, or time and size limits)

In addition, several policy template files exist that you can integrate in the Group Policies. You should also use logon scripts and registry changes to ensure that the following settings are valid:

- Adjust the CursorBlinkRate to 700 milliseconds to avoid display problems in Microsoft PowerPoint.

- Set the Office Assistant to Stillogo.acs as the Help Assistant, which is disabled by default.

- Set the %UserName% and %DomainName% default values for Exchange authentication.

- Install missing foreign language dictionary programs at a later time.

Note   Do not install the *Microsoft Office 2000 Resource Kit* on the terminal server itself. It is much safer to install it on a reference computer (for example, one running Windows XP) and transfer the required data from there to the target platform.

Microsoft Office XP and Microsoft Project 2002

Like Office 2000, Office XP and Project 2002 are installed using an .msi package. However, the standard installation is already terminal server–aware and does not require a transform file. You can control the installation through a modified .mst file. To create the .mst file, you need the Microsoft Office Custom Installation Wizard from the *Microsoft Office XP Resource Kit*. Security-relevant settings are configured through Group Policies, using corresponding templates that are also contained in the *Microsoft Office XP Resource Kit*. Installing Office XP is very similar to installing Office 2000.

Note   There are certain differences between the installation CDs in the various languages of which you should be aware. For instance, the English CD contains spelling programs for English, Spanish, and French. In contrast, the German CD provides German, English, French, and Italian. If you need spelling checkers for other languages, you can add them from the CD that contains the Microsoft Office XP Proofing Tools. For international environments, the Multilingual User Interface is certainly of interest.

In Microsoft Office XP, the Microsoft Office Custom Installation Wizard provides new choices for setting security options. These apply in particular to the use of ActiveX control elements and Microsoft Visual Basic for Applications (VBA).

> **Note**   Do not install the *Microsoft Office XP Resource Kit* on the terminal server itself. It is a lot safer to install it on a reference computer (for example, one running Windows XP) and transfer the required data from there to the target platform.

Internet Explorer 6.0

Internet Explorer 6.0 is already part of Windows Server 2003. You configure it using the following Group Policies:

- Computer Configuration\Administrative Templates\Windows Components \Internet Explorer

- User Configuration\Windows Settings\Internet Explorer Maintenance

- User Configuration\Administrative Templates\Windows Components\Internet Explorer

The administrative template for Internet Explorer is located in the Inetres.adm file and can be modified.

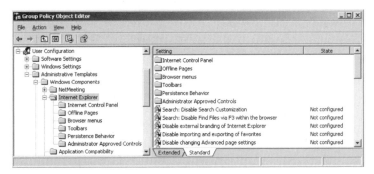

Figure 5-6   Configuring the Internet Explorer using Group Policies.

One interesting Internet Explorer option is located under Tools\Internet Options...\Advanced\Force offscreen compositing even under Terminal Server. Selecting this setting stops a Web page from flickering as it builds in Internet Explorer, which often happens on a terminal server. However, this option can significantly reduce Internet Explorer's speed.

> **Important** In any case, it is best to prohibit loading ActiveX Controls on terminal servers. Otherwise, users would be permitted to install software.

Netscape Navigator 7.*x*

Some companies use Netscape Navigator as an alternative Web browser. User configuration is done via different configuration files for Netscape Navigator. The global configuration files are located in the %ProgramFiles%\Defaults\Prefs directory. The individual user-based configuration file is saved at %AppData%\Mozilla\Profiles\%ProfilName%\pref.js.

To preconfigure user settings, you can adjust these JavaScript configuration files. Each configuration parameter represents a variable that contains a corresponding value. In the global scripts, you use the *pref* function; in the user-based script, you use the *user_pref* function. Comments in these files start with forward slashes (//). The following example shows a few changes to the All.js global configuration file.

Listing 5-1 The All.js Global Configuration File

```
pref("network.proxy.autoconfig_url","http://192.168.1.1/");
pref("network.proxy.type", 2);
pref("browser.cache.disk.enable", false);
pref("application.use_ns_plugin_finder", false);
pref("autoupdate.enabled", false);
pref("update_notifications.enabled", false);
pref("browser.activation.checkedNNFlag", true);
pref("browser.bookmarks.added_static_root", true);
pref("general.useragent.vendorComment", "Terminal Server");
pref("browser.startup.homepage", "http://www.microsoft.com");
pref("browser.toolbars.showbutton.mynetscape", false);
pref("browser.toolbars.showbutton.netscapeshop", false);
pref("xpinstall.enabled", false);
```

> **Note** You can review the entire configuration by entering **about:config** in the address line. This also indicates if the individual parameters are user-defined or set in a global configuration file.

Adobe Acrobat Reader

Adobe Acrobat Reader allows you to display the widely used documents in PDF format. After the standard installation, some configuration settings can be made. Some of these settings are computer-specific, while others are user-specific. If an administrator defines these settings, the terminal server should still be running in installation mode so that registry mapping enables user-specific settings for all users.

All settings that you can change from the default terminal server settings are as follows:

- Preferences\Update\Check for Updates: Manually

- Preferences\Options\Display PDF in Browser: Deactivate

- Preferences\Options\Check Browser Settings When Starting Acrobat: Deactivate

- Preferences\Options\Display Splash Screen: Deactivate

- Preferences\Options\Certified Plug-ins Only: Activate

- Preferences\Options\Use Page Cache: Activate

- Preferences\Options\Allow File Open Actions and Launching File Attachments: Deactivate

- Preferences\Options\Open Cross-Document Links In Same Windows: Deactivate

Note   You can create a preconfigured installation package with the Acrobat Enterprise Installation Tool. You will find additional information at *http://www.adobe.com/products/acrobat/deployment.html*.

WinZip 8.1

WinZip is a program used to compress and extract files. The installation program is named Setup.exe and requires that you answer several questions when it is executed. You should follow these steps when the terminal server is running in installation mode and answer the questions as follows:

1. Installation path: Type the path.

2. Welcome screen: Next.

3. Accept license agreement: Yes.

4. Quick Start screen: Next.

5. Select interface: The WinZip Classic interface is recommended.

6. Setup Type—Express Setup: Next.

7. The Installation is complete: Finish.

8. Screen with Tip of the Day: Do not show tip when program starts.

In this way, the application you install will run appropriately in most environments.

Developing Compatible Applications

Large corporate environments often need to provide more than just standard commercial applications. They frequently develop and program their own special applications for terminal servers. How do these applications need to be programmed so that they are compatible with Terminal Services? To answer this question, let us first turn to the application runtime environment.

In some ways, terminal servers are similar to the older, centralized host or mainframe environments, in which users log on, start programs, read and write to joint files, print on joint printers, and access joint databases. Due to the operating system, however, all terminal server sessions in a host environment are completely separate, which also applies to the applications. This is one difference between terminal servers and host environments. Because terminal servers use central operating system services, the separation of sessions can never be as strict as on a host, with its distinctive options for session virtualization.

Another obvious difference is the graphical nature of applications on terminal servers compared to purely text-based applications on hosts. Applications with sophisticated graphics or animation significantly increase data traffic between server and client. In addition, advanced user-interaction functions, such as using a mouse, need to be supported.

Host applications were generally designed to run in multiuser environments. This was not the primary goal in designing many Windows-based applications, yet they often need to run on terminal servers. This section will describe all the parameters for designing your own or testing commercial applications for successful use on terminal servers. Both conventional 32-bit applications and the new .NET Windows Forms applications are addressed.

In principle, both types of applications can produce performance bottlenecks that affect all terminal server users. The bottlenecks are usually due to one of the following four reasons:

- **Processor capacity**   On a terminal server, all users can open their own desktops and start all the applications installed. If just one application fails to cooperate, it might overload the existing processor resources.

- **Main memory**   Each user has an independent session in which he or she can start any installed application. Each application needs its own space in main memory that the operating system provides as a shared resource.

- **Hard drive access**   Access by multiple terminal-server users to run application files, DLLs, and virtual memory significantly increases demand for access to the hard drive. Additionally, multiple-user administration on a physical computer requires the operating system to access the hard drive frequently. If user-specific data are saved to the general areas of the local hard drive, collisions can hardly be avoided.

- **Network**   Naturally, the network plays a vital role for the terminal server. Every interactive user accesses his or her session over the network. This is accomplished by the extremely thin RDP protocol and normally does not result in bottlenecks. In turn, the terminal server accesses directory services, file, print, database, e-mail, and other servers. If these accesses consume all the network bandwidth, the user's connection is inevitably affected. One solution to this problem is to use several network adapters and a corresponding network segmentation.

These potential bottlenecks point to the design requirements for applications appropriate for terminal servers.

32-Bit Windows-Based Applications

There are a number of general conditions required to make conventional 32-bit Windows-based applications suitable for terminal servers, including design specifications and the corresponding development guidelines. Only if all these preconditions are met will the application run properly on a terminal server or terminal server farm.

Fundamental Design Standards

Here are all the design requirements of terminal server–compatible applications.

- **Ensure a consistent 32-bit architecture.**   The entire application logic is provided by 32-bit components; that is, both the executable program and DLLs or COM components must be created using 32-bit technology. The executable file must be in Portable Executable (PE) format. One component should be flagged shareable so that multiple users may work with the same instance of the loaded component.

- **Adhere to installation standards.**   Installation is performed using the default settings in the default directory for applications. It is important that you take the differences of the various language versions into account. The default directory for applications is %SystemDrive%\ProgramFiles. The %Program-Files% environment variable shows the correct installation directory for applications, even if it was modified. During installation, you need to make sure that all users—not only the installing administrator—can work with the application after you finish.

- **Avoid reboots.**   Installing an application should not require a reboot. This also simplifies automatic installation on terminal servers.

- **Follow the proper uninstallation procedure.**   An application including all its components, registry entries, and configuration files must be properly uninstalled.

- **Protect system files.**   An application should never try to replace system files (system drivers, fonts, and so on) during installation or operation. This could cause the operating system to become unstable and applications to behave unpredictably.

- **Protect shared components.**   Shared components, especially COM components and DLLS, cannot be replaced if they are protected by corresponding operating or file system mechanisms.

- **Personalized handling of user files.**   User data must be saved in an individual, configurable default path. The default path should be set in the %HomePath% environment variable. On standard systems, this variable usually points to the \Documents and Settings\<Username> directory, if no home directory was set up in the user profile.

- **Security configuration.**   An application needs to function properly even in a highly secure environment. The security measure used most often limits access to parts of the file system and the registry. You can also use Group Policies to protect the system.

- **Adhere to user interface standards.**   Default settings for size, colors, fonts, input devices, and output options of the user interface should be retained. The option to insert additional elements into the start menu and desktop can be disabled.

- **Use differentiated configuration settings.**   Generally valid and global configuration settings are saved at a central location in the registry or file system. User-specific data must be managed individually, for example through the user profile or the home directory.

- **Do not assume temporary files will persist.**   Files saved in the temporary directory during a user session might disappear by the next session. They could be deleted, or load sharing could start the next user session on a different terminal server in the farm.

- **Reduce graphics-intensive start screens.**   Product, company, or user information is often displayed when an application starts. This is not a problem in traditional Windows environments. On terminal servers, however, these start screens generate additional data streams that need to be transported to the client through the network. Therefore, start screens should be avoided as much as possible, or they should be configurable in a less resource-intensive version for terminal servers.

- **Reduce animation.**   Animation in an application consumes many processor resources. On terminal servers, the burden on the network from the constant transfer of animated objects is far from trivial. For this reason, animation should be executed on traditional Windows systems only. They should either be automatically disabled or kept to a minimum on terminal servers.

- **Use verified drivers.**   Some applications install and use their own drivers. All hardware drivers and drivers in kernel mode should be verified for Windows Server 2003 if they are to be used in environments with high stability requirements.

Developer Guidelines

What specifically should developers do to create terminal server–compatible applications? Adapting the application logic and using certain API calls is helpful. The following list presents the key developer guidelines.

- **Check the version.**   If the application is to run on certain target platforms only, you need to determine the version, usually through invoking the API function named *GetVersionEx*.

- **Personalize application settings.**   Saves all user-specific settings in the \My Documents folder, in the user profile, or in files that were saved to the home directory of the interactive, logged-on user. The advantage of saving to \My Documents is that it can be redirected to any physical location and be identified by application through the *SHGetFolderPath* API function. The administrator must be able to modify all the associated settings through Group Policies.

- **Create individual temporary files.**   Standard API calls (for example, *GetTempPath*) are best for saving temporary data. Hard-coded paths almost always cause serious problems in multiple-user environments.

- **Avoid .ini files.**   No Windows operating system built on Windows NT technology allows users to read or write to the Win.ini, System.ini, Autoexec.bat, or Config.sys files. Generally, .ini files should never be used. If you do use application-specific .ini files, they should be accessed through the respective API calls (for example, *GetPrivateProfileString*).

- **The computer name or IP address does not represent a user.**   Some applications assume that the computer name or IP address can be used for unambiguous user differentiation. This assumption is valid in traditional Windows environments, but not on terminal servers. On terminal servers, the same computer name or IP address is valid for all logged-on users. Therefore, this information cannot be used for checking a user license or for identifying a user.

- **Do not assume desktop access.**   Some applications assume that they will run on the desktop, thus giving them access to certain components and resources, such as Windows Explorer or Microsoft Internet Explorer. However, if a terminal server administrator decides to let the application run without the complete desktop, the application must support it.

- **Avoid memory leaks.** Applications that tie up memory resources without releasing them are known as *memory leaks*. They are hardly trivial even in traditional Windows environments and can easily become a major issue on terminal servers. If multiple users are working with an application that has a memory leak, the available memory rapidly decreases.

- **Determine system resources.** The installation routines of many applications verify the existing resources and processes running on the target system. On a terminal server, however, the resources found are not exclusively for one user. This often compromises the validity of the system analysis on the terminal server. Therefore, your installation routine should always take into account that the target platform is a terminal server.

- **Support UNC conventions.** The application must support long names and UNCs (universal naming conventions) for files and printers. Character strings need to be processed accordingly or default dialog boxes may be used for files and printers.

- **Exceptions when saving.** If access is denied when saving user data, the application must provide alternative options.

- **Identify the components.** All shared components must be identified, either in the installation log or the documentation.

- **Avoid direct access to graphics hardware.** To accelerate graphics output, some developers use functions or methods that allow direct access to the graphics hardware. This approach is used to combine images into one image in the application window (overlay) or to achieve fast animation sequences (double buffering). Such techniques usually cause unwanted results and are disruptive on terminal servers. For this reason, graphics should always be created first in a copy of the video memory of the normal main memory and transferred to the video system only when complete.

- **Channel user input through foreground applications.** User input should be managed through foreground applications only, not by background processes that applications use. Applications often "hang" on terminal servers while waiting for user input that was delegated to a background process.

Verifying Compatibility

So how do we verify if an application is compatible with terminal servers? The Windows Application Compatibility Toolkit is a big help. It contains several tools for testing conventional 32-bit applications with Windows Server 2003, Windows XP, and Windows 2000. This includes the application's potential use on terminal servers.

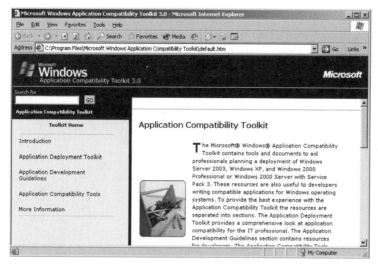

Figure 5-7   The Windows Application Compatibility Toolkit Version 3.0 startup window.

The Microsoft Application Compatibility Analyzer supports the administrator in a tedious task that must precede a terminal server project: taking inventory of the applications used in an existing environment. The collection of data on existing applications can be configured using command-line parameters. There are several ways to collect data from remote computers on the network: starting a network release, using a logon script, or using predefined user actions. The actual data collection usually takes no longer than one to two minutes per computer.

The Microsoft Application Compatibility Analyzer consists of these two components:

- The tool for collecting data (Collector.exe) runs on the client computer or on the terminal server.

- The tool for analyzing the collected data (Analyzer.exe) transfers the individual results to a database and allows evaluation of the results through a graphical interface.

Application Verifier (AppVerifier) is another tool in the Windows Application Compatibility Toolkit. It supports developers in verifying application compatibility under Windows Server 2003, Windows XP, and Windows 2000. AppVerifier focuses on reviewing typical problems related to application quality, especially heap errors, security gaps, drivers, system files, and access to certain registry areas. AppVerifier monitors the selected applications when they communicate with the operating system.

> **Note** AppVerifier marks a file so that it continues to be monitored even when AppVerifier itself is no longer running. To stop monitoring an application, you need to remove it from the list in AppVerifier.

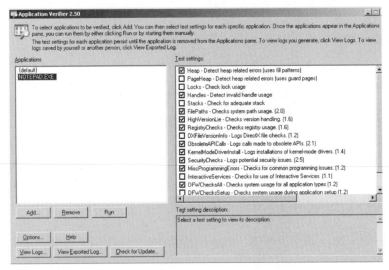

Figure 5-8 Application Verifier examining Notepad.exe.

Framework Applications

Much of what applies to 32-bit Windows-based applications is also true for .NET Windows Forms applications. However, the developer specifications and common language runtime make it much easier to adhere to the guidelines. Here are the reasons.

- **Consistent architecture** The entire application logic is provided by .NET components in Microsoft Intermediate Language format. Thus, these components run on all 32-bit and 64-bit platforms on which the common language runtime is available.

- **Installation and uninstallation** Framework applications are no longer registered on the system. Therefore, both installation and uninstallation are relatively uncomplicated. However, you need to make sure that only administrators have permission to perform these tasks. Use the policies for software restrictions for this purpose. (See Chapter 8.)

- **System files** Framework applications do not depend on system files, so system files are not modified when you install a Framework application.

- **Components**   Framework applications can use only those components that are provided exclusively or within the strictly controlled Global Catalog Cache.

- **Personalized handling of user files**   In Framework applications, user data needs to be saved in a specific, configurable default path. The default path should be linked to the \Documents and Settings\<User Name> folder.

- **Differentiated configuration settings**   Generally valid and global configuration settings are saved at predefined locations in the file system (normally in XML format). User-specific information needs to be managed individually, for example through the user profile or home directory.

- **Security configuration**   The .NET Framework has very strong security mechanisms that also apply on terminal servers.

- **Use of graphical and multimedia elements**   It is recommended that graphical start screens, animation, or other resource-intensive multimedia tasks be avoided for Framework applications if their target platform is a terminal server.

> **Note**   When this book was written, no formal development standards existed of .NET Windows Forms applications for terminal servers. Procedures based on real-world experience will no doubt be established in the months and years ahead. If, however, you want to experiment today, use the .NET Framework SDK and other sample applications. (See the CD that comes with this book.)

Terminal Server–Specific Applications

A special application variant directly accesses a terminal server's specific interfaces; this is the application programming interface, or API. This type of application is normally used for multiuser option administration on Windows Server 2003. It is also possible to use self-developed components to expand communication between the terminal server and RDP clients through virtual channels. The libraries and header files required to develop such applications or system components are known as *Terminal Server SDK*. The Terminal Server SDK is an integral part of the Platform SDK.

> **Note**   All terminal server–specific API functions are encapsulated in the Wtsapi32.dll file located in the Windows Server 2003 system directory.

Adjusting Server Dimensions

At the outset, the basic dimensioning and installation of a multiple-user platform on Windows Server 2003 differs little from other server scenarios in the Microsoft Back-Office environment. (See Chapter 1 and Chapter 2.) However, adjusting the hardware capacity relies heavily on the number and type of applications on the terminal server. The users, who can be grouped into different categories, are important as well. A user's working profile ranges from simple data input using just one application to simultaneous use of several resource-intensive applications.

The following questions need to be answered at this point: What is the maximum number of users that a server can handle? How many applications can be installed per server? How can applications and users best be distributed over several servers?

To find the answers, unfortunately, requires an in-depth investigation into the available server resources, user categories, and preferred applications. Ideally, we would have a table with the number of potential users in one column and the matching server configuration right next to it. However, individual user requirements and application characteristics are so different that it is impossible to create a table without setting fixed framework parameters.

> **Tip**   Every calculation model for server dimensions in multiuser environments is based on ideal assumptions. Previous experience with terminal server projects has taught us that there is no universally applicable formula to calculate the resources needed. For this reason, the calculation models produce rough estimates only, with ample wiggle room. It will never be possible to accurately predict to the megahertz (MHz) or the megabyte (MB) the necessary clock speed and main memory requirement—except for ideal environments.

Categorization

Before we can define users per server, applications per server, or applications per user, we need to categorize the specific parameters.

Note   This is precisely where we encounter one very sticky issue in preparing this book: Who exactly is the target group? Am I addressing managers, administrators, consultants, and system integrators who are planning to set up terminal server environments for 10, 100, 1000, or 10,000 users? Are we talking about 2, 10, 100, or 500 servers? Do we mean 2, 10, or 100 applications? To define each category would not be practical for environments with 10 or 20 potential terminal server users and a handful of applications. However, if more than 500 users need dozens of central applications, we cannot get around attempting an estimate. For large projects, you can, of course, "feel your way" toward the goal by buying servers until everything fits. However, this means planning has a high degree of uncertainty, which is unacceptable for most projects. My own project experience (including up to 140 applications for 5500 users) shows that thorough planning is needed to set environments with more than five servers if you want to avoid problems with administrators, users, and management. In Chapter 11, you will find additional information on using terminal servers in medium-sized and large companies.

User Categories

How do we categorize the users in the multiple-user environment? This question has prompted much controversy since the introduction of terminal servers. Three key user categories emerge, shown in the following table. However, they are fully out of context without application and server categories. We will use these categories in this book; yet keep in mind that they do not entirely match the "classic" definitions, which have proven inadequate in the past.

Note   Unlike many other server products, there are no general user classes or categories for terminal servers that are based on behavior studies of defined user groups. Surely, one of the reasons is that terminal servers are used for a broader range of tasks than e-mail or database servers, for example.

Table 5-1 The Three User Categories

User Category	Description
Users with low requirements: Light User	Starts one to three applications and prefers to use only one of them. Uses functions that go beyond the basic functions of the preferred application only. Enters data with an average speed of two characters or mouse pointer movements per second, thus producing a constant load. Has regular working hours and creates a continuous load.
Users with medium requirements: Medium User	Starts two to six applications and uses them alternately. Uses functions that go beyond the basic functions of at least two applications. Frequently exchanges data between the individual applications, thus increasing the average memory requirements by approximately 10 percent. Uses the applications with an average speed of three characters or mouse pointer movements per second in irregular patterns. Produces temporary peak loads.
Users with high requirements: Heavy User	Starts more than five applications and sometimes uses them simultaneously (for example, opening several large documents). Uses expert functions in many applications. Copies multimedia data from one application to the other, thus increasing the average memory requirements by approximately 25 percent. Uses the applications with an average speed of three characters or mouse pointer movements per second at all times, also beyond normal office hours. Produces irregular peak loads.

Naturally, these categories do not fully describe all users. In many user groups, not all users work simultaneously or continuously with the computer system. Overall, this means that many more users can work with the system than planned. The distinguishing feature is the typical length of time the application is in use, which differentiates the *part-time user* from the *full-time user*. On average, a significantly higher number of part-time users can work with the system than pure full-time users. On the other hand, the behavior of part-time users is a lot less predictable than that of full-time users. All the part-time users could want to work with a certain application at the same time, at month's end, for instance. In this case, they behave like full-time users. The terminal server environment should not reach its point of saturation precisely at that time, of course.

Application Categories

Many approaches to server dimensioning assume three categories of applications: 32-bit, 16-bit, and DOS applications. But the reality is different. For one thing, almost no DOS applications run on terminal servers anymore. Furthermore, typical 32-bit applications behave very differently from one another. An average user working with PowerPoint puts substantially more load on a terminal server than the average

Word user, mainly because PowerPoint produces much more graphical output, which the RDP protocol caching mechanism cannot support. Word, however, is used primarily to enter character strings, which can be easily optimized through the Glyph cache. The categories of applications listed in this table are a far better real-world representation.

Table 5-2   The Three Application Categories

Application Category	Description
Application with low requirements	Application with relatively low processor, memory, and graphics-output requirements. Uses no other components or processes, only text. Typical applications in this category are WinZip (moderate use) or text-based terminal emulation.
Application with medium requirements	Application with normal processor, memory, and graphics-output requirements. Uses additional components for specific tasks (for instance, COM components or assemblies) and sometimes accesses back-end network resources. Typical applications in this category are Microsoft Word (excluding macros), Microsoft Excel (excluding macros), Outlook, Internet Explorer (excluding ActiveX), Adobe Acrobat Reader, or simple database clients.
Application with high requirements	Application with high processor, memory, and graphics-output requirements. Uses additional components and accesses back-end network resources. Typical applications in this category include PowerPoint, graphics programs, development environments, modern ERP clients (for example, SAPGUI), or sophisticated database clients.

A more precise differentiation requires calculating a base value for resources used by each application at and just after startup. This base value includes the time span and processor load for the first instance of the application and for each additional instance—before any user interaction whatsoever. This initial estimate says a lot about what will happen if numerous users try to work with an application at the same time, such as at the beginning of the workday. At the very least, memory is later occupied even if a user is no longer working with the application.

The second key parameter is the additional processor and memory resources used when users are working with the particular application. This value depends on the user data that the application loads. For Word or PowerPoint, exceptional circumstances could generate additional data volume per user as high as 100 MB. The processor load also increases, but the higher load quickly dissipates in most applications.

Note   16-bit applications need approximately 30–50 percent more memory and processor power than comparable 32-bit applications because they use the Windows-on-Windows emulation layer.

To obtain a realistic estimate of the memory needed in a terminal server environment, we need to examine the application set, that is, all the applications combined. This will tell us the required maximum memory if every user launched every available application. The first number indicates the memory required for the applications without loaded user data only. The second calculation includes the loaded user data. Although both values are more or less theoretical, they do reveal both ends of the spectrum. It can never get any worse!

If you want similar values for processor and network load, you need to invest in extensive load testing, which is discussed in detail in Chapter 11. However, these tests are not as important for determining the required server resources as the memory requirements.

> **Tip**   DOS applications should definitely be avoided on production terminal servers. Because they use the emulation layer to execute and make (possibly) permanent keyboard requests, DOS applications put a much heavier load on terminal servers than comparable Windows-based applications. If a company needs DOS applications, they should be provided on a separate terminal server especially set up for this purpose.

Server Categories

Servers used in standard terminal server environments have the following subcomponents:

- **Computer power**   Between one and eight processors (CPUs) with clock speeds above one GHz.

- **Working memory**   Main memory expansion between 500 MB and above four GB.

- **Hard drive system**   Powerful hard drives (SCSI or E-IDE) providing between 20 to 100 GB, usually set up in a RAID-1 group (mirroring) for reliability reasons.

- **Network**   At least one network card (NIC) with transfer speeds between 100 megabits per second (Mbps) and 1 gigabit per second (gigabit/s).

Table 5-3 organizes the diverse server configurations into more or less four categories. Only the low-end server has an individual network card, which is used to communicate with clients and back-end servers. All other server categories have two network cards.

Table 5-3   The Four Server Categories

Server Category	Number of CPUs	Clock Speed	Main Memory	Hard Drives	NIC 1: To the Clients	NIC 2: To the Back End
Low-end server	1	1,4 GHz	1 GB	2 x 18 GB	100 Mbps	--
Standard server	2	1,4 GHz	2 GB	2 x 36 GB	100 Mbps	100 Mbps
Enterprise Server	4	1,4 GHz	4 GB	2 x 72 GB	100 Mbps	1 gigabit/s
Datacenter Server	8	1,4 GHz	8 GB	2 x 72 GB	1 gigabit/s	1 gigabit/s

Unfortunately, servers do not scale linearly as processors and main memory are added. Tests show that doubling the processors does not double overall capacity. This is valid for all types of processors that function with terminal servers. The rule of thumb is that increasing the number of processors from one to two raises capacity by 50–60 percent. Increasing the number of processors from two to four adds another 40–50 percent.

The overall performance of the selected processor configuration depends on two other factors: clock speed and second-level cache. The second-level cache is a memory space located directly on the processor. By caching, it eliminates slow main-memory accesses. The larger the cache, the lower the number of memory accesses needed. Doubling the second-level cache increases capacity by about 10 percent.

What about main memory? Settings (for example, */PAE* switch in the Boot.ini start configuration file) were already offered in Windows 2000 to enable access to over 4 GB of memory. Yet terminal servers with four or more processors often exhibited saturation behavior after occupying just over 2 GB of physical memory. This was not a problem of direct access to available main memory; the limits were the result of system-internal memory management. Related factors were the available free page table entries in memory and the limited size of the registry database containing system and user configuration data. If any of these factors pushed the terminal server environment to its resource limit, the whole system became unusable, so adding processors and physical memory made little sense. Therefore, rarely were terminal server environments configured for more than 200 simultaneous users. This is why limits on memory management had the greatest impact on the overall performance of systems utilizing large server platforms.

Windows Server 2003 either did away with such memory restrictions or increased the range substantially, making it highly unlikely that the free page table entries would restrict access to memory. The potential size of the registry database in main memory was also increased; the registry is now considered a file copy in memory (memory-mapped file). Nonetheless, initial tests on large server platforms still demonstrated limits in managing large numbers of simultaneous user sessions.

Improvements to the operating system kernel, however, did double the number of user sessions that can be managed with Terminal Services under Windows Server 2003 compared to Windows 2000 Server.

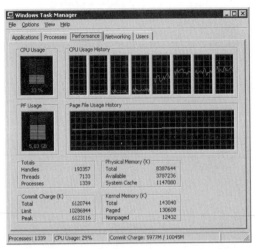

Figure 5-9 Test on a server platform with eight physical processors (Intel Pentium 4 XEON, 1.6 GHz clock speed, 1 MB second-level cache), 8 GB physical memory, and 132 open user sessions.

In Figure 5-9, each user has one document open in each of three applications (Notepad, Word, and Adobe Acrobat Reader), requiring approximately 60 MB per user session. The sharing of components saves about 2 GB of the total 8 GB required. It is very clear that more than 4 GB of physical memory was in use (total physical memory—available physical memory 4.5 GB). Users were not interacting with the applications at the time the data was captured; the applications are simply occupying memory. System-internal administrative tasks thus accounted for the full processor load! System reaction time to user actions in this scenario dropped noticeably from the time previously measured (dialog and window changes > 10 seconds).

Remember that the values obtained in these tests can differ widely in either direction depending on the application mix and the physical server platform. For accurate results, tests should be performed under actual conditions using the intended target platform. Because large servers tend to use resources poorly, however, the trend has been toward smaller server platforms using a maximum of four processors and 4 GB of main memory. This trend is supported by two newer technologies that might prove useful in terminal server environments.

■ **Blade servers** Server boards with one to four processors that can be inserted vertically in 19-inch racks housed in special cabinets. Because the boards are so small, a 19-inch rack can accommodate many servers.

- **Server virtualization**   Installing virtualization software on a guest system enables you to operate several virtual servers on one physical hardware platform. The virtual servers use predefined guest system resources. Typical examples of this software include Microsoft VirtualPC (formerly Connectix VirtualPC) or VMware by VMware, Inc.

These two technology trends might result in more farms with numerous smaller individual servers (physical or virtual). These scalability limits hampered most past terminal server projects from deploying large servers with more than four processors. In the future, a typical individual server on a terminal server farm will likely fall into the Standard Server or Enterprise Server category, as described in Table 5-3.

In further support, we also know that doubling the number of server processors usually more than doubles the price of the hardware platform. For large servers, the only potential savings lie in the price of the operating system license and automated installation of the terminal server environment. Even so, these issues will probably be resolved in the near future as well. Microsoft is already developing a licensing model that reflects the number of processors, and a number of manufacturers are offering powerful tools for mass installation.

The bottom line is that one-processor systems are generally too small and eight-processor systems are too large for use in terminal server environments. Naturally, there are always exceptions if special requirements or conditions apply.

> **Note**   A consistent 64-bit architecture can solve many scaling problems caused by the addressable main memory. Unfortunately, few user applications are available in 64-bit versions. If 32-bit applications are run on the 64-bit version of Windows Server 2003, memory accesses and system requests need to be channeled through an emulation layer. As mentioned previously, this technology already allows 16-bit applications to run on the 32-bit variants of Windows NT, Windows 2000, and Windows Server 2003. Unfortunately, the emulation layer consumes substantial system resources to access memory and convert system requests from 32 to 64 bits, essentially canceling out the potential advantages of 64-bit applications.

Dependencies Between the Categories

What are the dependencies between the categories? Only by viewing them in a relatively simple context can we make concrete estimates of resource requirements.

First, consider the impact of the minimum requirements of a certain user category on memory size. The resulting value is derived from the observation that user applications initially use 2–8 MB of main memory after startup.

Table 5-4   Minimum Main Memory Requirements for Each User Category

User Category	Minimum Main Memory Requirements
Users with low requirements (Light User)	A light user starts one to three applications and prefers using only one. Therefore, the minimum amount of memory that applications need is approximately 10 MB per user.
Users with medium requirements (Medium User)	A medium user launches two to six applications and uses them alternately. Therefore, the minimum amount of memory that applications need is approximately 20 MB per user.
Users with high requirements (Heavy User)	The heavy user launches more than five applications and sometimes uses them simultaneously (for example, opening several large documents). Therefore, the minimum amount of memory that applications need is approximately 30 MB per user.

Add to the values shown in Table 5-4 the 10 MB of memory for each user session on a terminal server (excluding applications). Ten MB is the total needed by Csrss.exe (approx. 2.5 MB), Ctfmon.exe (approx. 2 MB), Rdpclip.exe (approx. 2.3 MB), and Winlogon.exe (approx. 3 MB).

Note   Ctfmon.exe supports speech recognition, handwriting recognition, keyboard adjustments, and other alternative input technologies. Rdpclip.exe allows you to copy and paste files between a terminal server and a Terminal Services client.

The result is the following formula:

Memory requirement = Number of light users x (10 MB + 10 MB)
+ Number of medium users x (20 MB + 10 MB)
+ Number of heavy users x (30 MB + 10 MB)

To further refine the main memory requirements, we need to classify users not only by category, but also by the applications they use the most. Use the following matrix to help you with this additional estimate. In the calculations in this table, x users of a group need y MB main memory for their applications. A category-dependent percentage is added to the applications' memory requirement. This percentage covers the use of additional system resources.

Table 5-5   Allocation of Categories of Application Sets by Category of User Group

Application Category User Category	Applications with Low Requirements (+ 0%)	Applications with Medium Requirements (+ 10%)	Applications with High Requirements (+ 20%)
Light User (+ 0%)	X users (Y MB)	X users (Y MB)	X users (Y MB)
Medium User (+ 10%)	X users (Y MB)	X users (Y MB)	X users (Y MB)
Heavy User (+ 20%)	X users (Y MB)	X users (Y MB)	X users (Y MB)
Total	Result A	Result B	Result C

In Table 5-5, the application sets of a specific application category are allocated to user categories. The number of users and memory required are totaled per application category. Additional memory is required based on the application and user categories. This added percentage takes into account the average memory needed for additional components (COM components, assembly DLLs, clipboard, and so on). Depending on the environment, it might be necessary to adjust this percentage.

Before this table can be completed we need to know how much memory each application initially needs after start-up and the average memory required once user-specific documents are loaded. The first value represents the basic memory requirement after application start and the second includes the loaded user data.

Finally, the memory requirement is compared to the result in Table 5-6. This is based on the typical processing power needed for certain user categories. We assumed a clock speed of 1.4 GHz and a second-level cache of 256 KB.

Table 5-6   Estimate of the Average Number of Users for Different Server Categories

Server Category	Low-End Server	Standard Server	Enterprise Server	Datacenter Server
Typical number of light users	50	80	150	200
Typical number of medium users	30	45	90	110
Typical number of heavy users	15	25	50	65

Doubling the processors' clock speed increases computing power by 25 percent; halving it decreases it by 25 percent. Doubling the second-level cache boosts computing power by 10 percent.

The four results of the different calculations are likely to vary. Nevertheless, they represent the range for which resources should be planned. The actual range will fall somewhere between the high and low end.

> **Note** These resource estimates are only preliminary, of course. Production environments do fluctuate from previous estimates. More accurate planning requires the load tests described in Chapter 11. Always bear in mind that accurate planning for large terminal server environments requires substantial time and attention.

Calculating Resources

Let us move from the theory of user, application, and server categories and apply what we have learned to a concrete sample. The following fictional company produces and sells software products. It has 700 employees and plans to centralize some of its most frequently used applications on terminal servers. Employees are grouped as follows:

- Development, 100 employees: This division includes developers, product managers, quality assurance staff, test engineers, and technical writers. To keep it simple, we will also include administrators of internal computer systems and the network in this group. Compilers, special testing tools, and network monitoring products will remain on the local platforms. Employees in this group thus fall into the medium-user category.

- Support, 150 employees: Three shifts provide telephone and e-mail support, thus we need to include only 50 simultaneous user sessions in our calculation. The support task requires only a few applications, making these employees light users.

- Sales, 150 employees: This department comprises sales staff and sales assistants. They use a customer relationship management system and e-mail several times a day. This group is made up of medium users.

- System engineers, 200 employees: These employees install and configure the company's products at the various customer sites, where they use Internet or dial-up connections to access the terminal servers to generate project reports and view product documentation. Usually, only about half of them are logged on interactively, which equates to 100 simultaneous user sessions. The members of this group are medium users.

- Marketing, 50 employees: This division includes all employees who create marketing material and articles for publication. These tasks require different applications that frequently include high-resolution graphical elements, putting this group into the heavy-user category.

- Administration, 50 employees: Besides accounting, project coordination, and human resources, this group also includes company management. With a few exceptions, the members of this group are all medium users.

The preceding information is enough to allow us to make an initial rough estimate of the required resources. Seven hundred employees will need 500 simultaneous user sessions. We omitted vacation and sick leave from our calculation because it occurs irregularly, providing us with a bit of a buffer. The user categories are as follows:

- Fifty light users: support staff

- Four hundred medium users: staff in development, sales, and administration, plus the systems engineers

- Fifty heavy users: marketing staff

First let's calculate the base values for main memory and processor requirements:

$$
\begin{aligned}
\text{Memory requirement} \quad &= 50 \times 20\ \text{MB} + 400 \times 30\ \text{MB} + 50 \times 40\ \text{MB} \\
&= 1{,}000\ \text{MB} + 12{,}000\ \text{MB} + 2{,}000\ \text{MB} \\
&= 15{,}000\ \text{MB} \\
&= 15\ \text{GB}
\end{aligned}
$$

Now let's do the server calculation. First we need to determine the preferred hardware platform. For this example, let us assume that the terminal servers are installed on blade servers with two processors each. The processors have a clock speed of 1 GHz and a 256 MB second-level cache. One blade server thus corresponds to a standard server with approximately 10–15 percent less output due to the low processor clock speed, as in the reference model in Table 5-6. The basis for our calculation is as follows:

- Light users per blade server: 80 users − 10% = 70 users

- Medium users per blade server: 45 users − 10% = 40 users

- Heavy users per blade server: 25 users − 10% = 22 users

We now calculate the number of blade servers required:

$$
\begin{aligned}
\text{Number of servers} \ &= 50\ \text{light users}/70\ \text{users per server} \\
&+ 400\ \text{medium users}/40\ \text{users per server} \\
&+ 50\ \text{heavy users}/22\ \text{users per server} \\
&= 0.7 + 10 + 2.3\ \text{servers} \\
&= 13\ \text{servers}
\end{aligned}
$$

The initial result indicates that we need about 13 servers and at least 15 GB of main memory for the applications. Each server needs an additional 256 MB of main memory for the operating system. Therefore, the total requirement is 18.25 GB minimum. If we use blade servers with 2 GB of main memory each, the dimensioning should approximate the requirements.

To compare the initial calculation to the maximum, we need a list of the applications actually used. The memory required stated is an average value if several instances are invoked. If the overall conditions change, actual memory requirements might deviate significantly from the values provided.

Table 5-7   List of the Applications Used and Their Allocation to User Groups

Application	Application Category	Used By	Memory Req. (Excl./Incl. Documents)
Call center phone system (phones are connected to the RDP user session by virtual channels)	Low	Support	5 MB/6 MB
Terminal emulation (for accounting access to a mainframe computer)	Low	Administration	3 MB/3 MB
Microsoft Word 2000 (migration to Word XP planned)	Medium	Development Sales System engineers Marketing Administration	9 MB/15 MB
Microsoft Excel 2000 (migration to Excel XP planned)	Medium	Development Sales System engineers Marketing Administration	7 MB/10 MB
Microsoft Outlook 2000 (migration to Outlook XP planned)	Medium	Development Support Sales System engineers Marketing Administration	7 MB/10 MB
Adobe Acrobat Reader	Medium	Development System engineers Marketing Administration	18 MB/25 MB
Customer relationship management system (product from a small specialized manufacturer linked to Microsoft SQL Server and the call center system)	Medium	Support Sales Administration	6 MB/10 MB
Project planning system (developed in house and linked to Microsoft SQL Server)	Medium	Development System engineers Administration	4 MB/6 MB
Client for knowledge database (developed in house and linked to Microsoft SQL Server)	Medium	Development Support System engineers	4.5 MB/7 MB

Table 5-7   List of the Applications Used and Their Allocation to User Groups

Application	Application Category	Used By	Memory Req. (Excl./Incl. Documents)
CorelDRAW 10	High	Marketing	21 MB/26 MB
Microsoft PowerPoint 2000 (migration to PowerPoint XP planned)	High	Sales Marketing Administration	7.5 MB/12 MB

> **Note**   If you use different file editors in Outlook (such as Word to write e-mail messages), the initial memory per instance of Outlook might reach 60 MB. You need to adjust the calculation shown in Table 5-7 accordingly.

We can now figure the maximum application memory required per user category. We will assume that each user authorized to use the application has, in fact, started it.

This example shows the estimate for Outlook 2000 without user-specific documents:

Table 5-8   Memory Use When All Authorized Users Simultaneously Start Outlook 2000

Application User Category	Outlook 2000 (+ 10%)
Light User (+ 0%)	Support: (50 x 7 MB) + (0% + 10%) =350 MB + 35 MB =385 MB
Medium User (+ 10%)	Development: (100 x 7 MB) + (10% + 10%) =700 MB + 140 MB =840 MB
	Sales: (150 x 7 MB) + (10% + 10%) =1.050 MB + 210 MB =1.260 MB
	System eng.: (100 x 7 MB) + (10% + 10%) =700 MB + 140 MB =840 MB
	Administration: (50 x 7 MB) + (10% + 10%) =350 MB + 70 MB =420 MB
Heavy User (+ 20%)	Marketing: (50 x 7 MB) + (20% + 10%) =350 MB + 105 MB =455 MB
Total	Result: 4200 MB

If we do the calculation as shown in Table 5-8 for all applications of the fictional company, the result is approximately 28 GB without user-specific documents and 42 GB with them. The latter is the absolute maximum and reflects real resource requirements only under exceptional circumstances.

> **Note**   The CD included with this book contains a file with the full calculation of the memory requirements for the fictional company's applications. You can also use the file as a template for your own calculations.

The estimated minimum resources needed for the company's application and user mix indicates that 13 blade servers and 18.25 GB of main memory are required. Each of the blade servers provisioned can have 2 GB of main memory, 256 MB of which are needed for the operating system. Therefore, 13 x 1.75 GB = 22.75 GB are available for applications and user sessions. This even suffices if every user simultaneously started all the applications they are authorized to use. Using the 42 GB as a base maximum for applications and adding 10 MB for each user session, we arrive at approximately 27 blade servers. The calculation:

42 GB + (500 x 10 MB) = 42 GB + 5 GB = 47 GB

47 GB / 1,75 GB pro Server = 26,85 Server

The result indicates that 13 to 27 blade servers are required. The latter number is certainly impressive: 27 servers for 500 users! This equals fewer than 20 users per server. This extreme applies only to companies that want to protect their investment by ensuring that their terminal server environment never reaches its saturation point. Fifteen to twenty blade servers are adequate for most companies because the likelihood of every user starting every application is virtually nil. This number also includes migration to newer versions of applications (such as upgrading Office 2000 to Office XP).

Finally, let us examine the required network bandwidth. On average, terminal server access by one user requires a minimum of 20 kilobits per second (Kbps). In the best case, each user has 50 Kbps. With 500 users, this would result in a bandwidth requirement of approximately 25 Mbps in the direction of the Terminal Services clients. This should not be a problem for the servers as long as the network infrastructure is powerful enough. Only file server access can significantly increase bandwidth requirements. It should therefore be calculated separately.

> **Note**   This method of calculation was the result of much heated debate among experienced terminal server specialists. At some points, it contradicts the general school of thought expressed in many white papers. However, the methodology was validated in major real-life projects and is probably a very realistic approach to server dimensioning.

The calculation methods introduced here do not apply if a terminal server farm is supplying many applications to numerous users. In this instance, many other statistical methods and techniques for user modeling are needed than are covered in the previous relatively simple example. A discussion of this topic, however, is beyond the scope of this book. The financial and organizational effort to support a very complex model also bears little relation to the results. It is often more cost-effective to buy too many servers than to finance a sophisticated model. Therefore, these types of environments usually favor a multiphase model. In the first phase, the resources needed are roughly calculated using a method similar to the one described above. In the second phase, test users from all the target groups work on a test system that provides the basic number of required applications. This provides an initial estimate of resource needs per user. In subsequent steps, the number of users is incrementally increased as the terminal server environment expands. In this way, calculation errors can be quickly identified and eliminated. Even so, the fact that we do not know the amount of resources actually needed in the end is problematic. It might also be necessary to distribute server purchases over several phases. You can find additional information on calculating costs and planning terminal server projects in Chapter 15.

Alternatively, you can also perform automated tests to identify the required hardware resources. These tests do take different user categories into account, although they tend to be very inflexible. Nevertheless, they can provide an initial estimate even if the analysis and modeling of concrete user groups is very complex. You can find more detailed information about terminal-server load testing and related tools in Chapter 11.

Chapter 6

Registry

This chapter focuses on the registry as the central point for system configuration. We will, of course, examine in detail those registry topics that are relevant to Terminal Services. This chapter includes the following:

- An introduction to the registry and its particular significance for terminal servers

- An in-depth excursion into the specific registry settings for terminal servers

- Specifics on the special mode for installing applications, which often modifies the registry database

- Information on how and when to use compatibility flags in the registry

The registry is an essential configuration instance for Microsoft Windows Server 2003. Under Microsoft Windows 2000, the system did not allow the registry to grow larger than 376 megabytes (MB). This was, of course, a major issue for large terminal servers with many user sessions and an equal number of user profiles. In Windows Server 2003, the registry is managed as a file within the main memory (*memory-mapped file*), rendering the former size limitation invalid. The registry's system-specific hive alone can now handle up to 200 MB or one-quarter of the available physical memory—whichever value is smaller. In Windows 2000, the limit for this hive was 12 MB.

> **Important**   To directly change the values in the registry as described in this chapter always harbors a certain amount of risk. You need to take the utmost care in performing this task. It is, therefore, inadvisable to modify the registry of a production system directly. You should *always* test registry settings on a test system before you implement the results on a production system (using scripts or Group Policies).

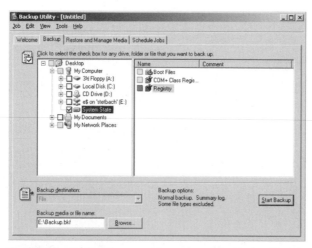

Figure 6-1   Saving the current system status using the backup program.

The Registry—A Brief Introduction

The Windows Server 2003 registry is a central instance and, as such, contains numerous configuration data about the operating system. Without basic knowledge of the registry's hierarchical administration element, it is very difficult to understand solutions to the problems described in later sections of this chapter. These problems might occur during application installation and system behavior optimization.

The registry concept evolved during the development of Microsoft Windows NT. The registry was applied as a successor to .ini files that were used in Windows for Workgroups (WfW) and Windows 3.1. The reason for this change in design was that .ini files had (and still have) a number of disadvantages. For instance, they are significantly limited in terms of size (64 kilobytes), there is no standard layout, access is comparably slow, and they cannot be used across the network. Additionally, the different .ini files have an immense number of parameters.

A registry already existed in principle under Windows 3.1. It managed dynamic data exchange (DDE), object linking and embedding (OLE), and file manager extensions. For Windows NT and all later systems, this registry was significantly expanded and still forms the heart of the operating system. However, because Windows Server

2003 is backward-compatible to existing 16-bit applications, .ini files are still supported even though their use is not recommended. They are normally found in the %SystemRoot% or %SystemRoot%\System folders.

Applications that are based on the Microsoft .NET runtime environment usually don't require use of the registry. (See Chapter 5.) The corresponding configuration parameters were normally saved in the registry are now stored in XML files. In this way, Microsoft returns to a design that, in contrast to the registry, is easier to read and manage. The effort required to install multiple applications is also reduced as the install program simply copies the executable program and configuration files in ASCII format. Under Windows Server 2003, the registry still plays a key role in system settings and conventional applications (that don't use the .NET runtime environment).

> **Note**   In this book, applications that are not based on the .NET runtime environment are usually called *conventional Windows-based applications*. In specialized literature (that is, technical books, articles, white papers, or articles from knowledge databases), an application written in Microsoft Visual Studio .NET that runs under the .NET common language runtime (CLR) is described as a *managed application*. In contrast to managed applications, *unmanaged applications* do not run under the .NET CLR. It is probably inaccurate to refer to conventional applications as legacy applications because they are still widely used. It will probably take a few more years before most applications are based on .NET and established in the market.

Registry Structure

Each change in the system, each installation of conventional software, and each modification to the user environment cause the registry to be accessed. Areas of the registry can be generated, changed, or deleted. In this way, the registry handles user, system, and application settings during system runtime. It also determines which drivers and services need to be loaded when the operating system is started.

The registry hives (or just hives) in the root of the hierarchy have preset names and meanings (hive key, or HKEY). Each *hive* is constructed as a branch of the registry in which applications find individual keys and their related individual values.

> **Caution**   When you shut down the system, many system settings are saved in the registry. For this reason, you should never simply switch off Windows Server 2003.

Registry Hives

The registry can more or less be divided into two areas. One area contains the system-wide information, including hardware data. The other area comprises settings for individual users. For simplification, the branches of these two registry areas are assigned special names or abbreviations. These will be used in further documenting the registry entries.

- **HKEY_LOCAL_MACHINE (HKLM)**   This hive contains entries for hardware configuration and system-wide data on software installed on the local computer. It also includes the paths required to load application components. If you change individual keys, you might irreversibly destroy the system. The most important entries for a terminal server's software configuration are located here as well, most settings are found under HKLM\System\Current-ControlSet and HKLM\Software.

- **HKEY_USERS (HKU)**   This hive contains all currently loaded user profiles, including the default profile. Each user profile is identified by a security identifier (SID) and includes individual application settings, paths, configuration data, temporary directories, desktop settings, environment variables, network connections, or printers. The specific software configuration for a user profile is usually located in the \Software subhive. This branch has priority over HKLM\Software.

The HKLM and HKU root hives have many more branches. Three of these subhives are so important that they have their own abbreviated names in the registry editor described in the following section. Due to the arrangement of these subhives in the registry hierarchy, it looks as if there were five root hives. In reality, there are only three root hives within HKLM and HKU that can easily be identified.

- **HKEY_CURRENT_USER (HKCU)**   This hive contains data on the session currently running. However, you need to bear in mind that on a terminal server, the information in this registry hive is represented in the context of the observing user. If an administrator looks at this hive, he or she sees only his or her own settings. The administrator cannot view or modify the settings of another user who is logged on. It is therefore easy to see that HKCU is an HKU subhive. HKCU data originates in the profile file of the corresponding user and is loaded when that user logs on.

- **HKEY_CLASSES_ROOT (HKCR)**   This hive allocates file extensions and programs, that is, it lists the file association or application for each file type. It also saves OLE data. Physically, HKCR is a reference to the HKLM\Software\Classes hive.

- **HKEY_CURRENT_CONFIG (HKCC)** Contains configuration data for the current hardware profile. Hardware profiles reflect only changes in the default system configuration. The changes themselves are located in the HKLM software and system hives. Physically, HKCC is a reference to the HKLM\SYSTEM \CurrentControlSet\Hardware Profiles\Current file.

Keys and Values

In principle, the hives listed consist of hierarchically arranged keys that can be assigned subkeys or values (data). Subkeys themselves can have subkeys or values, too. Each key has an additional default value (without a name).

The values possess a value name, data type, and data. A value can have different data types. However, only the first five data types in this list are commonly used.

- *REG_BINARY* A data field of any length that can be stated in binary or hexadecimal notation.

- *REG_DWORD* A numerical value of four bytes (32 bits) that can be stated in binary, decimal, or hexadecimal format.

- *REG_SZ* A single character string that ends in a zero byte.

- *REG_MULTI_SZ* A multiple character string or sequence divided by zero bytes.

- *REG_EXPAND_SZ* A dynamically expandable character string or sequence.

- *REG_RESOURCE_LIST* A series of linked data fields that can save a resource list. This type of list can be used for device drivers or the connected devices themselves. In the registry editor, this type of data is displayed as a binary value.

- *REG_RESOURCE_REQUIREMENTS_LIST* A series of linked data fields that enable you to save a list of possible hardware resources for a device driver. This type of data is displayed as a binary value in the registry editor.

- *REG_FULL_RESOURCE_DESCRIPTOR* A series of linked data fields that are used to save a resource list and can be used by a physical device. This type of data is displayed as a binary value in the registry editor.

- *REG_NONE* Data of no special type. This type of data is displayed as a hexadecimal value in the registry editor.

- *REG_LINK* A character string that represents a symbolic link.

- *REG_QWORD* A numerical value of eight bytes (64 bits).

Each value can be assigned data according to its data type. The data is usually arranged and set by an installation program. Applications have the ability to dynamically modify registry data during runtime. Through specific programming commands, applications read and write to the registry values.

Each key or value can be assigned an access control list. An access control list determines the read or write permissions for individual users or user groups.

New Registry Entries

During their installation, most conventionally programmed 32-bit applications create a number of entries in the registry. For some large application packages, this can be considerably more than 10,000 entries. The entries are located either in the system-wide or user-specific part of the registry. For this reason, it is imperative to control the registry in order to manage user settings and applications.

> **Note** When you uninstall some programs, not all entries that were made during installation are undone. It is therefore recommended that you back up the registry before you install a new application. This allows you to restore the registry's original state, if need be.

If the HKLM (system-wide data) and HKCU (user-specific data) registry hives have the same keys but differing values, the HKCU values have priority. When you install an application for all users of a terminal server, you need to make sure that you enter the application-specific entries in the registry for all users (HKLM) and not for the installing user alone (HKCU). However, this is difficult, especially with older applications, because there is often no user control of the target of registry entries via installation scripts delivered with the application.

Remote or automated access to the registry is granted either through special registry tools, script concepts, user profiles, or Group Policies. The latter, however, no longer represent classical remote access, but are based on transferring remote data to the local system, where that data is then used to modify the registry.

> **Note** Profiles are the individual user settings on a computer running Windows 2000, Windows XP, or Windows Server 2003. A Group Policy is a set of registry settings that describes those computer resources that are available for individual users, user groups, or the entire computer. See Chapter 4 for more information.

Corresponding Files

By default, the individual registry hives are saved as files in the %System-Root%\System32\Config directory. It contains a number of files representing the respective hive. Table 6-1 shows the significance of the individual files.

Table 6-1   Registry Trees and System File Assignments

Registry Structure	File Name
HKEY_LOCAL_MACHINE\SAM	Sam, Sam.log
HKEY_LOCAL_MACHINE\Security	Security, Security.log
HKEY_LOCAL_MACHINE\Software	Software, Software.log, Software.sav
HKEY_LOCAL_MACHINE\System	System, System.log, System.sav
HKEY_CURRENT_CONFIG	System, System.log, System.sav
HKEY_USERS\.DEFAULT	Default, Default.log, Default.sav
(not associated with a structure)	Userdiff, Userdiff.log
HKEY_CURRENT_USER	Ntuser.dat, Ntuser.dat.log (in the user-specific subdirectories)

Under Windows Server 2003, the individual configuration of a user session and the user interface display is called a *user profile*. These profiles are saved in the %Systemdrive%\Documents and Settings folder on the local system's hard drive or on a central network share. The individual registry settings for a user are located in the binary Ntuser.dat file. When a user logs on, the data contained in Ntuser.dat are loaded and added as entries in HKCU. (See Chapter 4.)

If a user logs on to a terminal server for the first time, his or her profile is created using the hidden %Systemdrive%\Documents and Settings\Default User directory as a template. In addition to the user-specific profile data, the generally valid settings saved under %Systemdrive%\Documents and Settings\All Users are used as well. Therefore, the resulting profile is a combination of individual and general settings.

Regedit—The Registry Editor

The administration programs that were introduced in the previous chapters are used to properly change certain values in the registry. In addition, there is a graphical tool for general changes to the registry. This tool is included with the standard system installation and is called the *registry editor* (*Regedit.exe*). It allows you to access the registry database at a system-core level, including targeted changes to registry keys or values. You can use this tool to back up parts or all of the registry, as well as to reconstruct it.

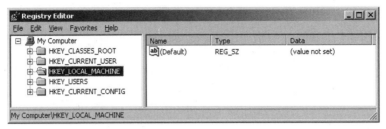

Figure 6-2 Regedit, the registry editor.

Important You can invoke Regedit by selecting Run under the Start menu and then typing in **regedit**. Even a minute change in the registry through the registry editor can be fatal for a terminal server. It can lead to the terminal server refusing to reboot, which, in some cases, might require reinstalling the complete system.

History of Registry Editors

Under Windows 2000, there were two different registry editors: Regedt32.exe and Regedit.exe. From a historical point of view, Regedt32 was the older program. Its user interface still adhered to the graphical style of Windows 3.*x* or Windows NT 3.1. However, in contrast to Regedit, Regedt32 allowed comprehensive security settings in terms of access permissions for the registry keys.

The Regedit program was introduced later and was based on the Windows 98 registry editor. It had several functions that Regedt32 did not have. For instance, only Regedit was able to perform recursive searches for keys, values, and data. In general, Regedit was far easier to handle and always displayed the current position within the registry in the status bar.

Due to its history, Regedit encountered several limitations under Windows 2000. The most problematic restriction was that it did not support all data types for registry values. Particularly, *REG_MULTI_SZ* data was automatically converted to *REG_SZ* data when it was modified with Regedit. This, in turn, could lead to massive problems with programs accustomed to receiving multiline character strings from the registry that suddenly receive only one line.

As you can imagine, using two different registry editors was problematic under Windows 2000. When do you use which? The new Regedit program on Windows Server 2003 is the result of a combination of the earlier versions of Regedit and Regedt32. It makes an administrator's life much easier, because now there is only one tool to directly manipulate the registry.

Note   On Windows Server 2003, the **Regedt32** command at the prompt starts the Regedit program. The Regedt32.exe executable file in the %SystemRoot%\System32 directory is only 5 KB and serves as a reference to the actual registry editor, Regedit.exe in the %SystemRoot% directory.

Regedit Functions

Regedit's central role is to generate, modify, and delete keys and values in the registry. This happens either via the context menu of a key or value, that is, through right-clicking with the mouse and selecting the corresponding option in the menu that appears. Alternatively, you can get to these options via the Edit menu item in the main window.

Additionally, Regedit allows you to import and export the entire registry or a selected substructure. The following data formats are supported:

- **Registry file**   Current Windows format of registry information can be viewed and modified with any ASCII editor (for example, Notepad).

- **Registry structure file**   Binary format that can be processed only by Regedit.

- **Text file**   Structured ASCII file, very suitable for documentation purposes.

- **Win9*x*/NT4 registry file**   Older Windows format of registry information can be viewed with Notepad.

Regedit also provides command-line options to import and export without any graphical user interface. These options are therefore suitable for scripts or batch processing programs, also.

- **Saving registry keys**   regedit /e Dateiname.reg.

- **Recovering registry keys; importing subtrees or subkeys**   regedit /i Dateiname.reg.

- **Recovering registry keys; the entire registry is overwritten by a .reg file**   regedit /c Dateiname.reg.

Certain registry structures can be loaded, if needed, using File\Load Hive or be removed using File\Unload Hive. You can do this only at the root level of HKU and HKLM. The respective Ntuser.dat profile file of logged-off users can be opened, for instance, to modify individual keys and values and save the results. In this way, it is possible to correct a faulty configuration or create a template for a mandatory profile. The source data does not have to be from the same computer as the target registry editor.

With the corresponding permissions, Regedit is very effective for viewing a remote computer's registry and modifying it, if required.

Regedit inherited a very important function from Regedt32: the possibility to modify the security settings of keys and values. The corresponding dialog boxes are reminiscent of the NTFS file system permission mechanisms on Windows Server 2003. They include different permission levels for users and groups, as well as monitoring and ownership options.

You can add frequently used areas of the registry to a list of favorites. This often helps in your daily routine by eliminating the need to navigate through the deeply nested hierarchy. We will now take a closer look at the preferred locations for terminal servers.

Registry Monitor

For several years, Windows experts Mark Russinovich and Bryce Cogswell have been publishing a lot of interesting data on Windows operating systems on their Web page System Internals at *http://www.sysinternals.com*. This Web site also offers a number of very powerful administration tools for free downloading. They even provide source code for some of the tools. One essential tool for examining the registry is the *Registry Monitor*.

> **Note** Only administrators can start the Registry Monitor; other users do not have the required permissions. If you want to examine accesses in the context of a user, you need to start a corresponding Terminal Services session while an administrator starts the Registry Monitor on the same physical server.

The Registry Monitor is a combination of a graphical application and a special device driver (filter driver). This combination enables the recording and displaying of all accesses to a registry of a Windows Server 2003 system. With integrated filter and search functions, the Registry Monitor is a powerful tool for investigating the relevant registry entries of a terminal server.

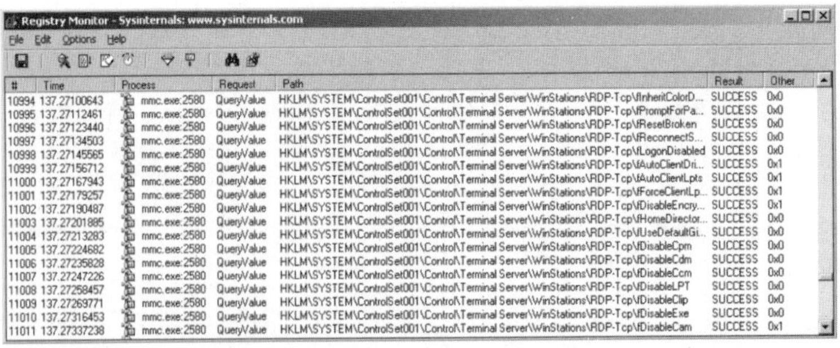

Figure 6-3 Analyzing accesses to the registry using Terminal Services configuration in Microsoft Management Console.

The graphical user interface of the Registry Monitor is mostly a list of registry accesses. Each access is displayed on one line with different fields. The fields comprise sequence number, process name, type of access, registry path, access result, and additional information. The access result and the complete path are particularly important, as is the additional information that can contain read or written registry values, for example.

A terminal server's registry analysis procedure is quite simple. An administrator starts the Registry Monitor and performs the desired actions. All accesses to the registry are collected in the Registry Monitor. The information presented is usually quite comprehensive. It is therefore practical to hide part of the list using filters you set via the Options\Filter\Highlight... menu item. You can use the * as a wildcard for any character strings.

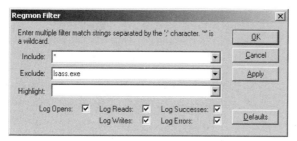

Figure 6-4   Configuring a filter in Registry Monitor.

Note   If you are patient enough, you can analyze very complex procedures on terminal servers using the Registry Monitor. For instance, the initial start of a terminal server session by a completely new local user generates approximately 60,000 accesses to the registry! However, the filter driver of the Registry Monitor slows the session start, which is why this type of analysis should never be performed on a production system. Analyzing the resulting log data is definitely hard work, but it gives you a very detailed look at the way terminal servers function.

Registry Keys for Terminal Services

The relevant configuration options for terminal servers, terminal server sessions, users, and clients can be found in different places in the registry. The administration tools and Group Policies, described in the previous chapters, usually change several registry values. The following section provides you with information on their paths and default values.

Note This section is a general overview of those registry keys that are essential for Terminal Services. A full documentation of all relevant keys would probably be a book in its own right. However, if you know where to find the "interesting" locations, there is nothing to prevent you from doing your own experiments on a test system. Experiments have produced many tips for optimizing system performance by modifying the registry, just as described in this book.

General Settings

We will first examine those areas of the registry that are vital to the global configuration of the terminal server and its sessions. These areas are located in the HKLM root hive.

One of the central HKLM root hive areas can be found under SYSTEM\Current-ControlSet and SYSTEM\ControlSet00n. The numbered ControlSet001 and ControlSet002 subkeys contain control information that is needed to start and keep Windows Server 2003 running. One of these two numbered subkeys is the original; the other is the backup copy. On startup, the system determines which one of the keys is the original and saves the result under HKLM\SYSTEM\Select. The last successful set of control information is saved in HKLM\SYSTEM\CurrentControlSet. The three sets of control information are for the most part identical, but only one is valid and used by the system.

Note In the following, we assume that ControlSet001 contains the valid control information used by the system. On your system, it could be ControlSet002.

The HKLM\SYSTEM\ControlSet001HKLM\SYSTEM\ControlSet001\Control\Terminal Server hive allows you to configure general settings, just as you can under Terminal Services configuration or Group Policies. Some of the values described here will be discussed in detail later in this chapter.

Table 6-2   Registry Values in the HKLM\SYSTEM\ControlSet001HKLM\SYSTEM\ControlSet001\Control\Terminal Server Hive

Value Names	Data Type, Default Value	Description
DeleteTempDirsOnExit	DWORD: 0x1	Deletes temporary session directories when the user logs off. Possible values are 0 or 1. Change this value using the Delete temporary directories on exit server setting in Terminal Services configuration.
fAllowToGetHelp	DWORD: 0x0	Disables or enables remote assistance on this computer. Possible values are 0 or 1. Usually, this setting is established in the Remote tab of the Control Panel's system properties.
fDenyTSConnections	DWORD: 0x0	Allows or denies connecting to Terminal Services. Possible values are 0 or 1.
FirstCountMsgQPeeks-SleepBadApp	DWORD: 0xF	Default value of the compatibility flag for applications. (See "Compatibility Flags" section later in this chapter.)
fSingleSessionPerUser	DWORD: 0x1	Each user can be limited to one session to save server resources or facilitate session recovery. Possible values are 0 or 1. Change this value using the Restrict each user to one session server setting in Terminal Services configuration.
fWritableTSCCPermTab	DWORD: 0x1	Allows write-protection of the Permissions tab in the Terminal Services configuration RDP connection settings. Possible values are 0 or 1.
IdleWinStationPoolCount	DWORD: 0x0	Sessions started in the background are assigned to new users. The default value for this setting is 0. For application servers, you can select different values, which might reduce login times for new user sessions.
Modems With Bad DSR	MULTI_SZ	List of modems that have a problem with Data Set Ready (DSR).
MsgQBadAppSleep-TimeInMillisec	DWORD: 0x1	Default value of the compatibility flag for applications. (See "Compatibility Flags" section later in this chapter.)
NthCountMsgQPeeksSleepBadApp	DWORD: 0x5	Default value of the compatibility flag for applications. (See "Compatibility Flags" section later in this chapter.)

Table 6-2 Registry Values in the HKLM\SYSTEM\ControlSet001HKLM\SYSTEM \ControlSet001\Control\Terminal Server Hive

Value Names	Data Type, Default Value	Description
PerSessionTempDir	*DWORD: 0x1*	Each user session receives its own temporary directory. Possible values for this setting are 0 or 1. Change this value using the Use per session directory server setting in Terminal Services configuration.
ProductVersion	*SZ: 5.2*	Version number of the terminal server.
SessionDirectoryActive	*DWORD: 0x0*	Indicates whether the session directory for this server is active. Possible values for this setting are 0 or 1.
SessionDirectoryCLSID	*SZ*	Class ID, needed by the session directory.
SessionDirectoryExCLSID	*SZ*	Another class ID that the session directory needs.
SessionDirectoryExposeServerIP	*DWORD: 0x1*	Indicates whether the server's IP address is exposed with the activated session directory. Possible values for this setting are 0 or 1.
TSAdvertise	*DWORD: 0x1*	Indicates whether the server advertises itself as the terminal server. Possible values are 0 or 1.
TSAppCompat	*DWORD: 0x1*	Indicates whether the system is running in application compatibility mode. Possible values are 0 or 1.
TSEnabled	*DWORD: 0x1*	Indicates whether basic Terminal Services functions are enabled. Possible values are 0 or 1.
TSUserEnabled	*DWORD: 0x0*	Indicates whether users can log on to the terminal server. Possible values are 0 or 1.

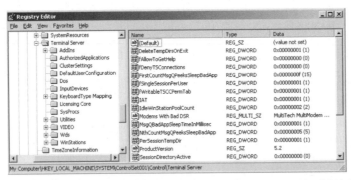

Figure 6-5 Registry values in the HKLM\SYSTEM\ControlSet001\Control\Terminal Server hive.

In addition to individual values, this path holds several subkeys that, in turn, contain keys and values for Terminal Services configuration.

Table 6-3   The Most Important Subkeys in the HKLM\SYSTEM\ControlSet001HKLM \SYSTEM\ControlSet001\Control\Terminal Server Registry Hive

Subkeys	Description
AddIns	Configuration of the redirection of clipboard and client ports (redirector)
AuthorizedApplications	Option to configure a list of applications that can be run on the terminal server
ClusterSettings	Configuration of the session directory
DefaultUserConfiguration	All default Terminal Services configuration settings, for example, automatic logon data, time limits, initial program, etc.
Dos	Adjusts DOS shell concerning query of keyboard events
KeyboardTypeMapping	Adjusts keyboard driver for unusual shortcuts or special hardware
SysProcs	A list of system programs that run in the system context (0) or in the user context (1)
Utilities	Adjusts the specific commands for the prompt: **Change logon**, **Change port**, **Change user**, **Change winsta**, **Query appserver**, **Query process**, **Query session**, **Query user**, **Query winsta**, **Reset session**, and **Reset winsta**
VIDEO	Device paths for graphics redirection
Wds	Configuration of TCP/IP log settings, for example, delays, buffer attributes, port number, service name, and so on
WinStations	Specific configuration for each type of connection and the console session

Log and User Session Settings

In Table 6-3, the last elements listed are the Wds and WinStations keys. They play a key role in configuring the RDP protocol and user sessions. Because some keys might exist in several hives, they should be explained in more detail. It is impossible to list and explain all keys in this book, so the following tables show only a selection of the most important configuration options. They can be found in one or more of these registry hives:

- HKLM\SYSTEM\ControlSet001\Control\Terminal Server\Wds\rdpwd

- HKLM\SYSTEM\ControlSet001\Control\Terminal Server\Wds\rdpwd\Tds\tcp

- HKLM\SYSTEM\ControlSet001\Control\Terminal Server\WinStation\Console

- HKLM\SYSTEM\ControlSet001\Control\Terminal Server\WinStation\Console \RDP

- HKLM\SYSTEM\ControlSet001\Control\Terminal Server \WinStation\RDP-Tcp.

The values here are changed through the tool Terminal Services Configuration.

Table 6-4 lists the so-called *flags*. Flags are binary values that make a statement true (1) or false (0).

Table 6-4 List of Flags Under HKLM\SYSTEM\ControlSet001HKLM\SYSTEM \ControlSet001\Control\Terminal Server \Wds and \WinStations Data Type

Value Names (*DWORD*)	Description
fAutoClientDrives	Connect to client drives upon logon.
fAutoClientLpts	Connect to client printers upon logon.
fDisableCam	Disable client audio mapping.
fDisableCcm	Disable client COM port mapping.
fDisableCdm	Disable client drive mapping.
fDisableClip	Disable clipboard mapping.
fDisableCpm	Disable Windows client printer mapping.
fDisableEncryption	Disable encryption.
fDisableExe	Disable program start upon connection.
fDisableLPT	Disable use of printers.
fEnableWinStation	Enable remote user sessions.
fForceClientLptDef	Use client main printer by default.
fInheritAutoClient	Inherit the setting on the terminal server to reset the connection when the connection was ended from another source.
fInheritAutoLogon	Inherit the setting on the terminal server to use the client's logon information for automatic logon from another source.
fInheritCallback	Inherit the setting on the terminal server that a modem calls back from another source.
fInheritCallbackNumber	Inherit on the terminal server the phone number for modem callback from another source.
fInheritColorDepth	Inherit the setting on the terminal server for color depth from another source.
fInheritInitialProgram	Inherit the setting on the terminal server to start an initial program upon logon from another source.
fInheritMaxDisconnection-Time	Inherit on the terminal server the maximum time after which disconnected sessions are ended from another source.
fInheritMaxIdleTime	Inherit on the terminal server the maximum idle time for user sessions from another source.
fInheritMaxSessionTime	Inherit on the terminal server the maximum session time from another source.
fInheritReconnectSame	Inherit the setting on the terminal server whether a new connection can be made only from the same client from another source.

Table 6-4   List of Flags Under HKLM\SYSTEM\ControlSet001HKLM\SYSTEM \ControlSet001\Control\Terminal Server \Wds and \WinStations Data Type

Value Names (*DWORD*)	Description
fInheritResetBroken	Inherit the setting on the terminal server, whether the session is ended upon reaching a session limit or upon disconnection from another source. If you do not set this flag, the session will be simply disconnected.
fInheritSecurity	Inherit the security setting on the terminal server.
fInheritShadow	Inherit the setting on the terminal server for remote control from another source.
fLogonDisabled	Selecting this flag disables logon.
fPromptForPassword	Makes entering a password obligatory.
fReconnectSame	You can reconnect from the same client only as you did previously. This value becomes effective only if you set the *fInheritReconnectSame* flag.
fResetBroken	The session ends when a session limit is reached or the connection is broken. If this flag is not set, the session is simply disconnected. This value becomes effective only if you set the *fInheritResetBroken* flag.
fUseDefaultGina	Always use the default Windows component to authenticate users.

Table 6-5 lists the most important keys with the *REG_DWORD* data type. These are often directly related to one of the flags listed in the preceding table.

Table 6-5   The Most Important Keys of the *REG_DWORD* under HKLM\SYSTEM \ControlSet001HKLM\SYSTEM\ControlSet001\Control\Terminal Server\Wds and \WinStations Data Type

Value Names (*DWORD*)	Description
Callback	Set modem callback. This value becomes effective only if you set the *fInheritCallback* flag to 0.
ColorDepth	Default color-depth setting.
DrawGdiplusSupportLevel	Support options for graphics elements output with GDI+.
InputBufferLength	Input buffer length for the RDP connection in bytes. Default value is 2048.
KeyboardLayout	Set keyboard layout.
MaxConnectionTime	Maximum session time in seconds. This value becomes effective only if you set the *fInheritMaxSessionTime* flag to 0.
MaxDisconnectionTime	Maximum time in seconds after which disconnected sessions are ended. This value becomes effective only if you set the *fInheritMaxDisconnectionTime* flag to 0.

Table 6-5 The Most Important Keys of the *REG_DWORD* under HKLM\SYSTEM \ControlSet001HKLM\SYSTEM\ControlSet001\Control\Terminal Server\Wds and *WinStations* Data Type

Value Names *(DWORD)*	Description
MaxIdleTime	Maximum idle time in seconds for user sessions. This value becomes effective only if you set the *fInheritMaxIdleTime* flag to 0.
MinEncryptionLevel	Set the minimum value of encryption level.
OutBufDelay	Maximum waiting time in milliseconds until the output buffer for the RDP connection is emptied.
OutBufLength	Output buffer length for the RDP connection in bytes.
PortNumber	Port for network communication using the RDP protocol. Default value is 3398.
Shadow	Remote control configuration. This value becomes effective only if you set the *fInheritShadow* flag to 0. 0: Deny remote control. 1: Obtain user permission and interact with the session. 2: Do not obtain user permission and interact with the session. 3: Obtain user permission and display session. 4: Do not obtain user permission and display session.

Finally, Table 6-6 shows the most important keys of the *REG_SZ* data type.

Table 6-6 The Most Important Keys of the *REG_SZ* under HKLM\SYSTEM \ControlSet001HKLM\SYSTEM\ControlSet001\Control\Terminal Server\Wds and *WinStations* Data Type

Value Names *(SZ)*	Description
CallbackNumber	Set a phone number for modem callback. This value becomes effective only if you set the *fInheritCallbackNumber* flag to 0.
Comment	Comment string in the administration tool.
Domain	Set a default domain name on logon of a user session.
InitialProgram	Initial program that is started when a user logs on. This value becomes effective only if you set the *fInheritInitialProgram* flag.
NWLogonServer	Set a NetWare logon server.
Password	Set a default password when logging on to a user session. The password is encrypted and saved here.
UserName	Set a default user name for logon to a user session.
WorkDirectory	Working directory that is set on user logon and initial start of an application.

Drivers and Services

The HKLM\SYSTEM\ControlSet001\Services\TermDD hive contains the attributes of the Termdd.sys terminal device driver. However, do not change these attributes. You can find the device driver's path and start option here.

An adjoining hive, called HKLM\SYSTEM\ControlSet001\Services\TermService, hosts both the configuration of Terminal Services within the generic Svchost.exe Windows service and of the Services.exe process. The keys you find there include, for example, the display name, description, complete path, or start options as also listed under services administration. The subkeys show license settings and parameters for the performance indicator object of the system monitor.

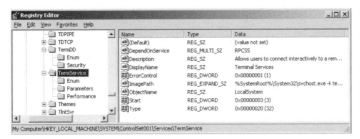

Figure 6-6   Drivers and services for terminal server functions.

Note   The UseLicenseServer key under \Parameters is used by Windows NT 4.0, Terminal Server Edition. Windows Server 2003 no longer needs this key. It remains in the registry for compatibility reasons only.

Logon

If you log registry access in a focused manner during logon of a user session, you will gain interesting insights into the corresponding initialization processes. For example, which areas relevant for terminal servers does the Winlogon.exe logon process access?

One piece of information needed during logon concerns creating or loading the user profile. HKLM\SOFTWARE\Microsoft\Windows NT\CurrentVersion\ProfileList. These keys contain the default paths for a default user (DefaultUser), general user (AllUsers), and individual user profiles. Furthermore, you can find a list of all users who have logged on to the system here. If a user logs on to the terminal server for the first time, he or she inherits both the normal default user settings and the default values for the terminal server session. They are saved under HKLM\SYSTEM\ControlSet001HKLM\SYSTEM\ControlSet001\Control\Terminal Server\DefaultUserConfiguration.

Another relevant area is located under HKLM\Software\Microsoft\Windows NT\CurrentVersion\Winlogon. It includes the AppSetup key that defines a special script file called UsrLogon.cmd. This script file is executed along with a possible logon script on startup of each terminal server session. (See Chapter 7.) The same location also contains the WinStationDisabled key that either denies (0) or allows (1) new terminal server users to log on, regardless of the protocol. At the prompt, you can modify this value using the **Change logon /enable** or **Change logon /disable** prompts.

The HKLM\Software\Microsoft\Windows NT\CurrentVersion\Winlogon \Notify\termsrv area is also needed for logon. It defines a specific logic as a response to system events.

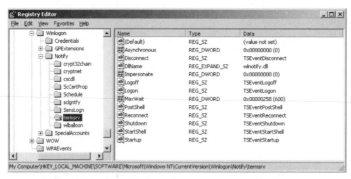

Figure 6-7   Determining the response to system events.

When a user logs on, even driver configuration is accessed. The area reserved for terminal servers is located under HKLM\SOFTWARE\Microsoft\Windows NT\CurrentVersion\Drivers32\Terminal Server\RDP. The video driver configuration plays a certain role for the user session, too. For instance, Explorer.exe needs the corresponding data that is located here: HKLM\SYSTEM\ControlSet001HKLM\SYSTEM\ControlSet001\Control\Terminal Server\VIDEO\rdpdd under the \Device\Video0 key.

If local Group Policies for Terminal Services settings were established, these must be loaded at the right time, of course. This happens during logon with keys found under HKLM\SOFTWARE\Policies\Microsoft\Windows NT\Terminal Services and the EnableAdminTSRemote key under HKLM\SOFTWARE\Policies\Microsoft\Windows\Installer. However, these areas can be fairly empty if no or just a few local Group Policies were predefined.

> **Note**   Basically, the settings for local Group Policies are located under HKCU\Software\Policies and HKLM\SOFTWARE\Policies. Users have only read-access rights to these two hives. Therefore, Group Policies cannot be modified at the user level.

Printing

Connecting and managing printers for terminal servers is a very complex topic. (See Chapter 4.) This fact is also quite evident in the registry. The general configuration of the printers used and the associated driver information are located under HKLM\System\CurrentControlSet\Control\Print.

You will find references to the currently installed printer drivers of the terminal server under HKLM\SYSTEM\ControlSet001\Control\Print\Environments \WindowsNTx86\Drivers\Version-3\<*Printer name*>. This correlates with the files under %SystemRoot%\system32\spool\drivers\w32x86\3. The user-specific settings for the printers are located in the registry under HKCU\Printers.

Note   Information for the printer drivers for the Windows Server 2003 64-bit versions is located under HKLM\SYSTEM\ControlSet001\Control \Print \Environments\WindowsIA64\Drivers.

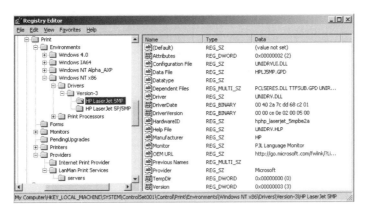

Figure 6-8   Configuring the print environment.

If you do not want to install printer drivers from sources that might not be controllable, you have the option of choosing a binding path. This path is called a *trusted printer driver path*. To configure this behavior, you need to add the following keys to HKLM\SYSTEM\ControlSet001\Control\Print\Providers\LanManPrintServices\servers:

- Name: LoadTrustedDrivers; type: REG_DWORD; value: 1

- Name: TrustedDriverPath; type: REG_SZ; value: *Server name*\Share folder

It is important that the structure of the *Server name*\Share folder mirror the %SystemRoot%\system32\spool\drivers\w32x86 folder. If all the data was properly entered, printer drivers can be installed only from the predefined source, allowing complete control of the printer drivers used.

User-Specific Configuration

The registry's user-specific section also contains keys that are relevant to the terminal server. For example, the HKCU\Software\Microsoft\Windows NT\CurrentVersion\Terminal Server hive has the key called LastUserIniSyncTime. This key indicates the last system time a user-specific .ini file was synchronized to its corresponding system-wide .ini file (discussed later in this chapter).

If a user has administrator permissions, there is an additional key called TSADMIN here, containing several subkeys. These subkeys allow access to attributes for connection options, alerts, refresh rates, keyboard shortcuts for remote control, server list options, and display values for system processes in the Task Manager.

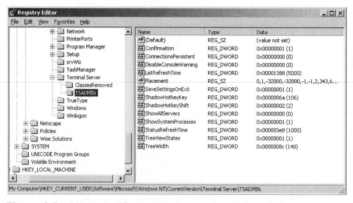

Figure 6-9   User-specific terminal server settings for an administrator.

After a user session has been established, it has its own ID (SESSIONNAME). It is located next to the client name (CLIENTNAME) and the logon server name (LOGONSERVER) in the HKCU\Volatile Environment section of the registry.

Use the following registry sections to define all relevant user folders in which to save data about the applications, desktop, local settings, personal files, network environment, print environment, or start menu:

- HKCU\SOFTWARE\Microsoft\Windows\CurrentVersion\Explorer \User Shell Folders

- HKLM\SOFTWARE\Microsoft\Windows\CurrentVersion\Explorer \User Shell Folders

Application-Specific Registry Modifications

Providing and adjusting applications is, of course, essential on terminal servers. The corresponding registry section is found under HKLM\SOFTWARE\Microsoft \Windows NT\CurrentVersion\Terminal Server. The key hierarchy starting here determines compatibility and application installation options, as well as security settings.

Configuration of the subkeys in \Compatibility and \Install\Software has an impact on essential system processes and will be described in detail later in this chapter. Table 6-7 gives you an initial overview.

Table 6-7   Meaning of the Keys under HKLM\SOFTWARE\Microsoft\Windows NT \CurrentVersion\Terminal Server

Subkey	Description
Compatibility	Sets compatibility options for individual applications, .ini files, and registry entries.
Install\Change User Option	Lists application and system components installed. Components with the value DWORD 0x1 run in system context, those with the value 0x0 run in user context.
Install\Software	Shadow copy: This area is loaded when a user logs on. If required, it adds necessary keys and values that are not contained in HKCU\SOFTWARE.
Security	Sets the level of security.

Installation Mode and Registry Mapping

During the installation of a conventional 32-bit application, a number of entries are made in the registry's HKLM\SOFTWARE section. These entries are used for initialization purposes when a user starts the application. Individual changes to the applications result in entries under HKCU\SOFTWARE and therefore affect the user profile.

> **Note**   The default installation directory for applications is defined under the HKLM\SOFTWARE\Microsoft\Windows\CurrentVersion\ProgramFilesDir key. This key is identical to the %ProgramFiles% environment variable.

As described in detail in Chapter 5, installing applications on a terminal server differs from the corresponding installation routines under Windows XP for only one interactive user. The reasons for this are found in the application parameters that are managed by the registry and occasionally .ini files. There are two potential problems that can occur that are particularly associated with registering:

1. When an application is installed, registry keys needed by all users are not defined globally in HKLM\SOFTWARE, but individually in HKCU\SOFTWARE. Thus, important data is located exclusively in the administrator's profile.

2. Necessary registry keys are not set up in HKCU\SOFTWARE during installation. They are entered only when the user runs the application for the first time. However, it might be necessary for the administrator to predefine certain values.

To solve both problems, terminal servers have two modes: the installation mode for application installations, and the execution mode for standard operation. What role does the registry play? If the terminal server is running in installation mode, all user-specific registry entries saved under HKCU\SOFTWARE are also copied to the HKLM\SOFTWARE\Microsoft\Windows NT\CurrentVersion\Terminal Server\Install\Software registry hive. Therefore, this hive is also called the *shadow copy*.

> **Note**   An application that adheres strictly to terminal server development standards will not, of course, create any critical entries in HKCU\SOFTWARE during installation. Therefore, the shadow copy is irrelevant for this type of application.

Users will later launch applications that might anticipate initial entries in HKCU\SOFTWARE. However, these entries do not exist in the user profile nor in HKCU\SOFTWARE. Nonetheless, the application will still try to read these entries and might produce errors if it cannot. To avoid this problem, the information in the shadow copy overlays the user's profile. This is known as *registry mapping*.

So how do user profiles and registry mapping create the resulting configuration where applications are concerned? When a user logs on, the session profile is built in multiple steps. First, system-wide configuration parameters for applications are loaded from HKLM\SOFTWARE. The entries in the user's profile file are added subsequently. If the values of a certain application key are different in HKLM\SOFTWARE than the profile file, the individual profile file has priority. The system-wide configuration of application parameters should therefore be viewed as a suggestion or a default value. Group Policy is the better source for reliable central parameters. This overlies the existing configuration when the user profile is loaded. On a terminal server, the HKCU\SOFTWARE registry hive is also superimposed by the mirrored HKLM\SOFTWARE\Microsoft\Windows NT\CurrentVersion\Terminal Server\Install\Software section generated during active installation mode.

> **Note**   To create user-specific entries in the ...\Terminal Server\Install registry hive, the hive might have to be modified through environment variables (for example, with %UserName%). This implies using the *REG_EXPAND_SZ* data type to convert the environment variable to a valid character string when the registry is read. Unfortunately, not all applications interpret this conversion correctly and sometimes produce errors. Therefore, it is often necessary to elicit the desired behavior through logon scripts. (See Chapter 7.)

Automatic Application Execution

Windows Server 2003 offers the option to configure applications or scripts in the registry using different keys. These scripts run automatically if a certain event occurs. This mechanism can be used to perform initialization tasks required on terminal servers. However, to do so requires an understanding of the corresponding keys. The following list presents them in detail.

- HKCU\SOFTWARE\Microsoft\Windows\CurrentVersion\Run: Entered programs are executed upon each user logon.

- HKCU\SOFTWARE\Microsoft\Windows\CurrentVersion\RunOnce: Entries made by executable programs are deleted after being processed.

- HKCU\SOFTWARE\Microsoft\Windows NT\CurrentVersion\Windows\Run: Entered programs are executed upon each user logon.

- HKCU\SOFTWARE\Microsoft\Windows NT\CurrentVersion\Windows\Load: Entered programs are executed upon each user logon.

- HKLM\SOFTWARE\Policies\Microsoft\System\Scripts: Usually configured through Group Policies.

- HKU\.DEFAULT\SOFTWARE\Microsoft\Windows\CurrentVersion\Run: Default user is used as a template for new user profiles.

- HKCU\SOFTWARE\Microsoft\Windows\CurrentVersion\Run: Entered programs are executed upon each user logon.

- HKLM\SOFTWARE\Microsoft\Windows\CurrentVersion\RunOnce: Entries made by executable programs are deleted after being processed.

- HKLM\SOFTWARE\Microsoft\Windows\CurrentVersion\RunOnceEx: Entries made by executable programs are deleted after being processed.

- HKLM\SOFTWARE\Microsoft\Windows NT\CurrentVersion\Terminal Server \Install\Software\Microsoft\Windows\CurrentVersion\Run: Shadow copy.

- HKLM\SOFTWARE\Microsoft\Windows NT\CurrentVersion\Terminal Server \Install\Software\Microsoft\Windows\CurrentVersion\RunOnce: Shadow copy.

- HKLM\SOFTWARE\Policies\Microsoft\Windows\System\Scripts\Startup: Usually configured using Group Policies.

If an application or a script is to be run when a user logs off, the following key is used:

- HKLM\SOFTWARE\Microsoft\Windows NT\CurrentVersion\Winlogon\LogoffApp: Lists applications and scripts, separated by commas.

> **Note** If only a script is to be run when a user logs on, configuration takes place under computer administration or the domain based on the Profile tab of the corresponding user account. (See Chapter 4.)

Compatibility Flags

Different compatibility flags in the registry provide the terminal server with specific data for optimum handling of certain applications, registry paths, or .ini files. The flags are set in the HKLM\Software\Microsoft\Windows NT\CurrentVersion \Terminal Server\Compatibility registry hive.

Several entries already exist right after a terminal server's system installation and affect frequently used standard applications or .ini files. Administrators can add new entries or modify existing ones to achieve a certain system behavior.

> **Note** There is no standard graphical tool to view or change these entries. You always need to use the registry editor or third-party tools. However, you should make changes only if applications do not function properly. Use utmost caution when modifying the registry.

Applications

You can control the execution of an application on terminal servers via compatibility flags in a special section in the registry. They are located in the HKLM\Software\Microsoft\Windows NT\CurrentVersion\Terminal Server\Compatibility\Applications\App hive. *App* is the name of the executable file of the corresponding application.

Supplementing existing entries is relatively easy. You just need to create a new key with the application's file name (excluding the .exe ending) as a character string. You can now add values with data to this key.

Figure 6-10   Microsoft Access compatibility flags.

The Flags Value

Probably the most important value is known as *flags* and has the *DWORD* data type. Entries are bit masks and therefore allow combining several defaults for the application. However, the number of possible combinations—as shown in Table 6-8—is a problem. For each application, you need to find out which flags will solve possible runtime problems.

Table 6-8   Compatibility Flags for Applications in the Terminal Server Registry

Value (*DWORD*)	Description
0x00000001	DOS-based application. This entry helps the system unambiguously identify the application characteristics for DOS platforms.
0x00000002	OS/2-based application. This entry helps the system unambiguously identify the application characteristics for OS/2 platforms.
0x00000004	Windows-based 16-bit application. This entry helps the system unambiguously identify the application characteristics for platforms under 16-bit Windows.
0x00000008	Windows-based 32-bit application. This entry helps the system unambiguously identify the application characteristics for platforms under 32-bit Windows.
0x0000000C	Windows-based 16- or 32-bit application (combination of the flags *0x00000004* and *0x00000008*, hexadecimal sum).
0x00000010	The terminal server responds to the **GetComputerName** API command with %UserName% instead of %ComputerName%. This function is needed for applications that identify with the computer name when they communicate with each other. When these applications run on a terminal server, conflicts occur. For this reason, identification occurs via the user name.
0x00000040	Ini mapping: synchronizes the user's .ini file in the %UserProfile%\Windows directory with the system version of the .ini file in the %SystemRoot% directory. This is needed particularly for 16-bit applications to function properly.
0x00000080	Ini mapping: Prevents replacement of the system-wide \Windows directory for the user by the corresponding directory in the user's profile path or basic directory.
0x00000100	Disables registry mapping of mirrored data from HKLM to HKCU for application registry keys. If a user starts this type of application, the mirrored registry values are used, but not written to HKCU.
0x00000200	Normally, objects are also marked with the user's connection identification. If this flag is set, the corresponding application is declared as system-wide. In this case, the application behaves like an operating system component. This option is needed for some server applications installed on the terminal server.

Table 6-8   Compatibility Flags for Applications in the Terminal Server Registry

Value (*DWORD*)	Description
0x00000400	The terminal server responds to the **GetWindowsDir** command with the system's %SystemRoot% directory instead of the user's \Windows directory. This is required for applications that need to have read access to global files from the %SystemRoot% directory.
0x00000800	Responds to the **GlobalMemoryStatus** command by limiting the return value for physical memory. The given application can request only reduced memory below the default value of 32 MB. In this way, the application does not affect other applications.
0x20000000	Prevents application freezing in case of unsuccessful keyboard polling (only for 16-bit Windows-based applications).

Bad Applications Values

In addition to the Flags value, you can set three other application values to optimize it for the terminal server. All value names contain the *BadApp* character string, which indicates an adaptation of *bad* applications. The *MsgQ* character string represents a connection to the message queue, which is responsible for transmitting system commands to the applications.

- FirstCountMsgQPeeksSleepBadApp (default value: 0xF): This value determines how many times an application will try to read the message queue before the terminal server deems it a bad application. If you lower this value, the application "sleeps" more frequently, thus using less CPU time. If you increase the value (for example, to 0xFF), the application usually becomes faster.

- MsgQBadAppSleepTimeInMillisec (default value: 0x1): If the terminal server deems an application bad, the application is put to sleep for the number of milliseconds defined here. If you increase the value, the application uses less CPU time. If you set the value to zero, the query recognition related to the message queue is switched off, often improving application speed.

- NthCountMsgQPeeksSleepBadApp (default value: 0x5): If the system deems the application bad, this value defines how many times the application will retry to access the message queue before it is "put to sleep" again. If you lower this value, the application uses less CPU time. If you increase the value (for example, to 0xFF), the application usually becomes faster.

While you are adjusting these parameters, make sure to check the results using the System Monitor, because processor use has been changed. Improved application response time generally results in more intense use of processor resources.

> **Note** Compatibility flags similar to the message queue also exist for the clipboard. However, there is currently no official information available on *ClipboardFlags*, *OpenClipboardInMilliSecs*, and *OpenClipboardRetries* flags. The only thing you can do is experiment—for example, by using the Microsoft Excel (program name: Excel.exe) compatibility flags.

Registry Paths

The following compatibility flags control the use of registry options in particular. They are located in the HKLM\Software\Microsoft\Windows NT\CurrentVersion \Terminal Server\Compatibility\Registry Entries\RegPath hive. *RegPath* is a key under HKCU\Software.

Table 6-9 Compatibility Flags for Registry Paths

Value (*DWORD*)	Description
0x00000008	Windows-based 32-bit application. This entry helps the system unambiguously identify the application characteristics for platforms under 32-bit Windows.
0x00000100	Disables registry mapping of mirrored data from HKLM to HKCU for application registry keys. If a user starts this type of application, the mirrored registry values are used but not written to HKCU. No registry values are deleted for the user, even if they no longer exist system-wide.

The typical value of an entry for disabling registry mapping of a preset path is 0x108.

> **Note** If an application's registry entries are not located directly under HKCU\SOFTWARE but in its own key hierarchy that starts here, this structure is also evidenced in the compatibility flags. For instance, if an application's parameters are saved under HKCU\SOFTWARE\Directory\Application, the path name for registry options is also \Directory\Application.

.ini Files

The following compatibility flags stipulate the use of .ini files, and they are located in the HKLM\Software\Microsoft\Windows NT\CurrentVersion\Terminal Server \Compatibility\IniFiles\IniFile file, in which *IniFile* is the name of the .ini file (without the .ini suffix).

Table 6-10   Compatibility Flags for .ini Files

Value (*DWORD*)	Description
0x00000004	Windows-based 16-bit application. This entry helps the system unambiguously identify the application.
0x00000008	Windows-based 32-bit application. This entry helps the system unambiguously identify the application.
0x00000040	Synchronizes the user's .ini file in the %UserProfile%\Windows directory with the system version of the .ini file in the %SystemRoot% directory. New entries in the central .ini file are mapped to the user-specific .ini file without deleting any entries there. By default, the user-specific .ini file is completely overwritten if it is older than the central .ini file. This is particularly needed for 16-bit applications to function properly. This flag is often called INISYNCbit.
0x00000080	Prevents replacement of the system-wide \Windows directory for the user by the corresponding directory in the user's profile path or basic directory.

Typical values for the changed synchronization behavior related to a 16-bit application .ini file are 0xC4 or 0x44.

If an application tries to read from an .ini file that does not exist in the user's home directory, the terminal server looks for the file in the system's root directory. If the .ini file is there, it is copied to the \Windows subdirectory of the home directory (%UserProfile%\Windows). If the application queries the Windows directory, the terminal server returns the home directory's \Windows subdirectory.

When a user logs on, the terminal server checks to determine if the system .ini file is more recent than the individual .ini files. If the system version is more recent, the user's .ini file is replaced with the newer version, or the more current entries in the system version are integrated in the user-specific .ini file. Which of the two procedures is used depends on whether the 0x40 INISYNC bit is set for this .ini file. The older version of the user-specific file is renamed; the file name becomes Inifile.ctx. If the system's registry values under the \Terminal Server\Install key are more recent than the version saved under HKCU, the version of that key is deleted and replaced with new keys under \Terminal Server\Install.

Chapter 7

Scripting

This chapter deals with terminal server *scripting*. It includes not only the default command shells, but also different extension options. You will learn about the following:

- Details of shell's commands and relevant scripts

- The shell extension offered by the KiXtart command interpreter

- Windows Script Host functions and their usage on a terminal server

- The most up-to-date possibilities that .NET Common Language Runtime offers for logon procedures

Experienced Microsoft Windows 2000 and Microsoft Windows Server 2003 administrators might find information and techniques here that they already know. Scripting always used to be an important concept for managing large Microsoft Windows NT environments and was thus a well-established mechanism. The technology was improved for Windows 2000 and was well-documented in many help files and publications. For Windows Server 2003, including the .NET Framework and its powerful options, even more scripting options are available. Therefore, this chapter summarizes the most pertinent information, always with a view to terminal server operation.

> **Important** Scripts can be a very powerful administration mechanism for terminal servers. However, scripts require a high degree of maintenance when the newest versions need to be installed on each terminal server in a large farm. Therefore, when planning scripts, bear in mind that the scripts might need to be started from a network share, as well.

Shell Commands

The Windows Server 2003 command prompt still leads to a number of misunderstandings. Many users—and administrators—do not really take it seriously because it reminds them a lot of DOS. However, this former "DOS box" is a fully developed 32-bit command-line interpreter (or *shell*) with the option of using several language elements.

Especially with terminal servers, the command prompt options offer powerful system access that can also be automated, including direct shell commands as well as different scripting concepts. Scripts allow access to files, directories, printers, user accounts, security settings, and the registry. For older applications in particular and for terminal server–specific modifications of the user environment at logon, scripts are an essential tool. For this reason, it will definitely be worth the effort in some environments if terminal server administrators take the time to learn about the relevant technical basics—even if it is their first contact with programming.

At first glance, it does not seem likely that Windows Server 2003 comes with an especially powerful command and scripting language. Basically, the direct command-line language is a leftover of the historic MS-DOS batch language scope that was used to create batch-processing programs. Command-line options were greatly expanded when the Windows Script Host and the .NET Frameworks were introduced, as will be described later in this chapter. However, learning to apply these new concepts requires a substantial amount of time. In the following section, we will take a look at the standard shell commands and language elements that are important for operating a terminal server and managing its users.

Selected Standard Commands

Scripts are an essential concept of operating a terminal server and its applications. The most important commands for administrators that are needed at the command prompt or in a script file are listed in this table. Some of these command options must be executed by a user with administrator permissions to work properly.

Table 7-1   A Brief Description of Selected Windows Server 2003 Standard Commands

Command	Description
At	Controls the scheduling of commands and programs to run at a specified time and date.
Attrib	Displays or modifies file attributes.
Cacls	Displays or modifies file access control lists (ACLs).
Call	Calls a batch-processing program from another batch-processing program without stopping the parent batch-processing program. The **Call** command also accepts labels as targets for jumps within the batch-processing logic.
Comp	Compares the content of two files or sets of files byte by byte.
Date	The **Date** command without parameters displays the current date and prompts you to type a new date. Using the Enter key keeps the current date. The **Date** command supports the /T option that displays the current date without prompting for a new date.
Fc	Compares two files and displays the differences between the two.
Find	Searches for a string of text in one or more files.
Findstr	Searches for patterns of text strings in files. This command uses regular expressions and has several parameters that make it very powerful.
Net	Command group for displaying and configuring network functions.
Set	Displays, sets, or deletes environment variables for the current environment settings of the opened command interpreter.
Sort	Reads input, sorts data, and displays the result on the screen, saves it to a file, or writes it to another device.
Start	Creates a new command prompt window to execute a program or command. It is also used for determining and setting the process priority of any selected program.
Systeminfo	Displays detailed configuration information about a computer and the operating system.
Time	The **Time** command without parameters displays the current time and prompts you to type a new time. Using the Enter key keeps the current time. The **Time** command supports the /T option that displays the current time without prompting for a new time.
Type	Displays the content of a text file.
Xcopy	Copies files and directories including subdirectories. With specific parameters, the **Xcopy** command supports the administration of security setting.

Windows Server 2003 extensions as related to Terminal Services do not apply only to graphical tools, but also to additional command-line tools. These tools are listed and described in the following table. More detailed information can be found in the Windows Server 2003 Help and Support Center's command-line reference A-Z.

Table 7-2   Brief Introduction of the Specific Terminal Services Commands

Command	Description
Change logon	Uses the following parameters to enable or disable client session logons and displays the current logon status. This utility is useful for system administration. The abbreviation for this command is **Chlogon**. */enable*: Enables user logon from clients, but not from the console (default setting). */disable*: Disables subsequent logons from clients. Does not affect users who are already logged on. */query*: Displays the current logon status.
Change port	Changes the mapping logic for serial ports to be compatible with MS-DOS applications. The abbreviation for this command is **Chgport**.
Change user	Uses the following parameters to change the mapping of .ini files and the registry for the current user during application installation. The abbreviation for this command is **Chguser**. */execute*: Enables the mapping of .ini files to the home directory (default setting). */install*: Disables the mapping of .ini files to the home directory during application installation. */query*: Displays the current setting.
Flattemp	Enables or disables a common (flat) temporary folder (temp mapping). */enable*: Enables common temporary folders. */disable*: Disables common temporary folders. */query*: Displays the current setting.
Logoff	Terminates a user session.
Msg	Sends a message to one or more users.
Query process	Displays information about the processes of all user sessions on a terminal server. This command includes parameters for further specification of the desired information, such as process ID, user name, session name, session ID, program, or server name.
Query session	Displays information about the sessions running on a terminal server. This command includes parameters for further specification of the desired information, such as user name, session name, session ID, program, or server name.
Query termserver	Lists all terminal servers running on the network. This command includes parameters for further specification of the desired information, such as server name or domain.
Query user	Displays information about the users logged on to a terminal server. This command includes parameters for further specification of the desired information, such as user name, session name, session ID, program, or server name.

Table 7-2   Brief Introduction of the Specific Terminal Services Commands

Command	Description
Query winsta	Same as the **Query session** command.
Reset session	Resets a user session to initial values. This command includes parameters for further specification of the desired information, such as session name, session ID, or server name.
Rwinsta	Same as the **Reset session** command.
Shadow	Allows the monitoring of the terminal server session of another user. This command includes parameters for further specification of the desired information, such as session name, session ID, or server name. All information displayed on the shadowed computer session is also displayed on the target computer.
Tscon	Attaches the client or user to an existing terminal server session.
Tsdiscon	Disconnects the client or user session from the terminal server.
Tskill	Terminates a selected process using its process ID or its name in combination with the server name and the session ID. Administrators can use this command for all processes; users can use it only for their own processes.
Tsprof	Copies the configuration information of a Terminal Services user to the configuration data of another user. You can also use the **Tsprof** command to update a user's profile path.
Tsshutdn	Allows an administrator to shut down the terminal server in a controlled manner. After starting **Tsshutdn**, no programs can be executed anymore. The session of the user who started **Tsshutdn** is still active, but all session information will have read-only permissions.

In particular, commands starting with **Query** are able to transfer many functions of the Terminal Services Administration graphical tool to the command line. (See Chapter 4.)

Language Syntax

Regrettably, the command-line language at the Windows Server 2003 command prompt provides only a few options for dynamic responses and structured programming. The basic elements a script developer might use within a simple language syntax are as follows:

- **The For command**   The **For** command executes a command for each file that is part of a set of files.

- **The Goto command**   In a batch-processing program, the **Goto** command invokes a jump to a tagged line. The tag is identified by a colon (:). When the script finds the tag, it processes the commands following in the subsequent line.

- **The If command**   The **If** command processes expressions with conditions in a batch-processing program.

The language syntax also includes command symbols and filter commands. Redirection symbols (for instance, >, <, or >>) determine where the command obtains its information and where the information will be sent. By default, Windows Server 2003 receives input from the keyboard and sends output to the monitor. However, sometimes it can be advantageous to redirect input or output to a file or a printer. For instance, a directory list can be redirected from the monitor to a file.

Filter commands help with sorting, viewing, and selecting individual parts of the command. Information generated through a filter command is divided, extracted, or resorted. Windows Server 2003 contains three filter commands: **More**, **Find**, and **Sort**.

> **Note** Please see the Windows Server 2003 Help and Support Center command-line reference for detailed information on command-line or batch-processing programs.

Examples

The following examples take the command prompt's language syntax to solve seemingly simple tasks. These are usually related to the runtime environment of terminal servers.

Dynamic File Names

In this example, a file is created with a dynamic name that relates to date and time. This type of file is often used for saving log data.

Listing 7-1: Creating a File with a Dynamic Name

```
@echo off
for /f "tokens=1,2, delims= " %%i in ('date /t') do (set day=%%i) & (set date=%%j)
for /f "tokens=1 delims= " %%k in ('time /t') do set time=%%k
for /f "tokens=1,2,3 delims=/" %%l in ('@echo %date%') do set file1=%%l_%%m_%%n
for /f "tokens=1,2 delims=:" %%p in ('@echo %time%') do set file2=%%p_%%q
set filename=%day%-%file1%-%file2%.log
@echo Command1 > %filename%
@echo Command2 >> %filename%
```

Lines 2 and 3 create the day, date, and time variables from the current date and time. Lines 4 and 5 use the result to create the file1 and file2 variables that replace the special characters / and : with _ to improve legibility. Line 6 creates the final file name: *Filename.log*, representing a summary of day, file1, and file2. The last two lines are examples for redirecting commands to the target file.

With this script, the weakness inherent to the language syntax of command-line scripts is obvious: the solution to a relatively simple problem is very complicated. Language elements are evidently not suitable for easy processing of dynamic information.

Logon Scripts

One of the most frequent terminal server requirements is creating logon scripts, often used for linking network shares or printers to a user session. It might also be necessary to write user-specific values to the registry database. Unfortunately, the options for these tasks are not very comprehensive in batch-processing scripts. Usually, the logon logic is set up around the **Net** command. Additional functions can be implemented only through additional command-line tools (for example, from the Windows Server 2003 Resource Kit).

Listing 7-2 shows a simple logon script.

Listing 7-2: A Simple Logon Script

```
if not exist u:\. net use u: \\fileserver\%username% /user:%username%
cscript login.vbs
```

So how is the logon script linked to the user account? The Active Directory Users and Computers tool handles the domain user, and the local user account is handled by Computer Management. On the Profile tab of the selected user account, a relative path (for example, **employee\sales.cmd**) is entered as the logon script.

The final question now is where to save the logon script physically on the file system. For domain users, the starting point for the relative logon path is located under %Systemroot%\SYSVOL\sysvol\<*Domainname*>\scripts on the server that handles authentication. For local users, the %Systemroot%\System32\Repl\Imports\scripts folder handles this task. It should be shared under the name of *netlogon* for all users. If the local folder does not exist yet, it is recommended that you create it exactly under the path described earlier.

Note Users and server operators should have permissions only to read and execute in folders with logon scripts. Full access is recommended for administrators only.

Analysis Scripts

The last example is an analysis script that can be executed on a terminal server after an installation. The script archives many settings that are saved in text files. The analysis script can be executed again at a later time. The corresponding script results allow easy comparisons between installation statuses.

The analysis script performs the following tasks:

- Creating a log file called *Inspect.log*
- Writing date and time in Inspect.log
- Logging the system information with the **Systeminfo** command

- Logging the network configuration with the **Ipconfig** command

- Logging the IP network statistics with the **Netstat** command

- Logging the NetBIOS over TCP/IP statistics using different options of the **Nbt-stat** command

- Logging the routing table with the **Netstat** command

- Logging the ARP cache for name resolution using the **Arp** command

- Logging the network environment using different options of the **Net** command

- Logging Terminal Services using different options of the **Query** command

The script can be supplemented by analyses relating to the registry (Regedit /e), the file structure of selected directories (Dir /s /o:n), or the security of directory trees (Cacls).

Note   The display of a text message in the command prompt can be suppressed by adding >NUL: 2>&1 to a command. >NUL: represents the redirection of the default output to the null device, that is, into nothing. 2>&1 directs all error output to the default output that points to the null device. As a result, neither default output nor error messages of the corresponding command are displayed.

Listing 7-3: The Analysis Script

```
@echo off
echo Processing system inspection...
echo System Inspection > %temp%\inspect.log
date /t >> %temp%\inspect.log
time /t >> %temp%\inspect.log
echo. >> %temp%\inspect.log

echo --- [ Systeminfo ] --- >> %temp%\inspect.log
systeminfo >> %temp%\inspect.log
echo. >> %temp%\inspect.log

echo --- [ IP Configuration ] --- >> %temp%\inspect.log
ipconfig /all >> %temp%\inspect.log
echo. >> %temp%\inspect.log

echo --- [ Netstat ] --- >> %temp%\inspect.log
echo [ netstat -e -s ] >> %temp%\inspect.log
netstat -e -s >> %temp%\inspect.log
echo [ netstat -a ] >> %temp%\inspect.log
netstat -a >> %temp%\inspect.log
echo. >> %temp%\inspect.log
```

```
echo --- [ Nbtstat ] --- >> %temp%\inspect.log
echo [ nbtstat -a %computername% ] >> %temp%\inspect.log
nbtstat -a %computername% >> %temp%\inspect.log
echo [ nbtstat -c ] >> %temp%\inspect.log
nbtstat -c >> %temp%\inspect.log
echo [ nbtstat -n ] >> %temp%\inspect.log
nbtstat -n >> %temp%\inspect.log
echo [ nbtstat -r ] >> %temp%\inspect.log
nbtstat -r >> %temp%\inspect.log
echo [ nbtstat -S ] >> %temp%\inspect.log
nbtstat -S >> %temp%\inspect.log
echo [ nbtstat -s ] >> %temp%\inspect.log
nbtstat -s >> %temp%\inspect.log
echo. >> %temp%\inspect.log

echo --- [ Routing ] --- >> %temp%\inspect.log
netstat -r >> %temp%\inspect.log
echo. >> %temp%\inspect.log

echo --- [ ARP Cache ] --- >> %temp%\inspect.log
arp -a >> %temp%\inspect.log
echo. >> %temp%\inspect.log

echo --- [ Net Command ] --- >> %temp%\inspect.log
echo [ net accounts ] >> %temp%\inspect.log
net accounts >> %temp%\inspect.log
echo [ net config server ] >> %temp%\inspect.log
net config server >> %temp%\inspect.log
echo [ net use ] >> %temp%\inspect.log
net use >> %temp%\inspect.log
echo [ net session ] >> %temp%\inspect.log
net session >> %temp%\inspect.log
echo [ net view ] >> %temp%\inspect.log
net view >> %temp%\inspect.log
echo. >> %temp%\inspect.log

echo --- [ Terminal Services ] --- >> %temp%\inspect.log
echo [ query termserver ] >> %temp%\inspect.log
query termserver >> %temp%\inspect.log
echo [ query session ] >> %temp%\inspect.log
query session >> %temp%\inspect.log
echo [ query user ] >> %temp%\inspect.log
query user >> %temp%\inspect.log
echo [ query process ] >> %temp%\inspect.log
query process * >> %temp%\inspect.log
echo. >> %temp%\inspect.log

echo System inspection finished >> %temp%\inspect.log

echo.
echo System inspection finished
```

Note You probably wonder why you should bother with these quite obsolete batch script concepts at all. The answer lies with the compatibility scripts that are described in the following section. It is hard to believe, but despite the availability of much more advanced scripting technologies, those scripts are still based on the batch-processing mechanisms described in this section, even on Windows Server 2003.

Application Compatibility Scripts

Adjusting different applications to a terminal server often requires the use of scripts or command files. Scripts and command files offer a suitable scripting language syntax to perform repeat administrative tasks by sequencing default commands. Basically, applications can be adjusted during two procedures: application installation and user logon.

The changes performed directly after an application is installed on a terminal server often cover known problems. Specifically adapted scripts result in automated system environment adjustment to improve the execution of the application. Therefore, scripts comprise different actions, most of which are documented in relevant articles (for example, in the Microsoft Knowledge Base):

- Changing paths that lead to wrong directories
- Moving executable programs and DLLs to system-global areas
- Adjusting compatibility flags

The second option for starting scripts correctly is to invoke them during user logon. On a terminal server, it is possible to assign each user a standard logon script and a terminal server logon script. Furthermore, each terminal server holds a systemwide logon script (**UsrLogon.cmd**). This script can perform global configuration changes that might be required on a multiple-user system. Due to the dependencies of the installed applications regarding the changes, the systemwide logon script invokes application-specific scripts for the changes.

Both solutions are based on compatibility scripts, which will be described in detail in the following section.

Note Compatibility scripts used to be a frequently used way to adjust older applications for their use on terminal servers. The newer applications no longer require this method and make use of more modern concepts. Nevertheless, it is worth checking out compatibility scripts, especially when the user environment needs to be optimized for stubborn applications that were never designed to run on terminal servers.

Compatibility Scripts for Installations

Many user session modifications with the purpose of improving applications can be performed by using special scripts. Each terminal server has several installation scripts located in the %SystemRoot%\Application Compatibility Scripts\Install directory. It might be necessary to adjust some of these scripts manually before they are executed—for instance, modifications related to default paths that are selected during application installation.

> **Note**   The compatibility scripts delivered for the installation of applications are just examples. They will still need to be adjusted for many environments.

A compatibility script's logical sequence requires many interdependent script modules. The reason for this is the missing ability of individual command-line scripts to appropriately handle dynamic data, conditional branches, and user input.

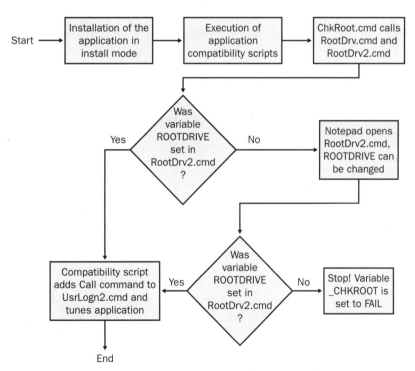

Figure 7-1   Logical sequence of a compatibility script.

ChkRoot, UsrLogon, RootDrv, and RootDrv2

When an installation script is executed on a terminal server for the first time, the script asks the administrator to enter a default letter for the home directory of each user. A file called **RootDrv2.cmd** is generated in the %SystemRoot%\Application

Compatibility Scripts directory. This file handles the allocation of drive letters and home directories. **ChkRoot.cmd** is the script responsible for this initial behavior. It is also located in the %SystemRoot%\Application Compatibility Scripts directory.

The **ChkRoot.cmd** script works according to the following logic:

- Using the **RootDrv.cmd** script to verify whether the %RootDrive% environment variable has already been set. If yes, it jumps to a label at the end of **Chk-Root.cmd**. If not, the script continues to execute.

- Generating the **RootDrv2.cmd** script in the %SystemRoot%\Application Compatibility Scripts directory. The script is called up in Notepad to assign the user's home directory to a fixed drive letter.

- Invoking **RootDrv.cmd** again to see if the definition of the drive letter was successful.

- Calling up the **UsrLogon.cmd** logon script to assign the home directory to the defined drive letter. In this way, the generated drive letter can be used during the installation of the application.

> **Note**   The main goal of this script is to ensure that a drive letter is assigned to a user's home directory. The status is verified with **Root-Drv.cmd**. The home directory can be located either locally under %System-Drive%\Documents and Settings\\<UserName> or on a network resource. The drive letter makes sure that even older applications can access a home directory that was defined by a UNC name or is based on long paths. Regarding application file access, the drive letter is the smallest common denominator for execution on a terminal server.

A reference to application-specific tasks that need to be executed during user logon is created in a script named **UsrLogn2.cmd** by the compatibility scripts logic.

> **Note**   To reset changes made by installation scripts, please refer to the %SystemRoot%\Application Compatibility Scripts\Uninstall directory when uninstalling an application. This directory supplies a number of uninstallation scripts.

The %RootDrive% Environment Variable

Let us assume that an authorized user *Admin* installs the application *App* on a terminal server. The application was programmed at a time when it was still unusual to access directories through the UNC name convention or with long path names.

However, the installation program determines the user's home directory by evaluating the %HomeDrive% and %HomePath% environment variables. The result is entered in the registry to define the paths for App for loading and saving data. It is highly possible that the long names lead to errors in the old applications.Two of the most important tasks of the scripts **ChkRoot.cmd** and **RootDrv2.cmd** introduced earlier are creating or verifying the %RootDrive% environment variable. Why is this environment variable so important for the applications on a terminal server? Let us take a look at a simple example to answer this question.

Assuming that the Admin's home directory is on a file server on the network, the path could be X:\Admin. The home directory in the Admin's account is determined by the assignment of \\Server\Share\Admin to the X: drive letter. On a terminal server, however, this entry is assigned to each user, which is not very plausible. Each user should have his or her own path for access to working files for App.

There can be users who do not have their home directory on the network. They use the Windows Server 2003 default setting. Their home directory is located under %SystemRoot%\Documents and Settings\%UserName%. For the user *Tina*, this would be C:\Documents and Settings\Tina. This, of course, looks completely different than X:\Admin. Table 7-3 shows the differences.

Table 7-3   Home Paths of Different Users

User	%HomeDrive%	%HomePath%
Admin	X:\	Admin
Tina	C:\	Documents and Settings\Tina

Even though no obvious mistake was made, the result is useless. If during the installation of App, the correct path (X:\Admin) is saved in the registry under, for example, the HKCU\Software\App\DefaultPath key, and this registry setting is mirrored in HKLM because of the installation mode, this data cannot be accessed by any other user.

The solution to this problem is the %RootDrive% environment variable. It represents a drive letter that can be freely selected and that has never been used by any other user before. The drive letter is fixed systemwide and is thus the same for all users. When a user logs on, his or her individual home directory %HomeDrive%%HomePath% is automatically assigned to the %RootDrive% drive letter.

When selecting the default drive letter W:\ as the %RootDrive% value, this entry must be saved in the HKCU\Software\App\DefaultPath registry value during the installationof an application. From that point on, each user accesses his or her home directory via the W:\ drive letter. The conflict is thus solved, and the old application needs to handle only one drive letter, W:\.

For the two users in the preceding example, the situation is now as follows:

- Admin: W:\ = X:\Admin

- Tina: W:\ = C:\Documents and Settings\Tina

%RootDrive% is linked to the user-specific home directory in the **Usr-Logon.cmd** script that will be described in further detail later. The corresponding commands are **Subst** and **Net**. The latter is used only to cancel an already existing assignment of the drive letter to a shared network resource.

Listing 7-4: Linking %RootDrive% to the User's Home Directory

```
Net Use %RootDrive% /D >NUL: 2>&1
Subst %RootDrive% "%HomeDrive%%HomePath%"
if ERRORLEVEL 1 goto SubstErr
goto AfterSubst
:SubstErr
Subst %RootDrive% /d >NUL: 2>&1
Subst %RootDrive% "%HomeDrive%%HomePath%"
:AfterSubst
```

> **Note** With alternative script environments, such as Windows Script Host, some of these programming approaches will be easier. However, the behavior described here still needs to be rebuilt to achieve a correct behavior of many old Windows-based applications. If you prefer to work without an additional drive letter, you need to automate all user-specific path entries in the registry during logon for all applications installed.

If there is a home directory for each user on the network already, the following procedure is recommended: Format the part of **Usrlogon.cmd** shown in Listing 7-4 as comments and set the letter for the home directory through the %RootDrive% variable in **RootDrv.cmd**. Further adjustments of the logon script subsequently have to ensure that all directories and files needed for the applications are located in the user's home directory and not in the user's profile.

Compatibility Scripts for User Logon

Whenever a user logs on to a terminal server, a drive letter must be assigned to the user's home directory to ensure proper operation of many applications. Additionally, the following application-specific tasks might need to be performed:

- Generating subdirectories in the user's home directory
- Copying files from a central source to the home directory
- Setting changed access permissions for certain files

All these tasks can be executed during user logon through the **UsrLogon.cmd** script. Each terminal server provides a number of application-specific standard logon scripts that are located in the %SystemRoot%\Application Compatibility Scripts\Logon directory.

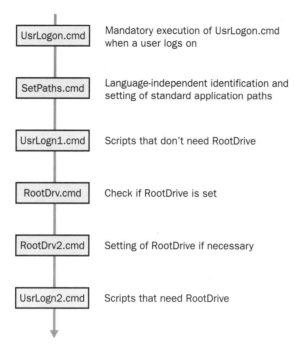

UsrLogon.cmd	Mandatory execution of UsrLogon.cmd when a user logs on
SetPaths.cmd	Language-independent identification and setting of standard application paths
UsrLogn1.cmd	Scripts that don't need RootDrive
RootDrv.cmd	Check if RootDrive is set
RootDrv2.cmd	Setting of RootDrive if necessary
UsrLogn2.cmd	Scripts that need RootDrive

Figure 7-2 User logon script sequence.

Tip   You can verify or change the mandatory execution of the Usr-Logon.cmd script in the registry under HKLM\Software\Microsoft\Windows NT\CurrentVersion\WinLogon\Appsetup. Other keys for automated execution of scripts after predefined system events (such as user logon or user logoff) are listed in Chapter 6.

The UsrLogon Script

The **UsrLogon.cmd** command file is a specific solution for terminal servers. It is located in the %SystemRoot%\System32 directory and runs at the time of each user logon. **UsrLogon.cmd** mainly ensures that other scripts are called up that are needed for the adjustment of individual applications. This script also assigns each user a so-called "RootDrive" under a previously selected drive letter.

This script is all but trivial, so let me briefly list its individual functions:

- Invoking the **SetPaths.cmd** script in the %SystemRoot%\Application Compatibility Scripts directory. This script generates environment variables from some registry entries so that the other scripts can be executed without hard-coded system paths. The scripts are thus independent of the system language. This particularly applies to start menus, autostart options, and the locations of system-specific files, templates, and applications. When it is done, **SetPaths.cmd** returns to **UsrLogon.cmd**.

■ Invoking the **UsrLogn1.cmd** script in the %SystemRoot%\System32 directory, if this directory exists. This script is responsible for all commands that are not dependent on the %RootDrive% environment variable and returns to **Usr-Logon.cmd** when it is done.

■ Invoking the **RootDrv.cmd** script in the %SystemRoot%\Application Compatibility Scripts directory. In combination with the **RootDrv2.cmd** script, this script handles the assignment of a user's home directory to a drive letter. When they are done, the scripts return to **UsrLogon.cmd**.

■ Assigning a user's home directory to a drive letter that is defined through the %RootDrive% environment variable. The default home directory is the local user profile directory. If the home directory is located on the network, manual changes need to be performed in the **UsrLogon.cmd** script.

■ Invoking the **UsrLogn2.cmd** script. It contains commands that depend on the %RootDrive% environment variable. In particular, the installation scripts of applications write command sequences in **UsrLogn2.cmd**, defining necessary adjustment tasks that will be executed upon user logon.

Right after a terminal server is installed, some of the scripts described earlier do not exist yet. So how do they get on the system? How is the %RootDrive% environment variable that handles invoking other scripts generated? This is what the installation scripts described earlier are needed for: they generate scripts that can be invoked right then. This concept is not really the most intuitive way to create such a configuration, but it is compatible with many older Microsoft Windows versions and programs.

> **Note** The logical sequence of the **UsrLogon.cmd** script is not easy to understand. Nevertheless, it is important to implement the required function for older Windows-based applications through default scripts. Here the differences between applications that are already compatible with Windows 2000 or Windows Server 2003 come to light because they do not need this type of scripts (for example, Microsoft Office 2000). Older applications need to be adjusted for Terminal Services first. The differences are so substantial that the complicated script mechanisms are needed to balance out the system.

Supporting Scripts

For both application installations and user logon on a terminal server, scripts are invoked that call other scripts. The most important supporting scripts are briefly described in the following section.

SetPaths.cmd

While the other scripts already existed in the Windows NT 4.0 Terminal Server Edition, at least in some initial version, the **SetPaths.cmd** script was introduced only with Windows 2000. It still exists under Windows Server 2003 and handles the correct setting of environment variables during installation and user logon.

RootDrv.cmd and RootDrv2.cmd

The drive letter for a user's home directory is selected through the **RootDrv.cmd** script, as shown in Listing 7-5. This script is executed during application installation and user logon.

Listing 7-5: The RootDrv.cmd Script

```
If Exist "%SystemRoot%\Application Compatibility Scripts\RootDrv2.Cmd" Call
"%SystemRoot%\Application Compatibility Scripts\RootDrv2.Cmd"
```

Listing 7-5 seems to be very confusing. It shows the lack of power of the default commands in the command-line shell and the resulting tricks to work around this problem. The **Rootdrv.cmd** script is called from different places in other scripts, and it is used only to verify the existence of yet another script.

The real assignment of a letter to the %RootDrive% environment variable is done by the **RootDrv2.cmd** script, which is invoked by **RootDrv.cmd**, if it exists. Only through this cascaded invoking of scripts can conditional branches be achieved with default commands. Specifically because of such a complicated script hierarchy, the **RootDrv2.cmd**'s syntax is relatively simple.

Listing 7-6: The Dynamically Created RootDrv2.cmd Script

```
Set RootDrive=W:
```

After invoking **RootDrv.cmd** through the **Call** command, **UsrLogon.cmd** verifies if the letter is assigned to the %RootDrive% environment variable.

Listing 7-7: Querying the RootDrive Environment Variable in the UsrLogon.cmd Script

```
If "A%RootDrive%A" == "AA" End.Cmd
```

If this is the case, the letter in %RootDrive% is used for the user's home directory. If not, the script ends immediately.

Additional Tools for Compatibility Scripts

It is easy to imagine that the default prompt commands are insufficient for powerful scripts, such as the ones that meet the demands of compatibility scripts described here. This is why a number of additional command-line tools must be set up to achieve the required modifications in the registry, file system, and security settings. Some of these tools were developed especially for the terminal server; some have been known for a longer time from earlier Windows Resource Kits. The supporting tools are introduced in the following table.

Table 7-4   Commands Needed for the Support of Compatibility Scripts

Tools	Description
Acregl.exe	This tool determines whether a predefined key and value exist in the registry. The result is redirected to a file that includes an environment variable and the associated registry value with a leading set command. The value must be a character string.
Acsr.exe	This tool performs simple search-and-replace actions in texts. It reads from an input file and writes to an output file. Each parameter can contain an environment variable.
Aciniupd.exe	This tool is used for .ini file updates.
Regini.exe	This tool is located in the %Systemroot%\System32 folder. It reads key files and uses its values to modify registry keys.

Extending Functionality with KiXtart

KiXtart is an independent script language developed by Ruud van Velsen of Microsoft Benelux. You find KiXtart at *http://netnet.net/~swilson/kix/download.htm*. It contains a logon script processor and a script language extension for Windows Server 2003. KiXtart lets you query information, set environment variables, modify the registry, and access the file system using a free-form language syntax with many functions that the default command-line prompt does not have.

The KiXtart package comprises several files. Only the main program (Kix32.exe) is needed for Windows Server 2003. It is recommended that the Kix32.exe program file be saved in a system directory that is already linked to the default path. In principle, Kix32.exe can be saved in the same directory as a KiXtart script to be executed. That is all the installation effort required.

KiXtart scripts are simple text files that can be invoked from the local hard drive or a network drive. If KiXtart is used for global logon scripts, Kix32.exe should be located in a network directory.

KiXtart is started by entering **Kix32** in the command line or referencing **Kix32** as a logon script. One or more script files can be set as *Kix32* parameters.

Core Components

The KiXtart script language has three core components: commands, functions, and macros. It also uses basic operators and special syntax characters. All these are described in the KiXtart documentation delivered with the product.

KiXtart has a free-form language that is independent of capitalization. However, it has become customary to differentiate the core components by spelling—for example, capital letters for commands, initial caps for functions, and all lowercase for macros.

Commands

KiXtart commands perform actions such as deleting screen contents, setting text colors, changing font size, or connecting network drives. For instance, the **Use** command connects and disconnects a network resource.

Expressions for conditional situations are supported by command sequences, such as If--Else--Endif or Select--Case--Endselect. KiXtart supports nested *If* conditions. To control execution flow, the **While—Loop** and **Do Until** commands loop instructions until defined abort conditions are met causing the execution loop to be exited.

Additionally, **Gosub** or **Goto** commands can be used for jumping subroutines. The **Run** command allows executing external programs, and the **Call** command enables invoking of further KiXtart scripts, similar to the language syntax of standard command-line scripts.

Functions

Functions exceed command possibilities and usually need one or more expressions for parameters. The character strings can be included in single or double quotation marks.

Most functions return a character string or a numerical value. They also set the @error value to indicate possible problems that might prevent a script from running properly.

Let us now look at some functions that can handle important tasks for terminal servers.

- *AddPrinterConnection, DelPrinterConnection*   Adds or deletes printer connections
- *SetDefaultPrinter*   Determines a user's default printer
- *AddProgramGroup, AddProgramItem*   Adds program groups and program icons
- *EnumLocalGroup, EnumGroup*   Determines the local and global groups to which a user belongs
- *InGroup*   Verifies whether a user belongs to a group
- *AddKey, DelKey*   Adds and deletes registry keys
- *LogEvent*   Writes messages in the systemwide Event Viewer log file
- *LogOff*   Forces a user to log off
- *MessageBox*   Displays a message box
- *CompareFileTimes, GetFileVersion*   Supports input and output at file level
- *SendMessage*   Sends a message to another computer

If a KiXtart script runs in user context, only personal program groups or user-specific areas of the registry can be modified. Only an administrator has extended permissions granted for relevant scripts.

Macros

KiXtart macros provide information such as network addresses or logon servers. The following table lists the most important macros.

Table 7-5   The Most Important KiXtart Macros

Macro	Description
@address	Network interface card address.
@date	Date in YYYYMMDD format.
@day	Day of the week.
@fullname	Full name of the current user.
@ipaddressx	The TCP/IP address. The *x* in the macro references the number of the network interface card. The value can be 0-3. *@ipaddress0* references the first network card. The return value consists of a character string in the decimal-point notation for IP addresses. Each octet can have a value from 000 through 255 (for example, 192.100.101.102).
@ldomain	Logon domain.
@lserver	Logon server.
@primarygroup	Primary group to which the current user belongs.
@pwage	Age of the current user's password.
@time	Current time.
@userid	User ID of the current user.
@wksta	Name of the computer.

Basic Operators and Special Syntax Characters

KiXtart supports the logical operators *AND* and *OR*. You can also use these conditional operators: < (smaller than), <= (smaller than or equal), > (larger than), >= (larger or equal), = (equal), and <> (not equal).

Under KiXtart, several special characters can be used to mark special syntactic constructions. For instance, the dollar sign ($) is used to mark a variable, the at sign (@) specifies a macro, and the percent sign (%) indicates an environment variable.

Generating a Script

A brief example can illustrate how a logon script is generated. We are going to verify which group a user belongs to during the logon procedure. Depending on the group, we will assign the file server for the home directory, and we will connect the default printer.

Listing 7-8: KiXtart Script for Assigning a Home Directory and a Default Printer

```
; Check group membership and set the $server variable
IF InGroup("marketing")
 $server = "FILESRV1"
ENDIF

IF InGroup("development")
 $server = "FILESRV2"
ENDIF

; Assign drive letter u to home directory
USE U: "\\$server\@userid"
; Set printer parameters
addprinterconnection (\\PRINTSRV\HPLJ22)
setdefaultprinter (\\PRINTSRV\HPLJ22)
```

For the script to run during user logon, it needs to be assigned to the relevant account properties or to be invoked from a conventional logon script. If the KiXtart script is named **Klogin.src**, the following line applies:

```
kix32 klogins.src
```

> **Note**   KiXtart is not officially supported by Microsoft, despite the fact that it was developed by a Microsoft employee. For this reason, the corresponding mechanisms should not be used on critical systems that depend on fast Microsoft support. However, KiXtart can be a very powerful tool in a terminal server environment if you know how to work with it.

Logon Scripts Using Windows Script Host

In the long term, batch-processing files are not the solution of choice for complex scripting tasks. Therefore, Microsoft developed the Windows Script Host (WSH) concept. The WSH technology was introduced with Windows 2000 and seamlessly fit into the Microsoft component architecture strategy before the .NET Framework was introduced. Windows Server 2003 comes with Windows Script Host 5.6 and can therefore easily handle complex administrative tasks.

The command prompt uses the WSH and the existing Component Object Model (COM) interfaces to automate applications. The underlying script interpreters have been in use since Microsoft Internet Explorer version 3.0, particularly the two language dialects, Microsoft Visual Basic Script (VBScript) and JScript (a variant of Netscape Java-Script). Third-party manufacturers offer additional WSH scripting languages.

To execute scripts, systemwide available COM components are used. The Windows Server 2003 operating system manages and provides these components. Communication is handled by COM interfaces as in many conventional applications.

The COM components are based on different libraries that define constants, functions, objects, and events that, in turn, can be used by other applications or scripts. In this way, these scripting engines supply functions for interpreting scripts in a defined language syntax. Scripting engines are realized as ActiveX components that can be used by the Windows Script Host.

WSH Runtime Environment

The command prompt's script language can easily be expanded with this concept. The user or administrator uses object-oriented options for generating powerful console scripts and for controlling the entire user interface with command-line programs.

Windows Script Host can either run in a Windows mode (Wscript.exe) or in a command-line mode (Cscript.exe). There are three ways to run scripts with corresponding file extensions on a terminal server:

- Double-clicking script files or their icons on the desktop

- Using the Run... option in the Start menu by entering the complete script name

- Executing Wscript.exe via the Run... option and the optional entry of parameters and arguments

If you run scripts in the command-line–based mode, use the following syntax:

```
Cscript [Parameters] Scriptname.Extension [Options] [Arguments]
```

The host parameters enable or disable different Windows Script Host options. These parameters always begin with a double slash (//). The script name is indicated by its extension—for example, **Chart.vbs** for a Visual Basic script. Script parameters (options and arguments) always begin with a single slash (/).

The most important host parameters of the **Cscript** command are listed in Table 7-6.

Table 7-6 Host Parameters of the *Cscript* Command

Parameters	Description
//I	Interactive mode (opposite of *//B*).
//B	Batch mode. Suppresses display of script errors and user queries.
//T:nn	Time limit in seconds. Maximum time for running a script (default value: unlimited). Suppresses uncontrolled script processes for an extended period of time.
//logo	Shows a WSH logo message at execution time (default setting, opposite of *//nologo*).
//nologo	Suppresses display of WSH logo message.

Table 7-6 Host Parameters of the *Cscript* Command

Parameters	Description
//H:Cscript or Wscript	Defines Cscript or Wscript as the default application to run scripts (default setting: Wscript).
//S	Saves the current command-line options for the current user.
//D	Enables debug mode.
//X	Executes the script in the debugger.
//job:	Specifies a job that is executed within the script. Different jobs are defined in XML syntax.
//?	Displays help information. Corresponds to running **Cscript** without parameters.

The easiest way to generate scripts is by using Notepad, but Microsoft Script Debugger and Microsoft Script Editor are much more powerful.

Object-Oriented Programming Model

What exactly is an object? This is the question many administrators ponder if they have never had to do object-oriented programming before. First of all, an object is simply a thing with a set of characteristics and attributes that describe the object. In principle, objects are divided into several categories, all relating to different units: users, groups, computers, printers, networks, or applications. Each of these objects has a set of properties that describes it in detail. Furthermore, each object can perform actions using methods. You might, for instance, look at a user object with these properties: user name, ID, and password. It might have methods to create, delete, or modify passwords. However, you need to create the user object before you can interact with it.

Before accessing an object's properties and methods, a corresponding instance needs to be created using two methods provided in the WSH runtime environment: *CreateObject* and *GetObject*. The concept of calling up a method within an object is radically different from using tools in batch-processing scripts as described previously. *CreateObject* is also a function in VBScript, which somewhat simplifies its use. As a result, the easiest syntax for creating an object instance is this:

```
set ObjectRef = CreateObject ("strApp.strObject" [, "strServerName"])
```

The *CreateObject* function returns the object instance that is to be used. The most important parameter for creating the object instance is *ProgID* (*strApp.strObject*, for example Scripting.FileSystemObject or Wscript.Shell). Using both object reference and point operator, the appropriate method can be found.

```
ObjectRef.ObjectMethod Parameter1, Parameter2
```

A special *Wscript* object library that comes with Windows Script Host allows access to the registry, file links, system folders, system properties, network drives, and network printers. The library can be invoked in the WSH Windows mode using *Wscript* and in the command-line mode using **Cscript**. Most of its objects are limited to the computer where the WSH script runs. This is why Windows Script Host is particularly suitable for logon scripts and standardized administration tasks.

The *Wscript* object has a number of properties and methods. These relate to Windows Script Host or the script being executed. Table 7-7 lists the most important methods in alphabetical order.

Table 7-7   The Most Important *Wscript* Object Methods

Methods	Description
AddWindowsPrinter	Adds printers
CreateObject	Creates an object and sets up system event processing
DisconnectObject	Disconnects an object from Windows Script Host
Echo	Displays the parameters in a window or in the command prompt
GetObject	Gets an automation object from a file
Sleep	Stops the script for the duration of n seconds
Sendkey	Controls older applications that do not have a COM interface by simulating keyboard input
StdIn/StdOut	Supports input and output via the command prompt
Quit	Ends the script execution

The Windows Script Host environment has additional COM-based libraries: *WshNetwork*, *WshShell*, and *WshController*. *WshNetwork* is used for network and printer connection access, while *WshShell* is suited for access to the desktop, environment variables, and the registry. The *Collection, Environment, Shortcut, Special-Folder*, and *UrlShortcut* objects are not directly available. Instead, they are supplied by the methods of the other objects. Special Windows Server 2003 objects allow access to the Active Directory system information (ADSI) and Windows Management Instrumentation (WMI). The properties and methods of all these objects represent the entire functionality of Windows Script Hosts. Expansions through additional COM automation objects are possible at any time.

Note   Using Windows Script Host requires solid knowledge of object-oriented programming. Normally, VBScript is the program language that is easiest to understand for beginners. JScript, on the other hand, is very well suited for administrators who are already familiar with Java, C, or C++. The objects available on the system, including all methods, can be analyzed with the OleView.exe tool.

Examples

In the following section, we will look at some WSH scripts that provide simple functions. Building on that information, new scripts can be created—for instance, for user logon, file administration, and adjusting the registry on a terminal server. In particular, we will highlight the possibility of performing very complex manipulations of character strings and modifying a user's desktop settings.

Environment Variables

The **Showvar.vbs** script is used for displaying all environment variables. The *shell* object is needed to determine the data, and the *echo* method is needed to display the result.

Listing 7-9: The Showvar.vbs WSH Script

```
'
' Display all environment variables
' Origin: Showvar.vbs, Microsoft Corporation
'
CRLF = Chr(13) & Chr(10)

Dim WSHShell
Set WSHShell = WScript.CreateObject("WScript.Shell")

Sub show_env(strText)
 WScript.Echo "WSH--Environment Variables", CRLF, strText
End Sub

intIndex = 0
strText = ""
intNumEnv = 0
For Each strEnv In WshShell.Environment("PROCESS")
 intIndex = intIndex + 1
 strText = strText & CRLF & Right(" " & intIndex, 4) & " " & strEnv
 intNumEnv = intNumEnv + 1
Next

If intNumEnv >= 1 Then Call show_env(strText)
```

This is an excellent example of showing how results are processed in a character string.

Network and Registry Access

Administrative scripts often need to access network resources. The *WshNetwork* object provides many methods for this purpose. The most popular one is mapping a shared network drive using *MapNetworkDrive*.

```
WSHNetwork.MapNetworkDrive strDrive, strShare
```

Another requirement for the administration of terminal server environments is the adequate access to the registry, including creating, modifying, and deleting registry keys and values. Listing 7-10 shows a sequence that creates and then deletes a key in the registry.

Listing 7-10: Creating and Deleting a Registry Key

```
Dim WSHShell
Set WSHShell = WScript.CreateObject("WScript.Shell")
WSHShell.RegWrite "HKCU\MyRegKey\", "Top level key"
WSHShell.RegWrite "HKCU\MyRegKey\Entry\", "Second level key"
WSHShell.RegWrite "HKCU\MyRegKey\Value", 1
WSHShell.RegWrite "HKCU\MyRegKey\Entry", 2, "REG_DWORD"
WSHShell.RegWrite "HKCU\MyRegKey\Entry\Value1", 3, "REG_BINARY"
WSHShell.RegDelete "HKCU\MyRegKey\Entry\Value1"
WSHShell.RegDelete "HKCU\MyRegKey\Entry\"
WSHShell.RegDelete "HKCU\MyRegKey\"
```

Verifying the Group

Finally, we pick up the KiXtart example introduced earlier to verify a user's group during logon. Depending on the group, the server containing the home directory is then assigned. This is a frequently performed action on terminal servers.

Listing 7-11: Verifying a Group

```
' Creation of required objects
Set WshNetwork = CreateObject("Wscript.Network")
Set UserObj = GetObject("WinNT://" & WshNetwork.UserDomain & "/"
& WshNetwork.UserName)

' Check group
For each GroupObj in UserObj.Groups
 select case GroupObj.Name
 case "marketing"
 WshNetwork.MapNetworkDrive "U:", "\\FILESRV1\home\" & WshNetwork.UserName
 case "development"
 WshNetwork.MapNetworkDrive "U:", "\\FILESRV2\home\" & WshNetwork.UserName
 End Select
Next
```

The same concept can be used to modify the user's terminal server settings. This example performs only two changes; the comments include additional options.

Listing 7-12: Changing a User's Terminal Server Settings

```
' Creation of required objects
Set WshNetwork = CreateObject("Wscript.Network")
Set UserObj = GetObject("WinNT://" & WshNetwork.UserDomain & "/"
& WshNetwork.UserName)

' Changing terminal server settings
UserObj.TerminalServicesInitialProgram =
"C:\Program Files\Internet Explorer\iexplore.exe"
UserObj.TerminalServicesWorkDirectory = "C:\windows"
' UserObj.ConnectClientDrivesAtLogon = 1
' UserObj.ConnectClientPrintersAtLogon = 1
' UserObj.DefaultToMainPrinter = 1
' UserObj.TerminalServicesProfilePath = "\\FILESRV1\profiles\" & WshNetwork.UserName
' UserObj.TerminalServicesHomeDirectory = "\\FILESRV2\home\" & WshNetwork.UserName
' UserObj.TerminalServicesHomeDrive = "U:"
```

```
' UserObj.AllowLogon = 1
' UserObj.MaxDisconnectionTime = 30
' UserObj.MaxConnectionTime = 0
' UserObj.MaxIdleTime = 120
' UserObj.BrokenConnectionAction = 0
' UserObj.ReconnectionAction = 0
' UserObj.EnableRemoteControl = 1
UserObj.SetInfo
```

It is easy to combine the script fragments introduced in this section with powerful tools. The diverse potential possibilities can, of course, only be hinted at in this book.

Using WMI

With Windows Management Instrumentation (WMI), Windows Server 2003 administrators have a powerful tool to perform many administrative tasks quickly and efficiently. WMI functions allow access to inventory data for hardware and software, system settings, and configuration data. WMI determines the required basic data from resources such as registry, drivers, file system, or Active Directory. Administrators can use WSH scripts to view and manipulate all information provided by WMI. Regrettably, these scripts are usually difficult to create and require a deeper understanding of object-oriented programming with Windows Script Host.

WMI from the Console

For the reasons described earlier, Windows Server 2003 comes with a new script interface, *Windows Management Instrumentation Command-line* (WMIC). WMIC uses aliases that provide primary WMI data. You do not necessarily need to have knowledge about WMI-specific concepts. Following are the key aliases for terminal servers:

- ***Printer*** Administration of printers using these methods: *AddPrinterConnection*, *CancelAllJobs*, *Pause*, *PrintTestPage*, *RenamePrinter*, *Reset*, *Resume*, *SetDefaultPrinter*, and *SetPowerState*.

- ***Process*** Process administration using these methods: *Create*, *GetOwner*, *SetPriority*, *Terminate*, and more.

- ***Rdaccount*** Permission management of terminal server connections using these methods: *Delete*, *ModifyAuditPermissions*, and *ModifyPermissions*.

- ***Rdnic*** Network adapter management using these methods: *SelectAllNetworkAdapters*, *SelectNetworkAdapterID*, and *SelectNetworkAdapterIP*.

- ***Rdpermissions*** Setting permissions for a certain terminal server connection using the methods *AddAccount* and *RestoreDefaults*.

- ***Rdtoggle*** The monitoring thread for terminal server connections is switched on or off remotely using the *SetAllowTSConnections* method.

■ ***Registry*** Registry management. Only the recommended registry size can be modified.

■ ***Service*** Windows services management using *StartService*, *StopService*, and other methods.

The following example shows a command-line string that uses WMIC to change the terminal server configuration. First, the terminal server connections are disabled. This works only if the administrator is logged on locally to the relevant terminal server.

```
WMIC rdtoggle where AllowTSConnections=1 call SetAllowTSConnections 0
```

If the administrator is logged on to a remote computer, it is slightly more difficult to call up the same WMIC functionality:

```
WMIC /Node:"<Servername>" /User:"<Domainname\Username>" /Password:"<Password>"
rdtoggle where AllowTSConnections=1 call SetAllowTSConnections 0
```

The following command lets the locally logged-on administrator view the current printer queue settings on a terminal server:

```
WMIC service where Name="Spooler"
```

After verifying the printer queue status, the administrator can stop the corresponding Windows service with this command:

```
WMIC service where Name="Spooler" call StopService
```

Finally, all priority 13 processes are displayed every five seconds in a list. This allows monitoring of certain system statuses.

```
WMIC process where Priority="13" list brief /every:5
```

Even these few examples show that the WMIC command-line extensions allow one to perform complex administrative tasks. Alternatively, it is possible to open a console using Wmic.exe without parameters. The console offers comprehensive help (using /?) for each alias and all methods. Furthermore, commands can be executed in the console, which leads to output results in a better format.

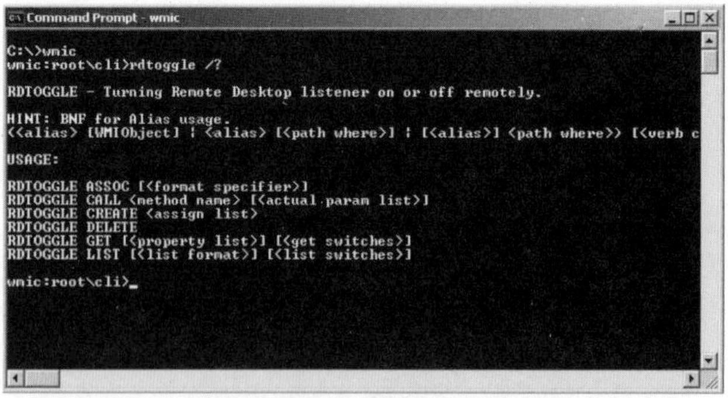

Figure 7-3 The WMIC console.

It is quite evident that WMIC allows local and remote access to the properties and configuration settings of terminal servers using the command line. The individual WMIC calls can, of course, also be used within batch-processing scripts.

> **Note**   To use the functionalities described in this section, you must be a member of the administrators group or have the corresponding Active Directory permissions.

WMI Properties and Methods

It is not easy to understand WMI properties and methods—not even with the possibilities offered by WMIC. WMI CIM Studio provides great help. It can be downloaded from the Microsoft Web server at *http://www.microsoft.com*. In the *Root\CIMV2* default namespace, WMI CIM Studio shows all of the details of all classes and instances within WMI. A search using Terminal or TS character strings leads to all relevant classes for terminal servers.

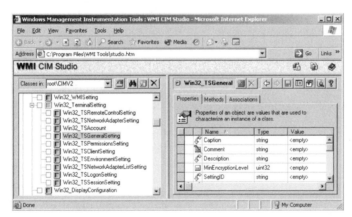

Figure 7-4   WMI CIM Studio shows properties and methods of the *Win32_TSGeneralSettings* class.

WMI queries, such as the one described earlier involving the WMIC console, are written in WMI Query Language (WQL). This language is reminiscent of SQL, which is normally used for database queries. Further information about WQL is located in the WMI area of the Platform SDK.

> **Note** Only if you are a member of the administrator group can you have full access to all WMI functions. Members of the local user group have only read access in the entire WMI namespace.

Logon Procedures Using the .NET Framework

Surely the most spectacular method to develop and execute logon procedures on Windows Server 2003 is by using the .NET Common Language Runtime. The .NET Framework can be used as a replacement or supplement for Windows Script Host and batch-processing scripts. So how does this work? So far, we have looked at the .NET Framework as a development platform for ASP.NET Web Forms, XML Web Services, and .NET Windows Forms applications. (See Chapter 5.) And how do the previously described script concepts fit into the picture? The answer is very simple: Executing a .NET Framework application using the command prompt is a special variant of a .NET Windows Forms application. .NET Windows Forms applications have their own namespaces in the .NET Class Library. This type of program is named Console Application and has a number of advantages over scripts:

- A .NET Console Application is compiled and thus offers advantages of speed over an interpreted script.

- The program logic is embedded in a compiled executable and thus helps to protect the developer's intellectual properties.

- It is not easy to change a .NET Console Application without a lot of effort if the source code is unavailable.

How is a console application for Windows Server 2003 created that can be used as logon procedure? Don't we need a development environment like Microsoft Visual Studio .NET? Naturally, Visual Studio .NET is the preferred development tool for this purpose, but the .NET Framework SDK will work, too.

The .NET Framework SDK can be downloaded for free in different languages from the Microsoft Web site on the Internet. The .NET Framework SDK contains compilers, debugger, help tools, libraries, examples, and a comprehensive documentation—thus, a complete development environment. Installing the .NET Framework SDK is very easy and does not even require selecting a target folder. It does not need to be installed on all target platforms; one development platform is sufficient. The .NET Common Language Runtime for executing the development results is automatically included in each installation of Windows Server 2003.

Listing 7-13 shows the simplest example of a console application written in Visual Basic .NET. And how do you develop a simple .NET console application? First of all, you need to enter the source code—for example, with the Notepad editor. The most difficult decision is which programming language to use. Options primarily include Visual Basic .NET and C#. Visual Basic .NET is easier for administrators who have some experience with Visual Basic. C#, however, is more appealing to C, C++, and Java programmers. The only difference between the two languages is their syntax. They use the exact same .NET library classes.

Listing 7-13: Console Application Written in Visual Basic .NET

```
Class ConsoleApplication
 Shared Sub main()
 System.Console.WriteLine(".NET Console Application")
 End Sub
End Class
```

Listing 7-14 shows the same simple console application written in C#:

Listing 7-14: Console Application Written in C#

```
Class ConsoleApplication {
 Static void Main() {
 System.Console.WriteLine(".NET Console Application")
 }
}
```

The .NET class library is quite extensive. For this reason, it is not easy in the beginning to gain an overview of the classes that are available. Fortunately, the .NET Framework comes with an excellent documentation, including help files and examples in SDK.

How can a sample application be compiled from source code to an executable program? The command-line compilers handle this task: Vbc.exe for Visual Basic .NET and Csc.exe for C#. In its simplest form, the compiler needs only the name of the source code as an argument. The classes used are included from the Mscorlib.dll default library. The compiler command line at the command prompt looks like this:

```
Vbc vbConsole.vb
```

If required classes are located in other library files, they can be referenced through additional compiler arguments. It is also possible to select an alternative output file name if you do not want the file name of the source code to be the name of the executable program. All these options can easily be determined by entering Vbc /? or Csc /?.

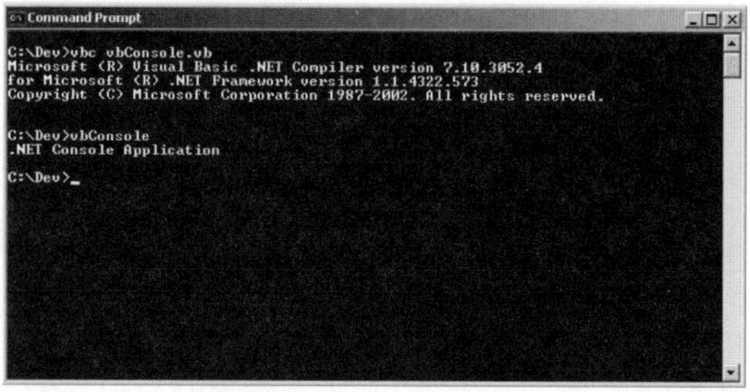

Figure 7-5   Compilation and execution of the vbConsole .NET console application using the .NET Framework SDK 1.1.

A compiled .NET console application is saved in an executable file that can be copied to any platform with the .NET runtime environment. So if you copy the console application to Windows Server 2003 with Terminal Services activated, you can call it up from a script during logon. This might look like this:

Listing 7-15: Logon Script Invoking a .NET Console Application

```
@echo off
echo Calling a .NET Console Application
ConsoleApp.exe
```

> **Tip**   It is, of course, also possible to reference the .NET console application in a suitable key in the registry to be automatically executed when certain system events occur. (See also Chapter 6.)

Now that we have laid the foundation for developing a .NET console application, we will briefly look at the namespaces and classes that are relevant for terminal servers.

Table 7-8 **.NET Framework Namespaces and Classes That Are Relevant for Terminal Servers**

Class	Description
System.IO.Directory	Provides static methods for creating, moving, and listing files in folders and subfolders.
System.IO.File	Provides static methods for creating, copying, deleting, moving, and opening files. This class also supports creating *FileStream* objects.
System.IO.FileStream	Allows synchronous and asynchronous read and write processes for files.
Microsoft.Win32.Registry	Supplies the basic registry keys that access values and subkeys in the registry.
Microsoft.Win32.RegistryKey	Provides a registry node at the key level. This class represents an encapsulation of the registry.

It would go beyond the scope of this book to describe the possibilities .NET console applications offer. Therefore, I would like to refer you to Charles Petzold's book, *Programming Microsoft Windows with C#* (Microsoft Press, 2002). He describes in detail many of the concepts touched on only briefly here, and much more.

Chapter 8

Security and Stability

A terminal server's security and stability are important to its success in a corporate environment. This chapter will therefore focus on security and shed some light on different security aspects. Naturally, a system configuration that has been optimized for security significantly contributes to system stability. For this reason, some procedures that enhance system stability will be described at the end of this chapter, as well. This chapter will enable you to do the following:

- Find out about the most important mechanisms for safe terminal server operation.

- Examine the different Microsoft Windows Server 2003 logon processes and options, especially as they relate to Terminal Services.

- Get acquainted with the powerful concepts that have been developed in the context of terminal server security policies, including both Local Computer Policy and Group Policies in an Active Directory domain.

- Discover how to secure access to a terminal server's desktop and applications in such a way that no unauthorized activities can take place, taking into account software restriction policies and how the AppSense Application Manager can assist you in this respect.

- Learn about the file system security options that exist to protect a terminal server, supported by SysInternal's File Monitor tool.

- Look at the connection options between a terminal server and its clients from a different angle—network security.

- See how modern concepts (such as firewalls, virtual private networks, public-key infrastructure, Internet protocol security, and smart cards) enable powerful access control on terminal servers at the network level.

- Find out about important relevant hardware components for configuring a stable terminal server environment.

Security Options

The initial Microsoft Windows NT developers had the chance to realize a completely new operating system. This gave them the opportunity to integrate several security options that they did not have to take into account previously. As the most recent successor with many extensions and improvements, Windows Server 2003 also benefits from this heritage. As a result, Windows Server 2003 includes many modern security concepts. Even though these concepts often exceed expectations, they do not limit the use of standard applications. Understanding the Windows security system is an important factor in properly configuring a terminal server environment. This is especially true for an environment in which users work with applications that are critical for the company.

Definition of Security

What exactly is security? Here, security means preventing people from any unauthorized access to a networked computer system and protecting the computer from both intentional and unintentional damages. This includes both local access and access via the network. An attacker or a negligent user normally changes or deletes data in a way that is not permitted on the target system by either modifying data directly or by changing it via an inserted program. Obviously, security in this chapter does not mean mirroring hard drives or regular data backups.

A number of mechanisms help ensure secure terminal server operation:

- **User identification, authentication**   Registered users must have an individual account and log on securely by providing a password. Alternatively, they can identify themselves with certificates (for example, on smart cards). All subsequent user action will then be linked to the logon information provided.

- **Authorization, access control**   A special system component controls which users have access to what data. This includes the file system, registry database, logical drives, and printers. The system uses access control lists (ACLs) to manage the access to each data object. Each data object has an owner who created the object and who can modify the ACL unrestrictedly.

- **Encryption**   Encryption options involve both local data and data streams flowing through the connected network. The relevant encryption algorithms ensure that all information is kept confidential and remains intact (integrity).

- **User permissions and administration**   To keep the system running, a number of administrative tasks must be performed. For this reason, a group of users (administrators) exists that has privileged system access. All other users have restricted permissions so that they cannot modify system settings.

- **Monitoring using a system protocol**   Users and administrators can make mistakes, even with the best intentions. A system instance logs many predefined activities to allow administrators to monitor the entire system and to conduct subsequent analyses. To detect and trace attacks by members of the administrator group, these audits should be conducted by others (internal auditors). Monitoring makes little sense if administrators can remove the traces of their forbidden actions from the system protocol.

Logon Procedures

The logon procedure on a terminal server client is basically the same as the procedure under Windows XP. However, a network connection between client and server is involved, and this can be critical from a security perspective. We will now take a closer look at some terminal server logon basics to gain a better understanding of the entire procedure.

Domains and the Secure Path

Logging on to a computer running Microsoft Windows XP or the local Windows Server 2003 console requires three keys to be pressed simultaneously: Ctrl, Alt, and Del. This keyboard combination activates a "secure path" that leads to the logon screen. At the logon screen, the user is asked to enter an account (= user name), password, and possibly a domain. The predefined behavior upon activation of this screen is very difficult to change. This makes it much harder for *Trojan horses* to be inserted—that is, programs that spy for passwords. Normally, one operating system cannot imitate the response of another operating system when the Ctrl, Alt, and Del key combination is entered and an Intel x86-compatible processor is used.

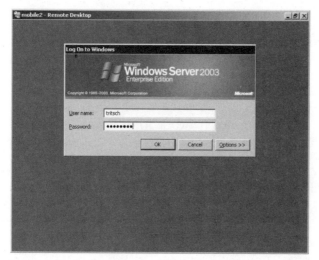

Figure 8-1 Logon screen for logon to a terminal server from a Terminal Services client.

Using terminal server clients in combination with terminal servers is, of course, problematic. The different client operating systems respond in different ways to the usual logon key combination. If the clients are Windows systems, the key combination will call up the local logon screen.

Starting a new Windows Server 2003 terminal server session naturally requires the same logon procedure as the local console session. This is why it is necessary to find an alternative for the secure path and the security screen. As a consequence, connecting to a terminal server leads directly to the logon screen in most cases.

> **Note** Windows Server 2003 now allows the use of smart cards for Terminal Services. If you use a Terminal Services client that supports this option (for example, under Windows XP), the corresponding logon data is transmitted to the terminal server via a virtual RDP channel and the user credentials are evaluated there. This is how authentication for terminal server environments becomes more secure.

The Security Screen

After logging on, users interact with their individual work environment until they log off or want to change a security-relevant feature of the environment. The secure path must always be available for activation from the client and must always lead to a security screen. For this reason, alternative key combinations, menu items, or special client programs are permitted.

Figure 8-2   On a Terminal Services client, the secure path is available through a special option in the Start menu (bottom right). This entry is visible only on the client, not on the local console session.

The security screen is displayed within the trusted context of a special session that does not permit any connection to other processes. The screen therefore allows a number of security-relevant actions with low risk of unauthorized access:

- Changing the password. The password can be either for a local or a network-based user account.

- Password-protected locking of the screen and all input devices. The secure path unlocks the screen and devices.

- Logging off the current user.

- Shutting down the computer. The user must have the corresponding permissions.

- Observing and modifying all processes the user works with.

> **Note**   Only an administrator can modify, to a limited extent, the appearance and responses of the security screen that receives the logon information. Most functions are, however, predetermined by the system.

The appearance and functionality of the security system are determined by a system component called graphical identification and authentication (GINA) DLL. The GINA DLL communicates with the security monitor, implements network access to user accounts, and handles password encryption. Msgina.dll, the standard GINA component, is, in part, freely available as source code so that relevant security algorithms can be verified independently. Many third-party system extensions that are relevant to the Windows Server 2003 security system and are often used with terminal servers use a modified GINA DLL. GINA DLL extensions can contain functions (such as single sign-on) to other systems or special authentication devices (such as fingerprint readers).

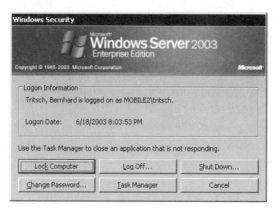

Figure 8-3 The Windows security dialog box on a Terminal Services client. Depending on permissions, the user will or will not be able to shut down the computer.

> **Tip** If security concerns exist when using alternative logon components that have been installed on the terminal servers at a later time, it is possible to enforce the use of the default Windows authentication through the Terminal Services Configuration tool.

> **Important** The Shut Down... button of the security screen holds unexpected functions in terminal services sessions, including, for instance, disconnecting the session or user logoff. The latter can, of course, also be done using the Log Off... button. However, a user who is not member of a group with the relevant permissions cannot shut down the system. The same is true for the Shut Down option in the Start menu. (See Figure 8-2.) The significance of this button in the security screen and the Start menu is therefore quite confusing for many users and will need to be explained before terminal server technology can be rolled out in an enterprise.

Local Logon Procedures and User Accounts

At the beginning of a local Windows Server 2003 logon procedure, the password entered together with the user name is encrypted and compared to a reference saved on the system. After successful authentication, the WinLogon process creates an access token based on the user's security identification (SID). Subsequently, an access control list is generated that has the same structure as the SID. WinLogon derives the access token from the security subsystem, which, in turn, is dependent on the Security Account Manager (SAM). As soon as the user is authenticated, WinLogon hands over the ACL and the access token to the Win32 subsystem.

Naturally, the Security Account Manager for local user accounts is an especially protected area of the registry. The security settings are basically reduced to two attributes: *Read* and *Full Access*. However, full access is granted only to the system; even administrators have very limited options. All other users and groups are totally excluded.

By taking a closer look at the extended security attributes of the registry, you will recognize the SAM database access options:

- *Query value*   system only
- *Set value*   system only
- *Create subkey*   system only
- *Enumerate subkey*   system only
- *Notify*   system only
- *Create link*   system only
- *Delete*   system only
- *Write DAC* **(access control list)**   system and administrators
- *Write owner*   system only
- *Read control*   system and administrators

Remote Logon

For logon via the network, the password is conveyed via multiple-encrypted transmission. Single encryption would allow the password to be intercepted and reused and is also a rather outdated method. Other very powerful encryption methods exist. One of the older methods is called *Challenge-Response*, formerly used for Windows NT and for the historic LAN Manager. The server transmits a single key to the client where a user requests authentication. With this key, the client creates a hash value of the password after default encryption and transmits it to the server, which waits for the hash value for a preset time. The server then creates the same hash value of the encrypted local password and compares the two. If they are identical, authentication is successful. Using the single key precludes the same (encrypted) password character string from being transmitted more than once over the network.

> **Note**   A *hash value* is a cryptographic fingerprint that unmistakably identifies a character string or file. It is impossible to reconstruct the original data from the hash value.

With the Active Directory came a much more powerful remote logon method: *Kerberos*. Kerberos is based on Internet RFC 1510, with the corresponding Kerberos service (Kdcsvc.dll) executed on a domain controller under Windows 2000 Server or Windows Server 2003. Kerberos uses TCP/IP port 88 for communication between clients and domain controller.

Kerberos is based on what is commonly called the *ticketing method*. A ticket master on a domain controller issues a user-specific ticket upon logon. This ticket is then used for authentication and authorization purposes on other computer nodes involved. The initial transmission of user name and password is similar to the Challenge-Response method. However, with Kerberos, information is not aligned with the Security Account Manager but with the user objects in the Active Directory. The instance that handles this process is the Active Directory Server (\Windows\System32\Ntdsa.dll) located on the domain controller.

After the user is authenticated, the local system verifies the user's access permission with the help of local policies. If the user does not have the necessary permissions for interactive logon, the process is aborted and a corresponding system message is displayed. If access is granted, the Lsass process adds all necessary security information and privileges to the user's access ID.

This is the point at which the user session is created (this is also true for local logon). In the registry, the Winlogon process reads the value from the HKLM \SOFTWARE\Microsoft\Windows NT\Current Version\Winlogon\Userinit key and starts all programs enumerated in this character string. The character string usually contains several executable files that are separated by commas. One of the default programs is Userinit.exe. This program deals with loading the user profile and generating the process that is located in HKLM\SOFTWARE\Microsoft\Windows NT \Current Version\Winlogon\Shell. In a standard environment, this would be Explorer.exe.

> **Note**   In terminal server environments, the value in the Shell key can be modified to prevent users from having full access to the desktop. This can apply to both clients and terminal servers. An alternative to Explorer.exe could, for instance, be Iexplore.exe. In this case, Internet Explorer would start instead of the regular desktop and all applications would need to be launched from a specially prepared HTML page.

However, there is one basic problem concerning all authentication procedures when using a terminal server. The user does not sit at the server hardware console and use the applications there; the applications are accessed through a Terminal Services client. The communication between client and terminal server always harbors a potential security risk. Communication does not necessarily include security-relevant data such as passwords in plain text. Rather, it transmits only the graphical representation of this information (for example, asterisks instead of the password) or the corresponding keyboard strokes that are encrypted before transmission. Only if the password is saved on the client and used for logging on to the terminal server is it possible to find the corresponding character strings in the data stream. For this reason, most communications protocols for connecting clients to a terminal server contain encryption options for the data stream. On the terminal server itself, the mechanisms described in this paragraph apply again when the terminal server accesses its local user database or a remote domain controller.

If, after successful authentication, the user wants to access an object—that is, a file, a directory, an application, and so on—the security subsystem requests the user's access token, verifies the relevant values, and supplies an object handle. The object handle allows the user to manipulate the object in line with his or her permissions.

Secondary Logon

In addition to the primary Windows Server 2003 logon methods described so far, there is another option of logging on to a remote system via the network. In contrast to terminal server sessions, secondary logon does not have the purpose of working interactively with the remote computer. Instead, this secondary logon usually serves to access shared resources of a remote server. If both computers involved are in the same domain and the network is accessed within the context of a domain user, logon takes place in the background, invisible to the user. Further access is regulated by the security structure based on the Active Directory. This type of access is crucial for terminal servers when it comes to connecting file or print servers.

Smart Cards

Smart cards are considered one of the most secure methods for logging on to a computer. This is because of their properties including a combination of hardware and a personal identification number (PIN). Unlike logging on with a user name and password, an unauthorized person must have the smart card and the PIN in their possession before he or she can initiate a successful attack on a user account.

The software components of an RDP client are able to transmit the information on a smart card to a terminal server for logon. This requires the client and the security policies to allow smart card information to be redirected to the terminal server.

Security Policies for Terminal Servers

Local security policies or certain areas of the Group Policies are used to configure the security settings on an individual computer. These settings include password policy, account lockout policy, audit policy, IP security policies, user permission assignment, software restriction policies, and other security options. The local security settings can be found in the Start menu under Administration\Local Security Policy, and they exist only on computers that are not domain controllers. If the computer is part of a domain, these settings might be overwritten by Group Policies. (See also Chapter 4.)

Note If you call up the local Group Policies with Gpedit.msc, the Computer Configuration\Windows Settings\Security Settings corresponds to the Local Security Policy tool that can be opened under Start\Administrative Tools\Local Security Policy.

Naturally, the Terminal Services-specific settings of the security policies play an important role for terminal servers and their users. This is why we will take a closer look at them now.

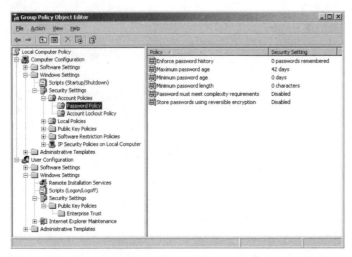

Figure 8-4   Security settings through the Local Computer Policy.

Account Policies

The account policy security settings apply to user accounts and contain attributes in the following categories:

- **Password Policy**   Determines settings for passwords for local or domain accounts. Comprises password history, complexity requirements for passwords, encryption options, maximum and minimum password age, and minimum password length.

- **Account Lockout Policy**   Determines conditions under which a local or a domain account can be locked to certain users. Comprises the number of invalid logons after which the account is locked, the duration an account is locked, and the option for resetting the account lockout counter after a preset time has passed.

- **Kerberos Policy**   Determines Kerberos-related domain account settings. Comprises, for instance, the validity period of Kerberos tickets.

Of course, no one can establish a universally applicable standard for all kinds of terminal server environments. However, it has proven beneficial to enforce a minimum password length of six characters and to require compliance with password complexity. This is done when enabling the Password by following the complexity requirements policy found under Password Policy. It is also recommended that the Account lockout threshold in the Account Lockout Policy be increased from 0 to 3. This also enables you to set the Account lockout duration and Reset account lockout counter. The recommended default value is 30 minutes for both settings.

> **Note**   To prevent a successful attack on the predefined Administrator account, it has proven effective to rename the account, for example, by using the security options. Alternatively, you can create a new system administration account with a different name. The Administrator account is then added to the Guests group and removed from the Administrators group. Then, even if a hacker is still able to guess the account password, little damage can be done. Additionally, since Windows Server 2003, another global system security default setting ensures that a user or administrator cannot open a terminal server session with a blank password, unless that user is physically at the server hardware console.

Local Policies

Local computer policies allow you to set audit policies, assign user permissions, and select advanced security options. Each of these areas has a direct impact on the terminal server's security settings.

Audit Policy

One of the central functions in a network operating system is monitoring access to servers and controlling server status through the Event Viewer. On a terminal server, this includes, in particular, user actions, system errors, and system load.

The audit policies are therefore vital to system security. They can be determined to be either local or central settings. The most important policies include monitoring logon events, logon attempts, use of permissions, and policy changes. Only for very secure systems is it necessary to also control access to the Active Directory and objects (such as files).

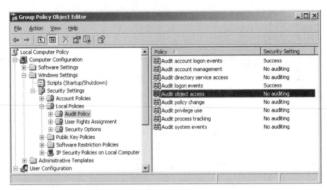

Figure 8-5   Default audit policy settings.

It is relatively easy to configure the monitoring functions within the policies. The individual functions can be adapted in the local or central security settings. For example, Figure 8-6 shows the configuration for monitoring object access attempts.

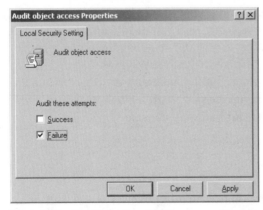

Figure 8-6   Modifying the object access attempt policy.

So what objects are monitored with this configuration? Basically, this setting involves files that can be monitored for access by predefined users or groups. If, however, a simple change in the audit policy results in monitoring all file accesses on a terminal server, the system will quickly reach its performance limits. For this reason, it is possible to precisely identify the directories and files to be monitored.

To configure a directory or file for monitoring purposes, you must first select the object in Explorer. Open the Security tab from the Properties directory or file. On the Security tab, activate the Advanced button to get to the Auditing tab. Continue to navigate by activating the Add... button. In the next dialog box, select a user or group. Click **OK** to get to the last dialog box, where you choose the monitoring entries. After these configuration tasks (which might take some time), the monitoring activities will be saved in the security log file of the Event Viewer.

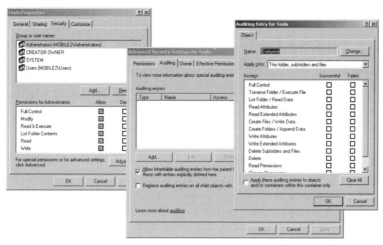

Figure 8-7   Determining a monitoring entry for a directory. There is a choice of two options: successful and failed access attempts.

In addition to directory and file accesses, a terminal server Event Viewer indicates the monitoring results of many functions and activities. For this, the auditing configuration needs to be linked to individual users or groups. It is recommended that the following list of monitoring functions be logged for all users of a secured terminal server.

- **Audit logon events**   Events that occur when a user logs on. This is where successful and failed attempts should be recorded.

- **Audit account logon events**   User logon action. This is where successful and failed attempts should be recorded.

- **Audit policy change**   Changes to the security settings. This is where only failed attempts should be recorded.

The Event Viewer's security log displays the result of the configuration. The other two Event Viewer functions, Application and System, allow further analysis of the terminal server environment. However, these logs can be viewed by quite a large user group and therefore allow individual configuration to a very limited extent only. The specific system log messages are explained in Chapter 4.

> **Note** A terminal server in a production environment should always have a minimum of extended security functions, as described earlier. Otherwise, the danger of misuse going unnoticed by administrators is too great.

The function of monitoring the system is assigned to the local group of administrators. Nevertheless, the last action of an administrator is always logged and stored for controlling and security purposes. This means that even if an administrator deleted all logged control data, this act would be the first entry in a new log.

Assigning User Permissions

This area of the security settings includes the tasks that a user on a computer system or in a domain can be permitted to perform—for example, logon permissions, saving files and folders, or shutting down the server. The relevant permissions can be assigned to groups or user accounts. However, it is recommended that only groups have the option to assign permissions.

Particularly on terminal servers, logon using Terminal Services merits special attention. The default setting allows only users who are members of the administrator group or the local group of Remote Desktop users to log on through Terminal Services. There is also an option to exclude certain users or groups from logging on using Terminal Services. Changing these settings might conflict with the Terminal Services configuration and its settings for RDP client connections (as discussed in Chapter 2), which could, of course, lead to unexpected results.

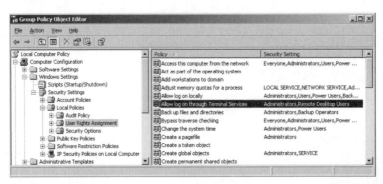

Figure 8-8 Assigning user permissions for logon using Terminal Services.

Security Options

The security options comprise a wide range of settings that are relevant for the security of domain controllers, domain members, devices, logon options, accounts, networks, and system objects. The following policies are of special interest when working with terminal servers:

- **Devices**   Prevent users from installing printer drivers: This security setting is very important for terminal servers because it allows only administrators and power users to install printer drivers on the local computer. This option is enabled by default.

- **Interactive logon**   Do not display last user name: When this policy is enabled, the name of the user who successfully logged on last does not appear in the Windows logon dialog box.

- **Interactive logon**   Require smart card: When this security setting is enabled, all users must have a smart card to log on.

- **Accounts**   Rename administrator account: This security setting determines whether a new account name is assigned to the administrator account's security ID (SID).

- **Accounts**   Limit local account use of blank passwords to console logon only: When this security setting is enabled, users with a blank password can log on only to the local console, but not via a Terminal Services session. In principle, blank passwords should not be allowed on terminal servers. (See earlier in the chapter.)

- **Network access**   Remotely accessible registry paths and subpaths: This is where, on a terminal server, the specific areas of the registry are released for remote access, regardless of the users and groups enumerated on the access control list.

Naturally, all other security options should be examined for their suitability in specific terminal server environments.

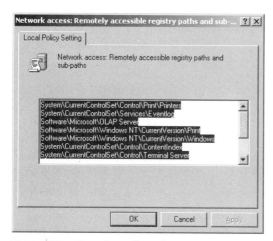

Figure 8-9   Security options for remote access to registry paths.

Desktop and Application Security

Administrators are known to say, "My terminal servers are safe and stable until users log on." Well, terminal servers do derive their right to exist from the fact that users log on and execute applications on them. How can desktop and application access be secured so that no unauthorized activities can be performed without impeding all other, permitted activities?

One big problem affecting terminal server stability is the fact that users with access to the Internet and e-mail also have the opportunity to download undesirable software. Undesirable software includes, for example, hacking tools, all sorts of games, animated screen savers, executable viruses, and many Microsoft Visual Basic scripts.

We should not, of course, forget that users might have the potential to install undesirable software locally. It is very difficult for a terminal server running with default settings to control downloads off redirected CD-ROMs, floppy disks, USB sticks, or digital cameras. A user who needs access to a CD-ROM drive for a supplier database can also use this method to install and use any application.

If the user installs illegal tools this way, he or she might obtain access to sensitive data. Unauthorized access often occurs through software that exploits the known weak spots of a terminal server. For instance, it is possible for password recovery and network monitoring tools to allow access to other users' IDs. Users who work with such tools can then pass themselves off as other users or can try to obtain extended permissions. The Internet makes it very easy for even non-administrator users to obtain these tools or permissions.

Securing the Desktop

Basically, there are two ways of securing the desktop:

- Through extensive limitation of all desktop functions that users could misuse for illegal activities.

- By replacing or expanding Explorer.exe as a desktop process, where an additional communication to the Terminal Services clients could be initiated.

The first method is easy to implement using Group Policies. The administrative templates for the user configuration allow adequate control of all objects on the desktop, in the Start menu, task bar, and system control, and on the system. The latter even contains preset buttons on the security screen that can be opened only via the secure path.

> **Note**   It is recommended that limiting the desktop functions through policies be performed through an organizational unit in the Active Directory, and through the local security policies only by exception.

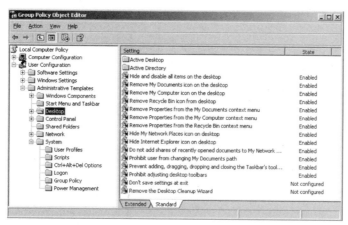

Figure 8-10   Limiting desktop objects through a local computer policy.

The problem with this method is that removing icons from the desktop or eliminating individual menu items from the Start menu does not prevent the users from opening the corresponding programs or elements in another way.

The second method described in the preceding paragraphs changes a value in the HKLM\SOFTWARE\Microsoft\Windows NT\Current Version\Winlogon\Shell registry key to start an alternative desktop process—for example, Internet Explorer with a specific start page containing all required applications. Or a self-developed program with the only task of providing users with secure access to their applications. This way, all unnecessary functions are no longer available. Another option is to extend the client platform functions to obtain the desired results.

However, the problem with this method is that users no longer access the applications via the interface they are used to. Furthermore, the seamless integration of user interface and terminal server operating system is lost. A combination of both methods is, of course, possible. This would require special policies and programs to modify desktop behavior.

> **Note** On the commercial market, special products address this problem in different ways. Solutions include, for example, desktop2001 by triCerat (*http://www.tricerat.com*), SoftGrid for Terminal Servers by Softricity (*http://www.softricity.com*), PowerFuse by Real Enterprise Solutions (*http://www.respowerfuse.com*), and EOL Desktop Manager by Emergent Online (*http://www.go-eol.com*).

Software Restriction Policies

A significantly more powerful method of securing a terminal server is controlling application execution. This function is provided by the Windows Server 2003 software restriction policies. These include not only executable programs, but also macros and scripts.

Setup

An administrator sets a software restriction policy in the local computer policies or in an organizational unit in the Active Directory. The software restriction policy is then enabled by activating the policy. If the policy applies to the computer, it is executed during the next system start. If the policy applies to the users, it becomes active during the next logon procedure. If a user then starts a program or script, the operating system or Script Host checks the relevant policy and ensures that the policy is executed.

If no software restriction policies are defined, the relevant Group Policies object appears as shown in Figure 8-10.

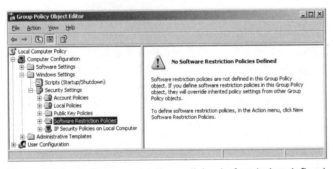

Figure 8-11 Software restriction policies before being defined.

If a new policy is defined via the Action\New Software Restriction Policy menu item, it allows controlled execution of unknown or suspect software. Basically, the administrator can choose between two software restriction security levels:

- If the administrator knows all applications to be started on the terminal server, he or she can list them on a positive list. Then it will not be possible to execute any other applications on the terminal server.

- If the administrator wants to prevent certain applications from being executed, he or she writes up a negative list.

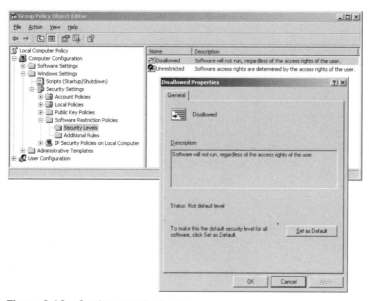

Figure 8-12   Setting security levels.

When drawing up a positive list, the basic question an administrator should ask first is: what applications do the users really need? Furthermore, should all users have access to all applications installed? Should there be exceptions for certain users or applications? Even these simple questions demonstrate that configuring software restriction policies is an enormously complex and time-consuming task.

Important   Software restriction policies apply only to conventional Windows applications—not to drivers, to programs within the system account context, to macros in Office documents, or to .NET Framework applications. The policies become effective only after the users log off and then log back on to their computers, thus updating the policy settings.

Configuration

Software restriction policies are relatively easy to configure. Using the *Enforce* object type, select the software and users to which the policies will apply. In addition to executable files, libraries (that is, DLLs) can be included in or excluded from the policies. However, including DLLs could result in significantly higher configuration effort and increased system load because the DLLs need to be verified during system start.

An administrator might want to prevent certain programs from being run. However, the administrator himself might need to retain permission to execute all programs. For this reason, software restriction policies can be applied to all users except the local administrator, if required. If the software restriction policies are created in an Active Directory Group Policy object, this should not apply to an object containing the administrator group.

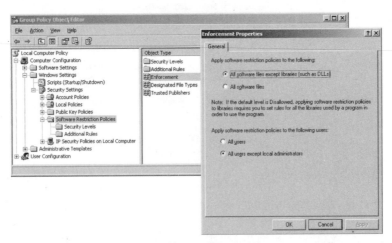

Figure 8-13 Configuring the software files and the corresponding users to be monitored.

It is now possible to determine the rules for limiting program execution. This is done using the Additional Rules option. This option already contains four default rules. Four methods exist to describe the application files in detail:

1. **Hash** This rule creates a cryptographical fingerprint of the file to clearly identify it. The hash algorithms used are MD5 or SHA-1 and the file name is not included in the hash value. Only if the file remains unchanged can it be executed by a user from any location in the file system—even under a different name.

2. **Certificate** Scripts or ActiveX controls with a valid certificate can be permitted through an individual rule. It is possible to prevent all other scripts and ActiveX controls from running.

3. **Path**   A rule based on the path to an executable file can contain either the folder only, or the program name as well. If the rule contains only the folder path, all programs in that folder and all its subfolders are affected. Environment variables and wildcards can also be part of the path name. Paths saved in the registry can be used for such a rule. The registry path format looks like this: %[Registry Hive]\[Registry Key]\[Value Name]%. All registry values involved must be either REG_SZ or REG_EXPAND_SZ. Furthermore, the abbreviations HKLM or HKCU are not allowed, only their real names: HKEY_LOCAL_MACHINE or HKEY_CURRENT_USER.

4. **Zone**   A rule can identify software by its Internet Explorer zone. These zones include Internet, local intranet, restricted sites, trusted sites, and local computer. However, this rule is currently used for only MSI installation packages.

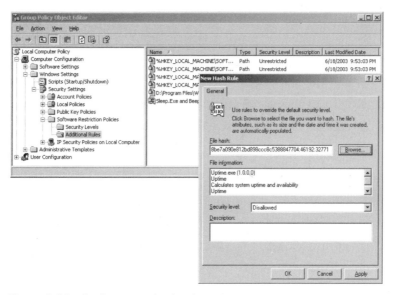

Figure 8-14   Setting a new hash rule.

Although each rule is quite easy to create in itself, one should not underestimate the complexity involved in securing a terminal server with this approach. For terminal server environments, it is particularly recommended that the software restriction policies be configured for a domain environment or organizational unit in the Active Directory and not for the local computer.

Several other problems exist with software restriction policies in larger environments:

■ It is not easy to find out which users might launch which applications. There is no tool that can help an administrator in this case. Many companies have software that is supposed to be used by only a few select persons. Reasons could include high license costs. However, it is quite difficult to define exceptions using the software restriction policies. The administrator has to create a new software restriction policy within the Active Directory and assign it to the relevant persons. This would have to be done for each user or application exception, which would significantly increase configuration and maintenance relating to these policies.

■ Other rules—for instance, applying a software restriction policy via a hash value—are equally problematic. If the administrator installs a service pack or hotfix for an application or the operating system, the hash values for these files will most probably change. The administrator has to redefine the hash for all updated applications to which the software restriction policies apply so that the users can work with the updated applications.

■ It is impossible to customize the message window. This means that the contents of this message window is fixed and cannot be changed.

■ A software restriction policy cannot recognize that a user is simply trying to open a self-extracting ZIP file. If a program is started in this way, the software restriction policy might prevent execution of the program. Complete control by administrators is therefore impossible because ZIP files can have different names and content. The software restriction policy is not able to register this and therefore prevents the files from being extracted.

■ Software restriction policies allow an administrator to search for relevant hints using only entries in the local Event Viewer of the terminal server being protected. There is no way to evaluate these events centrally.

Despite these limitations, which need to be viewed according to the target platform concerned, software restriction policies comprise a powerful tool for controlling applications, in particular on terminal servers. As soon as the software restriction policies have been established, the user receives a dialog box containing a default message after an attempt to start an application has been blocked.

Figure 8-15   Software restriction policies default message.

> **Important**   If the use of applications has been restricted through relevant
> policies, it is recommended that all scripts and programs be taken into
> account that might be needed for system start or user logon. If these are
> blocked, the system might not be able to function.

Security for .NET Framework Applications

Software restriction policies do not work for .NET Framework applications. On the contrary, the .NET Common Language Runtime introduces a new security model that is based on the evidence of the application code loaded on the system. In this way, the model called *Code Access Security* complements the operating system security mechanisms.

The .NET Framework application code features are linked to the relevant assembly. The security settings are aligned with the information on who published the assembly and where the assembly comes from. Examples of assembly features include the application directory, the *strong name*, an X.509 certificate, or the URL.

If the security settings of a .NET Framework application are to extend beyond the usual file options with their user and group assignments, they need to be established via the features described in the preceding paragraph. This is performed either directly in the code, through the functions invoked, or through the Common Language Runtime. The relevant runtime security policies apply to the organization, the computer, the users, or the application domain (that is, the code).

The basic security policy settings for accessing the code of .NET Framework applications in Windows Server 2003 are established using the Microsoft .NET Framework 1.1 Configuration, which is located under the Start\Administration menu item. However, describing all possibilities in this respect would go beyond the scope of this book.

AppSense Application Manager

AppSense Technologies Ltd. specializes in developing system tools for controlling security and resource capacity on Windows-based PCs. For instance, the AppSense Application Manager prevents undesirable applications from being launched. This tool is therefore an alternative to the software restriction policies. AppSense Application Manager uses *kernel-level filters* that control each program request. Unlike the software restriction policies, the Application Manager does not only verify the start path, name, hash, or signature of an application.

> **Note** The AppSense Application Manager principally addresses the same issue as the software restriction policies that we described earlier. However, the two technologies differ significantly when it comes to solutions. For this reason, the AppSense Application Manager can be considered to supplement the basic Windows Server 2003 functions for comprehensive terminal server installations.

Trusted Ownership Checking

The Application Manager builds on a technology called *trusted ownership checking*. If this mechanism is established on Windows Server 2003, a user can execute applications only if he or she is a *trusted owner* of this application. In principle, local administrators and the system account are always recognized as trusted owners. The list of trusted owners is freely configurable in the Application Manager. Even in its default settings, the Application Manager prevents execution of all applications that do not belong to an administrator. This function alone controls execution of undesirable applications very efficiently.

With the Application Manager, terminal server administrators are not required to make any changes to the security configuration when they install service packs or new software versions. This is because these later installations are still performed within the administrator accounts. For this reason, users can start working with the updated applications immediately.

But what does access restriction look like for critical tools that are included in the Windows Server 2003 standard scope? The operating system is always installed by an administrator; this means that the system tools are marked as being installed by a trusted owner. Without any further configuration, all users can therefore start the system tools. With the Application Manager, however, you can block even those applications with a trusted owner. The administrator can determine these and other settings using the Application Manager management console. In this way, filter rules are established that allow only predetermined users or groups to start applications and tools.

If a user attempts to start a restricted application, the Application Manager stops the attempt and displays a message that the administrator has defined through variables.

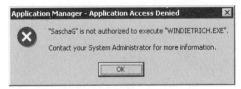

Figure 8-16 AppSense Application Manager message box.

Installation and Configuration

So how can these complex application access rules be distributed to any number of servers? The solution is similar to the Group Policies concept: Central server processes manage the configuration information that can be edited via a special administration console. Client elements that communicate with the server processes apply the filter rules in line with the central configuration.

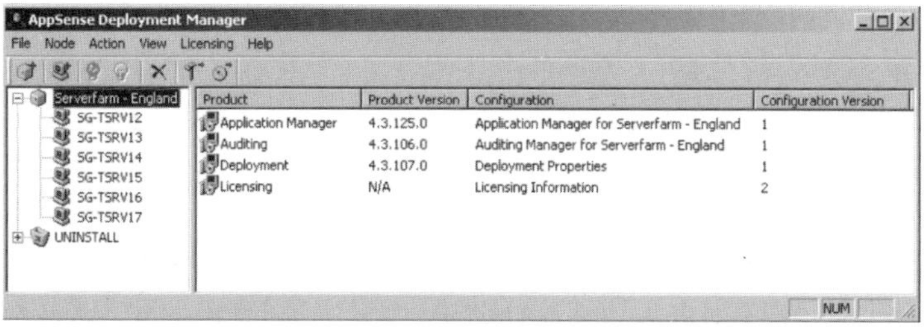

Figure 8-17   The AppSense Deployment Manager with six terminal servers in one node.

To simplify central distribution and administration of all AppSense products in corporate environments, an administrator works with the AppSense Deployment Subsystem. In addition to the tasks mentioned, this subsystem also handles license administration. The Deployment Subsystem includes these components:

- The *Deployment Server* provides the required client software and manages configurations.

- With the *Deployment Manager*, an administrator logically combines terminal servers into a node. All terminal servers in one node get assigned the appropriate AppSense software defined at the node level, including the configuration. This way, it is relatively easy for the administrator to distribute updated configurations to the terminal servers. The administrator configures the update cycle as well.

- *Deployment Agents* are installed with the help of Deployment Server components on all terminal servers (= AppSense clients) to be controlled. A Deployment Agent's tasks include downloading, installing, and updating client software and the corresponding configurations.

- All configuration data is saved in a central *database*.

A wizard controls the installation of the AppSense Application Manager on a server. The Application Manager is then available within the Deployment Manager as an additional component. The application access filter rules are configured by using a different management console. The main window of the Application Manager console consists of two parts. On the left, there is a list of the individual administration objects to be selected. On the right, are the relevant option windows for the configuration.

When installed, the Application Manager allows a number of configuration adjustments to administration objects, any of which might change their standard behavior:

- **Trusted owners** Defines the application owners that the Application Manager trusts. Two trusted owners are already listed by default: the system account and the local administrators group. The group of trusted owners is extendible.

- **User/group overrides** Application Manager restrictions do not apply to the users listed here. Users listed in this administration object may execute any application. By default, this administration object contains only the group of local administrators. The administrator can add new users or groups to the list.

- **Prohibited items (applications and directories)** This configuration object is needed to lock applications for all users. The administrator can explicitly add to the list the applications to be locked, or even entire directories. This function can be activated for both system tools and conventional end-user applications.

Figure 8-18 The AppSense Application Manager.

With the Application Manager objects described in the preceding list, an administrator is able to lock many applications for all users. The *Exceptions* administration object enables the administrator to grant certain users or groups access to individual applications. *Exceptions* includes several options:

- **Users** Only listed users can work with the application configured here.

- **User groups** Only users who belong to the listed groups can work with the application configured here.

- **Clients** Users can execute this application only if they log on to the terminal server from the client listed here.

In addition to the filter rules described so far, there are more useful options for terminal servers, including, for instance, limiting the number of application launches by a user. Or establishing a time during which applications may be used. Even more important is the validation of application files invoked indirectly—in particular, ActiveX controls, screen savers, Microsoft Windows Installer MSI packages, Windows Script Host script files, .reg files for registry changes, the Cmd.exe command interpreter, and self-extracting ZIP files. The owner of the indirectly invoked application files plays a key role here. All this results in improved control of terminal server environment security.

Secure File Access

The NTFS file system is superior to many other file systems due to its security concepts. For this reason, it is extremely important that a terminal server's essential hard drive partitions be formatted with NTFS. However, after installation of the terminal server and its applications, it is possible that not all relevant settings are adjusted for secure operation. This is why an administrator should know as much as possible about file system options if the environment requires advanced security.

An important precondition for securing the file system (and the registry database) is the selection of the Full Security permission compatibility setting in the Terminal Services Configuration Server Settings. Only if this option is selected do the terminal server users have the same limited permissions as the Users group members. This precludes access to certain registry areas and sensitive system files, even after a simple standard installation without any additional security configuration.

> **Note**   Encrypting a terminal server's file system using Encrypted File System is possible, but not common practice. This is because user data is usually saved in special file servers rather than on the terminal server. Furthermore, the existing processors require significant amounts of additional system resources for ongoing encryption and deciphering of local data.

File and Folder Properties

When using the NTFS file system, a file's properties include size, owner, and access permissions. The same is true for directories, where the basic permission is determined by a number of attributes.

The following file permissions exist: Full Control, Modify, Read & Execute, Read, and Write. The individual permissions each include one logical group of restricting permissions. The following table lists file permissions and the corresponding restrictions.

Table 8-1   Permission Groups and Corresponding Restricting Permissions

Restricting Permissions	Full Control	Modify	Read & Execute	Read	Write
Traverse Folder/Execute File	Yes	Yes	Yes	No	No
List Folder/Read Data	Yes	Yes	Yes	Yes	No
Read Attributes	Yes	Yes	Yes	Yes	No
Read Extended Attributes	Yes	Yes	Yes	Yes	No
Create Files/Write Data	Yes	Yes	No	No	Yes
Create Folders/Append Data	Yes	Yes	No	No	Yes
Write Attributes	Yes	Yes	No	No	Yes
Write Extended Attributes	Yes	Yes	No	No	Yes
Delete Subfolders and Files	Yes	No	No	No	No
Delete Folders	Yes	Yes	No	No	No
Read Permissions	Yes	Yes	Yes	Yes	Yes
Change Permissions	Yes	No	No	No	No
Take Ownership	Yes	No	No	No	No

Note   Groups and users with full access can delete all files in a folder, regardless of the individual file permissions.

The directories have the following permission options: Full Access, Modify, Read & Execute, List Folder Contents, Read, and Write. The individual permissions each include one logical group of restricted permissions. The only difference between the directories and files is the additional List Folder Contents group.

Note   When analyzing the options List Folder Contents and Read and Execute in detail, it seems that they have the same restricted permissions. However, these permissions are handled differently. The List Folder Contents permissions apply only to folders, not to files. This option should occur only when displaying folder permissions. On the other hand, with Read and Execute, the permissions apply to both files and folders. This option is available when displaying file or folder permissions.

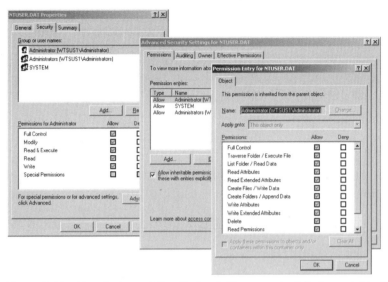

Figure 8-19 Permissions at the file level. The grayed attributes point to the fact that they were inherited by a parent object.

It is, of course, possible to assign different combinations of basic permission attributes to directories and files. However, this is common practice for system files only and requires in-depth understanding of the NTFS file system security concept.

The *Change Permissions* and *Take Ownership* attributes are of particular importance for a file system's security administration. Only users owning the attribute for changing directory or file permissions can actively modify the security settings. Only users owning the attribute for taking the ownership can assume ownership of a directory or file. The owner of a directory or file can always assign himself or herself the attribute for taking ownership and therefore change all other attributes, too. An administrator always has the right to become the owner of a directory or file. An administrator who owns a file or directory can assign himself or herself the attribute for changing permissions and therefore actively modify all other attributes as well. Administrators or users who own the attribute for taking ownership of a file or directory can assume ownership of this object, but they cannot actively return ownership to its original owner.

Note On Windows Server 2003, a user or administrator can only assume ownership of a directory or file actively. No one can transfer ownership to another person using standard methods.

To improve terminal server security, it is recommended that critical system files be protected as thoroughly as possible. This applies to the following file system areas in particular:

■ Start files in the system drive: Boot.ini, Ntdetect.com, or Ntloader

■ The different operating system directories (\WINDOWS)

■ User profile directories (\Documents and Settings)

■ Application-specific directories

Because of the improved default settings of Windows Server 2003 in comparison to its predecessors, the security of start files, system directories, and user data is ensured. However, installing applications that might change standard security settings can leave the security system vulnerable.

> **Important**   Whenever a new application is installed on a terminal server, it is recommended that all possible impacts on system security be checked. The default security settings of the new application can allow previously unauthorized users free access to the installation directory! Furthermore, many applications allow other programs to be launched indirectly, which might enable access to system-relevant settings.

Increasing system security after required applications are installed usually involves restricting permissions for standard groups, user groups, or even individual users within one administrator session. Subsequently, a test user logs on and the runtime system is monitored—for example, using file system access monitoring tools.

Windows Explorer or the Cacls.exe command-line program are recommended tools for modifying the security attributes of a directory or a file.

File Monitor

File Monitor is another tool developed by Mark Russinovich and Bryce Cogswell. It can be downloaded for free from the SysInternals Web site at *http://www.sysinternals.com*. File Monitor is a combination of graphical application and special device driver. It can record and display all file activities occurring on a Windows system. With its integrated filter and search functions, File Monitor is a powerful tool for examining a terminal server's file activities. It is particularly practical for tracing how applications use files and DLLs. This information can be used for delimiting and solving system- and application-related problems.

File Monitor's graphical user interface indicates each file access in an individual line. The line is divided into fields that include a sequence number, time, process name, access type, the file (including its path), access result, and additional information. The Result field is the most important means of analyzing errors that occur during file access. The Other field shows the relative position of read and write activity in the file. All file accesses logged can be easily viewed using the scroll bar.

#	Time	Process	Request	Path	Result	Other
664	9:55:41 PM	tsadmin.exe:3900	OPEN	C:\WINDOWS\system32\MSCTF.dll.re...	FILE NOT FO...	Options: Open Access: All
665	9:55:41 PM	tsadmin.exe:3900	CLOSE	C:\WINDOWS\system32\MSCTF.dll	SUCCESS	
666	9:55:41 PM	tsadmin.exe:3900	QUERY INFORMATION	C:\WINDOWS\system32\ntdll.dll	SUCCESS	Attributes: A
667	9:55:41 PM	tsadmin.exe:3900	QUERY INFORMATION	C:\WINDOWS\system32\imm32.dll	SUCCESS	Attributes: A
668	9:55:41 PM	tsadmin.exe:3900	OPEN	C:\WINDOWS\system32\imm32.dll	SUCCESS	Options: Open Access: Ex...
669	9:55:41 PM	tsadmin.exe:3900	OPEN	C:\WINDOWS\system32\imm32.dll.reloc	FILE NOT FO...	Options: Open Access: All
670	9:55:41 PM	tsadmin.exe:3900	QUERY INFORMATION	C:\WINDOWS\system32\imm32.dll	SUCCESS	Length: 108032
671	9:55:41 PM	tsadmin.exe:3900	CLOSE	C:\WINDOWS\system32\imm32.dll	SUCCESS	
672	9:55:41 PM	tsadmin.exe:3900	QUERY INFORMATION	C:\WINDOWS\system32\KERNEL32.dll	SUCCESS	Attributes: A
673	9:55:41 PM	tsadmin.exe:3900	QUERY INFORMATION	C:\WINDOWS\system32\tsadmin.exe...	FILE NOT FO...	Attributes: Error
674	9:55:41 PM	tsadmin.exe:3900	QUERY INFORMATION	C:\WINDOWS\WinSxS\x86_Microsoft...	SUCCESS	Attributes: D
675	9:55:41 PM	tsadmin.exe:3900	OPEN	C:\WINDOWS\WinSxS\x86_Microsoft...	SUCCESS	Options: Open Directory A...
676	9:55:41 PM	tsadmin.exe:3900	QUERY INFORMATION	C:\WINDOWS\system32\UxTheme.dll	SUCCESS	Attributes: A
677	9:55:41 PM	tsadmin.exe:3900	OPEN	C:\WINDOWS\system32\UxTheme.dll	SUCCESS	Options: Open Access: All
678	9:55:41 PM	tsadmin.exe:3900	OPEN	C:\WINDOWS\system32\UxTheme.dll...	FILE NOT FO...	Options: Open Access: All
679	9:55:41 PM	tsadmin.exe:3900	CLOSE	C:\WINDOWS\system32\UxTheme.dll	SUCCESS	
680	9:55:41 PM	tsadmin.exe:3900	OPEN	C:\WINDOWS\system32\tsadmin.exe...	FILE NOT FO...	Options: Open Access: All
681	9:55:41 PM	tsadmin.exe:3900	OPEN	C:\WINDOWS\system32\tsadmin.exe...	FILE NOT FO...	Options: Open Access: All
682	9:55:41 PM	tsadmin.exe:3900	QUERY INFORMATION	C:\WINDOWS\system32\Drivers\wdic...	SUCCESS	Attributes: A
683	9:55:41 PM	tsadmin.exe:3900	QUERY INFORMATION	C:\WINDOWS\system32\icacfg.dll	FILE NOT FO...	Attributes: Error
684	9:55:41 PM	tsadmin.exe:3900	QUERY INFORMATION	C:\WINDOWS\system32\icacfg.dll	FILE NOT FO...	Attributes: Error
685	9:55:41 PM	tsadmin.exe:3900	QUERY INFORMATION	C:\WINDOWS\system\icacfg.dll	FILE NOT FO...	Attributes: Error

Figure 8-20   File Monitor by SysInternals on a terminal server.

The File Monitor filter functions can be set to display the logs for selected processes or files only. The DASD (direct access storage device) path name is especially interesting because it indicates direct hard drive accesses that bypassed the file system.

Analyzing or securing a terminal server using the File Monitor is relatively simple. An administrator logs on, configures an application for maximum security for the file system, and starts File Monitor (if necessary, with a filter preset to reduce the resulting amount of data).

If the administrator now logs on with a second session, using a standard user account without administrator privileges, the administrator can verify if the application starts up as desired. Normally, this should not be possible with very strict security settings, and error messages will be displayed on the desktop.

Using the first session, the administrator now takes File Monitor to see which access errors were logged. The administrator can then view all files with access permissions that need to be changed. Entire files might be missing (such as DLLs or .ini files), which at that point becomes clearly evident.

Note   Only administrators can launch File Monitor because other users do not have the necessary permissions. If you want to examine accesses within user context, you need to start an RDP user session on a desktop that belongs to an administrator. By running File Monitor from this administrator session you will see system-wide activity including that of unprivileged sessions.

Securing Network Shares

Under Windows Server 2003, all drives are automatically shared through their logical name, that is, *driveletter$*, for example, C$ or D$. However, access permissions for these administrative shares are very restricted. Only if a user is a member of the Administrators or Backup Operators group is it possible for the user to access the administrative shares via the network. If the NTFS permissions for all objects of the administrative share are set accordingly, administrative access to their directories and files is unrestricted.

Important   Windows Server 2003 no longer supports access to an administrative share through an administrator account with a blank password. This significantly improves system security because it eliminates accidental loopholes due to incorrectly configured administrator accounts.

The following steps further improve the security of administrative shares:

- **Strong administrator password**   Assigning a strong password to the administrator account that is hard to guess. Windows Server 2003 security settings also allow settings that require increased password complexity (special characters, capitals, numbers) or minimum password length.

If the administrator password must remain weak, sharing can be blocked with these steps:

- **Disable server service**   If this service is disabled, directories can no longer be shared. This means that users can no longer connect to a drive or directory on this computer. Users working with this computer can still access shared directories on other computers. If server service is to be disabled permanently, the start type must be set to *Manual* or *Disabled*. Otherwise, the service relaunches automatically when the computer reboots.

- **Uninstall file and printer sharing for Microsoft Networks**   This option is located under the network and dial-up connection properties. Use the Uninstall button to remove this component (but not the check box File and Printer Sharing for Microsoft Networks).

Note   To temporarily block a drive from being shared, the context menu of the relevant drive must be opened. Under the Sharing and Security... menu item you will find the Do not share this folder option. However, you need to keep in mind that under Windows Server 2003, the drive will automatically be shared again after a reboot.

Connection and Client Security

Chapter 2 described the options for connecting a terminal server and its clients. Now we will take another look at network connections and clients, but this time with a view to security.

Encryption

A Terminal Services connection's data streams can be encrypted to minimize the risk of data being intercepted on its way from the server to the client. The default setting includes a 128-bit encryption that experts typically see as sufficiently secure. Furthermore, the data transmitted generally consists of user entries or fragments of the graphical representation of a desktop. Reconstructing a confidential document from this data is therefore no trivial feat, even when transmitted through an unencrypted channel. Only when users enter passwords or other critical character combinations is the potential for danger increased.

Some Terminal Services client versions do not support 128-bit encryption. This might be due to the clients being old or localized clients being subject to the legal stipulations of their target country where only lower encryption levels are allowed. In such cases, it is possible to activate the highest possible encryption level supported by the client.

There are four encryption levels:

- **Low**   This level provides 56-bit encryption of data transmitted from client to server, but not vice versa. Data transmitted from server to client is unencrypted.

- **Client-compatible**   With this setting, data transmitted between client and server is encrypted at the maximum level supported by the client.

- **High**   This level provides 128-bit encryption between client and server in both directions. The encryption algorithm is RC4. The Remote Desktop connection supports this encryption level as a default setting.

- **FIPS-compliant**   With this setting, data transmitted between client and server is encrypted in both directions with the help of the Federal Information Processing Standard, also known as Security Requirements for Cryptographic Modules. The standards FIPS 140-1 from 1994 and FIPS 140-2 from 2001 describe the federal requirements of hardware and software encryption methods used by the United States government. The corresponding cryptographic technologies are based on triple-DES for encryption, RSA for exchanging and authenticating keys, and SHA1 for hashing.

In high-security environments, it is recommended that the encryption level be as high as possible. However, this always takes away resources from encrypting and deciphering data on both clients and servers. Alternative encryption methods for the RDP data stream will be discussed later in this chapter.

Time Limits and Automatic Authentication Procedures

The RDP protocol creates the connections between a terminal server and the relevant clients. When these connections are established, data stream encryption usually provides sufficient network security within the corresponding user sessions. More problematic are situations in which time limits cause user sessions to behave in a predefined manner. Such situations occur, for instance, when a user session is disconnected after the user has been idle for a preset period of time, or when users need to identify themselves at the terminal server, either for logon or for logon to a disconnected session.

On terminal servers, it is possible to define how long active, disconnected, or idle user sessions will remain on the server. This helps prevent unlimited sessions that would, over time, consume too many system resources. Furthermore, these time limits help with security-relevant settings. For instance, in a high-security environment, it might be necessary for a disconnected session to be removed from the system immediately. (For configuration details, see Chapter 2.) This prevents a potential attacker from illegally reconnecting to the saved session using a stolen user ID.

The user session time limits mentioned in the preceding paragraph can be set through user configuration, Terminal Services configuration, or Group Policies. The time limits set in Terminal Services configuration are valid for all sessions using certain connections. With Group Policies, time limits can be entered in both computer and user configuration. Obviously, several options exist in the system for configuring the time limits centrally.

Terminal server default settings allow a disconnected session to be reconnected from any computer. However, it is possible to limit the number of users with permission to do this and to allow reconnection only from the computer where the session was originally executed. This requires the client to assign a serial number upon connection, as the Citrix ICA client does. (See Chapter 9.)

A new Windows Server 2003 functionality is the option to reestablish a connection after it is disconnected. The client encrypts and saves the user ID and password in its memory for the duration of the user session. After a short network connection failure, this data enables automatic reconnection to the user session. However, this option might be dangerous if the environment requires a high degree of security. Theoretically, at least, it is possible to imagine a scenario where hackers use harmful programs to steal a user's logon data from the client and use this information to gain unauthorized access.

Nonetheless, the options that allow the user ID for terminal server logon to be saved in the client software are much more problematic. Although data is saved and encrypted in the user profile, a significantly reduced security level is the price to pay for this convenience. For this reason, it is recommended that Terminal Services configuration or a Group Policy be set in such a way that the user ID always needs to be entered for user logon.

To optimally control user connections to terminal servers, only members of the local Remote Desktop Users and Administrators groups should have permission to log on. All users or global user groups who should have access to the terminal servers can be added to the groups mentioned above through computer administration. This way, each terminal server has a central location where the essential access configuration is handled. The permission settings in the Terminal Services configuration remain completely unchanged.

User Options on the Client Side

If we change perspective and look at the options from a user's point of view, two questions come to mind: First, how can Terminal Services users adjust the configuration? Second, what security-relevant communication options do these users have regarding other sessions?

Users can change the configuration within the Remote Desktop connection only if they are granted this option through the relevant settings in their account, through Terminal Services configuration, and through Group Policies.

- **Save my password**   The password for terminal server access can be encrypted and saved in the user profile if the client platform supports this option. Windows 95/98/ME and Windows NT 4.0 do not encrypt passwords and therefore can present a problem in this terminal server scenario.

- **Local Resources**   It is possible to access local drives from the terminal server session and therefore exchange documents and other data between client and server.

- **Reconnect**   Reconnect to the terminal server if the connection is interrupted.

As mentioned earlier, these options might cause problems in high-security environments. Only if the user account administrators, terminal server administrators, and Active Directory administrators prevent non-administrator users from changing these settings from the client side can these problems be avoided.

To prevent users from influencing other terminal server sessions, default settings do not give permission for remote control and sending messages. This can be changed on the Permissions tab in Terminal Services Configuration but is not recommended. The additional permissions mentioned in this paragraph should be available only to administrators and colleagues with special tasks (for instance, user support). Otherwise, it can become quite difficult to ensure adherence to corporate security and privacy policies.

Network Access Control

Now that we have taken a closer look at connection options and Terminal Services clients, let us focus on the network connection itself. What are the basic options for making the data transfer via RDP even more secure than with internal encryption alone?

Firewalls

A common means of controlling terminal server access is through a firewall—for example, Microsoft Internet Security and Acceleration Server (ISA Server). A firewall controls data traffic between computers in an unsafe zone and in a target system, and it defines source IP addresses, source ports, target IP addresses, and target ports. These are used to establish filter rules that control data traffic. If, for instance, you want to make a terminal server available from the Internet without exposing the terminal server to direct accesses, the firewall could be set up in the following configuration:

- Source IP address: All (that is, each IP address)
- Source port: All ports above 1024
- Target IP address: IP address of the terminal server
- Target port: 3389, the RDP port

When a terminal server session is established, the client uses any local port over 1024. The client uses that port and the target IP address to connect to the target port (3389). All other ports in the direction of the terminal server should be blocked to avoid attacks on the ports of other services. On Windows Server 2003 with Terminal Services activated in application mode, there are fewer ports than on any of its predecessors, which reduces the risk significantly. However, external communication should be allowed only through that one channel.

Nevertheless, a firewall does not provide complete protection! It only reduces the scope for attack. If a Windows service on a terminal server has a weakness, it could still be exploited despite the firewall. To avoid this effectively, additional authentication on the firewall can be required from the user attempting access—for example, by using RSA SecurID. Only after successful authentication does the port open up for a user session to be established. This gives the terminal server much more protection because it is invisible to anonymous users on the Internet. The terminal server is thus no longer a direct target for attack. Regrettably, this method is not suitable for all application scenarios.

Virtual Private Networks

An advanced method of protecting terminal servers is to use a virtual private network (VPN). A VPN is the extension of a private network into the normally unsafe public network connections or the Internet. However, data can be exchanged between computers via the public network or the Internet if a virtual, secured point-to-point connection is established. This secure connection is also called a *tunnel*.

There are several solutions for VPNs, either hardware-based (for example, by Cisco or Nokia) or software-based (for example, Smartgate by V-One or mVPN by PortWise). Hardware-based VPNs often work with firewalls; they require a special software to be installed on the local client. Software-based VPNs normally use port 443 (HTTPS). This port is open under most firewalls because it is needed for access to secure pages on the Web.

The following two examples describe possible scenarios where VPNs are used with terminal servers.

Hardware-Based VPNs

In this scenario, the terminal server is behind a firewall. If a user wants to connect to the server, he or she needs to pass through authentication at the VPN server (firewall) first. The software installed on the client connects to the firewall and in this way constructs a tunnel that is strictly limited to the client session. The data stream in the tunnel is often encrypted as well. Depending on the VPN server settings, the user might have access to the entire internal network or only to certain IP addresses and services. Terminal server access is transparent. Users do not notice that the server is not physically part of the local network.

Software-based VPNs

In this scenario, the terminal server and VPN server are behind a firewall. If an external client user wants to access the internal network with the terminal server, the user logs on to, for instance, a Web server with the relevant user name/password, smart card, or another authentication method. If the attempt is successful, tunnel software is downloaded in the form of an ActiveX control or Java applet and is locally installed on the client. The tunnel software then uses port 443 (HTTPS) to connect to the VPN server through the firewall, thereby establishing an encrypted tunnel.

The tunnel software modifies the communication path so that the Terminal Services client no longer communicates directly with the terminal server, but with the local tunnel software. The tunnel software packs the data stream in a HTTPS tunnel and directs it to the VPN server. The VPN server unpacks the data stream and establishes a connection to the terminal server. In this way, communication takes place through several stations. This method prevents direct terminal server access and guarantees that the identity of the user session remains the same. One possible bottleneck is the VPN server, specifically when it needs to manage all tunnels for many simultaneous user sessions.

Software-based solutions can usually be fine-tuned in terms of configuration and integrated into existing directory services. Depending on the user role, target systems can be allowed or blocked at the server, services, or user levels. As the tunnel software can be installed on the client later, this solution is universally applicable. For example, it is possible to access applications on the corporate network from an Internet café or Internet terminal at the airport, even though the target device does not usually allow installation of a VPN client.

> **Important**   When looking at a VPN in detail, do not forget that secure communication requires a secure client. Software and hardware can be installed on a terminal in an Internet café that logs user entries (such as keyboard key strokes or mouse moves). No VPN concept can protect these logs from unauthorized evaluation.

Public Key Infrastructure

A public key infrastructure (PKI) comprises the policies, standards, and software relating to certificates, and public and private keys. It includes a system of digital X.509 certificates, certification authorities, and other registration authorities that verify and confirm the validity of individual origin and destination points during an electronic transaction. If required, the Windows Server 2003 certification services and certification management tools can provide an independent public key infrastructure. This would be the basis for logon using smart cards, client authentication via Secure Socket Layer (SSL), or Internet Protocol Security (IPSec).

Smart Cards

Windows Server 2003 makes it possible to log on to a terminal server session using a smart card. Two conditions must apply: The client must recognize the smart card (Windows XP, Windows 2000, and Windows CE .NET), and smart card logon must be enabled on the server. All this requires a public key infrastructure, either by Microsoft or a third party.

For a third-party PKI, it is advisable to verify that the relevant root certificates are known in the Active Directory. A Microsoft CA (Certificate Authority) is already integrated in the Active Directory and does not require this verification. However, it is still necessary to integrate the relevant certificate templates for smart card logon into the certification point so that valid certificates can be generated for smart cards.

Secure Socket Layer

Secure Socket Layer (SSL) is a suggested and open standard for setting up a secure communication channel that aims to prevent unauthorized persons from intercepting critical information. This service is particularly suitable for transactions on the Web, but it can be used for other services as well. An X.509 certificate forms the basis for the transmission of user, device, or service identity. The public key for encryption of the data transmitted is linked to that certificate. The integrated encryption of the RDP protocol is very similar to the SSL concepts.

IPSec

Another option for defending your system against network attacks is Internet Protocol Security (IPSec). IPSec protects the contents of IP packages through encryption, package filtering, and enforcing trusted communication. All this is achieved through encryption technologies that are based on security services, security protocols, and dynamic administration of public and private keys. IPSec implementation comes with Windows 2000, Windows XP, and the Windows Server 2003 product family, based on established standards. IPSec is integrated through certification services and the Active Directory, and it uses Kerberos V5 for mutual authentication of the computers involved.

> **Note**   If the IPSec data traffic is directed through a firewall, you might need to perform additional configuration tasks.

In addition to encrypting and generating checksums, IPSec offers several filters that are relevant to Terminal Services. These filters serve to control data traffic—for example, allowing only certain IP addresses or subnets to communicate with the server. Furthermore, you can determine ports for exclusive server communication. In this way, you can define rules that allow communication with the server only from a certain subnet via port 3389. This could be useful for remote server administration using Terminal Services. It is, of course, also possible to determine dedicated clients that access a terminal server running in application mode. If the clients are set up in a certain subnet and if communication with the terminal server is allowed from there only, illegal client connections are almost impossible.

IPSec is an excellent alternative to the integrated encryption of the RDP protocol. RDP encryption uses an RC4 library by RSA. This library is based on the Secure Socket Layer concepts, but it is not an official industry standard. IPSec, on the other hand, is used in many companies and is often a preferred corporate solution because it is an industry standard.

Remarks on Stability

Terminal server administrators rely on their central components being as stable as possible. Here, this applies mainly to configuration and setting up hardware components. Creating backups in line with standard corporate strategy is an additional measure, but although this is touched on in Chapter 6, it is not discussed in detail in this book.

> **Important** Without adhering to clear-cut installation and backup strategies in combination with recovery processes, the stability of terminal server operation cannot be guaranteed in the long term. Even if hardware and software function properly and are stable, negligence or intentional sabotage might lead to the loss of important system or user files. Furthermore, even error-tolerant hard drive systems can be completely destroyed if certain events occur. For this reason, you must have a backup and a tried-and-tested disaster recovery procedure.

Avoiding System Failures

Tests have shown that an average company loses two to three percent of its sales within the first ten days after a failure in the IT system. If there is no disaster recovery plan and the network and computer infrastructure is not put back into operation within these first ten days, key corporate functions might be unavailable for more than five days. Half of all companies suffer permanent loss if they fail to get their IT up and running within these ten days. Without a disaster recovery plan, many companies end up bankrupt after a system breakdown. This is, naturally, all the more true for companies with businesses based exclusively on a properly functioning IT system.

In addition to the network, the individual servers play an important role for a company's IT infrastructure. If terminal servers are part of the strategic corporate platform, the administrator's topmost goal should be to increase their availability. However, the corresponding measures should always be in proportion to the potential damage a server failure could cause. That is why prioritizing individual servers and their services should always come before investing in availability-enhancing technology.

It is very interesting to check out some rough statistics and experiences relating to failure frequency of individual computer components. Securing those components that pose the most problems already significantly reduces the risk of system failure:

- Hard drive: Responsible for approx. 50 percent of all failures

- Power supply: Responsible for approx. 25 percent of all failures

- Fan, ventilation: Responsible for approx. 10 percent of all failures

- Memory: Responsible for less than 5 percent of all failures

- Controller: Responsible for less than 5 percent of all failures

- Other: Responsible for approx. 5 percent of all failures

Based on these statistics, computer availability can be improved by focusing on two weak points (for example, hard drive and power supply) and by placing a secondary focus on one additional weakness (for example, ventilation that affects CPU temperature and other important system components). Hard drives in particular require constant monitoring.

System Availability

The term *high availability* usually means using redundant and secured hardware combined with special software. Over the past few years, certain norms have become established to describe failure safety.

Table 8-2   Failure Safety Terminology

Availability Factor	Failure Times	Availability	Realization
99%	Approx. 3 days per year	Normal	Server system
99.9%	Approx. 8 hours per year	High	Cluster system
99.999%	Approx. 5 minutes per year	Error Tolerant	Special system

To make terminal server computer hardware as available as possible, the potential for failure of processors, memory, power supply, hard drive system, and network access must be minimized. This is an issue that should not be neglected, especially when it comes to processors and memory in a single-computer solution. However, double or triple power supplies, ventilators, hard drive controllers, and network cards in combination with hard drive RAID systems already provide relatively high redundancy. Passive back planes for individual processor cards and monitoring systems extend failure avoidance even more. Blade systems take the concept one step further by providing power supplies and other core system components in a centralized and redundant manner.

Redundant network lines in both the local and the wide area networks improve availability still more. Central, uninterruptible power supply should also be a standard solution for an environment with increased stability and security requirements.

Clusters and Load Balancing

Clusters dramatically increase failure safety. When Microsoft Cluster Service is used, a *cluster* represents a group of servers (nodes) that are linked with each other to work like a single system. An independent operating system instance runs on each node with additional communication functions for system synchronization. If one cluster node fails or is removed from the cluster for maintenance, the resources running on that node are transferred to the remaining nodes so they may assume that node's workload. Users are not aware of any changes if their server fails within one cluster, except perhaps a slight decrease in computing speed. Regrettably, Microsoft

Cluster Service solutions are not readily available for terminal servers. For this reason, alternatives for providing high availability must be developed. Microsoft Cluster Service is, however, highly suitable for file servers that save terminal server user and profile data centrally. This solution surpasses the possibilities that RAID load balancing offers for single servers, but it is, of course, much more expensive, as well.

Another option is *load balancing*, that is, combining two ore more identically configured terminal servers. In contrast to a cluster, load balancing ensures that a user is assigned to the server with the smallest load at the time of logon. If a server that is part of a load-balanced system fails, the sessions of the users logged on to this server are lost. However, the users can immediately log on again to the load-balanced system because the remaining servers are still available. Although downtime and some data loss are not completely avoided this way, they are at least minimized.

Terminal servers running Windows Server 2003 can use the integrated network load balancing service. This service allows the creation of a group of servers with a single virtual IP address and contains mechanisms for the dynamic distribution of user logons. Providing that user and profile data are saved on a dedicated file server, users can log on to and continue working on a load-balanced system even if their terminal server fails. Only data that was modified after it was last saved is lost. In Chapter 11, you will read more about configuring terminal servers in a load-balanced environment.

> **Note**   Constructing a fail-safe computer and network system for terminal servers is by no means a trivial task. You need comprehensive knowledge of configuring clusters, SANs, SCSI devices, hard drive RAID systems, and load-balanced systems. Nevertheless, there is a growing trend on the market to make this type of environment more and more powerful and easier to handle.

Stable Server Configuration

A terminal server should always be set up according to its purpose. Under no circumstances should such different devices as Microsoft BackOffice servers and Terminal Services be combined for the purpose of providing desktops on a physical server.

Terminal server operation is especially stable if the following points are observed as far as possible:

- Support by well-trained administrators who have sufficient practical experience and, ideally, have a test or reference environment at their disposal. Furthermore, a clear definition of an escalation path is recommended, all the way up to the decision-making bodies of a company, to address any serious problems that might arise.

- Use of sufficiently powerful and established standard hardware following at least one week of permanent test operation.

- Use of modern graphics cards and hard drive controllers with up-to-date and mature drivers.

- Connection of necessary peripheral devices only. Special peripherals that have nothing to do with the terminal server's function should be strictly avoided. It is recommended that keyboard, mouse, and monitor be set up to look unattractive to casual users to prevent them from being tempted to work interactively with the computer console.

- Avoiding backgrounds, screen savers, and animations because they use up a huge amount of a terminal server's resources when many users access these functions simultaneously. The result is slow responses and increased system instability.

- If at all possible, no additional installation of other server applications on a terminal server. This minimizes the risk of unfavorable mutual interference between individual applications. The application installation sequence might influence system stability and should therefore always be documented.

- Setting up servers in cool and secure rooms to avoid temperature problems and unauthorized hardware access.

- Use of uninterruptible power supply (UPS) to protect the system from network failure and power oscillation.

If it is absolutely necessary to install critical application programs, the server should be rebooted automatically on a regular basis (for example, weekly or monthly). This is especially true for terminal servers with several applications that have known problems relating to releasing main memory when the application is closed. These memory leaks can take away main memory from a terminal server until it becomes unstable.

Chapter 9

Citrix MetaFrame XP Presentation Server

Terminal Services in Microsoft Windows Server 2003 provides the functionality to connect to thin clients based on PCs and Microsoft Windows–based terminals by using the Remote Desktop Protocol (RDP) for communication purposes. Installing Citrix MetaFrame XP Presentation Server allows the establishment of additional system functionality and the introduction of ICA as a new communication protocol for terminal servers. This extends the technical options considerably—especially in larger environments. In this chapter, we will do the following:

- Learn about the concepts and the architecture of Citrix MetaFrame XP Presentation Server, which introduces extended functionalities.

- Take a thorough look at the concepts that stand behind the Citrix Independent Computing Architecture (ICA) and the Independent Management Architecture (IMA).

- Find out what makes the installation of a MetaFrame server a success.

- See the possibilities that can be opened in an enterprise environment when ICA clients are combined with the functionalities of the Program Neighborhood.

When planning the introduction of terminal servers in an enterprise, a thorough analysis is mandatory. During the decision process, the results of an analysis help to find out if the existing infrastructure requires extensions of the basic system. If server farms with load-balancing mechanisms, heterogeneous client platforms, or published applications are to be used, the Citrix products and solutions definitely deserve a closer look.

System Requirements and Architecture

The purpose of a terminal server is to provide centrally hosted Windows-based applications. The users of such a terminal server are able to make use of the RDP client Remote Desktop Connection to establish a user session over the network and to interact with their applications. Microsoft's RDP client is available for Windows Server 2003, Windows XP, Windows 2000, Microsoft Windows NT, Windows 95/98/ME, Windows CE, and Apple Macintosh.

However, the Microsoft RDP does not offer a solution when the clients are not based on a Windows operating system or if there is a need for individual applications to be provided in a centralized manner instead of a complete desktop. In these cases, the extension of terminal servers through the Citrix MetaFrame product lines is an appropriate option. An important constituent of the major Citrix product is the ICA protocol, which allows an improved support of enterprise-wide application scenarios using server-based client computing.

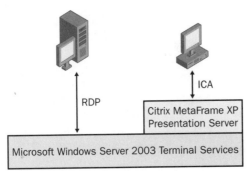

Figure 9-1   Citrix MetaFrame XP Presentation Server as an extension of Windows Server 2003 Terminal Services.

History and Product Lines

About 14 years ago, Citrix began the development of the technology that is the foundation of today's Windows Server 2003 Terminal Services. (See also Chapter 1.) This is the major reason why Citrix and Microsoft have been strategic partners since the beginning of the 1990s. Citrix develops its most important products for the Windows platform and has profound knowledge of Microsoft operating systems and application software. Today, Citrix is a Microsoft Global Gold Certified Partner, and Microsoft is a Premier Plus member of the Citrix Business Alliance Program.

In April 2003, when Windows Server 2003 was launched, Citrix introduced the newest version of their major products to the market: Citrix MetaFrame XP Presentation Server, Feature Release 3. This product extends the functionality of terminal servers and is certified for both Windows Server 2003 and Windows 2000 Server. The Citrix software complies with the strict requirement of the Microsoft program Certified for Windows and thus offers customers a high-quality product.

> **Note**   Until the market introduction of Feature Release 3, Citrix MetaFrame XP Presentation Server was known only as Citrix MetaFrame XP. Now Citrix uses the name *MetaFrame* as a branding for a complete line of products.

Citrix MetaFrame XP Presentation Server uses Windows Server 2003 as a basis and therefore profits from many of the new functionalities, such as Software Restriction Policies and improved scalability. MetaFrame XP Presentation Server enhances the Windows Server 2003 terminal server components in areas such as management, scalability, security, and flexibility. The extension of the basic terminal server functionalities results in the secure transfer of session data over the Internet, the access to applications and information from virtually every operating system, the management of distributed server groups from one central location, and the optimization of the terminal server scalability.

Citrix MetaFrame XP Presentation Server is available in three different versions, which address different customer needs:

- **Citrix MetaFrame XP Presentation Server, Standard Edition (XPs)**   This product is suitable for departments, work groups, or small organizations. It extends the functionalities of the Terminal Services in Windows Server 2003.

- **Citrix MetaFrame XP Presentation Server, Advanced Edition (XPa)**   This product is suitable for small to medium-sized organizations. Besides the features of the Standard Edition, it also contains load-balancing mechanisms.

- **Citrix MetaFrame XP Presentation Server, Enterprise Edition (XPe)**   This product addresses the needs of large server farms, large organizations, and multinational enterprises with extended requirements concerning management capabilities. Besides the features of the Advanced Edition, it contains additional tools for resource management, software installation, network management, integration into Microsoft Operations Manager (MOM), and extensions for the Web integration.

The components of the new integrated Citrix products named *MetaFrame Access Suite* offer additional value for MetaFrame installations on terminal servers. Citrix's change in strategy is evidenced in this product suite. Citrix is now offering solutions that go well beyond the capabilities of MetaFrame XP Presentation Server.

- **Citrix MetaFrame Secure Access Manager** This component provides Web-based user access to published applications and to any internal or external information sources, documents, or services. All these elements can be aggregated and made accessible in a structured and role-based manner using a Web browser interface. The Secure Socket Layer/Transport Layer Security (SSL/TLS) industry standard encryption provides secure ICA and HTTP/HTTPS data streams when used over the Internet. This solution allows secure Web access without the additional costs and implementation efforts of a conventional Virtual Private Network (VPN).

- **Citrix MetaFrame Conferencing Manager** This is the teamwork component of the MetaFrame Access Suite. Geographically distributed users can work on shared applications and documents using the MetaFrame Conferencing Manager. Technically, the Conferencing Manager is based on the mirroring functionalities for user sessions within Citrix MetaFrame XP Presentation Server.

- **Citrix MetaFrame Password Manager** This component provides a single sign-on for access to password-protected Windows-based applications and Web applications, as well as for access to proprietary or host-based applications. Passwords can be changed automatically, and the maintenance of the associated password list is completely invisible to the user.

- **Citrix MetaFrame Presentation Server for UNIX** This component is used to centrally provide and manage UNIX-based and Java-based applications in enterprises to Windows clients. Thus it is possible to combine heterogeneous enterprise server environments with MetaFrame XP Presentation Server for Microsoft Windows. The advantage of such a solution compared to the UNIX standard X11 is that the required network bandwidth of the ICA protocol for presentation and transmission of desktop contents is substantially lower than with X11. This creates the possibility of using the ICA protocol for X11 applications in relatively slow wide-area networks.

With its products, Citrix supports the Microsoft .NET strategy. MetaFrame XP Presentation Server can be used to centrally manage Windows-based applications, built on the .NET Framework, and deploy them on platforms in which the .NET Framework is not supported. The Citrix MetaFrame Access Suite and Windows Server 2003 complement each other in the implementation and management of .NET XML Web Services. In addition, the Citrix technology offers extended security features to users of browser-based Microsoft ASP.NET Web Form applications and .NET Framework Windows Forms applications because user data is not required to be transmitted to the client.

> **Note**   In the following chapters, Windows Server 2003 with installed Citrix MetaFrame XP Presentation Server will be referred to as *MetaFrame server*.

The Concepts

Similar to Windows Server 2003 Terminal Services, an environment based on Citrix MetaFrame servers consist of several components that can be organized into clients, communication protocol, and server areas. All three areas will be described in this and in the next chapter.

As a starting point, the following are some basic concepts that have a general significance for all three areas:

- **Published applications**   Applications that are installed on one or multiple MetaFrame servers. These applications are then made available for clients using a dedicated name. An ICA client can access any of these published applications after they have been configured properly on the server. Only published applications can take advantage of the load-balancing functionalities of a server farm.

- **Application groups**   The user's view on a group of applications that are published in a commonly managed farm of MetaFrame servers. The user must have the appropriate authorization to access all individual applications.

- **Server farm**   A group of MetaFrame servers that are defined and managed as one entity. Large server farms might be subdivided into multiple zones to achieve better scalability.

- **Load-balancing group**   Multiple closely associated MetaFrame servers that are grouped so that they can provide common applications. If a user wants to launch one of the common applications, the server with the smallest workload is detected by a load-balancer instance. According to the server selected by the load-balancer instance, the connection between client and server is established.

- **Seamless windows**   One or more published applications can be launched on a client without the surrounding server desktop. As a result, the application looks as if it were executed locally on the client. If certain parameters (such as encryption, bitmap cache, compression, mouse and keyboard buffer size, audio settings, and number of used colors) stay the same, authentication is needed only when the user launches the first application in a seamless window. Using seamless windows is sensible only if the client has its own fully functioning desktop including proper window management.

How do all these concepts fit together? This is best answered by presenting possible client scenarios of a MetaFrame environment.

Direct Access to a Desktop

The scenario of direct access to the MetaFrame server desktop is equivalent to the connection of an RDP client with an unmodified terminal server. If a user wants to display a remote desktop on the client, he or she selects the IP address or the logical name of the corresponding server. The appropriately authorized user can then launch and use all the installed applications on that desktop.

This access approach can also be used on simple clients that have no desktop or on client desktops with reduced functionalities (such as the Windows CE desktop). However, this approach is not well suited for a group of load-balanced servers because the user must specify a named server connection.

If all of a user's required applications are not installed on the same terminal server, that user will then create user sessions for each required application that exists on a different terminal server. This is supported by RDP or ICA clients allowing multiple parallel user sessions. For most users, the effect of accessing applications through multiple concurrent desktops is confusing, which often leads to increased support costs.

Automatic Program Start

If terminal servers are used, configuration options in Group Policies, connection type, user account, and MetaFrame server client allow the selection of an application that can be started automatically when a user logs on. After the logon, this application will provide the complete area of the server desktop that is displayed on the client. Configuration of this option is available to either a user on the client side, an administrator who is responsible for the user accounts or the terminal servers administrator. Administrators could simply predefine which application a user is allowed to use by setting up this configuration option in the Active Directory settings, the Group Policy Object Editor, the Terminal Services Manager, the Computer Management, or the MetaFrame server client.

Even if the desktop is not directly visible when the automatic program start option is used, the desktop functionalities are still available, which becomes obvious when the application is minimized to an icon. This approach is still very good for clients with limited local desktop functionalities. However, the restrictions concerning access to desktop elements stay exactly the same as if the user were accessing the desktop directly.

Published Applications

The scenario of a published application is only available in MetaFrame environments and resolves the requirement that the terminal server desktop should not be displayed on the client when a remote application is started. Publishing a

MetaFrame server hosted application to a desktop also requires the remote access software to supplement or replace the window manager components providing presentation of desktop elements. This allows the applications published by a Citrix server to be displayed in an individual window on the client desktop. This supplements the concept of seamless windows introduced earlier.

An application can be published from a server or a server farm by assigning a logical network name to the application. This allows the names of the individual servers hosting the terminal server application to lose their significance. Instead of trying to connect to a specific, named server for the application, the client will look for a network service that provides access to the desired application.

This concept of application access abstraction through a logical application namespace is perfectly suited for use on a load-balanced terminal server farm. Consequently, this approach represents a primary benefit for the extension of Windows Server 2003 with Citrix MetaFrame XP Presentation Server.

Published Desktops

The scenario of published desktops basically corresponds to published applications, with the difference that a published desktop contains a complete desktop from the terminal server. The primary reason for using a published desktop, instead of direct access to a desktop at a named server, is the requirement to abstract the access method. Again, this approach is very well-suited for load-balanced server farms because the published desktop is accessed by using a logical name and not by using the name of a physical server. As with Citrix application publishing, if a server farm is used, a mechanism is required to provide load-balancing access to the server farm.

Program Neighborhood

The *Program Neighborhood* is a concept that allows for the automatic provisioning of published applications and published desktops to clients. When the corresponding client software is launched, it provides a complete list of applications and desktops the user is allowed to access. This includes the presentation of the icons of applications installed on the servers without any manual modification of the client desktop settings. Specifically, when using published applications, a user can hardly tell whether an application is installed locally or if it is launched on a remote server. The integration of remote applications into high-end client desktops (such as Windows 2000 Professional or Windows XP) is very close to perfect. All these concepts of Program Neighborhood, published applications, server farms, and seamless windows introduced here will be highlighted from different viewpoint in both this chapter and in Chapter 10.

The Distinguishing Properties of MetaFrame Servers

Other than the concepts introduced earlier in this chapter, the installation of Citrix MetaFrame XP Presentation Server adds a number of specific features to Windows

Server 2003. However, these features must be considered separately from the features that are included in an unmodified terminal server, as described in the earlier chapters of this book.

- **Session shadowing**   This feature can be compared to the mirroring functionality using the remote control feature in Windows Server 2003. However, session shadowing is based on the mechanisms provided by Citrix MetaFrame XP Presentation Server. If shadowing is required, users who do not belong to the administrators group can initiate the shadowing. This scenario is often used when multiple users are supposed to cooperate in one session.

- **Encryption**   All data streams to and from a MetaFrame server can be encrypted using different encryption algorithms compared to the Remote Desktop Protocol. This includes a key length of up to 128 bits and therefore allows secure communication.

- **Color depth and screen resolution**   Sessions on a MetaFrame server support a color depth of up to 24 bits and a screen resolution of up to 64,000 by 64,000 pixels.

- **Support of multiple monitors**   As an enhancement of the multi-monitor support of Windows 98, Windows 2000, and Windows XP, the ICA Win32 client allows the concurrent use of multiple monitors. This functionality is often needed for computer-based workplaces—for example, in finance or in energy provider network environments.

- **Panning and scaling**   If the required resolution of a user session is larger than the physical resolution of a client's desktop, you can pan the session window around the client desktop. Additionally, shrinking the perceived size can scale a user session with a high resolution.

- **Content redirection**   This functionality defines whether a local or a remote application is to be started when files or links are opened. This content redirection makes it possible for an application that is available only on a MetaFrame server farm to open locally stored documents. MetaFrame servers allow the central management of content redirection in the same way as published applications are managed.

- **Mapping of local resources**   Citrix MetaFrame XP Presentation Server allows the redirection of local disk drives, ports, printers, and the clipboard to the remote user session. However, this feature is not very different from the corresponding mechanisms on an unmodified terminal server.

- **Centralized printer management**   Printer drivers and printer configurations can be replicated from one MetaFrame server to another MetaFrame server. Additionally, it is possible to "import" existing Windows print servers into MetaFrame servers.

- **Pass-through authentication**   The credentials of users who are already logged on to clients in the corporate network can also be reused for the automatic authentication on a MetaFrame server.

- **Automatic reconnection**   Selecting the appropriate server configuration allows the automatic reconnection of a user session when the client was disconnected unintentionally from a MetaFrame server. The underlying algorithm and the corresponding dialog boxes are different from those on an unmodified terminal server.

- **Administration delegation**   Any users can be assigned to a role where they are allowed to perform a subset of administrative tasks. This functionality is of great importance for larger environments.

- **Smart card support**   Supporting smart card readers on the client platforms allows the pass-through of logon credentials to the MetaFrame server using the ICA protocol and, thus, allowing access to published applications.

- **Microsoft Windows Installer support**   All software components coming with Citrix MetaFrame XP Presentation Server are delivered as .msi files.

Server Environment

Citrix MetaFrame XP Presentation Server is not an operating system; it is just a system extension. This extension consists of a number of Windows services and additional system tools. This is why Windows Server 2003 with Terminal Services activated in application server mode must be implemented on a server before the installation of Citrix MetaFrame XP Presentation Server is possible.

> **Note**   All functionalities of an unmodified terminal server as they were described earlier in this book will still be available after the installation of Citrix MetaFrame XP Presentation Server.

Citrix MetaFrame XP Presentation Server was developed to support multiple users logged on concurrently on Windows Server 2003. The prerequisites for MetaFrame server hardware is identical to what was already described in Chapter 1 for unmodified terminal servers. The quality of processors, hard drives, and memory is primarily responsible for the performance of a MetaFrame server.

The system architecture of a MetaFrame server is not very different from an unmodified terminal server. The main difference is the ICA communication protocol that is established in addition to RDP.

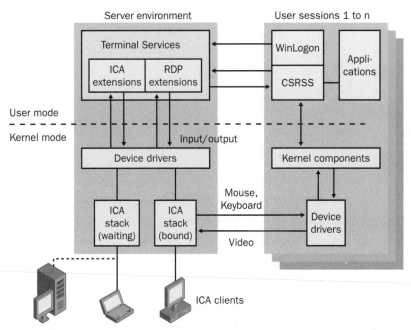

Figure 9-2   The basic architecture of a MetaFrame server.

Communication Protocol and Server Grouping

During the installation of Citrix MetaFrame XP Presentation Server, and in addition to the already available RDP, the ICA protocol is established to allow communication with ICA clients. Applying a new mechanism that requires a separate protocol allows the grouping of multiple MetaFrame servers with specific management functionalities (such as server features, user information, sessions, applications, and licenses). Both new Citrix protocols and their corresponding system components make up a MetaFrame server. This is why the two protocols are given a thorough examination in the following section.

Independent Computing Architecture

Citrix developed the ICA protocol to allow the remote presentation of and interaction with applications by providing multiple protocol channels. On a server, ICA separates the application logic from the user interface. In most cases, ICA only sends graphics elements to the client by using predefined protocol channels. On the client side, a user is able to see the graphics elements of the user interface. Each user interface interaction with mouse or keyboard is then transmitted to the server, again using certain protocol channels. As a rule of thumb, this communication requires between 10 kilobits per second (Kbps) and 20 Kbps of networking bandwidth. Additional functionalities that are based on the transmission of multimedia data streams or on the redirection of client resources are integrated into the ICA protocol by using specific virtual channels. Comparable to RDP virtual channels, ICA virtual channels are used to extend the supported feature set of the ICA protocol.

The network packets within the ICA protocol consist of one command and the optional data that follows. The data can be compressed and encrypted (using DES or RSA algorithms). The ICA protocol is highly optimized for the transmission of GDI system calls and can thus be also used for relatively slow network connections.

The features of the ICA protocol are summarized in the following list:

- Transparent support of standard Windows-based applications and DOS applications for almost any client platform.

- High performance for different network bandwidths, especially for slow connections between MetaFrame servers and ICA clients. This is achieved through strong compression algorithms applied to the ICA data stream.

- Minimal requirements for client platforms.

- Data encryption meeting the requirements of different security levels.

- Integration of local and remote clipboards for clients using a Windows operating system.

- Redirection of the client file system. This allows the use of client drives on MetaFrame servers (drive mapping).

- Redirection of client standard ports. This allows the use of devices physically connected to individual clients from the MetaFrame server (port redirection).

- Redirection of audio data streams between server and clients, allowing the playback of sound and music.

- Caching of bitmaps for the acceleration of the graphical output on the client side.

Note   Besides TCP/IP, the predecessor of Citrix MetaFrame XP Presentation Server also supported additional transport protocols, such as IPX/SPX, NetBEUI, or asynchronous mechanisms. These are no longer supported by Citrix MetaFrame XP Presentation Server for Windows Server 2003; TCP/IP is the only supported transport protocol for ICA.

In the past, the comparison between the two protocols, RDP and ICA, played a significant role in determining whether to acquire and use the Citrix products. Today, the protocols and most of their basic features are quite similar. This is why a direct feature comparison is no longer popular. The same is largely true for the bandwidth requirements of both protocols when their core functionalities are used.

The algorithms for the compression of the data streams between terminal servers or MetaFrame servers and their clients produce much the same network bandwidth. However, if the existing functionalities of the complete solutions provided by Microsoft on one side and Citrix on the other are compared, it becomes very obvious why the Citrix MetaFrame XP Presentation Server extensions are used in so many terminal server environments.

Table 9-1 shows the comparison of the functionalities and features of the Microsoft and Citrix solutions. Some of the listed items will be described in more detail later in this book.

Table 9-1   Comparison Between the Functionalities and Features of Solutions Provided by Microsoft and Citrix

Features and Functionalities	Terminal Services Based on Windows Server 2003	Extensions Provided by Citrix MetaFrame XP Presentation Server
Available clients	32-bit Windows platforms, Windows CE on Windows-based Terminals, Mac OS X	DOS, 16-bit Windows platforms, 32-bit Windows platforms, OS/2, Windows CE, Apple Macintosh, UNIX, Java, and many more
Bandwidth Control	Partially available in Remote Desktop Connection	Available for audio data stream and printer data stream
Remapping of server drive letters	Not available	Available
Program Neighborhood	Not available	Available
Published applications and seamless windows	Not available	Available
Remote control (shadowing)	From one source to one target	From one source to one target, from one source to multiple targets, from multiple sources to one target
Load balancing	Available, but independent of RDP; maximum of 32 nodes supported	Integrated into the ICA protocol; support of hundreds of nodes

Note   It is a requirement, of course, that some of the functionalities listed in Table 9-1 must be supported explicitly by their corresponding communication protocol (for example, bandwidth control, published applications, or seamless windows). However, it is also true that the capabilities of both protocols have not hit any natural limits so far. This means that there is abundant room for additional functionality. The "virtual channels" that are available for both RDP and ICA serve as a technical basis to extend the functionality of the communication protocols.

Independent Management Architecture

Besides the communication between the MetaFrame server and its clients over the ICA protocol, a mechanism is needed for communication between MetaFrame servers. Citrix introduced the *Independent Management Architecture* (IMA) to address this need. IMA consists of the following two components:

- A central IMA database (IMA data store), used to store MetaFrame server configuration information. This configuration information contains load-balancing rules, security settings, printer configurations, published application settings, and available licenses.

- The IMA protocol for the exchange of variable parameters between the MetaFrame servers. These parameters contain the current load, the logged on users, the existing sessions, and the licenses in use.

The IMA service is executed on each MetaFrame server, providing IMA communication with the IMA database and with the other MetaFrame servers. Additionally, the Management Console for MetaFrame XP is able to exchange information and control commands through the IMA service.

MetaFrame Server Farms

With the help of IMA, individual MetaFrame servers can be united to create large farms with hundreds of servers. Such server farms allow the central configuration and the control of all nodes involved. The servers of the farm do not need to be at the same physical location; they can be completely distributed with regard to location. An important prerequisite for a distributed environment is an adequate network connection between the individual locations. It is also possible that multiple MetaFrame server farms can be managed within one Windows domain. A method that has not stood the test of time is the establishment of a MetaFrame server farm spanning multiple domains of an Active Directory directory service—even if it is possible from a technical standpoint. The management of authorizations and the communication paths during user logons tend to become very complex and therefore are inefficient in such an environment.

To be able to segment larger farms into smaller units, Citrix introduced the concepts of *zones*. Zones help to solve the problem of the over-proportional growth of communication overhead between individual servers as soon as a critical farm size is reached. The delegation of administrative tasks is also much easier within zones, as compared to a single farm.

Another alternative that is being considered in many large MetaFrame projects is, of course, the creation of more than one server farm. This allows a completely independent configuration and tuning of each farm. But common changes that must be applied to all farms have to be done separately on each farm. It should also be considered that a user needs one valid license for each farm to which he or she connects. Still, this multi-farm option is feasible when the server farms are set up at different physical locations and the users log on to the MetaFrame server farm that is closest to their physical locations or meets their requirements best. In such a scenario, it might well happen that central file, print, and directory services are provided from a location that is remote to some of the MetaFrame server farms.

> **Note** Many concepts of the Independent Management Architecture might remind you of the domain and authorization structure in Active Directory. But IMA and Active Directory are completely independent. Currently, no common recommendations can be given as to whether it is better to set up one large MetaFrame server farm or to set up multiple smaller server farms to service a large enterprise network. The reasons for this are the differences in network structures, user management, operations concepts, and purchase requirements for licenses in different companies. As a rule of thumb, the internal communication overhead of the IMA protocol increases relatively with the size of the server farm. Experiences with large MetaFrame environments have resulted in a best-practice approach of creating and operating individual and non-segmented farms with fewer than 100 servers.

Zones in MetaFrame Server Farms

The required network bandwidth of the IMA communication within a server farm is a function that depends on the number of servers, the number of published applications, the number of users, and the number of managed printer drivers. A MetaFrame server farm can be divided into multiple zones, as introduced in the preceding section. Using zones helps to influence the function parameters of the IMA communication overhead that is related to the size of a server farm. A server farm with properly dimensioned zones can include many more servers than a farm without zones; this is because each zone can easily contain several hundreds of servers, at which point it is recommended to create a new zone. In most cases, because of organizational reasons, numerous published applications or many managed printer drivers, new zones will be created before the limit of several hundreds of servers is reached.

> **Caution** The official Citrix documentation of server farms and zones does not indicate any number of servers as a fixed technical limit. However, experience with large MetaFrame project has indicated that very high numbers of servers, published applications and managed printer drivers in one zone substantially increases the probability that one or more components involved will show behavioral signs of saturation. This often results in unacceptable response times of the MetaFrame environment. The scalability of MetaFrame servers and the resulting numbers of servers in farms and zones will be discussed in more detail in Chapter 10.

If multiple MetaFrame servers are grouped into a farm, an initial zone is created automatically in this farm. An administrator can create a new zone in the farm and assign servers to it. During their operation, all MetaFrame servers monitor different local parameters of a global relevance. The related global information contains events such as starting up and shutting down a server, logging on and logging off users, connecting and disconnecting sessions, modifications in the published applications settings, and changes in the load conditions. An additional monitoring task keeps track of the used licenses. All resulting dynamic information is sent to a central instance within the zone—to the Zone Data Collector (ZDC). The ZDC keeps most of the communication inside the zone. Only ZDCs are able to establish a communication beyond zone boundaries and synchronize their information with other ZDCs. That is why server farms with different zones are defined primarily by their ZDCs.

But which server within a zone plays the role of a ZDC? The solution is rather simple: Predefined system events such as the startup of a new server or the shutdown of the ZDC initiate an election if there is more than one MetaFrame server in the farm. This automatic election determines which server will be the ZDC. The election criteria are as follows:

- The newest software version represents the highest priority during the election of a new ZDC. This is why the newest version of Citrix MetaFrame XP Presentation Server always automatically becomes the ZDC when it is installed in an existing zone.

- If the newest software version is installed on more than one server, the preference for the election of the ZDC can be assigned manually. This is done in the Management Console for MetaFrame XP. (See also Chapter 10.)

- If the preference is the same for more than one server, a random number generated when the MetaFrame server is installed determines which server will be elected to be the ZDC.

The load of the ZDC grows as the zone grows. If the difference in the average load of the ZDC compared to the other MetaFrame servers of the farm is so significant that user sessions on the ZDC are affected negatively, it is recommended that a dedicated ZDC to be created. To do this, the selected MetaFrame server is configured so user sessions are not started; this server then receives the highest preference to become a ZDC. Additionally, it is very important that the newest version of the Citrix MetaFrame XP Presentation Server software is always installed first on the dedicated ZDC. This also includes Feature Releases and Service Packs.

Tip Never install a new version of Citrix MetaFrame XP Presentation Server in a production environment without previous testing. Following the rules described earlier, the new MetaFrame server will adopt the role of a Zone Data Collector immediately. This can lead to unpredictable results, specifically if the "new" server is switched off after some testing and the remaining environment has to automatically fall back into the initial state that existed before the new server was installed. In many cases, this process might fail.

The IMA Database

Whereas the ZDCs are responsible for the management of dynamic information within the zones, the IMA database stores the more static configuration information of a MetaFrame server farm. Changes in the static configuration can be applied by using the Management Console for MetaFrame XP. (See also Chapter 10.) The initial configuration can be found in the associated IMA database right after the installation of the first MetaFrame server of a server farm. The IMA database can be installed on one of the following database platforms: Microsoft Access (Microsoft Jet Engine), Microsoft SQL Server 2000 Desktop Engine (MSDE), Microsoft SQL Server 2000, Microsoft SQL Server 7 SP2 or later, Oracle 7.3.4 or later, and IBM DB2 7.2 FixPak 5 or later.

A MetaFrame server can access the IMA database server in a direct or an indirect manner. The second mode means that a MetaFrame server provides the access to the IMA database by using another MetaFrame server. In this configuration, one dedicated MetaFrame server takes over the role of a *gateway* to the database platform. If the IMA database is implemented using Microsoft Access, the indirect access is mandatory and not an option. The option of the indirect access is also recommended for MSDE because MSDE allows only five concurrent open database connections. All other database platforms allow both the direct and the indirect access option. As a rule, the direct access method is preferable because of performance and stability reasons.

Note The Citrix MetaFrame XP Presentation Server installation routine will create the Microsoft Access database automatically. To create a blank database in the right format for the other platforms, these platforms must already be available and the appropriate database setup routines must be executed before the MetaFrame installation is started.

During the startup phase of a MetaFrame server, the server accesses the IMA database using the IMA service. The MetaFrame server loads its individual configuration information, but it ignores the information that belongs to the other servers. After this initial contact, the MetaFrame server checks the IMA database every 30 minutes for any change of its configuration settings. The interval is configurable via the registry to accommodate larger farms. If changes occur, they are transmitted to the MetaFrame server.

Each MetaFrame server caches its individual configuration information in a local database named *Local Host Cache* (LHC). The LHC increases the performance substantially during read operations to the required data because no network communication to the IMA database is needed. The LHC is also responsible for maintaining proper MetaFrame server functionality even if the connection to the IMA database has been cut off. This is the case as long as the loss of connection to the IMA database does not exceed 96 hours. This time span is hard-coded in the product and cannot be changed. If no connection can be established to the IMA database during this time, after 96 hours the locally cached licenses are deactivated and users can no longer log on to this MetaFrame server.

> **Tip**   The Local Host Cache of a MetaFrame server can be manually synchronized with the IMA database by using the **Dsmaint refreshlhc** command.

Combining the Components

Independent Computing Architecture (ICA) and Independent Management Architecture (IMA) can both be found on each MetaFrame server. An interesting topic is the combined functionality of these two components. This includes which ports of the TCP/IP protocol are being used for the ICA and IMA communication.

Table 9-2   The Communication Channels of a MetaFrame Environment

Description of the Communication Channel	TCP/IP Port(s)
Citrix XML service providing published application information after a client request. (Port can be changed during installation, from the Management Console for MetaFrame XP, or by using the Ctxxmlss command.)	80 (TCP)
Communication between MetaFrame servers and Microsoft SQL Server or Oracle server.	139, 443, 1433
Citrix SSL Relay to forward ICA data streams over Secure Socket Layer.	443 (TCP)
ICA communication between MetaFrame servers and their clients. (Port can be changed by using the **Icaport** command.)	1494 (TCP)
Communication of older ICA clients with the ICA browser service.	1604 (UDP)
IMA communication between the IMA services on the MetaFrame servers and the Zone Data Collectors. (Port can be changed by using the Imaport command.)	2512 (TCP)
IMA communication between the IMA services and the Management Console for MetaFrame XP. (Port can be changed by using the **Imaport** command.)	2513 (TCP)

Figure 9-3 shows the results of combining the information about the concept of Independent Computing Architecture, Independent Management Architecture, and the associated communication channels.

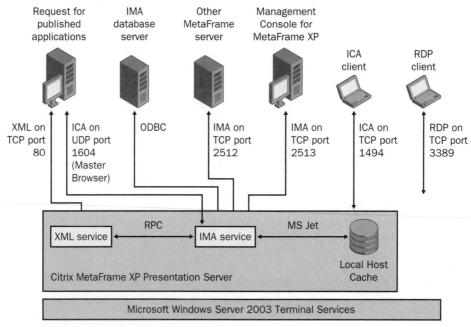

Figure 9-3   ICA, IMA, and the associated communication protocols.

Installing a MetaFrame Server

This section describes the installation of Citrix MetaFrame XP Presentation Server. This includes the establishment of the components described earlier in this chapter and the initial configuration steps.

Installation Prerequisites

The installation of Citrix MetaFrame XP Presentation Server and the associated communication protocol ICA requires the logon of a user with local administrator permissions on an existing terminal server. If the use of Novell NDS is required, the Novell client must be installed and configured on the target server first.

To install Citrix MetaFrame XP Presentation Server on Windows Server 2003, the Terminal Services must be configured in application server mode. Depending on the configuration type, the additional system files of a MetaFrame server consume up to 250 megabytes (MB) of disk space. The Management Console for MetaFrame

XP requires additional 50 MB, and the complete set of all ICA client software modules consumes another 150 MB.

> **Note**   If the drive letters have to be changed on the server, this can be done from the autorun screen of the installation routine or from the separate program DriveRemap.exe. Changing server drive letters will be described later in this chapter.

If you wish to use Microsoft Access (Microsoft Jet Engine) as the IMA database, during the installation of the first MetaFrame server of a farm, the installation process is able to create the Access database automatically. Otherwise, if one of the other supported database engines is desired, the IMA database has to be generated manually. For all other supported database platforms, a fully operable installation must be provided on a dedicated server. Creating the new database for the server farm requires appropriate permissions. This is why the login credentials of the database owner must be available during the installation of the first MetaFrame server of a farm. Depending on the database platform, some additional requirements must be met.

- **Microsoft SQL Server 2000 Desktop Engine (MSDE)**   MSDE must be present on the same server where Citrix MetaFrame XP Presentation Server is installed. It is very important to follow the installation instruction very carefully to comply with requirements concerning instance name and password of the MSDE service. If the instructions are followed, the database will be created properly during the installation of the MetaFrame server.

- **Microsoft SQL Server 2000 or Microsoft SQL Server 7 SP2 or later**   The Microsoft Data Access Components (MDAC) 2.61 SP1 or later and the ODBC driver version 3.70.08.20 or later must be present on the target server where Citrix MetaFrame XP Presentation Server is installed.

- **Oracle 7.3.4 or later**   The Oracle client must be present on the target server where Citrix MetaFrame XP Presentation Server is installed.

- **IBM DB2 7.2 FixPak 5 or later**   On the target server where Citrix MetaFrame XP Presentation Server will be installed, the DB2 run-time client must be present and FixPak 5 must be applied. In addition, FixPak 5 must also be applied on the database server.

Tip If one of the components mentioned in the preceding list was installed during the target platform preparation, a system reboot is recommended before installing Citrix MetaFrame XP Presentation Server.

The exact description for the generation of the IMA database on different platforms will not be given in the context of this book. The installation manual that comes with the product Citrix MetaFrame XP Presentation Server highlights this topic in great detail.

During the installation of a MetaFrame server that is supposed to join an existing farm, the following information is needed:

- To establish an indirect connection to the IMA database, the administrator needs to know the name of the MetaFrame server that serves as a gateway.

- The logon information for read and write permissions on the IMA database is required.

- The logon information of a fully privileged MetaFrame administrator is needed to be able to join the existing farm.

Important It is definitely not recommended to install Citrix MetaFrame XP Presentation Server on a dedicated database server or on a Windows Domain Controller. A user without administrator permissions should never be able to log on interactively on any of these platforms. With the standard setting, the security policies on servers prevent users from performing such a logon. If, however, a database server or a Windows Domain Controller takes on an additional role as a MetaFrame server, the security settings have to be modified massively. This modification will result in substantially reduced stability of the system.

Going Through the Installation

If all prerequisites described earlier are met and all needed information is available, the installation process can start. After inserting the MetaFrame installation CD, the start screen is loaded automatically, or it must be initialized manually by the starting the Autorun.exe program. As an alternative, you can also install the Microsoft Installer package of Citrix MetaFrame XP Presentation Server (MFXP001.msi) by using the Msiexec.exe command. The MSI file for 32-bit Windows platforms is located in the \MetaFrame\NET32 folder on the MetaFrame CD.

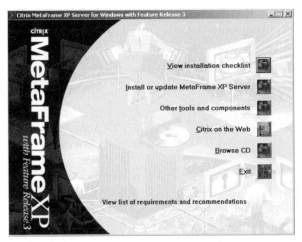

Figure 9-4   The start screen for the installation of Citrix MetaFrame XP Presentation Server.

Following is a list of all installation steps when the Install or update MetaFrame XP Server option is selected from the start screen. Choosing this option opens a new window where you can select to the option of installing Service Pack 3 or Feature Release 3. Only the selection of Feature Release 3 leads to a reasonable result for Windows Server 2003 because there was no predecessor of the Citrix product that could be installed on this platform.

1. The first window of the installation wizard for Feature Release 3 contains a welcome message, a recommendation to stop all other programs, and a copyright message.

2. The next step shows a license agreement. To continue the installation, you have to confirm that you agree with the stated conditions.

3. The following window allows the selection of the product family levels: XPe (Enterprise Edition), XPa (Advanced Edition), or XPs (Standard Edition).

4. According to the available license, a product type can be selected. Besides regular licenses, this can also be an evaluation license.

5. At this point, the list of components is shown, which depends on the product family level selected previously. If you want to, you can prevent individual components from being installed, as shown in Figure 9-5.

6. If the ICA Win32 pass-through client is to be installed on the MetaFrame server, that option can be selected here. This client allows the pass-through of logon credentials to another MetaFrame server and is mandatory for shadowing functionality used in user sessions. These settings may also be modified after installation. This will be described later in this chapter in the section "ICA Clients and Program Neighborhood."

7. The next window offers the choice of creating a new server farm or of having this server join an existing farm.

8. Depending on the selection in the last window, all required information to create a new farm or to join an existing farm is now collected. This also includes the configuration of zones.

9. The next window asks for the logon information of the first farm administrator. In most cases, this will be an existing user with administrator permissions.

10. At this point, a window appears that contains the basic configuration options for shadowing functionalities. If shadowing is prohibited in this window, you won't be able to change this setting later. Additionally, remote control can be prohibited, notification of a user before his or her session is shadowed can be enforced, and logging can be activated here.

11. With standard settings, the Citrix XML service uses port 80 to communicate with clients. At this point of the installation, the standard port number can be changed. Changing this setting will also affect other settings in a MetaFrame environment, which also will need to be changed.

12. A final configuration window summarizes all selected settings and allows the final initialization of the installation process.

13. After the installation completes successfully, a message window shows the final status.

14. Now the former terminal server needs to be rebooted to become the new MetaFrame server.

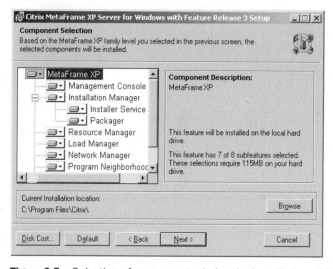

Figure 9-5 Selection of components during the installation of Citrix MetaFrame XP Presentation Server, Enterprise Edition.

> **Important**   It is possible to completely install Citrix MetaFrame XP Presentation Server without a valid user license. However, in this case it might be impossible to connect to the MetaFrame server from an ICA client. The behavior depends on whether the newly installed MetaFrame server joined a farm with valid pooled licenses or if it is the first server of a farm. A more accurate description of Citrix licensing will follow in Chapter 10, in which the Management Console for MetaFrame XP will be introduced.

System and Start Menu Modifications

If the installation of a MetaFrame server was successfully accomplished, no obvious changes are apparent after restart except for the existence of some new tools in the Start menu. Only a more exacting analysis evidences additional MetaFrame components.

The new MetaFrame processes are found in the Task Manager, as either system or a user context. Some of the processes that run in the system context represent Windows services. Here's a closer look at the MetaFrame system services.

- **Independent Management Architecture (ImaSrv.exe)**   The IMA service controls all communication that uses the IMA protocol.

- **MetaFrame COM Server (Mfcom.exe)**   The COM Server service offers access to a MetaFrame farm by providing a standardized programming interface. On the basis of this interface, and with the help of a Software Development Kit (SDK) provided by Citrix, new tools to control MetaFrame server can be developed.

- **Citrix WMI Service (Ctxwmisvc.exe)**   This Windows service provides the Citrix WMI classes. Accordingly, WMI calls allow the control of MetaFrame servers from command-line scripts.

- **Citrix XML Service (Ctxxmlss.exe)**   This Windows service handles all XML data requests originating from Citrix components. This service is used by all clients that need information about the current settings of MetaFrame servers, such as published applications for certain users or user groups.

- **ADF Installer Service (AgentSVC.exe)**   This Windows service provides support for the installation of ADF packages, which can be created by using the Citrix Packager.

- **Encryption Service (Encsvc.exe)**   This Windows service ensures a secure communication between ICA clients and a MetaFrame server by applying an RC5 128-bit encryption.

- **Resource Manager Mail (MailService.exe)**   This Windows service provides e-mail support for the Citrix Resource Manager. If configured accordingly, it can send out administrator messages, which are created automatically after predefined system events.

Depending on product family and configuration, not all of these Windows services are present on a MetaFrame server. Even if they are installed on the server, not all Windows services will be started automatically during the system initialization.

Besides the Windows services, drivers responsible for client drive mapping, session administration, compression, encryption, and keyboard support are also copied into the %SystemRoot%\system32 folder. Additionally, the appropriate files are copied onto the system for the specific treatment of printers and the required modification of the Microsoft Graphical Identification and Notification (GINA) DLL.

Note The Wfshell.exe process is executed for each user in its own security context. It affects the behavior of the desktops or the behavior of individual desktop elements (named *Shell*). Moreover, the process is responsible for control of the virtual channels of the ICA protocol. In this context, an adaptation of the associated desktop elements in the background is necessary to allow published applications in seamless windows. Even if not visible, the Windows Manager of the MetaFrame server still controls each of the published applications. If the user changes the size of the published application window, this results in a modification of the size of the desktop behind it.

Apart from the system environment changes on a terminal server, the installation of Citrix MetaFrame XP Presentation Server also creates several new items in the Start menu. These new items refer to the necessary administrative tools.

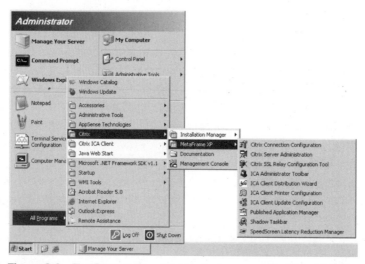

Figure 9-6 The Start menu of a terminal server with Citrix MetaFrame XP Presentation Server installed.

Items in the Citrix menu group will be listed here briefly. A more detailed description of all important tools from this list will be provided in Chapter 10.

- **Management Console**   The Management Console for MetaFrame XP is the central management tool for MetaFrame environments.

- **Installation Manager\Packager**   Packaging utility for the installation management.

- **MetaFrame XP\Citrix SSL Relay Configuration Tool**   Utility to create and configure a Secure Socket Layer (SSL)) or Transport Layer Security (TLS) relay for the ICA protocol.

- **MetaFrame XP\Citrix Connection Configuration**   Modified version of the Terminal Services Configuration administration tool, which provides additional options for the characteristic MetaFrame features.

- **MetaFrame XP\Citrix Server Administration**   This tool is not suitable for the administration of the Citrix MetaFrame XP Presentation Server. It is here only to ensure compatibility with preceding versions (such as MetaFrame 1.8). All functionalities of the Citrix Server Administration are also contained in the Management Console for MetaFrame XP.

- **MetaFrame XP\ICA Administrator Toolbar**   Launches a toolbar with the frequently used MetaFrame administration tools. With standard settings, the toolbar is launched automatically if you log on with an administrator account. This, however, can be changed by using the Exit option in the context menu.

- **MetaFrame XP\ICA Client Distribution Wizard**   This wizard allows the installation and the update of ICA client images, the ICA client update database, and the ICA pass-through client.

- **MetaFrame XP\ICA Client Printer Configuration**   Administration of ICA printers with respect to their creation and connection process.

- **MetaFrame XP\ICA Client Update Configuration**   Control of the automatic distribution of ICA client software to the individual client devices. This includes the use of the ICA client update database.

- **MetaFrame XP\Published Application Manager**   This program cannot be used any longer under the Citrix MetaFrame XP Presentation Server. All associated functionalities are now contained in the Management Console for MetaFrame XP.

- **MetaFrame XP\Shadow Taskbar**   Controls the shadowing of a user session to other user sessions.

- **MetaFrame XP\SpeedScreen Latency Reduction Manager**   Tool for the reduction of user session latencies by configuring local event handling.

Drive Mapping

During a user's connection initialization, a MetaFrame server can automatically map the logical names of client drives into the user session. However, in principle, a naming conflict exists between the logical names of the client drives and the names of the server drives. To avoid this conflict, the mapping of logical drive names must be adapted accordingly; specifically, each drive receives its own drive letter. For this reason, the DriveRemap.exe program allows the configuration of the mapping of a logical drive letter either before or directly after the installation of Citrix MetaFrame XP Presentation Server.

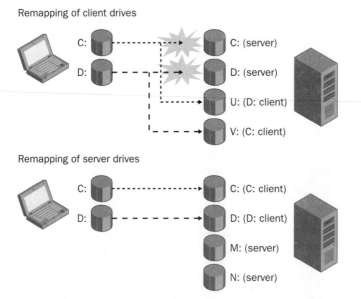

Figure 9-7   The options of mapping drive letters with Citrix MetaFrame XP Presentation Server.

Unmodified terminal servers also provide the RDP feature of automatically connecting to the local client drives. But the RDP functionality does not use letters for the logical drive names. This is, however, less intuitive for the user of a terminal server session if he or she has to access data on the local client drive C over the logical drive name \\TSCLIENT\C. Conversely, no conflicts in the name assignment arise when the Microsoft concept is applied. Here the concepts of Microsoft and Citrix behind drive-naming conventions are clearly different, although they provide the same functionality.

Caution   Logical drive letter mapping assignment decisions require planning. In most cases, a decision to change the logical naming convention cannot be changed without problems because it affects many configurations' path settings. This is why all applications should be installed only after DriveRemap.exe is executed and after Citrix MetaFrame XP Presentation Server is installed on the target server platform. If DriveRemap.exe is executed after the installation of applications, it is likely the applications will not function properly.

Remapping Client Drives

The unmodified standard settings of a MetaFrame server change the assignment of the client drive letters within the user session. The server uses the logical name sequence C:, D:, E:, and so on, for its own drive resources. This is very important for applications that require the availability of drive letter C: for their installation.

The client drives are mapped into the user session using the logical names V:, U:, T:, and so on—that is, backwards in the alphabet, starting with the letter V. The drive letters of the client floppy disk drives (that is, A: and B:) are not included; client drive mapping applies only to non-removable disks and CD drives.

The mapping of the client drive letters described is defined in the standard settings of the MetaFrame installation. The appropriate mapping is shown in Table 9-3.

Table 9-3   Standard Settings of Drive Mapping, Where the Associated Client Drive Letters Are Changed

Local Drive Letters	Mapping of Drive Letters Within an ICA Session
Client Drive	
A	A
B	B
C	V
D	U
Server Drive	
C	C
D	D
E	E

Remapping Server Drives

The reassignment of the server drive names makes it possible for the ICA client users, on certain hardware platforms, to continue using the standard logical client drive names (C:, D:, E: and so forth). This requires the execution of the Citrix utility program DriveRemap.exe, which allows the creation of new drive letter assignments on the Citrix server and is shown in Figure 9-8. The standard setting of this utility program suggests the use of drive letter M: for the first server drive (formerly driver letter C:). The next server drives are assigned the subsequent letters of the alphabet.

> **Important** The reassignment algorithm of the utility program Drive-Remap.exe does not work properly if the server drive letters are not in a correct alphabetical sequence, such as C:, D:, V:.

To prevent a possible collision between MetaFrame server drive letters, ICA client drive letters, and predefined network shares, the beginning of the enumeration of the new server drive letters can be set to another letter.

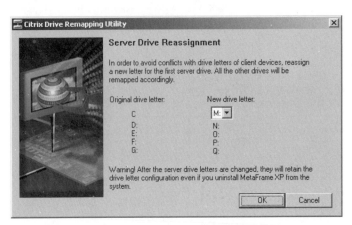

Figure 9-8   Reassignment of server drives using DriveRemap.exe.

The new mapping of the drive letters might be configured as shown in Table 9-4.

Table 9-4   Setting of Drive Mapping After a Reassignment

Local Drive Mapping Before the Reassignment Was Established	Drive Mapping Within the ICA Session After a Reassignment of Drive Letters
Client Drives	
A	A
B	B
C	C
D	D
Server Drives	
C	M
D	N
E	O

The decision to reassign drive letters has visible and lasting effects on the server organization. During the reassignment process, appropriate changes at the registry database are made and some environment variables are modified. Such modifications cannot be rolled back very easily, not even by uninstalling Citrix MetaFrame XP Presentation Server.

> **Important**   If the drive letter reassignment on a MetaFrame server was done according to Table 9-4, all applications should be installed only after this change. Otherwise, problems will occur during the resolution of application paths.

ICA Clients and Program Neighborhood

After the installation of Citrix MetaFrame, the core functionalities of a terminal server, in principle, behave the same as before. The main difference, however, lies in the support of ICA clients. Besides RDP clients, ICA clients handle the input and output of remote user interactions. The spectrum of supported client platforms is much larger for ICA than for RDP.

The basic functionalities of all ICA clients for the different platforms are the same, although naturally there are platform-dependent differences. Also, the configuration of the different clients cannot be identical because of the differences between the target platforms. All ICA clients allow the configuration of certain basic parameters, such as network settings, bitmap caching, supported color depth, window size, user authentication, and initially started applications. In addition, some clients allow the integration of audio, encryption, and remote software updates.

Available ICA Clients

The ICA client is the component used to display the graphical output of MetaFrame sessions, accept user input, and communicate with MetaFrame servers over the ICA protocol. At the time this book was written, ICA clients were available in the following versions:

- **32-bit Windows**   ICA client 7.0 for Windows Server 2003, Windows XP, Windows XP Embedded, Windows 2000, Windows NT, and Windows 95/98/ME. The ICA client for 32-bit Windows is used independently of the start up method of a user session or of a published application—either from the Program Neighborhood, from the Program Neighborhood Agent, from Microsoft Internet Explorer, or from Netscape Navigator. The ICA client contains all standard features including automatic printer recognition, universal printer drivers, and remapping of all clipboard standard formats. Compared with its predecessors, this version offers user-defined window shapes (such as rounded corners on applications in seamless mode), a Program Neighborhood Agent administration tool, automatic client reconnection improvements, dynamic client name support, and support for certificate revocation list checking.

- **16-bit Windows**   ICA client 6.3 for Windows 3.1 (in Enhanced Mode) and Windows 3.11. The ICA client for 16-bit Windows does not support the seamless mode for applications, universal printer drivers, or the Program Neighborhood.

- **Windows CE for Windows-based Terminals**   ICA client 6.3 for Windows CE. This ICA client does not support the seamless mode for applications and universal printer drivers and does support a reduced version of Program Neighborhood.

- **DOS**   ICA client 4.21 for 32-bit DOS and ICA client 4.0 for 16-bit DOS. These ICA clients support only basic functionalities to access desktops and published applications. The 32-bit version contains an integrated DOS extender, which reduces the amount of conventional memory used.

- **Java**   ICA client 7.0 for all platforms with an installed Java Virtual Machine (JVM). Java Development Kit (JDK) 1.0 and 1.1 are supported. The ICA client for Java includes almost all standard features except for universal printer driver support, and RTF and graphics exchange via clipboard.

- **OS/2**   ICA client 6.012 for OS/2. This ICA client does not support the seamless mode for applications and universal printer drivers and does support only a reduced version of Program Neighborhood.

- **UNIX**   ICA client 6.3 for Sun Solaris (SPARC), HP-UX, IBM AIX, Silicon Graphics IRIX, and Linux. The ICA clients for these platforms include almost all standard features except for universal printer driver support and Program Neighborhood.

- **Macintosh**   ICA client 6.3 for Mac OS X. The ICA client for Macintosh does not support the seamless mode for applications, universal printer drivers, or the Program Neighborhood.

- **Pocket PC, Symbian, and EPOC**   The ICA clients for these platforms do not support the seamless mode for applications, universal printer drivers, or even the reduced version of Program Neighborhood (except for Pocket PC).

The Program Neighborhood Concept

The ICA client, which is used under 32-bit Windows, can be integrated into a more general ICA environment. This environment makes all necessary interaction elements available for users who want to work on a client platform and want to start an ICA user session. Citrix calls the associated concept *Program Neighborhood*, a name that reminds one of the well-known term *Network Neighborhood*. The ICA client is not visible onscreen initially in the Program Neighborhood environment; it is only a user interface that includes the icons for published desktops and published applications. Only if an ICA user session is started by clicking one of these icons does the associated ICA client open.

The core component of the 32-bit Windows ICA client is represented by the Wfica.exe executable file. The ICA client is completed by accompanying DLLs providing optional functionalities and a set of .ini files with configuration parameters. Only the additional components provide the complete set of functionalities—in the maximum version this is the full Program Neighborhood. There are, however, additional variants of the ICA client environment, which serve different purposes.

- **Full ICA Win32 Program Neighborhood client**   With the help of this client environment, a user logs on to a MetaFrame server farm only once. Afterward, the user can see all desktop icons and published application icons for which he or she has the appropriate permissions. To support this functionality, the client takes advantage of a dedicated program that includes a number of options to control the organization and combination of the desktop and application icons.

- **Program Neighborhood Agent**   This client environment does not allow any modification by the user, but it contains all the functionalities of the full Program Neighborhood. All default settings come from an administrator exclusively. The references to all assigned desktops and published applications are placed in the Start menu hierarchy or on the client desktop.

- **Web client**   This client environment contains only the "raw" ICA client, which can be used from a predefined Web page from within a portal. All functionalities for the graphical presentation of desktop icons or published application icons are missing. The use of the Web client will be described in more detail in Chapter 13.

But why did Citrix introduce such a complicated client concept? The answer can be derived from the two most important tasks an ICA client environment performs: First, this Citrix client has to locate and to aggregate all application resources on the MetaFrame servers that are available to the logged on user. Second, the client has to establish a remote user session using the ICA protocol. This results in significantly extended requirements concerning the Program Neighborhood when compared to a standard ICA client, which accesses only the desktops of predefined servers. The Program Neighborhood focuses particularly on the user-specific graphical presentation of available desktops and published applications. This is the reason why the user interface of the Program Neighborhood primarily concentrates on the localization and aggregation requirements. Thus, the organization of the connection options is highlighted in the Program Neighborhood while the pure ICA connections have a lower relevance.

Configuration Files

All configuration settings of the Program Neighborhood presented in the following discussion are stored in .ini files, not the registry. This is the case for both global and user-specific settings. The following list gives a rough overview of the configuration files and their location in the system folder hierarchy.

The following configuration files are stored in the user profile of each individual user:

- **Appsrv.ini**   Located in the %UserProfile%\Application Data\ICAClient folder: This file contains all settings of the user-defined ICA connections.

- **Pn.ini**   Located in the %UserProfile%\Application Data\ICAClient folder: This file stores the application sets of the server farms. However, this file does not exist if the Web client or the Program Neighborhood Agent is used.

- **Wfclient.ini**   Located in the %UserProfile%\Application Data\ICAClient folder: This file contains the General page settings accessed from Tools\ICA Settings menu item in the full Program Neighborhood client. Additionally, this file allows the modification of the settings for the color depth, the window size, and the remapping of the client COM interfaces.

- **Uistate.ini**   Located in the %UserProfile%\Application Data\ICAClient folder: This file stores information concerning the window parameters of ICA session. Whenever an ICA session is finished, the data in this file is modified.

The following configuration files are stored on the client platform:

- **Module.ini**   Located in the %ProgramFiles%\Citrix\ICA-Client folder: This file contains all information concerning the required client modules and drivers that must be loaded to comply with the predefined functionalities of the Program Neighborhood and the ICA client.

- **Wfcname.ini**   Located in the %SystemDrive% folder: This file contains the ICA client name. This information is also stored in the registry key HKLM\Software\Citrix\ICA Client\ClientName. Version 7 of the ICA clients neither creates this file nor writes this client name to the registry key if the option to support dynamic client names was selected.

- **Webica.ini**   Located in the %Windir% folder: This file controls the access to local drives.

These .ini files make it easy to create predefined settings before the Program Neighborhood is installed on a client platform. The Appsrv.ini, Module.ini, and Pn.ini configuration files are specifically well-suited for this purpose. The sources for these configuration files are included in the ICA client installation packages and have the file extension .src. During installation, the .src files are used to create the .ini files.

The Full Program Neighborhood Client

A full Program Neighborhood client allows the configuration and the launch of both user-defined ICA connections and published applications that were installed on individual MetaFrame servers or server farms. The use of seamless application windows can also be initiated over this client. The full Program Neighborhood client can also display all enterprise-wide published applications to the users authorized accordingly and arrange the application icons into groups. One more feature of this client is the option to place remote application icons on the client desktop and to create references to remote applications in the client Start menu.

Note   Over time, probably all client platforms supported by Citrix will be able to take advantage of the concept of the Program Neighborhood as far as technically possible. Nevertheless, older ICA clients will also be able to cooperate with modern MetaFrame servers because most older ICA clients include the core functionalities to access published applications.

Now, which concrete functionalities are provided by the Program Neighborhood? It allows displaying the icons of application sets, which are made available for users or user groups over different MetaFrame server farms. In addition, users can manually create custom ICA connections to individual published applications or to the desktops of selected servers within the full Program Neighborhood.

From a technical perspective, Program Neighborhood clients have to contact the zone data collector of the desired server farms to receive the associated user-specific information about published applications. For this purpose, the Program Neighborhood client addresses any of the MetaFrame servers within the farm. This MetaFrame server redirects the communication request to the responsible data zone collector, which holds all information about published applications and authorization structures. The answer to the client request contains the list of all applications, including the associated icons and the user permissions. The data flow of the feedback is directed through the same network nodes as the initial request.

If a user initiates the start of a published application, the zone data collector must be contacted again. After all, it is possible that the selected application will not be started on the same MetaFrame server that was involved in the initial communication. This can occur if the selected application is not published on this server (but on any other MetaFrame server within the farm) or if the load-balancing algorithm selects another server. Only the zone data collector decides which server within the farm answers the published application connection request. When all this preparation work is done, the real ICA connection can be established to the target server and the user session is started. The user session can be either a complete desktop or a published application in seamless mode.

Installation

After the Citrix MetaFrame XP Presentation Server is installed and the ICA Client Distribution Wizard is executed, the ICA client software package will be located in the %SystemRoot%\System32\Clients\ica server folder. The required source files can be found on the MetaFrame XP Component CD. As an alternative, the installation packages can also be made available on a network share.

Basically, three different formats of installation packages are available for the Program Neighborhood client: an executable installation file (Ica32.exe), a CAB file (Ica32.cab), and a Microsoft Installer package (Ica32.msi). There is no functional difference between the packages; they are, however, suitable for different installation procedures. The size of the installation packages lies within the range of 3 MB.

A wizard controls the installation of a 32-bit Windows Program Neighborhood client, and it is accomplished quite quickly. The only dialog box, which requires substantial input, is related to the assignment of an unambiguous client name and the decision on whether local user information is used to open user sessions automatically (pass-through authentication).

As described in the section "Going Through the Installation" earlier in this chapter, during the installation of a MetaFrame server it is possible to select whether the Program Neighborhood client is installed with the pass-through authentication option activated. But does it make any sense to install the ICA client environment on a MetaFrame server? The answer is quite simple: There are situations where a MetaFrame server should behave like a Program Neighborhood client.

Even if this statement seems a contradiction in terms, the explanation is easy to understand. In a load-balancing group of MetaFrame servers, some applications might affect the individual servers in a negative way. This can occur with 16-bit applications or very resource-intensive 32-bit applications. To make matters even worse, the MetaFrame server memory management might hit a limit if a large number of different applications are executed at the same time on the same server. It can also be a basic requirement for some environments that only remote applications may be used on a MetaFrame server, but not its complete desktop.

In these cases, administrators have the opportunity to install the critical applications or to give access to a critical desktop on a separate multi-user server. The applications or the desktop can then be published via the Citrix ICA protocol; thus, they can be made available for other computers with an installed ICA client. The standard MetaFrame server in such a scenario simply provides desktops for the clients. Besides server-local applications icons, these desktops used within an ICA user session might also contain published applications icons from other MetaFrame servers.

The published applications run physically on the MetaFrame server on which they are installed. They export only the application's graphical user interface to another desktop. This can be either a client desktop or another MetaFrame server, which provides the desktop for a client. This multilayer concept permits a very effective distribution of processor load over several platforms.

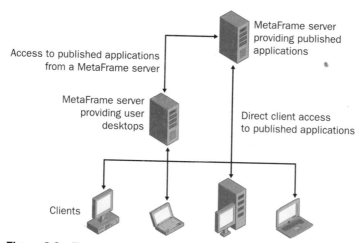

Figure 9-9   The concept is to integrate published applications into different desktops. These published applications can, of course, be used by multiple independent MetaFrame servers.

This concept of "ICA-in-ICA" makes it necessary that logon information from MetaFrame servers with the desktops are passed through to the MetaFrame server with the separated published applications. For this reason, the pass-through functionality can also be installed on MetaFrame servers and not only on client platforms.

Create Custom ICA Connections

After standard installation, the full Program Neighborhood client provides the mechanism of creating ICA connections. Afterward, a double-click with the mouse is sufficient to initiate the connection to a server and start a user session.

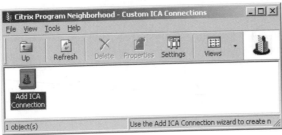

Figure 9-10   The main window of the Program Neighborhood client, which is almost empty after the initial installation.

The configuration of a new user session is done with the help of a wizard. Its sequence of dialog boxes begins with the selection of the connection type that is to be used for the new ICA connection. The options available are the local area network (LAN), a wide-area network (WAN), standard dial-up networking (PPP/RAS), or ICA dial-in.

The next dialog box permits the input to a freely selectable description for the new ICA connection. In addition, it allows the selection of network protocols for the exchange of control data, which are needed before the selected desktop or published application can be started. The options include TCP/IP + HTTP, SSL/TLS + HTTPS, TCP/IP, IPX, SPX, and NetBIOS. The last three entries of the list, however, are not relevant for Citrix MetaFrame XP Presentation Server on Windows Server 2003 because these protocols are not supported there any more. However, the Program Neighborhood client must also be able to cooperate with previous versions of the MetaFrame product line. As the last point of the second dialog box, the MetaFrame server or the published application can be selected. If it is necessary to provide the name of the MetaFrame server, this can either be its host name or its network address.

Tip   If the TCP/IP + HTTP protocol suite is selected for the control data, the Program Neighborhood client with standard settings tries to resolve the name *ica* into an IP address. If no server with this predefined name exists in the network concerned, an alternative configuration for the global or the individual settings should be accomplished. This will be described later in this chapter when the configuration of global Program Neighborhood settings is introduced.

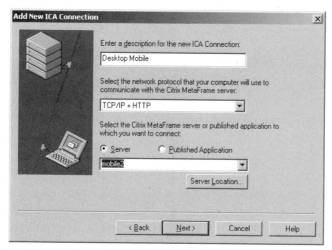

Figure 9-11   Creation of a new connection to the desktop of a server.

In the preceding dialog box, the encryption level can be selected, which allows a secure connection of the client to the MetaFrame server. Afterward, it is possible to provide user name, associated password, and, if required, the domain name. If the text fields are not filled in, a logon screen asking for user credentials appears during the initial connection phase. As an alternative, the local user information can be used for the logon when the pass-through functionality is activated. After the user credentials have been requested, the number of window colors and the window size are parameters queried by the wizard. The default values are 256 colors and 640 x 480 pixels, but these can also be increased.

The next dialog box, shown in Figure 9-12, is of central importance. If a filename is entered in the text field Application, it indicates which application is to be executed as soon as the user is successfully logged on to the MetaFrame server. To work properly, the drive letter and the complete path of the program must be entered completely, followed by the necessary command-line parameters. The field must be left free if the entire Windows desktop is to be launched instead of the individual program. The Working Directory text field allows the optional specification of a working directory, which can be used in relation to the individual application configured in the Application text field.

Note   The configuration of an application in the dialog box in Figure 9-12 is completely independent of the concept of a published application. This configuration lets the desktop disappear behind the application in full screen mode within the user session. This behavior was already described in Chapter 2 when the environment tab in the RDP properties of the Terminal Services Configuration system tool was introduced.

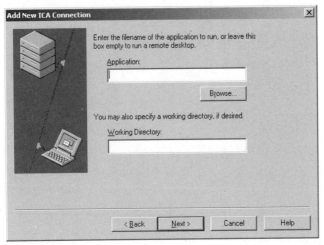

Figure 9-12   Option to enter the file name of an application, if the configuration of a complete remote desktop is not required.

After the steps described here, the new ICA connection is configured. If the associated icon is selected later, it provides all information needed to start the ICA client window and to establish the associated user session.

But these quite complex options needed for the manual configuration mechanism of ICA connections are actually one of the weaknesses of the full Program Neighborhood client. Many users just cannot handle the variety of the options, or they are tempted to play around with the environment in an unproductive manner. Therefore, the connection settings should be preconfigured by using the Appsrv.ini and Pn.ini configuration files or their installation source files Appsrv.src and pn.src.

Application Groups

The main window of the Citrix Program Neighborhood client allows you to move upward in the hierarchy if you click the Up button. As a result, two new symbols appear. The first symbol has the title *Find New Application Set,* and the other has the title *Custom ICA Connection*. If the second symbol is selected, the view jumps back to the configuration wizard icon, allowing the manual configuration of ICA connections, as described earlier.

But what are the application sets that you can find with the help of the first symbol? An application set contains a preconfigured group of applications, which an administrator can make available specifically to only certain users or user groups. Only the published application of a server farm may be organized in such a set of application icons. (See also Chapter 10.)

Figure 9-13   On the left side of the full Citrix Program Neighborhood main window is the symbol to find a new application set.

An administrator can define an application set with the help of the Management Console for MetaFrame XP. Within a subnet, this application set is added automatically to the Program Neighborhood structure. MetaFrame XP Presentation Server automatically populates a user's Program Neighborhood with the application set information if it is set to interoperability mode. If the application sets are not located inside the desired subnet, a user might have to configure the connection to the application set by manually selecting the server location. The server location configuration contains the definition, specifying which server (network address) can be reached by using which network protocols.

> **Note**   Application icons and application references can be displayed within the graphical user interface of the Program Neighborhood client, or they can be placed on the client desktop and in the client Start menu. This is done by using the File\Create Desktop Shortcut menu item of the Citrix Program Neighborhood client. Exactly the same action can be accomplished automatically through the administrator's default settings applied by the Program Neighborhood Agent.

For the application sets, the same arguments are valid as for the custom ICA connections described earlier: The manual configuration of these options is also complex for most users and should therefore be predefined before the installation of the Program Neighborhood clients. Controlled modifications of the configuration files in the user profile can be accomplished by logon scripts, a method that helps to reduce the time spent doing manual configuration.

Changing Individual Properties

If necessary, the properties of each application set and the user-defined ICA connections may be modified by a user. To change these properties, a right mouse button click to the selected ICA connection icon will open the context menu. Another method is to select the menu group File in the Program Neighborhood client main window. Both context menu and main menu provide access to the Properties for custom ICA connections, which are exposed through a dialog box with four tabs.

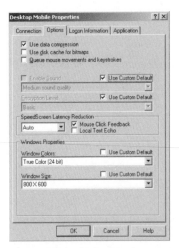

Figure 9-14 Changing the properties of a custom ICA connection.

The individual tabs for custom ICA connections contain the following options for changes in the configuration settings:

- **Connection** Connection type (LAN, WAN, PPP/RAS, or ICA dial-in), name of the server or of the published application, and configuration of the server location. The latter includes the selection of the network protocol for the exchange of control data and the option to add available MetaFrame servers for the associated communication. Different changes in the configuration settings used for the integration of firewalls can be initiated from this tab as well. (See also the next section in this chapter.)

- **Options** Data compression, caching of bitmaps, buffering of mouse movements and keystrokes, sound enabling, data encryption, screen latency reduction, window colors, and window size (including the seamless window option).

- **Logon Information** Selection among pass-through authentication, smart card integration, and logon using conventional user-specific credentials (user name, password, and domain).

- **Application** Application initially started after the connection was established, including path, working directory, and associated icon.

The following three tabs are for changes in the application set settings:

- **Connection**   Connection type (LAN, WAN, PPP/RAS, or ICA dial-in) and server location, including network protocol for the exchange of control data, server group, and address list.

- **Default Options**   Data compression, caching of bitmaps, buffering of mouse movements and keystrokes, desktop integration for the application set, sound enabling, data encryption, screen latency reduction, window colors, and window size (including the seamless window option).

- **Logon Information**   Selection among pass-through authentication, smart card integration, and logon using conventional user-specific credentials (user name, password, and domain).

Configuration of Global Settings

Besides the individual settings of application group and custom ICA connections, global default settings for the Program Neighborhood can also be configured. The configuration of the predefined global settings is done by selecting the File\Custom Connection Settings menu item.

The Connection tab in the custom connection setting dialog box defines the global default server location.

- **Network Protocol**   The Network Protocol dropdown field instructs the Program Neighborhood as to which protocol to use to exchange control information concerning location of and connection to the MetaFrame server. The selected protocol must be installed and must be supported by the MetaFrame server concerned.

- **Server Group**   The Server Group and Address List text fields are used to create lists of primary and backup servers designated for connecting to application sets. A maximum of one primary group and two backup groups can be defined, which a client might contact during the attempt to establish a connection. Each of the groups can contain up to five servers. Backup server groups provide business recovery for the client device if it cannot contact any server in the primary group.

- **Firewall**   A button with the label *Firewall* leads to an additional dialog box, which allows the configuration of an alternative address outside firewall or the use of the Web browser proxy settings. In addition, this dialog box contains the options to activate the use of SOCKS, of HTTPS, or of the Citrix Secure Gateway.

The Standard Options tab allows the configuration of the global settings concerning audio, encryption level, window colors, and window size.

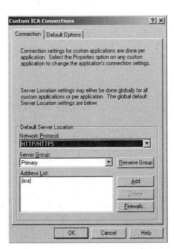

Figure 9-15 Global default settings for the configuration of custom ICA connections.

Tip Both individual applications and application groups within the Program Neighborhood offer the option of selecting one or more server addresses explicitly. This is used if the connection initialization to a MetaFrame server is done via routers or gateways. If problems occur during the establishment of connections, troubleshoot by experimenting with these options.

Additional global settings for the Program Neighborhood client are made by using the Tools\ICA Settings... menu item, which again leads to a dialog box with a number of tabs. The first tab is named General and provides access to the following fields:

- **Client Name** The Client Name field allows the change of the client name. The MetaFrame server uses the client name to uniquely identify resources, such as printers and disk drives, associated with a dedicated client computer. The client name must be unique for each computer running the Program Neighborhood client. Starting with version 7, the Program Neighborhood client optionally supports the activation of dynamic client name creation. If this feature is enabled, the ICA client name is changed automatically whenever the client device name is changed.

- **Keyboard Layout** Allows specifying the keyboard layout of the client computer. The MetaFrame server uses the keyboard layout information to configure the ICA user session according to the keyboard present at the client. The default value (User Profile) uses the keyboard layout specified in the user profile.

- **Keyboard Type**   Allows specifying the keyboard type of the client computer. The MetaFrame server uses the keyboard type information to configure the user session for the appropriate keyboard type.

Additional check boxes allow the selection if a dialog box is displayed before making dial-in connections, if a terminal window is displayed when making dial-in connections, if automatic client updates are allowed, if pass-through authentication is available, and if local credentials can be used to log on.

The second tab of the ICA settings dialog box is named *Bitmap Cache*. It is used to configure the bitmap cache directory and to determine the minimum size of bitmaps that will be cached. The caching of bitmaps results in storing commonly used graphics objects on a local disk drive and thus allows fast access to these objects when they are required again. If the bandwidth of the network is limited, the activation of this option increases the system performance. If the client is located in a high-speed network, however, the bitmap cache should be set to zero.

The Hotkeys tab allows the configuration of the assignment of certain standard tasks and standard key combinations on a local desktop to alternative key combinations used from the remote session. This is a very important functionality to coordinate the cooperation of the local and the remote window manager.

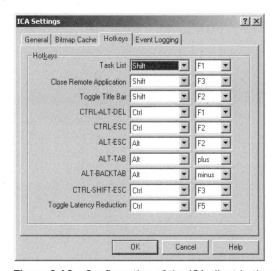

Figure 9-16   Configuration of the ICA client hotkeys.

The last tab, named *Event Logging*, instructs the Program Neighborhood client, including the ICA client, on how to keep a log of various events in the ICA environment.

The integration of devices locally attached to the client is also handled through ICA protocol, which usually is related to the mapping of the serial and parallel interfaces and the printers attached to them. The result of the mapping of client devices and server devices can easily be verified in Windows Explorer. All remapped devices besides the client drives in the network neighborhood can be seen there. Because they all represent network resources for a MetaFrame server, they are symbolized accordingly.

Figure 9-17 Remapped drives and devices in the Windows Explorer of an ICA session. You can see the remapping convention of Microsoft (\\Client\DevideName) and Citrix (renamed drive letter).

The Program Neighborhood Agent

The Program Neighborhood Agent was developed by Citrix to provide administrators a completely centrally manageable ICA client environment. The Program Neighborhood Agent compensates for the weakness of the full Program Neighborhood client, namely its high complexity for most users. All important configuration parameters of the Program Neighborhood Agent are centrally stored in an XML file on a Web server, but not on the client platform or in the user profile. On the desktops or in the Start menus of the target client platforms, all references to published applications are thus strictly given according to the rules in the XML file. As a consequence, users cannot create their own ICA configurations for the connection to individually selected servers with published applications or desktops. This feature makes the Program Neighborhood Agent very attractive for MetaFrame environments, in which the liberties of the users have to be limited for cost and efficiency reasons. Instead of having to modify individual .ini files on the client platforms, now the change of the central XML file is sufficient to set up general configuration defaults.

For the installation of the Program Neighborhood Agent, an executable installation file (Ica32a.exe) and a Microsoft Installer package (Ica32a.msi) is provided. Again, there exists no functional difference between the packages. Also, their size is only a little smaller than the installation packages for the full Program Neighborhood client.

How can the Program Neighborhood Agent know after an installation on a target client platform where the central XML configuration file is located? One option to configure the default location setting is to let the installing user type in the needed address to the Web server. But this is an awkward procedure, which again leads to errors. It is much better to preset the parameters. This leads to the second configuration option, which requires the extraction of the installation package (for example, with WinZip) and the modification of the Install.ini configuration file.

The contents of the unmodified Install.ini file is shown in Listing 9-1.

Listing 9-1: Contents of the Install.ini configuration file

```
[install]
;ServerURL=http://pnagent
;SetMachineNameClientName=DCN
;Location=<PROGRAM_FILES>\Citrix\PNAgent
;StartMenu=Citrix PNAgent
;InstallSingleSignOn=no
;AcceptClientSideEULA=no
```

Removing the semicolon at the beginning of the line can activate the individual options of the Install.ini configuration file. Before the options listed in Table 9-5 are valid for a given environment, correct values must be entered. After storing the configuration file, a new installation package can be compiled by using an appropriate tool.

Table 9-5   The Options of the Install.ini Configuration File

Options	Description
ServerURL	Specifies the address of the Web server with the XML configuration file, which can be found under the predefined \Citrix\PNAgent\config.xml link folder
SetMachineNameClientName	Specifies the client name
Location	Specifies the installation folder of the Program Neighborhood Agent
StartMenu	Specifies the folder in the Start menu where the icon of the Program Neighborhood Agent is placed
InstallSingleSignOn	Specifies if the pass-through authentication is activated (yes) or not (no)
AcceptClientSideEULA	Specifies if the start screen with the license agreements is displayed (yes) or not (no)

To activate the Config.xml configuration file with the correct settings requires that it be provided over the predefined Web server. The easiest way to configure, maintain, and provide the Config.xml file is to use the Web Interface for MetaFrame XP. (See also Chapter 13.) The access to the Web-based administration tool is done over *http://<Servername>/Citrix/PNAgentAdmin*.

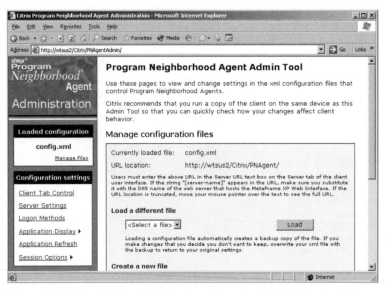

Figure 9-18   The Program Neighborhood Agent administration tool.

The configuration file contains a number of parameters used for the global setting of what users of the Program Neighborhood Agent are allowed to see and if they may change certain settings. This includes the options to change the settings in the following Program Neighborhood Agent tabs:

- **Server settings**   Configuration of Server URL, refresh interval, SSL/TLS settings, and logon methods.

- **Application display**   Configuration of published application links in the Start menu, on the desktop, and in the taskbar.

- **Application refresh**   Configuration of the settings on when and how often the client requests a current list of published applications from the server hosting the Web Interface for MetaFrame XP.

- **Session options**   Configuration of window size, color depth, and audio quality.

Note   The Config.xml file allows the hiding of complete Program Neighborhood Agent tabs, but not the blocking of individual setting options within a tab.

After the Program Neighborhood Agent launches and the user authentication takes place, all published application icons will be displayed on the desktop, in the Start menu, or in the taskbar, according to the configuration in the central Config.xml file. The Program Neighborhood Agent executable itself hides behind a little icon in the taskbar notification area (that is, on the right side of the taskbar). The

Properties context menu item of this icon opens a dialog box. This dialog box allows the modification of the parameters that the user is allowed to change according to the configuration defined by the Program Neighborhood Agent administrator. The tabs in the Program Neighborhood Agent can include the setting of the server URL, the logon mode, the application display, and the session options.

Figure 9-19   Setting the Program Neighborhood Agent properties on a client.

The Web Client

If ICA sessions are to be launched over a Web page rather than using a client's Windows desktop or Start menu, the management functionalities of the Program Neighborhood are no longer necessary on the client. Only the basic functionalities of an ICA client are needed in such an environment. The associated parameters can be passed from the Web server to the ICA client before it requests the establishment of a connection to a MetaFrame server. Fairly recently, Citrix provided special clients for this purpose. It is, however, much easier to use the same basic ICA client engine for Web environments that is used for the Program Neighborhood clients. For this reason, Citrix still provides special ICA Web client installation packages for Windows-based platforms, but they do not contain an explicit Web client anymore. On the contrary, each current ICA client for Windows can be registered as a COM component on a client platform and then can be started over a link on a Web page. (See also "Web Interface for MetaFrame XP" and "Citrix MetaFrame Secure Access Manager" in Chapter 13.)

The special Web installation packages for 32-bit Windows clients with no Program Neighborhood client software show some minor differences from the standard installation routine. This difference can be explained primarily by the fact that little user interaction is desired for installation over the Web only, and not all functionalities of the full Program Neighborhood client are needed. That's why there are no differences between core functionalities of the ICA Web client and the Program Neighborhood client. However, the installation of the Web client does not create a Program Neighborhood icon on the client's desktop or Start menu. Furthermore, no help files are copied to the client platform. All this reduces the size of the associated Web installation packages Ica32t.exe and Wficat.cab, which are only about 2 MB large.

The same .ini files as for the full Program Neighborhood clients are used for the configuration of the Web clients. Because of the automatic Web client installation process, it might be necessary to adapt the parameters of the .ini configuration files in the installation packages according to the given requirements before they are deployed.

Program Neighborhood Connection Center

The Program Neighborhood Connection Center gives you an overview of all remote desktops and published applications started in a 32-bit Windows ICA client. As soon as the first ICA connection is established, the little Connection Center icon is displayed on the right side of a client's taskbar.

Clicking with the right mouse button or double-clicking with the left mouse button on the Program Neighborhood Connection Center opens a dialog box. It shows all active ICA connections and allows a number of actions: disconnect a session, log off a user, terminate an application, change the security settings, and display the properties.

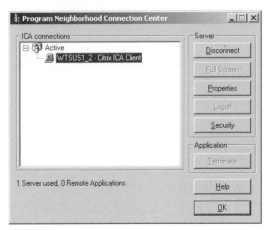

Figure 9-20   The Program Neighborhood Connection Center with one active MetaFrame desktop.

The dialog box with the properties of an ICA session contains information about encryption and produced network traffic. The Security button leads to a dialog box that controls the access to local client files. For a selected connection, it is possible to configure no access, read-only access, or full access to the local file system. Furthermore, this dialog box allows the decision if the security configuration will be applied globally to the client or per connection, or if it just applies to the selected application or desktop.

After this chapter's introduction of the Citrix MetaFrame XP Presentation Server architecture and communication mechanisms, the next chapter will highlight the associated administration tools and operation concepts.

Chapter 10

Administration of Citrix MetaFrame Servers

The Citrix MetaFrame XP Presentation Server extends the functionality of terminal servers considerably. This chapter covers the tools and concepts that come into play after the installation of the MetaFrame server and the corresponding ICA clients have been completed. In this chapter we'll do the following:

- Get to know the MetaFrame administration tools that configure the connections, handle the day-to-day administrative tasks, and set up licenses.

- Learn what published applications, desktops, and content are needed and how to set them up.

- See how Citrix approaches the problematic issue of printing and offers practical solutions.

- Read about the extensive scalability of MetaFrame environments and about their limitations.

- Examine the options for making a MetaFrame environment secure.

MetaFrame Administration Tools

MetaFrame administration tools are the programs that the administrator uses on the server side to configure and manage the Citrix MetaFrame server. These tools are integrated into the terminal server, and they allow ICA clients remote access to the complete desktop or to published applications. The MetaFrame settings are therefore carried out in different standard tools that are similar in many ways to the corresponding administration programs for Microsoft Windows Server 2003 Terminal Services. In some cases, particularly for MetaFrame-specific configurations, the work can be done even with Windows Server 2003 standard tools.

Citrix Connection Configuration

An ICA connection is the logical access that a MetaFrame server provides to its clients. Citrix Connection Configuration is the tool used for setting up the ICA protocol after the installation and during the operation of MetaFrame. It has many of the configuration options that Terminal Services Configuration provides. (See Chapter 2.)

Adjustable Parameters

In the same way as for RDP connections, various parameters for ICA sessions can be configured for the connection, the user, or the clients. Settings for the connections relate to all users and clients that communicate with the server in a predefined manner—for example, using a specified network card in a server that has more than one network card installed. These settings are established in the ICA Connection Configuration. User settings relate to an individual user or user group, and the connection type is irrelevant. The corresponding configuration is carried out through the extended properties fields in user administration. The client configuration was covered in the "Program Neighborhood" section in Chapter 9. It concerns mostly the default settings for screen size, screen colors, logon information, security, and compression.

> **Tip** Citrix Connection Configuration allows a range of parameters to be set up differently for various types of connections on the MetaFrame server. For many of these settings, the possibility exists to overwrite user-specific or client-specific values. This indicates that the connection-specific settings have a higher priority status.

The hierarchy of the ICA connection settings is very similar to the familiar RDP connection configuration hierarchy (also discussed in Chapter 4) of a terminal server with no extensions and is as follows:

- **Policies** The standards defined by the Management Console for MetaFrame XP have the highest priority. However, it is important not to confuse these policies with the Group Policies in the Microsoft Active Directory directory service.

- **Connection configuration** The settings can overwrite both client and user-specific settings, but is still subject to the predefined policies.

- **User configuration**   The settings at the user and group level that can be carried out in computer administration to overwrite the client settings.

- **Client configuration**   The settings for a user on the respective ICA client have the lowest priority.

Selecting a Configuration

When the Citrix Connection Configuration interface is launched, a rather unassuming window appears. It primarily lists the installed communication protocols, including their key parameters. However, when this window is compared with the Terminal Services Configuration, a small difference in the start views becomes apparent. In fact, after the installation of Citrix MetaFrame, the settings for the ICA parameters can be set, almost without exception, by using Terminal Services Configuration. The Terminal Services Configuration was developed as an MMC snap-in, which is contrary to the Citrix Connection Configuration. This explains the major differences in appearance that emerge as one works with the two tools.

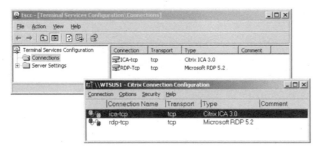

Figure 10-1   Comparison of the main windows of Terminal Services Configuration (left) and Citrix Connection Configuration (right front).

> **Tip**   It is even possible to create a new ICA connection within the Terminal Services MMC. If the Connections list item is enabled in the left-hand window, the main menu will display the option Action\Create New Connection. By clicking here, a wizard is launched that allows a new ICA or RDP connection to be defined.

By selecting the ICA protocol in the Citrix Connection Configuration interface, its respective parameters can be configured. The start dialog allows the connection name, connection type, and transport protocol to be viewed and the comments to be modified. In the local network, the LAN adapter and the maximum number of ICA connections for the chosen adapter can also be selected.

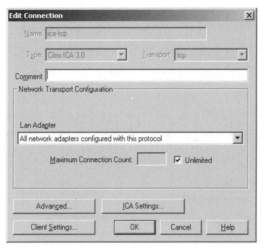

Figure 10-2   The Citrix Connection Configuration start dialog for modifying the ICA protocol.

Important   The Security menu item in the main Citrix Connection Configuration interface window can be used to set the access permissions for individual users or groups for the type of connection selected. This includes the same options as for RDP, which are described in Chapter 2.

Client Settings

If the Client settings are configured through this interface, a number of options can be set in the corresponding dialog box, some of which are specific to ICA. These control the settings for local interfaces, printers, maximum color depth, clipboard, and system sounds. Again, there is a corresponding tab in the Terminal Services Configuration MMC for the same settings.

Client assignments for local drives, printers, LPT and COM interfaces, clipboard, and audio support can be individually enabled or disabled for each connection configuration. If the client's drive assignment is not disabled, the client drive assignments will automatically be re-created during the session logon procedure. The logical order of the drive letters follows the convention selected at the time of MetaFrame installation.

If the client's printer assignment and the LPT connection assignment are not disabled, the printer connected to the client will automatically be integrated during the session logon procedure. If the client's default printer is also to be used as the default printer for the session on the MetaFrame server, this option can also be selected at this point. It is even possible to completely block out the server's printer. To minimize the time it takes to generate the assigned printers during logon, it is possible to assign the client's default printer only.

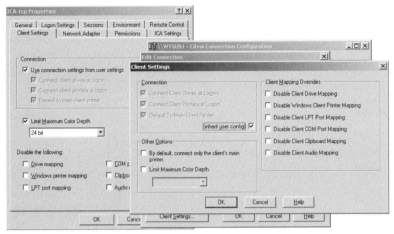

Figure 10-3   The respective dialog boxes for configuring client settings in Terminal Services Configuration (left back) and in Citrix Connection Configuration (right front). The check box By Default, Connect Only The Client's Main Printer that is missing in the Terminal Services Configuration can be found there in the ICA Settings tab.

Multimedia Bandwidth

The ICA protocol may be configured for better audio data stream control than with RDP. It is, for instance, possible to transmit audio at various quality levels within ICA.

If the ICA settings button is selected in the Citrix Connection Configuration start dialog, a dialog box appears that allows audio quality to be modified. The same ICA parameters can also be set up in Terminal Services Configuration, where there is an additional tab for the purpose. This tab is also called ICA settings. Figure 10-4 shows a direct comparison of the two configuration tools.

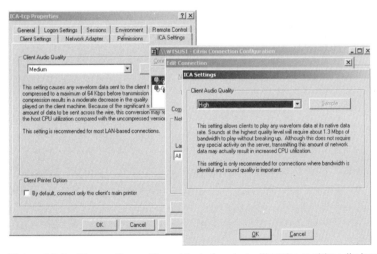

Figure 10-4   The audio quality settings for controlling the multimedia bandwidth. Highlighting the corresponding tabs in Terminal Services Configuration (left back) and the dialog field in Citrix Connection Configuration (right front).

The three possible quality levels for audio data streams can be set as follows:

- **Low**   In this setting, the audio data sent to the client is compressed to a maximum of 16 kilobits per second (Kbps). This substantially impairs the audio quality, but allows for acceptable performance in connections with very low bandwidth.

- **Medium**   This setting is recommended for most LANs. All audio data sent to the client is compressed to a maximum of 64 Kbps. This impairs the sound quality slightly, but it is acceptable in most cases.

- **High**   For this setting, the server must have a lot of bandwidth and available high processor performance. The transmission of audio data to the client requires about 1.3 megabits per second (Mbps), but results in a sound quality comparable to that of a CD. However, the clients are often unable to render this sound accurately.

Advanced Connection Settings

By far the widest possibilities for configuring an ICA connection are available in the Citrix Connection Configuration under the Advanced... button in the start dialog. Apart from a few differences, the parameters of the ICA protocol are the same as those of the RDP protocol. For details, please refer to Chapter 2, which contains a description of the individual functions in connection with Terminal Services Configuration. The only additional options available in Citrix Connection Configuration are Only Run Published Applications and Disable Wallpaper.

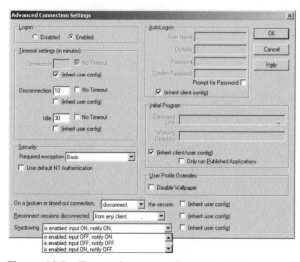

Figure 10-5   The configuration of all major ICA parameters. In this example, many settings are already predetermined by the server administrator.

The user interface in Citrix Connection Configuration is considered by most administrators to be less intuitive than that of Terminal Services Configuration. On the other hand, with Citrix Connection Configuration, almost all settings can be carried out in one dialog box, without having to switch between tabs.

It can take a little while to get used to the naming conventions for shadowing in the Citrix Connection Configuration. For this reason, remote assistance options are compared to shadowing options in the following list:

- *Is Disabled in the Citrix Connection Configuration* is the same as *Do Not Allow Remote Control in Terminal Services Configuration.*

- *Is Enabled: Input OFF, Notify ON in the Citrix Connection Configuration* is the same as *Use Remote Control With The Following Settings: Check Require User's Permission and Select View The Session in Terminal Services Configuration.*

- *Is Enabled: Input OFF, Notify OFF in the Citrix Connection Configuration* is the same as *Use Remote Control With The Following Settings: Uncheck Require User's Permission and Select View The Session in Terminal Services Configuration.* Because of privacy protection reasons, this option is prohibited in some countries.

- *Is Enabled: Input ON, Notify OFF in the Citrix Connection Configuration* is the same as *Use Remote Control With The Following Settings: Uncheck Require User's Permission and Select Interact With The Session in Terminal Services Configuration.* Because of privacy protection reasons, this option is prohibited in some countries.

- *Is Enabled: Input ON, Notify ON in the Citrix Connection Configuration* is the same as *Use Remote Control With the Following Settings: Check Require User's Permission and Select Interact With The Session in Terminal Services Configuration.*

Management Console for MetaFrame XP

After an environment based on Citrix MetaFrame XP Presentation Server is successfully installed and configured, the issue of administration needs to be considered. The Management Console for MetaFrame XP is a centralized tool available for this purpose.

The Management Console for MetaFrame XP is a Java application and therefore requires a suitable Java Virtual Machine. This is established on the target server automatically when Citrix MetaFrame XP Presentation Server is installed. However, it is possible in principle to install the Management Console for MetaFrame XP and the Java Virtual Machine on any other suitable computer in the network.

> **Tip**   The Management Console for MetaFrame XP can be directly invoked using the command line, if required. To do so, you need to go into the \Programs\citrix\administration folder and to enter **java –jar tool.jar** in the command prompt. The same command can also be used to publish the Management Console.

When the Management Console for MetaFrame XP is launched through Start\All Programs\Citrix\Management Console or by using the command line, the first thing that appears is a dialog box, which can be used to log on to a suitable server. It is possible to log on to any server in a MetaFrame server farm because they all access the same set of data and configuration options through the common zone data collector (ZDC). However, to consume less network bandwidth and also to improve the response time of the Management Console, it is best to log on to the MetaFrame server that contains the zone data collector. This is directly connected to the IMA database server. The configuration information for the IMA database server can be viewed and modified through the Management Console.

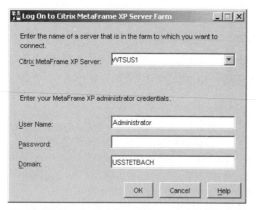

Figure 10-6   The logon dialog for launching the Management Console for MetaFrame XP. If the pass through authentication is selected when the Management Console is invoked the first time, next time the logon occurs automatically if the user is already working on the MetaFrame server console.

> **Tip**   As few instances as possible of the Management Console for MetaFrame XP should be opened in parallel because they cause quite a large permanent stream of data. In addition, this often leads to problems if several administrators modify the same objects at the same time.

Farms and Server Properties

If the main window of the Management Console for MetaFrame XP is opened after a successful logon, all relevant information concerning the MetaFrame server farm can be accessed. The list of elements on the left-hand side is known as the console structure and displays a hierarchy of objects underneath a root object. The object in the topmost position in the management console structure is the server farm. Under it are positioned the administration functions and components.

> **Note**   The access to the objects of the console structure is controlled by the delegated administrator options described under "Administrators" later in this chapter."

If the topmost object in the list containing the name of the server farm is enabled, the related properties can be modified in a corresponding dialog box. Several options are available here:

- **Connection Limits**   Determines the maximum number of connections and log options.

- **ICA Keep-Alive**   Offers the possibility to set a heartbeat that is sent from a server to the client devices to determine if a connection is open.

- **ICA Settings**   Configures the ICA display and the automatic reconnection of clients.

- **Information**   Contains connection information, published resources, and zone information.

- **Interoperability**   Configures the compatibility with the earlier version, MetaFrame 1.8.

- **MetaFrame XP Settings**   Responds to ICA broadcasts, client time zones, DNS address resolution for the XML service, enables content redirection, and allows remote connection to the Windows Server 2003 console session.

- **SNMP**   Enables and configures the SNMP agents on all servers.

- **SpeedScreen Browser Acceleration**   Optimizes the screen output and defines the handling of the Macromedia Flash Player.

- **Zones**   Displays all zones in the server farm; the individual servers can be prioritized for the election of the zone data collector.

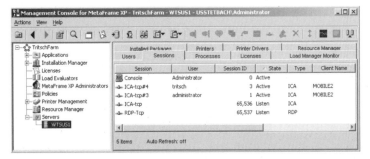

Figure 10-7   The Management Console for MetaFrame XP viewing the current sessions of a server within a farm.

So, the settings for each server in a farm can be viewed and modified. The current status of the server is displayed on the right-hand side in various categories. These contain information categorized by users, sessions, processes, licenses, printers, printer drivers, and other aspects, depending on the version installed. Different actions belong to each category of server properties. In the User and Session categories, for instance, it is possible to connect sessions, disconnect them, shadow them, reset them, query the status, log off, or send messages.

The general configuration of the server can be accessed through Properties in the Actions menu item. As with the server farm, a separate dialog box is used, which categorizes the configuration options based on the following (depending on the product version, you might not be able to see all the options):

- **Hotfixes**   List of all installed service packs and hotfixes.

- **ICA Keep-Alive**   Selection of the option to use the farm-wide configuration of ICA Keep-alive or to configure a server's keep-alive settings individually.

- **ICA Settings**   Configuration of the farm settings or the individual settings of the ICA display, and the automatic reconnection of clients.

- **Ignored Processes**   List of processes that are not monitored if the Resource Manager is installed; in the default settings these are system processes.

- **Information**   Information on the version of MetaFrame installed, the operating system, and the network port used.

- **MetaFrame XP Settings**   Dialog box containing some important configuration options. Here, the system can be made compatible with earlier versions of MetaFrame and the ICA browsers available there. This affects browser lists using UDP and the response to ICA broadcasts. Furthermore, server logon and shadowing logs can be enabled or disabled. There is also the option to change the selected ports for communications with the XML service and for the client-to-server content redirection of documents.

- **Metric Summary Schedule**   Defines when the Resource Manager data is summarized into a report, if the Resource Manager is installed.

- **Printer Bandwidth**   Available client printer bandwidth and setting of an upper limit (in Kbps) for the bandwidth used by client print jobs.

- **Published Applications**   List of published applications. For improved clarity, the list can be divided into groups. These groups are, however, independent of the configured applications grouping in the Program Neighborhood client.

- **Reboot Schedule**   In combination with the Resource Manager, it is possible to set times when the system should automatically reboot.

- **Resource Manager Alerts Recipients**   Configuration of recipients of e-mails or text messages with warnings that can be sent from the Resource Manager, as long as the latter is installed on the system.

- **SNMP**   General Simple Network Management Protocol (SNMP) configuration of the farm settings or individual activation and configuration of SNMP agents. This is used to allow communication with a system that allows the MetaFrame server to be managed using SNMP.

- **SpeedScreen Browser Acceleration**   Improves the response times for published applications that generate HTML output. This includes Microsoft Outlook, Microsoft Outlook Express, or Internet Explorer version 5.5 or later. Can, if required, optimize integrated output through Macromedia Flash Player.

The data display in the Management Console for MetaFrame XP can be updated in two ways: manually and automatically. Manual updating is the default setting and can be invoked by pressing F5. Automatic updating for user and license data can be selected by going to View\Preferences... in the menu. However, this setting is not recommended because it uses up a lot of network bandwidth.

If the number of servers in a farm increases and it becomes difficult to maintain an overview of them, the servers can be logically grouped in folders. Go to Actions \New\Folder to create a new folder. This can also be achieved by simply right-clicking the Servers node in the left-hand pane and from that menu selecting New Folder. Please note that grouping servers logically in this way has no effect on their functionality.

Although this represents only a rough overview of the possibilities of the management console, it is easy to see that it offers centralized access to a wide range of configuration options. This chapter goes on to outline more specific possibilities of the Management Console for MetaFrame XP.

> **Note**   All available options of an enabled list object can be accessed in the left-hand window of the management console by clicking on Actiions. The same is true for selecting the available actions through the context menu of a list object.

Policies

The policies in the management console are completely independent of the Group Policies in Active Directory and therefore represent a separate infrastructure of permissions for MetaFrame settings. The policies allow selected settings for the Citrix MetaFrame XP Presentation Server to be assigned to certain users or user groups. New policies can be created easily by going to Action\Policy\Create Policy or by using the context menu. Existing policies can have user accounts and a relative priority with respect to other policies assigned to them.

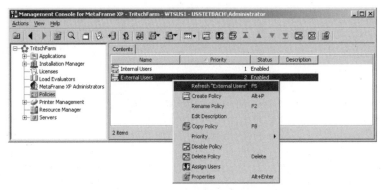

Figure 10-8   Configuring a policy using the context menu.

The configuration options within a policy are quite extensive. They allow exceptions to the default settings to be defined for certain users or user groups. It is possible, for instance, to define a rule for a user group that uses a higher encryption level. Rules in a policy with higher priority override policies of lower priority.

Policies can always be used whenever the basic settings of the Management Console for MetaFrame XP are not to apply to all users equally. This is often the case in large companies or organizational structures. Individual users or user groups are assigned to the policies that should apply to them.

Figure 10-9   Defining a rule within a policy.

Administrators

MetaFrame administrators manage the settings of server farms. In the case of large-scale installations, it can be helpful to delegate individual tasks to different persons at different hierarchical levels. For example, it is often desirable to give an administrator the responsibility for adding and removing servers to and from the farm only, therefore allowing this administrator to perform only this task. That is why the Management Console for MetaFrame XP has the option of assigning user-defined permissions.

Through the context menu of the MetaFrame XP Administrators list object or the Actions\New\MetaFrame XP Administrator... menu item, it is possible to open a wizard to add a new administrator. After an existing user account or group has been selected, the permissions for all objects can be defined. This applies especially to user policies, printers, licenses, servers, sessions, and published applications. Depending on the version of Citrix MetaFrame XP Presentation Server used, there might be other objects in the list as well.

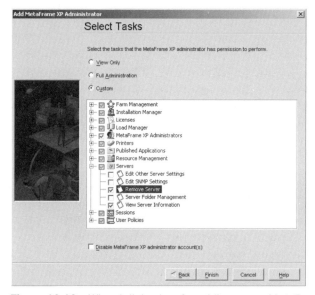

Figure 10-10   Wizard dialog box for adding a new MetaFrame XP administrator.

MetaFrame administrators with user-defined access rights can execute all of the tasks assigned to them without requiring full access to the farm configuration. If one of these administrators picks up an object for which he or she does not have per-missions, the right-hand side of the console remains empty.

Licensing

Using Citrix MetaFrame XP Presentation Server requires Citrix licenses. It is, of course, also essential to have Microsoft licenses for the terminal server, as described in Chapter 2. The Citrix licenses allow access to the extensions that a MetaFrame server offers when compared with an unmodified terminal server.

There are two types of Citrix licenses:

- **Product licenses**   Required for the different types of Citrix products. In the case of MetaFrame XP Presentation Server, these are the product licenses for the different versions of XPs, XPa, XPe, Feature Release 1, Feature Release 2, or Feature Release 3. As of Feature Release 3, Feature Release levels require an additional license separate from the product license. For each version of Citrix MetaFrame XP Presentation Server, only one product license is required per server farm. An unlimited number of servers can be added to the farm. Each product license includes a single connection license so that an administrator can always log on to do any necessary configuration work. The only exception to this licensing model is the demonstration version of the MetaFrame XP Presentation Server, which requires a license for every server.

- **Connection licenses**   Required for users who log on to the servers in a farm using an ICA connection. The number of connection licenses required corresponds to the number of *concurrent users*. The Citrix licensing model therefore differs considerably from the Microsoft licensing model, which is based on one license *per named user* or *per device*. (See Chapter 2.) The connection licenses for a MetaFrame server farm are dependent on the product version; however, connection licenses for a higher or robust version can be used with a lower or more simple version. The Citrix connection licenses are managed in a common pool that can be used for all servers in the farm.

All licenses for the Citrix MetaFrame XP Presentation Server are managed at the farm level and stored in the IMA database. Each MetaFrame server knows which license it needs and retrieves it from the IMA database, providing the latter is available, at the start of the IMA service. Each server's local host cache obtains a copy of the license information to enable it to remain functioning if the connection to the IMA database is lost. The licenses are monitored at run time by the zone data collector.

The connection licenses are usually kept in a common pool and are therefore available to all MetaFrame servers in the farm. However, it is possible to tie connection licenses to an individual MetaFrame server. Some environments require this for organizational reasons.

Important   If a MetaFrame server in the farm loses the connection to the IMA database, users will still be able to log on to it for a maximum of 96 hours. After this time period has elapsed, it will be impossible to log on without a connection to the IMA database.

License Components

To make both license types manageable for different product versions, the licenses consist of several components. Knowledge of these components is helpful in understanding the administrative tasks connected with licensing.

- **Product Code**   An eight-digit number that gives a MetaFrame server its product identity. Citrix distinguishes between XPs, XPa, and XPe and between versions for sale, not for resale, for evaluation, for demonstration, and for beta tests. Additionally, there are the feature release versions that generate their own resulting product code in combination with a product identity. With this number, the MetaFrame server knows which license(s) it has to request from the IMA database when the IMA service is launched.

- **Serial Number**   Each MetaFrame server license consists of a 25-digit serial number. This number is entered using the Management Console for MetaFrame XP either during the installation or during administrative tasks. Using its unique serial number, a MetaFrame server can identify which product licenses and how many connection licenses were purchased. It might be necessary to enter several serial numbers to establish all product and connection licenses on the MetaFrame server farm.

- **Machine Code**   A randomly generated eight-digit number that is added to a license's serial number during the installation. This prevents a license number being used for other server farms. The serial number and the machine code together are often called the license number.

- **Activation Code**   Before the licenses added to a MetaFrame environment by keying in the corresponding serial numbers can be used permanently, they need to be activated. This involves registering the serial numbers and the corresponding machine code with Citrix, whereupon they will be assigned to a fixed owner. To be activated, both the serial number and the machine code must be sent to Citrix, who will then generate a unique 10-digit activation code. This code must then be keyed in to the respective MetaFrame server. The easiest way to do this is to request an activation code via the Citrix portal at *http://www.citrix.com /mycitrix*. The MetaFrame environment can be used for a limited period without activating the license. For most Citrix licenses, this is 35 days. After this time, the environment will stop working if it hasn't been activated.

Citrix offers other types of licenses that are suitable for migration, upgrading, or for large companies. For the latter in particular, it can be very time-consuming to activate a large number of MetaFrame servers. This is why Citrix provides the **Mlicense** command, which allows the process of activation to be automated.

License Management

License management is done through the Licenses list object in the Management Console for MetaFrame XP. All license information can be viewed or modified in four tabs on the right-hand side of the management console.

- **Summary**   This tab provides an overview of the licenses installed, focusing on the product codes.

- **Connection**   Displays all available connection licenses. Double-clicking any listed license brings up a dialog box in which the corresponding properties can be modified. This also includes adding, activating, and deleting licenses.

- **Product**   Displays all available product licenses. Double-clicking any listed license brings up a dialog box in which the corresponding properties can be modified. This also includes adding, activating, and deleting licenses.

- **License Numbers**   This tab displays all license numbers that are installed. The status of the license numbers is shown by the words Not Activated or Activated. Double-clicking a license brings up a dialog box displaying an overview of the license sets and the combination of serial number and machine code.

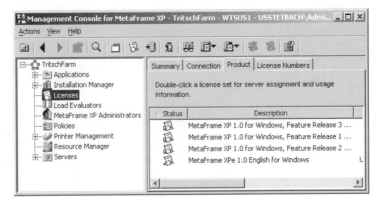

Figure 10-11   The product licenses view.

The Actions\License menu item can be used to add, activate, or delete licenses or to copy them to the clipboard. It can also be used to create a new server-related assignment of licenses so that the licenses are no longer available in the common pool.

Shadow Taskbar

The actions of other users can be monitored by redirecting or shadowing their sessions. The session being shadowed is displayed in the session of the person executing the command. The session being shadowed can be controlled from the other session using the mouse and keyboard. Under the default settings, the shadowed user is asked to allow or reject the shadowing of the session. The mouse, keyboard, and notification options can be controlled for connections by the Terminal Services Configuration or Citrix Connection Configuration utility programs, or by the user administration for individual users.

> **Note**   A shadowing session must support the screen resolution used in the respective shadowed session. The system console cannot be shadowed, and within a console session no other sessions can be shadowed.

The Shadow Taskbar allows shadowing from one location to begin following correct authentication. After activating the Shadow button, you can choose which user session should be shadowed in the environment of the user initiating the shadowing.

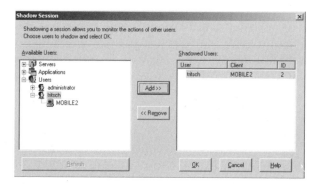

Figure 10-12   Selecting a user session to shadow.

To facilitate a better overview of the shadowed sessions, each is represented in the Shadow Taskbar by a separate button. These buttons can be used to switch quickly between the open shadowed sessions.

For security reasons, the start and the end of the mirroring icon bar can be logged in the Event Viewer. The same applies to the start and end of shadowing sessions. This function is enabled through the context menu of the Shadow taskbar. Furthermore, a shadowed user can terminate the shadowing of the respective session at any time through a special dialog box.

Figure 10-13   The option to terminate shadowing of a user session.

SpeedScreen Latency Reduction Manager

A frequent point of criticism from users is the time lag that occurs between entering an instruction and the session responding to the corresponding mouse action or keyboard input. This time lag is known as latency. Depending on the performance level of clients, network, and server, and the signal runtime between the involved components, latency might create unsuitable conditions for the productive use of a terminal server environment.

To resolve this situation, Citrix developed SpeedScreen technology and the Latency Reduction Manager. SpeedScreen makes it possible to precalculate a local reaction to user input based on the available information at the client level and to display the result. Any minor deviations to the image calculated by the server are corrected when the server is contacted and returns the real image. The slow reaction speed of the human eye means that the corrections between the precalculated and the real image are usually not noticed.

Note   This technology existed with traditional green terminals, as well. It was called the *local echo*. This name is still used today for the reduction of latency times with terminal servers. Because green terminals do not use graphical elements and use only certain determined font types, the technology was relatively simple to realize in that environment. In a terminal server environment, the term local echo refers to entering letters in a character string only and not to the whole SpeedScreen functionality. The client uses the same or a type as close as possible to the font type that is locally available to represent the letter in advance after the user has entered it. Only when the MetaFrame server has answered with the real letter is the display adjusted where applicable and the correct letter displayed.

The SpeedScreen Latency Reduction Manager allows global settings for immediate mouse-click response and local text echoing. This can also be enabled for individual applications and their input boxes. This is relatively time-consuming, however, because each individual application window and all of the desired input boxes need to be incorporated separately. The only connections that will generally benefit from this are those with small bandwidths or long signal runtimes between geographically distant locations.

ICA Client Update Configuration

A common problem in large network environments is the management of the clients and their software versions. Basically, this is also true of the MetaFrame environment. A special tool has therefore been provided that allows the ICA clients to be updated as smoothly as possible. The starting point for this tool is a server-based database with the necessary ICA client software and the corresponding updating functionality located on the ICA clients. A corresponding service is established on the server that copies the new files onto the client with an existing ICA connection.

The database on the server contains all of the installation files that belong to the supported ICA clients. Each ICA client has a unique product, model, variant, and version number that allow it to be identified. If a new version of the installation files for an ICA client is incorporated into the database, the update takes place the next time older clients are connected. The administrator can determine whether a user can intervene in this process. A central database therefore allows all of the ICA clients to be updated.

Client software is added and deleted using the options provided in the Client menu item. New clients to be incorporated into the database can be downloaded from Citrix via the Internet.

Note   An update using the ICA Client Update Configuration tool can be performed only for clients of the same model. This means it does not allow migrating a 16-bit client to a 32-bit client.

New client models can be added using a corresponding menu item. To do this, the path to the installation files must be entered. Then the display shows the name, product, version, model, variant, and icon for the client. Finally, the updating options on the client platform are determined.

The database might contain several clients with the same details concerning product, model, variant, and version. However, only one client can be enabled for each category. This client is the one used for the automatic update.

Note   Under the default settings, the client update database is located in the %SystemRoot%\ICA\ClientDB directory. A new database can be set up on the local server's hard disk or on a shared network drive.

The ICA Client Update Configuration has some shortcomings, which is why many administrators of production environments do not use it. Its inability to support Multicast mechanisms or compression procedures means that more suitable software distribution tools often need to be applied, as described in Chapter 5.

Additional Functions and Commands

Besides the standard functions described earlier, Citrix MetaFrame XP Presentation Server also contains integrated components for the specific support of large server environments. This includes the management of resources on the one hand and the automated installation of applications on the other. Some of the Resource Manager's properties were implied in the descriptions earlier. A more precise description can be found in Chapter 11. The Installation Manager allows applications to be distributed to MetaFrame servers in different package formats. In this respect, the underlying concepts are similar to those of commercial tools for software distribution, as presented in Chapter 5. This is why we will not cover the Citrix Installation Manager in more detail.

In addition to the graphical tools for system administration, Citrix MetaFrame XP Presentation Server comes with a large number of command line extensions. In particular, they allow system parameters to be changed and the runtime environment to be analyzed. The following table lists the special MetaFrame commands individually.

Table 10-1 The MetaFrame Commands

Command	Description
Acrcfg	Configures the settings for automatically reconnecting clients to a MetaFrame server or a MetaFrame server farm.
Altaddr	Specifies an alternative IP address, which a MetaFrame server relays to the client if it requests one. This function is feasible for MetaFrame servers behind firewalls.
App	Secure script interpreter as a simple alternative to Windows Script Host for executing commands before an application is launched. The **App** commands consist of the elements *Copy, Delete, Deleteall, Execute, Path,* and *Workdir.*
Apputil	Adds another server to a published application.
Auditlog	Generates logon and logoff reports in the security log of the Event Viewer. The output can also be redirected into a file.
Change client	Displays the assignment of hard disks, COM connections, and LPT connections on client devices and allows them to be modified. All parameters of the **Change** command (such as *Logon, Port,* or *User*) are part of the standard scope of Windows Server 2003 and not of Citrix MetaFrame XP Presentation Server.
Chfarm	Allows the membership of a MetaFrame server to be changed to a different farm.
Clicense	Used for adding, deleting, requesting, and managing licenses on MetaFrame servers in a farm.
Cltprint	Sets the number of printer queues for clients.

Table 10-1   The MetaFrame Commands

Command	Description
Ctxxmlss	Changes the connection port of the Citrix XML service.
Driveremap	Changes the assignments of drive letters on a MetaFrame server. This command should never be executed after applications have been installed on the MetaFrame server.
Dscheck	Checks the consistency of the IMA data store.
Dsmaint	Configures the IMA data store for a MetaFrame server farm.
Icaport	Configures the connection port for TCP/IP that is used by the ICA protocol. The default port is 1494.
Imaport	Configures the connection port for TCP/IP that is used by the ICA protocol. The default port for accessing the management console is 2512 and for the accessing the IMA database it is 2513.
Migratetomsde	Migrates the IMA data store from Microsoft Access to Microsoft SQL Server 2000 Database Engine (MSDE). The **Migratetomsde** service program should be executed from the Support\MSDE folder on the CD provided with the MetaFrame XP Presentation Server.
Mlicense	This command is used for adding and activating several licenses on a MetaFrame server including the creation of a backup copy. Text and XML files containing the license numbers and other required information provide the basis for the automated execution of this task.
Query farm	Displays farm information.
Query process	Displays process information.
Query server	Displays the status of the available MetaFrame server in the network.
Query session	Displays session information.
Query termserver	Displays information on the terminal server.
Query user	Displays user information.
Twconfig	Allows the configuration of display settings that affect the graphical output for ICA clients.

Published Applications

Small companies might find it sufficient to access the desktop of a MetaFrame server using ICA clients. Larger and more complex environments, however, require more far-reaching concepts for the provision of individual applications.

Publishing applications is precisely the function that allows an ICA client to launch applications on a MetaFrame server without having to load the entire desktop. This allows users without in-depth knowledge of the Windows Server 2003 desktop to work with the Microsoft Windows applications installed on it. Moreover, this method also allows Windows applications or user sessions to be launched without the user knowing the name of the corresponding MetaFrame server or having to do any configuration work on the client. Instead of connecting directly to a MetaFrame server, the name of which might change, the user looks for a published application and launches it. In doing so, the user is also shielded from the operating mechanisms of the MetaFrame server environment.

Applications published on a MetaFrame server farm have the following properties:

■ Published application icons and links are automatically distributed for users of Program Neighborhood clients or Program Neighborhood Agents. No additional configuration of the client is required.

■ The applications are bundled in application groups for Program Neighborhood users. This gives the administrators greater control over how the application is provided to users.

■ For applications published in a server farm, the connection properties are preconfigured—for example, window size and color for the session, the supported encryption levels, and audio settings. Depending on the application's minimum requirements in terms of client capability, they might or might not be available in a user's Program Neighborhood.

■ When publishing an application, the administrator can create a shortcut to the published application in the start menu or on the desktop. For this to work, a Program Neighborhood client or a Program Neighborhood Agent is required.

■ The applications can be made accessible to certain explicit users, or user groups, only. This means it is possible to ensure that the application icons appear on the desktops or in the start menus only of those users who are actually allowed to use the applications.

Applications, Desktops, and Contents

As indicated in Chapter 9, the MetaFrame server can publish not only applications, but also desktops. But what is the point of this option? The answer is relatively simple. Only published desktops can be addressed with a logical name within a server farm. The client or its user no longer need to know the name or the IP address of the MetaFrame server. In addition, on several MetaFrame servers, a published desktop is an essential prerequisite for establishing load balancing. The underlying concepts of load balancing are described in more detail in Chapter 11.

Using the Program Neighborhood, the shortcuts to published applications and desktops can be displayed for each user specifically at different positions on the client: in the main window of the Program Neighborhood, in the Start menu, or on the desktop. When applications are launched, these shortcuts are usually displayed in the kind of windows that are also common for local applications. Because no special frame indicating the remote nature of the applications is displayed around the window of the published applications, Citrix calls this mode *seamless windows*. Behind the window for an application of this kind, there is still something like the desktop of the corresponding MetaFrame server, but it is never visible. It is always exactly the same size as the application window itself, even if the user increases or decreases the size of this window.

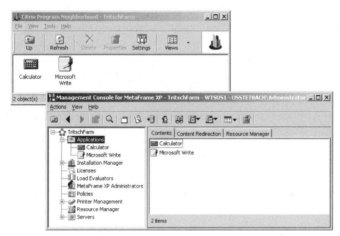

Figure 10-14   Parallel view of published applications in the Program Neighborhood (top) and in the Management Console for MetaFrame XP (bottom).

Before publishing applications and desktops, it is essential to consider which users or user groups are to be allowed to access these applications. There are two basic types of access that can be determined when setting up the published application: explicit access through user accounts or anonymous access through guest accounts.

> **Note**   Even many of the older ICA clients support the launching of published applications and desktops. However, full functionality is available only with the Program Neighborhood clients or the Program Neighborhood Agents.

Just as it is possible to publish applications and desktops, a MetaFrame server also offers options for publishing contents. This is how an administrator provides access to documents, multimedia files, or Web sites. The links to the published contents are presented to a user in exactly the same way as the links to published applications. The published contents are opened and displayed either by corresponding local client applications or by the corresponding published applications of a MetaFrame server. In this way, certain user groups can be given access to links to documents located on the central servers.

To configure a user environment with published applications, desktops, and content, two steps must be taken. The first concerns the MetaFrame server, the second relates to the ICA client. The necessary server settings are described in the following section; the ICA client configuration was presented in Chapter 9.

> **Important**   More so than for most other concepts, there must be an accurate resolution of computer names via DNS if published applications, desktops, and contents are to interact correctly with the Program Neighborhood. (See Chapter 3.) The complex communication patterns between MetaFrame server, IMA data store, zone data collector, XML service, and ICA clients mean that even minor mistakes in the configuration of the name resolution can lead to unsatisfactory results.

Setting Up Published Applications and Contents

Publishing applications is a central function of the Citrix MetaFrame XP Presentation Server. A published application is set up with the help of a corresponding list object in the management console for MetaFrame. To do this, the administrator should proceed as follows:

1. Open the wizard for publishing an application by going to the Actions\New \Published Application menu item.

2. Enter the display names and application description.

3. Determine the object to be published. This can be an application, a desktop, or content. For an application, enter the command line and the working directory. For a desktop, enter the server name, and for content, enter the document source.

4. Enter the settings for launching the application or the desktop in the Program Neighborhood. This includes the creation of the name of the Program Neighborhood folder in the Start menu and the creation of shortcuts in the Start menu or on the client desktop.

5. Set the size, color depth, and title bar for the session window. If the application is launched in seamless mode, the settings for size and title bar will be ignored.

6. Determine the ICA client requirements relating to audio, encryption, and print options.

7. Enter the application limit that relates to the maximum number of application instances per server farm or per user. It is also possible to select a level of priority for launching the application.

8. Select the servers upon which to publish the application or the desktop.

9. Determine the users or user groups that have permission to access the application or desktop. It is also possible to allow anonymous access to the published application.

10. Enter a file type assignment if client-to-server content redirection is going to be defined. This allows local files to be opened with a published application of the MetaFrame server.

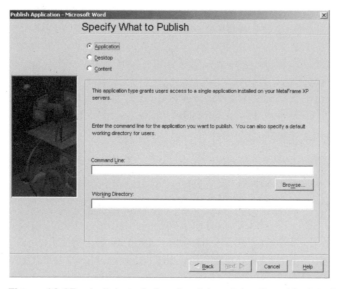

Figure 10-15   A dialog window for determining the object to be published in the corresponding wizard.

Note   Anonymous access is based on special local accounts that are created automatically during the installation of the Citrix MetaFrame XP Presentation Server. In terms of security, these accounts are comparable to the Guests user group under Windows Server 2003 and do not save a profile. Using these accounts, users log on to the system without entering an individual user name or password. This feature is especially intended to allow the system to be accessed via the Internet, although it is essential to respect the licensing terms of the application concerned. It is important to note, however, that these very user accounts will not be available if the Citrix MetaFrame XP Presentation Server, against all the recommendations, is installed on a domain controller.

Publishing contents via the MetaFrame server allows documents to be assigned to users in the same way as applications and desktops are. The documents are then displayed through the Program Neighborhood clients or the Program Neighborhood Agents. The addresses of the respective document can link up with Web servers, FTP servers, or file servers with shared folders.

As with the servers, the application display can become very disorganized if there are a large number of entries. This is why the applications can be bundled in folders. A new folder can be added by going to Actions\New\Folder. These folders have nothing to do with the order of icons in the Program Neighborhood that was determined within the Program Neighborhood folder properties.

Printing

A very important function for many MetaFrame server users is printing. Printers can be integrated into user sessions in various ways, which makes the issue a complex and somewhat problematic one:

- Printers that are physically connected to the client device.

- Shared printers that are connected to the client operating system through the network and possibly also through a print server.

- Virtual printers that are used to redirect document data in files with specific formats on the client device. The file formats can be, for example, PostScript, Adobe Portable Document Format (PDF), or Hewlett-Packard Printer Control Language (PCL).

- Printers that are physically connected to the MetaFrame server. However, this is not a very common option in real-world environments.

- Shared printers that are connected to the MetaFrame server through the network and through a print server. These are often the same printers that a client can access through the network.

Some of the system constellations described here might result in bottlenecks due to the network bandwidth they require for printing. Mapping the printers connected to the client devices locally in a MetaFrame server user session is also no simple task because of the possible differences between client and server platforms. The assignment of the desired printers is another aspect that requires some explanation if it is to be done by users themselves. That is why the Citrix MetaFrame XP Presentation Server provides a range of mechanisms and tools for managing printers.

Managing Printers

When a connection is established between an ICA client and a MetaFrame server, an attempt is made to create a connection between the local printer configuration and the user session (the same as with an unmodified terminal server). When the user logs on, the print drivers that are installed on the client are dynamically loaded on the MetaFrame server side and will later be removed again. In other words, the server is basically asking the client which drivers it has installed and is integrating them locally in the user session. Users can therefore print on local printers without any extra effort, even though they might be working in a user session that is physically being executed on the MetaFrame server. However, the necessary print drivers must exist on the MetaFrame server, and the information about the printer on the client must be complete. (See Chapter 4 for more details.) An automatically created printer within a user session will have the name \\Clientname#\Printername.

> **Tip**   The properties of an automatically created printer should never be modified manually. The proper functioning of the printer assignment is based on certain predetermined, and also automatically created, information.

The basic tasks involved with managing printers can be performed through the Printer Management list object in the Management Console for MetaFrame XP. The properties of this list object lead to a dialog box that allows the configuration of standards for the automatic creation of client printers. This includes how printer properties, print jobs, and printer selection are handled during the user logon procedure.

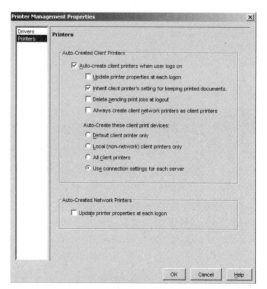

Figure 10-16   Configuring the behavior when creating client printers.

Furthermore, selecting the Printer Administration list object allows access to three tabs that can be used to modify the basic settings of the print system:

- **Content** This displays the objects Printers and Drivers, which can also be seen in the structure under the Printer Administration list object. Besides displaying the installed printers and assigning printers to users, this feature is also used to configure the automatic replication of installed print drivers to other MetaFrame servers. This is done in the subordinated tab called Drivers accessed through the context menu of the individual print drivers listed.

- **Network Print Server** Here, network print servers can be listed and added using the menu item Actions\Printer Management\Import Network Print Server. It is, of course, also possible to delete network print servers and update the corresponding information.

- **Bandwidth** This feature allows the bandwidth of the print data stream to be defined for each server in the farm. This prevents user sessions from being negatively affected when the network is experiencing a heavy load from large print jobs. However, for each server it is possible to define only settings that are the same for both LAN and WAN. In this case, the corresponding printers in the LAN might function at full capacity.

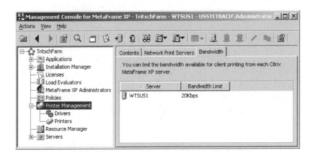

Figure 10-17 Managing the printer configuration.

Most of these printer settings can also be conducted in the Server list object, but they will then apply only to individual MetaFrame servers.

How are client printers assigned to print drivers on the MetaFrame server? When a user logs on, the name of a print driver on the client will be transmitted to the MetaFrame server over the ICA protocol. The MetaFrame server checks whether it also has a driver of the same name installed. If it does, this is the driver that is used for creating the print data streams. However, there will always be cases when the identical printer name is not available on the client and the MetaFrame server. There could be any number of reasons for this: the client and server platforms are too different, the print model on the client was installed using an OEM driver, or some default print drivers were removed from the server. The solution to the problem is to logically map the respective print drivers using the menu item Actions\Printer

Management\Mapping... in the Management Console for MetaFrame XP. In the corresponding dialog box, the *exact* names of the client print drivers (including all spaces and special characters) can be mapped to the corresponding names of the server print drivers.

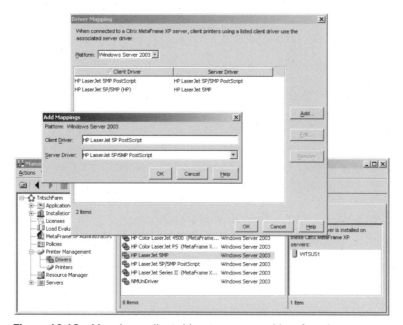

Figure 10-18   Mapping a client driver to a server driver for printers.

The result of the mapping will be saved in the Wtsprnt.inf file, which is located in the %Systemroot%\system32 folder. It is also possible to execute additional mapping information in the %Systemroot%\System32\Wtsuprn.inf file, which, however, is applied at user level. A template called Wtsuprn.txt is placed in the Programs\Citrix \System32 folder when the installation of Citrix MetaFrame XP Presentation Server is completed.

Listing 10-1: Wtsprnt.inf Following the Mapping of Some Print Drivers

```
;
;          WTSPRNT.INF -- DO  NOT  CHANGE
;
;This file is supplied by Citrix as a reference and best guess for
;client printer selections.  The file wtsuprn.inf is the user file
;for client printer mapping and takes precedence over this file.
;An example file, wtsuprn.txt is supplied as a template.
;
;This file is changed automatically when the admin makes changes to
;the MetaFrame farm wide driver mapping settings.
;This file may be overwritten during software upgrades!
```

```
[Identification]
OptionType=PRINTER
[ClientPrinters]
"HP LaserJet 5P/5MP (HP)"="HP LaserJet 5MP"
"HP LaserJet 5MP PostScript"="HP LaserJet 5P/5MP PostScript"
"HP LaserJet 5P PostScript"="HP LaserJet 5P/5MP PostScript"
```

Universal Printer Drivers

The Citrix MetaFrame XP Presentation Server comes with universal printer drivers that are used to address printers on the clients using a default print format. In many cases, this prevents having to install a large number of specific print drivers. Naturally, the universal printer drivers with their general data formats cannot support all of the properties of the various printer products on the market, but they do represent a common denominator. For higher requirements, the specific drivers are still needed. Buying, testing, installing, and managing a large number of specific drivers is, however, extremely time-consuming.

So how do you print with a universal printer driver? The universal printer driver on the MetaFrame server creates the print data stream in a universal format. This print job is directed to the ICA client over the spooler. There, the client printer outputs the print data stream directly, providing that it correctly interprets the universal data format. If it does not, the client's local printer drivers generate a specific data stream from the universal print data format that the selected printer can understand.

Citrix supplies three universal print drivers with the MetaFrame XP Presentation Server:

- **PCL4** Understood even by older ICA clients and allows black and white printing to a resolution of 300 dots per inch (dpi).

- **PCL5c** Understood only by 32-bit Windows and Macintosh clients of version 7.0, but it does offer color and black and white printing to a resolution of up to 600 dpi.

- **PostScript** Can be used with version 7.0 of the UNIX client. PostScript-compatible printers and emulators also understand this format directly.

If the client printers are created automatically, it is also possible to specify whether universal or native print drivers should be used. This is done by going to Drivers in the properties under Printer Administration in the Management Console for MetaFrame XP.

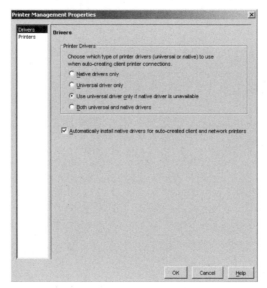

Figure 10-19   Choosing when to use universal printer drivers.

The following options are available for using universal printer drivers:

■ **Native drivers only**   The use of universal printer drivers is disabled. If a specific printer driver is not available on the server when the user logs on, the client printer cannot be created on the MetaFrame server.

■ **Universal drivers only**   Only the universal drivers are used, not the native drivers.

■ **Use universal driver only if native driver is unavailable**   The native drivers are the drivers of choice. Only if a native driver is not available on the MetaFrame server is a universal printer driver used.

■ **Both universal and native drivers**   Both options can be used in parallel. However, the user must be very skilled in selecting the right driver for a specific task.

■ **Automatically install native drivers for autocreated client and network printers**   This option allows the automatic installation of native print drivers, at which point the choice of printer can be set up through the driver compatibility list. This can be opened by going to Actions\Printer Management\Compatibility.

ICA Client Printer Configuration

The ICA Client Printer Configuration manages the mapping of client printers and can be used for this purpose by all users. For this reason, it might not be the best solution to combine it with the administration tools into the same menu structure. It cannot be invoked from the system console of a MetaFrame server; it can be invoked only from an ICA session.

When the ICA client printer configuration is launched, it displays the printers available on the client. The options provided by the ICA protocols to use not only the server printers, but also the local printers, mean that each client often has an individual list to select from. The connections for the client printers have their own naming conventions that take into account the local names of the printers.

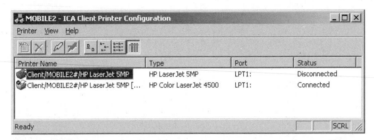

Figure 10-20 ICA client printer configuration. Here it identifies different printers on the client and suggests them for integration in the user session.

Scalability

If Citrix MetaFrame XP is intended for use in a large corporate environment, the issue of maximum scalability is bound to arise. It is important to bear the following point in mind when considering the details given later in this section: all extension products offered by Citrix for Windows Server 2003 are offered with the aim of increasing the scalability of terminal servers. Citrix products can therefore help achieve a scale among servers, clients, printers, and users in a farm that would otherwise be impossible to accomplish. The mechanisms employed in achieving this aim range from highly specialized load-balancing mechanisms and bandwidth control for multimedia data and print data streams to concepts for published applications, seamless windows, and the Program Neighborhood.

However, even Citrix products have their limits, mostly caused by the communication between clients, IMA services, zone data collectors, and the IMA database. Knowing and respecting these limits has proved useful during many a project. The details given in the following paragraphs should therefore be considered rough guidelines concerning the scalability of a MetaFrame farm.

When we speak of scalability here, often the only statements that can be made are relative ones made on the basis of sample implementations or extrapolations. It is vital that reference values be defined in order for this issue to be properly considered. Such reference values include specific statements about the acceptable response times in relation to certain occurrences. This means that an administrator or an architect of a future MetaFrame environment must consider the permissible times for a server to restart, for load-balancing information to be identified, for an application to be published, and for certain information to be opened to the Management Console for MetaFrame XP. Only then can the earlier mentioned relative statements truly be viewed in relation to the requirements. To round off the topic, extensive load tests should ideally follow to verify the forecasts made.

> **Important** With its products, Citrix is positioned primarily in the environment of companies above a certain size. Individual MetaFrame servers do not play as central a role as larger server farms do. The following points do not, therefore, relate to the bandwidth of the ICA protocol, the number of user sessions on individual servers, or the launch times of applications. For these parameters, the difference between an unmodified terminal server with RDP protocol and a MetaFrame server with ICA protocol is minimal. The relevant values and scalability factors were described in detail in Chapter 3 and Chapter 5. The points in the following section will be interesting to readers who want to build larger environments with MetaFrame servers.

Number of Servers in Farms and Zones

The maximum number of servers in a farm or a zone is determined by certain factors. First of all, there is a limit, set by Citrix, of 512 servers per zone. While it is possible to increase this limit by modifying the registry database, it is not advisable to do so. This is because it is not advisable to have more than a couple of hundred servers per zone that all communicate with their zone data collector and to which they transmit all of their information.

If there are several zones in a farm, the respective zone data collectors are in constant communication with each other. According to Citrix, this usually results in less than 1 kilobyte of data transfer for certain events, such as publishing an application, making a connection, ending a connection, reconnecting, and logging off a user. If printer drivers are replicated as well, the volume of data passing to the zone data collectors and moving between the zones naturally increases.

The Management Console for MetaFrame XP reads all of the data from the IMA database that it displays. The response time for displaying the various information also depends very much on the number of servers involved. In very large server farms, it might – depending on the number of published applications and the printer configuration – take longer than usual for all of the required data to be made available.

Where there is already a large farm with a lot of applications published on all servers, a further bottleneck arises if a new server is added. This new server must be added to all of the published applications, which means accessing the IMA database every time. If this is done manually using the Management Console for MetaFrame XP, there is no apparent direct impact. However, if an automation script is used that publishes the applications via Citrix's MFCOM interface, it will result in considerably longer script runtimes, depending on the size of the farm.

Extreme scalability is a feature of the load-balancing mechanism of the Citrix MetaFrame XP Presentation Server and its predecessors. Even with a very large number of clients and servers in a farm, a client is always assigned quickly to the server with the greatest amount of free capacity. In this respect it is very unlikely to come up against any limitations in real production environments with fewer than 1,000 servers.

> **Note**   There has been little experience to date with installations of more than 1,000 servers in a logical network. Most large environments with more than 1,000 servers are organized in several separate farms that are not directly linked with each other. However, it is increasingly likely that in the future even farm constellations with considerably more than 1,000 directly linked nodes will be needed. Designing this kind of environment is sure to be a major challenge for administrators, architects, and system integrators.

Number of Applications and Printer Drivers

Having looked at the number of servers in a MetaFrame farm, we will now consider the published applications and the replicated printer drivers.

> **Note**   Citrix improves the scalability of its products with each new generation. The numbers cited in the following paragraph should therefore be viewed with caution, as they represent a moment in time in a test environment. In particular, the introduction of the Feature Release 3 for MetaFrame XP, which corresponds to the current version of MetaFrame XP for Windows Server 2003, has implemented major improvements in IMA database access.

The more information a MetaFrame server requires from the IMA database, the longer it and the respective IMA service will take to start up. Problems arose in two different test scenarios. In one test there were 50 published applications and 500 servers. Another test involved up to 1,500 published applications and 140 servers.

When the servers were started up during the tests, all of the required information from the IMA database was competing to be read. When the MetaFrame servers were started up simultaneously, in the first test scenario the initial SQL database server with two CPUs achieved a state of saturation with 100 percent processor load over a long period. Only when an eight-way system and sufficient main memory were employed did the situation improve. In this case, the network was the limiting factor.

In the second test scenario, it was impossible to start up the servers simultaneously. Here, the servers had to be started up successively to achieve acceptable times. Also, by the end of the second test scenario, the time delays in publishing additional applications from the Management Console for MetaFrame XP had increased considerably. But the system did remain fully functioning.

Naturally, the results of the two tests should be viewed only in correlation with the hardware employed and cannot be directly transferred to a general context. However, the results do highlight a certain tendency in terms of the dimensions of MetaFrame environments. If a company really wants to operate several hundred servers with more than 1,000 published applications in a single farm, major problems could be expected in performing certain administrative tasks. It is therefore advisable to segment the farm and the applications into smaller units.

Note   Even in cases in which, due to farm size, the time it takes to start up the IMA service under Windows Server 2003 is so long that it provokes an error message, the system, generally speaking, will still function properly.

Another critical parameter is the return of the list of published applications if a client requests it. Tests show that the time required depends on the number of published applications, not on the number of servers. Only when the number of applications goes beyond 1000 will the response time exceed 2 seconds. What is certainly a problem here, however, is a scenario where a very large number of users almost simultaneously requests information on all the published applications they are entitled to. This might occur, for example, if all of a company's employees start work at the same time and log on via the Program Neighborhood. If all of the queries go through the same MetaFrame server, saturation problems are very likely to arise.

The replication of print drivers is another aspect that can reach its limitations in large environments. A single queue for the driver replication should have no more than 1,500 entries. The number of entries is calculated by multiplying the number of servers with the number of drivers. So if a farm consists of 100 servers, there should be no more than 15 printer drivers in the queue. The sheer volume of data required for transmitting the drivers themselves makes it unwise to replicate printer drivers during the core working hours of the users.

> **Note**   The number of replicated printer drivers influences the startup times of the IMA service. The same is true if many different license numbers in the IMA database need to be supplied. All of this information needs to be transmitted when the MetaFrame server starts up, and therefore the transmission leads to delays.

Finally, the following formula is a means of calculating the total approximate volume of data in kilobytes that a MetaFrame server receives from the IMA database when it is starting up.

```
IMA data = 402 + 6.82*(servers-1)
```

```
In this formula, the variable »servers« represents the number of MetaFrame servers in
the farm
```

Security

The issue of security is definitely an important one for Citrix MetaFrame XP Presentation Server. There are three main options for securing the data streams exchanged between the MetaFrame server and the ICA clients: ICA encryption, SSL Relay, and Secure Gateway. These complement the security mechanisms presented in Chapter 8.

ICA Encryption

ICA encryption allows the data connection between a MetaFrame server and an ICA client to be made secure. During the configuration of the ICA client or when publishing applications and desktops, it is possible to set the desired encryption options. The encryption level for the ICA protocol can be set through the extended connection settings of Citrix Connection Configuration or through the Terminal Services Configuration properties. It is also possible to set the required encryption of an ICA connection using a rule in the policies. The methods described in the following list progress from the weakest level of encryption to the strongest.

The available options for the encryption levels are as follows:

- Basic encryption based on a non-RC5-conform algorithm that does not provide complete protection from deciphering the data.

- RC5 encryption with 128 bit for authentication only; the ICA connection is encrypted with the basic procedure.

- RC5 encryption with 40 bit for the whole ICA data stream.

- RC5 encryption with 56 bit for the whole ICA data stream.

- RC5 encryption with 128 bit for the whole ICA data stream.

In principle, ICA encryption is a means of making it difficult or impossible for an unauthorized user to intercept data from an ICA communication and to display it in a comprehensible form without going to an excessive amount of trouble. An attacker could see, at most, meaningless screen commands, but he or she would be unable to extract any sensitive information.

ICA encryption is primarily used for internal communication within a corporate network. It is supported by almost all versions of the ICA client software. ICA encryption presents some problems if the communication is on public networks (the Internet) or across perimeter networks (demilitarized zones).

> **Note**   A *perimeter network* uses firewalls to establish special network segments that do not belong to the internal or the external network. This is done using package filtering mechanisms. These perimeter networks (also known as DMZs, demilitarized zones, and screened subnets) contain particularly endangered components that can be addressed only from the intranet or extranet through special connection ports. The separation of servers with certain particularly exposed services usually increases the security of a corporate network considerably.

Citrix SSL Relay

The Citrix SSL Relay ensures consistent encryption through Secure Socket Layer (SSL) or Transport Layer Security (TLS) between appropriately configured MetaFrame servers and the ICA clients. (See Chapter 8.) The ICA data stream on the MetaFrame server is sent to the SSL Relay, which then encrypts the data following the standard procedure. Almost all ICA clients can then communicate with the MetaFrame server through the encrypted data stream.

It makes sense to use Citrix SSL Relay where only a small number of MetaFrame servers are concerned, no perimeter network is used, and the IP address of the MetaFrame server does not need to be hidden through Network Address Translation (NAT), but industry-standard consistent encryption between the MetaFrame server and ICA clients is required.

The basic prerequisite for using Citrix SSL Relay is that every MetaFrame server to be secured must have a server certificate installed under %Systemroot%\sslrelay \keystore\certs. Either an X.509 certificate can be bought from a certifying authority, or a certificate can be created through the company's own Certificate Authority. After this has been done, the further configuration can be carried out by the Citrix SSL Relay Configuration Tool, which is found under Start\All Programs\MetaFrame XP.

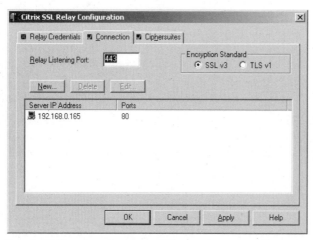

Figure 10-21   The Citrix SSL Relay Configuration tool.

Secure Gateway

A considerably more scalable means of encrypting the ICA data stream with SSL or TSL is the Citrix Secure Gateway. It establishes its own central instance in the network that can encode large numbers of ICA connections between MetaFrame servers and ICA clients. As with Citrix SSL Relay, the Secure Gateway uses server certificates.

The Secure Gateway encrypts the ICA data streams and the access to the MetaFrame server through a single point. This considerably simplifies the management of the certificates and means that the IP addresses of all of the involved MetaFrame servers do not need to be published. Only the Secure Gateway needs to have the MetaFrame server's address information.

Figure 10-22   The Secure Gateway for Citrix MetaFrame XP Presentation Server.

The problem here is that the ICA connection between the MetaFrame servers and the Secure Gateway is not secure. Only the connections between the Secure Gateway and the ICA clients are encrypted by SSL or TSL. It is therefore important in many environments to use the ICA encryption feature in combination with Secure Gateway.

Chapter 11

Resource Management in Server Farms

Previous chapters have focused on terminal servers individually or in small groups. Larger environments were really mentioned for the first time in Chapter 10, when Citrix MetaFrame XP Presentation Server was presented. In fact, terminal server environments have shown a recent tendency to increase in scope because they have become more commonly used as a strategic solution in companies with many tens of thousands or hundreds of thousands of workstations. Collections of farms with more than 100 terminal servers are nothing new these days, unlike just a few years ago. Furthermore, some of these farms are no longer used in pure Microsoft environments and need to inter-operate with other operating systems.

So what is the best way to deal with the technical requirements in large, mixed environments? On the one hand, installation procedures and operating concepts need to be highly standardized and automated, as described in previous chapters. On the other hand, it is, of course, necessary to design the large-scale terminal server environments with potentially heterogeneous infrastructures in such a way that they meet requirements concerning scalability, resource administration, and stability. For this reason, many of the issues described here relate only to Microsoft

Windows Server 2003, Enterprise Edition, or require the use of additional tools. This chapter will cover the following topics:

- Find out about load balancing and the Session Directory, which are the basic technologies for successfully distributing the application load and making terminal server environments scalable, with a focus on third-party products in particular.

- Learn how to plan, analyze, and manage the required resources for large terminal server environments with the help of appropriate tools from Microsoft and others. This section also touches upon the issue of automatically limiting resource allocation for individual user sessions or application programs.

- Become familiar with the concepts and the available tools for conducting meaningful load tests in a terminal server environment.

- Take a brief look at how third-party systems can be integrated into terminal server environments.

This chapter focuses on the strengths of the Windows Server 2003 family because it represents a workable, stable, and scalable platform on which to build large-scale corporate environments. Microsoft provides a solution for all the issues raised in this chapter. However, where maximum scalability is the dominant consideration, add-on products by specialized manufacturers might be needed to meet all requirements. Using third-party add-on tools is intentional where the aim is to offer an appropriate solution to meet the special needs of certain customer segments with a general product, such as Windows Server 2003. Citrix provides particularly good solutions in this respect, as was demonstrated in previous chapters.

Load Balancing and the Session Directory

As soon as there is more than one terminal server in a corporate environment, the issue of load balancing at the server level arises. How can the system be set up such that users do not need to directly log on to one of the available terminal servers without knowing how heavy its load is at the time?

In an environment with several terminal servers, these servers can be grouped into logical units known as *server farms*. First, these server farms serve to create a logical connection between the individual servers to make it easier to manage them jointly. Second, load-balancing mechanisms can be established in server farms. A farm represents an individual logical unit with a unique name for one client. The point responsible for balancing the load within a farm uses an adequate algorithm to redirect the connection to the most suitable server in the load-balancing network.

There are several different technologies connected with load balancing on terminal servers. Each addresses different requirements relating to availability, scalability, and supporting special functions.

> **Important**   Most load-balancing mechanisms only function appropriately when the terminal servers in a farm are configured with identical software and hardware. If they are not identical, users experience inconsistent performance when using several differently configured terminal server connections. The installation of Windows Server 2003 and applications for terminal servers was described in detail in Chapter 2 and Chapter 5. In addition, for terminal servers to function in a load-balancing network, user data, user profiles, and home directories must be stored on dedicated file servers. None of the production terminal servers should assume additional tasks, such as those of Web servers, database servers, or print servers. Only then will the environment have the optimum configuration for a terminal server farm.

Network Load Balancing

By default, the first port of call when looking for a solution for load balancing between terminal servers is Microsoft. After all, the producer of Terminal Services ought to have an intimate knowledge of the elements required for establishing a server farm. Regrettably, however, there is no explicit function to fulfill this purpose. Only when you take a more "creative" approach to looking for a solution do you come across the Microsoft Windows cluster technology, which, at first glance, does not seem to have anything to do with terminal servers. On closer inspection, though, this technology offers at least a minimum solution for a terminal server farm.

The Windows cluster technology is an integrated option for raising the availability and scalability of system services. The various constellations of Windows Server 2003 products and versions contain three different cluster options. However, only the first of the options listed here is truly relevant for terminal servers:

- **Network Load Balancing Service (NLBS)**   Available in all versions of Windows Server 2003. The maximum number of servers is 32. It is commonly used for load balancing for TCP and UDP data traffic for terminal servers, Web servers, Internet Security and Acceleration (ISA) servers, Windows Media Servers, and Mobile Information Servers.

- **Component Load Balancing (CLB)**   Available in Microsoft Application Center 2000. The maximum number of servers is 12. This technology is used to establish an individual configuration and administration point for Web server farms. Nonetheless, the technology is irrelevant for terminal servers.

- **Server clusters**   Available in Windows Server 2003, Enterprise Edition or later. The maximum number of servers is eight. Special hardware components can be used to connect Microsoft SQL Servers, Microsoft Exchange Servers, file servers, or print servers so that, should one server fail, another will assume all of the required processes. Processes continue in the same status as prior to the failure. The cluster service is not compatible with the terminal server service and can only be used around the periphery of terminal servers.

The concept of server farms is extremely important for terminal servers—even though the Network Load Balancing Service is more effective with Web servers. Still, terminal servers installed in an identical manner can be integrated into one server farm using NLB. An incoming client request is then distributed to one server in the farm. The appropriate load for the individual servers in the farm can be configured in relatively coarse terms. If the total operational load increases over time, additional servers can be added to the farm. This reduces the load on the individual servers and means easy scalability for the entire environment.

If a server fails or is shut down unexpectedly, the respective user sessions are often lost. But, if they log on again, users are immediately redirected to another server available on the load-balancing network, where they can carry on working. Of course, for this to function, the user data must not be stored on the terminal servers; it must be managed by specialized data servers that are attached to the system, for example, a file server or database server. Only then will all of the data entered before the last time the save function was used be available when the user logs back on. That is why it is always advisable when installing applications to make sure that the automatic save function is enabled for user data and set at relatively short intervals.

> **Note** In a traditional client/server model, both the failover capabilities of the user interface components and the administration complexity of the application layer are increased on servers in a Network Load Balancing Service environment. Generally terminal servers or Web servers are clustered with Microsoft Network Load Balancing Service. The data layer servers, on the other hand, are usually configured as server clusters. These two cluster solutions, that is, load-balanced servers and clustered servers, must not be confused. See Chapter 1 for common client/server models.

The mechanisms of the Microsoft Network Load Balancing Service are only relevant for terminal servers at the time of user logon. However, the actual load on the individual servers at the time is not measured by the Network Load Balancing Service, so a more appropriate name for the procedure might be *connection balancing*. Once the user session has been established via the conditional protocols, RDP or ICA, the communication between terminal server and Terminal Services client takes place without any further load balancing. The relevant dedicated network connection usually remains the same for the whole duration of the session. The user session therefore stays on the same server for its entire lifecycle, even if there happens to be other servers in the farm experiencing lower load at certain times; which would make them more suitable for more active client connections. Users who log off and log back on might be connected to another server by the Network Load Balancing Service.

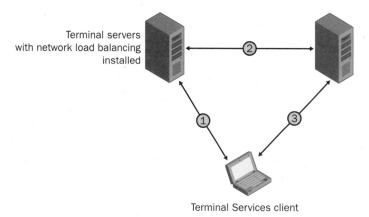

Figure 11-1   Communication channels for load balancing: (1) Terminal Services client connects with a terminal server to Network Load Balancing Service installed. (2) Network Load Balancing Service determines the terminal server that responds fastest. (3) The RDP connection is established with the selected terminal server.

An exception to this rule occurs when the connection is intentionally or unintentionally interrupted. In line with the preset configuration, the respective client session might remain open on its terminal server and be used again once the connection is re-established. Obviously, load balancing does not make sense here, because it is highly likely that a different server will be selected by the load-balancing service when the connection is re-established. That would result in a new user session being started on another terminal server while the interrupted user session remains active in the memory of another server. In that case, it would be impossible to open documents from the second user session even with the appropriate permissions if they were still being accessed in the first, no longer used, user session. To solve this problem, Microsoft developed the Session Directory with Windows Server 2003. (See later in this chapter for more details.)

System Requirements and Activation

With Windows Server 2003, the Network Load Balancing Service is executed with the default network driver. The latest version was designed to use Ethernet adapters at 10 megabits per second (Mbps), 100 Mbps, and 1 gigabit per second. It is not compatible with asynchronous transfer mode (ATM) or Token Ring. For optimum performance and easier configuration, it is advisable to install a second network adapter on each server. The first network adapter processes the usual network traffic using the Network Load Balancing Service and the cluster IP address, or the respective logical name of the server farm. The second network adapter enables direct communication for the other terminal servers in the farm, the application data layer servers and administrators, using the separate physical IP address.

The Network Load Balancing Manager, which is found under the Start\Administrative Tools menu group, is used to establish and enable a Network Load Balancing Service (NLBS) cluster. The cluster parameters include the virtual IP address, the subnet mask, and the full Internet name of the cluster. The port rules that determine the port area, protocols, and filter mode are also configured from this tool. After these settings are properly configured, the connection is established with the servers that are to become part of the new NLBS cluster.

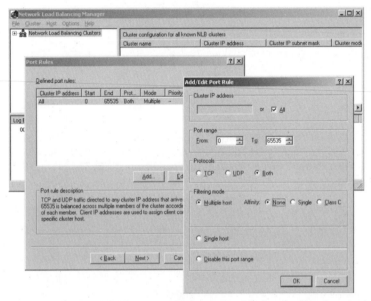

Figure 11-2   Establishing a new Network Load Balancing Service cluster.

If this configuration work is carried out on a server that has only one network card (Unicast mode), the Network Load Balancing Manager cannot configure and manage other servers from this server. Adding a new server to an existing cluster must then be done locally on that server.

If the configuration is to be done without the Network Load Balancing Manager, the properties of the Internet protocol (TCP/IP) are modified manually for the network adapter of each terminal server under Start\Control Panel\Network connections\LAN connections. In the process, an additional IP address is added, which is the virtual address of the cluster. Additionally, the Network Load Balancing Service for the network adapter must be enabled and properly configured. This must include the cluster parameters described earlier (such as virtual IP address, subnet mask, and Internet name), host parameters, and port rules.

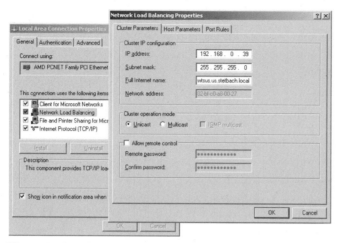

Figure 11-3   Configuring the Network Load Balancing Service using the properties of the LAN connection.

Note   The network adapter of a server that is to become a member of a Network Load Balancing Service cluster is not permitted to receive its IP address from a Dynamic Host Configuration Protocol (DHCP) server. The IP address must be statically assigned to guarantee that the connection will be made using the load-balancing mechanism.

Using the Network Load Balancing Service for Terminal Servers

The port rules in a Network Load Balancing Service cluster determine values for affinity and load weight within the filtering mode. Using the Single or Class C affinity options for multiple hosts, you can determine a rule requiring multiple requests of a particular client IP address to be always redirected to the same server in a cluster. Obviously, this is not very useful for terminal servers. With terminal servers, the None option with regard to affinity should be used to select the server experiencing the lightest load.

The load weight setting in the host properties determines the relative share of network traffic for each individual server on the network. The permissible values lie between 0 and 100. In this way, even servers with different performance levels can be included in a NLBS cluster. The actual share of data flow assigned to each server is calculated as the local load weight divided by the total load weight in the cluster.

Tip To make sure that the latest data is displayed after any configuration modifications, the cluster needs to be refreshed in the Network Load Balancing Manager.

If you study the descriptions of the Network Load Balancing Service in more detail, you will find that it was not developed for use with terminal servers, but for balancing stateless Web server connections. So for large terminal server farms, the Microsoft Network Load Balancing Service is clearly not the best solution. This is partly due to the NLBS only supporting up to 32 nodes. Another reason is that available hardware solutions or terminal server-specific software products for load balancing are more powerful than the general load-balancing functions of Windows Server 2003.

The Session Directory

The Session Directory is a new function introduced in Windows Server 2003. It allows users of a load-balanced terminal server farm to reconnect with a disconnected session in a manner that is reproducible and secure. For this reason, the Session Directory is compatible with the Network Load Balancing Service in Windows Server 2003. It also supports load-balancing technologies from third-party manufacturers, such as F5 Networks, Alteon, or Radware. These clearly hold greater potential than using Microsoft's Network Load Balancing Service.

Note In principle, the Session Directory service can be used with all versions of Windows Server 2003. However, to be able to participate in a Session Directory, Windows Server 2003 Enterprise Edition or Datacenter Edition must be installed on the target platform. This is true for both the 32-bit and the 64-bit versions.

Functionality

From a technical point of view, the Session Directory is a database. It manages a list of user names in correlation with the sessions in a terminal server farm. The database can be located on a terminal server in the farm or on a separate server on the network.

Following user authentication in the terminal server farm, the Session Directory is searched for the relevant user's logon name. If the database already contains a session for this user, the user will be redirected to the server that was holding the disconnected session. This remedies at least the most obvious weakness of a Network Load Balancing Service cluster in this situation. However, where this function becomes truly interesting is in connection with hardware solutions for network load balancing, where it is relatively easy to link the respective products from other manufacturers with the functions of a terminal server.

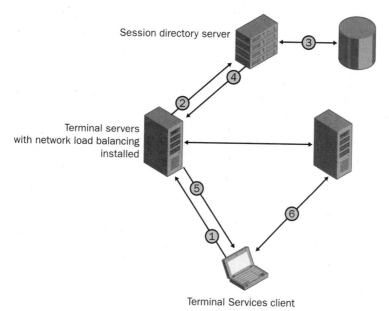

Figure 11-4   Communication pattern for reconnecting a user using the Session Directory: (1) User wants to establish a connection with a terminal server farm. (2) Terminal server asks the Session Directory server if it already has a session for this user. (3) Session Directory server searches its database. (4) User session is found and information is returned to the terminal server that made the request. (5) Terminal Services client receives the information. (6) Terminal Services client connects with the server holding the user session.

Two components are required to be able to use the Session Directory in a terminal server farm:

- **Session Directory server**   This is the server where the Session Directory service runs. It does not need to be a terminal server. The Session Directory service works with all editions of Windows Server 2003.

- **Client servers**   These are all terminal servers that request data from a Session Directory server. Client servers must be configured so that they link up with the Session Directory server. Only terminal servers running Windows Server 2003, Enterprise Edition or Datacenter Edition, can use the Session Directory.

> **Tip** If very high availability on the part of the Session Directory server services is required, it is advisable to set it up as a separate server cluster with two nodes. The Session Directory server service is compatible with Microsoft cluster technology in this respect. In this way, the probability of service failure can be considerably reduced. Additional information is available in the White Paper "Windows Server 2003: Session Directory and Load Balancing Using Terminal Server" which can be found on the companion CD-ROM of this book

Configuration

Tssdis.exe, the initially disabled Terminal Services Session Directory service, is installed on Windows Server 2003 by default. All that is required to make the function available permanently is for an administrator to set the start type on the selected Session Directory server to Automatic. For the initial configuration, it can be started manually, thus avoiding restarting the whole server.

After the Session Directory service has been launched, both the Session Directory server and the client server need to be configured. The first time the Session Directory service is launched, the empty, local security group named *Session Directory Computers* is automatically created on the Session Directory server, if it does not already exist. All terminal servers that need to be able to access the Session Directory must be in this group. Consequently, you need to include each of the servers concerned in this group, using the Local Users and Groups in the Computer Management tool.

> **Tip** If the Session Directory is launched on a domain controller, the group created, that is, the Session Directory Computers security group, will be a local group across the entire domain. This results in the configuration being assigned across all domain controllers, which is not recommended.

On the client servers, the configuration is carried out using the Terminal Services Configuration tool or Group Policies. The first option requires that the following properties be set under the Server Settings\Session Directory menu point:

- **Join Session Directory** Activates the Session Directory for a terminal server. If this option is selected, the cluster name and the server name for the Session Directory must also be entered.

- **Cluster name** Name of the Network Load Balancing Service cluster resolved through DNS.

- **Server name for Session Directory**   Name of the server on which the Session Directory service was launched.

- **Session Directory for network adapter and IP addresses should divert user to:**   Chooses the network adapter that the user's request for a new connection should be redirected to. This is required for terminal servers with more than one network adapter.

- **IP address redirection**   Provides the option to support load-balancing products from other manufacturers. Many of these products act as load balancer and router simultaneously. Where this is the case, it might no longer be possible to contact a terminal server through its direct IP address, and a routing token might be required, which will need to be redirected.

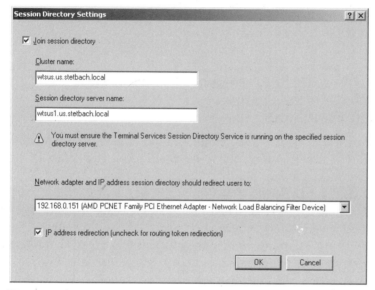

Figure 11-5   Session Directory Settings in Terminal Services Configuration.

All of the settings relating to the Session Directory can also be conducted through Group Policies. These can either be valid within an organizational unit in the Active Directory or for the local server only. If the Session Directory is to be used in a large-scale environment, it is recommended that the Active Directory options be configured.

The four relevant entries are located along the following path: Computer Configuration\Administrative Templates\Windows Components\Terminal Services\Session Directory. The settings here correspond to the configuration options in Terminal Services Configuration:

- **Merge Session Directory**   Corresponds to Join Session Directory in Terminal Services Configuration.

- **Cluster name of the Session Directory**   Corresponds to Cluster name in Terminal Services Configuration.

- **Session Directory server**   Corresponds to Server name for Session Directory in Terminal Services Configuration.

- **Terminal server IP address redirection**   Corresponds to IP address redirection in Terminal Services Configuration.

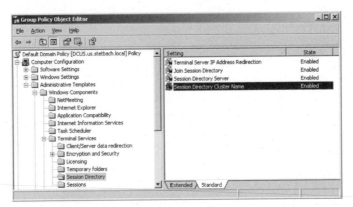

Figure 11-6   Conducting the settings for the Session Directory using Group Policies.

Citrix Load Evaluators

The Microsoft Network Load Balancing Service and the new Session Directory enable smaller terminal server farms to be established. The combination of the Session Directory and hardware products for load balancing expands the possibilities still further. But with these solutions, the effort required for the apparently simple task of load balancing is still very high. So what alternatives are available?

With the MetaFrame XP Presentation Server, Citrix also offers a very powerful component for load balancing, which integrates itself seamlessly into the concept of published applications, desktops, and content. The Citrix load evaluators allow the load to be balanced among different servers in a farm. The respective rules are set, monitored, and adjusted by the corresponding list object in the Management Console for MetaFrame XP.

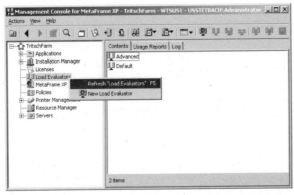

Figure 11-7   The Management Console for MetaFrame XP with the context menu for load evaluators.

In the default configuration, the Management Console for MetaFrame XP contains two load analysis programs, one named *Standard* and one named *Advanced*. They both contain predefined rules and neither can be modified or removed. However, other load evaluators can be defined, with specific sets taken from a total of 12 rules based on conditions or performance counters objects. The rules observe the following parameters:

- Number of users that access a certain published application

- Context switches on a processor when it changes from one process to another

- Utilization of the processor or the processors of a server

- Input and output of hard drive data volume

- Number of hard disk operations per second

- Range of the IP addresses where an accessing ICA client is located

- Number of available licenses on a server

- Proportion of a server's main memory utilization

- Number of page faults when a server accesses physical memory that has been flushed to disk

- Number of page swaps per second on a server when physical memory is moved to virtual memory on disk

- Weekly days and hours when a server should be available to the load-balancing network

- Number of users that access a server

These rules can be used in any combination to form a new load evaluator. Many rules allow you to determine threshold values for defining the condition of full load and no load. The number of users, processor utilization, page swaps, and the amount of memory used are the most important criteria for load balancing.

A load evaluator can be assigned either to a server or to a published application. To do this, go to Actions\Load Manager\Load Manage Server or Actions\Load Manager\Load Manage Application, providing the server or the application has already been activated. In this way, different published applications or desktops can be configured in a highly individual manner in terms of load-balancing behavior. However, it is sufficient for most environments to apply the two predefined load evaluators.

The configuration of the load evaluators with their rules is stored in the MetaFrame server farm's IMA data store, from where each server obtains the necessary data for the appropriate load-balancing settings when starting up. Taking the rules as the basis, the zone data collector selects a suitable server when a client requests a connection and returns the result to the client. The client is therefore able to connect to the server with the lightest load. If a session connection has already been established, each subsequent connection will be directed to the same server to allow applications to communicate.

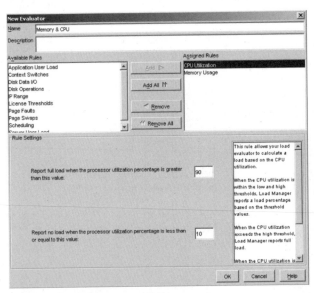

Figure 11-8 Adding a new load evaluator.

The load-balancing feature in a Citrix MetaFrame server farm is extremely powerful and can easily incorporate several hundred servers. This is why the solution is used in the majority of production terminal server farms.

Using Several Farms

Very large environments often require the use of several farms with different applications available on them. This might be for organizational or technical reasons. But problems can arise when a user works with several farms simultaneously and has a user profile that is stored on a central file server. Whenever the user closes the last published application or desktop in a farm, the user's profile is written back to the profile store on a file server. If this happens for several farms, data from the first farm might be overwritten by contradictory settings on a different farm. As an example, the settings for the default printer that a user modified might no longer be in the user's profile if the user closed the applications in the "wrong" order. An application on another farm would then have the old settings in the profile simply because it was closed there at a later time. At the next logon, the user will be surprised and annoyed to find that the modified printer settings have disappeared.

A common solution to this problem is to establish a separate profile folder for each server farm on the file server. These folders could be named *Farm1*, *Farm2*, and *Farm3*, for example, if there were three server farms in the load-balancing network. The servers in all farms would then require an environment variable (such as %FarmID%) containing details of which farm they belong to. The %FarmID% environment variable would then contain the value Farm1 for the first farm, Farm2 for the second farm, and Farm3 for the third farm. Through the properties of the user account, each user would then be assigned a profile path containing the name of the variable, e.g. \\File server\Share\%FarmID%\User name. The drawback here is that three profiles need to be stored for each user. This solution takes up a large amount of the hard disk resources and often causes the system to behave in a way that is confusing the users.

Another alternative is to use mandatory profiles. (See Chapter 4.) However, this data needs to be handled specially for authorized system modifications by the user to be stored and loaded at the next logon. Logon and logoff scripts are used for this purpose; some of them even requiring registry access. When a big number of different applications are concerned and the user is to have the greatest possible freedom to adjust settings, it takes a lot of effort to manage all user-specific changes to the runtime system regardless of the standard concept of server-based profiles.

For this reason, Citrix and certain system integrators working with terminal servers have, over time, developed a set of support tools that support a mixture of mandatory profiles and user-specific system data. The tools are generally complicated, are hard to explain, and are normally too much to handle for inexperienced administrators. They should therefore be seen as integration aids rather than products.

Adjusting a terminal server environment to the concepts of these hybrid profiles, flex profiles, jumping profiles, or advanced profiles requires precise knowledge of all application accesses to the registry database and the system files during startup and shutdown. Obviously the same requirement holds for common settings that apply to all applications. The task of keeping the respective configuration data up-to-date should not be underestimated, but in many cases excellent maintenance does enable significantly better user logon times and consistent configuration across farm boundaries.

A further improvement in logon times in large-scale environments with several terminal server farms can be achieved with the use of local policies instead of Group Policies. It is important to bear the one considerable drawback in mind, however, which is that it will no longer be possible to manage local policies centrally. In large-scale environments, this can only be seen as a workable solution if the policies can be distributed fully automatically to all terminal servers in a farm at the same time as the system and application installation.

Resource Management

The Network Load Balancing Service as described at the beginning of this chapter ensures that user sessions are shared out as evenly as possible between all the terminal servers available in a farm. Analyses of server resource utilization might guarantee the proper adjustment of the balancing algorithm, but the analyses are almost always based on a moment-in-time consideration of system load at the time of a connection request by a new user. But how can the scalability of a terminal server environment be increased further? How can you prevent one user using so much of the terminal server resources that other users are put at a major disadvantage? How can logical resources, such as a time zone or license server, be modified differently depending on the location of the user or server without the need for complicated system intervention? The following section aims to answer these questions.

Windows System Resource Manager

The utilization of a terminal server in large-scale environments can only be described through statistics. In a farm with 100 terminal servers, each with 100 applications installed and with 5000 potential users altogether, there will be a resulting standard resource utilization profile that represents an average value. But this is only statistics. Someone might be unlucky and might get logged on to a terminal server with many power users who just happen to be relatively inactive at that particular moment when the load balancer selected the server. Equally, someone might be unlucky when, another interactive user, sharing the same relatively lightly utilized terminal server, might launch an application that is particularly uncooperative, tying up a large amount of server resources. In either case, the experience with the terminal server technology will be extremely dissatisfactory for the user concerned.

This, however, is by no means an error, but is legitimate system behavior subject to the prevailing probabilities. Often, as a result of the mixture of user behavior and applications run in large terminal server farm environments, extreme load disparity is found between individual terminal servers. A user who becomes accustomed to high system performance one day might have to suffer applications with unacceptable response times the next. That is why there must be the option of monitoring the user sessions and their processes to see how many resources they consume throughout the entire duration of the runtime. This is particularly true for the use of processors and main memory. (See "Adjusting Server Dimensions" in Chapter 5.)

A technical solution to the problem of controlling resources on terminal servers is offered by the Windows System Resource Manager, which is an optional function with Windows Server 2003, Enterprise Edition or later. The Windows System Resource Manager (WSRM) is not part of the default installation package on Windows Server 2003, however. WSRM is available on the second CD supplied with the Enterprise Server and the Datacenter Server. If the administrator does not have the Windows Server 2003 installation CDs, WSRM can be downloaded from *http:// www.microsoft.com/windowsserver2003/downloads/wsrm.mspx.*

> **Note**   One alternative would be, of course, to enable a user session being run on one terminal server to be moved to another terminal server experiencing a lower load. This could be done automatically or at the request of a user. (The option could be called, "Find me a better terminal server.") However, to do this, the current system status and all applications launched in the user session would have to be frozen, transferred to the other terminal server, and re-enabled there. Also, the Terminal Services client would have to accept the change in the physical address of its communication partner while at the same time maintaining a consistent user interface. Such an approach can best be compared with that of a server cluster, albeit without all of the processes being launched on different servers in advance. Regrettably, such an approach has not even been attempted (yet)! But as you can see, there is considerable potential for terminal server technology to develop.

Functions and Installation

With the Windows System Resource Manager, administrators can control the assignment of CPU and main memory resources to applications, services, and processes. Managing resources in this way increases the system performance and reduces the risk of applications, services, or processes having a damaging impact on the rest of the system. Moreover, users find the behavior of applications and services executed on the computer more uniform and predictable.

From a technical point of view, WSRM consists of the Wsrm.exe service and an MMC snap-in as the administration interface. The service ensures the implementation of all the rules determined through the administration interface. The Windows System Resource Manager also contains a calendar function that is useful for planning resource assignment policies. Furthermore, it provides a system of recording resources that can be used to collate performance data and other relevant data.

It is fairly easy to install the Windows System Resource Managers on a terminal server. The only option that might need to be looked at in more detail is the option of installing server components (the WSRM service) and the administration interface separately on different computers.

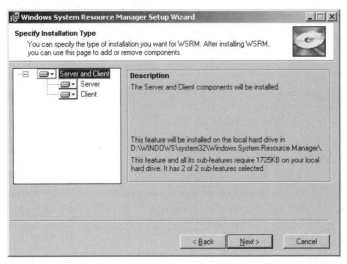

Figure 11-9   Installing the Windows System Resource Manager.

Using Windows System Resource Manager on Terminal Servers

The Windows System Resource Manager facilitates the resource management for several different applications and users on one terminal server. A dynamic management algorithm for process priorities is available that can help determine the assignment of system resources to numerous processes. Using this algorithm, administrators can draw up resource assignment policies incorporating several different resource assignments. The resource assignment itself includes process-matching criteria, a CPU consumption target, different memory allocation limits, or a processor assignment:

- **Process-matching criteria**   Mechanisms used to match running processes to a predefined policy assigning resource allocations.

- **CPU consumption targets**   Specifies a CPU target bandwidth for the assignment of resources. WSRM uses an algorithm for dynamic process priority allocation to limit, wherever possible, a process' CPU usage. This limit is defined by the consumption target stated in the selecting resource policies for the process.

- **Memory allocation limits**   Two values limiting main memory may be entered. The *working set memory* corresponds to the amount of the physical main memory assigned to the process by the operating system. The committed memory resides in the working set of a process or maps to a disk file. This value has a tendency to become larger over time if the process is not able to release certain memory section, which is often referred to as a memory leak. The value relates to the memory limitation per process and not to the entire process-matching criterion.

■ **Processor assignment**   On systems with more than one processor, a group of processors is entered here, on which the process will be executed exclusively. This is also known as *processor affinity* or *CPU affinity*.

Once a resource assignment is allocated to a process group, the Windows System Resource Manager service monitors the resource assignment of the individual processes. If the resource assignment of a process is exceeded, the service will attempt to reduce the resource utilization to the predefined target value.

The common procedure to define resource control rules for a terminal server requires the following steps:

1. Create a new process-matching criterion containing applications or user groups whose resources are to be controlled on the terminal server.

2. Create a new resource allocation policy, and add process-matching criteria to it. Here you can set the CPU consumption targets in percent, determine the memory allocation limits, and assign the available processors.

3. If there is more than one process-matching criterion in a resource assignment policy, you can modify their order and thereby their priority.

4. Set the desired resource allocation policy as a managing policy.

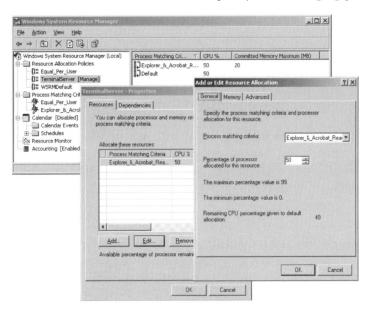

Figure 11-10   Configuring a resource allocation policy.

Within a resource allocation, a management rule can be set using the Advanced tab. This determines how CPU resources are allocated. You can select from the following three management rules:

- **Standard** The allocation of the CPU assignment to the selected processes is not managed by the Windows System Resource Manager. With this setting, suballocation of processor resources can also be determined.

- **Equal per process** The CPU assignment is the same for all processes selected.

- **Equal per user** The CPU assignment is the same for all users. The processes created by a user can consume as much of the user's total CPU assignment as necessary.

> **Note** By using the Wsrmc.exe command-line tool, Windows System Resource Manager can also be managed using the command prompt.

The WSRM provides some very interesting administration options for terminal servers. However, it is too new to be able to make any qualified statements on how it behaves in production environments. Furthermore, it does not really allow for intuitive configuration, and the results can be dramatic when the predetermined limits are reached. For example, application processes might be shut down without warning or might not start again. This is not a welcome result when managing resources in terminal server environments.

AppSense Resource Management Tools

AppSense Technologies' Performance Manager and Optimizer products take a somewhat different technical approach to managing resources than does Microsoft's Windows System Resource Manager. But they still address the issue of optimizing the allocation of processor capacity and main memory to the different applications of a terminal server such that the number of unexpected system bottlenecks is kept to an absolute minimum.

> **Note** Products from manufacturers like Real Enterprise Solutions (*http://www.respowerfuse.com*), Emergent OnLine (*http://www.go-eol.com*), and many others also cover some aspects of terminal server resource management, as described in this section with the AppSense resource management tools as an example.

AppSense Performance Manager

Like the Windows System Resource Manager, the AppSense Performance Manager does not stop at simply logging the resources consumed. It, too, takes a proactive approach to resource distribution. It focuses in particular on applications that sometimes display "damaging" behavior on terminal servers as a result of particular constellations. Often, this behavior can be traced back to the fact that many applications were not developed for use on terminal servers. (See "Applications in Multiple-User Mode" and "Developing Compatible Applications" in Chapter 5.)

> **Note**   The Windows System Resource Manager guarantees a minimum of resources that will be made available to a process at any given time. Conversely, the AppSense Performance Manager defines a maximum of resources that represent the limit for a process. Predefined actions are taken once this limit is reached. The possibilities and the system impact of the two tools therefore differ in this respect, but they also complement each other in some cases.

So how do the bottlenecks on terminal servers arise that can unexpectedly lead to a dramatic deterioration in response times and thus affect all user sessions on a server? In particular, very large data imports, data exports, or calculation tasks, using old 16-bit or DOS applications, and loading certain components or active Web pages in Web browsers often result in as much as 100 percent of processor capacity being consumed at a given time. A simple example for such a misbehaving process can even be a poorly programmed macro for Microsoft Excel. If a user executes this in a terminal server session, the sessions of other users will suddenly slow down dramatically. The user who caused the problem is not aware of being the culprit—the user will believe that the system was used correctly.

Similar effects arise if the system's memory experiences excessively heavy use. Both processor and memory bottlenecks are two things that make users extremely unhappy. If these problems occur for no apparent reason and seem to follow no visible pattern of behavior, the system administrator is left searching for the cause. In many cases, the "simplest" solution is chosen, whereby more servers are attached to an existing farm without all of the available resources being used optimally.

The AppSense Performance Manager allows effective policies for controlling processor utilization and memory use to be easily set up. After the Performance Manager software components have been installed by a wizard on the central Deployment Server, the system administrator can use an administration console to configure the Performance Manager. (See Chapter 8 for a description of the AppSense Deployment Subsystem.)

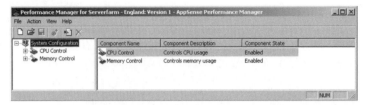

Figure 11-11   The main administration console window of AppSense Performance Manager.

The main window consists of two sections. On the left, the individual administration objects are listed and can be selected. On the right is the options window for the configuration. The system administrator has two administration objects available: CPU Control and Memory Control.

The CPU Control administration object offers two options. The first option is named *Application Limits* and allows the system administrator to define a CPU limit for one or more applications. Once the CPU limit has been set, all combined instances of this application cannot use more processor resources than allowed by the system administrator. In this way, the amount of resources consumed by problematic applications can be limited or applications that are not critical to company operations can be given a lower priority in terms of resource consumption.

The *Intelligent Process Management* option monitors the processor utilization of processes and threads on a continuous basis. If excessive load is identified, the Performance Manager steps in to actively reduce it. The permissible amount of processor utilization can be adjusted, and the number of controlled processes and threads modified. The corresponding control model is based on a few simple parameters that enable the applicable factors to be precisely adjusted (for example, the allowed incremental processor utilization). By modifying user or group-specific factors, a defined group of users who need to carry out particularly processor-intensive tasks can be assigned a higher proportion of processor resources. Furthermore, individual applications can be assigned a set percentage of processor resources, which enables purposeful control of applications that use up a disproportionately high share of processor resources.

The Memory Control administration object allows the memory used at the application and the user level to be limited. Limiting memory utilization is a two-step process. If the memory utilization exceeds the warning level, a warning message flashes up on the user's screen stating that too much memory is being used. If the memory utilization exceeds the blocking level, all requests to start up a new application or to use up more memory will be blocked. The user is told the reason why it is being blocked in a message box. The user concerned will only be able to use additional memory after freeing up some memory by closing other applications or files. The text in both of the message boxes described here can be modified by the administrator.

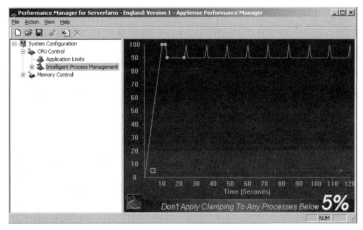

Figure 11-12   Configuring the Intelligent Process Management: the maximum processor load is limited to 90 percent. Regular checks are performed to see if the limitation is still necessary.

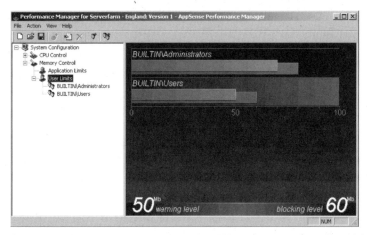

Figure 11-13   Limiting the memory for different user groups. The highlighted user group is on a warning level of 50 MB and a blocking level of 60 MB per user session.

Additionally, the Performance Manager enables you to monitor many events and performance indicators relating to processor and memory utilization. This allows detailed reports to be compiled on sessions, users, and applications. The data can then be analyzed using the available report templates.

AppSense Optimizer

Many applications are still not designed or developed with Terminal Services in mind, which can lead to performance and functionality problems when they are deployed in a multi-user environment. Even if an application functions correctly, it is rare that it has been optimized to make the most efficient use of a server's resources. These problems often go unnoticed in a desktop environment, where only a single user runs the application. However, in a multi-user environment, where many instances of the same application are running concurrently, these inefficiencies can have a severe effect on server scalability and the number of users supported.

There is little that can be done to solve many of the inefficiencies caused by applications, other than asking the software vendors to improve their applications, which is rarely an option. Fortunately, there is a particular inefficiency that can be solved without the intervention of the original software vendor. This is the excessive virtual memory that is often allocated during the loading of Dynamic Link Libraries (DLL), which can be avoided by performing suitable optimizations.

Many applications require one or more DLLs to be loaded to provide their functionality. These include common system DLLs, to provide access to the Window's kernel objects and GUI components, such as Kernel.dll and User32.dll. In addition, application and vendor specific DLLs are usually loaded, to provide common application functionality. ActiveX controls (OCX) and Control Panel utility applications (CPL) are specialized versions of DLLs.

When a DLL is loaded it is usually shared across all processes that require it, avoiding duplication in virtual memory. This sharing is particularly beneficial in a Terminal Services environment, where many instances of the same DLL will be loaded because it can be shared across sessions. Only the data sections in a DLL need to be private to each application instance, whereas the program code can be shared because it does not need to change from one instance to the next. Unfortunately, this sharing of code in memory can only occur if each DLL successfully loads into memory at its preferred load address. If a DLL fails to load at its preferred load address, because the memory address range is already in use, the operating system must move it to an alternative address in memory during loading.

In the 32-bit version of Windows Server 2003 each process has a 4 gigabyte (GB) virtual address range. Most of the lower 2 GB address range is available for code and user data and is private to each process. With the exception of a few system DLLs, each DLL is loaded into the lower 2 GB address range. If the preferred load address of a DLL would cause it to load into a set of memory pages that are not free, a load address collision occurs. The operating system must relocate the DLL to an alternative address, which requires address fixups to be performed on the code pages. The process of performing fixups not only results in a slower load time, but also causes an increase in pagefile usage.

AppSense Optimizer endeavors to eliminate the inefficient use of virtual memory by modifying the loading behavior of DLLs. This is done in the following three phases:

- **Analysis phase** The analysis phase is usually scheduled to run periodically and may also be triggered manually from the management console. It analyzes the applications currently in use and identifies any applications that have had one or more DLLs relocated, due to load address collisions. It continually monitors the applications in use because many applications load DLLs on demand, dependent on the functionality being used by the users.

- **Optimization phase**   The optimization phase creates optimized versions of the DLLs identified by the analysis phase. This optimization process is similar to the process performed by the operating system during load address collision, but instead of saving the fixups to the pagefile, a separate version of the DLL is created on disk in an optimization cache. The original application DLLs are left intact during optimization. In addition, the optimization process takes into account that a DLL might be loaded by different applications, as opposed to different instances of the same application. The address fixups in the DLL are performed to be compatible with both situations.

- **Kernel-level optimization loader**   Once a DLL has been optimized, it needs to be loaded by the application. The optimization loader does this by intercepting the application's request to load its DLLs at kernel level, and then automatically loading an optimized version from the optimization file cache. This process is completely seamless to the application and results in the application avoiding load address collisions and the expensive relocations that would otherwise occur.

> **Note**   Depending on the constellation of the applications deployed and the quality of their corresponding DLLs, the results of this optimization might be very different. It is therefore advisable to conduct extensive tests in a production environment prior to using the AppSense Optimizer.

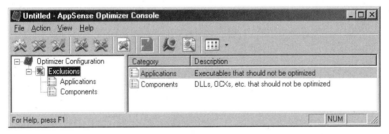

Figure 11-14   The AppSense Optimizer console window.

The AppSense Optimizer is integrated into the same architecture as the other AppSense products. In the corresponding administration console, particular applications and components can be excluded from the optimization, although this should not be necessary in most cases. What is more important in terms of settings is that the analysis and optimization phases be planned as one-time or regular events. One of the really interesting functions of the AppSense Optimizer is the possibility to disable the loading of the optimized DLLs as required and to re-enable it at a later date. Consequently, it is easy to compare the two settings. During system repair work, it might also be necessary to stop the optimization, which this function allows.

Citrix Resource Management

Citrix Resource Management is a component of the Citrix MetaFrame XP Presentation Server, Enterprise Edition. It is directly integrated in the Management Console for MetaFrame XP. The MetaFrame XP Presentation Server Resource Manager basically enables several MetaFrame servers in a network to be monitored. It has performance indicators and metrics that allow server performance, application utilization, and user activities to be recorded and displayed. It is possible to display all relevant data graphically in 15-second intervals. Furthermore, each MetaFrame server saves all data it recorded in the past 96 hours. For longer-term data storage, data can be archived on an external database server, which is named a summary database. All of the data collated can, of course, be used to compile meaningful reports on the resource utilization of a MetaFrame server farm. Unlike the Windows System Resource Manager and the AppSense Performance Manager, the Citrix Resource Management only allows the relevant performance object metrics to be observed; it does not facilitate predefined and proactive intervention in system behavior.

The Resource Management tool is present at various points in the object hierarchy in the Management Console for MetaFrame XP:

- **Resource Manager** A separate object that enables the analysis of the recorded performance indicators and the basic configuration for the reaction when predefined limits are met. This can be through various tabs. The object also sends a report to administrators or an administration instance by SMS, SNMP, or e-mail message.

- **Applications** For each published application, metrics for the Resource Manager can be added or removed using the context menu of the object hierarchy. The only available metric for applications is *Count*, which contains the number of users that have opened the relevant published application. The status of a metric can be viewed for each application using the Resource Manager tab.

- **Server** For each server in a farm, metrics for the Resource Manager can be added or removed using the Resource Manager tab's context menu. Here, too, the status of a metric can be viewed for each server.

Note All configuration data in the Citrix Resource Management is stored centrally in the IMA database.

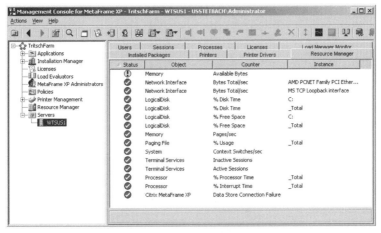

Figure 11-15   Predefined server counter objects representing metrics in the Citrix Resource Manager.

Threshold values that determine the status can be set for each metric and predefined actions can be performed once a certain status is achieved for a configured time interval. The status of the metrics is expressed as colors and can be any of the following:

- **Green**   The metric is within the boundaries of a functioning environment.

- **Yellow**   The metric has passed the first threshold for a predefined minimum time and, its status can therefore be considered as a warning. A warning message can be generated, if required.

- **Red**   The metric has passed the second threshold for a predefined minimum time, and its status can therefore be considered as critical. An alert message can be generated, if required.

- **Blue**   A new metric has been added but not yet configured. Only when the properties have been configured will it change to a different color.

- **Gray**   The metric has been stopped manually for a limited period and is therefore unable to send out a warning message. However, metric data continues to be collected and stored.

- **Black**   The metric has been stopped manually for an unlimited period and is therefore unable to send out a warning message. However, metric data continues to be collected and stored.

Configuring a metric involves determining the yellow and the red thresholds and the corresponding minimum time until the displayed status changes. It is also possible to configure warning and alert messages that notify you by SMS, SNMP, or e-mail message when a status change occurs. Only for the change to red status is it possible to configure a script that can be executed to launch countermeasures.

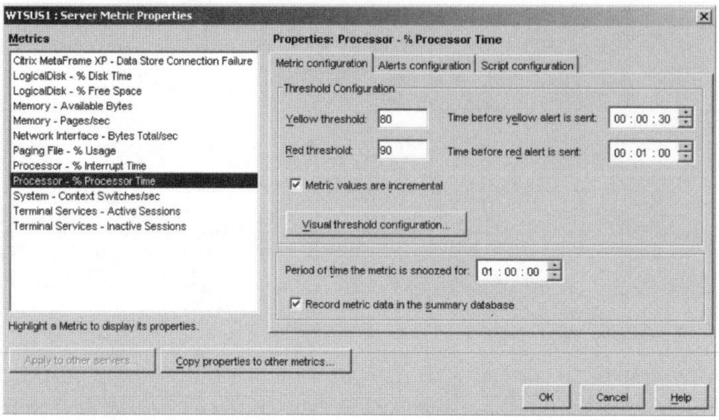

Figure 11-16   Dialog for configuring the server metric properties.

The status of each individual metric can only be viewed within the respective object structure. This concerns either published applications or server farms. However, you can obtain an overview of all metrics with yellow or red status using the Watcher tab in the *Resource Manager* object of the Management Console for MetaFrame XP. Alternatively, the Resource Manager—Show Resource Manager Watcher Window icon in the toolbar of the Management Console for MetaFrame XP allows you to open a separate window that displays the same status information on a permanent basis.

Unlike some of the resource management tools described above, the Citrix Resource Manager does not enable the configuration of preventive measures for resource bottlenecks, with the exception of a script when the status of a metric changes to red. Instead, the Citrix Resource Manager's purpose is to monitor the utilization of resources, to archive, and to inform administrators when thresholds are overstepped. Neither the correct configuration of thresholds nor the launching of appropriate countermeasures to deal with resource bottlenecks are automated and both depend to a large degree on the experience of the administrators. This tool is therefore not suitable for large-scale environments in which different groups of people with different knowledge bases are responsible for setting up and operating the MetaFrame servers. For small environments or highly skilled administrators, though, it does represent a powerful tool.

One special feature of Citrix Resource Management is the option to generate billing information including fee profiles and cost centers from the metrics data. This can be used to map the costs of a MetaFrame environment onto users, groups, and cost centers through charging profiles according to the principle of causality.

Managing Logical Resources

Using the Windows Server 2003 Group Policies, it is possible, without the use of any other tools, to assign a range of logical resources in a way that can be properly used in a large-scale terminal server environment. One of these logical resources is the time zone. In geographically dispersed environments, it might be necessary to avoid using the server time zone and to redirect the client's time zone onto the user session. This is particularly important in cases when not only are applications accessing the terminal server, but local client applications are also accessing a common file server. If the time zone is not redirected, a file's creation and modification dates might become inconsistent if they are changed by different applications on the terminal server and on the client.

The time zone redirection function in Windows Server 2003 is enabled through the settings under Computer Configuration\Administrative Templates\Windows Components\Terminal Services\Client\server Data Redirection\Allow Time Zone Redirection in the Group Policy Object Editor. When the function is enabled, the clients with permission to perform a time zone redirection send the respective information to the server. The server's Greenwich Mean Time (GMT) is used to calculate the current session time. At present, the Remote Desktop Connection distributed with Windows XP and Windows Server 2003 and the RDP client in version 5.1 of Windows CE are the only clients capable of redirecting a time zone.

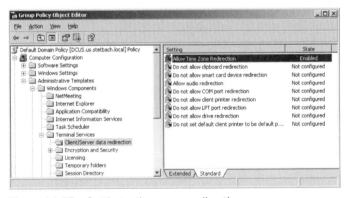

Figure 11-17   Setting a time zone redirection.

Note   If the settings for the time zone redirection are modified by an administrator, only new user sessions will display the corresponding behavior.

Another important setting for logical resources is located under Computer Configuration\Administrative Templates\Windows Components\Terminal Services\Licensing\License Server Security Group in the Group Policy Object Editor. This setting controls which servers are issued licenses. The default setting is that every computer that requests a license is issued with one. However, this can lead to undesirable side effects in large environments. For example, licenses might be issued to computers that are not part of the intended target group.

Enabling the setting for logical resources will automatically generate a local group named *Terminal server computers*. If the target computer of these settings is a domain controller, this group is located locally on the domain. If the administrator sets up a global group with the accounts of all terminal servers and license servers that belong together, the administrator can assign these to the local (or domain-local) group named *Terminal server computers*. As a result, licenses are issued within this group only. If the terminal servers continue to allow access by certain user and computer groups only, the logical resource Licenses is assigned in a highly dedicated manner. Consequently, differently assigned license servers can be operated across several domains within a corporate network.

> **Note** Three tools that can be used to analyze the license setting of a terminal server environment: the Terminal Server Licensing (Lsreport.exe) tool displays a list of license tokens assigned by a license server, the Terminal Server Client License Test (Tsctst.exe) queries details about license tokens on a given client, and the License Server Viewer (Lsviewer.exe) tool performs a license server discovery process. You can access these on the Microsoft Web site at *http://www.microsoft.com/windowsserver2003 /techinfo/reskit/resourcekit.mspx*.

Testing Terminal Server Environments

Comprehensive testing before launching a complex terminal server environment often helps avoid unpleasant surprises. So how are these tests performed and what are the key parameters for a test to succeed? These questions must be viewed in the context of the fact that tests are usually one of the more unpopular tasks involved in setting up terminal server environments. The normally technically minded person shows a rather muted excitement when it comes to testing. Reasons for the lack of enthusiasm include the following:

- Really meaningful tests, including thorough evaluation, usually require considerable time and effort and are thus often reduced to a minimum due to budget restrictions.

- Tests are normally performed at the end of a project. If the previous project phases overrun, tests are cut short or eliminated to meet the overall project deadline.

- There are only a few test tools that are suitable for complex terminal server environments.

- Performing a meaningful test is only half of the work. Evaluation and documentation are also important, and they require special skills on the part of the test engineers in charge.

- Conscientious test engineers will possibly be able to show consultants, developers, or system integrators system bottlenecks or even mistakes in the terminal server infrastructure, which then results in additional (troubleshooting) work. Although this sounds rather harmless, testing can be social dynamite in complex projects.

- According to general opinion, test engineers do not generate creative results but instead examine the results of technical creativity using formal methods.

To cut a long story short, testing tends to be viewed with reluctance because test engineers are not very well liked, they often do not have the right tools, they do not generate "creative" results, and their work is very expensive. These are common prejudices, although they are definitely unjustified!

So why are tests needed at all? Couldn't we just do without them? As you were able to see in Chapter 5, without meaningful tests it is very difficult to predict a terminal server environment's resource requirements. Furthermore, you can easily be accused of negligence in a project where no tests have been done to secure the results. For this reason, tests are indispensable in larger environments—especially where time and money are in limited supply.

Note   Testing is a discipline that is reminiscent of classic natural sciences. A test often cannot incorporate an entire target environment, so strong abstraction is necessary. Some tests, by their very nature, change the observed object so fundamentally that general statements are no longer possible. Sometimes, marginal parameters (for example, exact user behavior) are not known or can be mapped only roughly in statistical terms. Because no test environment is exactly like the target environment, tests are often performed with individual components. This, however, requires the components to be prioritized. The key rule here is: do it properly or don't do it at all. To obtain meaningful test results, all of the following tasks must be performed: measuring, creating statistics, documenting, evaluating, interpreting, and communicating.

Test Criteria

To perform a successful test, you first need to define the objectives. First, it is imperative to find out if terminal servers are the right corporate solution:

- Can all important applications be provided on terminal servers?

- How many users will be affected by a possible migration to terminal servers?

- What are the requirements relating to the terminal server environment's stability, availability, and scalability?

- How will the company and employees be affected if a terminal server fails?

- How easy will it be to increase system resources, if required?

These questions need to be answered in respect for business processes within the company in the first instance. If the answer turns out in favor of terminal servers, the same questions need to be answered with a view to the technical aspects. Tests are, of course, required to back up the entire argumentation. After all, the strategic introduction of terminal servers is quite expensive and is no easy task from a technical point of view.

This is exactly where the problems start: how to test? It is almost impossible to install a reference environment that corresponds to the planned target environment. Furthermore, it is usually counterproductive if the future users are asked to participate in internal beta testing. For these reasons, it is recommended that an independent test environment be defined and a simulation be performed that includes all suitable methods and tools. Many of the potential problems can be discovered at this early stage. Only in relatively small and undemanding environments is it possible to perform the relevant tests directly in a production environment, and only for a limited period of time.

Evaluating the terminal servers in a test environment helps make concrete statements on the expected operating conditions and limiting values. When evaluating the environment, several criteria must be taken into account:

- **Performance** Performance tests are used to evaluate an environment's individual areas in terms of speed. A test tool must therefore be able to simulate many simultaneous accesses to determine the respective response times of each area. The results can be integrated in the corresponding service level agreements. With this type of test, it is, for example, possible to determine the dialog change time of a terminal server application under different conditions.

- **Load** A load test subjects the environment to the kind of access and usage rate expected in routine operation. This requires the test to define the maximum response time for the individual system components and to align the response time with the existing state of technical implementation. The corresponding measurements need realistic load samples simulated by the test tool. The results show whether the response times are within the expected limits.

- **Stress**   Stress tests are simulated, mostly benign attacks that generate excessive loads in an environment. In reality, this type of test corresponds to a peak load that could be the result of certain conditions, such as the start of work, end of a quarter, or successful marketing activities. The main goal of a stress test is to find out when an environment starts generating errors and whether it reverts to normal after extreme stress.

- **Endurance**   An endurance test subjects an environment to a predefined load for some considerable time. During this period, the test examines whether certain parameters change significantly, for instance memory requirement, processor load, and response times. The results allow statements to be made on the quality of the programs and components used. This is especially important for an environment's long-term operation.

- **Scalability**   The term *scalability* does not say much about an environment's response behavior. It does, however, describe its behavior in relation to access times when the number of users is increased. A scalability test therefore delivers the values required for extending an environment and guaranteeing constant service quality with increasing numbers of users. The individual components are examined and evaluated as to their ability to be scaled up (that is, the relevant platform is updated) and scaled out (that is, the number of relevant platforms is increased).

Security is another criterion, but we will not cover this in detail here. Special tests help observe terminal server behavior in case of attacks on the security system. The basics are described in detail in Chapter 8.

> **Important**   If there is not an expert in your company with sufficient knowledge of Windows Server 2003 and networks, testing and productive operation of Terminal Services will be problematic. A terminal server requires, at least in the beginning, a high degree of competent maintenance, which takes a lot of time and effort.

Measurement Methods and Test Tools

In most cases, there are not enough "real" users for tests to take place under controlled conditions. Moreover, scenarios with test users are usually not really reproducible because the individual users behave differently from test to test. Therefore, typical user actions need to be simulated, which requires precise knowledge of user behavior and the type of application. However, it quickly becomes evident that only simple user activity can be simulated because complex behavior modeling takes too much time and effort.

In terms of automated and thus reproducible terminal server environment tests, it is necessary to distinguish between different concepts that relate to the location of the test logic. The test logic can either run on the server or be client based. Modeling the temporal processes of graphical user interaction is problematic due to the communication protocols, RDP and ICA, being stateful. This is why a terminal server test differs significantly from a Web server test with the stateless HTTP protocol.

If the logic for a terminal server test is set up on clients, the following constellation results: a script is able to simulate all user actions on an RDP or an ICA client. A suitable runtime environment that can perform mouse clicks and keyboard strokes like a human user needs to be installed on each client platform. The graphical display of applications is, however, only an image of the graphical application elements and does not represent the application elements themselves. The latter are created and managed on the terminal server only.

It is, of course, desirable that the test clients be controlled centrally and that multiple simultaneous instances of RDP or ICA clients be executed per client platform. In the best case scenario, the terminal server does not even "notice" that it is not a real user but a script logic requesting a session and interacting with the applications.

How to handle time and space requirements for the simulated user interaction is a problematic issue. Considerations include whether the script is able to "click" on the correct screen element at the right time or to enter a text into a dialog box only when the box actually appears on the screen. Graphical application elements that are not always displayed at fixed screen coordinates and increasing time delays for the graphical output when the server load increases often take scripts on the clients to their limits. This, in turn, results in a high number of failed simulated user sessions that freeze and thus distort the entire result.

The most successful test approaches based on client platforms involve special RDP or ICA clients. They concern the presentation layer of an application that is executed on a terminal server. It is therefore necessary either to program a modified client with massive support from Microsoft or Citrix, or the test runtime environment can control a normal client for the most part. Both options incur quite some effort in terms of developing the respective test environments.

An alternative to the client-side test is to use tools that automate user sessions on the server. This shifts the test activities from the presentation layer to the application layer. Macro tools for automating user actions are the best-known members of this product category. The problem with using macro tools is, though, that they change the server constellation. The macro tool itself is an auxiliary program that needs to be run during all tests. It thus distorts the result. Furthermore, events on the client play no role at all, which does not represent "normal" terminal server environment behavior.

Standardized benchmark tests that physically run on the terminal server are another option. However, for them to be displayed through several clients, they generally need to be launched manually in different terminal server sessions. These tests often contain popular application programs or representative screen output to model reality as closely as possible (such as Ziff-Davis benchmarks). Still, they are not really suitable for objective and individualized testing of a terminal server environment.

The continuous generation of processor load and the targeted occupation of memory resources is another way of testing terminal server performance. This procedure often helps obtain a first impression of the terminal server's behavior when using standard applications under different conditions.

There are a number of products and tools available for the options described here, but using them professionally usually entails relatively high expense. They all have one thing in common, though: they all extensively utilize the Windows Server 2003 System Monitor performance indicators for evaluations. The relevant performance indicators for terminal servers are described in detail in Chapter 4.

Note   Integrated tests that include access to terminal server environments through a Web interface, as described in Chapter 12 and Chapter 13, pose real problems. If you additionally want to include logon via certificates and virtual private networks in your tests, it will be even more difficult to obtain the relevant commercial test tools.

Objective assessment of the test results can be supported by the following methods:

- Measuring time using a stop watch or the system timers
- Comparing the results of the standardized load tests with reference environments
- Observing system activities with the System Monitor and the Network Monitor
- Evaluating the test results using statistical and analysis tools

Subsequently, the raw measurement data must be brought into a structured form to determine the utilization of all system resources. In this way, the basic cornerstones can be identified and analyzed to work out the key indicators of satisfactory system performance. Expensive test environments usually include powerful automated interpretation functions. These need to be set up manually when using the more cost-effective tools.

The goal after interpreting all test results is to be able to make an objective statement on the behavior of terminal server environments under set load conditions, clearly defining the limits pertaining to memory, processors, hard drive systems, and network. Furthermore, it should be possible to give an estimate of the maximum number of simultaneous terminal server users and the scalability of a load-balanced server farm.

Mercury Interactive

A rather expensive but very popular test tool is LoadRunner by Mercury Interactive (*http://www.mercuryinteractive.com*). Its functions were extended especially for use on MetaFrame servers, and this version is named LoadRunner for Citrix.

LoadRunner for Citrix's test logic is on the client side. A specially adapted ICA client allows the use of ICA functions for controlling tests via scripts. An external administration console centrally controls the clients. Powerful processing script tools facilitate highly realistic simulation of user sessions. The scripts support the dynamic import of server names, user names, passwords, domains, applications, and window parameters. The interaction of the simulated users comprises text entries and mouse events. The user session's synchronization with the control script focuses on the window name and the content of graphical elements.

LoadRunner's particular strength lies in its options for evaluating MetaFrame server tests. The relevant performance indicators, which can be displayed in many correlations and statistical views, allow detailed statements on the test results to be made.

Tevron

CitraTest by Tevron (*http://www.tevron.com*) is a purely client-side test environment, like LoadRunner for Citrix by Mercury Interactive. It is based on image comparison algorithms that are able to identify predefined bitmap images within an ICA client. The relevant script logic is coded in Microsoft Visual Basic 6 and determines the behavior when recognizing expected image patterns. In line with the predefined logic for finding the expected graphical application elements, the script generates mouse and keyboard events. A tool supplied with CitraTest records, saves, and, if necessary, modifies the reference images for pattern recognition.

Because an application's graphical output elements might differ depending on the user, CitraTest is able to handle variations in colors and character strings. Furthermore, integrated algorithms for optical character recognition (OCR) allow text output to be read and interpreted. The tests are evaluated based on the measurement of the response times caused by mouse and keyboard events on the client.

Scapa Technologies

StressTest for Thin Client by Scapa Technologies (*http://www.scapatech.com*) is based on an architecture that needs components on both the terminal server and the clients. The relatively thin server component starts and controls the execution of test scripts and coordinates this with the client interfaces. Communication with the relevant client component is integrated in the RDP or ICA communication protocols.

The Scapa StressTest client component allows the import of different standard scripts for coding the test logic. This includes process control, support of different user names, passwords, and dialog box entries. A separate component handles the controlling of test clients. It executes, controls, and evaluates the relevant scripts. Scapa StressTest is compatible with script tools such as Wilson WindowWare Win-Batch or TaskWare WinTask.

A Scapa StressTest specialty is the simultaneous support of the ICA and RDP communication protocols. Scapa StressTest also comprises functions that allow it to cooperate with Canaveral iQ by New Moon Systems, SoftGrid for Terminal Servers by Softricity, and Secure Access Manager by Citrix.

Script and Macro Tools

Script and macro tools help create automated process controls for user interfaces and Windows-based applications. The results can either be used as basic material for test environments such as Scapa StressTest or can be used directly for server-side application tests. The following list contains an overview of the most popular script and macro tools used on terminal servers:

- MacroExpress by Insight Software Solution (*http://www.macroexpress.com*) is a macro tool developed to support users in automating repeated tasks. MacroExpress includes hundreds of commands and the option to program responses to system events.

- Macro ToolsWorks by Pitrinec Software (*http://www.pitrinec.com*) is another common macro tool. It includes its own macro language with more than 150 commands, a graphical development environment, and several elaborate options to control the timing of the developed macros.

- WinBatch by Wilson WindowWare (*http://www.winbatch.com*) is a script and macro tool with a recording component and its own development environment.

- WinTask by TaskWare (*http://www.wintask.com*) is another script and macro tool whose programming language is very similar to Visual Basic. It includes a recording component for keyboard strokes, mouse movement, and Windows functions, which facilitates the creation of scripts. In addition, WinTask contains functions to control program timings, which make it highly suitable for maintenance tasks.

- AutoIt by Hiddensoft (*http://www.hiddensoft.com/autoit*) is a simple but free script tool.

Citrix

The Citrix Server Test Kit (CSTK) is an automated tool that a Citrix server administrator can use to configure and execute different load tests. It creates consistent and repeatable loads on different system configurations by using scripts that simulate application access without requiring user interaction. It also allows several sessions to be started from a single client. The test is controlled through a server console.

Once the CSTK is installed on a MetaFrame server, the CSTK client, the CSTK console, the System Monitor, and the documentation are all located in one program group. The CSTK client is also included in each user's auto-start group. For this reason, the CSTK is not suited for testing in production environments. When the CSTK console is started on the MetaFrame server, the simulation scripts can be imported on the server. These scripts have previously been generated with one of the script and macro tools mentioned in the previous section. Each script can be assigned to a normal user or a power user. The former user category can start individual scripts successively, while the latter can execute several scripts simultaneously.

When all test users have been set up with the CSTK console and all relevant test scripts have been set, the test can begin. Initially, it is started through the CSTK console, but at least one user must log on from an ICA client to start the test process. A special CSTK client program (Cstklaun.exe), located in the CSTK installation directory, enables the simultaneous start of several test user sessions on one ICA client platform.

Analyzing the results of a CSTK test is not easy. First of all, you need the results from the System Monitor. System Monitor collects all relevant data during the entire test on the MetaFrame server. This activity itself consumes quite a significant amount of system resources. Furthermore, each CSTK client instance that is executed in each test user session requires more than 2 MB of memory. This is why the CSTK can supply only a rough estimate of the performance situation on a MetaFrame server.

Microsoft Test Tools

The CD that comes with the Windows Server 2003 Technical Reference contains various tools that can be used for different tests on terminal servers.

Consume

Combined with various test scenarios, the Consume.exe command-line tool simulates a resource bottleneck. With this tool, it is possible to occupy physical memory, swap file, hard drive, processor, or kernel pool in a targeted manner. This helps developers and administrators estimate how applications might behave in many extreme situations.

The Consume.exe command-line syntax, shown here, is explained in Table 11-1.

```
Consume {-physical-memory | -page-file | -disk-space | -cpu-time | -kernel-pool} [-
time seconds]
```

Table 11-1   Consume.exe Command-Line Parameters

Parameters	Descriptions
-physical-memory	Consumes as much physical memory as possible.
-page-file	Consumes the swap file.
-disk-space	Consumes hard drive space.
-cpu-time	Consumes processor resources by starting up 128 threads with normal priority.
-kernel-pool	Consumes as many kernel pool resources as possible (non-paged pool).
-time seconds	Determines the time in seconds that the resources were occupied for. If this parameter is not set, resource occupation goes on until it is ended by pressing Ctrl+C on the keyboard.

Note   This program replaces the tools Cpustres.exe and Leakyapp.exe of the Windows 2000 Server Technical Reference. Cpustres.exe allows load generation through four separate threads that each contain individual priorities and activity levels. Leakyapp.exe behaves like an application with a memory leak. Both tools still work under Windows Server 2003.

Create File

The Create File command-line tool (Createfil.exe) generates files of a predefined size filled with blanks. It can therefore occupy hard drive space during a test or transmit defined amounts of data via the network.

Windows Program Timer

The Windows Program Timer (Ntimer.exe) command-line tool measures the time a program runs. Ntimer.exe launches the relevant program as a parameter. Subsequently, Ntimer.exe indicates the time that the program took overall, the time the program spent in user mode, and the time it spent in privileged system mode.

Terminal Server Scalability Planning Tools

Significantly more sophisticated terminal server test environments can be created using Terminal Server Scalability Planning Tools. They are included in a self-extracting installation file named Tsscalling.exe on the CD that comes with the Windows Server 2003 Technical Reference. When you run this program, the installation process creates a folder with a name of your choice and saves a number of tools, test scripts, and documents in it.

The test environment includes the following automation and test tools:

- **Robosrv.exe**   RoboServer is the central control tool with a graphical interface for testing the load on a terminal server. It is usually installed on a special control computer that controls a number of clients. RoboServer determines these settings: the number of user sessions per client platform, the number of clients in one group, and the time between certain test events.

- **Robocli.exe**   RoboClient is installed on each client platform and controls the test scripts that the clients execute on the terminal server. RoboClient receives the commands for how and when to start the test scripts from RoboServer. Together with RoboServer, RoboClient is responsible for automatically executing complete test scenarios. Before RoboClient can be launched, RoboServer must already be installed on the network.

- **Tbscript.exe**   Terminal Services Bench Scripting is a test tool and represents a script interpreter for Microsoft Visual Basic Scripting Edition scripts. It supports a number of specific extensions for controlling terminal server clients.

- **Qidle.exe:**   Query Idle is a test tool that is able to automatically identify user sessions on terminal servers that are idle for a long time. In test environments, this is the same as an interrupted script. As soon as Qidle.exe finds such a user session, it informs the administrator with a system sound.

Besides these tools, the test suite also includes pre-prepared test scripts and some quite comprehensive documentation on installing test environments, executing tests, and using the Tbscript.exe tool.

In addition to the scripts on the remote clients, RoboServer is also able to execute a local *canary script*. This script runs before the actual test and before adding a new group of client sessions. The duration of the execution of this script is logged and allows a statement to be made on the respective terminal server load before and during the test.

To start a test, the relevant clients must be selected using the user interface. The context menu then allows you to select the Run Script option.

Note   You can also run RoboServer from the command line. The syntax is as follows: `Robosrv -s:ServerName -n:ClientNumber`, where *ServerName* specifies the target server for RoboClient and *ClientNumber* specifies the number of initial connections to RoboServer. RoboClient can also be run from the command line; the syntax is: `Robocli -s:RoboServerName`.

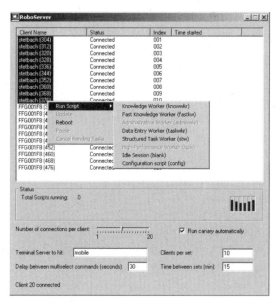

Figure 11-18   Test script execution options with RoboServer: two RoboClients with 10 user sessions each are connected with RoboServer.

In combination with Tbscript.exe, VBScript scripts do the actual load test work. This is based on an already installed version of the usual Windows 2000, Windows XP, or Windows Server 2003 RDP client. The relevant configuration is performed by the Smclient.ini file that sets all required parameters. Starting Tbscript.exe and the corresponding scripts then allows the automated execution of the following functions:

- Logging on, logging off, and ending a connection
- Launching applications
- Transmitting mouse and keyboard input
- Transmitting data and character strings
- Using the clipboard
- Executing loops and conditional jumps
- Using API calls in DLLs

All in all, using Terminal Server Scalability Planning Tools successfully implies quite considerable effort that should not be underestimated. Once you are acquainted with the tools, however, you will find they present a powerful method for helping administrators improve their knowledge of terminal servers and the way terminal servers behave when experiencing heavy load.

Integrating Third-Party Systems

Many companies today have heterogeneous networks, that is, networks with components by many different manufacturers and with different operating systems. Terminal servers are often integrated in these networks, most of which are not based on pure Microsoft platforms. Integrating third-party systems is very important in these environments but is not of central importance in this book. Third-party integration is covered by more general publications about Windows Server 2003. That is why we provide only a quick overview of this topic here.

Novell and UNIX

In heterogeneous terminal server environments, Novell or UNIX servers are especially popular. Mixed operation requires a connection through gateways, directory services, network-based file system, and the special implementation of Server Message Blocks. In some cases, the Network Information System (NIS) is also required as a name service.

For years, Novell NetWare has been an established and powerful network operating system in the PC world, competing with Windows 2000 and Windows Server 2003. With the growing use of Windows environments, many companies and institutions have been considering how to integrate an existing Novell network. Both Microsoft and Novell offer suitable solutions. Whereas the solutions supplied by Microsoft mostly focus on converting an existing NetWare environment to a Windows 2000 or Windows Server 2003 environment, Novell, of course, targets the integration of Windows systems in a NetWare centric environment. Particularly on terminal servers, it is possible to replace the existing authentication component (GINA-DLL) with an alternative that allows logon using Novell servers.

UNIX is a widely used operating system, albeit with no common standard. Various manufacturers, such as IBM, Sun, Hewlett-Packard, Silicon Graphics, and Apple offer their own UNIX derivates. These, however, are mostly bundled with hardware. Another option is to use the open-source UNIX variant named Linux that is supplied by different distributors. Linux is not owned by a commercial company but is developed by a global independent software community. Most traditional UNIX manufacturers also support the Linux software community and are increasingly adapting their products to Linux.

Most UNIX derivatives come with a graphical user interface based on the X11 standard. For terminal servers to access UNIX server file and print services, either Samba, the Network File System or the remote line printer (LPR) mechanism can be used. In principle, it is possible to start and use UNIX and Windows-based applications from a suitable client. This is, in fact, practiced by many companies that have Linux on the client platforms but terminal servers and ICA clients for a number of applications.

An interesting alternative to X11 for transmitting UNIX desktops and applications to remote clients is the Citrix MetaFrame XP Presentation Server for UNIX. This system replaces the X11 protocol with the ICA protocol, which is done by modifying the UNIX operating system. The advantage of this solution for transmitting screen content is that the bandwidth required by ICA is significantly lower than that needed by X11.

Mainframes

As in the client/server landscape, it is possible to connect mainframes to a terminal server by installing emulation tools for direct mainframe access. Another option is a gateway for the implementation of TCP/IP access methods for mainframe-specific communication protocols. A third option is middleware products that allow direct communication between the two rather contradictory computer worlds. Integrating terminal servers and mainframes can therefore be a very complex task that might even require specific adjustments to some software components. It is, for instance, very possible that, for Windows to access a mainframe, the middleware first needs to be adjusted for multiple-user operation before it can be used on terminal servers.

Now, we are again at a point where we started in the Preface of the book: looking at Mainframes and terminal server as central execution platforms for applications. The last 11 chapters showed, however, why terminal servers are not just another incarnation of mainframes but comprise many advanced concepts related to modern, centrally managed Windows-based applications. The next two chapters will show another, even more spectacular aspect of server-based computing: the combination of terminal servers and Web technologies. If mainframe computing represents the past, and pure terminal server environments stand for the present use of centrally managed Windows-based applications, the advantages of combining terminal servers and Web technologies might well be seen as a preferred enterprise application providing option in the near future. Microsoft Windows Server 2003, including the .NET Framework, Terminal Services and Internet Information Services, is a perfect platform for this option.

Chapter 12

Web Access to Terminal Server Applications

A client platform with a conventional Remote Desktop Protocol (RDP) client (such as the Remote Desktop Connection) is not always available for accessing terminal servers. However, many companies need users or administrators to be able to work with applications on terminal servers without prior manual installation of such an RDP client, if at all possible. A suitable solution is to integrate Terminal Services access into Microsoft Internet Explorer. This chapter will cover the following topics:

- Learn about the various strategies for Web integration of terminal servers. There are two options for this: embedding Terminal Services sessions in Web sites and providing Web icons for launching Terminal Services sessions.

- Become familiar with the Remote Desktop Web Connection that facilitates access to terminal servers via Internet Explorer.

Web Integration of Terminal Services

How is it possible to access terminal servers through Internet Explorer? After all, terminal server technology (RDP protocol) and Web server technology (HTTP protocol) are two completely different concepts. RDP is *state based*, which means that the network connection is maintained during the entire user connection between a terminal server and its client. This makes it easy to associate users and the corresponding status with the session. Should the communication break down due to a network failure, the user session must be stored in memory on the server and the connection to precisely this session must be resumed prior to a new interaction through the client.

Thus, RDP is a fairly rigid point-to-point connection that can achieve a certain dynamic only during its initialization phase by means of load-sharing mechanisms.

Web servers and the respective clients, on the other hand, function completely differently. The HTTP protocol is based on a *stateless* mechanism, which means a separate connection is opened for every element that the Web browser requests from the Web server, and the connection is maintained only for the time it takes to load the element. When all the elements have been loaded on the client Web browser, the user can interact with them without a network connection, until additional elements need to be loaded. The Web server does not automatically store any information about the users or the terminal equipment that have obtained data from it. Thus, managing individual user sessions involves additional complexities. The wide array of features of Web technologies in their pure forms makes them exceptionally suitable for anonymous server access from computer environments that are attached to networks whose quality varies significantly.

Thus, at first glance, it appears that these two conflicting worlds cannot be joined. However, quite the opposite is true. There are two possible ways to integrate: embedding Terminal Services sessions in Web sites and providing Web icons for launching Terminal Services sessions. We will take a closer look at both of these options below.

Web Technology Basics

The World Wide Web (WWW) project—today called simply the *Web*—originated in 1989 at the CERN (European Organisation for Nuclear Research) research laboratory in Geneva, Switzerland. The WWW project arose out of the need to offer the international teams working at the lab the possibility of using a structured approach to manage a rapidly changing collection of reports, blueprints, images, photos, publications, and other documents, and to link them in a logical manner. The results of the WWW project were used at the National Center for Supercomputing Applications (NCSA) at the University of Illinois in Urbana-Champaign and at the Massachusetts Institute of Technology (MIT) in Boston for a more advanced development of the Web concepts. Finally, this project led to commercial implementation of Web browsers and Web servers, starting the Internet hype in the 1990s.

The developers of the Web defined multiple protocols for the application layer, as well as a standard for publishing documents. The three traditional key concepts are URLs, HTML, and HTTP:

- **URLs** are Uniform Resource Locators (also known as *links*). Their primary function is to represent the extension of the complete path name for a data object on the Internet. This is what allows the data object to be uniquely identified.

- **HTML** (HyperText Markup Language) is the hypertext page description language that defines the content of documents on the Web. Such documents might contain not only pure text, but also links to multimedia elements to be included in the Web document.

- **HTTP** (HyperText Transport Protocol) describes the transport protocol that is needed to access remote Web documents. It is made up of a rather simple set of commands.

What is the typical setup of a Web environment using these key concepts? A typical Web server is listening on TCP port 80 for incoming HTTP connections from a Web browser (or another client). Once the connection has been established, the client sends a request and the server replies by sending either the requested HTML document or an error report (reply or response). Thereafter, the connection is terminated, corresponding to a stateless concept for communication between Web browsers and Web servers.

In addition to simple text, the static or dynamic HTML pages on a Web server typically also contain graphics, sounds, animations, or even entire videos. These multimedia page elements are loaded via separate network connections that are terminated when the loading process is complete. Some of the multimedia data are not displayed directly via the Web browser's built-in program logic, but instead require helper applications that are loaded and integrated as needed.

Many Web sites include, in combination with static graphics, forms or other interactive elements in which users can enter information. Typical Web applications use these elements intensively for the graphical user interface (GUI) design. The interactive elements are analyzed by the program logic, which is located either directly in the page description on the client or on the Web server. The latter, of course, requires a communication feedback channel to the Web server.

However, individualized or personalized communication between a Web browser user and a Web server reveals the disadvantage of stateless network communication. Managing user sessions and the corresponding status information requires a great deal of effort.

Embedding RDP Sessions in Web Pages

Most Web sites are made up of text and graphical elements that are displayed together. However, as mentioned earlier, the elements are transferred to the Web browser via separate network connections. The strings for the text on the requested Web site are combined with the links to the graphics and some associated parameters. The graphics and animation data are loaded later as separate files according to their links, and they are positioned on the page by the browser logic. Thus, it is even possible for the text information to come from a different Web server than the graphics elements.

The parameters linked to a graphic specify its position and size on the Web page, as well as the type of graphic. If the browser's programming logic includes the functions or methods for displaying the graphic type, it is quite easy to fulfill the request. However, if the browser does not recognize the graphic type, it can load additional display components if the Web page includes a link to the source of these components. Here, too, the source can be a Web server that is completely independent from the Web server on which the Web sites and the referenced graphics are located.

Looking now at an RDP session as an animated graphic or a video data stream, the solution concept for integrating terminal servers and Web servers is obvious: a Web page contains a link to an RDP multimedia element located on a terminal server. If a browser loads this Web page, it cannot display the RDP video by itself. Thus, it searches the Web page for information that will allow it to subsequently load a component to display RDP videos. Of course, this subsequently loaded component encompasses or references a complete RDP client that is also capable of accepting user interaction. For the Web browser, this embedded RDP client acts just like a video that is displayed at a particular location on the Web page. The network connection for this multimedia element is maintained until the end of the video. To establish and maintain the user session as a video, the RDP client in the Web browser must communicate with the associated terminal server by means of the RDP protocol. The communication situation on the browser is therefore as follows:

1. The browser loads a page from a Web server via HTTP. The Web page includes a link to an RDP element that points to a terminal server.

2. The browser first displays the Web page's text information.

3. If the browser does not recognize the RDP element type, it loads the corresponding display component from a source that is defined within the Web page. In doing so, it registers the linking of all RDP elements on Web sites with this new display component, which represents a complete RDP client.

4. The browser uses the embedded RDP client by transferring to it the parameters contained in the RDP element link.

5. The RDP client begins to communicate with the terminal server through RDP.

6. The browser ensures that the RDP output is positioned properly with the Web page's other elements.

7. The RDP client controls the data stream between the client and the terminal server while the corresponding user session is maintained.

If the user navigates from a Web page containing an embedded RDP client to another page, the corresponding RDP client session is removed from memory. This, of course, also terminates the connection to the terminal server. This is because Web browsers actively use only the display components for the elements on the current

Web page. Depending on the configuration of the terminal server environment, it might or might not be possible to restore the connection to this session.

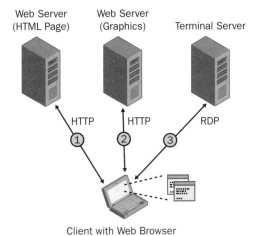

Web Server   Web Server
(HTML Page)   (Graphics)   Terminal Server

HTTP   HTTP   RDP

①   ②   ③

Client with Web Browser

Figure 12-1   Possible constellation with Web servers for HTML pages (1) and graphics (2) and for a terminal server (3) to generate a Web page with an embedded RDP session.

Note   Although the distribution of text and graphical information from Web pages to various Web servers is unusual, it is technologically possible. This clearly demonstrates the role of the terminal server, which provides a further data type for use on a Web page.

Providing Web Icons for RDP Sessions

A much easier alternative to embedding RDP sessions in Web pages is providing Web icons for RDP or ICA sessions. With this method, only the application icons, familiar from conventional desktops, are positioned on a Web page. Behind each application icon is a link to the terminal server with which the connection is to be made, and on which an application might even be scheduled for launch.

Technologically, the normal Remote Desktop connection or a conventional ICA client is started by using the icons on the Web page. Clicking an application icon creates an RDP or ICA file that launches the corresponding client and supplies the necessary parameters. Here, an ActiveX control is normally used to control the transfer of parameters from the Web page to the RDP or ICA client.

Unlike with embedding RDP sessions, the Web icons launch separate windows for the RDP or ICA user sessions. These are then completely independent from other user interactions in the browser.

> **Note** Although providing Web icons to launch Terminal Services applications does not at first appear to be particularly exciting, this technology offers enormous potential for the future. For this reason, we will look at it in greater detail in Chapter 13, "Application Access Portals."

Remote Desktop Web Connection

To offer embedded RDP sessions in Web pages with Microsoft Windows 2000, Service Pack 1 added the Windows Terminal Advanced Client (TSAC). The TSAC was a special RDP client that supported RDP version 5.0 and extended the terminal server technology to include the Web. To connect to a terminal server, clients merely needed to have Internet Explorer, a connection to an internal or external network, and authorization to use an ActiveX control.

Windows XP then included TSAC's successor, Remote Desktop Web Connection for RDP 5.1. Microsoft Windows Server 2003 comes with an updated version of this tool, but it must be specially installed. Although both versions of Remote Desktop Web Connection for Windows XP and Windows Server 2003 support the latest RDP functions, they are, of course, also backward compatible with RDP 5.0.

Installation

If Windows Server 2003 is playing the role of a Web application server (using Active Server Pages or ASP.NET), Internet Information Services (IIS) 6.0 is already installed. IIS is required to install Remote Desktop Web Connection. If IIS is not already installed, it can be added at any time using the server configuration wizard.

Unfortunately, it is not very easy to find the location for installing Remote Desktop Web Connection under Windows Server 2003. It is located in the software installation dialog window. To launch it, go to Start\Control Panel\Add or Remove Programs\Add/Remove Windows Components. Navigate from Application Server to Internet Information Services (IIS) and World Wide Web Service, and finally to Remote Desktop Web Connection. Click the Details button to move from one level of the component hierarchy to the next.

Remote Desktop Web Connection can be successfully installed under Windows Server 2003 after IIS has been installed with default settings. If need be, the current configuration of Internet Information Services can be changed at any time using Internet Information Services Manager under Start\Administrative Tools\Internet Information Services (IIS) Manager.

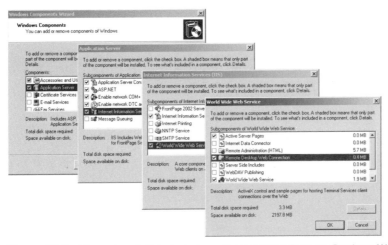

Figure 12-2   Hierarchy of dialog windows for installing Remote Desktop Web Connection.

Important   The Remote Desktop Web Connection versions are different for Windows XP and Windows Server 2003, although both can be installed with Windows Server 2003. The requirement for both versions is, of course, the prior installation of Internet Information Services. After installation, the Remote Desktop Web Connection files for Windows XP, as downloaded from the Microsoft Web site, are located at Inetpub \wwwroot\TSWeb. Installation via the Windows components of Windows Server 2003 includes more up-to-date versions of the files and is performed in the %Systemroot%\Web \TSWeb folder.

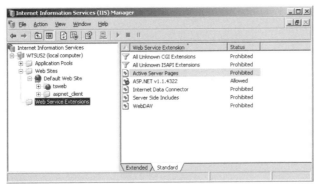

Figure 12-3   Internet Information Services Manager after installing Internet Information Services and Remote Desktop Web Connection.

Technical Mode of Operation

From a technological standpoint, Remote Desktop Web Connection is a Web application consisting of an ActiveX control and a connection page that serves as a sample page. If Remote Desktop Web Connection is distributed via a Web server, the client connection to a terminal server can take place through Internet Explorer and a TCP/IP connection.

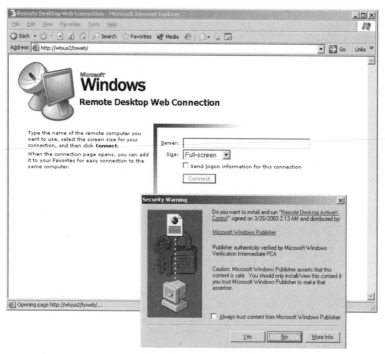

Figure 12-4 Log in using Remote Desktop Web Connection. Installing the signed ActiveX control element usually generates a security warning.

What components are needed to execute Remote Desktop Web Connection?

- A server platform running Windows Server 2003 and version 6 of the Internet Information Services.

- A client that can load and execute the ActiveX control element. This can be any client that has Microsoft Windows NT 4.0, Service Pack 4 or higher, and Internet Explorer version 4.01 or higher. Active scripting as well as loading and executing signed ActiveX control elements must be enabled in the relevant Internet Explorer security zone.

The Remote Desktop Web Connection sample page uses the Msrdp.cap installation file to supply the Msrdp.ocx RDP client. Depending on the configuration of the terminal server, this RDP client uses an RC4 encryption algorithm by RSA security, with a key length of 40, 56, or 128 bits. Like other RDP clients, this client uses TCP port 3389 for communication, which is an important restriction of usage across firewall boundaries.

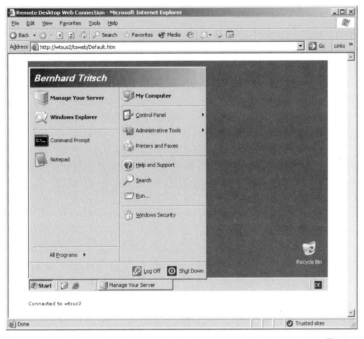

Figure 12-5   Executing an embedded user session in Internet Explorer.

Adapting the Sample Page

The logic of the sample page shows how the RDP ActiveX control is incorporated. This can, of course, also be used for other Web sites.

Listing 12-1: Incorporating the ActiveX Control and Transferring the Parameters for the Width and Height of the Terminal Services Session

```
<OBJECT language="vbscript" ID="MsRdpClient"
onreadystatechange="OnControlLoad"
CLASSID="CLSID:9059f30f-4eb1-4bd2-9fdc-36f43a218f4a"
CODEBASE="msrdp.cab#version=5,1,2600,1095"
WIDTH=<% resWidth = Request.QueryString("rW")
    if  resWidth < 200 or resWidth > 1600 then
        resWidth = 800
    end if
    Response.Write resWidth %>
HEIGHT=<% resHeight = Request.QueryString("rH")
    if  resHeight < 200 or resHeight > 1200 then
        resHeight = 600
    end if
    Response.Write resHeight %>>
</OBJECT>
```

Listing 12-1 shows how basic parameters are incorporated. The value for *WIDTH* is the width in pixels used to show the Terminal Services session in the Web site. A similar statement applies to the value *HEIGHT* and the height of the Terminal Services session. The *CODEBASE* value is the location where the file containing the Remote Desktop Web Connection code is stored. The name of this file is Msrdp.cab. It is located in the folder in which the ActiveX control element and the sample pages for Remote Desktop are installed. *PARAMNAME* is defined in at least one of the parameters supported in Msrdp.ocx.

The Remote Desktop ActiveX control element has a number of object parameters and methods with which it can be controlled. As an additional example, Listing 12-2 lists the preparatory commands for opening and also lists when the user session is to be started using the *Connect* method.

Listing 12-2: Invoking an Application That Is Launched Within a New User Session

```
if MsRdpClient.SecuredSettingsEnabled then
    MsRdpClient.SecuredSettings.StartProgram = "notepad.exe"
else
    msgbox
"Cannot access secured setting (startprogram) in the current browser zone"
end if
```

> **Note** Additional object parameters for the *Msrdp.ocx* ActiveX control element of Remote Desktop Web Connection can be viewed with a program such as Oleview.exe or with the Microsoft Visual Basic Object Browser.

The Remote Desktop Web Connection sample page shows only the basic possibilities of this technology. Additional object parameters of the ActiveX control and, above all, the possibilities for coding associated Web applications with ASP.NET make it possible to develop much more powerful start pages for Remote Desktop access.

Just providing rather simple Web pages to access centralized Windows-based applications is not suitable for most enterprise environments in which additional features are required. This is why the next chapter will introduce the concept of application access portals.

Chapter 13

Application Access Portals

Simple Web clients that allow Terminal Services sessions to be started only when the sessions are embedded in Web pages are not sufficiently capable to meet the requirements of many corporate environments. Only when functions are added to facilitate personalization and structured graphical presentation of Web pages with the application icons does this technology becomes attractive for the respective target group. Security and scalability of the appropriate infrastructure are also important issues in this context. Special Web applications for the creation of dynamic Web pages—application access portals—are one possible solution, enabling the integration of terminal servers in corporate environments.

This chapter covers the following topics:

- What are application access portals and what can they be used for? The first part of this chapter serves as an introduction to this topic and presents the features that should be included in an ideal portal environment for terminal servers.

- The second part details various portal products by Citrix and New Moon, including architecture, installation, configuration, and the relevant clients.

- Finally, we highlight available alternatives to the standard portal products and where the trend is moving in this respect.

A Web Portal for Terminal Server Applications

Solutions for centralized data, application, and process integration are becoming ever more popular—both on the Internet and within companies. The accompanying processes and products to these solutions use middleware, application servers, component models, communication standards, and database technologies. New standards, such as XML and SOAP, are used to an ever-increasing degree in the relevant integration environments, based on the Microsoft .NET Framework, for example. The term *portal* has become established as the overall name for these means of accessing information and applications. Portals are usually characterized by their ability to personalize user access and content. This necessitates auxiliary components for authentication and session administration.

The term portal is used in a wide variety of contexts. In corporate environments there are portals for content management, information management, document management, Enterprise Application Integration (EAI), Enterprise Resource Planning (ERP), and customer relationship management (CRM). What the different portal types have in common is the fact that they can be personalized, integrate processes or applications, and simplify user activities in networks. In most cases, portals access application servers with a process logic based on Web technologies. Microsoft ASP.NET and .NET Web services, in particular, provide the ideal basis for this. However, companies want to use portals in a corporate environment not only because of the enticing technical approach, but especially because of the opportunities a portal offers to cut costs. Costs can be reduced because all of the required applications and information are gathered at one central point. Users therefore spend less time finding the "right" applications or even installing them themselves, which usually gives rise to considerable subsequent costs. In the ideal situation, all needed information and all applications relating to the individual user roles will be available through the portal.

But what does all of this have to do with terminal servers? A portal becomes a valuable integration tool if the required application logic is not available as a Web application but still needs to be made available through a portal's centralized environment. What kind of Web pages on the portal allow access to applications that run on terminal servers? For these type of Web pages, it is not enough to simply provide the links to RDP or ICA client software components for the applications to be accessed through a Web browser. Instead, further technical features must be added to meet the requirements for the use of an application access portal across a company. This scenario, focusing on the personalized aggregation of links to Windows-based applications, is referred to as Windows Forms application integration. However, it should not be compared or confused with powerful concepts from the field of EAI portals. These portal environments are generally based on pure Web applications and usually include industry-specific modules for process and workflow modeling. Such functions do not play as prominent a role for application access portals in the context of terminal servers. What is much more important for these portals is that they can make available the links to terminal server applications and to Web applications simultaneously and in a manner to suit the specific users.

Users, therefore, can no longer directly see whether they are accessing a Microsoft Windows or a Web application through a state-oriented or stateless protocol. This allows the administrators in the background to migrate applications from one basic technology to another without passing on the link to the application to the end user through complicated distribution mechanisms. All they have to do is to change the logic behind the application icon in the portal. It is not necessary to install applications locally or to modify the local desktops on the client.

At this point it should be pointed out that centrally executed Web applications or terminal server applications are nothing new from a technical perspective. Even mainframe computers were, and still are, based on the same concepts: a centralized host provides its computing capacity to several users to execute the application logic. The interaction with the user is delegated to a remote computer via a special protocol. This computer can be a terminal, a Web browser, an RDP client, or an ICA client. The most significant differences between these client types are only their use of graphical elements and the possibility of using a mouse. In principle, Web browsers, RDP clients, and ICA clients are the modern variants of the more antiquated terminals or terminal emulators.

Note Conventional 32-bit Windows applications are now generally referred to as *Windows Forms* in a Windows environment using the .NET Framework. This new name separates them from Web applications, now known as *Web Forms*. Windows applications need not be integrated on a Web interface within a portal that specializes in this aspect only. It is also possible to use a portal that does not have the appropriate function as part of its standard scope. In this case, an additional component must integrate the access to the Windows applications. This component should have the same technical features as a special *Windows Forms application access portal*. In the same way, standard EAI or ERP portals can also be expanded to include the function that allows them to use conventional Windows applications on terminal servers. However, the adjustments required here are usually highly specific to the individual portal products, so we will not cover them in detail in this book.

Windows Forms Application Integration

To follow up on this rather abstract introduction to Windows Forms application access portals, we will now look at the practical requirements. This section lists the technical features of an ideal environment that would enable the optimum integration of Windows Forms applications. Generally speaking, however, no real product will fulfill all of these requirements optimally. The following list should therefore serve as more of a guide for comparison. We purposefully did not rate or prioritize the individual features because each environment has different requirements.

- Mapping the portal logic in a Web application (for example, as an ASP.NET application) that can present all of the icons required for terminal server applications in a structured manner. The traditional desktop is thereby shifted to the Web browser. To improve scalability and availability, the portal is ideally implemented so that it can be executed on several Web servers in parallel. This requires mechanisms to facilitate load balancing.

- A centrally configurable standard to a user interface with standard elements that comply with a company's standards (otherwise known as the *corporate design*). All of these elements should also be adjustable, to a limited extent. This applies, for example, to company logos, colors, navigation elements, font types, and font sizes. If more than one company or division within a company—each with its own corporate design—is to be included in the same portal, the portal must be able to support several separate user groups or organizational units with different features.

- Provision of a graphical user interface with syntactically and semantically consistent navigation mechanisms. Even though the environment should provide as much flexibility as possible, this requirement must still be considered to prevent the usability of the system from being jeopardized. Implementing this requirement requires a clearly determined set of atomic and integrated standard graphical elements that can be produced at high throughput using an abstract model. The accompanying technical solutions often follow the same pattern with respect to design and optimization as a well-known conventional graphical user interface—the Windows desktop.

- Avoidance of any overly long waits when a page loads and when changing masks. The reaction times should remain within predefined limits even at times of peak load, to prevent the interaction from tiring the user. This can be achieved for a predetermined maximum number of simultaneous users by optimizing the generation, rendering, and presentation of standard graphical elements.

- Administration of all user sessions to guarantee that users are identified when they access the stateless HTTP protocol for a second or subsequent time. This can be done using cookies or by adding a user-specific chain of characters in each HTML link. This task is far from trivial, so special session management components are often used; these are programmed independently of the rest of the portal logic and integrated by means of interfaces.

- Support of as many browser types and clients as possible for connection to the terminal server. This allows a company's previously independent organizational units with different IT environments to be integrated more easily. This feature is particularly important for large companies faced with repeated structural changes as a result of mergers or changes to the corporate structure.

- User and group-specific presentation of the portal interface and integrated graphical elements (such as application icons). This individualization of the graphical user interface is generally enabled by linking the portal logic with a directory service such as Microsoft's Active Directory directory service. Managing the status of each individual user session is particularly important here.

- The possibility for users who have logged on to change the portal interface to their taste. If these parameters are to be saved and reloaded the next time the user logs on, the mechanisms for managing a user profile must be integrated.

- A database system or configuration files for the centralized provision of portal content and as a basis for the portal logic. Further parameters for the creation of portal pages originate in the directory service and from information queries to the terminal server. In the optimum scenario, all portal pages are dynamically generated.

- Client software that can display the applications in full without the underlying desktop. This makes a remote application behave in exactly the same way as a local application. The individual applications must, however, have the possibility to run in the same logical user session. This allows the applications invoked to be linked through the old but still commonly used OLE or COM mechanisms, as long as they are executed on the same terminal server.

- Windows applications load-balancing mechanisms provided by terminal servers. The portal logic must incorporate the relevant output parameters of all the terminal servers concerned to select a suitable assignment when the first application request is made. Alternatively, it is, of course, possible to use other established load-balancing mechanisms. For all subsequent attempts to access the Windows applications, the portal logic or the load-balancing mechanism must, where necessary, make sure that only the initially selected terminal server can be accessed for predefined applications within a user session. A feature of the load-balancing mechanism might include saving the ID of the terminal server that the user worked with most recently.

- The potential to organize terminal servers in several separate units (that is, farms) that allow it to provide different sets of applications. This functionality improves the scalability and usability in larger companies. However, the complexity of the load-balancing mechanisms relating to individual farms might increase.

- The option of switching the portal interface between different languages. This applies both to text and graphical elements and to different terminal servers to which the portal refers via the application icons.

- Mechanisms to control the bandwidth used between the individual servers within the portal infrastructure. This includes the possibility to limit the resources requested so as to prevent overload in extreme situations.

These requirements can be used to draw up a list of specifications for an application access portal. However, the preceding requirements do not include any security mechanisms. Only with security mechanisms can a portal be operated in an environment that is subject to external influences and even, sometimes, to attacks.

Security Extensions

It is important to consider the subject of security in sufficient detail. We will therefore expand on the basic requirements to incorporate security considerations.

- Secure logon options from a Web browser with which the individualized portal interface and the integrated application icons can be launched. The possibility of user identification can range from anonymous logon to user names and passwords, or even to smartcards and certificates. Here, too, the connection to a directory service plays a central role. The logon information must be passed on securely to the terminal servers for the applications to start up.

- Different options for encrypting all data streams between the portal servers, terminal servers, and all other involved servers. This allows this technology to be used even in highly security-conscious environments, such as military bases, government bodies, banks, hospitals, or public administrations.

- The possibility to distribute certain services and programs to dedicated servers that can, if necessary, be located in different zones (often called *demilitarized zones*) of a perimeter network. This increases both the security and the scalability of the overall infrastructure. Even features that can analyze and control all data streams passing from one security zone to another within the perimeter network can be integrated where required.

So what would an ideal and secure application access portal look like in reality? Sadly, there is no simple and universal answer to that question. However, there are some products available on the market that attempt to fulfill at least some of the preceding technical requirements. Some of the products are so complex and powerful that each would merit a whole book of its own. Nevertheless, the following section presents the main portal solutions that integrate terminal servers and MetaFrame servers.

Web Interface for MetaFrame XP

The Web Interface for MetaFrame XP was developed by Citrix and was known until recently as NFuse Classic. It enables access to distributed information and applications provided by MetaFrame servers. Program Neighborhood, as described in Chapter 9, makes this function available on a conventional desktop, too. However, the Web Interface for MetaFrame XP extends the possibilities of the Program Neighborhood by providing application icons and information not through the desktop, but through a Web environment.

The Web Interface for MetaFrame XP creates dynamic HTML pages that display all the available resources of MetaFrame server farms in an individualized manner. It uses the Active Server Pages on Internet Information Services. When a user logs on to the Web Interface for MetaFrame XP from the start page, a new and dynamically generated Web page displays all applications and resources for which the user has rights. Using the Web Interface for MetaFrame XP thus allows a simple Web environment to be created for accessing the applications or forms the basis for the integration of published applications in a company's portal.

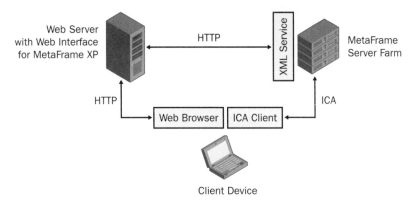

Figure 13-1   Outline of an environment with the Web Interface for MetaFrame XP.

Note   The Web Interface for MetaFrame XP can be based on an unmodified installation of Windows Server 2003 Internet Information Services, although the Active Server Pages Web services extension must be permitted. The respective program code of the Active Server Pages cannot directly access the interface with the Java component required by the Web Interface for MetaFrame XP. That is why Citrix supplies a COM component with the installation package, which provides a kind of shell around the Java component. This shell is called a *Java wrapper*. As a result, the information is accessed from the Active Server Pages through COM requests that are transformed by the Java wrapper into requests to the Java component. The Java component requests the required information from the XML service of a MetaFrame server and obtains an answer. The Java component then passes the information on to the Java wrapper, which provides it to the program logic in the Active Server Pages. However, there are an increasing number of developers that program their Web applications on the basis of ASP.NET. If you want to use the Java component of the Web Interface for MetaFrame XP for this programming model, too, you will need to access the Java wrapper via a corresponding .NET Framework interface, which is not always easy in managed code. Alternatively, you have the option of writing a *COM wrapper* under the .NET Framework, which in turn incorporates the accesses from the .NET Framework programming logic into the Java wrapper. With ASP.NET, however, it is no longer possible to use the sample code from the Web Interface for MetaFrame XP—reprogramming is unavoidable.

To transmit all relevant information through a MetaFrame server farm, the Web Interface for MetaFrame XP contains a Java component that communicates with a selected MetaFrame server in the farm. This communication is comparable with that of a Program Neighborhood client and therefore usually occurs via port 80 and the Citrix XML service on the MetaFrame server side.

Installation

The Web Interface for MetaFrame XP installation file called *NFuseClassic-IIS.msi* is located in the NFuse folder on the component CD supplied with the Citrix MetaFrame XP Presentation Server. The software can be installed on Windows 2000 with Service Pack 3 or on Microsoft Windows Server 2003. Both operating systems need to include Internet Information Services (IIS), version 5.0 or 6.0. Web Interface for MetaFrame XP also requires a Java Virtual Machine (JVM) to execute the Web server extension. If the JVM is not present on the target platform, the installation wizard will automatically install it on the system. This ensures the operability of Web Interface for MetaFrame XP on Windows Server 2003 even without the installation of other components in addition to Internet Information Services.

Web Interface for MetaFrame XP is installed by using the installation wizard accomplished by using the NFuseClassic-IIs.msi file in the %ProgramFiles%\Citrix \NFuse folder. ICA Web clients are copied into the \Citrix\ICAWEB folder, which is created under the document root directory of the Web server. This is usually located in the c:\inetpub\wwwroot folder. On Windows Server 2003 with Internet Information Services 6.0, the Active Server Pages Web service extension permits the installation wizard logic, even if it was prohibited before.

> **Note**   Web Interface for MetaFrame XP is still based on conventional Active Server Pages and not on ASP.NET. This is why the .NET Framework runtime environment is not a prerequisite.

To identify all of the information required to construct the user interface, Web Interface for MetaFrame XP must communicate with the Citrix XML service on one of the MetaFrame servers in the farm. The selected server can be defined by its fully qualified name or by its IP address. The Web server and the MetaFrame server farm generally communicate through TCP port 80, although this can, if required, be changed on one or both sides. The MetaFrame server selected as the contact point is often called the *NFuse gateway*, even though the old name (NFuse) is no longer commonly used for Web Interface for MetaFrame XP. In the future, the name of the NFuse gateway will rather be Web Interface gateway. It is recommended that the NFuse gateway or Web Interface gateway also be the zone data collector in a zone within the MetaFrame server farm.

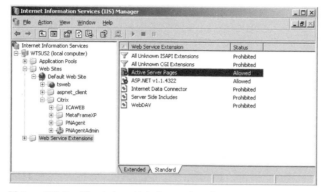

Figure 13-2   The Internet Information Services Manager after the installation of Web Interface for MetaFrame XP.

When you have installed all components on the server, you need to restart the system. After restarting, you can access the start page of the Web Interface for MetaFrame XP using the URL *http://<Webserver>/Citrix/MetaFrameXP*. *Webserver* should be replaced by the name of the Web server where the Web Interface for MetaFrame XP is located.

Configuration

There are two ways of configuring the Web Interface for MetaFrame XP: by using a Web-based administration tool, or by using a configuration file. The administration tool is simply a graphical user interface that makes it easier to access the configuration file. All relevant parameters for the Web Interface for MetaFrame XP are therefore physically located in the configuration file %ProgramFiles%\Citrix\NFuse\conf\NFuse.conf.

Administration Tool

Configuration using the Web-based administration tool is done via the special start page *http://<Webserver>/Citrix/MetaFrameXP/WIAdmin*. This page is established automatically when Web Interface for MetaFrame XP is installed on Windows Server 2003 with Internet Information Services. The start page can be accessed only from Internet Explorer version 5.0 or later.

When opening the start page for the Web-based administration tool, the user is asked to enter a user name and password. The user account must be an administrator's account for the tool to be accessed successfully and for the overview page of the administration interface to open.

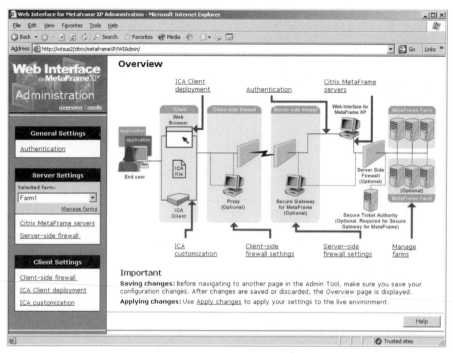

Figure 13-3 Web Interface for MetaFrame XP administration environment.

The administration tool allows access to various areas for configuration purposes:

■ **Authentication** Determines the authentication method used when a user logs on to the Web Interface for MetaFrame XP. The available options are smartcard, guest user with no user name or password, pass-through of desktop logon information, and explicit logon with user name and password. The latter also contains the option to require the use of RSA SecurID and to control the options available to a user to change the password.

■ **Manage farms** Several MetaFrame server farms can be listed and put in order of succession. This can be used for load sharing and for establishing error tolerances.

■ **Citrix MetaFrame servers** The administrator enters which MetaFrame servers are to be used as the NFuse gateway in what order, via which protocol, and through which port. The XML service on the servers listed here must be ready for communication through the port indicated.

■ **Server-side firewall settings** Settings for the use of the IP address, which might be defined as the default address, alternative address, network address translation (NAT), or by the Secure Gateway for MetaFrame.

- **Client-side firewall settings**   This is where the administrator configures if and how an existing proxy server is to be used for the communication between ICA client and MetaFrame server. The proxy server makes sure that system names used inside a firewall do not get outside of the firewall.

- **ICA client deployment**   Determines the deployment of the ICA clients via the Web Interface for MetaFrame XP. This includes the options for downloading the ICA clients, embedding applications in the window of the Web browser, and installing the Java client.

- **ICA customization**   Determines the settings that users can establish on their client. This includes window size, window color, and audio quality.

The settings must be saved when the configuration has been changed. The settings are entered in the NFuse.conf configuration file.

> **Note**   If the application icons for more than one server farm are displayed in Web Interface for MetaFrame XP, you need to install the Web Interface Extension for MetaFrame XP. However, this also changes the way various Web Interface for MetaFrame XP default options are handled. There is an exception to the need of installing the Web Interface Extension for MetaFrame XP if all the farms are in trusted domains.

The NFuse.conf Configuration File

The global configuration settings from the Web Interface for MetaFrame XP are saved in %ProgramFiles%\Citrix\NFuse\conf\NFuse.conf. All Web pages created by the Web Interface for MetaFrame XP use the values in this file. Changes to the values, therefore, affect all the corresponding Web pages in the first instance. It is possible, however, to overwrite some of the values in NFuse.conf for individual pages in the scripts handling the programming logic.

> **Important**   Changes in NFuse.conf become active only when Internet Information Services has been restarted. With Windows Server 2003 Internet Information Services, it is sufficient to restart the thread in which Web Interface for MetaFrame XP is executed.

Usage

Following installation, it is very easy to use Web Interface for MetaFrame XP without any further configuration. The start page located at *http://<Webserver>/Citrix*

/MetaFrameXP contains a logon dialog and provides the opportunity to download the required ICA client, if necessary. The ICA client can be installed properly only if the user has the necessary permissions on the client platform.

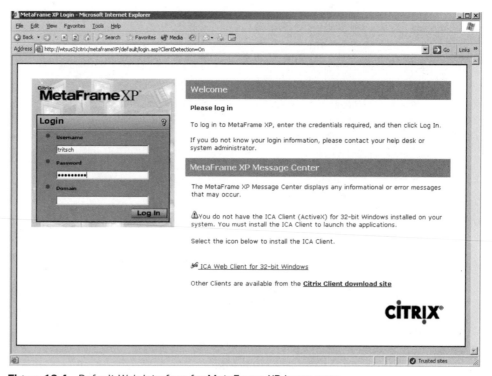

Figure 13-4 Default Web Interface for MetaFrame XP logon page.

For Web Interface for MetaFrame XP to work correctly with the end user devices, the following conditions relating to the Web browser and ICA clients must be met:

- **32-bit Windows** ICA client, version 6.1.963 or later; Internet Explorer, version 5 or later; Netscape Communicator, version 4.7x or later; Netscape Navigator, version 6.21 or later

- **Macintosh** ICA client, version 6.0.66 or above; Internet Explorer, version 5 or later; Netscape Communicator, version 4.7x or later; Netscape Navigator, version 6.21 or later

- **Unix for Solaris (SPARC)** ICA client, version 6.0.915 or later, and Netscape Communicator, version 4.7x or later

- **Redhat Linux** ICA client, version 6.3 or later, and Netscape Communicator, version 4.7x or later

The ICA Web client for 32-bit Windows includes a signed ActiveX control that allows access to the ICA client component and usually issues a warning message at the time of installation. It is therefore advisable for the ICA Web client to be installed in the corporate environment at the time the client environment is initially installed, or for the ActiveX control to be defined through Group Policy as a trusted component. However, it is also possible to use the full Program Neighborhood client or the Program Neighborhood Agent (see Chapter 9).

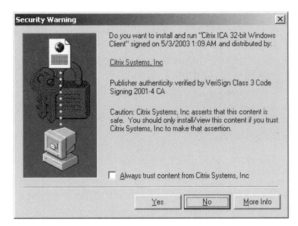

Figure 13-5   Warning during the installation of the signed Web Interface for MetaFrame XP ICA client.

When the user successfully logs on using Web Interface for MetaFrame XP, an individualized Web page appears that displays the icons for all published applications the user is allowed to work with. This corresponds exactly with the functions available to the user through the conventional Program Neighborhood client or the Program Neighborhood Agent.

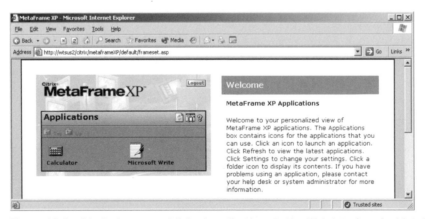

Figure 13-6   Displaying two published applications in the Web Interface for MetaFrame XP.

It is, of course, possible to adapt the programming logic and the appearance of the Web Interface for MetaFrame XP to company requirements. To do this, however, the corresponding server-side and client-side scripts in the c:\inetpub\wwwroot \citrix\MetaFrameXP\site folder need to be adjusted. This demands excellent knowledge of Internet Information Services, Active Server Pages, Jscript, and VBScript.

Important As described in Chapter 9, Web Interface for MetaFrame XP is also the preferred administration environment for the Program Neighborhood agents. The respective administration start page is located at *http: //<Webserver>/Citrix/PNAgentAdmin*.

Integration of Secure Gateway

Until recently, the Secure Gateway was a separate Citrix product. It has now been added as an extension to the Citrix MetaFrame XP Presentation Server and to the Citrix Secure Access Manager (see Chapter 10 and later in this chapter). The Secure Gateway contains components that provide secure communication via secure socket layer (SSL) or transport level security (TLS) between ICA clients and the MetaFrame server. This allows a so-called secure tunnel between the MetaFrame servers and the ICA clients to be established. Web Interface for MetaFrame XP supports the Secure Gateway and facilitates the relevant configuration via the page for server-side firewall settings in the administration tool.

As a prerequisite to use the Secure Gateway in combination with Web Interface for MetaFrame XP, a Secure Ticket Authority must be installed in advance and a valid server certificate provided. The Secure Ticket Authority provides the Secure Gateway with the information that a user has already been authenticated and has permission to access the server farm. From a technical standpoint, the Secure Ticket Authority is based on an Internet Server Application Program Interface (ISAPI) DLL that can be used on a server with Internet Information Services, version 5.0 or later. From its location, the DLL issues session tickets and verifies them when a page is accessed again with an existing ticket.

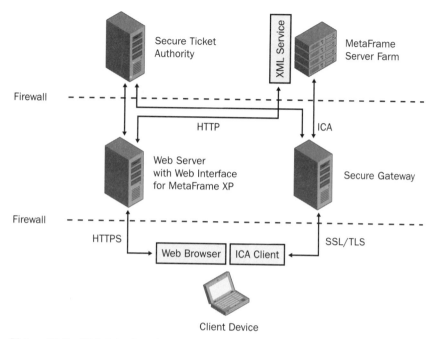

Figure 13-7   Web Interface for MetaFrame XP in combination with the Secure Gateway.

Citrix MetaFrame Secure Access Manager

Citrix MetaFrame Secure Access Manager is, historically speaking, the successor to Citrix NFuse Elite that had Secure Gateway as an additional extension component. Contrary to NFuse Classic, Citrix NFuse Elite could not only map the Program Neighborhood to the Web, but could also present external content that had been linked in. One of the major components of Citrix MetaFrame Secure Access Manager runs on the basis of Windows Server 2003 Internet Information Services. In combination with other components, Citrix MetaFrame Secure Access Manager establishes an environment with scalable access to centralized applications and information. So far its functions outstrip those of Citrix's Web Interface for MetaFrame XP.

The Citrix MetaFrame Secure Access Manager is based on the ISAPI extensions of Internet Information Services. The Internet Server API (ISAPI) is an application programming interface (API) on a server platform for initiating software services optimized for the Microsoft Windows operating system. ISAPI is an API for developing extensions for Internet Information Services (IIS) and other HTTP services supporting ISAPI.

Architecture

Citrix MetaFrame Secure Access Manager combines applications and information from all types of different server systems in a common interface. The applications might, of course, also originate in a MetaFrame server farm, but Secure Access Manager does not rely on such applications exclusively. Using Citrix MetaFrame Secure Access Manager, Web applications or static Web content can be made available through a secure connection. Due to its architecture, Secure Access Manager is suitable for small, mid-sized, and large companies. If required, the individual components can be installed on dedicated computers, thus increasing scalability. Some components allow for multiple installation to facilitate load balancing.

The architecture of Secure Access Manager is no simple matter because it includes a large number of components:

- A *state server* manages all access centers, which can be considered the highest administrative units. The state server thus manages all user profiles, session information, and access center configurations. The state server is a flat file system located in the %InstallDir%\CONFIG\STATE SERVER folder. Each Secure Access Manager server farm has only one state server. High availability levels for several state servers can be achieved using Microsoft's cluster services.

- The *repository* is the database for the Secure Access Manager and is based either on Microsoft SQL Server or Microsoft SQL Server 2000 Desktop Engine (MSDE). This database is used to store the basic data and a copy of the access center configurations as they exist on the state server. The database does not contain any user-specific information. Here, too, availability can be significantly improved by using a cluster solution.

- A *content delivery service* (CDS) manages and generates all access center information, including pages, users, roles, color schemes, and content delivery agents (CDA). The content delivery agents incorporate certain functions that are linked to other functions within the Secure Access Manager to a limited extent or not at all. The CDS receives incoming messages from the user's Web browser and identifies which pages are being requested by whom. It also checks the user's authentication. Finally, the page is created and transmitted to the Web browser for display.

- An *agent server* is where the content delivery agents (CDAs), DLLs, and the content delivery service (CDS) are installed. A Secure Access Manager server farm can consist of several load-balanced agent servers. However, there is only one CDS per agent server.

- The *Web server* houses the access center and is therefore the point of access to all information and applications. Each access center is created in the form of a virtual folder. After a new access center has been created and the system has been configured, the access center can be accessed through http://<Webserver> /<AccessCenterName>. The Access Manager ISAPI filter is also installed on the Web server. The filter converts the incoming HTTP requests into an XML data stream and removes the XML from the outgoing HTML reply documents. When such a request is made, the ISAPI filter invokes the load-balancing mechanism, which is a second added component on the Web server. The load-balancing mechanism communicates with the agent servers and identifies a server that can take the request. The most suitable agent server is identified based on its processor capacity.

- With the help of the *index server*, users can search documents and Web sites in the intranet and on the Internet. The index server indexes the content and delivers the search results in the form of links to the documents identified. The server assumes the existing security settings, allowing users to see only those documents for which they have read and write access.

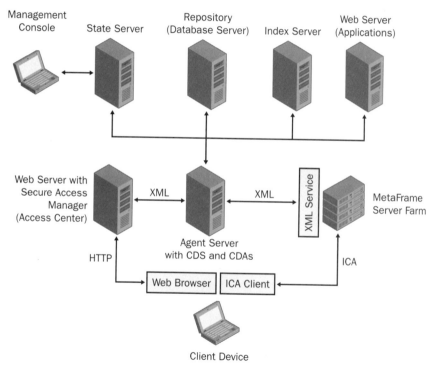

Figure 13-8 The architecture of an environment with Secure Access Manager. In addition to the potential of linking up MetaFrame servers, further application servers can also be integrated.

Following is an overview of the communication processes that take place in an environment with a Secure Access Manager when accessed by a user:

1. The Web browser on the client platform requests, via HTTP, a Web page from the Web server.

2. The Web server contacts the agent server and requests the page content. If the environment contains more than one agent server, an internal algorithm in the Web server ensures proper load balancing and selects the appropriate agent server.

3. The agent server contacts the state server and requests the configuration information.

4. The agent server generates the page with the required CDAs and sends it to the Web server in XML format.

5. The Web server converts the XML data stream into an HTML document, which is transmitted, via HTTP, to the Web browser on the client platform. The Web browser processes the incoming data stream and makes the resulting page available to the user.

Installation

The installation of Citrix MetaFrame Secure Access Manager on Windows Server 2003 requires that certain conditions be met.

- The target platforms should have at least 512 megabytes (MB) main memory.

- Internet Information Services must be installed using the Windows Server 2003 server configuration wizard, allowing the ASP.NET Web service extension.

- .NET Framework 1.0 with Service Pack 2 and Microsoft Data Access Components (MDAC), version 2.7 Refresh, must be installed.

- Under the Identity tab in the Application Pool's Properties dialog box, the service account that is to be used with the Secure Access Manager server farm must be determined. The service account must be in the domain administrator group if the Secure Access Manager is to be installed on more than one server.

> **Important** All of the preceding prerequisites must be in place before Citrix Secure Access Manager can be installed. All required components can be found on the installation CD containing Citrix Secure Access Manager.

The installation routine is wizard-based and follows the usual procedure. There are only two instances where it is possible to select options that have a major impact on the role of the future server. In the first instance, you are asked to choose whether to install the administration components for Secure Access Manager only, or to install the server components, too. In the second instance, you are given the possibility to join an existing farm or to create a new farm. All other options concern the target folder or service account only.

After the installation, certain settings need to be established before Secure Access Manager can be used on a target platform.

- The Host.dll component must be added to the Web services extensions in the Internet Information Services and be allowed. The Host.dll file is located in the \Bin folder in Secure Access Manager's installation directory.

- The ASP.NET v1.0.3705 Web services extension must also be added and enabled manually. The path %SystemDrive%\windows\microsoft.net\framework\v1.0.3705\aspnet_isapi.dll must be entered to provide access to the required files.

- If an access center has been created, the Default Application Pool must be linked to its assigned virtual directory.

All components of Citrix MetaFrame Secure Access Manager can be installed on a single server. However, distributing several instances of Secure Access Manager across separate servers is clearly the preferred option. This solution is scalable and more able to adapt to different requirements relating to user extension or processor load. The minimum configuration requires one Web server, two agent servers, one state server, and one database server. When selecting components during the installation process, it is possible to choose which components will be activated. However, the Web server and agent server components are always installed.

> **Note**   In addition to the index server, the Secure Gateway is also available as an optional component on the Secure Access Manager installation CD.

Administration and Display Concepts

Secure Access Manager is managed in the Access Management Console (AMC). The AMC is a Microsoft Management Console snap-in. Each node within the Access Management Console represents an administrative area. Menus can be displayed or the wizards launched by clicking on the AMC with the right mouse button. This makes the administration of the Secure Access Manager quite easy.

The name of the Secure Access Manager server farm is the same as the name of the state server. The state server is therefore always the primary server in a server farm. On the basis of the server farm name, it is now possible to add or import a new access center. The access center properties facilitate the administration of agent servers, Web servers, and index servers within the server farm.

The main menu entries within an access center are folders. They determine what information is found where and to whom this information will be made available. Web pages that the user may see are allocated to a folder. The CDAs that incorporate the information or application logic in a graphical area are positioned on a Web page. It is also possible to launch several instances of a single CDA on one page. This way, the user can see all the main information at a glance.

Figure 13-9 A Citrix Secure Access Manager page. Each window corresponds to a content delivery agent (CDA).

The role of the user, too, has a major influence on the personalized presentation of the information and application icons. A role defines a group of users by their function within a company or by the applications, data, and other resources they use. Roles are used to determine the following display features for users:

- The default color scheme
- The CDAs that a user can add to the current page
- The pages a member of a role group can see

Note   With its Developer Network (*http://www.citrix.com/cdn*), Citrix offers two development environments (software development kits, or SDKs) for generating CDAs. One of the SDKs is suitable for developing scripting CDAs that work on the basis of Microsoft Visual Basic script logic. The other SDK facilitates CDA development with the .NET Framework under Microsoft Visual Studio .NET (Web Forms). However, using these SDKs requires extensive knowledge of programming Web applications.

Integration of MetaFrame XP Presentation Server

Generally speaking, Secure Access Manager does not need a MetaFrame XP Presentation Server to work, nor is the latter required for the installation to be successful. However, to provide users with more than just information from different data sources, the Secure Access Manager offers the opportunity to access the published applications of a MetaFrame server farm through a corresponding Program Neighborhood CDA. The appearance of the application links is the same as that of Web Interface for MetaFrame XP. No modifications on the MetaFrame servers are required in this respect. Rather, Secure Access Manager is based on the corresponding existing infrastructure of MetaFrame servers.

Note   Just as with Web Interface for MetaFrame XP, it is also possible to use Secure Gateway for Secure Access Manager to make the communication between the various communication transmission points secure. The main difference is that, with Secure Access Manager, the Web server is usually located in the secure company network and not in the demilitarized zone between the firewalls. Architectures with several demilitarized zones are also possible, but these clearly go beyond the focus of this book.

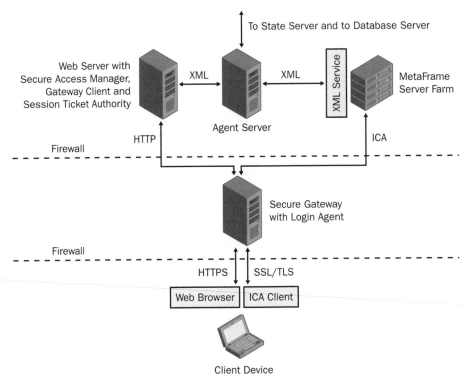

Figure 13-10 Integrating Secure Gateway in Secure Access Manager.

When a user starts an application from the Program Neighborhood CDA, the procedure is as follows:

1. The user logs on to the access center. In line with his or her relevant role, the user has permission to use the Program Neighborhood CDA.

2. When the Program Neighborhood CDA is loading, it asks the MetaFrame server farm to transmit the list of applications the user will have access to.

3. The user starts an application by selecting the appropriate icon. Using the XML service of a MetaFrame server and the load-balancing mechanism, the Program Neighborhood CDA determines which MetaFrame server to use for executing the application.

4. The Program Neighborhood CDA contacts the session ticket authority and receives a ticket for the internal server address.

5. The ticket is positioned in the ICA file for the application start. Next, the server address is replaced by the address of the Secure Gateway in the ICA file.

6. The ICA file is transmitted to the client.

7. The ICA client opens an SSL connection to the Secure Gateway. Inside the SSL tunnel, there is a normal ICA connection.

8. The Secure Gateway contacts the session ticket authority and validates the ticket transmitted by the client via SSL. If the ticket is valid, the Secure Gateway receives the IP address of the relevant MetaFrame server.

9. The Secure Gateway passes on the ICA connection to the relevant MetaFrame server. The ICA session is now established.

The Program Neighborhood CDA thereby allows published applications to be integrated into the Citrix MetaFrame Secure Access Manager relatively easily. However, it is clear that the Secure Access Manager is not focused on the integration of MetaFrame servers alone, but rather on providing a general portal environment.

> **Note**   The Secure Gateway that comes with the Citrix MetaFrame Secure Access Manager has greater functionality than the Secure Gateway of the Citrix MetaFrame XP Presentation Server. The additional functions pertain in particular to tunneling HTTP data streams.

New Moon Canaveral iQ

Canaveral iQ by New Moon (*http://www.newmoon.com*) offers an environment for distributing and managing central Windows applications. This is done by extending the RDP protocol and providing a portal environment for application access and central system configuration. Canaveral iQ therefore competes against Citrix products, even though the two producers' technical approaches differ considerably.

> **Note**   New Moon was taken over by Tarantella (*http://www.tarantella.com*) in May 2003. Tarantella was created in 2001 in the wake of the spinoff of Santa Cruz Operation (SCO), a company that is particularly well known in the UNIX world. Tarantella Enterprise is a middleware product that translates different standard protocols into the proprietary Adaptive Internet Protocol (AIP). Through a Unix server running Tarantella Enterprise, computer platforms with an appropriate AIP client software can use the applications of terminal servers (via RDP), Web servers (via HTTP), UNIX servers (via Telnet and SSH), mainframe computers (via 3270), and AS/400 hosts (via 5250). With regard to a terminal server, Tarantella Enterprise acts like a client with several RDP connection instances. However, the output is not displayed, but converted into an AIP data stream. User interaction goes from the AIP client via the Tarantella server to the terminal server. The acquisition of New Moon has made it possible for Tarantella to offer a complete solution for managing centralized terminal server applications in a pure Windows environment, too.

Architecture

New Moon Canaveral iQ comprises two groups of components, with one responsible for the server side and the other responsible for the client side. We will look at the server side first. Servers can be grouped into what New Moon calls *teams*. Within a team, the individual servers can take on one or more roles:

- **Web servers** The aim of this server role is to provide a Web-based user interface for the end users and administrators of Canaveral iQ. In addition, DCOM components for linking and managing applications, domains, licenses, and database access are established on a server with this role. A Web server in Canaveral iQ is roughly comparable with the Citrix Web Interface for MetaFrame XP combined with the Management Console for MetaFrame XP.

- **Load balancers** These components handle the sharing of the available resources when a client accesses the terminal servers. This role can be assumed by several servers to raise scalability and failure safety. A comparable component is also installed on the Citrix MetaFrame XP Presentation Server.

- **Relay servers** The Canaveral iQ Single Port Relay bundles and secures RDP connections via SSL port 443. This prevents other ports on the firewall from having to be opened in cases where RDP communication with Canaveral clients beyond the intranet needs to be enabled. The SSL connection requires certificates, which might originate from New Moon, another certificate service, or an official certifying authority. Establishing this role is not absolutely necessary to operate a Canaveral environment. The role can, however, be assumed by several servers in parallel to account for load or redundancy considerations. In this case, some of the functions are similar to those of the Citrix Secure Gateway.

- **Application servers** The components that belong to this role allow Canaveral iQ to control terminal servers and the applications installed upon them. To fulfill this task, the New Moon solution does not modify the terminal servers as much as Citrix does with its MetaFrame XP Presentation Server; however, it also does not achieve quite the same performance level.

The Canaveral administration console on the Web server allows an administrator with the requisite permissions to control the application servers. This also involves identifying the installed applications and providing them, when required, as published applications to defined user groups. It is also possible, of course, to share entire desktops in this way. How, though, can users access these desktops and applications? First of all, the relevant icons are placed on an application access portal that has the capacity to be personalized. A normal RDP client, however, does not understand these links. For this reason, New Moon supplies Canaveral iQ with a special RDP client with extended functionality.

The name of this extended client is *Canaveral Connection Center*. It incorporates the RDP client components with standard functions and adds a kind of shell containing additional features. These include the potential to display published applications in seamless windows on the client desktop. Furthermore, the Canaveral Connection Center is able to place the application icons on the desktop and in the Start menu of the client platform. Additional functions include assigning document types on the client to remote applications on terminal servers by means of their file type and providing a universal print driver based on exchanging print data in EMF format (Enhanced Meta File). New Moon uses the virtual channels of the RDP protocol for all of these extended functions.

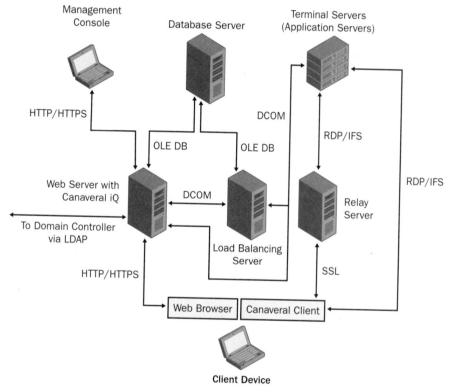

Figure 13-11   The architecture of a Canaveral environment where all roles are assumed by dedicated servers. The combination of several server roles on one platform simplifies the architecture considerably.

Communication between the different servers and the clients in a Canaveral environment takes place via a number of ports. These are listed in Table 13-1.

Table 13-1   The Communication Channels in a Canaveral Environment

Description of the Communication Channels	TCP/IP Port(s)
Transmission of Web pages, downloading software via the HTTP protocol, and queries to the load-balancing servers.	80 (TCP)
Communication with the Microsoft SQL Server.	139, 443, 1433
Access to a domain controller's information via the Microsoft Active Directory Service Interface (ADSI) or the lightweight directory access protocol (LDAP).	389 (TCP)
SSL and HTTPS communication via the Web server and the relay server.	443 (TCP)
Connections via the RDP protocol. The Iqtsachost.exe and Mstscax.dll client components communicate with the terminal servers via RDP. The relay server can pack this protocol into an SSL tunnel.	3389 (TCP)
The Canaveral IFS protocol for integrating client hard drives and printers. In particular, the Iqclntmgr.exe program uses IFS to communicate with the terminal servers. The relay server can pack this protocol into an SSL tunnel.	4660 (TCP)
Communication via DCOM. No predetermined port is used here, which is why this type of communication cannot take place beyond the boundaries of a firewall. All servers that communicate with each other via DCOM must therefore be located in a common security zone.	many

Note   With Canaveral iQ, the connection properties of RDP sessions are not saved in RDP files. Instead, both the general RDP parameters and the specific Canaveral features of a user session are stored in the database, making them available centrally.

Installation

A Canaveral iQ environment usually consists of a server team and a group of client platforms that are linked through a network. When the Canaveral software is installed on the first team server, some of the fundamental features of the environment are determined using the installation wizard. This includes, in particular, the configuration of the database and the name of the team. The first server always has the role of Web server and load balancer at least. It can therefore be used as the administrative instance for the server team.

When the first server is established, an administrator can install the Canaveral software on further servers or distribute it there using the administration console. When a new server is installed, only the basic Canaveral base component is set up if the server is being added to an existing team. However, the role of the new server has not yet been determined. An administrator still needs to assign the role using the administration console.

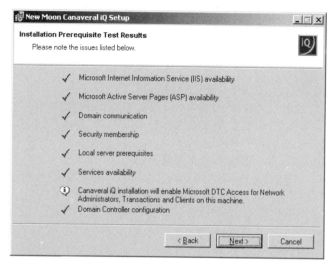

Figure 13-12   New Moon Canaveral iQ installation wizard dialog box, checking whether all of the installation prerequisites have been met on the target platform.

The following conditions must be in place for the successful installation of Canaveral iQ on Windows Server 2003 and for the assignment of servers to roles:

- The target platform should be located in an existing domain based on Microsoft Windows NT 4.0 or Microsoft Active Directory. Another option is installing Canaveral iQ on an independent server, but in this case, all components would necessarily be on a single server, which does not provide any opportunity for extension or load balancing.

- Internet Information Services must be installed on the platforms for the Web server role with Active Server Pages enabled.

- As a database system, either Microsoft SQL Server 2000, Microsoft SQL Server 7, or Microsoft SQL Server Desktop Engine (MSDE) is required. MDAC 2.6 or MDAC 2.7 must be installed on all Canaveral servers to ensure access to the database.

- To set up the Canaveral software on platforms that will take on the role of application server, Windows Server 2003 Terminal Services will naturally be required.

The Web server role is, of course, of great importance for Canaveral iQ. The Web server is responsible for supplying the application access portal pages (http://<Webserver>/LaunchPad) and the administration environment (http://<Webserver>/Console). Moreover, it also provides a depot containing all the files required for the installation of Canaveral functions on other client or server platforms. These files are accessed from the application access portal and the administration environment.

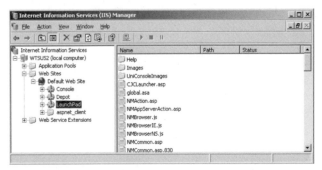

Figure 13-13   Structure of the New Moon Canaveral iQ Web site in the Internet Information Services Manager.

Administration

Canaveral iQ's administration console facilitates the configuration of all major parameters via the start page http://<Webserver>/Console. The following tabs are available for grouping and subgrouping administration functions:

- **Home**   Provides an overview of the configuration and product licenses, provides the logon screen and options for downloading components, and displays administrative messages.

- **Manage**   Options for managing applications, servers, groups, organizational units, users, domains, client groups, connection settings, and administrator roles. Most of the activities that administrators perform in an environment with Canaveral iQ can be handled centrally on the Manage tab.

- **Monitor**   Monitors all session parameters relevant for operating Canaveral iQ. These include the current values for connections, load balancing, the database server, and other system components. In this view, the administrator console regularly requests updated information from the components that it is monitoring.

- **Reports**   Compiling reports on sessions, applications, users, clients, servers, and product licenses. This enables the subsequent analysis of all activities on the system.

- **Options**   Options for changing the default settings for the user interface, load balancing, backing up the database, connection security, and general system properties. This is where the administrator decides how the system should act and look in a target environment.

The most important tasks executed with the help of the administration console following installation consist mostly of published applications, defining default values for user sessions, and grouping users in an appropriate way. During the operation of a server environment with Canaveral iQ, frequent activities include the setting of thresholds and time limits that use certain criteria to determine when sessions should no longer be permitted or should be ended. Managing active sessions and logged-on users, as well as controlling the load balancing, are other frequent tasks.

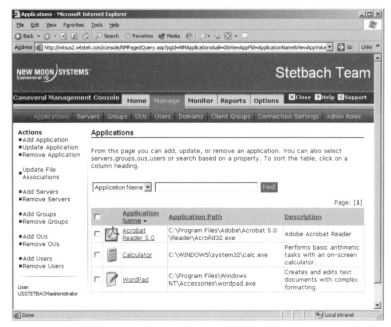

Figure 13-14   The New Moon Canaveral iQ Management Console in the process of configuring published applications.

These activities differ only slightly from those carried out for Terminal Services configuration and Terminal Services administration in a conventional terminal server environment. The tasks for managing the specific functions relating to published applications, for instance, are quite similar. It is therefore not surprising that a number of the relevant administration options can also be found in the Citrix Management Console for MetaFrame XP with only slight modifications.

User Access and Client Environment

The Canaveral client software has two different tasks to fulfill to meet the requirements for supporting seamless published applications via the RDP protocol. First, the available application resources of the integrated terminal servers must be positioned on the client desktop or in the client Start menu to offer alternative access possibilities in addition to the Web pages of the application access portal. This also involves linking locally managed document types with the remote published applications on the terminal servers. Diverting client resources to the Terminal Services session of the user who is logged on also comprises one of the tasks of this Canaveral client component. New Moon calls this component the *Canaveral Connection Manager* (Iqclntmgr.exe). The Canaveral Connection Manager receives all necessary information through a link to the Canaveral database whose data sets are determined by an administrator using the administration console described earlier. A small icon to the right of the task bar on the client desktop indicates that the Canaveral Connection Manager has been launched and allows access to its current settings via the context menu.

The actual Canaveral client with the extended RDP functions is a signed ActiveX control (Iqtsachost.exe), which in turn incorporates the Microsoft ActiveX control with the normal RDP client (Mstscax.dll). The Canaveral client is opened either from the application access portal with the start page http://<Webserver> /LaunchPad or from the Canaveral Connection Manager. If the Canaveral client is not yet available on the client platform when the initial access is made, it can be downloaded and installed via the Web server. The complete installation package for the client environment is about 5 MB in size.

So how does the personalized Web environment for accessing the application icons that New Moon calls *Canaveral Application Launch Pad* appear to a user who has successfully logged on? The user sees a relatively simply structured Web site with the icons of the available applications and some links to additional Web sites. Depending on the configuration by the administration console, these links are either enabled (visible) or disabled (not visible):

- **Favorites** Page with the application icons that the user needs most frequently. The link to this page can be enabled or disabled under the user options located in the Management Console.

- **Applications** Page with a list of all application icons available to the user currently logged on.

- **Connections** Displays the current user's active and terminated connections. The link to this page can be enabled or disabled under the user options located in the Management Console.

- **Options** Options for individually modifying the parameters that determine how the application icons are displayed, what the link settings are, and which application icons are located in the Favorites window, on the desktop, or in the Start menu. The user's access to the individual options can be enabled or disabled in the Management Console.

- **Download Client** Page with a link to the installation package of the Canaveral client environment on the Web server.

- **About** Information about the product and the manufacturer, New Moon.

When the first application is launched with default settings from the Canaveral Application Launch Pad, a window opens up that shows the connection as well as the logon procedure on the terminal server selected by the load-balancing mechanism. The RDP session is displayed in full-screen resolution of the client platform. When the logon procedure is completed, the RDP session is no longer displayed on the client desktop and the launched application appears in a seamless window. Simultaneously, an icon for this application is created in the task bar on the client desktop, and the Canaveral Connection Manager is informed of the current status of the session. At this point, it is not as easy to distinguish between the published application of the RDP session and a local application.

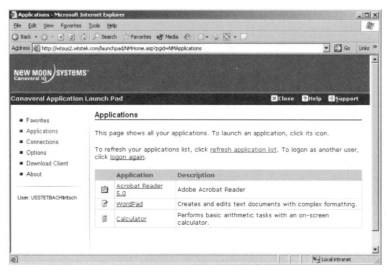

Figure 13-15   User view of the New Moon Canaveral iQ application access portal. The view shows the window with the list of all applications that have been published for the current user.

If you look at the RDP connection in the Terminal Services Manager, you will notice that, regardless of the number of published applications that have been launched, only one session is visible per user. The corresponding information shows that the initial RDP window determines the parameters. The now "invisible" session in the background serves to manage the individual applications, thereby replacing the corresponding desktop functions of the Windows Manager on the terminal server.

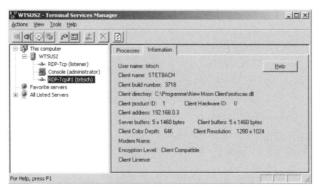

Figure 13-16   Displaying the connection to an RDP client in Canaveral iQ.

Microsoft SharePoint Portal Server and Other Alternatives

The products for the application access portal environment that have been described so far in this chapter represent the most common solutions available on the market for the Web-based and personalized provision of application icons. However, when compared with the desired features of an ideal portal from the very top, it becomes clear that these common solutions do not meet all of the requirements. This is why there are also alternative solutions, although it must be said that the specific conditions these require put them in a niche market for terminal server projects.

One particularly prominent example is the Microsoft SharePoint Portal Server. This product was initially developed and marketed as a means of managing documents and information in a corporate environment. It is not difficult to imagine that the links to terminal server applications—as well as the links to Web applications—could be integrated into the pages of a SharePoint Portal Server. This would be an easy way of expanding the functionality of the SharePoint Portal Server, especially in terms of providing programs for viewing various document types.

However, the lack of possibilities for managing published applications and seamless windows with an unmodified RDP client had soon pushed such approaches to the limits of their capabilities. At several conferences recently, Microsoft has declared that it will realize this functionality by the time it releases the next version of Windows XP (codename *Longhorn*) and will also allow the integration of such functionality in the new version of the SharePoint Portal Server.

Producer and system integrator, visionapp (*http://www.visionapp.com*), takes another approach, which emerged as a result of a terminal server project for a major European bank. To meet the requirements of this internationally operating key account with more than 10,000 workstations, the system had to satisfy the highest standards of security, be able to switch between languages while the system is running, and integrate the corporate design of several organizational units in a single environment. The solution visionapp came up with was based on Citrix MetaFrame XP on the application servers and the Java component of Citrix NFuse Classic (now Citrix's Web Interface for MetaFrame XP) on load-balancing Web servers. Through the application servers, the Java component supplied all information to an application access portal that had been completely developed using ASP.NET. An abstraction model maps the published applications to the relevant organizational units and user groups.

The system integration business was also the origin of the software named Panther (*http://www.pantherpowered.com*), whose functions make it more of an alternative to Citrix's products. Similar to New Moon's Canaveral iQ, Panther's administration tools for terminal servers, proprietary solutions for load balancing, and the support of seamless windows in RDP sessions play a dominant role.

As these few examples show, the possibilities for terminal servers are not nearly exhausted. The integration of remote applications into a personalized Web environment opens up a completely new perspective, hinting at the development of further high-performance solutions in the future.

Chapter 14

Optimization and Troubleshooting

Optimizing the runtime environment and analyzing errors and flawed conditions are key tasks when operating a platform as complex as Microsoft Windows Server 2003 with Terminal Services in application server mode. Little hints often suffice to identify a weakness and eliminate it quickly and efficiently. Of course, strategies that help to avoid certain errors from the start are even better. This chapter describes common problem areas and relevant troubleshooting methods:

- Find out what changes are necessary to optimize the operating system.

- Learn about solutions to problems with applications.

- Discover possibilities for network optimization.

Terminal servers are, of course, under particular scrutiny when they are used as central instances to provide applications. Like unstable domain controllers or inadequate resolution of network names, terminal servers that function unreliably lead to highly dissatisfied users and unwarranted costs. The stability of a terminal server environment depends very much on the skill and competence of the administrators in charge.

A terminal server resembles a classic mainframe environment in many respects. Administrators, who often come from the traditional PC environment, need to take special care to avoid some acquired habits—in particular, to stop executing routine tasks under a privileged account on the console of a production server in a terminal server environment. When an administrator interacts with the terminal server, even the smallest mistakes can negatively affect many other user sessions.

To avoid and overcome crises involving terminal servers, administrators need to consider not only the technical, but also the social, element. A set of rules applies and each person involved with this type of environment should adhere to these rules.

- No one except explicitly authorized persons must perform changes on the terminal server including hardware, operating system, and applications.

- New system software and applications should be installed using automated routines that have previously been tested on a reference system.

- Each action relating to hardware and software changes must be 100 percent documented with the relevant tools.

Discipline is a must for the persons in charge because a terminal server merges two worlds that used to be strictly separate: Microsoft BackOffice (that is, Windows Server 2003) and front-end applications (that is, direct user interaction). In conventional environments, no administrator would dare to even imagine that users could log on to a server interactively. Who knows what ways they would find to change the system! Another reason for maintaining strict discipline is that, among administrators, experience with terminal servers is not as broad as with standard installations of Microsoft Windows systems.

Note   When this book was written, there was very little experience in operating Windows Server 2003 Terminal Services in large production environments. Still, this chapter includes a list of optimization recommendations for commonly known issues and might be useful for troubleshooting terminal servers in well-managed environments. For additional information check the Microsoft Knowledge Base and the other Web resources introduced in the "About This Book" section, regularly.

Operating System

For a terminal server, an optimized operating system means improved performance and no crashes. This is why the methods described in the following section are recommended for optimizing performance or troubleshooting.

Frequent System Starts

If applications with well-known memory leaks are used on a terminal server, it might become necessary to reboot the system frequently. This would clean the memory and lead to improved stability.

The **Tsshutdn** command is suitable for rebooting and includes a number of parameters. The most important ones are */reboot* for rebooting the server (that is, not only shutting it down) and the waiting time in seconds. When that time has passed, all user sessions will be disconnected. Out of basic courtesy, users should be informed of the imminent reboot. The **Tsshutdn** command does this automatically, using the following syntax:

```
TsShutdn 120 /reboot
```

With the help of the **At** command, it is possible to configure the system for frequent reboots. The Task Scheduler service must be started because it handles the time-controlled execution of commands. In the following example, the server is restarted every Sunday at 11:00 P.M.

```
At 23:00 /every:Su "TsShutdn 120 /reboot"
```

User Logon

If users fail to log on to a terminal server, this can be for many reasons. It is important to know that under Windows Server 2003 there is a clear distinction between local logon and logon via Terminal Services, and that Windows Server 2003 does not behave like Windows 2000 in this respect.

If a user fails to log on to a terminal server, it makes sense to check the following settings:

- **User group**   Verify whether the user or user group is part of the local Remote Desktop Users group, which is a standard requirement for using Terminal Services. It is possible to add the user to another group that is defined in the Policy for the local computer or in Group Policy under Computer Configuration\Windows Settings\Security Settings\Local Policies\User Rights Assignment\Allow log on through Terminal Services. Alternatively, it is possible to add groups including the user concerned.

- **User properties in Computer Management or in Active Directory**   Activate the Allow logon to terminal server setting on the Terminal Services Profile tab.

- **Guest or user access**   Using Terminal Services Configuration, a user or group can be granted guest or user access if the corresponding settings have been changed in the Permissions tab of the Connection properties.

Overwriting User Settings

The Windows Server 2003 registry allows a system-wide configuration for overwriting unwanted user settings. In particular, these settings involve certain graphical output generated in user sessions. The relevant keys are located in the registry under HKLM\SYSTEM\CurrentControlSet\Control\Terminal Server\WinStations \<*Connectionname*>\UserOverride\Control Panel\Desktop, where <*Connectionname*> is the name of the connection (that is, RDP-Tcp or ICA-Tcp).

Table 14-1   Registry Entries for Optimizing Graphical Output in User Sessions

Value Name	Data Type, Default Value	Description
CursorBlinkRate	SZ: -1	The cursor does not blink permanently and thus does not create data traffic between terminal server and client.
DragFullWindows	SZ: 1	Only the window's outline is visible when dragging it.
MenuShowDelay	SZ: 10	Time before a menu opens after moving the mouse over it.
WaitToKillAppTimeout	SZ: 20000	Time in milliseconds that the system waits for a response after an application was ended by the Task Manager using the End Task button.
SmoothScroll	DWORD: 0x0	Moving window elements without delay using the scroll bars.
Wallpaper	SZ: (none)	Users cannot use background images on their desktops.
WindowMetrics\MinAnimate	SZ: 1	Minimizing windows without animation.

Connection and Logon Limits

As with Windows 2000 Server Terminal Services, it is possible to prevent clients from establishing user sessions to Windows Server 2003 when specific conditions are met. These conditions are not based on available licenses, but on preset maximum connection configuration values. These values were originally set to prevent a denial-of-service attack on the server. During such an attack, an enormous amount of data packages provokes overload. However, on a terminal server, these limits are often reached, under normal conditions, and can thus lead to unwanted results. This is usually caused by programs that send a large amount of connection requests per user session to a server (for example, Lotus Notes).

The behavior described in the preceding paragraph can be changed through two values in the registry, *MaxWorkItems* and *MaxMpxCt*. In an unmodified installation of Windows Server 2003, these values do not yet exist in the registry and therefore need to be created. Nevertheless, their standard behavior has already been predefined in the system. The keys to both values are located in the registry under HKLM\System\CurrentControlSet\Services\LanmanServer\Parameters. For a terminal server environment, the value for *MaxWorkItems* should be set to DWORD: 8192, and the value for *MaxMpxCt* to DWORD: 500. *MaxWorkItems* determines the number of input buffers that a server can provide simultaneously. *MaxMpxCt* sets the maximum number of client requests that a server can process. You can find more detailed information on this topic in article 232476 in the Microsoft Knowledge Database at *http://support.microsoft.com*.

Printing

Printing documents from Terminal Services sessions is a frequent source of problems and errors because of the different print options and rather complex paths for creating print data streams, as described in Chapter 4 and Chapter 10. For this reason, the following section deals with solutions that will enable the user to avoid some of these system-based problems before they have a chance to occur.

Local Client Printers

A frequent scenario in large terminal server environments is that of users wanting to connect a new printer to their Terminal Services client and, of course, wanting to use it to print from their user sessions. To automate this process, the terminal server needs a driver that corresponds to the printer driver on the client. So how can the administrator ensure that only the wanted printer drivers are on the terminal server, and no other drivers that might have been imported without the administrator's knowledge? The solution is installing all permitted printer drivers manually via Start\Printers and Faxes. If the relevant files are in line with the Windows 2000 or Windows Server 2003 specifications, they are saved in the %Systemroot%\system32\spool\drivers\w32x86\3 folder. Furthermore, all relevant configuration data is generated in the registry under HKLM\System\CurrentControlSet \Control\Print and HKLM\SYSTEM\CurrentControlSet\Control\Print\Environments \Windows NT x86\Drivers\Version-3*<Printer Name>*. (See Chapter 6.) If the reference to the printers under Printers and Faxes is deleted later, the driver files and the relevant data remain intact on the system. This becomes obvious when you attempt to install the same printer driver during a new installation because the system asks if you want to keep the existing driver.

If the client is part of a corporate network and has access to a print server, users may configure their client environment in a way that they can work with network printers via the print server. The necessary drivers are installed either manually or automatically. It is basically impossible for user sessions running on a terminal server or Citrix MetaFrame XP Presentation Server to differentiate between these network printer drivers and a local client printer driver.

If a client with locally configured drivers connects to a terminal server and if the system was configured accordingly, both print subsystems will try to link up automatically. If this works out because the printer drivers already exist in the system, only the administrator group and this particular user will have access to the resulting printer resource. If, however, the character strings between client printer and all printer drivers installed in %Systemroot%\system32\spool\drivers\w32x86 \3 on the terminal server or Wtsprnt.inf for MetaFrame servers do not match, the Ntprint.inf file for terminal servers will help to perform a corresponding allocation through an installation at a later time. Ntprint.inf contains a list of all printer drivers that are part of the standard Windows Server 2003 scope of delivery. The printer drivers, including all relevant driver files, can be installed at a later time using the

Driver.cab file located in the %Systemroot%\Driver Cache folder. This later installation will be in system context with maximum access permissions, even if the process was initiated by a user with standard access permissions. In contrast to Ntprint.inf, Wtsprnt.inf contains a list only of printers actually installed that are managed by Citrix MetaFrame XP Presentation Server.

If an original equipment manufacturer (OEM) driver is installed for a new printer model that is not covered by the Driver.cab file, Ntprint.inf also changes. Thus, an OEM printer driver behaves just like an installed default printer driver when it comes to linking Terminal Services sessions. Of course, it is also possible to manually remove the references to printers that are not to be used in a corporate environment from Ntprint.inf. If the list in Ntprint.inf comprises only the preinstalled printer drivers, no new driver will be installed automatically on the terminal server. The driver already exists on the system—even if it was invisible under Printers and Faxes.

Note You might find an instance when the files are on the system and the driver is registered on the system, but the reference is not visible in the standard printer admin tool "Printers and Faxes". This happens if you uninstall a printer driver: the files and some registry keys remain on the system. This is why the system "remembers" that this driver has already been here when you try to reinstall this driver.

If a driver is not properly assigned to a client printer in Ntprint.inf, the client printer will not be available for the user session, and a corresponding message will be generated. For this reason, it is an advantage to have many tested and preinstalled printer drivers on a terminal server with a modified Ntprint.inf file because they will ensure the desired functionality and increase stability.

Tip The OEM driver is a driver that is not included in the standard distribution CD of the operating system. The OEM driver comes with the device on a companion CD.

A MetaFrame server expands the printer management logic slightly. (See Chapter 10.) On the one hand, Citrix MetaFrame XP Presentation Server allows automatic distribution of printer drivers over an entire server farm so that the same printer drivers are installed anywhere on the farm at any time. On the other hand, it is possible to assign all unknown printers to a common, universal printer driver. This method is definitely more favorable than allowing untested OEM drivers on a production terminal server! If the driver installation behavior is controlled by universal printer drivers, the system will be more stable—in the end, it is undetermined as to the damage an untested printer driver that was installed in system context could cause on a terminal server. Only the Group Policy that prevents Microsoft Windows NT 4–compatible drivers from being installed can provide a little additional security in this context.

> **Note** In addition to Citrix, the most popular manufacturers of universal printer drivers are ThinPrint (*http://www.thinprint.com*), Charon Systems with UniPrint (*http://www.uniprint.net*), Tricerat with Screwdrivers (*http://www.tricerat.com*), and Emergent Online with EOL Universal Printer (*http://www.go-eol.com*). These solutions are suitable both for unmodified terminal servers and with Citrix MetaFrame XP Presentation Server.

If several client printers are linked to one user session, error messages might be written to the Event Viewer. This is often caused by removing the relevant printer queues in the wrong sequence. Error messages numbered 1109 are caused by this issue and may be ignored.

Network Printers

Another option for printing from user sessions is a set of network printers that can be accessed directly from terminal servers. However, the printer drivers still have to be assigned both on terminal servers and print servers. Each user can individually configure the print server printers available on the network. The corresponding settings are saved in each user's terminal server profile.

This concept will work fine as long as the printer drivers on terminal servers and print servers are identical. If there are differences between the versions, users will receive a message saying that they will not be able to print on the printer they selected. This is because an automatic update of driver versions for network printers requires write access. However, a normal user has only read and execute permissions in the relevant %Systemroot%\system32\spool\drivers\w32x86\3 folder.

If the user notifies an administrator of the situation, and the administrator subsequently tries to reproduce the error with his or her account, the administrator will not receive the error. This is because the administrator has full access to %Systemroot%\system32\spool\drivers\w32x86\3 and thus may synchronize the drivers automatically—possibly without even knowing it. This will correct the incompatibility and the user will be able to print on the terminal server in question because the needed printer driver is now there. The problem will disappear and the Administrator might not understand how this issue was corrected.

However, if the terminal server in this scenario is part of a farm, this process will result in the individual servers of the farm having different printer configurations. The problems with individual printer configurations will be difficult to predict because user connections will depend on a load-balancing mechanism; and users will be randomly redirected to different servers upon logon. The more administrators help to resolve the problem described earlier, the greater the chaos relating to the installed printer driver versions.

One solution is denying administrators write permission for %System-root%\system32\spool\drivers\w32x86\3. This limitation needs to be lifted for a short time only, when new and tested printer drivers are installed on all servers of a farm. Alternatively, it is recommended that new printer drivers for larger environments be installed through special, automated installation environments and a suitable services account. Instead of the drastic limitation of administrator permissions, it is possible to use the Citrix MetaFrame XP Presentation Server print functions. They easily synchronize printer drivers with those of the print server and automatically distribute them over the entire MetaFrame server farm.

Client Connections

Even if the Restrict each user to one session option was selected in the Terminal Services Configuration server settings, it is still possible that a user could log on to the server more than once. This happens if the user starts a Remote Desktop connection with an initial program and launches another connection without an initial program. The terminal server interprets these two sessions as individual sessions and thus allows this unexpected behavior.

Specific logon scripts may be used to prevent a user from logging on to the terminal server or terminal server farm with several sessions. With these scripts and their relevant commands, a list is created enumerating the users who are logged on, current user names are compared, and the second session is terminated immediately. (See Chapter 7.)

With Citrix MetaFrame XP Presentation Server and its Program Neighborhood settings, it is significantly easier to prevent a user from logging on more than once.

System Optimization

Although the Active Desktop allows interesting graphical effects, it usually consumes too many system resources on terminal servers and should therefore be disabled in the Terminal Services Configuration server settings.

To improve the security of conventional logon scripts through batch processing programs, it is recommended that these scripts be executed invisibly on terminal servers—for example, by setting a corresponding system policy under Computer Configuration\Administrative Templates\System\Scripts. Third-party tools are also available for this purpose; for example, Runh.exe. This program can be found on the Web site *http://www.scripthorizon.com*.

If user profiles are centrally saved, roaming users can be supported. (See Chapter 4.) A terminal server saves local copies of each profile on the local file system while the user is logged on. Normally, changes to settings (such as application or printer configuration settings) are saved in the local copy of the profile first. When the user logs off, all changes to the local profile are synchronized with the profile saved on the server. This makes a lot of sense if there are only a few terminal servers because the possibility that a user will log on to the same terminal server is relatively high. If the locally cached profile is still current, it does not need to be downloaded from the central location, which, of course, saves network bandwidth and ensures quick processing.

However, in large, load-balanced terminal server environments, this behavior is quite counterproductive. In time, profiles will collect on each server because almost all users will have worked on each server. The possibility that one user will log on to the same server twice is fairly low. This means that local hard drive space will be consumed by the user profiles saved on the servers, even though the profiles will still be loaded from the central location. Because terminal servers—just like other computers—do not respond too positively to full hard drives, it is recommended that local profiles be deleted when users log off. The way to do this is by using the DWORD: 0x1 value in the *DeleteRoamingCache* key located in the HKLM\SOFTWARE\Microsoft\Windows NT\CurrentVersion\Winlogon registry path. If needed, this key must be generated manually. However, this setting can also be established through the system policies under Computer Configuration\Administrative Templates\System\User Profiles.

Protection from Viruses

As with all operating systems, a terminal server responds extremely sensitively when it is attacked by viruses, especially script and macro viruses. To protect the terminal server from viruses, it is necessary to take action. An antivirus program suitable for Windows Server 2003 and multiple-user environments will definitely help. This type of program is usually designed as a service and therefore works in the background. If several terminal servers within a Windows environment need to be checked for viruses, it is possible to deploy specific antivirus programs that consist of a server and a client component. The server program initiates the examination by the client program and notifies the administrator if a virus has indeed been found.

Nevertheless, it is often even better to protect the peripherals from viruses instead of the terminal server itself. If e-mail and file servers are properly protected from viruses and if suitable protection mechanisms are deployed on firewalls, routers, and gateways, it is not necessary to use antivirus programs on terminal servers. Tools such as the AppSense Application Manager offer additional protection. (See Chapter 8.)

Applications

Not only the system settings, but also the application environment configuration should be adapted to running on terminal servers. The following section describes some common modifications.

Program Start Errors

A terminal server's permission compatibility is set to Full Security or Relaxed Security via the server settings of Terminal Services configuration. If the low security level is selected, each user who starts a Terminal Services session receives an additional permission that allows extended access to certain areas of the registry database and the file system. In the registry, this involves HKLM\Software, HKLM\Software\Microsoft\Tracing, HKLM\Software\Microsoft\Windows\CurrentVersion\App Paths, HKLM\Software\Microsoft\Windows\CurrentVersion\Explorer\MyComputer\NameSpace, HKLM\Software\Microsoft\Windows\CurrentVersion\SharedDLLs, HKLM\Software\Microsoft\Windows\CurrentVersion\Uninstall, and redirecting accesses from HKLM\Software\Classes. In the file system, extended access to .inf files and the files located in %SystemRoot%\help is granted.

If full security was selected for permission compatibility and an application needs to access the system areas concerned, error messages will occur because of the restricted permissions. This setting might even cause the program start to be aborted. Settings for individual aspects of permission compatibility are located in the registry under HKLM\Software\Microsoft\Windows NT\CurrentVersion\Terminal Server\RegistryExtensionFlags. Nevertheless, it is recommended that the basic permission compatibility be changed to relaxed security only if errors occur when an application is launched, and only by modifying the Terminal Services Configuration server settings.

Dr. Watson

Dr. Watson is the application debugger that automatically starts if errors occur in applications and if these errors cannot be handled by a default procedure. For instance, Dr. Watson is often launched when an application accesses memory improperly. This requires exception handling; and if such an exception occurs, Dr. Watson is launched and saves all relevant data. However, this type of behavior is not desirable on terminal servers, except for targeted error analyses.

For this reason, Dr. Watson should be disabled on production systems by deleting the HKLM\Software\Microsoft\Windows NT\CurrentVersion\AeDebug\Debugger registry key and the drwtsn32 –P %ld –e %ld –g value. By deleting this key, Dr. Watson is disabled. Dr. Watson can also be deactivated by deleting the HKLM\Software\Microsoft\DrWatson key.

Microsoft Office

After Microsoft Office applications are installed on standard clients, they contain a little tool called *SysInfo*. This tool can be started from a menu entry. It displays system information and allows access to other system resources. If Office 2000 or Office XP is installed with the help of the transformation file for terminal servers, SysInfo is disabled by default. This should not be changed, because SysInfo represents a potential danger on terminal servers.

Because the Microsoft Word grammar check gobbles up enormous system resources, it should be disabled on terminal servers. Depending on the different versions of Word, the corresponding setting can be found at different places in the registry. However, searching for the AutoGrammar key will lead you to the right place in HKCU. It is recommended that the value of this key be set to zero either for the default user before creating new profiles, or through a logon script.

Network

The network is a central resource for a terminal server. If the network does not perform properly or fails, many users will no longer be able to work.

Optimizing the Network Connection

The properties of the network adapters can be changed through Start\Control Panel\Network Connections and the properties of the appropriate LAN connection. The configuration of the physical adapter should not include an autodetect of the network speed or automatic negotiation of duplex options. These settings must be preset to avoid errors that can cause a significantly reduced network connection.

If network communication bottlenecks occur, it is recommended that the File and Printer Sharing for Microsoft Networks properties of the network connection be adjusted. Changing the Maximize data throughput for file sharing to Maximize data throughput for network applications often improves the terminal server's performance.

Standard Troubleshooting Tools

In addition to the standard graphics tools, Windows Server 2003 includes a number of troubleshooting programs to handle network problems. The following overview lists the available tools, their purpose, and their areas of use.

- **Arp**   Displays the Address Resolution Protocol (ARP) table on the local computer. *Arp -a* shows the current IP cache resolution cache.
- **Hostname**   Indicates the current computer name.

- **Ipconfig**   Displays and updates the current TCP/IP configuration. *Ipconfig/all* shows all relevant network parameters.

- **Nbtstat**   Reviews the status of NBT connections (NetBIOS over TCP/IP). *Nbtstat -c* displays the local cache, including the IP addresses of the NetBIOS names.

- **Netstat**   Displays log statistics and the status of all current TCP/IP connections. *Netstat -a* shows active TCP/IP connections, *Netstat -r* indicates active routes.

- **Nslookup**   DNS server query to verify data records, aliases, and other services.

- **Ping**   Verifies the TCP/IP configuration and connection to other computers. *Ping -a <Computername>* translates the address into a name.

- **Route**   Output and modification of routing tables. *Route print* displays active routes.

- **Tracert**   Verifies the route to a remote computer.

Skillfully sequencing these commands and output of the results into a file can bring about amazingly powerful analysis tools.

Accelerating RDP and ICA

If remote users are able to type very quickly, screens on Terminal Services clients sometimes tend to hang. This is true for both the RDP and the ICA protocol. To improve terminal server response times, it is possible to change the time that the terminal server waits until it transmits buffered data packages. The shorter this time is, the smaller the data packages are. The time is set via the OutBufDelay registry value. This method increases the frequency with which the data packages are sent. However, this change also gives rise to a slightly increased network load.

The output buffer settings are always related to a protocol as it was created in the Terminal Services Configuration. For RDP, these two registry paths are relevant: HKLM\System\CurrentControlSet\Control\Terminal Server\Wds\Rdpwd\TDS \tcp\OutBufDelay and HKLM\System\CurrentControlSet\Control\Terminal Server \WinStations\rdp-tcp\OutBufDelay. The parameters specify the number of milliseconds that a terminal server buffers data before transmitting it to the client. The default value is 0x64; half of that value should improve overall system response.

The ICA protocol registry entries are saved under HKLM\System \CurrentControlSet\Control\Terminal Server\Wds\Icawd\TDS\tcp\OutBufDelay or HKLM\System\CurrentControlSet\Control\Terminal Server\WinStations\ICA-tcp \OutBufDelay.

Chapter 15

How to Plan Production Environments

A centrally managed Microsoft Windows system with centrally available applications on thin clients for professional users: this was the demand that led to the development of Microsoft Windows Server 2003 Terminal Services. However, there is still much uncertainty regarding how it is best used. Is a terminal server only suited for large companies, or can small and medium-sized enterprises benefit from it, too?

Looking at the degree of complexity in terminal server technology, it is no surprise that global-environment solutions usually are not targeted. Rather than projects with extremely large scope, it is usually preferred to approach Terminal Services in small scopes and detailed analyses. Smaller experimental environments lead to more concrete results. These analyses are usually followed by a project consisting of several phases to establish a terminal server–based environment. In particular, the integration of terminal servers into an existing client/server network environment is a tedious task and needs to be prepared thoroughly.

This chapter leans on the previous technical chapters of this book and will focus on explaining how a production terminal server environment should be planned. Successful project approaches will also be described. The following issues will be covered:

- Analyzing and planning terminal server target environments

- Calculating total costs of a terminal server–based system

- Realizing terminal server projects and finding out how to avoid mistakes

Analyzing the Infrastructure

A suitable terminal server infrastructure contains not only existing technology components, but also accompanying consolidation measures and the integration into an overall architecture. The following section will deal with these issues from a somewhat abstract point of view.

Infrastructure Assessment

Before setting up a terminal server–based environment, the existing infrastructure needs to be analyzed and documented. In addition to comprehensive tests, this analysis is essential for installing a terminal server without running into major problems.

First, infrastructure analysis will provide an integrated view of terminal servers and their clients, within the framework of a business plan. The result will then be adapted to a three-layer model to show the general error tolerance options in a terminal server environment. The layers are structured as follows:

- **Layer 1**   Central domain controllers, file servers, or database servers (backend servers) that need to be configured using different methods to ensure failover protection. This layer handles data storage and provides central network services.

- **Layer 2**   Load-balanced terminal servers. If one server fails, the user can immediately log on to another server. The user's profile and data are not located on the terminal server; instead they are stored on the domain controller and file server. This layer hosts the application execution environment.

- **Layer 3**   Thin clients for user interface. If the network or client hardware fails, the user can reconnect to the session and continue working from another client. This layer visualizes the user interface and connects input devices (mouse, keyboard, and so on).

Redundancy and scalability considerations make this type of environment superior to most other concepts. If the existing application servers are no longer adequate, new servers may be added. Thus, fewer users work on each server, which increases the amount of resources available per user. Smart load-balancing mechanisms also allow different server generations to be mixed.

To integrate this type of environment into a corporate network, the existing infrastructure must be analyzed. The following list contains a number of issues that need to be clarified to prepare the necessary documentation and evaluate the infrastructure. The results should be taken as a precondition for planning the integration of terminal servers into the system.

- **Server**   Manufacturer, BIOS version, motherboard (including processor versions), number of processors supported, main memory, disk capacity, disk access speed and peripherals.

- **Infrastructure**   Computer naming conventions, names of the domains or work groups, backup systems, emergency plans, and procurement details.

- **Local network**   Transport protocols used, server and client bandwidth available, physical LAN aspects such as topology or active components (such as routers or switches), IP addresses assigned to the terminal servers, subnet masks and standard gateways, name resolution (DNS, WINS), address assignment (static or via DHCP), and file server access protocols.

- **Wide area network**   Connecting remote corporate locations, including the available bandwidths, backup data lines, and existing routers or firewalls, as well as filter rules and modem dial-up options.

- **Backend systems**   Domain setup, connection to third-party systems (that is, UNIX, Novell, or others), file servers, supported file systems, database servers, and Internet connection including possible regulations.

- **Printers**   List of printers and print servers needed.

- **User environment**   User names, group assignments, logon scripts, profiles, and Group Policies.

- **Administration and monitoring**   Administration tools used (Microsoft Systems Management Server, Microsoft Operation Manager, CA UniCenter, HP Openview, or others).

- **Applications**   Commercial applications, applications with special hardware requirements, and proprietary applications developed for your company's business requirements.

- **Security**   Public key infrastructure and smart cards.

- **Clients**   3270 terminals, 5250 terminals, VT-100 terminals, Windows-based terminals, network computer, X terminals running under UNIX, PCs running under a 16-bit Windows operating system, PCs running under a 32-bit Windows OS, and browser-based clients.

Referring to this list will help the project manager or the person in charge of the system evaluate the potential terminal server target environment.

Project Integration and Corporate Architecture

Experience shows that the introduction of terminal servers and their related application access portals often follows a specific pattern. These projects usually succeed if simple rules are adhered to, especially rules related to the above-mentioned technical requirements of the potential target environment and other existing framework conditions.

So what is the ideal sequence in which terminal server technologies should be introduced in a company? The following phases have been identified time and again in successful terminal server projects:

1. **Backend server consolidation** Terminal servers usually rely on central services. (See Chapter 3.) Therefore, file, database, and e-mail servers as well as other backend server services should be centralized before terminal servers are set up. For this reason, successful terminal server projects are launched only after a backend consolidation process has been launched and completed.

2. **Terminal server environment setup** Following successful tests, a large terminal server environment is planned and introduced. During this time, administrators and users need to be prepared and trained intensively so that they will be able to work within the environment. In this phase, the terminal server environment is accessed through conventional clients' desktops or thin clients.

3. **Application access portal launch** To further cut conventional clients and their desktop administrative costs, an application access portal is placed on the intranet; this occurs after the terminal servers have successfully been set up. The application access portal centralizes functions such as authentication or personalized administration of application icons.

4. **Concept expansion to external users** As soon as a terminal server environment and application access portal have been launched on the intranet, the concept can be expanded to external users if appropriate security mechanisms are in place. The group of external users can include people who are not part of the company and have limited access to the environment. However, this group can also consist of employees who need to access the environment from outside the company network, possibly from unsecured locations.

In some (very ambitious and very complex) projects, these phases take place simultaneously. For these projects to succeed, it is absolutely essential that the requirements and framework conditions be distinctly planned in advance because the project goal must be accurately defined. The following six points help define the project objective:

- **What?** What data should be generated or managed within the scope of the terminal server project? Are databases, file system documents, or other data sources required? What data model will be used? Is better data or an improved data generation workflow expected to be the result of the terminal server project? Does data need to be saved as it relates to the organizational unit, and is it necessary to include a revision stage?

- **How?** Which corporate processes will be involved in the terminal server project? Which application architecture is affected? Which individual applications need to be integrated in the environment? How are the applications installed in the terminal server environment? Are all applications installed on one farm with identical terminal servers, or will there be an individual terminal server farm for each small group of applications? What are the consequences for the existing security infrastructure? Do agreements on definition and grade of service need to be drawn up?

- **Where?** What is the existing corporate environment, and how does it need to be modified to fit terminal server requirements? To answer this question, it makes sense to use the preceding questions for analyzing infrastructure.

- **Who?** Which individuals and organizational units will be affected by the terminal server environment? Is there a clear-cut organizational chart including roles and skills? Will end users and management be sufficiently involved in the process of introducing terminal servers? Do training concepts for all employees exist?

- **When?** What is the key timing factor for the terminal server launch? How does the time of launch fit into the overall business plan of the company? When does the terminal server environment need to be available for everyday operations? What are the time-related dependencies between business processes and applications on the terminal servers? What are the maximum downtimes for terminal servers before a situation is reached that could endanger business?

- **Why?** What is the reason for introducing a terminal server environment? Is the overall objective cost reduction or the introduction of new technologies, or does technical necessity caused by a problematic vintage system call for a new one? How do these objectives fit with overall business goals? Does the corporate strategy need to be modified as a result of the introduction of terminal servers?

Answering these questions before a terminal server project is kicked off helps avoid misunderstandings regarding goals and procedure. Nevertheless, the answers to these questions contain some high-risk elements that should be addressed.

Calculating Operating Costs

Why should a company trust in a technology such as terminal server technology? What are the problems with conventional PC environments? Before PCs were networked, they were the most cost-efficient computers. Through networking and identification of hidden maintenance and training costs, this point of view has changed drastically. The term *total cost of ownership* (TCO) is used to describe the total cost incurred by a system during its entire life.

In the past, the sheer number of Microsoft Windows concepts and applications meant that networking greatly improved computer systems. On the other hand, however, it was and still is challenging (and may be expensive) to introduce and maintain networked systems. This is true despite the fact that corporate administration tools such as Microsoft Systems Management Server were developed at great expense and effort. Unfortunately, these tools are not always the optimum choice, particularly for heterogeneous network environments.

In these cases, terminal servers can be a great alternative, especially because the existing infrastructure (network, server, clients) does not necessarily have to be replaced. Terminal servers are a central instance that can be managed comparatively easily, even if different clients need to be integrated. Nevertheless, before terminal servers are accepted for some business units or even for the entire company, the profitability of this solution still needs to be justified in detail.

Cost Categories

The following section deals with individual cost items and how to categorize them as they relate to terminal servers. The exact costs depend on the target environment and will not be stated in absolute figures, but rather in qualitative terms.

Investment Costs

Investments are those costs that need to be incurred for the initial purchase of hardware and software. They are mainly made up of central components, infrastructure, decentralized components, hiring staff, and costs of location:

- **Central components**　Hardware, peripheral devices, operating systems, user authentication software, file servers, central printing, e-mail servers, database servers, Web servers, CD servers, and backup tasks.

- **Infrastructure**　Network, including cables, routers, switches, and firewalls.

- **Decentralized elements**　Hardware, peripherals, operating systems, and software for clients that the end users will work on.

- **Staff**　Costs incurred in finding and hiring suitable personnel.

- **Location**　Air conditioning, uninterruptible power supply, security, and fire protection.

When terminal servers come into play, investment in decentralized elements and infrastructure usually decreases. It is not necessary to modernize an existing network including clients to achieve improved application performance. Only the connection between the servers should be as fast as possible, which might require some investment in suitable network components.

Expenses for central elements will increase because terminal servers require powerful hardware. As this hardware requires a lot of space, fitting out the location will be quite expensive. Even though less staff will be necessary to manage the clients, more personnel will be needed for administration. However, the larger an installation, the lower the administration cost per workstation.

When a conventional environment reaches a certain size, it requires central administration and installation tools. The cost of these tools must be considered when comparing a conventional environment with a terminal server environment. However, central installation assistants or cloning processes will be needed for very large terminal server environments as well.

In general, the investment costs incurred by a conventional PC environment and those incurred by terminal servers are basically the same, or are perhaps, if anything, a little more favorable for terminal servers. Terminal server environments do not allow for major savings yet. Nevertheless, it is important to see that the costs of client/server hardware often represent less than 15 percent of the total cost incurred in providing applications.

Fixed Current Costs

Fixed current costs regularly arise for the environment's general operation. These costs include administrative tasks, personnel costs, training activities, end user support, siting costs, expendables, maintenance agreements, and frequent hardware disposal:

- **Administrative tasks**   User administration, installation and administration of applications, performance management, security, licensing and data administration (availability, security, and virus protection).

- **Personnel costs**   Salaries, rent, administration, and expenses.

- **Training activities**   Administrator and end user training, training material, and management information.

- **End user support**   Troubleshooting, hotline, helpdesk, and task logs.

- **Siting costs**   Rent for server rooms, power and communication charges for clients, server, and network.

- **Expendable**   Procurement, storage, and management of data carriers, literature, and spare parts.

- **Maintenance agreements**   Frequent hardware component maintenance, and software support agreements.

- **Disposal**   Removing and disposing of client and server hardware at the end of its useful life.

Administrative tasks on terminal servers are highly centralized and therefore require less effort, which, of course, results in significantly lower personnel costs. This fact can be realized especially when working with low-maintenance clients.

In regard to training activities, there are almost no differences between terminal server and conventional environments. However, the difference is extreme when it comes to end user support. A homogeneous and central environment simply does not require as much support for configuration and applications.

Siting costs are higher with servers; thin clients require considerably less space and power. Compared to a conventional PC client environment, expenses remain about the same. The same goes for expendables. Even though fewer variations of material are needed, the amount required makes up for any difference.

Basically, terminal server maintenance agreements are quite simple because they encompass only a few components. However, depending on the number of client types, the bandwidth of their individual maintenance agreements can still be fairly comprehensive. On the other hand, the hardware replacement is less often because both clients and servers work a lot longer on server farms than before.

All in all, current fixed costs are considerably decreased when terminal servers are used, thus presenting obvious savings potential.

Note Some fixed current costs stay the same while administration costs, support, and disposal costs are reduced. These are *fixed* current costs because you have to pay the system administration staff and the support staff, even if there is less work in system administration and support. Typically, the income of a supporter is not a variable cost for the company because they have to pay his salary even if he has to answer fewer support calls. You cannot fire "half" a support person. You can reduce your support personnel, and thus the related fixed current costs, if you find out that your average number of support calls remain on a reduced level after the introduction of terminal servers.

Variable Current Costs

Because variable current costs are exceptions, they are not easy to calculate. They are incurred by unplanned downtime, necessary changes to the runtime environment, and user support.

- **Unplanned downtime** System failures, work interruption, and failed cases of user self-help.

- **Changes to the runtime environment** Evaluation of new software, piloting, project management, software distribution, and changes to application configurations.

- **User support** Help for new users and after introduction of new software versions.

Central, well-managed servers reduce downtime in terminal server environments. Even mistakes caused by self-help in conventional environments are no longer important because users have no opportunity to interfere with terminal servers.

In a production terminal server environment, software components are usually not changed without prior tests. However, it is relatively easy to integrate a test system with new operating system or application software components into the existing environment and let selected users test it. This allows risk-free installation of new software versions. Downtimes are reduced to a minimum through new operating system versions and application configurations. One definite precondition for this is that a test environment be available where the new runtime parameters can be determined prior to general installation.

User-support expenses are also significantly reduced in terminal server environments. All terminal server users work with the applications selected by the administrators, and users no longer have the opportunity to manipulate applications. Another advantage is remote control. It enables the administrator to take over control of a user session and guide the user through solving the problem.

All in all, terminal server environments incur considerably fewer variable current costs than conventional environments. Nevertheless, this calculation strongly depends on the quality of both the server installation and the organization of the administrators in charge.

Application Costs

The cost qualification model described above focuses on hardware. If networks and computer systems already exist in the target environment, other criteria play a more important role, especially the costs incurred by owning and providing applications for use on heterogeneous networks and clients. For this reason, the preceding cost analysis is adjusted accordingly and thus becomes *total cost of application ownership* (TCA).

Cost Structure
These four factors influence costs relating to applications:

- **Where is the location of the application executable?** If an application executable is located on a client rather than on a central server, costs for administration, installation, and configuration are higher.

- **Where is the application executed?** If an application runs on the client, the client needs the corresponding attributes. This might even imply a physical exchange or extension of client hardware when a new application version is installed. This is even true for applications that run partly on the client and partly on the server, or whose executable files are first loaded by the server. Executing the application on the server allows central adjustment of hardware for many users.

- **Where is the data saved?**   User data saved on the client is a risk when it comes to security and availability. For this reason, user data should be located on a central server.

- **What is the user location and type of connection?**   Distributed user locations and the bandwidth of the network connection impact costs depending on the different models. Support costs and the necessary infrastructure play an important role, too.

The terminal server model is optimal regarding all four factors: applications are saved and executed on the server. Data is saved on a server. Clients are no longer relevant and can be located anywhere. The network connection requires a relatively low and easy-to-provide bandwidth.

However, the disadvantages of a terminal server environment also need to be considered. They include reduced flexibility for the user, extreme dependency on a network that functions continuously, and problems with processing local data (for example, printing or scanning documents).

Conclusion

Using terminal servers reduces the overall costs for providing applications for the entire company. It is possible to use the existing infrastructure without subjecting it to substantial changes. Framework conditions include powerful server components and a minimum network bandwidth of 10 to 20 kilobits per second for each client. Furthermore, well-trained administrators are the basis for stable and thus cost-effective operation of this type of environment.

Realizing Terminal Server Projects

Just as for other complex technologies, the introduction of terminal servers fails in many companies. Frequently, it is not technical issues but rather the organizational issues that result in unsatisfactory solutions. Still, users do not care about the reason for failure—they care about the impact on their everyday work. If production work becomes impossible, system administrators and management will be affected, too. Acceptance can drop to zero, even for a technology with a great concept. This failure can even cast doubt on an entire corporate strategy.

To help avoid organizational or conceptual mistakes, we will briefly examine project planning and, the selection of a system integrator plus we will discuss establishing guidelines to avoid mistakes.

Project Planning

So what is the difference between a successful and a failed terminal server project? The technology itself works, as has been proved, just not under all circumstances. No one expects a sports car to be perfectly suited to all tasks in construction or manufacturing. A four-wheel-drive truck would be a lot better for these tasks, although their basic structure (a vehicle with four tires and a steering wheel) doesn't differ much from a sports car. The same is true for terminal servers. They are better suited for some tasks than for others. Finding out which areas of a company terminal servers can be effectively used and implementing successfully, from a technical point of view is the objective of a terminal server project.

Terminal server projects are typically divided into five phases. Either an internal or an external service provider normally handles the implementation of such a project.

- **Pre-study, including test**   In this phase, the service provider analyzes the target environment, the IT terminal server strategy is defined, required core applications are defined, the total cost of ownership (calculating the total costs) is determined for different operation models, and the test environment is installed. The test environment outlines the basic feasibility of any future project. After all pre-study activities have been completed, you will have an analysis document describing the actual situation, a rough concept describing the target situation, an estimate of all costs, and presentation material for all business units involved. Do not forget that the results of the pre-study might lead to the conclusion that terminal servers are not recommended for a particular implementation. If desired, a corporate concept can be drawn up during the pre-studies for a future production environment based on terminal servers.

- **Planning phase**   After the successful pre-study, a complete technical concept and set of specifications are drawn up. The technical concept describes the technical procedures, such as selecting hardware and operating system components, how to integrate the terminal servers in the existing infrastructure, and installing all required applications. The specifications explain the formal processes during the project, for example, decision making, time schedules, measurable results and milestones, approval procedures and criteria, exit scenarios, and escalation mechanisms. Both documents are absolutely essential for the successful conclusion of the entire project. Therefore, changes to the technical concept or specifications during the project should always be checked and approved by all project partners involved. During the planning phase, the customer will receive some initial training, if this has not been done before, to establish a common basis for know-how and terminology.

- **Pilot phase**   In this phase, there will be a so-called "clean room installation" with no direct connection to the existing production target network environment. This procedure helps prove the basic functionality of the project concept. It could even require separate network components and individual domain controllers, file servers, print servers, database servers, and so on. Only if very extensive third systems (for example, mainframe computers or comprehensive databases) need to be connected should compromises to the clean room installation be made. As a result of this phase, there will be documented tests in line with the specifications, which will help determine reference parameters.

- **Field-test phase** This project section deals with transitioning and integrating the clean room installation into the existing production environment. The focus lies on establishing connections to existing user accounts, backend servers, and legacy systems. Furthermore, it is often necessary to adapt logon scripts, profiles, and policies. Sometimes, complete strategic corporate processes for network, user, and server administration are questioned during this phase. Test users and approval procedures ensure that the installation is qualified. The last part of this phase sees the composition of approval protocols, project documentation, and, if applicable, complete operational concepts.

- **Production phase** In this phase, the end users start to work with the system productively. In the beginning, the service provider will offer on-site assistance. If this results in essential changes in the users' work routines, there will be acceptance difficulties for some time. Continuously informing end users and setting up a special help desk will help make the people involved more willing to cooperate. Furthermore, operations and maintenance concepts will start to be effective and assure uninterrupted operation of the terminal servers.

Each of the above phases is concluded with a milestone. This milestone represents the end of the phase and determines whether the project will go on or be aborted. All criteria regarding the following step need to be set in the specifications from at least the planning phase on.

If weaknesses in the project concept become evident during the pilot or field-test phase, it will be necessary to backtrack to the planning phase. Even though this might lead to deadline attainment problems, this procedure will prevent a system that does not work properly from being transitioned to the production phase. Once in the production phase, conceptual mistakes can no longer be corrected and usually lead to catastrophic results.

> **Important** Mistakes happen in every project! The earlier they are identified and solved, the less problematic they are. For this reason, efficient escalation management is essential for the success of a project. Determining corresponding procedures and defining project abortion criteria in the specifications is therefore essential.

Selection of the System Integrator

What is the difference between a TV and a toaster on one hand, and a corporate server and a mainframe computer on the other? The former category can be used by untrained persons without any technical introduction. The latter category is based on technology that needs to be explained and should therefore be set up and operated only by specialists. These specialists must have undergone extensive training and acquired a great deal of experience.

Naturally, the world is not black and white. There are so many nuances, and this also goes for the technological categories described earlier. Skillful operation of a sophisticated VCR or motor vehicle requires comprehensive studying of manuals or attending special practical training. After completing their studies and/or training, normal people can use these devices. Due to improved user interfaces, setting up and using a PC is becoming common knowledge. However, in large companies, this can lead to a fatal mixture: untrained staff operating seemingly easy-to-use but at the same time company-critical technology that actually needs to be explained.

The "self-made administrator problem" is especially obvious in corporate networks with terminal servers. Because of its graphical administration tools, an application server configured as a terminal server at first glance seems to be easy to operate. However, this computer as a host that has many terminals connected to it requires relevant in-depth knowledge. If several terminal servers are combined for load balancing to provide an environment for multiple users, the corresponding administration task is anything but trivial. For this reason, system integrators assist with installing, training administrators, and operating a terminal server environment.

So what services should be considered for the introduction and production use of this type of environment? What does a good system integrator offer? Usually, five selection criteria are essential: consulting, installation, support during operation, training sessions, and support tools combined with effective project management. Let us take a closer look at these criteria.

- **Consulting**   Before project start, the target environment needs to be analyzed in detail, involving not only the existing and planned technology, but also the potential acceptance of the system by management, users, and administrators. Additionally, a plausible concept plays a major role. The overall objective is to draw up technical specifications to ensure proper project process of the terminal server environment installation. Tests can also be part of this pre-phase of the project. However, a suitable reference environment (for example, a test lab) needs to be available to conduct these tests.

- **Installation**   Installing a complex terminal server environment is the most critical part of a project and requires extensive experience and conscientiousness. Specially trained system engineers will help avoid mistakes by keeping strictly to the specifications and the time schedule. An experienced project manager should support them. The project manager must always be informed of the latest developments and check installation progress on site frequently. At the end, there will be an approval protocol and follow-up support in case of problems that might occur. The customer is presented with a well-functioning and well-documented production environment.

- **Support during operation**   After a new production terminal server environment is installed, technical problems may occur. They are usually caused by certain system software weaknesses or insecurity on the part of the administrators in charge. For this reason, each system integrator should operate a proper customer support hotline for a certain time after the actual project is finalized. Several invoicing methods might be implemented for this service. In addition to calling phone numbers subject to a charge (for example, 900 numbers), so-called call-IDs may be purchased and used as coupons for calling the hotline. Another type of hotline support is the call-by-call method, meaning that one technical question can be asked for a certain charge. This method has the advantage of involving no further contractual obligations and requiring that the answer must be presented within a certain time frame. Large companies in particular, however, prefer paying an annual fee that allows them as many technical inquiries as they need (premier support). The relevant modalities are all agreed upon in a contract. Of course, support inquiries should be possible not by phone only, but also by e-mail or fax. All inquires should be processed by the system integrator at a central helpdesk. All helpdesk staff have access to a database-supported system that archives all problems and documents all solution approaches and answers (tracking system). This method also simplifies time and content control by a superior escalation instance. Frequently asked questions should be made available to the customer on the Internet or on a document or data carrier that the users can subscribe to.

- **Training sessions**   A system integrator who offers the installation of a technology as complex as the terminal server should also be able to provide the customer with the required training. Proper training makes handing over the installed production environment to the customer and possible cooperation with a help desk much easier for everyone involved. Staff training with a fixed date, location, and content should come first. Another option is exclusive training for selected participants. Special training with individualized content would round off this service. Workshops including extensive practical exercises generally result in the participants' ability to understand the technology and safely work with it.

- **Support tools**   A system integrator can usually present a number of reference projects relating to the required technology. This implies that the system integrator has built up an internal knowledge base that will help deal with all aspects of the issues described above, including all activities before project start (pre-sales, consulting), during the project (installation), and after the project (post-sales, support). Furthermore, the system integrator develops special products, tools, mechanisms, or procedures before or during the project, thus ensuring quick and smooth work in follow-up projects. This so-called "toolbox" is similar to the toolbox of a skilled craftsman. It usually consists of automated analysis and measurement tools, support tools for system installation, configuration aids, and defined research options for troubleshooting.

Implementation of the criteria listed earlier often requires highly specialized personnel to reach the targets set for the installation of terminal servers. Before you decide on your terminal server project provider, ask all potential system integrators about their products and general conditions relating to the preceding issues and about the availability of the required personnel. Only when suitable staff can cover all relevant areas is the probability of project success high enough to warrant implementation. Also, it is always legitimate to ask a system integrator for on-topic publications and strategic partnerships with the producers of the system software.

Tip   When drawing up a server-based computing concept for your company, always focus on the *human aspect*. This includes the management, administrators, and, of course, the users. If these three groups do not accept the strategy, even the best technical concept can only lead to unsatisfactory results. If these people do not sufficiently accept the solution offered, achieving the discipline initially required for the use of Windows terminal servers will be difficult. System stability will never be reached if the exclusive administration of the Windows terminal server by trained administrators and the terminal server's explicit treatment as a vital corporate component are not ensured.

Index

Dr. Bernhard Tritsch

As Chief System Architect for visionapp GmbH in Frankfurt, Germany, Bernhard Tritsch is responsible for the development and the adaptation of terminal server and application access portal products for the commercial market. visionapp was founded when the Dresdner Bank terminal server project *starship* and the German terminal server system integrator asp4you were merged into a new company. Today, visionapp has offices in Germany and in England, and it belongs to the Dresdner Bank Group and the Allianz Group.

Before joining visionapp, Bernhard Tritsch was Director of Software Development and New Technologies for the Group Technologies AG business unit asp4you in Karlsruhe, Germany, from July 2001 to October 2002. Under his leadership, the system integrator asp4you started with the development of products derived from large terminal server projects. This resulted in a very close cooperation with the developers from the project *starship* at Dresdner Bank. At that time, *starship* was one of the most spectacular terminal server projects in Europe, including 250 terminal servers with 140 published applications for 5,500 international users.

Prior to that, from 1999 to 2001, Bernhard Tritsch held the position of a Technical Director at GTS-GRAL in Rossdorf, Germany. Leading 40 highly-skilled systems engineers in the United States and in Europe, he and his team were reponsible for consulting, system integration, and customer support in the field of server-based computing solutions for enterprises.

Bernhard Tritsch joined the Fraunhofer Institute for Computer Graphics in Darmstadt, Germany, where he worked in research as Windows developer (C, C++) and project leader for international computer graphics projects for four years. After receiving an equivalent to a Ph.D. in Computer Science in 1996 from the Technical University in Darmstadt, Germany, Bernhard Tritsch was the group leader responsible for the introduction and the administration of more than 400 PCs under Windows NT at the Fraunhofer Institute and its affiliated research institutes in Germany, Portugal, Singapore, and the United States until the end of 1998. During that time he was also leading a test and development laboratory for Windows NT in heterogeneous networks, which was supported by Microsoft. The goal of this laboratory was to work out enterprise solutions based on Windows NT, Active Server Pages, Terminal Servers and Citrix MetaFrame.

Previously, Bernhard Tritsch received an equivalent to an M.S. degree in Physics from the University in Freiburg, Germany, after finishing his master's thesis at the European Organization for Nuclear Research CERN in Geneva, Switzerland.

Over the last 12 years, Bernhard Tritsch gave some 200 presentations in Europe and in the United States, published more than 24 articles, and wrote four books in German; three of them were about terminal servers. This is his first book in English.

When he is not in multi-user Windows mode, Bernhard Tritsch enjoys the time he shares with his wife, his two sons, and the teammates from his volleyball team. They are the ones who keep him going.

Get a **Free**
e-mail newsletter, updates,
special offers, links to related books,
and more when you

register online!

Register your Microsoft Press® title on our Web site and you'll get a FREE subscription to our e-mail newsletter, *Microsoft Press Book Connections.* You'll find out about newly released and upcoming books and learning tools, online events, software downloads, special offers and coupons for Microsoft Press customers, and information about major Microsoft® product releases. You can also read useful additional information about all the titles we publish, such as detailed book descriptions, tables of contents and indexes, sample chapters, links to related books and book series, author biographies, and reviews by other customers.

Registration is easy. Just visit this Web page and fill in your information:

http://www.microsoft.com/mspress/register

Microsoft

- -

Proof of Purchase

Microsoft® Windows Server™ 2003 Terminal Services
0-7356-1904-2

CUSTOMER NAME

Microsoft Press, PO Box 97017, Redmond, WA 98073-9830